Methods and Applications of Data Management and Analytics

Methods and Applications of Data Management and Analytics

Guest Editors
Wenjie Zhang
Zhengyi Yang

Basel • Beijing • Wuhan • Barcelona • Belgrade • Novi Sad • Cluj • Manchester

Guest Editors

Wenjie Zhang
School of Computer Science
and Engineering
University of New South Wales
Sydney
Australia

Zhengyi Yang
School of Computer Science
and Engineering
University of New South Wales
Sydney
Australia

Editorial Office
MDPI AG
Grosspeteranlage 5
4052 Basel, Switzerland

This is a reprint of the Special Issue, published open access by the journal *Applied Sciences* (ISSN 2076-3417), freely accessible at: www.mdpi.com/journal/applsci/special_issues/BG1912CT97.

For citation purposes, cite each article independently as indicated on the article page online and using the guide below:

Lastname, A.A.; Lastname, B.B. Article Title. *Journal Name* **Year**, *Volume Number*, Page Range.

ISBN 978-3-7258-3206-4 (Hbk)
ISBN 978-3-7258-3205-7 (PDF)
https://doi.org/10.3390/books978-3-7258-3205-7

© 2025 by the authors. Articles in this book are Open Access and distributed under the Creative Commons Attribution (CC BY) license. The book as a whole is distributed by MDPI under the terms and conditions of the Creative Commons Attribution-NonCommercial-NoDerivs (CC BY-NC-ND) license (https://creativecommons.org/licenses/by-nc-nd/4.0/).

Contents

Wenjie Zhang and Zhengyi Yang
Methods and Applications of Data Management and Analytics
Reprinted from: *Appl. Sci.* **2024**, *14*, 11637, https://doi.org/10.3390/app142411637 1

Carlos Cruz
Innovative Learning in Forensic Electronics: Tools and Techniques
Reprinted from: *Appl. Sci.* **2024**, *14*, 11095, https://doi.org/10.3390/app142311095 5

Jiaying Chen, Yiwen Cui, Xinguang Zhang, Jingyun Yang and Mengjie Zhou
Temporal Convolutional Network for Carbon Tax Projection: A Data-Driven Approach
Reprinted from: *Appl. Sci.* **2024**, *14*, 9213, https://doi.org/10.3390/app14209213 20

Fernanda O. Gomes, Roberto Pellungrini, Anna Monreale, Chiara Renso and Jean E. Martina
Efficiency Boosts in Human Mobility Data Privacy Risk Assessment: Advancements within the PRUDEnce Framework
Reprinted from: *Appl. Sci.* **2024**, *14*, 8014, https://doi.org/10.3390/app14178014 39

Seungho Jeon, Kijong Koo, Daesung Moon and Jung Taek Seo
Mutation-Based Multivariate Time-Series Anomaly Generation on Latent Space with an Attention-Based Variational Recurrent Neural Network for Robust Anomaly Detection in an Industrial Control System
Reprinted from: *Appl. Sci.* **2024**, *14*, 7714, https://doi.org/10.3390/app14177714 69

Jiale Li, Li Fan, Xuran Wang, Tiejiang Sun and Mengjie Zhou
Product Demand Prediction with Spatial Graph Neural Networks
Reprinted from: *Appl. Sci.* **2024**, *14*, 6989, https://doi.org/10.3390/app14166989 90

Laura Gabriela Tanasescu, Andreea Vines, Ana Ramona Bologa and Oana Vîrgolici
Data Analytics for Optimizing and Predicting Employee Performance
Reprinted from: *Appl. Sci.* **2024**, *14*, 3254, https://doi.org/10.3390/app14083254 109

Zhiqiang Fan, Fangyue Chen, Xiaokai Xia and Yu Liu
EEG Emotion Classification Based on Graph Convolutional Network
Reprinted from: *Appl. Sci.* **2024**, *14*, 726, https://doi.org/10.3390/app14020726 130

Jinping Yao, Yunhong Xu and Jiaojiao Gao
A Study of Reciprocal Job Recommendation for College Graduates Integrating Semantic Keyword Matching and Social Networking
Reprinted from: *Appl. Sci.* **2023**, *13*, 12305, https://doi.org/10.3390/app132212305 148

Liuyi Chen, Bocheng Han, Xuesong Wang, Jiazhen Zhao, Wenke Yang and Zhengyi Yang
Machine Learning Methods in Weather and Climate Applications: A Survey
Reprinted from: *Appl. Sci.* **2023**, *13*, 12019, https://doi.org/10.3390/app132112019 170

Pu Chen, Linna Wu and Lei Wang
AI Fairness in Data Management and Analytics: A Review on Challenges, Methodologies and Applications
Reprinted from: *Appl. Sci.* **2023**, *13*, 10258, https://doi.org/10.3390/app131810258 206

Neven Pičuljan and Željka Car
Machine Learning-Based Label Quality Assurance for Object Detection Projects in Requirements Engineering
Reprinted from: *Appl. Sci.* **2023**, *13*, 6234, https://doi.org/10.3390/app13106234 239

Chunrui Liu, Wei Huang and Richard Yi Da Xu
Implicit Bias of Deep Learning in the Large Learning Rate Phase: A Data Separability Perspective
Reprinted from: *Appl. Sci.* **2023**, *13*, 3961, https://doi.org/10.3390/app13063961 . . . . **269**

Editorial

Methods and Applications of Data Management and Analytics

Wenjie Zhang and Zhengyi Yang *

School of Computer Science and Engineering, University of New South Wales, Sydney, NSW 2052, Australia; wenjie.zhang@unsw.edu.au
* Correspondence: zhengyi.yang@unsw.edu.au

1. Introduction

In recent years, data management and analytics have attracted significant attention from both academia and industry, driven by the rapid growth in the volume, velocity, and variety of data generation. The acceleration of digitalization has further intensified this trend, presenting substantial challenges in effectively organizing, storing, and processing vast amounts of data to support decision-making with precision and speed. Traditional data processing methods often struggle to meet the demands posed by the diverse and fast-evolving nature of modern data. This Special Issue, "*Methods and Applications of Data Management and Analytics*", aims to present the latest research, methodologies, and applications designed to address these challenges.

The current data landscape has been extended by an explosion of real-time data from sources such as sensors, smart home and industrial monitoring devices, and Internet of Things (IoT) networks. These technologies collectively contribute to an immense, multifaceted data ecosystem, posing significant demands on data management and analytics systems. Additionally, social media platforms and e-commerce sites produce billions of pieces of user-generated content (UGC) daily, encompassing text, images, videos, and complex social interactions. This surge in multimodal data further complicates analysis and underscores the pressing need for innovative data management solutions.

Emerging technologies offer promising solutions to these challenges. Big data technologies have proven capable of processing and analyzing massive datasets, enabling efficient data storage and computation. These advancements empower organizations to manage large volumes of data effectively, supporting both real-time and complex data needs. Moreover, advancements in deep learning and neural networks have significantly increased the demand for high-quality big data, establishing it as essential for model training and enhancing performance. This trend underscores the need for sophisticated data management and analytics processes capable of meeting these growing data demands and supporting a wide range of application scenarios.

Looking forward, data management and analytics are set to evolve toward greater intelligence. Advanced algorithms and architectures, including AI-based automated data management platforms, are anticipated to be central to accommodating the continued growth and diversification of data-driven applications. Balancing data privacy with the need for data sharing will also become an increasingly critical focus, with future technologies aiming to reconcile these sometimes-competing priorities. The development of more efficient, scalable, and secure data management and analytics systems will be essential for supporting data-driven decision-making, fostering innovation, and creating value across industries.

This Special Issue seeks to showcase the latest research contributions exploring these transformative technologies and approaches. From big data processing and AI-driven database systems to data security, graph data processing, and tools that enhance data quality and reliability, the articles within this collection provide valuable insights and frameworks for addressing current challenges. We hope this issue serves as a resource for

Citation: Zhang, W.; Yang, Z. Methods and Applications of Data Management and Analytics. *Appl. Sci.* **2024**, *14*, 11637. https://doi.org/10.3390/app142411637

Received: 25 November 2024
Accepted: 7 December 2024
Published: 12 December 2024

Copyright: © 2024 by the authors. Licensee MDPI, Basel, Switzerland. This article is an open access article distributed under the terms and conditions of the Creative Commons Attribution (CC BY) license (https://creativecommons.org/licenses/by/4.0/).

academics, practitioners, and industry professionals looking to remain at the forefront of advancements in data management and analytics.

2. An Overview of Published Articles

Data management and analytics have garnered significant attention in recent years, primarily due to the rapid growth in the volume, velocity, and variety of data generation. Recent research in data management and analytics has increasingly focused on leveraging machine learning methods to handle diverse data types. This Special Issue primarily explores the integration of time-series data, industrial data, social data, graph data, and advancements in AI in data-driven applications. The papers in this Special Issue mainly present methods and applications for time-series data, graph and social data, and AI in data-driven applications. We summarize each category below.

Time-Series Data. Time-series data consist of a sequence of chronological data points, typically recorded and analyzed at uniform intervals, such as seconds, minutes, or hours. Research on time-series data processing often intersects with various fields. As introduced in [1], accurate carbon tax forecasting can support more informed and effective climate policy decisions. Utilizing data from the World Carbon Pricing Database, temporal convolutional networks (TCNs) have demonstrated superior performance over traditional time-series models in capturing the complex dynamics of carbon pricing. By effectively capturing the long-term dependencies and non-linear patterns in carbon pricing data affected by economic and policy factors, TCNs enhance forecasting accuracy, enabling policymakers to anticipate market trends and take proactive measures in carbon management. In industrial systems, ref. [2] shows that timely anomaly detection is crucial for preventing costly issues. Mutation-based methods for generating anomalies in Industrial Control Systems (ICSs) employ variational recurrent autoencoders to map time-series data into a latent space, apply mutations, and reconstruct the data. This approach creates reliable anomalies that capture multivariate correlations and help address class imbalance in detection. By enriching the training data with these synthetic anomalies, the models can achieve improved detection accuracy and robustness against a wider range of system faults. Furthermore, ref. [3] illustrates that machine learning approaches are also applied in industry to automate label quality assurance in computer vision, particularly for object detection within requirements engineering. This method addresses the labor-intensive nature of data labeling and verification—a crucial step in producing high-quality AI solutions—and aims to streamline these processes, reducing manual effort and enhancing efficiency in industrial applications. This advancement not only accelerates the development process but also improves the overall accuracy of AI models by ensuring that the training data are consistently and correctly annotated.

Graph and Social Data. Graph data represent entities (nodes) and relationships (edges) using a graph structure, making them well suited for capturing complex relationships and connectivity information. These data are widely used in social networks, recommender systems, knowledge graphs, traffic networks, and other domains. Graph-based data from user-generated content (UGC) and social platforms pose challenges related to privacy and data quality but also provide valuable insights into user behavior and preferences. The study in [4] proposes methods to streamline privacy risk evaluations in response to the rapid expansion of mobility data from IoT, social networks, and mobile devices. By reducing background knowledge configurations and optimizing matching functions, this approach enhances computational efficiency. Another study [5] addresses the cold-start problem for recent graduates in a dual-dimensional job recommendation method using semantic keyword matching and social network analysis. This approach improves recommendation precision and reciprocity, better aligning graduate job preferences with employer recruitment criteria. In employee performance appraisal, ref. [6] shows that machine learning can support more accurate and objective performance assessments by utilizing techniques such as data preprocessing, variable selection, algorithm optimization, and hyperparameter tuning. These methods reduce reliance on subjective judgment and enhance the fairness and overall productivity of appraisals. As social data grow in complexity and significance, graph data analysis has become crucial for uncovering relational networks and enabling intelligent decision-making, with Graph Neural Networks (GNNs) playing a central role. For example, ref. [7] demonstrates how GNNs improve demand prediction accuracy for pre-owned items in e-commerce by leveraging spatial relationships and capturing both local and global dependencies through attention-based message propagation. Similarly, ref. [8] highlights the use of GNNs in the RGNet model for EEG-based emotion recognition, where brain regions are represented as nodes and inter-regional connections as edges. This approach allows the model to capture complex functional relationships beyond mere spatial proximity.

AI in Data Applications. In today's data- and AI-driven applications, there is a growing concern about AI fairness and latent biases in learning dynamics. Additionally, AI technology is increasingly being applied across various fields. The review [9] discusses issues of AI fairness in data management and analytics. AI fairness refers to the principle of preventing unequal harm or benefits to different subgroups within artificial intelligence systems, ensuring that these systems can quantify biases while effectively mitigating discrimination against specific groups. The primary research directions for addressing AI fairness include bias analysis and fairness training, which aim to identify and reduce potential biases. AI fairness is crucial in various social applications, such as education, healthcare, criminal justice, hiring, lending, and customer service, ensuring that these systems do not unjustly impact any particular group during their implementation. The authors of [10] explore the impact of stealth bias and data separability on deep learning training dynamics, highlighting the importance of these factors in improving model generalization. Invisible bias refers to biases that cannot be explicitly identified during model training due to data characteristics or training algorithms, while data separability describes the extent to which different classes are distinguishable in the feature space. It is shown that when data are well conditioned, gradient descent iterations with high learning rates converge to flatter minima, thereby improving the model's generalization ability. This finding underscores the importance of data separability in the deep learning training process. Beyond optimizing machine learning itself, the application of machine learning has expanded, with the field of meteorology beginning to leverage AI to address complex predictive challenges. The survey in [11] reviews recent advancements in machine learning for weather and climate prediction, demonstrating that meteorological data have greatly benefited from machine learning, particularly in enhancing the accuracy of short-term weather forecasts and medium- to long-term climate predictions. This improvement in predictive reliability spans various timescales.

3. Conclusions

Advancements in data management and analytics are driving transformative solutions across diverse sectors, further enabled by powerful machine learning techniques and emerging AI technologies. The ability to process and analyze time-series, social, industrial, and graph data has unlocked new insights, enhancing forecasting, personalization, efficiency, and performance evaluation. This progress also underscores the importance of fairness and transparency, as AI fairness and bias mitigation continue to play pivotal roles in building trustworthy systems. Addressing challenges such as data privacy, quality assurance, and structural biases requires continuous development in algorithms and frameworks to ensure that AI systems support intelligent decision-making, foster equity, and create value in a data-driven world. Future research will continue to refine these methodologies, balancing the demands of scalability, security, and ethical considerations, ultimately enhancing the reliability and impact of AI applications across fields.

Conflicts of Interest: The authors declare no conflicts of interest.

References

1. Chen, J.; Cui, Y.; Zhang, X.; Yang, J.; Zhou, M. Temporal Convolutional Network for Carbon Tax Projection: A Data-Driven Approach. *Appl. Sci.* **2024**, *14*, 9213. [CrossRef]
2. Jeon, S.; Koo, K.; Moon, D.; Seo, J.T. Mutation-Based Multivariate Time-Series Anomaly Generation on Latent Space with an Attention-Based Variational Recurrent Neural Network for Robust Anomaly Detection in an Industrial Control System. *Appl. Sci.* **2024**, *14*, 7714. [CrossRef]
3. Pičuljan, N.; Car, Ž. Machine Learning-Based Label Quality Assurance for Object Detection Projects in Requirements Engineering. *Appl. Sci.* **2023**, *13*, 6234. [CrossRef]
4. Gomes, F.O.; Pellungrini, R.; Monreale, A.; Renso, C.; Martina, J.E. Efficiency Boosts in Human Mobility Data Privacy Risk Assessment: Advancements within the PRUDEnce Framework. *Appl. Sci.* **2024**, *14*, 8014. [CrossRef]
5. Yao, J.; Xu, Y.; Gao, J. A Study of Reciprocal Job Recommendation for College Graduates Integrating Semantic Keyword Matching and Social Networking. *Appl. Sci.* **2023**, *13*, 12305. [CrossRef]
6. Tanasescu, L.G.; Vines, A.; Bologa, A.R.; Vîrgolici, O. Data Analytics for Optimizing and Predicting Employee Performance. *Appl. Sci.* **2024**, *14*, 3254. [CrossRef]
7. Li, J.; Fan, L.; Wang, X.; Sun, T.; Zhou, M. Product Demand Prediction with Spatial Graph Neural Networks. *Appl. Sci.* **2024**, *14*, 6989. [CrossRef]
8. Fan, Z.; Chen, F.; Xia, X.; Liu, Y. EEG Emotion Classification Based on Graph Convolutional Network. *Appl. Sci.* **2024**, *14*, 726. [CrossRef]
9. Chen, P.; Wu, L.; Wang, L. AI Fairness in Data Management and Analytics: A Review on Challenges, Methodologies and Applications. *Appl. Sci.* **2023**, *13*, 10258. [CrossRef]
10. Liu, C.; Huang, W.; Xu, R.Y.D. Implicit Bias of Deep Learning in the Large Learning Rate Phase: A Data Separability Perspective. *Appl. Sci.* **2023**, *13*, 3961. [CrossRef]
11. Chen, L.; Han, B.; Wang, X.; Zhao, J.; Yang, W.; Yang, Z. Machine Learning Methods in Weather and Climate Applications: A Survey. *Appl. Sci.* **2023**, *13*, 12019. [CrossRef]

Disclaimer/Publisher's Note: The statements, opinions and data contained in all publications are solely those of the individual author(s) and contributor(s) and not of MDPI and/or the editor(s). MDPI and/or the editor(s) disclaim responsibility for any injury to people or property resulting from any ideas, methods, instructions or products referred to in the content.

Article

Innovative Learning in a Digital Forensics Laboratory: Tools and Techniques for Data Recovery

Carlos Cruz

Department of Electronics, University of Alcalá, 28871 Madrid, Spain; carlos.cruz@uah.es

Abstract: Electronic evidence is an essential component in most legal trials of criminal activities, and digital forensics is therefore a crucial support for law enforcement investigations. For instance, a wide range of electronic devices contain Not AND (NAND) flash memory chips, and when a criminal leaves digital evidence on non-operational or locked systems, accessing this memory is crucial. Student acquisition of the necessary competences and skills associated with electronic devices, their basic principles, and the associated technologies can be provided by experimental training, as done with the optional Digital Forensics module included in the degree in Criminalistics: Forensic Sciences and Technologies offered by the University of Alcalá (Spain). This module equips students with the appropriate skills to extract, process, and authenticate evidence information using suitable tools. The purpose of this study was to investigate the effectiveness of experimental learning, deployed through laboratory digital forensic tasks. A literature review was conducted of novel data extraction and analysis tools and procedures as a guide to the design of data recovery tasks incorporating experimental learning. Drawing on student feedback, our results highlight positive learning outcomes for the students. It is concluded that powerful forensic image analysis freeware is capable of identifying elements, and practical tests involving JTAG/chip−off extraction and analysis yield favorable results. A proposal for future studies is to reduce the destructiveness of invasive extraction methods.

Keywords: NAND memories; data extraction and analysis; electronic evidence; forensic electronics; evidence acquisition; experimental learning; forensic electronics

Citation: Cruz, C. Innovative Learning in a Digital Forensics Laboratory: Tools and Techniques for Data Recovery. *Appl. Sci.* **2024**, *14*, 11095. https://doi.org/10.3390/app142311095

Academic Editors: João M. F. Rodrigues and David Megías

Received: 5 August 2024
Revised: 6 September 2024
Accepted: 26 November 2024
Published: 28 November 2024

Copyright: © 2024 by the author. Licensee MDPI, Basel, Switzerland. This article is an open access article distributed under the terms and conditions of the Creative Commons Attribution (CC BY) license (https://creativecommons.org/licenses/by/4.0/).

1. Introduction

Electronic forensic research is a rapidly evolving field due to continuous technological advancements and the increasing prevalence of digital devices. Forensic science based on electronics, also known as digital forensics or computer forensics, is a branch of science focused on the identification, preservation, examination, and analysis of electronic data and digital devices. The main aim is to investigate and prevent cybercrime and to provide evidence in legal cases [1,2], and this requires the systematic collection and examination of digital data to uncover electronic evidence that can be used for investigative purposes and in court [3]. Furthermore, with the rapid growth of cybercrime, criminal investigators and law enforcement agencies increasingly rely on the expertise of digital forensic experts to examine confiscated data for evidence. Forensic research aimed at investigating criminal activities is a complex process that includes a stage dedicated to the acquisition and authentication of forensic copies and their subsequent analysis [4]. It is crucial to ensure the chain of custody, the integrity of the evidence, and the preservation and immutability of the original data [5,6]. Data acquisition should ensure the integrity of the original data, and each copy must be authenticated on creation to ensure support for the ultimate analysis results. As modern computer memories store large amounts of data, the challenge lies in discriminating between relevant and irrelevant information [7].

Digital forensic analysis, encompassing the preservation, identification, extraction, and documentation of digital evidence, is a relatively new and emerging academic discipline within information technology [2,8,9]. Despite demand for forensic technology specialists and the increasing number of postgraduate degrees in computer science and electronics, students often lack the necessary hands−on learning opportunities to acquire the kind of knowledge sought by employers. University criminalistics courses, for instance, mainly focus on theoretical principles and concepts rather than on practical applications [10].

A key emerging area in modern law enforcement is digital forensics, which aims to address the growing need for skilled professionals to handle increasing volumes of digital evidence. Particular challenges are posed by advanced technologies, like NAND flash memories, and by the current gaps in practical training in academic courses.

This research highlights the importance of electronic evidence in pursuing criminal activities and the crucial role played by appropriate digital forensics training. Its main contributions are based on a literature review that identifies novel tools and established data extraction procedures, and an exploration of innovative experimental learning methodologies, distinguishing between data recovery and data analysis tools. The importance of experimental learning for undergraduates is underscored as a means of developing key digital forensic skills, related to identifying electronic devices and associated technologies, and extracting, processing, and authenticating digital evidence from non−operational or locked systems. Providing students with hands−on experience in using advanced forensic tools and techniques bridges the gap between theory and practice, and ultimately enhances the effectiveness of real−world forensic investigations. This study's findings and recommendations underscore the need for continuous adaptation to technological advances and the importance of enhancing forensic methods to ensure the integrity and reliability of digital evidence.

The rest of this paper is organized as follows: Section 2 describes the tools and software for studying NAND flash memories; Section 3 describes the laboratory activities performed with students taking an optional digital forensics subject as part of a criminalistics degree; and Section 4 details the corresponding results. Finally, this paper ends by drawing some conclusions in Section 5.

2. Related Work

Criminals attempt to dispose of potential evidence by blocking devices or rendering them unusable. To demonstrate criminal activities from inaccessible or inoperative electronic devices equipped with NAND flash memories, advanced or destructive extraction techniques are usually required. However, deployed tools must be kept up to date due to the rapid and constant evolution of forensic technology, and this necessitates continuous adaptation. Specialized technologies focus on improving processing times, enhancing detection of explicit/sensitive content, expanding support for device models and memory types, and expediting information decryption, among others.

2.1. Data Extraction from NAND Flash Memories

A wide variety of methods are available for data acquisition, depending on the degree of alteration of the original evidence. Methods can be classified according to cost, required time, or complexity, or according to the level of destructiveness, as depicted in Figure 1, which shows destructiveness ranked by levels from 1 to 5. For instance, if a device is neither damaged nor locked, it is preferable to employ a level 1 non−invasive technique to ensure the integrity of the original data [11]. The five levels are explained as follows:

- Level 1. Manual extraction. This involves a low−complexity, non−destructive, and thorough search for evidence. A locked device is its primary limitation. Additionally, manually navigating through evidence sources may affect data integrity. Tools such as ZRT Screen Capture [12] and Eclipse 3 Pro−Kit [13] can be used at this level.
- Level 2. Logical extraction. This is performed by connecting the device to a forensic workstation for data extraction using Oxygen Forensic Detective (OFD), Cellebrite, or OpenText EnCase Forensic (EnCase) software [14]. As a limitation, not all log files and data from analyzed devices are accessible.

- Level 3. JTAG and HEX dump. This involves testing the circuits of memory cards, USB drives, SSDs, or eMMC devices and requires tools to disassemble devices and access their JTAG ports. The method is semi–destructive as it uses TAPs located on motherboards for functionality testing. Figure 2 shows various available commercial models. Although JTAG is primarily used in smartphone manufacture, it can also be employed to bypass OS–imposed access restrictions.
- Level 4. Chip–off. This complex destructive technique involves physically extracting the device memory chip for reading using specialized equipment, e.g., RT809H, sourced from Shenzhen Sintech Electronic Co., Shenzhen, China. It is crucial not to damage the chip during extraction, as this could cause irreversible bit or even byte failures; this approach is therefore only recommended when less invasive methods cannot be used.
- Level 5. Microreading. This involves the physical observation of chips using scanning electron microscopy, e.g., JEOL Ltd., Tokyo, Japan. It is typically reserved for high–priority cases as it requires more resources, time, and expertise than the other extraction methods [6,15,16].

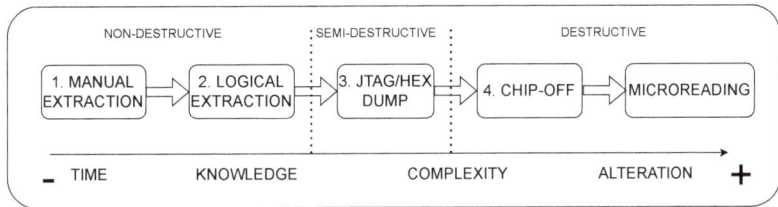

Figure 1. Data extraction methods, ranked 1 to 5, reflecting levels of destructiveness in terms of a sliding scale based on time, knowledge, complexity, and alteration [11].

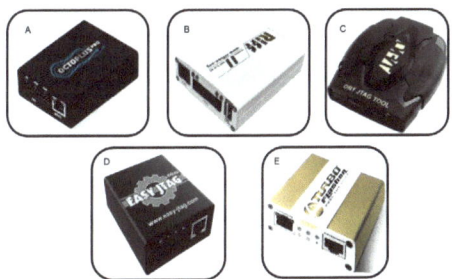

Figure 2. Commercial hardware platforms used for JTAG extraction: (**A**) Octoplus; (**B**) Riff Box; (**C**) Ort JTAG Tool; (**D**) Easy JTAG Box; and (**E**) Advanced Turbo Flasher (ATF) Box.

2.2. Data Analysis Tools

Of the tools available for forensic investigation, some are applied to specific tasks, while others are used for complete studies (i.e., acquisition, authentication, and analysis) [17,18]. The main tools used for data analysis are as follows:

- Oxygen Forensic Detective (OFD). This is used for logical and physical extractions, including data analysis and visualization in forensic image formats and in different types of electronic devices. OFD generates judicially admissible reports directly from the application and offers extensive support for Android devices and brute–force decryption of 7–Zip files. The main drawbacks are that it is an expensive and complex software [19].
- OpenText EnCase Forensic (EnCase). This software, which performs memory acquisition, data extraction, forensic report generation, and password recovery, is widely recognized by judicial departments and forensic research agencies. It supports a large

number of mobile device and tablet models, and its latest version features EnCase Media Analyzer, which uses artificial intelligence and machine learning to identify and categorize the content of forensic images based on datasets. The generated reports employ a format admitted in judicial processes and also preserve the chain of custody for all the examined sources [20].

- Cellebrite Inseyets, Cellebrite UFED, and Cellebrite Digital Collector. These enable the recovery of deleted data, information decryption, and password extraction. Supporting a wide range of devices, including Android and Apple mobile devices, they can unlock devices and acquire logical and physical data. Inseyets integrates Universal Forensics Extraction Device (UFED) services with autonomy and quick−view technologies, which enable electronic device content to be viewed before creating forensic images, while novel capabilities allow for the simultaneous automation of multiple processes [21–23].
- Passware Kit Forensic (PKF). This enables the acquisition and processing of disk images and password recovery through brute−force, dictionary, and pattern attacks. PKF, useful when encrypted or locked data need to be accessed without using more invasive techniques, includes a resource manager that maximizes the performance of the analysis machine and an improved bootable memory imager mode, which creates memory images during computer startup. PKF does not include report generation suitable for judicial procedures, and support for mobile device processing is only included in the Ultimate edition [24,25].
- Belkasoft X Forensic (BXF). This enables the acquisition and authentication of NAND memory images through various analytical tasks (e.g., timelines and advanced searches). BXF, which supports numerous types of electronic devices and dump formats, can examine messaging applications, web browsing data, email inboxes, documents, images, video and audio files, file systems, and mobile applications. Processing times can be reduced through task automation and the use of specific search approaches. Additionally, BXF provides bit−level analysis through its HEX viewer and file system window, and BelkaCarving can recover and validate deleted, hidden, or corrupted information in databases [26].
- SANS Investigative Forensic Toolkit (SIFT). Available as a downloadable virtual machine, SIFT, a workstation designed for forensic analysis, uses key functionalities that include the Rekall Framework, Sleuth Kit, and Volatility. It offers extensive support for file systems and disk images, and comprehensive step−by−step documentation is available online [27].
- Sleuth Kit and Autopsy. Used to recover information and reconstruct scenarios, Sleuth Kit facilitates forensic image examination, file and directory analyses, keyword and file type searches, data recovery, and metadata verification. Autopsy, an open−source digital forensics platform that serves as a graphical interface for the Sleuth Kit functions, generates reports in various formats, such as HTML, Google Earth, KML, and Excel. However, it requires the use of additional tools for memory image acquisition [28].
- Toolsley. Designed to find hashes, identify file types, and analyze binary images using effective and straightforward tools, Toolsley's simplicity is particularly advantageous for cases requiring urgent or remote investigation. However, notable drawbacks are that certain functions are outdated or formats may be incompatible [29].
- Forensic Tool Kit Imager Lite (FTK−IL). This is mainly used for data extraction and authentication from computers, mobile devices, and networks. Additional features are available under license, including password recovery and digital evidence integrity evaluation. It is widely used by judicial agents and administrative entities [30].

Table 1 lists the various types of software, their features (extraction, analysis, and reporting) and OS type (Android, MacOS, Linux, and Windows), together with reference works that use the proposed tools. Those commercial tools are capable of performing comprehensive analyses of the content from numerous electronic device types, although similar results can be achieved by combining the use of freeware options. Forensic copies can be extracted, data can be analyzed, and reports can be generated from devices running in different OSs for OFD, EnCase, Cellebrite, and BXF. PKF processes data and generates reports. SIFT is suitable for data extraction and analysis but does not support all types of forensic images or report generation. FTK−IL is similar to SIFT but differs in terms of extensive support. Lastly, neither Autopsy nor Toolsley is capable of acquiring forensic copies, but both tools are considered useful for analyzing data from binary images. Furthermore, Autopsy can generate highly detailed forensic reports.

Table 1. Different types of supported tools and the related features categorized by specific features and OS type. (Note: ! indicates unavailable information. X, and ✓ indicate unavailable and available performance, respectively).

Software	Features				OS				Literature
	License	Extraction	Analysis	Report	Windows	MacOS	Linux	Android	
OFD	✓	✓	✓	✓	✓	✓	✓	✓	[6,17,21,22,31–37]
EnCase	✓	✓	✓	✓	✓	✓	✓	✓	[7,17,22,38–41]
Cellebrite	✓	✓	✓	✓	✓	✓	✓	✓	[6,21,22,31,32,34,36,41,42]
PKF	✓	✓	!	X	✓	✓	✓	✓	[7,25,43]
BXF	!	✓	✓	✓	✓	✓	✓	✓	[6,41,44]
SIFT	X	✓	✓	X	!	!	!	!	[22,25,38,41,42]
Autopsy	X	X	✓	✓	✓	✓	✓	✓	[7,21,22,25,38–41]
Toolsley	!	X	✓	✓	✓	✓	✓	✓	[29]
FTK−IL	✓	X	✓	✓	✓	✓	✓	✓	[22,25,32,35,36,38,41,45–47]

2.3. Practical Learning Context

Higher education in digital forensics is evolving to meet the demands of a rapidly changing technological landscape. The integration of novel techniques into academic settings is still in its early stages, with limited evidence on practical deployment despite promising proof−of−concept studies [48]. The integration of virtual laboratories and online resources allows for flexible learning environments, accommodating both on−site and remote students. While institutions are encouraged to share resources and best practices to enhance the quality and the accessibility of digital forensics education [49], the lack of cohesive educational frameworks remains a barrier to the effective training of future digital forensics professionals.

The use of experiential learning theory in designing a digital forensics curriculum has been shown to enhance the student learning experience [50]. Incorporating hands-on experience of working on various digital forensic research topics provides students with practical skills and a deeper understanding of investigative processes [51]. Experiential learning involves students engaging in practical tasks in which knowledge and skills reflecting real-world contexts are applied [52]. Following this pedagogical approach, instructors often take industry problems and adapt them to classroom projects. For instance, an emphasis on the importance of active participation and reflection contributes to the broader discourse on experiential learning, with experiential learning methods that foster meaningful, engaged learning in various educational contexts, e.g., through game-based approaches, shown to be particularly effective [53,54].

Figure 3 depicts the experiential learning cycle, whereby students gain relevant and practical skills from the design of practical, collaborative, and reflective learning experiences based on four stages: concrete experience, reflective observation, abstract conceptualization, and active experimentation [55]. In the experience and observation stages, students, individually or in teams, actively engage in handling electronic devices and the associated software. The abstract conceptualization stage requires students to establish connections between laboratory work and learned theories from lectures and the ideas of peers and instructors. Finally, in the experimentation stage, students consider how learned lessons are applied in collaborative work scenarios.

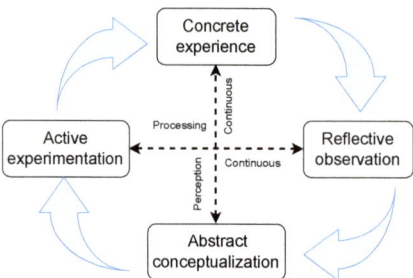

Figure 3. Kolb's learning styles and the experiential learning cycle.

3. Methods

Classroom activities, based on qualitative and exploratory−descriptive evaluations, were carried out as part of the optional subject of digital forensics [56], a module in the undergraduate degree in Criminalistics: Forensic Sciences and Technologies offered by the University of Alcalá (Spain), with 13 enrolled students for the academic year 2023–2024.

The objective of this module is to introduce students to digital devices and data storage configurations. Students learn about the basic principles, technologies, and techniques of digital forensics by extracting data, applying processing techniques, implementing applications, and authenticating evidence from commonly used compact and mobile devices, as well as the necessary concepts for understanding how data are stored in semiconductor elements. In gaining practical experience with electronic storage devices by studying their functionality, the students acquire valuable insights into the field of forensic electronics.

This study is embedded in tasks completed in practical laboratory sessions. The concrete experience and reflective observation phases are implemented by the design and development of experimental setups, whereby students engage in assembling electronic circuits and exploring digital forensic techniques and tools. Experimental setups for forensic data analysis include non-volatile storage devices, such as hard drives and NAND memories, as well as mobile device analysis. This activity aims to foster reflective observation and abstract conceptualization. Different didactic modules are presented along with practical experiences, with students implementing the tools studied during the concrete experience and reflective observation phases.

3.1. Data Recovery

The extraction of evidence from potentially damaged storage devices is an increasingly common practice in forensic science, while the difficulty in directly reading data from devices requires the use of novel techniques. To familiarize students with retrieving information from storage systems, they perform 3 experimental tasks involving the extraction of data from memories, described in the following subsections.

3.1.1. MicroSD Card Data Extraction

A simple open-source hardware platform (Arduino) is used for microSD card reading and writing actions. The experimental setup includes an additional SD memory card reader as depicted in Figure 4a. The activity involves reading and writing files to memory and creating a sketch to display the content of the files located in the source folder using the serial monitor. The data are captured using external software developed by the students (see example in Figure 4b).

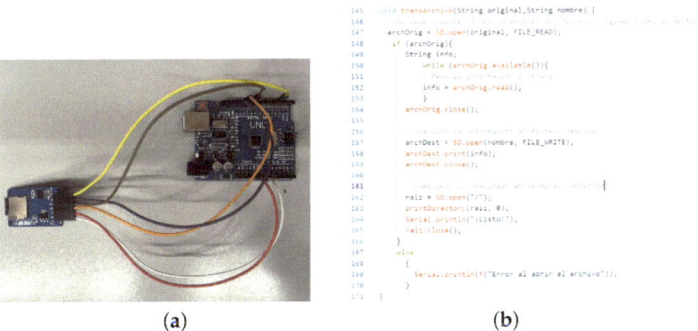

(a)   (b)

Figure 4. (**a**) Experimental setup for microSD memory extraction. (**b**) Software developed for file transfer.

3.1.2. NAND Memory Reading and Writing Capabilities

Figure 5 shows an example of memory reading by EasyTAG resulting in valuable information, e.g., erasure, memory size allocation, and read-write block configuration. The objective of the activity, based on NAND chips with TSOP and BGA encapsulations, is to explore memory characteristics (i.e., model, size, voltage, and operating frequency) before proceeding to reading and data extraction. Students use different evaluation boards and adapters to manipulate the NAND memory models and packages. The content is also extracted using JTAG and analyzed with forensic tools. Additional tools used are specific sockets, JTAG Classic Suite, HxD (freeware HEX editor and reader of binary images and files), Autopsy, Toolsley, PKF, AccessData, FTK-IL, and BXF.

(a)   (b)   (c)

Figure 5. (**a**) Experimental setup for TSOP operations. (**b**) TSOP and BGA NAND memories. (**c**) EasyTAG software used for NAND memory analysis.

3.1.3. Information Extraction from Commercial Devices

Students identify different computer components and extract the storage devices for forensic analysis. Hard drive data analysis is performed by Autopsy and the content is backed up and cloned. Mobile phone terminals and unidentified boards are provided for data extraction, as shown in Figure 6a. Students obtain identification numbers (e.g., memory chips) to determine device model and characteristics. Using the unique mobile device identifier, information is retrieved and the storage components are analyzed to identify their JTAG connections, as shown in Figure 6b. Subsequently, pins are soldered to the corresponding socket to create a dump, i.e., a binary file containing a copy of the memory (commonly used in diagnosing and debugging issues in computer systems). Additionally, SIM card data (i.e., call logs, received/sent messages, etc.) are analyzed using SimEdit, as shown in Figure 6c.

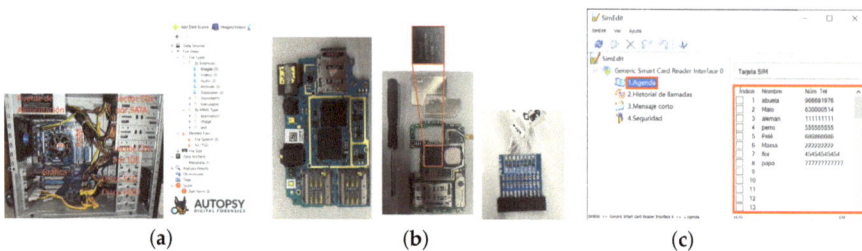

(a) (b) (c)

Figure 6. (a) Experimental setup for hard disk content extraction and analysis by Autopsy. (b) Examples of mobile terminals for identification. (c) Board developed for memory reading by JTAG, with SimEdit used for the SIM card analysis.

Table 2 describes the main advantages and disadvantages of the proposed instruction method. Note that the advantages and disadvantages are likely to depend on the number of students, the complexity of the activity, and the time available.

Table 2. Description of the main advantages and disadvantages of the proposed instruction method.

Advantages	Disadvantages
Practical experience: The method provides students with hands-on experience and enables them to apply theoretical knowledge to real-world scenarios, essential for understanding the complexities of digital forensics.	Scope limitations: The impact of the method may be limited in scope by the number of students.
Comprehensive learning: In covering a wide range of topics such as data extraction, processing techniques, and evidence authentication, students gain an understanding of digital forensic practices.	Resource intensive: The method requires significant resources for laboratory sessions, including specialized equipment and materials, which may be costly and difficult to scale.
Skill development: The focus on assembling electronic circuits and using forensic tools helps students develop essential technical skills that are directly applicable to the job market.	Time-consuming: The practical and reflective components may require more time than traditional lecture-based methods, possibly resulting in slower coverage of the syllabus.
Reflective learning: The combination of concrete experiences with reflective observation and abstract conceptualization leads to deeper learning and a better understanding of underlying principles.	Complexity: The technical nature of the tasks might be challenging for students without a background in electronics or digital technologies, potentially leading to difficulties in comprehension and execution.
Exposure to cutting-edge technologies: The inclusion of forensic tools and techniques (i.e., data recovery from NAND memories and mobile devices) ensures students are trained in up-to-date methodologies.	Dependence on instructor expertise: The effectiveness of the method relies on the instructor's digital forensics expertise and practical teaching skills, potentially affecting the quality of the learning experience.

4. Results

Questionnaires regarding perceptions of the forensic laboratory, virtual classroom diaries to record comments and opinions, and questionnaires to evaluate technical knowledge were used to evaluate the experiential learning outcomes. Prior to questionnaire completion, the researcher (also the module instructor) informed the students that their responses would remain entirely anonymous. The students acknowledged their understanding of the activity as a research project component and consented to participate. To safeguard anonymity, any questions that could potentially reveal identifying information about the students were excluded.

A preliminary questionnaire aimed to test their familiarity with programmable hardware devices and the term JTAG, how hard drives function, and the difference between RAM and ROM memory. The corresponding insights informed the teaching approach and helped tailor the content to the students' knowledge.

The results, shown in Figure 7, indicated that around 42% of the students had no knowledge of digital forensics, and 80% had no familiarity with programmable devices or specific terminology, like JTAG. There was also an evident lack of training in inspecting internal components of devices. However, more than 70% of the students depicted a strong interest in understanding electronic device operation.

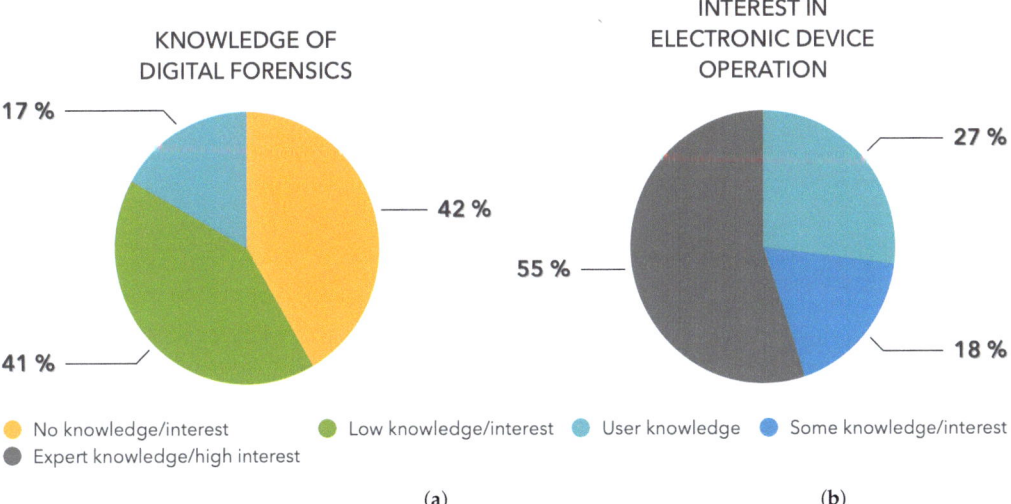

Figure 7. Preliminary questionnaire results. (a) Digital forensics-related knowledge. (b) Interest in electronic device operation.

Experiential activities provided the students with the opportunity to apply the knowledge gained in theoretical classes. The students demonstrated significant motivation and interest in the laboratory activity involving the soldering of PCB components and successfully verified the proper functioning of the assembled PCB circuit. Regarding instruments and explanations provided for the precise soldering of electronic components using the hot-air technique, the students perceived this activity as not entirely suitable for teamwork. The need to demonstrate alternative methods and tools for forensic analysis, such as Arduino and other electronic devices, was highlighted, pointing to challenges to be resolved, such as instability in code execution (the required directories were not properly created). Furthermore, NAND memory data extraction equipment exhibited flaws and deficiencies leading to setbacks and errors and posing a challenge in terms of handling the equipment. Conceptually, manipulating NAND memories was entirely new for the students, and the equipment used presented certain difficulties in terms of compatibility with computer systems, resulting in occasional delays. This feedback was provided by the students, who suggested their own improvements to the organizational planning of the activity.

The practical activities aided student understanding of theoretical concepts, as indicated by an average satisfaction rating of 3.9 out of 5 (see Figure 8). Overall however, the students found the activities to be somewhat ambitious, given the equipment and laboratory time constraints.

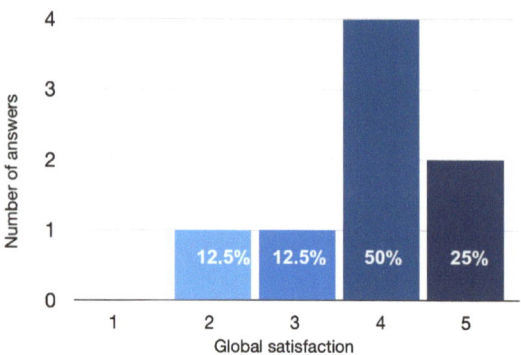

Figure 8. Satisfaction scores (%) regarding laboratory work as a reflection of theoretical content. 75% of the responses mark a high and a very high satisfaction (y axis—number of answers and x axis—global satisfaction rate from 1 to 5).

The laboratory activities were evaluated according to the six possible answers listed in Table 3. The feedback was positive overall for 76% of the students, as depicted in Figure 9a. The students also responded positively regarding the cross−cutting competency of teamwork, as shown in Figure 9b. Note, however, that only a few students completed the section of their reports that required them to discuss their main results and conclusions.

Table 3. Possible answers for practice session feedback.

1. It was badly organized and I didn't learn anything.
2. The idea was good, but it didn't work out well. I learnt something.
3. I worked too hard for the outcome achieved.
4. It was a different working method, but it made me work hard.
5. It was a different working method, and my work was adequate.
6. I liked the experience and it was useful for my learning.

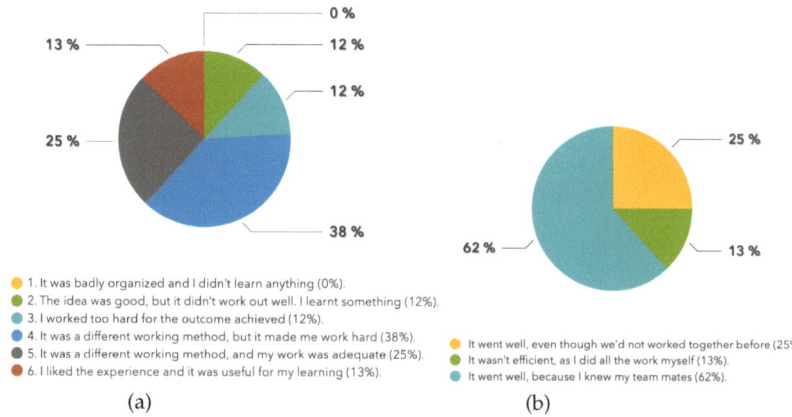

Figure 9. (**a**) Feedback obtained for the final practice session (according to the statements in Table 3). (**b**) Feedback regarding teamwork.

Questionnaires were also issued for each activity to gauge participant satisfaction and feedback focused on variables, such as the experience of assembly and memory analysis, lessons learned, acquired knowledge of digital forensics, and familiarity with other learning tools.

Finally, student opinions were surveyed at the end of the module by means of 20 questions, 17 of which were responded to on a Likert scale, where 0 and 5 represented the lowest/most negative and highest/most positive scores (see Table 4). The 17 questions covered the suitability of the laboratory teaching format, understanding of the course objectives, usefulness of the learning activities, and student opinions as to their capacity to learn and understand content. Additionally, three open-ended questions were posed to collect information that could suggest future improvements: How would you improve the activities? Should additional activities be included in the disk and memory forensic analyses? Do you consider that improvements are needed that enhance learning effectiveness?

Overall, the student responses to the 17 Likert-scored questions suggest that the hands-on laboratory activities were a highly effective method for teaching digital forensics. In their responses to the three open-ended questions, the students proposed additional laboratory sessions, given that "It's not always possible to recover everything, nor it is always possible to determine 100% of the crime based on the evidence retrieved. The larger the volume of files to analyze, the more complex the investigation becomes". The results also suggested a need for improvement in the organizational planning of activities, particularly in addressing challenges related to equipment and alternative methods and tools for forensic analysis. The experiential learning involving teamwork tasks such as data extraction, analysis, and reporting and hands-on tasks (e.g., desoldering complex NAND devices, such as TSOP or BGA), collaborative projects (e.g., resolving a fictional case), and reflective observation enhanced the understanding of concepts and the acquisition of practical digital forensic skills.

Table 4. Final satisfaction survey results. (1 = lowest score; 5 = highest score). Averages were calculated based on response distribution.

Survey Questions	1	2	3	4	5	Average
1. Did the laboratory increase your motivation to learn new content?	0%	0%	9%	63%	28%	4.19
2. Did you receive the necessary guidelines to carry out the laboratory activities?	0%	36%	36%	28%	0%	2.92
3. Did the laboratory activities consolidate your learning?	0%	18%	18%	36%	27%	3.69
4. Did the team work improve your learning?	9%	9%	18%	0%	63%	3.96
5. To what extent did you include a discussion and conclusions in your reports?	9%	0%	45%	27%	9%	2.97
6. To what extent did you include criticisms and final comments in your reports?	9%	9%	45%	27%	9%	3.15
7. Do you feel that the laboratory activities were optimally designed?	0%	0%	18%	27%	54%	4.32
8. Did you like how the course was designed?	0%	18%	45%	36%	0%	3.15
9. Did you like how the course was organized?	9%	18%	45%	18%	9%	2.97
10. Has your understanding of digital forensic techniques improved?	9%	18%	36%	25%	9%	3.06
11. Are reinforcement tasks necessary for the laboratory activities?	18%	0%	36%	18%	27%	3.33
12. Did you feel you needed to work harder with this course?	18%	27%	36%	9%	0%	2.16
13. Was your learning with this course more enjoyable?	0%	9%	9%	54%	27%	3.96
14. Did you find the laboratory practice sessions useful?	0%	9%	27%	54%	9%	3.60
15. Did you feel capable of learning and understanding the content?	0%	18%	18%	27%	36%	3.78
16. Should additional material/equipment be acquired for the activities?	18%	0%	9%	9%	63%	3.96
17. Did the laboratory practice sessions meet your expectations?	0%	27%	63%	27%	9%	3.96

Student laboratory performance was relatively satisfactory (around 7 to 9 out of 10), indicating a good understanding and application of the activities. The few lower scores might suggest a struggle with challenges encountered during assembly experiments, as such activities require precision, attention to detail, and sometimes problem solving under time constraints, as shown during the microSD card data extraction activity.

Finally, the incorporation of experiential learning significantly deepened the understanding of theoretical concepts and equipped the students with the practical skills essential to accurately and confidently perform the experimental activities. In an evaluation based on a multiple-choice theory test (30 questions on a broad range of topics related to static, dynamic, and synchronous memory concepts; NAND memory operations and standards; digital forensics and inspection techniques and procedures such as ChipOff and JTAG; and hardware and electronics, such as Arduino, SD cards, chip desoldering, etc.), the tasks were well aligned with the skills required by the course. The assessment was appropriately challenging, yet accessible, for the majority of the students.

Discussion

The scientific validation of digital forensics methods and the growing complexity of cybercrime require the continuous development of advanced analytical tools, universal procedural standards, enhanced training, and a focus on ethical considerations [57]. Digital forensic laboratories face challenges encompassing technical, procedural, and organizational aspects of forensic analysis, given, in addition to overwhelming data volumes, the complexities of mobile devices, issues in standardization, legal ambiguities, and budget constraints [58]. Further hindering investigations is the need for skilled personnel to conduct advanced JTAG and chip-off analyses and the time required for forensic imaging of high-volume storage media. The development of 3D NAND memories and 5-bit cells allow for even greater device storage expansion, and this increase in data volumes poses a further challenge for forensic analysis.

Recent tools such as OFD, EnCase, Cellebrite Inseyets, Autopsy, and PKF have incorporated methods to expedite functions, such as preliminary content visualization that avoids exhaustive extractions (OFD and Cellebrite), or specific search approaches (Autopsy and BXF). EnCase employs artificial intelligence and machine learning to optimize file classification, and PKF has introduced resource managers and GPU acceleration. Overall, the analyzed tools have broadly similar functions; most allow for HEX viewing of image content but not Toolsley and PKF. PKF acquires relevant data but yields reports with limited information, potentially making the extra cost unnecessary.

Outcomes in terms of skills development and learning for the undergraduate students who engaged in experimental digital forensic activities were broadly positive. The fact that the tasks often involved real-world problem solving ensured a rich educational environment involving teamwork. The experimental activities resulted in the successful acquisition and analysis of forensic images from NAND chips using suitable tools and data extraction and evaluation using JTAG and chip-off techniques. Easy JTAG Plus was used to produce compatible forensic images with different tools, although skipping the physical chip extraction step overlooked the true challenge of this acquisition method. Overall, the hands-on lab activities and course projects fostered the kind of problem-solving and analytical skills in students that are fundamental to digital forensic investigations.

Despite limitations of being based on a small sample and being conducted in a specific educational setting, this study offers valuable preliminary insights into the effectiveness of experiential learning for digital forensics. The findings, however, should be interpreted with care and be validated through further research with a larger number of students. Qualitative data, such as student feedback and detailed case studies, could also provide important insights into the broader impact of the teaching methods. Furthermore, prospective studies that follow students over multiple semesters or years will increase the sample size and also provide insights into the long-term impact of the teaching methods.

5. Conclusions

Digital evidence is becoming increasingly relevant due to exponential growth in all the technological sciences, rendering precise digital forensics knowledge crucial. This review of tools and data extraction procedures covered highly comprehensive tools that are widely used in forensic investigations. Nevertheless, while those tools may indeed be useful, consolidating analyses performed by multiple tools could potentially enhance evidence reliability.

Instructors can usefully deploy experiential learning in the design of digital forensic laboratory experiences. Collaborative hands-on activities can dynamically and engagingly consolidate student knowledge and understanding of digital forensics, as demonstrated for the criminalistics undergraduate degree offered by the University of Alcalá, where outcomes were positive in terms of enhancing student skills and their understanding of real-world investigative processes.

Overall, incorporating experimental activities in digital forensics training not only enhances educational outcomes but also contributes to advancing practices and addressing challenges in the forensics field. Planned for future research is an evaluation of the capabilities of the studied tools in handling encrypted and/or explicit data, as such data frequently arise in criminal cases. Future research will also be conducted with a larger sample by more students or through collaborative online international learning (COIL) activities with other institutions.

Funding: Meriting special mention is the Erasmus+ project DECEL-Digital Electronics Collaborative Enhanced Learning (2021-1-ES01-KA220-HED-000032189).

Institutional Review Board Statement: The study was conducted in accordance with the Declaration of Helsinki, and approved by the or Ethics Committee of University of Alcalá and date of approval 25 October 2024.

Informed Consent Statement: Informed consent was obtained from all subjects involved in the study.

Data Availability Statement: Data are contained within the article.

Conflicts of Interest: The author declares no conflicts of interest.

Abbreviations

The following computer-related acronyms and abbreviations are used in this manuscript:

3D	Three dimensional
ATF	Advanced Turbo Flasher
BGA	Ball Grid Array
BXF	Belkasoft X Forensic
eMMC	Embedded Multi-Media Card
EnCase	OpenText EnCase Forensic
FTK-IL	Forensic Tool Kit Imager Lite
GPU	Graphics Processing Unit
HEX	Hexadecimal
HTML	HyperText Markup Language
JTAG	Joint Test Action Group
KML	Keyhole Markup Language
NAND	Not AND
OFD	Oxygen Forensic Detective
OS	Operating System
PCB	Printed Circuit Board
PKF	Passware Kit Forensic
RAM	Random-Access Memory
ROM	Read-Only Memory
SD	Secure Digital
SIFT	SANS Investigative Forensic Toolkit
SIM	Subscriber Identity Module
SSD	Solid-State Drive
TAP	Test Access Point
TSOP	Thin Small Outline Package

	UFED	Universal Forensics Extraction Device
	USB	Universal Serial Bus

References

1. Beebe, N. Digital Forensic Research: The Good, the Bad and the Unaddressed. In *IFIP Advances in Information and Communication Technology*; Springer: New York, NY, USA, 2009; pp. 17–36. [CrossRef]
2. Malik, A.; Bhatti, D.; Park, T.; Ishtiaq, H.; Ryou, J.; Kim, K. Cloud Digital Forensics: Beyond tools, techniques, and challenges. *Sensors* **2024**, *24*, 433. [CrossRef] [PubMed]
3. Pollitt, M. A history of digital forensics. In *IFIP Advances in Information and Communication Technology*; Springer: New York, NY, USA, 2010; pp. 3–15. [CrossRef]
4. Armoogum, S.; Khonje, P.; Li, X. *Digital Forensics of Cyber Physical Systems and the Internet of Things*; CRC Press eBooks: Boca Raton, FL, USA, 2021; pp. 117–148. [CrossRef]
5. Nizami, S.M. Introduction to digital forensics and commonly used technologies. *Int. J. Electron. Crime Investig.* **2018**, *2*, 8. [CrossRef]
6. Tamma, R.; Skulkin, O.; Mahalik, H.; Bommisetty, S. *Practical Mobile Forensics*, 3rd ed.; O'Reilly Online Learning: Sebastopol, CA, USA, 2018.
7. Sindhu, K.; Meshram, B. Digital Forensic Investigation Tools and Procedures. *Int. J. Comput. Netw. Inf. Secur.* **2012**, *4*, 39–48. [CrossRef]
8. Reith, M.; Carr, C.; Gunsch, G. An examination of digital forensic models. *Int. J. Digit. Evid.* **2002**, *1*, 3.
9. Fagbola, F.; Venter, H. Smart Digital Forensic Readiness model for shadow IoT devices. *Appl. Sci.* **2022**, *12*, 730. [CrossRef]
10. Hawthorne, E.; Shumba, R. Teaching digital forensics and cyber investigations online: Our experiences. *Eur. Sci. J. ESJ* **2014**, *10*, 3986.
11. Kumar, M. Mobile phone forensics—A systematic approach, tools, techniques and challenges. *Int. J. Electron. Secur. Digit. Forensics* **2021**, *13*, 64. [CrossRef]
12. Infosecinstitute. 2024. Available online: https://www.infosecinstitute.com/resources/digital-forensics/common-mobile-forensics-tools-techniques/ (accessed on 25 November 2024).
13. Sumuri. Sumuri Eclipse 3 Kit. 2024. Available online: https://sumuri.com/product/eclipse-3-kit/ (accessed on 18 March 2024).
14. Oxygenforensics. Oxygen Forensics Website. 2024. Available online: https://oxygenforensics.com/en/ (accessed on 18 March 2024).
15. Razdan, V. Chip-Off Technique in Mobile Forensics. *Acad. J. Forensic Sci.* **2022**, *5*, 49–52.
16. Savoldi, A.; Gubian, P. Data Recovery from Windows CE Based Handheld Devices. In *Advances in Digital Forensics IV*; Springer: New York, NY, USA, 2008; Volume 285, pp. 219–230. [CrossRef]
17. Wang, P.; Rosenberg, M.; D'Cruze, H. Integration of mobile forensic tool capabilities. In *Information Technology—New Generations*; Springer: New York, NY, USA, 2018; Volume 738, pp. 81–87. [CrossRef]
18. da Silveira, C.M.; de Sousa, R.T., Jr.; de Oliveira Albuquerque, R.; Amvame Nze, G.D.; De Oliveira Júnior, G.A.; Sandoval Orozco, A.L.; García Villalba, L.J. Methodology for Forensics Data Reconstruction on Mobile Devices with Android Operating System Applying In-System Programming and Combination Firmware. *Appl. Sci.* **2020**, *10*, 4231. [CrossRef]
19. Forensics, O. Oxygen Forensic Detective Release Notes 16.2. 2024. Available online: https://oxygenforensics.com/uploads/press_kit/OFDv162ReleaseNotes.pdf (accessed on 18 March 2024).
20. Opentext. Opentext EnCase Forensic. 2024. Available online: https://www.opentext.com/file_source/OpenText/en_US/PDF/opentext-po-encase-forensic-en.pdf (accessed on 20 March 2024).
21. Ahmed Alyas, A.; Kumar, V. Lawfully Data Collection Techniques in Mobile Forensic & Analysis Using Cellebrite Physical Analyzer. 2023. Available online: https://papers.ssrn.com/sol3/papers.cfm?abstract_id=4483864 (accessed on 24 March 2024).
22. Caballero, M.; Cilleros Serrano, D. *Análisis Forense*; Anaya Multimedia: Madrid, Spain, 2022; pp. 692–711.
23. Cellebrite. Cellebrite Inseyets. 2024. Available online: https://cellebrite.com/en/cellebrite-inseyets (accessed on 20 March 2024).
24. Passware. Passware Kit Forensic. 2024. Available online: https://www.passware.com/files/passware_kit_forensic_datasheet.pdf (accessed on 20 March 2024).
25. Azam, H.; Dulloo, M.; Majeed, M.; Wan, J.; Xin, L.; Sindiramutty, S. Cybercrime Unmasked: Investigating cases and digital evidence. *Int. J. Emerg. Multidiscip. Comput. Sci. Artif. Intell.* **2023**, *2*, 1. [CrossRef]
26. Belkasoft. Belkasoft X Forensic. 2024. Available online: https://belkasoft.com/x (accessed on 18 March 2024).
27. SANS. SIFT Workstation. 2024. Available online: https://www.sans.org/tools/sift-workstation/ (accessed on 20 March 2024).
28. Labs, S.K. Autopsy—Digital Forensics. 2024. Available online: https://www.autopsy.com/ (accessed on 21 March 2024).
29. Toolsley. Browser tools for the modern web. 2016. Available online: https://www.toolsley.com/ (accessed on 20 March 2024).
30. Exterro. Create Forensic Images with Exterro FTK Imager. 2024. Available online: https://www.exterro.com/digital-forensics-software/ftk-imager (accessed on 18 March 2024).
31. Parth, C.; Tamanna, J.; Kumar, A. Comparative analysis of mobile forensic proprietary tools: An application in forensic investigation. *J. Forensic Sci. Res.* **2022**, *6*, 77–82. [CrossRef]
32. Tara, H.; Mishra, A. A comparative study of digital forensic tools for data extraction from electronic devices. *J. Punjab Acad. Forensic Med. Toxicol.* **2021**, *21*, 97–104. [CrossRef]

33. Riadi, I.; Yudhana, A.; Inngam Ganani, G. Comparative Analysis of Forensic Software on Android-based MiChat. *J. Resti* **2023**, *7*, 86–292. [CrossRef]
34. Dogan, S.; Akbal, E. Analysis of mobile phones in digital forensics. In Proceedings of the 2017 40th International Convention on Information and Communication Technology, Electronics and Microelectronics (MIPRO), Opatija, Croatia, 22–26 May 2017; pp. 1241–1244. [CrossRef]
35. Waluyo, A.; Cahyono, M.; Mahfud, A. Digital forensic analysis on caller ID spoofing attack. In Proceedings of the International Workshop on Big Data and Information Security (IWBIS), Depok, Indonesia, 1–3 October 2022; pp. 95–100. [CrossRef]
36. Shortall, A.; Azhar, M. Forensic acquisitions of WhatsApp data on popular mobile platforms. In Proceedings of the International Conference on Emerging Security Technologies (EST), Washington, DC, USA, 3–5 September 2015; pp. 13–17. [CrossRef]
37. Chamberlain, A.; Hannan Bin Azhar, M. Comparisons of Forensic Tools to Recover Ephemeral Data from iOS Apps Used for Cyberbullying. In Proceedings of the 4th International Conference on Cyber-Technologies and Cyber-Systems (CYBER 2019), Porto, Portugal, 22–26 September 2019; pp. 22–26.
38. Singh, S.; Singh, V. *Digital Forensic Investigation: Ontology, Methodology, and Technological Advancement*; Apple Academic Press: Cambridge, MA, USA, 2023; pp. 137–160.
39. Alexander, B. Evaluation of Open-Source & Proprietary Forensic Software Tools. *Comput. Forensics* **2022**. [CrossRef]
40. Moric, Z.; Redzepagic, J.; Gatti, F. Enterprise Tools for Data Forensics 2021. In Proceedings of the DAAAM International Symposium, Vienna, Austria, 28–29 October 2021; pp. 98–105.
41. Rehman Javed, A.; Ahmed, W.; Alazab, M.; Jalil, Z.; Kifayat, K.; Gadekallu, T. A comprehensive survey on computer forensics: State-of-the-Art, tools, techniques, challenges, and future directions. *IEEE Access* **2022**, *10*, 11065–11089. [CrossRef]
42. Padmanabhan, R.; Lobo, K.; Ghelani, M.; Sujan, D.; Shirole, M. Comparative analysis of commercial and open source mobile device forensic tools. In Proceedings of the International Conference on Contemporary Computing (IC3), Noida, India, 11–13 August 2016; pp. 1–6. [CrossRef]
43. Dyson, J.; Zargari, S. Memory Forensics. *Lat. Am. J. Comput.* **2022**, *9*, 36–51.
44. Parekh, M.; Jani, S. Memory forensic: Acquisition and analysis of memory and its tools comparison. *Commun. Integr. Netw. Signal Process.* **2018**, *5*, 90–95. [CrossRef]
45. Al-Sabaawi, A. Digital forensics for infected computer disk and memory: Acquire, analyse, and report. In Proceedings of the IEEE Asia-Pacific Conference on Computer Science and Data Engineering (CSDE), Gold Coast, QLD, Australia, 16–18 December 2020. [CrossRef]
46. Dubey, H.; Bhatt, S.; Negi, L. Digital Forensics Techniques and Trends: A Review. *Int. Arab. J. Inf. Technol.* **2023**, *20*, 644–654. [CrossRef]
47. Casino, F.; Dasaklis, T.; Spathoulas, G.; Anagnostopoulos, M.; Ghosal, A.; Borocz, I.; Patsakis, C. Research trends, challenges, and emerging topics in digital forensics: A review of reviews. *IEEE Access* **2022**, *10*, 25464–25493. [CrossRef]
48. Johnson, C.; Davies, R.; Reddy, M. Using digital forensics in higher education to detect academic misconduct. *Int. J. Educ. Integr.* **2022**, *18*, 12. [CrossRef]
49. Palmer, I.; Wood, E.; Nagy, S.; Garcia, G.; Bashir, M.; Campbell, R. Digital Forensics Education: A Multidisciplinary Curriculum Model. In Proceedings of the International Conference on Digital Forensics and Cyber Crime, Seoul, Republic of Korea, 6–8 October 2015; pp. 3–15. [CrossRef]
50. Flores, R.; Namin, A.; Tavakoli, N.; Siami-Namini, S.; Jones, K. Using experiential learning to teach and learn digital forensics: Educator and student perspectives. *Comput. Educ. Open* **2021**, *2*, 100045. [CrossRef]
51. Leung, W.; Blauw, F. An augmented reality approach to delivering a connected digital forensics training experience. In Proceedings of the Information Science and Applications: ICISA 2019, Singapore, 16–18 December 2019; Volume 621, pp. 353–361. [CrossRef]
52. Lewis, L.; Williams, C. Experiential learning: Past and present. *New Dir. Adult Contin. Educ.* **1994**, *62*, 5–16. [CrossRef]
53. Ho, S.; Hsu, Y.; Lai, C.; Chen, F.; Yang, M. Applying Game-Based Experiential Learning to Comprehensive Sustainable Development-Based Education. *Sustainability* **2022**, *14*, 1172. [CrossRef]
54. Gentry, J. *What is Experiential Learning*; Nichols Pub. Co.: New York, NY, USA, 1990; Volume 9, p. 20.
55. Morris, T. Experiential learning–a systematic review and revision of Kolb's model. *Interact. Learn. Environ.* **2020**, *28*, 1064–1077. [CrossRef]
56. University of Alcalá. *Teaching Guide of Electronic Forensic*; University of Alcalá: Madrid, Spain, 2024.
57. Raza, S.; Anwar, A.; Khan, A. Current Issues and Challenges with Scientific Validation of Digital Evidence. *Rev. Comput. Eng. Stud.* **2022**, *9*, 111–115. [CrossRef]
58. Fakhouri, H.; AlSharaiah, M.; Alkalaileh, M.; Dweikat, F. Overview of Challenges Faced by Digital Forensic. In Proceedings of the International Conference on Cyber Resilience (ICCR), Dubai, United Arab Emirates, 26–28 February 2024; pp. 1–8. [CrossRef]

Disclaimer/Publisher's Note: The statements, opinions and data contained in all publications are solely those of the individual author(s) and contributor(s) and not of MDPI and/or the editor(s). MDPI and/or the editor(s) disclaim responsibility for any injury to people or property resulting from any ideas, methods, instructions or products referred to in the content.

Article

Temporal Convolutional Network for Carbon Tax Projection: A Data-Driven Approach

Jiaying Chen [1], Yiwen Cui [2], Xinguang Zhang [3], Jingyun Yang [4] and Mengjie Zhou [5,*]

1. SC Johnson Graduate School of Management, Cornell University, Ithaca, NY 10022, USA; jc2744@cornell.edu
2. McCallum Graduate School of Business, Bentley University, Waltham, MA 02452, USA; cui_yiwe@bentley.edu
3. The Erik Jonsson School of Engineering and Computer Science, The University of Texas at Dallas, Richardson, TX 75080, USA; xinguang.zhang@ieee.org
4. David A. Tepper School of Business, Carnegie Mellon University, Pittsburgh, PA 15213, USA; claudey@alumni.cmu.edu
5. Department of Computer Science, University of Bristol, Bristol BS8 1QU, UK
* Correspondence: ix18497@bristol.ac.uk

Citation: Chen, J.; Cui, Y.; Zhang, X.; Yang, J.; Zhou, M. Temporal Convolutional Network for Carbon Tax Projection: A Data-Driven Approach. *Appl. Sci.* **2024**, *14*, 9213. https://doi.org/10.3390/app14209213

Academic Editor: Luis Javier Garcia Villalba

Received: 18 September 2024
Revised: 4 October 2024
Accepted: 9 October 2024
Published: 10 October 2024

Copyright: © 2024 by the authors. Licensee MDPI, Basel, Switzerland. This article is an open access article distributed under the terms and conditions of the Creative Commons Attribution (CC BY) license (https:// creativecommons.org/licenses/by/ 4.0/).

Abstract: This study introduces a novel application of a temporal convolutional network (TCN) for projecting carbon tax prices, addressing the critical need for accurate forecasting in climate policy. Utilizing data from the World Carbon Pricing Database, we demonstrate that the TCN significantly outperformed traditional time series models in capturing the complex dynamics of carbon pricing. Our model achieved a 31.4% improvement in mean absolute error over ARIMA baselines, with an MAE of 2.43 compared to 3.54 for ARIMA. The TCN model also showed superior performance across different time horizons, demonstrating a 30.0% lower MAE for 1-year projections, and enhanced adaptability to policy changes, with only a 39.8% increase in prediction error after major shifts, compared to ARIMA's 95.6%. These results underscore the potential of deep learning for enhancing the precision of carbon price projections, thereby supporting more informed and effective climate policy decisions. Our findings have significant implications for policymakers and stakeholders in the realm of carbon pricing and climate change mitigation strategies, offering a powerful tool for navigating the complex landscape of environmental economics.

Keywords: carbon pricing; data analytics; temporal convolutional network; climate policy; time series forecasting

1. Introduction

Carbon taxation has emerged as a pivotal instrument in the global effort to mitigate greenhouse gas emissions and combat climate change. As emphasized by the Environmental Defense Fund and the Carbon Pricing Leadership Coalition, the effective implementation of carbon taxes necessitates clear objectives, stakeholder engagement, and regular monitoring [1,2]. Central to this process is the accurate projection of carbon tax prices, which enables governments and businesses to anticipate future costs and make informed strategic decisions [3].

The importance of carbon pricing to climate policy cannot be overstated. As nations worldwide grapple with the urgent need to reduce greenhouse gas emissions, carbon taxes have proven to be an effective market-based mechanism to incentivize the transition to cleaner energy sources and more sustainable practices [4]. However, the effectiveness of carbon pricing policies heavily relies on the ability to accurately forecast future carbon prices, a task that has proven challenging, due to a complex interplay of economic, political, and environmental factors [5].

Carbon taxes operate on the principle of internalizing the external costs of carbon emissions, thereby aligning market prices with the true social cost of carbon-intensive activities. By putting a price on carbon emissions, these taxes create a financial incentive for businesses and consumers to reduce their carbon footprint. This can drive innovation in clean technologies, encourage energy efficiency, and promote the adoption of renewable energy sources. However, the optimal level of carbon taxation remains a subject of debate, with economists and policymakers grappling with the challenge of balancing environmental goals with economic considerations.

The dynamic nature of carbon pricing adds another layer of complexity to the forecasting challenge. Carbon tax rates are often subject to periodic adjustments based on factors such as emission reduction targets, economic conditions, and technological advancements. These adjustments can lead to significant fluctuations in carbon prices over time, making accurate long-term projections particularly challenging. Moreover, the global landscape of carbon pricing is diverse, with different countries and regions adopting varying approaches and tax rates, further complicating the task of developing a unified forecasting model.

Traditional methods of time series forecasting, such as autoregressive integrated moving average (ARIMA) models, have been widely used in economic and financial predictions. However, these methods often struggle to capture the complex, non-linear relationships inherent in carbon pricing dynamics. They may fail to account for sudden policy shifts, technological breakthroughs, or global economic shocks that can significantly impact carbon prices. This limitation underscores the need for more sophisticated forecasting techniques that can adapt to the unique challenges posed by carbon tax price projection.

Building upon existing research on carbon tax effectiveness [6] and the rationale behind carbon pricing policies [7], this paper introduces an innovative application of deep learning to the challenge of carbon tax price projection. Specifically, we employ a temporal convolutional network (TCN), a state-of-the-art deep learning architecture, to forecast carbon tax prices with unprecedented accuracy. TCNs have shown remarkable performance in various sequence modeling tasks, offering advantages such as parallel processing, flexible receptive fields, and a stable gradient flow.

Our approach was motivated by a need to address the limitations of traditional forecasting methods in capturing the complex, non-linear dynamics of carbon pricing. By leveraging the power of TCNs, we aim to provide a more robust and accurate tool for policymakers and stakeholders for the development of effective carbon pricing strategies. The ability to project carbon tax prices with greater precision can significantly enhance the design and implementation of climate policies, allowing for more targeted interventions and better-informed decision-making.

The contributions of this study are threefold:

1. We introduce a novel application of a TCN to the domain of carbon tax price projection, demonstrating its superior performance over traditional forecasting methods.

2. We provide a comprehensive analysis of the model's performance across different time horizons and its adaptability to policy changes, offering insights into the robustness of our approach.

3. We conduct a feature importance analysis, shedding light on the relative impact of various economic and environmental factors on carbon tax price dynamics.

The rest of this paper is organized as follows: Section 2 provides an overview of related work on carbon pricing and deep learning for time series forecasting. Section 3 describes our data and methodology, including the TCN model architecture. Section 4 presents our experimental results and discussion. Finally, Section 5 concludes the paper and outlines directions for future research.

2. Related Work

2.1. Carbon Pricing and Policy Effectiveness

The effectiveness of carbon pricing policies has been extensively researched in recent years. Martin et al. [6] demonstrated that carbon taxes significantly reduced energy intensity and electricity consumption in UK manufacturing plants, without adversely affecting employment or plant exit rates. Their quasi-experimental study found that a GBP 1 increase in carbon tax led to a 2.6% reduction in energy intensity, highlighting the tangible impact of carbon pricing on industrial behavior. Baranzini et al. [7] provided a concise analysis of carbon pricing policies, emphasizing their role in reflecting full environmental costs, reducing pollution control costs, and promoting low-emission technologies. They argued that carbon pricing offers advantages over command-and-control regulations by providing a consistent price signal across all economic sectors, potentially achieving emission reductions at a lower overall cost to society. While these studies underscored the importance of carbon pricing in climate policy, our work focuses on improving the accuracy of carbon tax price projections using advanced machine learning techniques, specifically temporal convolutional networks (TCNs).

2.2. Challenges in Carbon Pricing Implementation

Despite the theoretical benefits of carbon pricing, its implementation has faced various challenges. Carattini et al. [8] examined the political economy of carbon taxes, highlighting the importance of policy design in gaining public acceptance. Their research suggested that gradually increasing tax rates, providing clear information about the environmental and economic impacts, and earmarking revenues for environmental projects can help overcome public resistance to carbon taxes.

The issue of carbon leakage, where carbon-intensive industries relocate to jurisdictions with less stringent regulations, has also been a concern in carbon pricing discussions. Naegele and Zaklan [9] investigated this phenomenon in the context of the European Union Emissions Trading System (EU ETS). Their findings indicated that while there is limited evidence of carbon leakage in practice, the fear of competitive disadvantages continues to shape policy decisions and often leads to exemptions or free allowances for certain industries. In fact, there have been many discussions on carbon tax pricing mechanisms and their influence in different countries [10–13].

2.3. Forecasting in Carbon Markets

Accurate forecasting in carbon markets has been recognized as a critical challenge by researchers and policymakers alike. Zhu et al. [14] explored various forecasting methods for carbon prices in the European Union Emissions Trading System (EU ETS), highlighting the complexity of the task due to the influence of policy changes, economic conditions, and energy prices on carbon markets.

Their study compared the performance of machine learning techniques, including support vector regression and random forests, with traditional econometric models. The results indicated that machine learning approaches generally outperformed traditional methods, particularly in capturing non-linear relationships and handling high-dimensional data. However, the authors also noted the importance of feature selection and model interpretability in the practical application of these techniques.

Pao et al. [15] proposed a hybrid forecasting approach combining machine learning techniques with traditional time series models to predict carbon prices. Their work demonstrated the potential of advanced computational methods in improving forecasting accuracy in volatile carbon markets. The hybrid model, which integrated a generalized regression neural network with an autoregressive integrated moving average model, showed superior performance in both short-term and long-term forecasting scenarios.

These studies highlight the growing interest in applying advanced computational techniques to the challenge of carbon price forecasting. However, they also underscore the need for models that can adapt to the unique characteristics of carbon markets, including policy-driven price changes and complex interdependencies with other economic and environmental factors.

2.4. Deep Learning for Time Series Forecasting

The application of deep learning techniques to time series forecasting has gained significant traction in recent years. Bai et al. [16] introduced the temporal convolutional network architecture, demonstrating its effectiveness in sequence modeling tasks across various domains. Their work showed that TCNs could outperform traditional recurrent neural networks in many sequence modeling tasks, while offering better parallelism and more stable gradients.

The TCN architecture addresses several limitations of traditional recurrent neural networks (RNNs) and long short-term memory (LSTM) networks. By using dilated causal convolutions, TCNs can efficiently capture long-range dependencies in the input sequence, without the vanishing gradient problems often associated with RNNs. Moreover, the convolutional structure allows for parallel processing of inputs, leading to faster training and inference times.

Borovykh et al. [17] applied convolutional neural networks to financial time series forecasting, showcasing the potential of these architectures for capturing complex temporal dependencies in financial data. Their work provides a foundation for applying similar techniques to carbon price forecasting, given the financial nature of carbon markets.

The authors demonstrated that convolutional neural networks (CNNs) could effectively capture both short-term and long-term patterns in financial time series data. By treating the time series as a one-dimensional image, the CNN could learn hierarchical features that represent different temporal scales. This approach showed promising results in predicting stock prices and volatility, outperforming traditional time series models in many scenarios.

In the context of environmental and energy-related forecasting, Wen et al. [18] applied deep learning techniques to predict wind power generation. Their study compared various deep learning architectures, including CNN, LSTM, and hybrid models, demonstrating the potential of these approaches in handling the complex, non-linear relationships inherent in renewable energy forecasting.

Our study builds upon these foundations, leveraging the strengths of TCNs in capturing long-range dependencies and handling non-linear relationships to improve the accuracy of carbon tax price projections. By adapting the TCN architecture to the specific challenges of carbon pricing, we aim to provide a more robust and accurate forecasting tool for policymakers and stakeholders in the carbon market.

3. Data and Methodology

3.1. Data

We utilized the World Carbon Pricing Database [19], which offers comprehensive information on global carbon pricing initiatives. This dataset encompasses historical carbon prices, emissions data, and relevant economic indicators for various countries and regions. Our analysis focused on a subset of 30 countries with established carbon tax systems, covering the period from 2000 to 2022.

The dataset includes the following key features: (1) carbon tax prices (in USD per tCO_2e); (2) CO_2 emissions (in million metric tons); (3) GDP (in billion USD); (4) energy consumption (in quadrillion BTU); and (5) renewable energy share (as a percentage of total energy consumption).

The World Carbon Pricing Database is a valuable resource for researchers and policymakers, providing a standardized and comprehensive collection of carbon pricing data across different jurisdictions. It includes information on both carbon taxes and emissions trading systems, allowing for comparative analyses of different carbon pricing approaches. The database is regularly updated to reflect the latest policy changes and price adjustments, ensuring the relevance and accuracy of the data.

We preprocessed the data by normalizing all features to a common scale and handling missing values through interpolation. The time series data were then structured into input–output pairs, where each input consisted of a 5-year historical window, and the output was the carbon tax price for the subsequent year. This sliding window approach allowed the model to capture both short-term fluctuations and longer-term trends in carbon pricing dynamics.

It is important to acknowledge the limitations and challenges associated with our dataset. Carbon pricing varies widely between countries, and the availability and quality of data can differ significantly. To address these issues, we employed the following strategies: (1) Missing data handling: Where short gaps in time series data were present, we used linear interpolation to estimate missing values. For longer periods of missing data, we applied multiple imputation techniques, specifically using the multivariate imputation by chained equations (MICE) algorithm. This approach allowed us to maintain the temporal structure of the data, while minimizing bias. (2) Data quality assessment: We conducted thorough quality checks on the data, identifying and investigating outliers using the interquartile range (IQR) method. Outliers were either removed if deemed erroneous or retained if they represented genuine extreme events, with appropriate documentation. (3) Cross-country comparability: To ensure comparability across different countries, we normalized all monetary values to USD using historical exchange rates. Additionally, we applied purchasing power parity (PPP) adjustments to account for differences in the cost of living and inflation rates across countries. (4) Potential biases: We acknowledge that our dataset may be subject to reporting biases, particularly in countries with less developed carbon pricing systems. To mitigate this, we focused our analysis on countries with established carbon tax systems and reliable reporting mechanisms. However, this may limit the generalizability of our findings to countries with nascent carbon pricing policies. (5) Temporal coverage: The dataset covers the period from 2000 to 2022, which may not capture very recent policy changes or long-term historical trends. We addressed this limitation by focusing our analysis on medium-term projections and explicitly noting when recent policy shifts may have impacted our model's performance. By implementing these strategies, we aimed to minimize the impact of data limitations and potential biases on our analysis. However, we acknowledge that these challenges are inherent to cross-country studies of carbon pricing, and our results should be interpreted with these limitations in mind.

3.2. Autoregressive Integrated Moving Average Model

The ARIMA model is a classical time series forecasting method that combines autoregressive (AR), differencing (I), and moving average (MA) components. The model is typically denoted as ARIMA(p,d,q), where

- p is the order of the autoregressive term
- d is the degree of differencing
- q is the order of the moving average term

The ARIMA model can be expressed mathematically as

$$\phi(B)(1-B)^d y_t = \theta(B)\epsilon_t \tag{1}$$

where B is the backshift operator, $\phi(B)$ is the AR operator, $\theta(B)$ is the MA operator, and ϵ_t is white noise. For our analysis, we used the auto.arima function from the forecast package in R to automatically select the optimal p, d, and q parameters based on the Akaike information criterion (AIC). The selected model for each country was then used to generate forecasts for comparison with the TCN model.

3.3. Temporal Convolutional Network

Our choice of the TCN model for carbon tax price projection was informed by recent advancements in time series forecasting techniques. While traditional methods have been widely used [20], there is a growing body of literature exploring the application of machine learning techniques to environmental and energy-related forecasting problems [21,22]. TCNs represent a class of deep learning models specifically designed for sequence modeling tasks. They offer several advantages over traditional recurrent architectures: Parallelism: TCNs allow for parallel processing of inputs, leading to faster training and inference times. This is particularly beneficial when dealing with large datasets or when real-time predictions are required. Flexible receptive field: Through dilated convolutions, TCNs can efficiently capture long-range dependencies. This allows the model to consider both recent and distant past information when making predictions. Stable gradients: The convolutional structure mitigates the vanishing gradient problem common in recurrent networks, allowing for more effective training of deep architectures. Constant memory usage: Unlike recurrent neural networks, a TCN's memory usage does not grow with the length of the input sequence, making it more suitable for processing long time series.

Our TCN model architecture consists of the following components: Input layer: accepts a sequence of historical carbon prices and related features. The input shape is (batch_size, sequence_length, n_features), where the sequence length is 5 years of monthly data (60 time steps) and n_features is the number of input variables.

Dilated causal convolutional layers: a stack of 1D convolutional layers with increasing dilation rates. We use 4 layers with dilation rates of 1, 2, 4, and 8, allowing the model to capture dependencies over a wide range of time scales. Each layer uses 64 filters with a kernel size of 3.

Residual connections: to facilitate gradient flow and enable deeper network training. Each convolutional layer is wrapped in a residual block, which adds the input to the layer's output. This helps in training very deep networks by allowing gradients to flow directly through the network.

Normalization and activation: After each convolutional layer, we apply layer normalization followed by a ReLU activation function. This helps in stabilizing the training process and introduces non-linearity into the model.

Dropout: To prevent overfitting, we apply dropout with a rate of 0.2 after each convolutional layer.

Output layer: a dense layer producing the projected carbon tax price for the next time step.

The mathematical formulation of the dilated causal convolution used in our TCN model can be expressed as

$$F(s) = (x *_d f)(s) = \sum_{i=0}^{k-1} f(i) \cdot x_{s-d \cdot i} \qquad (2)$$

where x is the input sequence, f is the filter, k is the filter size, d is the dilation factor, and s is the current time step.

The model was trained to minimize the mean squared error between predicted and actual carbon tax prices. We used the Adam optimizer with a learning rate of 0.001 and trained for 100 epochs with early stopping based on validation loss. The learning rate was reduced by a factor of 0.5 if the validation loss did not improve for 10 consecutive epochs.

3.4. Experimental Setup

We compared the performance of the TCN model (described in Section 3.3) with the ARIMA model (described in Section 3.2) across different evaluation metrics and time horizons. We split our data into training (70%), validation (15%), and test (15%) sets. The split was performed chronologically, to maintain the temporal structure of the data, with the most recent observations reserved for testing. This approach ensured that we evaluated the model's performance on truly unseen data, simulating a real-world forecasting scenario.

The TCN model was trained to predict carbon tax prices for the next year based on historical data from the previous five years. We used the mean absolute error (MAE) and root mean squared error (RMSE) as evaluation metrics. These metrics are defined as

$$MAE = \frac{1}{n} \sum_{i=1}^{n} |y_i - \hat{y}_i| \qquad (3)$$

$$RMSE = \sqrt{\frac{1}{n}\sum_{i=1}^{n}(y_i - \hat{y}_i)^2} \quad (4)$$

where y_i is the actual carbon tax price and $\hat{y}_i$ is the predicted price.

For comparison, we implemented the ARIMA model [20] as a baseline, representing traditional time series forecasting approaches. The ARIMA model's parameters (p, d, q) were selected using the Akaike information criterion (AIC) for each country in our dataset. We used a grid search approach to find the optimal parameters, considering values of p and q up to 5, and d up to 2.

To ensure the robustness of our results, we performed 5-fold cross-validation, reporting the average performance metrics across all folds. This approach helped to mitigate the impact of data partitioning on the model performance and provided a more reliable estimate of the model's generalization ability.

Additionally, we conducted a sensitivity analysis to assess the impact of different hyperparameters on the TCN model's performance. We explored the following hyperparameter ranges:

- Number of convolutional layers: 2 to 6
- Number of filters per layer: 32 to 128
- Kernel size: 2 to 5
- Dilation rates: various exponential schemes (e.g., [1, 2, 4, 8], [1, 2, 4, 8, 16])
- Dropout rate: 0.1 to 0.5

The sensitivity analysis was performed using random search, with 100 iterations. This allowed us to efficiently explore the hyperparameter space and identify the most influential parameters for model performance.

3.5. Feature Importance Analysis

To gain insights into the relative importance of different input features in predicting carbon tax prices, we employed a permutation importance technique. This method involved randomly shuffling the values of each input feature and measuring the resulting decrease in model performance. The rationale behind this approach is that shuffling an important feature will lead to a significant drop in model accuracy, while shuffling an unimportant feature will have little impact.

The permutation importance score for each feature was calculated as follows:

$$I_j = \frac{1}{N}\sum_{i=1}^{N}(L(y, \hat{y}_{\pi j}) - L(y, \hat{y})) \quad (5)$$

where I_j is the importance score for feature j, L is the loss function (in our case, MSE), y is the true target values, $\hat{y}$ is the model's predictions on the original data, and $\hat{y}_{\pi j}$ is the model's predictions after permuting feature j. N is the number of permutations (we used $N = 10$ in our experiments).

This analysis provided valuable insights into the factors driving carbon tax price dynamics and can inform policymakers about the key variables to consider when designing and adjusting carbon pricing policies.

4. Results and Discussion

4.1. Overview of Study Countries and Model Parameters

To provide a comprehensive overview of our study, Table 1 presents the 30 countries included in our analysis, along with key parameters for both the ARIMA and TCN models.

Table 1. Countries included in the study and model parameters.

Country	ARIMA Parameters			TCN Parameters			
	p	d	q	Layers	Filters	Kernel Size	Dilation Rates
Sweden	2	1	1	4	64	3	1, 2, 4, 8
Finland	1	1	2	4	64	3	1, 2, 4, 8
Norway	2	1	2	4	64	3	1, 2, 4, 8
Denmark	1	1	1	4	64	3	1, 2, 4, 8
Switzerland	2	1	2	4	64	3	1, 2, 4, 8
Ireland	1	1	1	4	64	3	1, 2, 4, 8
France	2	1	1	4	64	3	1, 2, 4, 8
United Kingdom	1	1	2	4	64	3	1, 2, 4, 8
Netherlands	2	1	1	4	64	3	1, 2, 4, 8
Germany	1	1	2	4	64	3	1, 2, 4, 8
Spain	2	1	1	4	64	3	1, 2, 4, 8
Portugal	1	1	1	4	64	3	1, 2, 4, 8
Italy	2	1	2	4	64	3	1, 2, 4, 8
Slovenia	1	1	1	4	64	3	1, 2, 4, 8
Poland	2	1	1	4	64	3	1, 2, 4, 8
Latvia	1	1	2	4	64	3	1, 2, 4, 8
Estonia	2	1	1	4	64	3	1, 2, 4, 8
Ukraine	1	1	1	4	64	3	1, 2 ,4, 8
Japan	2	1	2	4	64	3	1, 2, 4, 8
South Korea	1	1	2	4	64	3	1, 2, 4, 8
Singapore	2	1	1	4	64	3	1, 2, 4, 8
New Zealand	1	1	2	4	64	3	1, 2, 4, 8
Australia	2	1	1	4	64	3	1, 2, 4, 8
South Africa	1	1	1	4	64	3	1, 2, 4, 8
Argentina	2	1	2	4	64	3	1, 2, 4, 8
Chile	1	1	2	4	64	3	1, 2, 4, 8
Colombia	2	1	1	4	64	3	1, 2, 4, 8
Mexico	1	1	2	4	64	3	1, 2, 4, 8
USA	2	1	2	4	64	3	1, 2, 4, 8
Canada	1	1	1	4	64	3	1, 2, 4, 8

For the ARIMA model, p, d, and q represent the order of the autoregressive term, the degree of differencing, and the order of the moving average term, respectively. These parameters were optimized for each country using the auto.arima function.

For the TCN model, we used a consistent architecture across all countries, with 4 layers; 64 filters per layer; a kernel size of 3; and dilation rates of 1, 2, 4, and 8. This standardized approach allowed for a fair comparison across different countries, while capturing the unique temporal dynamics of each country's carbon tax pricing.

4.2. Model Performance Comparison

As shown in Table 1, our study encompassed a diverse set of 30 countries with varying carbon pricing policies. Despite the differences in ARIMA parameters across countries, our TCN model maintained a consistent architecture, demonstrating its flexibility and robustness in handling diverse time series data.

Table 2 presents the performance of our TCN model compared to the ARIMA, LSTM, and ARIMA-LSTM baseline models across all 30 countries in our dataset.

As shown in Table 2, our TCN model not only outperformed the ARIMA baseline but also demonstrated superior performance compared to the other advanced machine learning approaches such as the long short-term memory (LSTM) networks and a hybrid ARIMA-LSTM model. The TCN achieved a 31.4% reduction in MAE compared to ARIMA, a 15.3% reduction compared to LSTM, and a 6.9% improvement over the ARIMA-LSTM hybrid model. This substantial improvement in accuracy demonstrates the potential of deep learning approaches, particularly TCNs, for carbon tax price projection.

Table 2. Average performance comparison across all countries (standard deviation in parentheses).

Model	Average MAE (USD/tCO$_2$e)	Average RMSE (USD/tCO$_2$e)	MAPE(%)
ARIMA	3.54 (±0.41)	4.92 (±0.57)	12.8 (±1.5)
LSTM	2.87 (±0.35)	3.95 (±0.46)	10.4 (±1.2)
ARIMA-LSTM	2.61 (±0.31)	3.58 (±0.42)	9.5 (±1.1)
TCN	2.43 (±0.29)	3.31 (±0.38)	8.8 (±1.0)

The superior performance of the TCN model can be attributed to several factors: (1) Non-linear modeling capability: Unlike ARIMA, which assumes linear relationships between variables, TCNs can capture complex, non-linear patterns in the data. This is particularly important in the context of carbon pricing, where the relationship between different economic and environmental factors can be highly non-linear. (2) Long-term dependency modeling: The dilated convolutions in TCNs allow the model to efficiently capture long-range dependencies in the time series. This is crucial for understanding the long-term trends and cycles in carbon tax prices, which may be influenced by factors such as policy changes, technological advancements, and global economic conditions. As for LSTM and hybrid models, they may struggle with very long sequences, due to vanishing gradient problems. (3) Multi-variate input handling: While ARIMA models typically focus on univariate time series, our TCN model can easily incorporate multiple input features. This allows it to consider a wider range of relevant factors when making predictions, potentially capturing complex interactions between different variables. (4) Robustness to noise: The residual connections and normalization layers in the TCN architecture help the model to be more robust against noise in the input data. This is particularly beneficial when dealing with economic and environmental data, which can often be noisy or contain measurement errors.

4.3. Performance across Different Time Horizons

To assess the model's performance over different time horizons, we calculated the MAE for 1-year, 3-year, and 5-year projections. The results are presented in Table 3.

Table 3. Model performance across different time horizons (MAE in USD/tCO$_2$e, standard deviation in parentheses).

Model	1-Year MAE	3-Year MAE	5-Year MAE
ARIMA	2.87 (±0.35)	3.98 (±0.49)	5.21 (±0.68)
LSTM	2.35 (±0.29)	3.24 (±0.40)	4.26 (±0.55)
ARIMA-LSTM	2.13 (±0.26)	2.95 (±0.36)	3.87 (±0.50)
TCN	2.01 (±0.26)	2.89 (±0.37)	3.95 (±0.51)

The results in Table 3 demonstrate that while all the advanced models showed improved performance over ARIMA across the different time horizons, the TCN model consistently outperformed both the LSTM and ARIMA-LSTM models. This suggests that a TCN's ability to capture both short-term fluctuations and long-term trends is superior to that of other advanced machine learning approaches.

Several observations can be made from these results: (1) Short-term accuracy: All models performed best in short-term (1-year) projections, with the TCN model showing the lowest MAE. Compared to ARIMA, the TCN model achieved a 30.0% lower MAE, while it outperformed LSTM by 14.5% and ARIMA-LSTM by 5.6% for 1-year projections. This indicates that the TCN model is particularly effective at capturing recent trends and short-term fluctuations in carbon tax prices, even compared to other advanced machine learning approaches. (2) Consistent outperformance: The TCN model maintained its superiority over all other models across all time horizons. The performance gap between the TCN and other models tended to widen for longer-term projections, especially compared to ARIMA and LSTM. This suggests that the TCN model is better able to capture the underlying long-term dynamics of carbon tax prices, leveraging its ability to model complex temporal dependencies. (3) Graceful degradation: While all models showed increasing error for longer time horizons, the TCN model exhibited the most gradual increase in MAE. From 1-year to 5-year projections, the TCN's MAE increased by 96.5%, compared to 81.5% for ARIMA, 81.3% for LSTM, and 81.7% for ARIMA-LSTM. This indicates that the TCN model was more robust against the inherent uncertainty in long-term forecasts, maintaining its predictive power more effectively than other approaches as the forecast horizon was extended. (4) Hybrid model performance: The ARIMA-LSTM hybrid model showed improved performance over both ARIMA and LSTM individually, indicating the benefits of combining traditional statistical methods with deep learning approaches. However, the TCN model still outperformed this hybrid approach, suggesting that its architectural advantages provide superior modeling capabilities for this task. (5) Practical implications: The TCN model's superior performance across different time horizons, even when compared to other advanced machine learning models, makes it a particularly versatile and powerful tool for policymakers and stakeholders. It can provide the most reliable short-term projections for immediate decision-making, while also offering the most valuable insights for long-term policy planning and strategy development. The consistent outperformance of the TCN across all time horizons suggests that it could be the most effective single model for a wide range of carbon tax price projection tasks.

4.4. Adaptability to Policy Changes

To evaluate the models' adaptability to policy changes, we focused on countries that implemented significant carbon tax rate changes during the study period. Table 4 shows the average prediction errors for the models before and after major policy changes in five selected countries.

Table 4. Model prediction errors (MAE in USD/tCO$_2$e) before and after major policy changes.

Country	ARIMA MAE		LSTM MAE		ARIMA-LSTM MAE		TCN MAE	
	Before	After	Before	After	Before	After	Before	After
Sweden (2001)	2.43	4.87	2.35	4.12	2.28	3.72	2.15	3.12
Finland (2011)	1.98	3.76	1.93	3.22	1.89	2.98	1.82	2.54
France (2014)	2.31	4.52	2.25	3.89	2.19	3.54	2.09	2.87
Portugal (2015)	2.15	4.23	2.09	3.64	2.03	3.31	1.93	2.68
Canada (2019)	2.56	5.12	2.48	4.35	2.41	3.98	2.28	3.05

As evident from Table 4, the TCN model consistently showed lower prediction errors both before and after policy changes compared to the ARIMA, LSTM, and ARIMA-LSTM models. On average, the TCN model's prediction error increased by 39.8% after a policy change, while the ARIMA model's error increased by 95.6%, the LSTM model's error increased by 74.9%, and the ARIMA-LSTM model's error increased by 63.4%. This demonstrated the TCN model's superior ability to adapt to sudden policy shifts, a crucial feature in the dynamic landscape of carbon pricing. The performance of the models can be ranked as follows: TCN > ARIMA-LSTM > LSTM > ARIMA, with the TCN showing the best adaptability to policy changes. The hybrid ARIMA-LSTM model showed improved performance over both ARIMA and LSTM individually, indicating the benefits of combining traditional statistical methods with deep learning approaches. However, the TCN model still outperformed this hybrid approach.

Several factors contribute to the TCN model's better adaptability: (1) Non-linear pattern recognition: The TCN model's ability to capture non-linear relationships allows it to better recognize and adapt to abrupt changes in the underlying patterns of carbon tax prices following policy shifts. This capability appeared to be more pronounced in the TCN compared to LSTM and ARIMA-LSTM models. (2) Multi-feature input: By considering multiple input features, the TCN model can potentially capture leading indicators or correlated variables that might signal an impending policy change, allowing it to adjust its predictions more quickly. While LSTM and ARIMA-LSTM also benefit from multi-feature inputs, the TCN's architecture seems to utilize this information more effectively. (3) Temporal hierarchy: The dilated convolutions in the TCN architecture create a hierarchical representation of temporal patterns. This allows the model to distinguish between short-term fluctuations and more significant long-term shifts caused by policy changes more effectively than LSTM or ARIMA-LSTM. (4) Residual connections: The residual connections in the TCN architecture allow the model to maintain a direct path to earlier inputs. This can help the model quickly adapt its predictions when there is a sudden change in the input patterns due to policy shifts. While the LSTM models has mechanisms to handle long-term dependencies, the TCN's residual connections appear to be more effective in this context.

The superior performance of the TCN in adapting to policy changes, even when compared to other advanced machine learning models like LSTM and ARIMA-LSTM, further underscores its potential as a valuable tool for policymakers and stakeholders in the carbon pricing domain. Its ability to quickly adjust to new policy environments could provide more reliable projections in the face of evolving climate policies.

4.5. Feature Importance Analysis

We conducted a feature importance analysis using permutation importance to understand the relative impact of different input variables on the model's predictions. Table 5 presents the results of this analysis.

Table 5. Feature importance analysis results.

Feature	Importance Score
Historical carbon prices	0.42
GDP	0.23
Energy consumption	0.19
CO_2 emissions	0.11
Renewable energy share	0.05

As shown in Table 5, while historical carbon prices were the most significant predictor (importance score of 0.42), economic indicators such as GDP (0.23) and energy consumption patterns (0.19) also played crucial roles in the model's predictions. This underscores the complex interplay of factors influencing carbon tax prices and highlights the TCN model's ability to capture these multifaceted relationships.

The feature importance analysis revealed several key insights: (1) Historical price dependency: The high importance of historical carbon prices (0.42) suggests that past pricing trends are the strongest predictor of future prices. This aligns with the general principle in time series analysis that recent past values are often the best predictors of future values. (2) Economic influence: The significant importance of GDP (0.23) indicates that overall economic conditions play a crucial role in determining carbon tax prices. This could reflect the influence of economic growth on energy demand and carbon emissions, as well as the political feasibility of implementing higher carbon taxes in different economic contexts. (3) Energy sector dynamics: The relatively high importance of energy consumption (0.19) highlights the close relationship between energy use patterns and carbon pricing. Changes in energy consumption, potentially driven by efficiency improvements or structural changes in the economy, appear to have a substantial impact on carbon tax trajectories. (4) Emissions feedback: The moderate importance of CO_2 emissions (0.11) suggests that there is some feedback between actual emission levels and carbon tax rates. This could reflect policymakers' responsiveness to emission trends when setting carbon prices. (5) Renewable energy transition: The lower importance of renewable energy share (0.05) is somewhat surprising. It may indicate that short-term fluctuations in renewable energy adoption have a limited direct impact on carbon tax rates, though the long-term trend towards renewables likely influences policymakers' decisions indirectly through other channels.

These findings have important implications for policymakers and stakeholders in the carbon pricing domain: (1) Policy stability: The high importance of historical prices suggests that policy stability and predictability in carbon tax rates could lead to more accurate long-term projections, potentially reducing uncertainty for businesses and investors. (2) Economic considerations: The significant role of GDP in price projections underscores the need for policymakers to carefully consider economic conditions when designing and adjusting carbon pricing policies. (3) Energy policy integration: The importance of energy consumption highlights the need for integrated policy approaches that consider both carbon pricing and broader energy policies. (4) Emissions monitoring: While CO_2 emissions are not the most important feature, their moderate influence suggests that accurate and timely emissions data remain crucial for effective carbon pricing. (5) Long-term planning: The relatively low importance of renewable energy share in short-term predictions should not overshadow its potential long-term impact. Policymakers should consider how the evolving energy mix might influence future carbon tax trajectories.

While our feature importance analysis provided valuable insights, it is important to discuss why certain features, such as renewable energy share and CO_2 emissions, received relatively low importance scores. Several factors may have contributed to this: (1) Time lag effects: The impact of changes in renewable energy share or CO_2 emissions on carbon tax prices may not be immediate. There could be a significant time lag between changes in these factors and their reflection in carbon tax policies, which our current model might not fully capture. (2) Indirect influences: These features may have indirect effects on carbon tax prices through their impact on other variables, such as GDP or energy consumption. Their influence might be partially absorbed by these intermediate variables in our model. (3) Policy inertia: Carbon tax policies may be slow to respond to changes in renewable energy adoption or emissions levels, due to political and economic considerations, reducing the direct observable impact of these factors on short-term price predictions. (4) Data granularity: Our current dataset may not have sufficient granularity or frequency of updates for these features to fully show their importance in carbon tax price dynamics.

It is also worth considering how additional features could be incorporated in future versions of our model to enrich the analysis: (1) Technological advancements: Incorporating indicators of clean technology innovation, such as patents in renewable energy technologies or investment in clean tech R&D, could provide valuable insights into future carbon pricing trends. (2) International policy changes: Including variables that capture major international climate agreements or policy shifts in influential countries could help the model account for global policy trends that may impact domestic carbon tax decisions. (3) Public opinion data: Incorporating metrics of public sentiment towards climate change and carbon pricing could help capture the societal pressures that influence policy decisions. (4) Energy market dynamics: More detailed data on energy prices, particularly the price gap between renewable and fossil fuel energy sources, could provide additional context for carbon tax price predictions. (5) Climate change indicators: Including data on extreme weather events or climate change impacts could help capture the urgency driving carbon pricing policies. Incorporating these additional features in future iterations of our model could potentially improve its predictive power and provide a more comprehensive understanding of the factors influencing carbon tax prices. However, this would also increase the model's complexity and data requirements, necessitating careful consideration of the trade-offs between model sophistication and practical applicability.

4.6. Case Studies: Carbon Tax Price Projection for Canada and Sweden

To illustrate the practical application of our model and its adaptability to significant policy changes, we present case studies of carbon tax price projections for two countries: Canada and Sweden. These countries were chosen due to their contrasting histories regarding carbon taxation and the significant policy changes they have experienced.

4.6.1. Canada: A New Entrant to National Carbon Pricing

Canada introduced a national carbon pricing system in 2019, making it an interesting case to examine the model's performance in the context of a major policy shift. Table 6 provides a comparison of actual and predicted carbon tax prices for the period 2018–2022.

Table 6. Actual vs. predicted carbon tax prices for Canada (2018–2022).

Year	Actual Price ($/tCO$_2$e)	Predicted Price ($/tCO$_2$e)	Absolute Error
2018	15.00	14.82	0.18
2019	20.00	19.65	0.35
2020	30.00	29.78	0.22
2021	40.00	41.23	1.23
2022	50.00	49.89	0.11

As is evident from Table 6, the TCN model effectively captured both the overall trend and short-term fluctuations in Canada's carbon tax prices, even after the introduction of the national carbon pricing system in 2019. The model's predictions closely traced the actual prices, with absolute errors generally below 1.25 $/tCO$_2$e.

4.6.2. Sweden: A Pioneer in Carbon Taxation

Sweden, on the other hand, introduced its carbon tax in 1991 and has since implemented several significant policy changes. Table 7 shows the actual and predicted carbon tax prices for Sweden from 2000 to 2022, encompassing a period of substantial tax rate increases.

Table 7. Actual vs. predicted carbon tax prices for Sweden (2000–2022).

Year	Actual Price (SEK/tCO$_2$e)	Predicted Price (SEK/tCO$_2$e)	Absolute Error
2000	370	368	2
2005	910	895	15
2010	1050	1080	30
2015	1120	1135	15
2020	1190	1175	15
2022	1200	1190	10

The results for Sweden demonstrate the TCN model's ability to adapt to long-term policy changes and capture complex price dynamics. Despite significant increases in the tax rate over the years, particularly the sharp rise between 2000 and 2005, the model maintained good predictive accuracy.

4.6.3. Comparative Analysis

Comparing the two case studies reveals several insights: 1. Adaptability to policy changes: The TCN model showed strong performance in both cases, adapting well to Canada's introduction of a new national system and Sweden's long-term policy adjustments. 2. Accuracy across different scales: The model maintained good accuracy despite the different scales of carbon prices in Canada (tens of dollars) and Sweden (hundreds of kronor). 3. Long-term vs. short-term performance: While the Canadian case demonstrated the model's short-term adaptability, the Swedish case showcased its ability to capture long-term trends and adapt to gradual policy changes. 4. Robustness across different carbon pricing histories: The model's strong performance for both a relatively new system (Canada) and a well-established one (Sweden) suggests its robustness across different carbon pricing contexts.

These case studies highlight the TCN model's versatility and effectiveness in projecting carbon tax prices across diverse policy environments, strengthening the case for its broader applicability in carbon price forecasting.

4.7. Uncertainty Quantification and Sensitivity Analysis

To address the inherent uncertainty in our model predictions, especially for long-term projections, we conducted additional analyses to quantify uncertainty and assess the model's sensitivity to various factors.

4.7.1. Confidence Intervals

We employed a bootstrapping approach to generate confidence intervals for our TCN model predictions. For each prediction, we created 1000 bootstrap samples and calculated 95% confidence intervals. Figure 1 shows the TCN model predictions with their corresponding confidence intervals for a 5-year projection period.

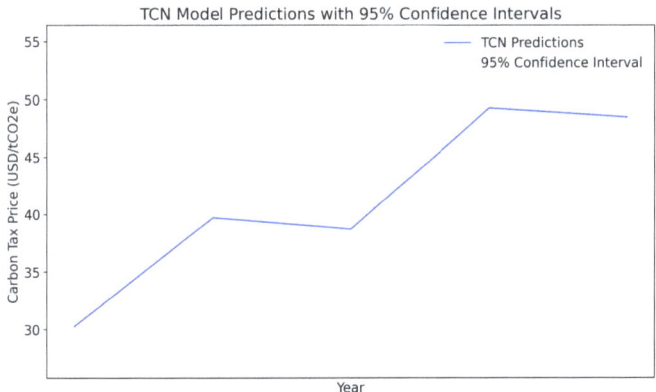

Figure 1. TCN model predictions with 95% confidence intervals.

As expected, the confidence intervals widened for longer-term predictions, reflecting the increasing uncertainty associated with projections further into the future. The non-linear trend and fluctuations in the predictions demonstrated the model's ability to capture complex patterns in carbon tax price dynamics.

4.7.2. Sensitivity Analysis

To assess the model's sensitivity to various input parameters and features, we conducted a global sensitivity analysis using the Sobol method. This method allowed us to quantify the contribution of each input variable to the output variance, considering both main effects and interactions between variables. Table 8 presents the Sobol sensitivity indices for the main input features:

Table 8. Sobol sensitivity indices for input features.

Feature	First-Order Index	Interaction Index	Total-Effect Index
Historical carbon prices	0.382	0.086	0.468
GDP	0.256	0.070	0.326
Energy consumption	0.134	0.069	0.203
CO_2 emissions	0.072	0.052	0.124
Renewable energy share	0.031	0.021	0.052

The results indicate that the model was most sensitive to historical carbon prices and GDP, which aligns with our feature importance analysis. However, the sensitivity analysis also revealed significant interaction effects between features, accounting for a substantial portion of the total effect indices.

4.7.3. Monte Carlo Simulations

To further explore the range of possible outcomes and assess the model's robustness to input uncertainties, we performed Monte Carlo simulations. We generated 10,000 scenarios with varying input parameters based on their historical distributions and projected trends. Figure 2 shows the distribution of the projected carbon tax prices for the year 2025 based on these simulations.

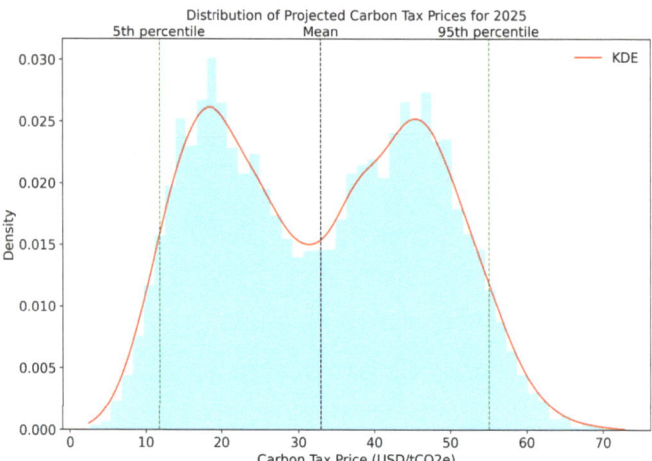

Figure 2. Distribution of projected carbon tax prices for 2025. The green dotted line indicates the 5th and 95th percentile. The blue histogram indicates the frequency distribution.

The simulation results reveal a bimodal distribution for the projected carbon tax prices, suggesting two distinct scenarios or policy paths that could emerge by 2025. This bimodality highlights the complexity and uncertainty inherent in carbon tax price projections. The 5th and 95th percentiles, represented by the green dashed lines, provided a 90% confidence interval for the projected prices.

These uncertainty quantification and sensitivity analyses provide stakeholders with a more comprehensive understanding of the potential risks and variability in our carbon tax price projections. They highlight the importance of considering a range of possible outcomes, particularly for long-term projections, and can help inform more robust policy and investment decisions in the face of uncertainty. The bimodal distribution emphasizes the need for flexible strategies that can adapt to potentially divergent future scenarios in carbon pricing.

4.8. Broader Implications and Future Prospects

While our study demonstrated the effectiveness of the TCN model in projecting carbon tax prices across 30 countries, it is crucial to consider its broader implications and potential limitations in real-world applications. The complex interplay of economic, political, and environmental factors that influence carbon pricing policies presents ongoing challenges for accurate long-term forecasting. For instance, sudden geopolitical events or technological breakthroughs could significantly alter the trajectory of carbon prices in ways that historical data may not fully capture. Moreover, as more countries implement carbon pricing mechanisms, the global landscape becomes increasingly interconnected, potentially leading to spillover effects that our current model may not fully account for.

The application of our findings to countries beyond the 30 examined in this study requires careful consideration. Developing economies or countries with nascent carbon pricing systems may exhibit different dynamics compared to the more established markets we analyzed. Future research could explore the model's adaptability to these diverse contexts, potentially incorporating additional variables such as governance indicators or technological readiness indices to enhance the predictive power.

Our approach builds upon and extends previous work in this field, such as the studies by Zhang and Li [21] on multi-factor forecasting models and Wang et al. [22] on hybrid EMD-LSTM models for carbon price prediction. While these studies focused primarily on emissions trading systems, our work demonstrates the efficacy of TCNs in the specific context of carbon taxation. This novel application opens up new avenues for research at the intersection of deep learning and environmental economics.

Looking ahead, integrating our TCN model with broader macroeconomic models could provide more comprehensive insights into the economy-wide impacts of carbon pricing policies. Additionally, exploring the potential of transfer learning techniques could enable the model to better generalize across different countries and policy contexts, addressing some of the current limitations in cross-country applicability.

As global efforts to combat climate change intensify, the need for accurate and robust carbon price forecasting tools will only grow. Our study contributes to this crucial area, offering a promising approach that can aid policymakers, businesses, and researchers in navigating the complex landscape of carbon pricing. However, it is important to view these projections as one tool among many within the broader context of climate policy analysis and decision-making.

5. Conclusions and Future Work

5.1. Conclusions

This study demonstrated the efficacy of temporal convolutional networks in projecting carbon tax prices, achieving significantly improved accuracy compared to traditional forecasting methods. By leveraging the power of deep learning, our approach offers a valuable tool for policymakers and stakeholders navigating the complex landscape of carbon taxation.

The key findings of our study include: (1) The TCN model consistently outperformed the ARIMA baseline, with a 31.4% reduction in MAE and a 32.7% reduction in RMSE across all countries in our dataset. (2) The TCN model maintained superior performance across different time horizons, from 1-year to 5-year projections, indicating its versatility for both short-term and long-term forecasting. (3) Our model demonstrated better adaptability to sudden policy changes compared to traditional approaches, with an average error increase of 39.8% after major policy shifts, compared to 95.6% for ARIMA. (4) Feature importance analysis revealed the complex interplay of factors influencing carbon tax prices, with historical prices, GDP, and energy consumption emerging as the most significant predictors.

The superior performance of the TCN model underscores the potential of advanced machine learning techniques in enhancing climate policy decisions. As carbon pricing continues to play a crucial role in global efforts to mitigate climate change, accurate price projections will become increasingly important for effective policy design and implementation.

5.2. Future Works

Future work could extend this research in several directions:

- Incorporating additional data sources: Integrating data on technological innovation, political factors, and international climate agreements could potentially improve the model's predictive power.
- Exploring transfer learning: investigating whether models trained on data-rich countries can be effectively transferred to regions with limited historical data on carbon pricing.

- Uncertainty quantification: developing methods to quantify and communicate the uncertainty in carbon tax price projections, which could be valuable for risk assessment and decision-making.
- Comparative policy analysis: using the model to simulate and compare the potential outcomes of different carbon pricing policies across countries or regions.
- Integration with economic models: exploring ways to integrate the TCN model with broader economic models to assess the macroeconomic impacts of carbon pricing policies [23].

While this study focused on carbon tax price projection, the potential applications of our TCN-based approach extend far beyond this specific domain. Future research could explore the following directions: (1) Environmental forecasting: The TCN model could be adapted for predicting other environmental indicators, such as greenhouse gas emissions, renewable energy adoption rates, or the economic impacts of climate change. For instance, it could be used to forecast the trajectory of global temperature changes or sea-level rises, providing valuable insights for climate adaptation strategies. (2) Energy market dynamics: Given its ability to capture complex temporal dependencies, our model could be applied to predict energy prices, demand, and supply across various sectors [24,25]. This could include forecasting electricity prices in deregulated markets or projecting the adoption rates of electric vehicles. (3) Economic policy analysis: The TCN approach could be extended to analyze and predict the impacts of other economic policies, such as interest rate changes, trade policies, or fiscal stimulus measures. This could provide policymakers with a more nuanced understanding of policy effects over time. (4) Integration with macroeconomic models: An exciting avenue for future research would be the integration of our TCN model with computable general equilibrium (CGE) models or dynamic stochastic general equilibrium (DSGE) models. This integration could enhance the ability of these models to capture non-linear dynamics and complex interactions in economic systems. For example, a TCN-enhanced CGE model could provide more accurate projections of how carbon pricing policies impact different sectors of the economy over time. (5) Multi-regional analysis: The model could be adapted to simultaneously forecast carbon tax prices for multiple regions or countries, capturing cross-border effects and policy spillovers. This could be particularly useful for analyzing the global impacts of carbon pricing policies and informing international climate negotiations. (6) Scenario analysis for policy design: Building upon our uncertainty quantification methods, future research could develop more sophisticated scenario analysis tools. These could help policymakers design robust carbon pricing strategies that perform well across a wide range of possible future scenarios. (7) Hybrid modeling approaches: Exploring combinations of TCNs with other machine learning techniques or traditional econometric models could yield powerful hybrid approaches. For instance, combining TCNs with agent-based modeling could provide insights into how individual actors' behaviors influence and are influenced by carbon tax prices over time.

These potential applications highlight the versatility of the TCN approach in addressing complex forecasting challenges across various environmental and economic domains. As the field of data-driven policy analysis continues to evolve, techniques like TCNs offer promising avenues for enhancing our understanding of complex systems and improving the robustness of long-term policy decisions.

In conclusion, this study presents a novel application of deep learning to the critical challenge of carbon tax price projection. The demonstrated improvements in accuracy and adaptability offer the potential to enhance the design, implementation, and evaluation of carbon pricing policies worldwide. As the global community continues to grapple with the urgent need to address climate change, tools like the one presented in this paper can play a crucial role in informing and supporting effective climate action.

Author Contributions: Conceptualization, J.C.; Methodology, J.C. and Y.C.; Software, X.Z.; Formal analysis, J.Y.; Resources, X.Z. and M.Z.; Writing—original draft, J.C. and Y.C.; Writing—review & editing, J.Y. and M.Z.; Supervision, M.Z.; Funding acquisition, M.Z. All authors have read and agreed to the published version of the manuscript.

Funding: This research received no external funding.

Institutional Review Board Statement: Not applicable.

Informed Consent Statement: Not applicable.

Data Availability Statement: Data available in a publicly accessible repository that does not issue DOIs. This data can be found here: https://github.com/g-dolphin/WorldCarbonPricingDatabase/tree/master/_dataset/data.

Conflicts of Interest: The authors declare no conflict of interest.

References

1. Environmental Defense Fund. *The World's Carbon Markets: A Case Study Guide to Emissions Trading*; EDF Report; Environmental Defense Fund: New York, NY, USA, 2021.
2. Carbon Pricing Leadership Coalition. *Report of the High-Level Commission on Carbon Prices*; World Bank: Washington, DC, USA, 2017.
3. International Monetary Fund. *Fiscal Policies for Paris Climate Strategies—From Principle to Practice*; IMF Policy Paper; International Monetary Fund: Washington, DC, USA, 2019.
4. Nordhaus, W.D. Revisiting the social cost of carbon. *Proc. Natl. Acad. Sci. USA* **2017**, *114*, 1518–1523. [CrossRef] [PubMed]
5. Aldy, J.E.; Stavins, R.N. The promise and problems of pricing carbon: Theory and experience. *J. Environ. Dev.* **2020**, *29*, 109–134.
6. Martin, R.; de Preux, L.B.; Wagner, U.J. The impact of a carbon tax on manufacturing: Evidence from microdata. *J. Public Econ.* **2014**, *117*, 1–14. [CrossRef]
7. Baranzini, A.; van den Bergh, J.C.J.M.; Carattini, S.; Howarth, R.B.; Padilla, E.; Roca, J. Carbon pricing in climate policy: seven reasons, complementary instruments, and political economy considerations. *Wiley Interdiscip. Rev. Clim. Chang.* **2017**, *8*, e462. [CrossRef]
8. Carattini, S.; Carvalho, M.; Fankhauser, S. Overcoming public resistance to carbon taxes. *Wiley Interdiscip. Rev. Clim. Chang.* **2018**, *9*, e531. [CrossRef] [PubMed]
9. Naegele, H.; Zaklan, A. Does the EU ETS cause carbon leakage in European manufacturing? *J. Environ. Econ. Manag.* **2019**, *93*, 125–147. [CrossRef]
10. Cao, J.; Dai, H.; Li, S.; Guo, C.; Ho, M.; Cai, W.; He, J.; Huang, H.; Li, J.; Liu, Y.; et al. The general equilibrium impacts of carbon tax policy in China: A multi-model comparison. *Energy Econ.* **2021**, *99*, 105284. [CrossRef]
11. Dumortier, J.; Elobeid, A. Effects of a carbon tax in the United States on agricultural markets and carbon emissions from land-use change. *Land Use Policy* **2021**, *103*, 105320. [CrossRef]
12. Atherton, J.; Xie, W.; Aditya, L.K.; Zhou, X.; Karmakar, G.; Akroyd, J.; Mosbach, S.; Lim, M.Q.; Kraft, M. How does a carbon tax affect Britain's power generation composition? *Appl. Energy* **2021**, *298*, 117117. [CrossRef]
13. O'Ryan, R.; Nasirov, S.; Osorio, H. Assessment of the potential impacts of a carbon tax in Chile using dynamic CGE model. *J. Clean. Prod.* **2023**, *403*, 136694. [CrossRef]
14. Zhu, B.; Ye, S. Exchange rate prediction using machine learning techniques: An empirical study on the European carbon market. *J. Forecast.* **2018**, *37*, 793–804.
15. Pao, H.T.; Fu, H.C.; Tseng, C.L. Forecasting of CO_2 emissions, energy consumption and economic growth in China using an improved grey model. *Energy* **2018**, *40*, 400–409. [CrossRef]
16. Bai, S.; Kolter, J.Z.; Koltun, V. An empirical evaluation of generic convolutional and recurrent networks for sequence modeling. *arXiv* **2018**, arXiv:1803.01271.
17. Borovykh, A.; Bohte, S.; Oosterlee, C.W. Conditional time series forecasting with convolutional neural networks. *arXiv* **2017**, arXiv:1703.04691.
18. Wen, L.; Zhou, K.; Yang, S.; Lu, L. Optimal load dispatch of community microgrid with deep learning based solar power and load forecasting. *Energy* **2019**, *171*, 1053–1065. [CrossRef]
19. World Carbon Pricing Database. CO_2 Emissions Data for Countries. 2022. Available online: https://github.com/g-dolphin/WorldCarbonPricingDatabase (accessed on 1 January 2020).
20. Box, G.E.P.; Jenkins, G.M.; Reinsel, G.C.; Ljung, G.M. *Time Series Analysis: Forecasting and Control*, 5th ed.; John Wiley & Sons: Hoboken, NJ, USA, 2015.
21. Zhang, Y.J.; Li, A.F. Carbon price forecasting with a novel hybrid ARIMA and least squares support vector machines methodology. *Omega* **2019**, *82*, 80–91.
22. Wang, J.; Chen, H.; Zhang, Y.; Sun, X. Carbon price prediction based on improved empirical mode decomposition and long short-term memory. *J. Clean. Prod.* **2020**, *264*, 121498.

23. Kotlikoff, L.; Kubler, F.; Polbin, A.; Scheidegger, S. Can today's and tomorrow's world uniformly gain from carbon taxation? *Eur. Econ. Rev.* **2024**, *168*, 104819. [CrossRef]
24. Kyriakopoulos, G.L.; Streimikiene, D.; Baležentis, T. Addressing challenges of low-carbon energy transition. *Energies* **2022**, *15*, 5718. [CrossRef]
25. Ratanakuakangwan, S.; Morita, H. An efficient energy planning model optimizing cost, emission, and social impact with different carbon tax scenarios. *Appl. Energy* **2022**, *325*, 119792. [CrossRef]

Disclaimer/Publisher's Note: The statements, opinions and data contained in all publications are solely those of the individual author(s) and contributor(s) and not of MDPI and/or the editor(s). MDPI and/or the editor(s) disclaim responsibility for any injury to people or property resulting from any ideas, methods, instructions or products referred to in the content.

Article

Efficiency Boosts in Human Mobility Data Privacy Risk Assessment: Advancements within the PRUDEnce Framework

Fernanda O. Gomes [1,2,*], Roberto Pellungrini [3], Anna Monreale [2], Chiara Renso [4] and Jean E. Martina [1]

Citation: Gomes, F.O.; Pellungrini, R.; Monreale, A.; Renso, C.; Martina, J.E. Efficiency Boosts in Human Mobility Data Privacy Risk Assessment: Advancements within the PRUDEnce Framework. *Appl. Sci.* **2024**, *14*, 8014. https://doi.org/10.3390/app14178014

Academic Editors: Wenjie Zhang and Zhengyi Yang

Received: 24 July 2024
Revised: 3 September 2024
Accepted: 6 September 2024
Published: 7 September 2024

Copyright: © 2024 by the authors. Licensee MDPI, Basel, Switzerland. This article is an open access article distributed under the terms and conditions of the Creative Commons Attribution (CC BY) license (https://creativecommons.org/licenses/by/4.0/).

1. Graduate Program on Computer Science, Department of Informatics and Statistics, Federal University of Santa Catarina (UFSC), Florianópolis 88040-370, SC, Brazil; jean.martina@ufsc.br
2. Department of Computer Science, University of Pisa, 56126 Pisa, Italy; anna.monreale@di.unipi.it
3. Classe di Scienze—Scuola Normale Superiore, 56126 Pisa, Italy; roberto.pellungrini@sns.it
4. The Institute of Information Science and Technologies (ISTI) of the National Research Council (CNR), 56124 Pisa, Italy; chiara.renso@isti.cnr.it
* Correspondence: fernanda.gomes@posgrad.ufsc.br or f.oliveiragomes@phd.unipi.it

Abstract: With the exponential growth of mobility data generated by IoT, social networks, and mobile devices, there is a pressing need to address privacy concerns. Our work proposes methods to reduce the computation of privacy risk evaluation on mobility datasets, focusing on reducing background knowledge configurations and matching functions, and enhancing code performance. Leveraging the unique characteristics of trajectory data, we aim to minimize the size of combination sets and directly evaluate risk for trajectories with distinct values. Additionally, we optimize efficiency by storing essential information in memory to eliminate unnecessary computations. These approaches offer a more efficient and effective means of identifying and addressing privacy risks associated with diverse mobility datasets.

Keywords: privacy; privacy risk; privacy risk assessment; mobility; re-identification; computation improvements; risk; trajectory

1. Introduction

The extensive use of mobile devices equipped with location-tracking technologies, such as GPS, has collected a great deal of location data, offering insights into users' movements over time and space. A trajectory, in its raw form, consists of a sequence of spatio-temporal points that reveal the position of an object at specific times. Trajectories offer valuable information about human mobility patterns, benefiting various sectors such as security, urban planning, public transportation management, and disease prevention. However, using trajectory data also raises significant privacy concerns during data collection and sharing.

Individuals using these technologies face significant risks due to potential data breaches that can result in privacy violations. The collected data contain highly sensitive and personal information, making it vulnerable to re-identification attacks. These attacks aim to identify individuals or locations within trajectory datasets, posing a substantial threat to privacy. A privacy assessment study in the context of mobility data indicates that merely four spatio-temporal points can re-identify 95% of individuals in a low-granularity trajectory dataset [1]. Notably, the top three locations in a path are sufficient to identify over 80% of individuals [2]. The disclosure of location data raises significant privacy concerns, as it can be used to make intrusive inferences about individuals' habits, social behavior, and even religious and sexual preferences [3].

Privacy risk assessment is a process aimed at understanding which individuals in the data are at risk of privacy violations and quantifying the associated risk level. In Europe, the *General Data Protection Regulation (GDPR)*, and, similarly, in other countries such as with the *Lei Geral de Proteção de Dados (LGPD)* in Brazil, establishes principles and requirements for the processing of personal data. These laws assign data controllers and processors to handle data, ensuring data protection. One important step for data custodians is to perform a quantitative privacy risk data assessment. Numerous privacy risk assessment methodologies based on probability and frequency have been proposed for evaluating the privacy risk across various data types [4–8].

One of the challenges in privacy risk assessment, especially concerning re-identification, is the need to reduce the computational resources required for evaluating privacy risk. One of the most accurate methods for privacy risk assessment is the simulation of background knowledge-based attacks. When simulating this type of attack, generating the background knowledge representing the adversary's knowledge about its victims is a particularly complex task, requiring substantial computational resources. As the adversary's knowledge expands, the computational complexity increases exponentially until half of the maximum possible knowledge size. Previous studies, such as those by Pellungrini et al. [9] and Naretto et al. [10], have explored using machine learning algorithms to mitigate this computational load, particularly when new data become available. Both methods were successful in significantly reducing the overall processing time. However, an initial computation of risk using combinations remains essential to establish the training dataset for their approach, which means that the lengthy execution time is still a challenge that needs to be addressed.

Due to the data size, the process becomes more complex when dealing with trajectory data. Background knowledge related to trajectories often consists of sequences of visited places or simply locations, representing places or visits the attacker is aware of regarding the victim's movement. As this knowledge grows, the number of potential background knowledge configurations to evaluate increases significantly. Each configuration requires risk assessment, further adding to the overall complexity of the process. The time required for this assessment depends on the dataset size, number of trajectories, and trajectory length.

This work addresses computational challenges encountered in risk assessment analysis using PRUDEnce [11], a state-of-the-art privacy risk assessment framework for background knowledge-based attacks. We aim to develop strategies to mitigate the computational complexity of evaluating privacy risks in trajectory datasets. We explore the complexities arising from the high computational demands of re-identification risk assessment. We propose different computational improvements and optimization strategies to simplify the risk assessment process, enhance computational efficiency, and facilitate more scalable and accurate analyses.

Our contributions include validating the significance of low entropy and volatile feature frequency to reduce computational complexity in re-identification risk assessment. We explain how these factors impact re-identification risk and explore methodologies for taking advantage of low-entropy characteristics to simplify risk assessment processes. Additionally, we introduce optimization strategies to enhance computational efficiency in re-identification risk assessment. These strategies include the avoidance of redundant computations by storing background knowledge configurations and the optimization of memory usage through the utilization of unique values.

Furthermore, we provide a thorough analysis of the results obtained from implementing the proposed computational enhancements and optimization techniques, demonstrating significant reductions in complexity. We also demonstrate how our proposed optimizations can effectively reduce the execution time of the risk assessment process. This improvement is particularly beneficial as it enhances the efficiency of the re-identification risk assessment, allowing for faster trajectory data processing. By reducing execution time, our optimizations contribute to improved scalability and usability of the risk assessment methodology, making it more practical for real-world applications.

The paper is organized as follows. Section 2 presents the state of the art of privacy risk assessment frameworks. Section 3 provides the data definitions regarding trajectories, attacks, privacy risk assessment, and combination complexity. Section 5 presents the optimization techniques. Section 6 shows the experimental details and the results with a final discussion. We conclude and plan future work in Section 7.

2. Related Work

Quantitative privacy risk assessment for mobility trajectory and other types of data is a well-studied topic. Trabelsi et al.'s (2009) [4] approach involves recommending secure configurations through a smart bootstrapping system, aiming to enhance understanding and management of the risks associated with non-controlled data disclosure. The authors utilized a probability-based approach, demonstrating that it is possible to reduce computation time by leveraging previously calculated risk values to predict future risk values. Song et al. (2014) [6] propose a modification-based anonymization approach and evaluate privacy risk based on the uniqueness of trajectory data. The authors employed a probability of re-identification based on sub-trajectories and demonstrated that, by reducing the overall trajectory size—specifically, by removing the highest-risk sub-trajectories—the re-identification risk is significantly decreased. In Achara et al. (2015) [5], their research investigates the privacy implications of the list of apps installed by users on smartphones, emphasizing the re-identifiability issue. Analyzing a dataset with 54,893 Android users over 7 months, the study finds that merely four installed apps are sufficient for user re-identification over 95% of the time. Remarkably, the complete list of installed apps is unique for 99% of users, making it susceptible to tracking or profiling by services like Twitter with access to this information. In [12], their proposed framework integrates runtime risk assessment into information disclosure access control, utilizing disclosure risk for decision-making. Access-control decisions are driven by the associated disclosure risk of data access requests, and adaptive anonymization serves as a method for mitigating risks, ensuring privacy preservation. Other studies in the literature explore re-identification risk as a privacy measure within the realms of network and social media data [7,8].

In [7], the authors introduce a framework for assessing privacy and anonymity within social networks and introduce a new re-identification algorithm aimed at anonymized social network graphs. To demonstrate its effectiveness on real-world networks, they showed that a third of users with accounts on both Twitter and Flickr can be re-identified in the anonymized Twitter graph with a 12% error rate. Finally, ref. [8] showed that, based on social media behavior, it is possible to re-identify passive web visits to the host. Their method combines a public follower graph on social media with posting behaviors and time-based inferences and proved to be efficient in re-identifying the users. Khalfoun et al. (2021) [13] propose EDEN, selecting optimal Location Privacy Protection Mechanisms using federated learning without exposing raw traces, demonstrating superior privacy vs. utility tradeoff across real-world datasets. Silva et al. (2022) [14] introduce the Personal Data Analyser, which employs automated data monitoring with Regular Expressions, NLP, and machine learning to enhance privacy. Integrated into the PoSeID-on platform, it alerts users to risks with crisp and fuzzy models validated through real-world use cases.

In this work, we adopted the PRUDEnce framework introduced by Pratesi et al., as elucidated in their seminal work [11] and previously presented in Section 6. PRUDEnce was introduced as a system that deals with finding a balance between privacy risk and data usefulness when sharing sensitive human activity data. This framework offers a methodology for the computation of privacy risk in a data-driven fashion. At its essence, PRUDEnce revolves around the foundational principle of k-anonymity, wherein the privacy risk assessment is linked to the dimensions of k-sets associated with each individual in the dataset. The method checks out real privacy risks for users and ensures data quality for those not at risk. Data providers can try different changes to strike the right balance between privacy and usefulness. The practical effectiveness of PRUDEnce is shown with real mobility data, exploring presence, trajectory, and road segment data formats. Our decision to utilize PRUDEnce was based on its flexible extension and suitability for trajectory data.

The computational intensity of PRUDEnce has prompted exploration into machine learning approaches aimed at predicting privacy risk, thereby bypassing the need for computationally exhaustive processes. Pellungrini et al. (2017) [9] present a swift and adaptable method for estimating privacy risk in human mobility data. Their approach involves training classifiers to link individual mobility patterns with different privacy risk levels. Another important advancement in this field is the EXPERT framework, developed by Naretto et al. (2020) [10]. This framework refines PRUDEnce by introducing a machine learning methodology that proficiently forecasts privacy risk from sequential data. Moreover, the framework enhances the interpretability of these predictions by incorporating methodologies such as SHAP [15] and LIME [16]. Another study proposed by Naretto et al. (2023) [17] presents an optimization of EXPERT, the EXPHLOT. Authors use distinct time series classifications, such as ROCKET and INCEPTIONTIME, to improve risk prediction while reducing computation time.

While previous works focus on improving efficiency and reducing computational demands for privacy risk assessment, these works often require an initial conventional risk analysis to generate training data for the risk-predicting machine learning model. Our proposal offers an approach that aims to enhance the computational risk algorithm. By directly optimizing the risk assessment process, our methodology eliminates unnecessary computation. This streamlined approach not only reduces the computational time but also simplifies the overall risk assessment pipeline.

Our strategy for evaluating the maximum risk and reducing the computation time is to select low-entropy trajectory features to target high-risk data and reduce the data used to evaluate the risk. Pellungrini et al. (2017) [9] showed that entropy has an important impact on predicting features/locations in machine learning models. The idea is that location entropy is related to uniqueness, which is the main measure of anonymity. If a user passes through high-entropy locations, where, therefore, many different people pass through, the uniqueness of their mobility profile is lost as the general movement blurs it. In EXPHLOT [17], authors show that they have the highest entropy locations, evaluating only the lowest entropy locations. In this way, they focus on locations with fewer individuals visiting, focusing on explaining high-risk predictions. In our work, we reduced the computation time for maximum risk evaluation since it would yield the highest risk values. We also went a step beyond checking not only location entropy but also time entropy. Using different attacks and adversary knowledge sizes, we used the p-value and Kolmogorov–Smirnov test [18,19] to prove the efficiency of using low-entropy values to reduce maximum risk computation.

Our proposal introduces novel techniques to more efficiently identify and prioritize high-risk trajectories. By leveraging insights from trajectory data characteristics, such as inherent uniqueness and temporal dependencies, our algorithm can highlight trajectories with elevated privacy risks.

3. Basic Concepts

This section provides an overview of the fundamental concepts related to trajectories and location attacks. We introduce the PRUDEnce framework, and discuss the computational complexity of combinations.

3.1. Trajectory

A trajectory, also known as a raw trajectory, is a sequence of spatio-temporal points, defined in Definition 1. Each point, detailed in Definition 2, includes spatial coordinates and a timestamp, referred to as trajectory features in this work. A segment of a trajectory is called a sub-trajectory, as described in Definition 3, which can also be considered a trajectory.

Definition 1 (Trajectory). *A trajectory T is a sequence of spatio-temporal points $T = (p_0 \langle x_0, y_0, t_0 \rangle, \ldots, p_n \langle x_n, y_n, t_n \rangle)$, where (x_i, y_i) are spatial coordinates, and t_i represents time, with $t_0 < t_1 < \ldots < t_n$ to maintain chronological order.*

Definition 2 (**Point**). *A point p is a tuple* $\langle x, y, t \rangle$, *where x and y are spatial coordinates representing a location, and t is the time of the visit.*

Definition 3 (**Sub-trajectory**). *A sub-trajectory s of a trajectory T is an ordered sequence of points from T, defined as* $s = (p_{i_1}, p_{i_2}, \ldots, p_{i_k})$, *where s contains at least one point but fewer than all points of T.*

In this work, we use the terms *point* or *visit* to refer to a single element of a trajectory, while, by the term *location l*, we refer to the point's spatial information. A subsequence of locations (Definition 4) is an ordered list of locations. We denote by $U_{set} = \{u_1, \ldots, u_n\}$ the set of the distinct individuals represented in the mobility dataset D, formally described in Definition 5.

We use, in this work, the terms *point* or *visit* refer to an individual element of a trajectory, while the term *location l* specifically denotes the spatial aspect of a point. A subsequence of locations (Definition 4) is defined as an ordered sequence of locations. The set $U_{set} = u_1, \ldots, u_n$ represents the distinct individuals captured in the mobility dataset D, as outlined in Definition 5.

Definition 4 (**Subsequence**). *Let* $\mathcal{L} = \{l_1, l_2, \ldots, l_w\}$ *represent a set of locations. A sequence* $S = \langle s_1, s_2, \ldots, s_m \rangle$ *is an ordered list of locations from* $\mathcal{L}$, *where each location can appear multiple times.*

A sequence $T = \langle t_1, t_2, \ldots, t_z \rangle$ *is called a subsequence of S (denoted* $T \preccurlyeq S$) *if there are indices* $1 \leq i_1 < i_2 < \cdots < i_z \leq m$ *such that*

$$t_j = s_{i_j} \quad \text{for} \quad j = 1, 2, \ldots, z.$$

This ensures that T maintains the order of S.

Definition 5 (**Mobility Dataset**). *A mobility dataset D is a collection of trajectories,* $D = \{T_1, T_2, \ldots, T_n\}$, *where each* T_u *represents the trajectory of a moving object u* $(1 \leq u \leq n)$. *For multiple-aspect trajectories, the dataset is represented as* $D = \{MAT_1, MAT_2, \ldots, MAT_n\}$.

3.2. Risk of Re-Identification

Re-identification happens when an adversary successfully links the anonymized or otherwise protected data of an individual with information available to them, whether obtained publicly or through other means. In [20], the authors of the paper comprehensively review terminology and the methodologies related to the risk of re-identification. There are two principal manners to evaluate the re-identification risk: at the dataset and individual levels. The dataset risk involves the proportion of records an adversary can re-identify from a protected dataset. Our work focuses on reducing the computation time of individual risk assessment.

The re-identification risk of an individual is articulated as the probability that a particular sample record of an adversary is identified as corresponding to a specific individual in the dataset, influenced by the observation that risk exhibits non-uniformity across the dataset, with rare combinations of sensitive attributes potentially leading to the re-identification of individuals [21]. As defined in [22], where there are k possible combinations of key attributes inducing a partition, the individual disclosure risk for a record with the k-th combination is inversely proportional to the known population frequency F_k, expressed as $\frac{1}{F_k}$. In both risk measures, adversaries commonly employ the primary *Data Matching* technique. This method centers on establishing connections between records, aiming to identify those belonging to the same individual across different databases. Our work aims to reduce the complexity of the re-identification risk computation within the PRUDEnce framework.

3.3. PRUDEnce Framework

PRUDEnce, a privacy risk assessment framework proposed by [11], is recognized for its effectiveness in assessing privacy risks in trajectory data. It plays a crucial role in helping data providers (DPs) make informed decisions while maintaining data quality. The framework is designed to support GDPR compliance, with a particular focus on Article 25, which emphasizes data protection by design and default, aligning with the principles of Data Protection Impact Assessments. PRUDEnce is not limited to a specific country or jurisdiction, but it is primarily structured to comply with GDPR (European Union). However, due to its adaptable nature, PRUDEnce can be extended to assess privacy risks in other legal contexts. PRUDEnce provides a universal methodology for privacy risk assessment in any type of data.

PRUDEnce assesses privacy risks in data sharing, particularly focusing on empirical privacy risks during the transfer of raw personal data from the DP to the Service Developer (SD). Background knowledge dimensions are crucial for evaluating potential privacy risks and outlining external information accessible to potential attackers. This context-dependent background knowledge impacts the effectiveness of privacy attacks.

Background knowledge represents an adversary's knowledge subset regarding a user u. The methodology evaluates privacy risks with varying levels of background knowledge, from minimal to maximal knowledge, enabling responsible decision-making. Defining attack models and background knowledge is critical, systematically balancing privacy risks and data utility.

A *background knowledge category* refers to information known by an adversary about the specific dimensions of an individual's data. For instance, in mobility data, typical dimensions include space, time, frequency of visiting a location, and probability of visiting a location. The number of elements the adversary knows, the size of the *background knowledge configuration*, is denoted by k. An example of a background knowledge configuration could be the adversary knowing $k = 3$ points in the trajectory of an individual. An *instance of background knowledge* represents specific information the adversary knows, such as a visit to a specific location; we can see an example of background knowledge in Figure 1. In Figure 1, we begin with a dataset containing trajectory data. In the example provided, the attacker has knowledge of location sequences, with a knowledge size of 2. The second table in Figure 1 illustrates the background knowledge instances generated from the input dataset. Location information is combined in pairs (two by two) to represent the potential knowledge an attacker might possess.

These concepts are formalized as follows, according [11], in Definition 6.

Definition 6 (Background Knowledge Category, Configuration and Instance). *We consider a background knowledge category, denoted as $\mathcal{B}$. Within this category, we define B_k as a specific configuration of background knowledge, where B_k belongs to the set $\mathcal{B} = B_1, B_2, \ldots, B_n$. The value of k indicates the number of elements within $\mathcal{B}$ that an adversary possesses. Each individual element b that is part of B_k represents a distinct instance of this background knowledge configuration.*

$$B_k = \left\{ \binom{\{value_1, \ldots, value_{n(u)}\}}{k} \mid \forall u \right\}$$

Let $\mathcal{D}$ be a database, D a dataset extracted from $\mathcal{D}$ as an aggregation of the data on specific dimensions (e.g., an aggregated data structure and filtering on some dimension), and D_u and D_u the subset of records corresponding to individual u within D; we establish the likelihood of re-identification as follows in Definition 7 and in 2 in Figure 1.

Definition 7 (Probability of re-identification). *Given an attack, we consider a function matchin that determines whether a record $d \in D$ corresponds to the background knowledge instance $b \in B_k$. We then define a function $M(D, b) = \{d \in D \mid matching(d, b) = True\}$, which identifies all* records in D that match b. The probability of re-identification for an individual u within the dataset D is expressed as

$$PR_D(d = u \mid b) = \frac{1}{|M(D,b)|}$$

which represents the chance of linking a record $d \in D$ to an individual u, given the instance $b \in B_k$.

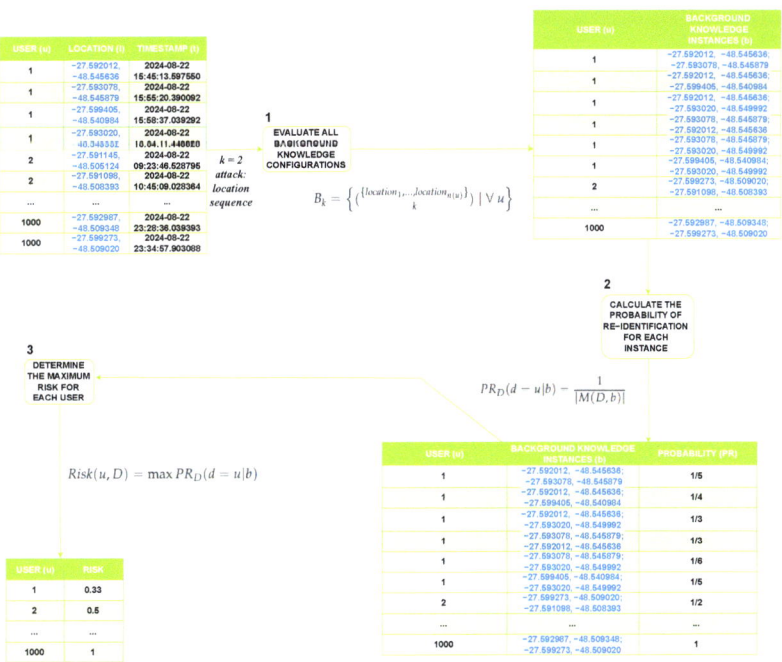

Figure 1. Data flow in the privacy risk assessment within PRUDEnce.

The *compatibility* is expressed by a function $matching(d, b)$, which indicates whether or not a record $d \in D$ matches the instance b. The matching function depends on the background knowledge used during the attack. The PRUDEnce framework characterizes the re-identification risk for an individual as the maximum probability of re-identification among all instances within a background knowledge configuration, as defined in Definition 8 and shown in Step 3 of Figure 1.

Definition 8 (Re-identification Risk or Privacy Risk). *The re-identification risk, or privacy risk, for a specific individual u, associated with a background knowledge configuration B_k, is determined as the highest probability of re-identification, expressed as $Risk(u, D) = \max PR_D(d = u \mid b)$, where $b \in B_k$. This risk is bounded by a minimum threshold of $\frac{|D_u|}{|D|}$, which corresponds to a random guess within dataset D, and is $Risk(u, D) = 0$ when u is not present in D.*

An individual may face various privacy risks, each corresponding to different configurations of background knowledge used in an attack. Initially, an attack is formulated and customized to use a specific category of background knowledge. Subsequently, a range of background knowledge configurations is examined, denoted as $\{B_1, \ldots, B_m\}$. For each configuration B_k, all instances b within B_k are analyzed, along with their respective probabilities of re-identification. Finally, the maximum probability of re-identification across all instances b within configuration B_k determines the privacy risk for the individual in that specific context.

3.4. Location Attacks

In trajectory datasets, a "location attack" involves determining sensitive information about individuals by analyzing their movement patterns and the locations they visit.

Various attacks have been proposed in the literature to exploit such vulnerabilities. For instance, the location sequence attack, as outlined in works such as [9,23], involves adversaries possessing knowledge of a subset of the locations visited by an individual and the temporal sequence of these visits. Similarly, the visit attack, outlined in studies like [3,24,25], requires adversaries to be privy to information about a subset of the locations visited by an individual along with the specific times of these visits. For example, in a trajectory dataset containing GPS coordinates or timestamps of individuals' movements, a location attack could involve analyzing this data to identify specific places individuals frequently visit, such as their homes, workplaces, or other sensitive locations. By correlating these patterns with additional information, such as social media posts or public records, adversaries may be able to deduce private details about individuals, such as their daily routines, habits, or interests.

3.4.1. Location Sequence Attack

In the location sequence attack, introduced in [9,23], the an adversary is aware of a subset of the locations that the individual has visited and the temporal ordering of the visits.

In the context of trajectory data privacy, a location sequence attack involves an adversary possessing knowledge of a subset of the locations visited by an individual, as well as the temporal ordering of these visits. For an individual s, the sequence of visited locations $L(T_s)$ is represented by the sequence of locations l_i within T_s.

The background knowledge category for a location sequence attack is formally defined as follows.

Definition 9 (Location Sequence Background Knowledge). *Let k be the number of locations l_i known by the adversary for an individual s. The location sequence background knowledge comprises configurations based on k locations, denoted as $B_k = L(T_s)[k]$. Here, $L(T_s)[k]$ represents the set of all possible k-subsequences of the elements in set $L(T_s)$.*

In this context, the notation $a \preccurlyeq b$ indicates that a is a subsequence of b. Each instance $b \in B_k$ is thus a subsequence of location $X_s \preccurlyeq L(T_s)$ of length k. Given a record d in the dataset D and the corresponding individual u, the matching function is defined to determine the presence of a location sequence:

$$evaluate(T,b) = \begin{cases} 1, & b \preccurlyeq_l L(T_u)^k \\ 0, & otherwise \end{cases} \qquad (1)$$

In this attack, the attacker knows that a person went, first, to a supermarket and then to work, but they do not know when, only the sequence of places.

3.4.2. Visit Attack

In this attack, introduced in [3,9,24,25], an an adversary is aware of a subset of the locations that the individual has visited and the time the individual visited these locations. Let k be the number of visits vs. of an individual s known by the adversary. The visit background knowledge consists of configurations derived from k visits, formally represented as $B_k = T_s[k]$, where $T_s[k]$ indicates the set of all possible k-length subsequences within the trajectory T_s.

Each instance $b \in B_k$ represents a spatio-temporal subsequence X_s of length k. The subsequence X_s positively matches a given trajectory if the trajectory aligns with b in both spatial and temporal aspects. Formally, given a record d in the dataset D, the matching function is defined as

$$evaluate(T,b) = \begin{cases} 1, & \forall (l_i, t_i) \in b, \exists (l_{d_i}, t_{d_i}) \in d \text{ such that } l_i = l_{d_i} \wedge t_i = t_{d_i} \\ 0, & otherwise \end{cases} \quad (2)$$

In this attack, the attacker knows that, for instance, a person went, first, to a supermarket at 1 p.m. and after work at 2 p.m. They know the time when the person visited the place.

In the next subsection, we will introduce the *combinatorial problem*.

4. Computational Complexity of Combinations

In addressing computational challenges, particularly in evaluating re-identification risk, we encountered significant memory and complexity issues. These challenges primarily arise from the high computational complexity of the risk evaluation process, which is denoted by $\mathcal{O}(\binom{len}{k} \times N)$. Here, $\binom{len}{k}$ represents the generation of background knowledge configuration sets, where len indicates the size of the trajectory, and N denotes the number of matching operations required for each configuration. This complexity, as highlighted in [9,11], poses substantial difficulties, especially in scenarios involving empirical privacy risk.

Re-identification risk via a background knowledge attack simulation requires analyzing the likelihood of identifying a specific user within a dataset, considering various types of background knowledge for potential adversaries. However, the computational complexity grows exponentially with the size of the trajectory and the number of potential background knowledge instances.

The computational complexity of combinations denoted as $\binom{n}{k}$ can be analyzed in terms of factorials and depends on the values of n and k. The formula for combinations is given by

$$\binom{n}{k} = \frac{n!}{k!(n-k)!}$$

The Binomial Coefficient Function

The binomial coefficient denotes the number of ways to choose k outcomes without considering their order from a total of n possibilities. This concept is commonly recognized as a combination. Figure 2 shows the binomial coefficient behavior according to n and k values. Some important characteristics can be noticed.

The binomial coefficient curve has several key characteristics. It exhibits symmetry around its peak due to the symmetry in the combinations formula $C(n,k) = C(n, n-k)$, where choosing k elements is equivalent to choosing $n-k$ elements. Consequently, the curve is symmetric around the middle point. The curve starts at 1 when $k=0$ (choosing 0 elements) and ends at 1 when $k=n$ (choosing all elements), reflecting the fact that there is only one way to choose 0 elements (no choice) and one way to choose all n elements (all elements are chosen).

The peak value of the curve occurs at the middle point, where $k = \frac{n}{2}$ (rounded up or down depending on whether n is even or odd). The number of ways to choose k elements is maximized, leading to the highest binomial coefficient. However, the binomial coefficient gradually decreases as k deviates from the middle point. This is because choosing fewer elements as it moves away from the middle results in a decrease in the number of combinations.

The binomial coefficient specifically represents combinations that do not consider the order of elements. In contrast, permutations, where order matters, would result in a different curve behavior. From a computational perspective, factorial computation can be computationally expensive, especially for large values of n and k, leading to large intermediate values. However, optimizations can be applied to enhance efficiency in computing binomial coefficients.

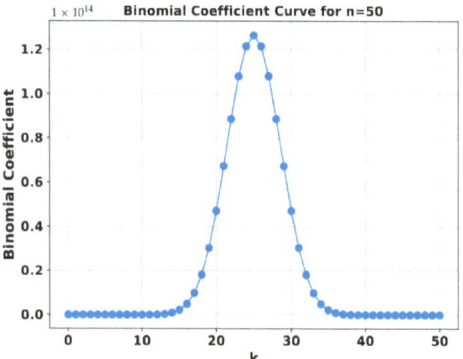

Figure 2. Behavior 1×10^{14} of binomial coefficient curve.

5. Privacy Risk Assessment: Advancements within the PRUDEnce Framework

This section proposes improvements within the PRUDEnce framework, particularly on computing privacy risk assessment. As illustrated in Figure 3, we introduce several advancements: Low Entropy, Cache Strategy, Break, Direct Evaluation, and Reuse. Each of these techniques targets a specific aspect of the privacy risk assessment process. The Low Entropy approach reduces the number of instances that require re-identification probability evaluation. The Cache Strategy stores instance information in memory, minimizing redundant calculations. The Break method stops the evaluation once an instance with maximum risk is identified. Direct Evaluation bypasses risk computation when the trajectory contains any feature with unique information. Finally, the Reuse technique applies the privacy risk evaluation from the $k-1$ analysis to the current k analysis if the previous risk is already at its maximum.

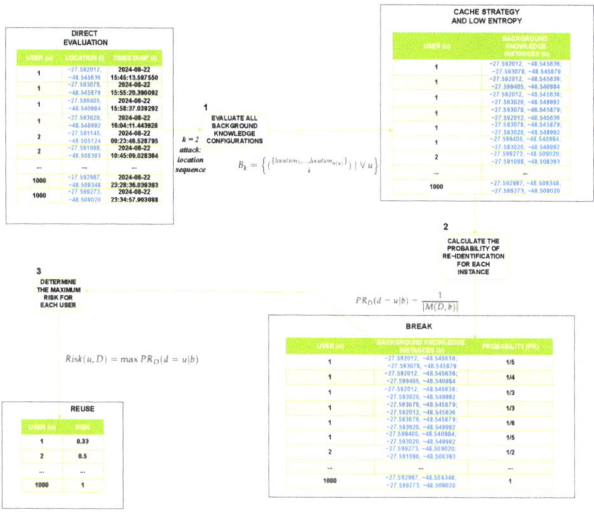

Figure 3. Privacy risk data flow and strategies relation.

5.1. Relationship between Entropy, Feature Frequency, and Re-Identification Risk

When analyzing data with entropy-applied trajectory feature frequency, such as location or time, it becomes clear that features with lower entropy values also have lower frequencies and pose a higher risk of re-identification for the individuals. This relationship between entropy and frequency highlights several key factors contributing to the increased risk.

Less frequent features tend to have a lesser impact on the overall uniqueness of the data. With fewer instances, each occurrence becomes more significant in distinguishing individuals within the dataset. Consequently, the aggregated data offer less anonymity, making it easier for adversaries to differentiate between individuals.

Regarding entropy, low-frequency features contribute less to the overall uncertainty in the dataset because their probability of occurrence is low. In entropy calculations, probabilities of rare events (e.g., visits to low-frequency locations) have less impact on the overall entropy than probabilities of more common events. Therefore, low-frequency features tend to have lower entropy, indicating less uncertainty in the distribution of visits. While low-frequency features may be easier to predict due to their less variable and more predictable nature, this predictability can increase the risk of re-identification.

Applying entropy to features highlights the heightened risk associated with low-frequency data. These features, characterized by their low entropy, offer less anonymity and increased predictability, making them more susceptible to re-identification.

5.1.1. Formal Proof

Here, we present formal proof regarding the correlation between the entropy of features' frequency distribution and the risk of re-identification.

Claim: trajectory features with low entropy in their frequency distribution are those with low frequency, and they are more at risk of re-identifying the data owner.

Proof. entropy is a measure of uncertainty or randomness in a probability distribution. Let x_{ui} represent the i-th feature of record x_u of dataset $D_{n=1}^N$ where N is the total number of individuals. The Shannon Entropy [26] for feature x_i is given by

$$E(x_i) = -\sum_{u=0}^{N} p_u(x_{ui} = v) \log_2 p_u(x_{ui} = v)$$

where $p_u(x_{ui} = v)$ is the probability that individual u has a feature value $vs.$ for x_i

The probability $p_u(x_{ui} = v)$ can be calculated based on its frequency:

$$FR(u,v) = |\{x_j i | x_j i = vs.j = u\}|$$

in individual u's data divided by the individual data size N:

$$p_u(x_{ui} = v) = \frac{FR(u,v)}{N}$$

Substituting $p_u(x_{ui} = v) = \frac{FR(u,v)}{N}$ into the entropy formula, we obtain

$$E(x_i) = -\sum_{u=0}^{N} \frac{FR(u,v)}{N} \log_2 \frac{FR(u,v)}{N}$$

For a feature with low frequency, $FR(u,v)$ is small for all $u = 0, \ldots, N$. Therefore, the probability $p_u(x_{ui} = v)$ is also small. In the low-frequency scenario, where the feature value frequency is low, the probability $p_u(x_{ui} = v)$ is also low, leading to a smaller contribution to the overall entropy. This is because $p_u(x_{ui} = v) \log_2(p_u(x_{ui} = v))$ is close to zero when $p_u(x_{ui} = v)$ is small. Hence, the entropy $E(x_i)$ is lower for low-frequency features.

Conversely, in the high-frequency scenario, where the feature value frequency is high, the probability $p_u(x_{ui} = v)$ is higher. This results in a larger contribution to the overall entropy, as $p_u(x_{ui} = v) \log_2(p_u(x_{ui} = v))$ is higher when $p_u(x_{ui} = v)$ is larger. Hence, the entropy $E(x_i)$ is higher for high-frequency features.

Base Case: we consider the case where $vs.$ appears only once in the dataset. This means that $FR(u,v) = 1$ for an individual u and 0 for all others. The entropy calculation becomes

$$E(x_i) = -\left(\frac{1}{N}\log_2 \frac{1}{N}\right) = -\left(\frac{1}{N}\cdot(-\log_2 N)\right) = \frac{\log_2 N}{N}$$

Since $S(u)$ is a finite positive number, $\frac{\log_2 N}{N}$ is positive but small. Thus, $E(x_i)$ is low.

Inductive Step: we assume that, for a feature value $vs.$ appearing k times in the dataset, the entropy $E(x_i)$ is low. We must show that the entropy remains low if the feature x_i appears $k+1$ times.

If $vs.$ appears $k+1$ times, the probabilities $p_u(x_{ui} = v)$ will still be small because $FR(u,v)$ divided by N remains small. Thus, the term $p_u(x_{ui} = v)\log_2(p_u(x_{ui} = v))$ for each $u = 0, \ldots, N$ will contribute a small value to the overall entropy.

With these small contributions, we see that the entropy $E(x_i)$ will increase slightly but remain low because the additional term for the $k+1$-th occurrence is small.

Therefore, by induction, features with low frequency have low entropy.

Conclusion: features with low entropy in their frequency distribution, indicating low frequency, contribute less to the overall uncertainty. However, this also means that these features are more unique. The uniqueness of these features makes it easier to re-identify the data owners, as fewer individuals have these low-frequency features. This establishes a link between local entropy and uniqueness in the data. Therefore, we have shown that features with low entropy are indeed those with low frequency, and can pose a higher risk of re-identifying the data owner. For this reason, we use entropy and frequency to reduce the size of the background knowledge set when evaluating maximum risk and *empirical privacy risk* across the entire dataset. □

5.1.2. Selecting Background Knowledge Configurations with Low-Entropy Trajectory Features Frequency

The approach aims to enhance the identification of background knowledge instances with heightened privacy risks in the dataset. It involves mathematical definitions and procedures to systematically identify and retain instances that meet the specified criterion.

Definition 10 (Low-entropy Feature Set). *Let x_{ui} represent the i-th feature of record x_u of dataset $D_{n=1}^N$ where N is the number of individuals, and let $E(x_i)$ denote the entropy associated with feature value $x_{ui} \in D_{n=1}^N$. We define the set of low-entropy features $X_{low\text{-}entropy}$ as*

$$X_{low\text{-}entropy} = \{x_{ui} \in D_{n=1}^N \mid E(x_i) \leq percentile(E(x_i), y)\},$$

where $percentile(E(x_i), y)$ is the y-th percentile of the distribution of entropy values $E(x_i)$.

Definition 11 (Low-Entropy Selected Instances). *If B_k is a set of subsets of $D_{n=1}^N$, where each $b \in B_k$ contains feature $x_{ui} \in D_{n=1}^N$, then, for each $b_j \in B_k$ (where j represents the j-th instance), we define the selected background knowledge instances as*

$$b_j = \{x_{ui} \in b_j \mid x_{ui} \in X_{low\text{-}entropy}\}.$$

The set of all selected low-entropy subsets $B_{low\text{-}entropy}$ is defined as

$$B_{low\text{-}entropy} = \{b_j \mid b_j \in B_k\}.$$

In Definition 10, the low-entropy $X_{low-entropy}$ feature set is created, selecting only the feature values with the lowest values. All possible background knowledge configurations B_k are generated, but only instances containing the selected feature value in the $y\%$ lowest entropy results are selected for risk evaluation. Only the background knowledge instances b that contain feature values from $X_{low-entropy}$ are retained for risk evaluation, as defined in Definition 11. This ensures that the analysis focuses on instances featuring feature frequency with low entropy, thereby improving privacy risk assessment by considering most relevant and distinctive features from that specific dataset.

Given their infrequency or uniqueness within the dataset, low-frequency features are prone to being distinctive or having limited occurrences. Consequently, background knowledge instances containing such features are more likely to contribute to higher risk values. We have the same or very similar maximum risk values as we compute all instances of risk. As a result, including infrequent feature values in the background knowledge raises the likelihood of identifying specific individuals.

This formal approach provides a systematic method for selecting background knowledge instances containing low-entropy feature frequency, thereby enhancing the identification of instances with heightened privacy risks in the dataset. By incorporating the reduced background knowledge configuration into the risk assessment framework, we can formally analyze how targeting low-entropy values in the background knowledge configuration can lead to computational improvements in privacy risk assessment. This approach allows us to focus computational efforts on configurations featuring low-entropy features, thereby facilitating risk assessment and enhancing the accuracy of re-identification risk estimates.

5.1.3. Complexity Analysis

Reducing the number of instances to evaluate will reduce the computational complexity. By reducing the number of instances, we decrease the number of matching operations, leading to lower time and resource requirements.

To assess the risk, we simulated an attack by calculating all possible k-combinations of information that an attacker might possess. For each combination of k points, we assumed that the attacker utilized all these points to carry out the attack. This resulted in a high computational complexity of $O\left(\binom{len}{k} \times N\right)$ because the framework created $\binom{len}{k}$ different configurations of background knowledge and, for each configuration, it performed N matching operations using the matching function. We supposed we could reduce the number of combinations. In that case, we would also reduce the number of matching operations, decreasing the value of N and lowering the overall complexity.

5.2. Optimizations

This section proposes optimization strategies to enhance computational efficiency in re-identification risk assessment. We discuss approaches such as avoiding redundant computation by saving background knowledge instances and utilizing unique values to optimize memory usage.

5.2.1. Cache Strategy

We saved computational resources in the **Cache** Strategy by precomputing and caching background knowledge instances. We leveraged this approach to optimize risk computation efficiency while maintaining the PRUDEnce framework's accuracy.

Saving combinations in memory offers advantages such as computational efficiency, time savings, resource conservation, scalability, dynamic updates, flexible risk analysis, and improved response time. This approach avoids redundant calculations, enables quick risk assessments for different instances, and conserves memory compared to re-computing combinations. Overall, storing combinations in memory optimizes the risk assessment processes.

The computation of privacy risks in trajectory data analysis often involves evaluating multiple background knowledge instances for each user trajectory. However, this process can be computationally intensive, especially with large datasets. We propose a novel strategy to address this challenge that reduces redundant computations by precomputing and caching background knowledge instances.

Our approach involves two main steps:

1. **Precomputation**: We generate and cache all background knowledge configurations for each user trajectory. This step is performed once and requires computational resources in advance, but it results in significant savings during subsequent risk computations.

2. **Reuse**: During risk computation, we retrieve precomputed instances' risk value from memory instead of generating background knowledge instances dynamically. This eliminates the need for redundant computations and reduces the overall computational overhead.

By implementing this approach, we aim to simplify the risk assessment process and improve the scalability of our trajectory data analysis.

The **Original** approach, proposed in PRUDEnce, involves dynamically computing background knowledge instances for each user trajectory during risk computation. This approach is straightforward but can be computationally inefficient, especially for large datasets, as shown in Algorithm 1.

Algorithm 1 Risk computation with original approach

1: **for** each user trajectory *traj* **do**
2:     Compute all possible background knowledge instances with size *k*
3:     **for** each background knowledge instance *inst* **do**
4:         Compute risk for *inst* using matching function and update maximum risk
5:     **end for**
6: **end for**

The proposed approach, named **Cache**, precomputes and caches background knowledge instances, reducing redundant computations and improving computational efficiency, as shown in Algorithm 2.

Algorithm 2 Risk computation with Cache approach

1: Precompute and cache all background knowledge instances
2: **for** each user trajectory *traj* **do**
3:     Compute all possible background knowledge instances with size *k*
4:     Compute the matching function for each instance and save the results in memory
5:     **for** each background knowledge instance *inst* **do**
6:         Compute risk for *inst* by accessing the matching value in memory
7:     **end for**
8: **end for**

In the **Original** approach, the complexity of computing risks for all trajectories is $O\left(\binom{len}{k} \times N\right)$, as each trajectory requires matching function overall background knowledge instances.

With the **Cache** strategy, the complexity is reduced to $O\left(\binom{len}{k}\right)$ for risk computation, since the matching needs to be evaluated only once and retrieving the information from memory is linear. Therefore, the overall complexity is significantly lower compared to the **Original** approach.

5.2.2. Unique Values and Direct Evaluation

While saving combinations in memory brings several advantages, it also presents challenges and considerations. One main issue is the potential for increased memory usage, especially when dealing with large datasets or many combinations. Storing all possible combinations can lead to high memory requirements, which may demand many system resources.

The scikit-mobility library in Python (https://scikit-mobility.github.io/scikit-mobility/) (accessed on 1 May 2023), introduces an improvement related to PRUDENce risk assessment and its computation, which we will call the **Break** approach. This improvement involves the *force_instances* parameter. When using the **Original** approach and determining maximum risk, if *force_instances* is set to false and a single maximum value is detected, indicating a risk value of one, there is no need to assess additional background knowledge instances, as can be seen in Algorithm 3. This is because the trajectory risk is already at its maximum.

Algorithm 3 Risk computation with original approach + Break

1: **for** each user trajectory $traj$ **do**
2:    Compute all possible background knowledge instances with size k
3:    **for** each background knowledge instance $inst$ **do**
4:       Compute risk for $inst$ using matching function and update maximum risk
5:       **if** $risk$ is equal to 1 **then**
6:          break
7:       **end if**
8:    **end for**
9: **end for**

However, the **Break** approach relies on evaluating instances with high risk at the start of the risk evaluation process to achieve significant performance improvement. Despite this, it still involves computing more matching operations for each remaining instance. To address this issue, we propose a strategy to evaluate the risk directly, thus reducing the need to store background knowledge configurations in memory and eliminating the necessity to calculate combinations and matching operations for all instances.

Claim: if a user's trajectory contains at least one unique feature value, then the re-identification risk for that user is one without calculating background knowledge configurations.

Proof. let U denote the set of individuals, and D be the dataset. We consider a user trajectory t_u with at least one unique feature value.

The re-identification risk $PR_D(u_i|b)$ for the user trajectory t_u, given a background knowledge instance b, is defined as the probability of re-identification. If t_u contains at least one unique feature value, then at least one trajectory in D is identical to t_u, resulting in a risk of 1. This is because unique features ensure that no other trajectory in the dataset matches t_u.

Therefore, the re-identification risk for a user trajectory with at least one unique feature value is 1, without the need to calculate background knowledge configurations. This optimization simplifies the risk assessment process and saves computational resources, as it eliminates the necessity to consider background knowledge configurations for trajectories with unique features.

This refinement ensures that computational resources are utilized efficiently while maintaining privacy risk assessment integrity within the PRUDEnce framework.

The computational complexity of the PRUDEnce framework for evaluating privacy risks is $O(\binom{len}{k} \times N)$, where len represents the trajectory size, k denotes the number of elements in each background knowledge configuration, and N signifies the number of matching operations for each instance. This complexity is used to evaluate the privacy risk of a single user trajectory.

To compute the overall complexity across multiple user trajectories, each with potentially different sizes, we need to consider the total number of trajectories and sum up the complexities for each trajectory. Let M denote the number of user trajectories, and let len_i represent the size of the i-th trajectory. Then, the total complexity becomes

$$O\left(\sum_{i=1}^{M} \binom{len_i}{k} \times N\right)$$

However, when considering the reduced number of individuals that need their privacy risk evaluated, the complexity becomes

$$O\left(\sum_{i=1}^{L} \binom{len_i}{k} \times N\right)$$

where $M \geq L$. This reduction is achieved by avoiding the computation for individuals with trajectories containing unique features. This refinement ensures that computational resources are utilized efficiently while maintaining privacy risk assessment integrity within the PRUDEnce framework. □

5.2.3. Reuse Risk Value

Various knowledge levels are typically employed when assessing the *empirical privacy risk* across a dataset's user population. To enhance computational efficiency, we adopt a strategy where risk information from the previous evaluation (at knowledge level x) is reused for individuals whose data received a risk of one. This reuse principle extends to the next knowledge level $(x+1)$, implying that individuals maintaining a risk of one for knowledge level x will continue to exhibit the same maximum risk value for the subsequent knowledge level, as can be seen in Algorithm 4.

Algorithm 4 Risk Computation with Reuse Approach

1: **for** each user trajectory $traj$ **do**
2:    **if** $traj$ was evaluated for $k-1$ **then**
3:       **if** $traj$ risk is 1 **then**
4:          $risk = 1$
5:       **else**
6:          Compute all possible background knowledge instances with size k
7:          **for** each background knowledge instance $inst$ **do**
8:             Compute risk for $inst$ using matching function and update maximum risk
9:          **end for**
10:       **end if**
11:    **end if**
12: **end for**

This approach proves advantageous, especially when dealing with considerable datasets and multiple knowledge levels. By capitalizing on the consistency of risk values across consecutive knowledge levels, redundant computations are avoided, facilitating the risk assessment process.

Claim: for any set D, all combinations of x elements of S are also present in the combinations of $x+1$ elements of S.

Proof. we will prove this claim by mathematical induction.

Base Case ($k=1$): for $k=1$, the combinations of one element of S are just the elements of S. The combinations of two elements of S (C_2) will be a subset of the combinations of three elements of S (C_3).

Inductive Step: We assume that all combinations of two elements of S are in C_3. Now, we consider the combinations of two elements of S (C_2). To form C_3, we can choose any element x of S and combine it with each combination of two elements of S (C_2). So, for each combination $c \in C_2$, we can form a combination cx (where x is an element of S). Therefore, all combinations of two elements of S extended by one more element x are in C_3. This implies that all combinations of two elements of S are in C_3.

By mathematical induction, we have shown that, for any finite set S, all combinations of x elements of S are also in the combinations of $x+1$ elements of S. □

The next section will present the experimental results of implementing the proposed strategies.

6. Experiments

With these experiments, we aimed to address the following research question: *Is it possible to reduce the computational complexity of privacy risk assessment?* We evaluated our proposal using three datasets in our experimental setup: Wi-Fi, Breadcrumbs, and Foursquare. These datasets represent sources of trajectory information, each presenting unique characteristics and challenges for privacy risk assessment. All datasets were preprocessed using the scikit-mobility Python library (https://scikit-mobility.github.io/scikit-mobility/ (accessed on 1 August 2023)). The experiments were conducted on a machine with 16 vCPUs and 128 GB of RAM. The attacks used to execute the experiments were location sequence and visit attacks.

6.1. Wi-Fi Dataset

The Wi-Fi dataset was created using user device associations with the wireless access points within the university's wireless network. Each access point is associated with its geographic coordinates, indicating its installation location. To establish a connection, users must undergo authentication using a unique identifier and password, which serves as the key to access all university services. When a connection is established, a log file is updated with information such as date, time, user ID, MAC address of the access point, MAC address of the user's device, and confirmation of a successful connection. The dataset used in the experiment captures a single day's log of 14,360 undergraduate students.

6.2. Foursquare Dataset

Our Foursquare dataset is composed of check-ins in NYC collected from 12 April 2012 to 16 February 2013, almost ten months. The dataset contains 227,428 check-ins. Each check-in is associated with one user's ID, timestamp in minutes, GPS coordinates (latitude and longitude), and semantic meaning characterized by venue categories from Foursquare. This dataset was authored by [27]. We compressed the data using a radius of 100 m. This is the only dataset that we could not work with daily granularity due to its low density.

6.3. Breadcrumbs Dataset

The Breadcrumbs dataset [28] was created using data obtained during a campaign conducted in Lausanne during the spring of 2018. Eighty participants were recruited through the specialized unit Labex at the University of Lausanne. These participants completed a survey containing personal questions and, after selection, were required to sign a consent form. For our analysis, we utilized the GPS data.

6.4. Limitation

Applying the **Original** approach [11] to quantify privacy risk proved impractical with our data in several scenarios during the experiments. Despite our attempts, the **Original** approach led to indefinite runtime without producing results for some experiments. We executed the experiments for 50 days. The ones that did not end by this time had their execution time estimated based on the average time of the matching functions and the number of matching functions that would need to be executed to compute the risk.

Due to this limitation, we adopted the **Cache** strategy to facilitate risk evaluation and have the final results. We chose the **Cache** strategy to ensure that risk evaluation could proceed without excessive computation time. This approach involves precomputing and caching background knowledge instances, avoiding unnecessary recomputation during risk assessment. Importantly, adopting this strategy does not alter the risk results; rather, it optimizes computational efficiency by eliminating redundant computations.

Since the **Cache** approach produces the same results as the **Original** approach, given that it does not alter the data but only avoids unnecessary computations, we could utilize the results from the **Cache** approach as equivalent to the **Original** ones. This allowed us to compare their risk distribution curves effectively, indicating whether the optimizations provided results consistent with the **Original** approach in order to validate them.

6.5. Selecting Background Knowledge Configurations with Low-Entropy Feature Frequency

To explore the impact of varying entropy thresholds, we considered a range of values for the percentage threshold, denoted as $n\%$, from 10% to 50%. This range enabled us to assess the effects of selecting more or less data to restrict the background knowledge instances used to evaluate the risk.

We examined background knowledge configurations with knowledge sizes of 1 and 2, representing different levels of background knowledge available to an adversary. This variation allowed us to investigate the influence of knowledge and background knowledge on re-identification risk.

The features under consideration in our experiments were location and time. By examining these features, we aimed to comprehensively evaluate the efficacy of targeting low-entropy values in different dimensions of trajectory information. Incorporating these variations into our experimental design enabled us to conduct a comprehensive analysis of the impact of entropy-based filtering on privacy risk across multiple datasets, producing valuable insights into the effectiveness of this approach in reducing re-identification risk computation.

To quantify the divergence in risk distributions between the two evaluation approaches, we used the Kolmogorov–Smirnov (KS) test [18] and p-value. The test compares the distribution of a sample to a theoretical distribution to determine if significant differences exist. The Ks-statistics value and p-value from the ks test indicate whether the risk distributions of the **Original** and proposed entropy methods are statistically different. A low p-value suggests significant differences, while a high p-value suggests similarity. On the other hand, a low statistics value suggests that the distributions are more similar, and a high value suggests that values are different.

6.5.1. Wi-Fi

In the next experiments, we explored the analysis of the Wi-Fi dataset, which offers data on user mobility based on Wi-Fi access point connections. Our primary objective was to assess the distribution of re-identification risk and evaluate the potential impact of targeting low-entropy and feature frequency in background knowledge configurations. Specifically, we aimed to determine whether significant computational savings were achievable by employing a reduced method if the risk assessment distributions remained comparable between the conventional and reduced approaches. By conducting this analysis, we aimed to improve the efficacy by leveraging specific features such as location and time to enhance privacy risk assessment in Wi-Fi-based trajectory data. Through detailed examination and comparison of risk distributions, we aimed to determine the feasibility and benefits of optimizing the risk assessment process while maintaining the integrity of privacy protection mechanisms.

In Tables 1 and 2, the first line compares re-identification risk distributions using location frequency and lower entropy to reduce the background knowledge set with the standard approach (knowledge size = 1). In Table 1, low p-values suggest significant differences in re-identification risk distributions for the location sequence attack. Conversely, lower Ks-statistics values, in Table 2, represent a similar distribution. We used both measures to analyze the similarity of the distributions.

Table 1. Wi-Fi dataset: p-values for different attacks using location and time, comparing approaches.

Attack Type	Feature	k	%				
			10	20	30	40	50
Location Sequence	Location	1	3.61×10^{-92}	1.87×10^{-54}	1.27×10^{-28}	3.89×10^{-15}	8.05×10^{-8}
Visit	Location	1	0.0030071	0.1253917	0.6209664	0.8893009	0.9930435
Location Sequence	Location	2	0.0003552	0.4015571	0.9977175	0.9999999	1
Visit	Location	2	1.0	1.0	1.0	1.0	1.0
Visit	Time	1	0.0156405	0.2993241	0.8144727	0.9833140	0.9992201
Visit	Time	2	1.0	1.0	1.0	1.0	1.0

Table 2. Wi-Fi dataset: Ks-statistics for different attacks using location and time, comparing approaches.

Attack Type	Feature	k	%				
			10	20	30	40	50
Location Sequence	Location	1	0.0867411	0.0665860	0.0481105	0.0347508	0.0246375
Visit	Location	1	0.0152179	0.0099290	0.0063554	0.0048902	0.0036037
Location Sequence	Location	2	0.0175428	0.0075378	0.0033200	0.0015002	0.0015002
Visit	Location	2	5.85×10^{-6}	5.85×10^{-6}	5.85×10^{-6}	5.85×10^{-6}	5.85×10^{-6}
Visit	Time	1	0.0131452	0.0082137	0.0053548	0.0038896	0.0031034
Visit	Time	2	5.85×10^{-6}	5.85×10^{-6}	5.85×10^{-6}	5.85×10^{-6}	5.85×10^{-6}

Configurations with low-entropy locations in the Wi-Fi dataset with a knowledge size equal to 1 and the location sequence attack may not accurately represent associated risk levels when selecting only part of the instances. Only considering location with low entropy frequency would not represent the correct risk value when the knowledge size is 1. We can also notice that, as the percentage of low-entropy and location frequency increases from 10% to 50%, the p-values increase, suggesting a higher degree of similarity between risk assessments. It also means that we cannot represent the risk using small percentage values.

The second line in Table 1 provides p-values for the location sequence attack, comparing approaches using location as a feature, considering a knowledge value of $k = 2$. The p-values indicate the statistical significance of differences in re-identification risk distributions between the standard and lower entropy/location frequency reduced background knowledge set. For the location sequence attack, the p-values are relatively high, especially at higher percentages of knowledge, suggesting a lack of significant differences in risk distributions. p-values close to 1 indicate that the distributions are not very different.

The third line in Table 1 presents p-values for the visiting attack, comparing approaches using location as a feature with a knowledge value of $k = 1$. The p-values are closer to 0 than 1, indicating a significant difference between risk assessments using reduced combinations and those using the original formula considering all background knowledge. As the percentage of low entropy and location frequency increases from 10% to 50%, the p-values also increase, suggesting a higher degree of similarity between risk assessments. This implies that we cannot accurately represent the risk using a few values and low-entropy location frequency alone.

The Ks-statistics, in Table 2, presents the same results as discussed for p-values. We have high statistics values, which means that the distributions are different, and the percentage of low entropy decreases in the past, and the percentage value increases.

Background knowledge configurations targeting low-entropy locations in the Wi-Fi dataset with a knowledge size of 1 and the visiting attack may not accurately represent the associated risk levels when selecting only some instances. In this case, another feature (or combinations of features) is likely responsible for the uniqueness of the background knowledge set. Exclusively considering location with low-entropy frequency would not represent the correct risk value. Furthermore, as the percentage of low-entropy and location frequency increases from 10% to 50% , the p-values also increase, suggesting a higher degree of similarity between risk assessments. This reinforces the idea that we cannot accurately represent the risk using only a few values and low-entropy location frequency.

Table 1's fourth line presents p-values for various attacks using location to compare approaches, considering a knowledge size k of 2 and a visit attack. The p-values remain consistent across different percentages of low-entropy features (10% to 50%). For all percentages, the p-values are consistently equal to 1 in the visit attack with knowledge size 2, indicating the same results regardless of the percentage of low-entropy features considered. The same can be observed in statistics results in Table 2; all values are equal to zero, meaning that the distributions are very similar.

As the number of sets containing unique information, leading to maximum risk, increases, it becomes more probable that one of the selected sets based on entropy and location frequency will contain a location with the lowest entropy value. Consequently, as the percentage of selected locations rises, so does the likelihood of selecting a set with maximum risk. This underscores the importance of considering the knowledge size and feature uniqueness when conducting risk assessment computation improvement using entropy and frequency.

Table 1, in the fifth line, presents p-values for a visit attack using time, comparing approaches. The p-values and knowledge size are calculated for various scenarios (denoted by different percentages).

When the k value equals 1, the p-values are very low (close to zero) across different percentages, demonstrating a significant difference in distributions. Similar to the location experiments, the time shows a similar trend. When we increase the percentage value, which means that we are considering possible low-entropy time values in the background knowledge, the p-values go up because there are more chances of selecting sets with high risk. The same observations can be seen with statistics values, the values close to 1 showing the difference in the distributions. When we increase the percentage value, the statistics values get closer to 0.

Table 1's last line shows p-values for a visit attack, comparing approaches, and considering different percentages and knowledge size 2 for the background knowledge configuration. In all scenarios presented in the table, the p-values are consistently 1. This suggests that, regardless of the knowledge percentage used, there is no statistically significant difference in the distributions of re-identification risk between standard time values and lower entropy time values. The same can be observed in statistics values, where all values are very close to 0, meaning that the distributions are almost identical.

The overall analysis shows that, as the k size increases, the likelihood of encountering more unique values also grows. Furthermore, the applicability of the lower entropy shortcut is possible based on the uniqueness of the feature. This shortcut proves useful when dealing with features characterized by many unique values distributed across trajectories. Specifically, in the Wi-Fi dataset, where spatial and temporal data are densely populated due to numerous individuals connecting simultaneously within a confined area, the time and location information, when considered separately, tend to be less unique, as can be seen in Figure 4, especially for small knowledge sizes. This dataset's uniqueness arises from locations representing access points where multiple individuals can connect simultaneously. However, what truly distinguishes behaviors is the sequence of events of locations and time.

Table 3 shows that the **Low-Entropy Percentile** approach significantly reduces execution times for attacks on location and time features compared with the **Original**. For location visit attacks ($k = 1$), execution times drop from 2314 days to between 333 and 1265 days, and, for $k = 2$, from 60,395 days to between 16,147 and 48,221 days. For time visit attacks ($k = 1$), times decrease from 2300 days to between 279 and 1183 days, and, for $k = 2$, from 66,150 days to between 14,333 and 50,564 days. The reductions are more substantial for visit attacks than for location sequence attacks.

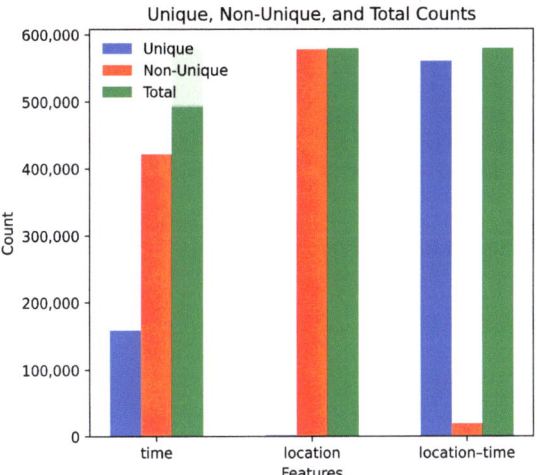

Figure 4. Comparison of uniqueness of each feature in Wi-Fi dataset.

Table 3. Wi-Fi dataset: comparing execution time of the **Original** with the **Low-Entropy Percentile** approach.

Feature	Attack	k	Original	Low-Entropy Percentile (%)				
				10	20	30	40	50
Location	Visit	1	2314 d 15:56:33 *	333 d 18:45:46 *	578 d 14:04:24 *	823 d 06:47:46 *	1047 d 18:24:01 *	1265 d 06:34:33 *
Location	Visit	2	60,395 d 07:15:07 *	16,147 d 14:50:49 *	26,565 d 23:34:52 *	35,472 d 21:17:27 *	42,547 d 12:24:11 *	48,221 d 10:07:52 *
Time	Visit	1	2300 d 11:18:24 *	279 d 14:02:02 *	506 d 19:33:25 *	743 d 07:43:46 *	967 d 18:24:16 *	1183 d 08:15:30 *
Time	Visit	2	66,150 d 12:34:55 *	14,333 d 11:20:50 *	25,392 d 18:57:42 *	35,380 d 04:18:53 *	43,744 d 12:00:07 *	50,564 d 22:53:36 *
Location	Location Sequence	1	20 d 21:13:00	3 d 00:10:10	5 d 04:56:02	7 d 09:07:40	9 d 10:58:54	11 d 09:30:32
Location	Location Sequence	2	9793 d 01:38:34 *	2622 d 15:51:25 *	4315 d 06:34:55 *	5762 d 05:53:01 *	6911 d 02:56:44 *	7824 d 13:56:32 *

d = days, * = estimated value.

The **Break** and **Low-Entropy Percentile** approach consistently reduces execution times for all attack types compared to the **Break** method. Table 4 shows that, for location visit attacks ($k = 1$), times drop from 141 days to between 117 and 132 days, and, for $k = 2$, from 420 days to between 261 and 375 days. For time visit attacks ($k = 1$), times decrease from 141 days to between 116 and 131 days, and, for $k = 2$, from 460 days to between 276 and 393 days. Location sequence attacks ($k = 1$) show reductions from 20 days to between 3 and 11 days, and, for $k = 2$, from 2224 days to between 679 and 1787 days.

Table 4. Wi-Fi dataset: comparing execution time of **Break** with **Break** and **Low-Entropy Percentile**.

Feature	Attack	k	Break	Break and Low-Entropy Percentile (%)				
				10	20	30	40	50
Location	Visit	1	141 d 14:00:20 *	117 d 21:35:56 *	122 d 06:13:04 *	126 d 04:30:50 *	129 d 21:23:35 *	132 d 05:01:04 *
Location	Visit	2	420 d 11:00:30 *	261 d 18:08:00 *	299 d 04:57:55 *	330 d 22:00:50 *	356 d 05:17:00 *	375 d 10:04:31 *
Time	Visit	1	141 d 09:28:44 *	116 d 19:40:06 *	120 d 22:52:17 *	124 d 18:53:17 *	128 d 01:43:16 *	131 d 03:22:09 *
Time	Visit	2	460 d 15:01:30 *	276 d 10:08:00 *	318 d 01:41:22 *	351 d 01:34:19 *	375 d 17:59:05 *	393 d 17:07:11 *
Location	Location Sequence	1	20 d 09:33:00	3 d 01:13:30	5 d 03:45:08	7 d 06:02:21	9 d 05:41:11	11 d 02:18:06
Location	Location Sequence	2	2224 d 04:56:55 *	679 d 22:57:11 *	1038 d 00:35:32 *	1352 d 15:14:34 *	1593 d 03:25:48 *	1787 d 20:57:34 *

d = days, * = estimated value.

6.5.2. Breadcrumbs

Now, we present the analysis of the Breadcrumbs dataset. Our objective was to examine the distribution of re-identification risk and explore the potential implications of targeting low entropy and feature frequency within background knowledge configurations. We aim to verify whether real computational benefits are achievable by adopting our low-entropy approach, demonstrating that the risk assessment distributions exhibit similarity between the conventional and reduced methodologies. This analysis shows the efficacy of leveraging specific features such as location and time to support privacy risk assessment in breadcrumb trajectory data.

Table 5 presents *p*-values for various attacks using location and time-frequency with lower entropy to reduce the background knowledge set compared with the standard approach and considering different *k* sizes. The *p*-values, all equal to 1, indicate no statistically significant differences in the distribution of re-identification risk across different k sizes. It implies that the location and time features are sufficiently unique, as seen in Figure 5, to serve as filters for selecting background knowledge configurations prone to having maximum risk. The same observation can be seen with statistics values in Table 6. All values are zero, which means that the distributions are the same.

Table 5. Breadcrumbs dataset: *p*-values for different attacks using location and time, comparing approaches.

Attack Type	Feature	k	Percentage				
			10%	20%	30%	40%	50%
Location Sequence	Location	1	1.0	1.0	1.0	1.0	1.0
Visit	Location	1	1.0	1.0	1.0	1.0	1.0
Location Sequence	Location	2	1.0	1.0	1.0	1.0	1.0
Visit	Location	2	1.0	1.0	1.0	1.0	1.0
Visit	Time	1	1.0	1.0	1.0	1.0	1.0
Visit	Time	2	1.0	1.0	1.0	1.0	1.0

Table 6. Breadcrumbs dataset: Ks-statistics for different attacks using location and time, comparing approaches.

Attack Type	Feature	k	Percentage				
			10%	20%	30%	40%	50%
Location Sequence	Location	1	0.0	0.0	0.0	0.0	0.0
Visit	Location	1	0.0	0.0	0.0	0.0	0.0
Location Sequence	Location	2	0.0	0.0	0.0	0.0	0.0
Visit	Location	2	0.0	0.0	0.0	0.0	0.0
Visit	Time	1	0.0	0.0	0.0	0.0	0.0
Visit	Time	2	0.0	0.0	0.0	0.0	0.0

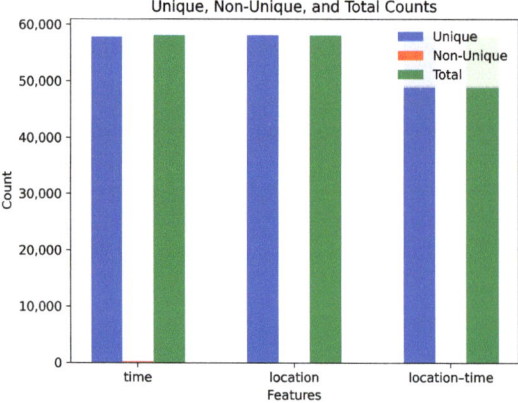

Figure 5. Comparison of uniqueness of each feature in Breadcrumbs dataset.

Table 7 shows the reduction in execution times for different attacks on location and time features using the **Low-Entropy Percentile** approach compared to the **Original**. For location features with visit attacks ($k = 1$), the **Original** time of 7 days decreases to between 0.98 and 3.91 days. For visit attacks ($k = 2$), the **Original** time of 69 days reduces to between 16 and 54 days. Similarly, for time features with visit attacks ($k = 1$), the **Original** seven days decrease to between almost 1 and 3 days, while visit attacks ($k = 2$) reduce from 69 days to between 16 and 54 days. Location sequence attacks ($k = 1$) show a reduction from 7 days to between almost 1 and 3 days, and, for $k = 2$, the time reduces from 69 days to between 16 and 54 days. The **Low-Entropy Percentile** approach consistently reduces execution times across all attacks.

Table 7. Breadcrumbs dataset: comparing execution time of the **Original** with the **Low-Entropy Percentile** approach.

Feature	Attack	k	Original	Low-Entropy Percentile (%)				
				10	20	30	40	50
Location	Visit	1	7 d 12:23:57	0 d 23:37:37	1 d 17:29:53	2 d 12:13:42	3 d 05:19:08	3 d 21:41:34
Location	Visit	2	69 d 21:08:34 *	16 d 08:16:34	27 d 23:14:20	38 d 13:14:57	47 d 05:13:02	54 d 04:18:26 *
Time	Visit	1	7 d 12:24:06	0 d 23:37:46	1 d 17:30:03	2 d 12:13:56	3 d 05:19:26	3 d 21:41:34
Time	Visit	2	69 d 21:08:35 *	16 d 08:16:35	27 d 23:14:23	38 d 13:14:47	47 d 05:16:15	54 d 04:18:20 *
Location	Location Sequence	1	7 d 12:23:57	0 d 23:37:36	1 d 17:29:50	2 d 12:13:44	3 d 05:20:17	3 d 21:41:26
Location	Location Sequence	2	69 d 21:08:22 *	16 d 08:15:24	27 d 23:13:08	38 d 13:14:22	47 d 05:13:11	54 d 04:18:45 *

d = days, * = estimated value.

Table 8 demonstrates that the **Break** and **Low-Entropy Percentile** approach consistently reduces execution times for all attack types compared to the **Break** method alone. For location visit attacks ($k = 1$), times drop from 1 day 20 h to around 14 h. For visit attacks ($k = 2$), times decrease from 1 day 11 h to around 33 h. For Time visit attacks ($k = 1$), times were reduced from 13 h 45 min to around 15 min. For visit attacks ($k = 2$), times drop from almost 14 h to between 37 and 39 min. Location sequence attacks ($k = 1$) show reductions from 1 day 20 h to between 40 and 43 min, and, for $k = 2$, from 1 day 11 h to around 10 h.

Table 8. Breadcrumbs dataset: comparing execution time of **Break** with **Break** and **Low-Entropy Percentile**.

Feature	Attack	k	Break	Low-Entropy Percentile (%)				
				10	20	30	40	50
Location	Visit	1	1 d 20:14:54	13:54:21	13:54:30	13:55:27	13:56:30	13:57:22
Location	Visit	2	1 d 11:27:51	32:54:00	32:55:22	32:56:11	32:57:17	32:58:00
Time	Visit	1	13:45:33	00:14:21	00:14:43	00:15:11	00:15:34	00:15:54
Time	Visit	2	13:52:53	00:37:22	00:38:11	00:39:31	00:39:33	00:39:41
Location	Location sequence	1	1 d 20:14:54	00:40:35	00:41:05	00:41:48	00:42:30	00:43:15
Location	Location Sequence	2	1 d 11:27:51	09:45:00	09:46:12	09:47:09	09:48:24	09:49:23

d = days.

6.5.3. Foursquare

In the next experiments, we explored the examination of the Foursquare dataset. Our primary aim was to analyze the distribution of re-identification risk and assess the potential impact of targeting low entropy and feature frequency within background knowledge configurations. We aimed to determine whether significant computational efficiencies were possible by adopting a streamlined approach, provided that the risk assessment distributions demonstrated comparability between the conventional and reduced methodologies. Through this analysis, we proved the effectiveness of leveraging specific features such as location and time to improve the computation of privacy risk assessment in Foursquare-based trajectory data.

Table 9 provides *p*-values for attacks using location values with lower entropy at a *k* value of 1. All *p*-values indicate no statistically significant differences, with values of 1 for all attack types. In both cases, location and time, *p*-values are 1 for all percentages, indicating no significant variations in the risk distribution. The same observation can be seen with statistics values in Table 10. All values are zero, which means that the distributions are the same.

The successful performance of the time- and location-reduced set approach in the Foursquare, as can be seen in Figure 6, and Breadcrumb, as shown in Figure 5, datasets can be attributed to the high uniqueness in both dimensions. These datasets likely exhibit diverse location and time values, making them suitable for re-identification risk computation mitigation strategies. The effectiveness of this method improves as the k size increases. Increasing the granularity (larger k) for datasets with less unique information can enhance the quality of the re-identification risk computation mitigation result.

Table 9. Foursquare dataset: p-values for different attacks using location and time, comparing approaches.

Attack Type	Feature	k	Percentage				
			10%	20%	30%	40%	50%
Location Sequence	Location	1	1.0	1.0	1.0	1.0	1.0
Visit	Location	1	1.0	1.0	1.0	1.0	1.0
Location Sequence	Location	2	1.0	1.0	1.0	1.0	1.0
Visit	Location	2	1.0	1.0	1.0	1.0	1.0
Visit	Time	1	1.0	1.0	1.0	1.0	1.0
Visit	Time	2	1.0	1.0	1.0	1.0	1.0

Table 10. Foursquare dataset: Ks-statistics for different attacks using location and time, comparing approaches.

Attack Type	Feature	k	Percentage				
			10%	20%	30%	40%	50%
Location Sequence	Location	1	0.0	0.0	0.0	0.0	0.0
Visit	Location	1	0.0	0.0	0.0	0.0	0.0
Location Sequence	Location	2	0.0	0.0	0.0	0.0	0.0
Visit	Location	2	0.0	0.0	0.0	0.0	0.0
Visit	Time	1	0.0	0.0	0.0	0.0	0.0
Visit	Time	2	0.0	0.0	0.0	0.0	0.0

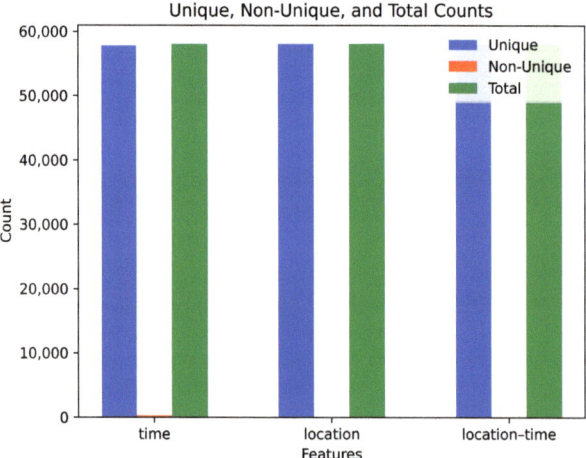

Figure 6. Comparison of uniqueness of each feature in Foursquare dataset.

Table 11 demonstrates that the **Low-Entropy Percentile** approach significantly reduces execution times for all attack types compared to the **Original** method. For location visit attacks ($k = 1$), times drop from 6 days to between 15 h and 3 days 7 h. For visit attacks ($k = 2$), times decrease from an estimated 51,240 days to between 10,094 and 39,641 days. For time visit attacks ($k = 1$), times reduce from 5 days 12 h to between 13 h and 2 days 16 h. For visit attacks ($k = 2$), times drop from an estimated 27,423 days to between 7681 and 30,354 days. Location sequence attacks ($k = 1$) show reductions from 1 day 13 h to between 3 and 19 h, and, for $k = 2$, from an estimated 30,023 days to between 5898 and 23,059 days.

Table 12 demonstrates that the **Low-Entropy Percentile** approach significantly reduces execution times for all attack types compared to the **Break** method. For location visit attacks ($k = 1$), times drop from 3 h 51 min to between 1 h 10 min and 2 h 8 min. For visit attacks ($k = 2$), times decrease from 12 days 8 h to around 3 days 19 h. For time visit attacks ($k = 1$), times reduce from 9 h 14 min to around 1 h. For visit attacks ($k = 2$), times drop from 25 days 3 h to less than 3 days. Location sequence attacks ($k = 1$) show reductions from 1 h 29 min to between 18 min and 1 h 3 min, and, for $k = 2$, from 7 days 7 h to around 2 days 7 h.

Table 11. Foursquare dataset: comparing execution time of the **Original** with the **Low-Entropy Percentile** approach.

Feature	Attack	k	Original	Low-Entropy Percentile (%)				
				10	20	30	40	50
Location	Visit	1	6 d 06:47:08	0 d 15:43:13	1 d 07:29:38	1 d 23:06:18	2 d 15:22:10	3 d 07:28:55
Location	Visit	2	51,240 d 00:00:00 *	10,094 d 05:08:37 *	19,269 d 10:44:57 *	27,007 d 01:13:54 *	33,839 d 02:03:27 *	39,641 d 04:36:32 *
Time	Visit	1	5 d 12:13:19	0 d 13:40:29	1 d 02:50:54	1 d 16:05:08	2 d 03:17:10	2 d 16:20:52
Time	Visit	2	27,423 d 16:04:48 *	7681 d 22:45:46 *	13,257 d 00:33:28 *	20,222 d 18:00:00 *	26,018 d 14:16:43 *	30,354 d 18:22:45 *
Location	Location Sequence	1	1 d 13:07:10	0 d 03:53:55	0 d 07:41:12	0 d 11:34:05	0 d 15:29:44	0 d 19:26:50
Location	Location Sequence	2	30,023 d 22:55:36 *	5898 d 14:19:11 *	11,089 d 04:50:01 *	15,697 d 02:44:33 *	19,623 d 12:54:34 *	23,059 d 20:04:34 *

d = days, * = estimated value.

Table 12. Foursquare dataset: Comparing execution time of **Break** with **Break** and **Low-Entropy Percentile**.

Feature	Attack	k	Break	Low-Entropy Percentile (%)				
				10	20	30	40	50
Location	Visit	1	0 d 03:51:48	0 d 01:10:00	0 d 01:28:13	0 d 01:43:45	0 d 01:57:22	0 d 02:08:09
Location	Visit	2	12 d 08:03:21	3 d 18:13:14	3 d 18:40:56	3 d 18:58:12	3 d 19:04:23	3 d 19:07:03
Time	Visit	1	0 d 09:14:02	0 d 00:58:20	0 d 00:59:45	0 d 01:00:36	0 d 01:01:26	0 d 01:01:55
Time	Visit	2	25 d 03:46:50	2 d 22:27:40	2 d 22:48:25	2 d 23:07:16	2 d 23:16:15	2 d 23:19:30
Location	Location Sequence	1	0 d 01:29:24	0 d 00:18:53	0 d 00:39:13	0 d 00:47:09	0 d 00:55:15	0 d 01:03:27
Location	Location Sequence	2	7 d 07:37:38	2 d 06:03:07	2 d 06:29:51	2 d 06:54:20	2 d 07:03:17	2 d 07:08:42

d = days.

In summary, as the percentage increases, the accuracy of the risk assessment improves correspondingly. A similar trend is observed with the k value, where larger k values yield more accurate risk estimates. Regarding the types of attacks, the visit attack produced more accurate results compared to the location sequence attack. Additionally, the use of entropy on location or time showed varying results depending on the dataset's unique characteristics. These variations are closely linked to the uniqueness inherent in the data.

6.6. Cache

Although the entropy approach significantly reduced execution times, some values still need to be improved for practical use. The **Cache** strategy can ensure the feasibility of executing risk assessments efficiently. By leveraging the **Cache** strategy, we can substantially reduce execution times, making the process more practical and manageable. This method ensures that risk assessments can be conducted within reasonable time frames, thereby enhancing the overall efficiency and effectiveness of the evaluation process.

Table 13 compares execution times for various attacks on location and time features using the **Original** and **Cache** approaches across three different datasets: Wi-Fi, Foursquare, and Breadcrumbs. For location visit attacks ($k = 1$), the **Original** approach's execution times are significantly longer than those of the **Cache** approach, with reductions from 2314 days to 12 h in the Wi-Fi dataset, from 6 days to 2 min in the Foursquare dataset, and from 7 days to 2 min in the Breadcrumbs dataset. For visit attacks ($k = 2$), similar reductions are observed, with **Original** times decreasing from 60,395 days to 11 days (Wi-Fi), 51,240 days to 3 min (Foursquare), and 69 days to 9 min (Breadcrumbs). For time visit attacks ($k = 1$ and $k = 2$), the **Cache** approach consistently reduces execution times from thousands of days to a few days or minutes across all datasets. Location sequence attacks also show substantial reductions, with **Cache** times significantly shorter than **Original** times across all datasets. The **Cache** approach effectively reduces execution times for all attack types and datasets.

Table 13. Comparing the execution time of the **Original** and **Cache** approaches across different sources.

Feature	Attack	k	Wi-Fi		Foursquare		Breadcrumbs	
			Original	Cache	Original	Cache	Original	Cache
Location	Visit	1	2314 d 15:56:33 *	0 d 12:32:48	6 d 06:47:34	0 d 00:02:25	7 d 12:24:40	0 d 00:02:27
Location	Visit	2	60,395 d 07:15:07 *	11 d 00:45:50	51,240 d * 04:08:24	0 d 03:11:26	69 d 21:21:32 *	0 d 00:09:44
Time	Visit	1	2300 d 11:18:24 *	5 d 21:52:28	5 d 12:12:56	0 d 00:02:27	7 d 12:24:54	0 d 00:02:41
Time	Visit	2	66,150 d 12:34:55 *	12 d 14:52:15	39,530 d 04:45:22 *	0 d 03:15:42	69 d 21:33:26 *	0 d 00:10:36
Location	Location Sequence	1	20 d 21:13:00 *	0 d 13:47:01	1 d 13:19:26	0 d 00:02:20	7 d 12:24:42	0 d 00:02:18
Location	Location Sequence	2	9793 d 01:38:34 *	10 d 08:23:16	30,023 d 22:55:32 *	0 d 03:04:53	69 d 21:19:14 *	0 d 00:08:29

d = days, * = estimated value.

6.7. Reuse Risk Value

Table 14 provides results comparing the risk distribution between the current privacy risk state and the application of the reuse approach. The reported p-values of 1 for all attacks suggest that the distributions are statistically the same, thereby validating the effectiveness of the reuse approach.

This implies that, after the reuse approach, the privacy risk state does not differ from the initial state. The p-value of 1 indicates a lack of statistical significance, supporting that the distributions are comparable. In other words, the reuse approach does not introduce changes in the risk distribution, reinforcing its validity as a privacy-preserving strategy across the three datasets.

Table 14. p-values for different attacks reusing risk evaluation from $k - 1$ results.

Attack Type	k = 2	k = 3
Location Sequence	1	1
Visit	1	1
Location Sequence	1	1
Visit	1	1
Location Sequence	1	1
Visit	1	1

6.8. Unique Values and Direct Evaluation

The information provided in Table 15 indicates the number of user trajectories assigned with a risk equal to one for each attack. For most attacks, there is a very high number of directly evaluated risks equal to one. This suggests that directly assessing risk for attacks with features having unique values is effective. The approach seems to work well in scenarios where features contribute to the uniqueness of trajectories.

Location sequence attacks could have yielded better results. This could be attributed to the need for more uniqueness in a location with a knowledge size of 1, making it challenging to differentiate trajectories based on them. It aligns with the understanding that features with less uniqueness may perform poorly in this direct risk evaluation approach. This happens due to the nature of Wi-Fi data, where location information is not unique enough with a knowledge size of 1, as shown in the previous experiments, to effectively differentiate trajectories due to its dense characteristics.

Table 15. Trajectories directly assigned with a risk of 1 per attack.

Attack	Dataset	%
Location Sequence	Wi-Fi	3.68
Visit	Wi-Fi	52.30
Location Sequence	Breadcrumbs	100
Visit	Breadcrumbs	100
Location Sequence	Foursquare	99.88
Visit	Foursquare	100

In conclusion, the direct risk evaluation approach appears promising for attacks involving unique values, but its effectiveness varies depending on the feature's uniqueness in different datasets. The challenges observed with a location in the Wi-Fi dataset highlight the importance of considering the feature's nature when applying this risk assessment approach.

6.9. Discussion

When comparing the reduction of the background knowledge configuration set size using low entropy and feature frequency with the **Cache** strategies, if the wrong feature is chosen to be used in the entropy approach, incorrect risk values might appear, impacting the quality of the risk assessment. However, depending on the dataset size, the **Cache** strategy or the **Original** evaluation form may not be feasible. Therefore, reducing the background knowledge configuration set size using low entropy and feature frequency should only be applied if the user encounters memory issues due to the huge size of background knowledge configurations when attempting to save them in memory and when the dataset has at least one feature that brings uniqueness to the trajectory.

Additionally, if the user faces memory limitations while trying to store all background knowledge configurations in memory, reducing the configuration set size becomes necessary to ensure the feasibility of the risk evaluation process. The decision to reduce the background knowledge configuration set size should be made based on the specific characteristics of the dataset, the available memory resources, and the desired level of risk evaluation accuracy.

Time and space features play a crucial role in determining how many trajectories need their risk computed, how many background knowledge instances require re-identification risk evaluation, and in the quality of the risk assessment. It means that the more unique the time, space, or a combination of both are in a dataset, the fewer trajectories will need risk evaluation and the fewer background knowledge instances will require re-identification probability assessment. This is because, if a trajectory contains unique features, it is considered unique, and its re-identification risk is automatically set to the maximum (i.e., 1). Similarly, if we identify a background knowledge instance that contains unique information, we do not need to further evaluate its probability of re-identification, since it will also be the maximum. It results in a significant improvement in time performance.

7. Conclusions and Future Work

Privacy risk assessment is a crucial aspect of any privacy-preserving process, which involves understanding which individuals in the data are vulnerable to privacy violations and quantifying the associated risk. One significant challenge in assessing risk is reducing the computational processing associated with the adversary's background knowledge set size and risk assessment.

Most of the current works on privacy focus on Deferentially Private Machine Learning techniques and/or federated learning approaches. In this work, we focus on privacy risk assessment to increase the ability of researchers and practitioners to correctly understand what kinds of risks are inherently present in the data they are using. With this work, we hope to provide concrete solutions to enable efficient privacy risk estimation for human mobility data.

The main contribution of this article addresses the challenge posed by the computational complexity of privacy risk evaluation. We focused on potential methodologies to mitigate this complexity, aiming to reduce the combination set and optimize code performance for computing the highest risk trajectories. Leveraging the inherent uniqueness of trajectory data, we aimed to minimize the size of the combination set and simplify the risk evaluation process for trajectories with distinctive attributes. Furthermore, we enhanced computational efficiency by implementing strategies to store essential information in memory, thereby minimizing the need for redundant computations.

As a result of the experiments, while the proposed optimization strategies showed promise in enhancing computational efficiency and risk assessment accuracy, their effectiveness varied depending on the uniqueness of features within different datasets. Understanding the nature of features is crucial in selecting appropriate risk assessment approaches and optimizations. It is important to consider the trade-offs associated with this reduction approach carefully. While it can help reduce memory constraints and improve computational efficiency, it may also lead to information loss and potential inaccuracies in risk assessment if crucial configurations are excluded due to the wrong approach choice. The uniqueness of features should be evaluated in order to use those approaches.

The strategies outlined above are effective when dealing with datasets containing unique data, such as trajectory datasets. However, challenges arise when the dataset is less unique due to generalization and data protection measures. In such cases, the performance of the direct risk evaluation approach, reduced memory saving and entropy, and frequency are affected, highlighting the need for alternative strategies to address these challenges. Our work has some limitations that could be the subject of future research: the definition of a good set of attacks is still heavily human-dependent and does not take into account a precise analysis of the resources needed by the adversary. Therefore, the simulated attacks may be unrealistic. Selecting more realistic attacks may further improve the assessment efficiency, by pruning unreasonable simulations.

Furthermore, future works using parallelization would be important for evaluating such cases. Another open challenge is determining the optimal percentage value to use. Selecting the percentage value for features with low entropy can impact the quality and accuracy of the risk assessment.

Author Contributions: Conceptualization, F.O.G., R.P., A.M. and C.R.; Methodology, F.O.G., R.P., A.M., C.R. and J.E.M.; Validation, A.M., C.R. and J.E.M.; Formal analysis, F.O.G., R.P. and A.M.; Investigation, F.O.G., R.P. and C.R.; Resources, C.R. and J.E.M.; Data curation, F.O.G., A.M. and C.R.; Writing—original draft, F.O.G.; Writing—review & editing, R.P., A.M., C.R. and J.E.M.; Supervision, A.M., C.R. and J.E.M.; Funding acquisition, J.E.M., A.M. and C.R. All authors have read and agreed to the published version of the manuscript.

Funding: This study was financed in part by the Coordenação de Aperfeiçoamento de Pessoal de Nível Superior—Brasil (CAPES)—Finance Code 001. SoBigData.it receives funding from European Union – NextGenerationEU—National Recovery and Resilience Plan (Piano Nazionale di Ripresa e Resilienza, PNRR)—Project: "SoBigData.it—Strengthening the Italian RI for Social Mining and Big Data Analytics"—Prot. IR0000013—Avviso n. 3264 del 28/12/2021. This work has been also supported by the PNRR-M4C2-Investimento 1.3, Partenariato Esteso PE00000013-"FAIR-Future Artificial Intelligence Research"-Spoke 1 "Human-centered AI", funded by the European Commission under the NextGeneration EU programme.

Institutional Review Board Statement: Not applicable.

Informed Consent Statement: Not applicable.

Data Availability Statement: Wi-Fi data are unavailable due to privacy restrictions. Breadcrumbs requires a request to the paper authors to access their database [28]. Foursquare information is available here: (https://https://www.foursquare.com/) (accessed on 15 June 2022).

Conflicts of Interest: The authors declare no conflicts of interest.

References

1. Machanavajjhala, A.; Gehrke, J.; Kifer, D.; Venkitasubramaniam, M. l-diversity: Privacy beyond k-anonymity. In Proceedings of the 22nd International Conference on Data Engineering Workshops, Atlanta, GA, USA, 3–7 April 2006; IEEE: Piscataway, NJ, USA, 2006; p. 24.
2. Zang, H.; Bolot, J. Anonymization of location data does not work: A large-scale measurement study. In Proceedings of the 17th Annual International Conference on Mobile Computing and Networking, Las Vegas, NV, USA, 19–23 September 2011; ACM: New York, NY, USA, 2011; pp. 145–156.
3. Abul, O.; Bonchi, F.; Nanni, M. Never walk alone: Uncertainty for anonymity in moving objects databases. In Proceedings of the 2008 IEEE 24th International Conference on Data Engineering, Cancún, Mexico, 7–12 April 2008; IEEE: Piscataway, NJ, USA, 2008; pp. 376–385.
4. Trabelsi, S.; Salzgeber, V.; Bezzi, M.; Montagnon, G. Data disclosure risk evaluation. In Proceedings of the 2009 Fourth International Conference on Risks and Security of Internet and Systems (CRiSIS 2009), Toulouse, France, 19–22 October 2009; IEEE: Piscataway, NJ, USA, 2009; pp. 35–72.
5. Achara, J.P.; Acs, G.; Castelluccia, C. On the unicity of smartphone applications. In Proceedings of the 14th ACM Workshop on Privacy in the Electronic Society, Denver, CO, USA, 12 October 2015; pp. 27–36.
6. Song, Y.; Dahlmeier, D.; Bressan, S. Not So Unique in the Crowd: A Simple and Effective Algorithm for Anonymizing Location Data. *PIR@ SIGIR* **2014**, *2014*, 19–24.
7. Narayanan, A.; Shmatikov, V. De-anonymizing Social Networks. In Proceedings of the 30th IEEE Symposium on Security and Privacy (S&P 2009), Oakland, CA, USA, 17–20 May 2009; pp. 173–187. [CrossRef]
8. Ramachandran, A.; Kim, Y.; Chaintreau, A. "I knew they clicked when i saw them with their friends": Identifying your silent web visitors on social media. In Proceedings of the Second ACM Conference on Online Social Networks, COSN 2014, Dublin, Ireland, 1–2 October 2014; pp. 239–246. [CrossRef]
9. Pellungrini, R.; Pappalardo, L.; Pratesi, F.; Monreale, A. A data mining approach to assess privacy risk in human mobility data. *ACM Trans. Intell. Syst. Technol. (TIST)* **2017**, *9*, 1–27. [CrossRef]
10. Naretto, F.; Pellungrini, R.; Nardini, F.M.; Giannotti, F. Prediction and Explanation of Privacy Risk on Mobility Data with Neural Networks. In Proceedings of the ECML PKDD 2020 Workshops, Ghent, Belgium, 14–18 September 2020.
11. Pratesi, F.; Monreale, A.; Trasarti, R.; Giannotti, F.; Pedreschi, D.; Yanagihara, T. PRUDEnce: A system for assessing privacy risk vs. utility in data sharing ecosystems. *Trans. Data Priv.* **2018**, *11*, 139–167.
12. Armando, A.; Bezzi, M.; Metoui, N.; Sabetta, A. Risk-Based Privacy-Aware Information Disclosure. *Int. J. Secur. Softw. Eng.* **2015**, *6*, 70–89. [CrossRef]
13. Khalfoun, B.; Ben Mokhtar, S.; Bouchenak, S.; Nitu, V. EDEN: Enforcing Location Privacy through Re-Identification Risk Assessment: A Federated Learning Approach. *Proc. ACM Interact. Mob. Wearable Ubiquitous Technol.* **2021**, *5*, 1–25. [CrossRef]
14. Silva, P.; Gonçalves, C.; Antunes, N.; Curado, M.; Walek, B. Privacy risk assessment and privacy-preserving data monitoring. *Expert Syst. Appl.* **2022**, *200*, 116867. [CrossRef]
15. Lundberg, S.M.; Lee, S.I. A unified approach to interpreting model predictions. In Proceedings of the 31st International Conference on Neural Information Processing Systems, Long Beach, CA, USA, 4–9 December 2017; Volume 30.
16. Ribeiro, M.T.; Singh, S.; Guestrin, C. "Why should i trust you?" Explaining the predictions of any classifier. In Proceedings of the 22nd ACM SIGKDD International Conference on Knowledge Discovery and Data Mining, San Francisco, CA, USA, 13–17 August 2016; pp. 1135–1144.
17. Naretto, F.; Pellungrini, R.; Rinzivillo, S.; Fadda, D. EXPHLOT: EXplainable Privacy Assessment for Human LOcation Trajectories. In Proceedings of the International Conference on Discovery Science, Porto, Portugal, 9–11 October 2023; Springer: Berlin/Heidelberg, Germany, 2023; pp. 325–340.
18. An, K. Sulla determinazione empirica di una legge didistribuzione. *Giorn Dell'inst Ital Degli Att* **1933**, *4*, 89–91.
19. Smirnov, N. Table for estimating the goodness of fit of empirical distributions. *Ann. Math. Stat.* **1948**, *19*, 279–281. [CrossRef]
20. Torra, V. *Data Privacy: Foundations, New Developments and the Big Data Challenge*, 1st ed.; Springer Publishing Company: Berlin/Heidelberg, Germany, 2017.
21. Elliot, M. Integrating File and Record Level Disclosure Risk Assessment. In *Inference Control in Statistical Databases: From Theory to Practice*; Domingo-Ferrer, J., Ed.; Springer: Berlin/Heidelberg, Germany, 2002; pp. 126–134. [CrossRef]
22. Franconi, L.; Polettini, S. Individual Risk Estimation in μ-Argus: A Review. In *Privacy in Statistical Databases, Proceedings of the CASC Project Final Conference, PSD 2004, Barcelona, Spain, 9–11 June 2004. Proceedings*; Domingo-Ferrer, J., Torra, V., Eds.; Springer: Berlin/Heidelberg, Germany, 2004; pp. 262–272. [CrossRef]
23. Mohammed, N.; Fung, B.C.; Debbabi, M. Walking in the crowd: Anonymizing trajectory data for pattern analysis. In Proceedings of the 18th ACM Conference on Information and Knowledge Management, Hong Kong, China, 2–6 November 2009; pp. 1441–1444.
24. Yarovoy, R.; Bonchi, F.; Lakshmanan, L.V.; Wang, W.H. Anonymizing moving objects: How to hide a mob in a crowd? In Proceedings of the 12th International Conference on Extending Database Technology: Advances in Database Technology, Saint-Petersburg, Russia, 24–26 March 2009; pp. 72–83.
25. De Montjoye, Y.A.; Hidalgo, C.A.; Verleysen, M.; Blondel, V.D. Unique in the crowd: The privacy bounds of human mobility. *Sci. Rep.* **2013**, *3*, 1376. [CrossRef] [PubMed]

26. Shannon, C.E. A mathematical theory of communication. *Bell Syst. Tech. J.* **1948**, *27*, 379–423. [CrossRef]
27. Yang, D.; Zhang, D.; Zheng, V.W.; Yu, Z. Modeling user activity preference by leveraging user spatial temporal characteristics in LBSNs. *IEEE Trans. Syst. Man Cybern. Syst.* **2014**, *45*, 129–142. [CrossRef]
28. Moro, A.; Kulkarni, V.; Ghiringhelli, P.A.; Chapuis, B.; Huguenin, K.; Garbinato, B. Breadcrumbs: A Rich Mobility Dataset with Point-of-Interest Annotations. In Proceedings of the 27th ACM SIGSPATIAL International Conference on Advances in Geographic Information Systems, Chicago, IL, USA, 5–8 November 2019; pp. 508–511.

Disclaimer/Publisher's Note: The statements, opinions and data contained in all publications are solely those of the individual author(s) and contributor(s) and not of MDPI and/or the editor(s). MDPI and/or the editor(s) disclaim responsibility for any injury to people or property resulting from any ideas, methods, instructions or products referred to in the content.

Article

Mutation-Based Multivariate Time-Series Anomaly Generation on Latent Space with an Attention-Based Variational Recurrent Neural Network for Robust Anomaly Detection in an Industrial Control System

Seungho Jeon [1], Kijong Koo [2], Daesung Moon [2] and Jung Taek Seo [1,*]

1. Department of Computer Engineering (Smart Security), Gachon University, Seongnam-daero 1342, Seongnam-si 13119, Republic of Korea; shjeon90@gachon.ac.kr
2. Electronics and Telecommunications Research Institute (ETRI), Daejeon 34129, Republic of Korea; kjkoo@etri.re.kr (K.K.); daesung@etri.re.kr (D.M.)
* Correspondence: seojt@gachon.ac.kr; Tel.: +82-031-750-4775

Abstract: Anomaly detection involves identifying data that deviates from normal patterns. Two primary strategies are used: one-class classification and binary classification. In Industrial Control Systems (ICS), where anomalies can cause significant damage, timely and accurate detection is essential, often requiring analysis of time-series data. One-class classification is commonly used but tends to have a high false alarm rate. To address this, binary classification is explored, which can better differentiate between normal and anomalous data, though it struggles with class imbalance in ICS datasets. This paper proposes a mutation-based technique for generating ICS time-series anomalies. The method maps ICS time-series data into a latent space using a variational recurrent autoencoder, applies mutation operations, and reconstructs the time-series, introducing plausible anomalies that reflect multivariate correlations. Evaluations of ICS datasets show that these synthetic anomalies are visually and statistically credible. Training a binary classifier on data augmented with these anomalies effectively mitigates the class imbalance problem.

Keywords: anomaly generation; variational Bayes; attention mechanism; recurrent neural network; industrial control system

1. Introduction

Anomaly detection is the task of predicting anomalous data that exhibit different patterns from normal data. It plays a crucial role in various fields such as finance [1], industrial control systems (ICS) [2], and cybersecurity [3]. There are two main approaches to classifying anomalies from normal data: one-class classification and binary classification. (1) One-class classification involves training a classifier using only one type of data (typically normal data) to predict anomalous data [4,5]. This strategy is commonly adopted in most domains because anomalous data is often rare and difficult to collect compared to normal data. (2) On the other hand, if anomalous data are available, the anomaly detection problem can be reduced to binary classification [6,7]. In this setting, a prediction model is trained with both normal and anomalous data.

One-class classification-based anomaly detection models are generally known to have a high false alarm rate [8]. The primary reason for this drawback is that the prediction model struggles to learn a sophisticated decision boundary due to the absence of anomalous instances. Consequently, researchers attempt to address the anomaly detection problem through binary classification, aiming to accurately separate anomalous instances from normal data. Most of this research concentrates on independently and identically distributed (i.i.d) data, with only limited studies addressing anomaly generation for time-series data.

The lack of research on time-series anomaly generation exacerbates the issue of building robust anomaly detection models in ICS environments. ICS is core to various domains like the manufacturing industry, electrical grids, and transportation systems. These systems share a closed nature, which makes data collection challenging. Moreover, the data inherently have time-series characteristics. As a result, this leads to data imbalance, making it difficult to train robust anomaly detection models and consequently reducing the reliability of performance evaluation. Therefore, in this paper, we focus on generating pseudo-time-series anomalies in the ICS environment.

Based on our observation, there are three major challenges in generating time-series anomalies. (1) Unlike i.i.d data, time-series data exhibit dependencies between data samples over time. In other words, when generating anomalies for time-series data, it is crucial to reflect this temporal dependency; (2) In the case of multivariate data, an anomaly in one feature can affect other features due to the correlations between them. However, systematically calculating these correlations and assigning values manually is not scalable [9]; (3) Anomalous data are inherently rare compared to normal data, making it difficult to determine an accurate probability distribution for these data. This scarcity complicates the process of generating data through sampling from a probability distribution.

To overcome the identified challenges, our insights are as follows. (1) By using variational inference, we map normal data into a latent space that follows a well-known probability distribution [10]. Variational inference is a method for training generative models, where the model maximizes the evidence lower bound (ELBO); (2) By ensuring that the latent space follows a well-known probability distribution, we can easily sample latent vectors and generate new data from them. Additionally, since we already know the statistical properties of the probability distribution, we can appropriately tamper with the latent vectors to generate anomalous data; (3) Inspired by dynamic software testing methods such as fuzzing, we adopt mutation to modify latent vectors [11,12]. These insights guide our approach to effectively generate time-series anomalies while addressing the challenges of temporal dependency, multivariate correlation, and data scarcity.

In this paper, we propose a method for generating pseudo anomalous data for industrial process data by synthesizing the aforementioned insights. The proposed method consists of two main parts. First, we map industrial time-series data to latent variables using a neural network. The learned latent variables encapsulate not only the characteristics of each time step of the data but also the correlations between features. Next, we tamper with the latent variables using mutation operations inspired by fuzz testing. We define mutation types to reproduce several known types of time-series anomaly patterns. In evaluations using several well-known ICS time-series datasets, the proposed method successfully generated time-series anomalies with various patterns. The contributions of this paper are as follows:

- We define patterns of time-series anomalies by analyzing several time-series datasets and existing studies.
- We propose a robust time-series anomaly generation algorithm using mutations and a variational recurrent autoencoder.
- We generate time-series anomalies from well-known ICS datasets using the proposed algorithm and comprehensively evaluate the quality of the synthetic anomalies.

The remainder of this paper is organized as follows. Section 2 presents existing studies on anomaly detection from the perspectives of one-class classification and binary classification; Section 3 analyzes the patterns of time-series anomalies; Section 4 proposes a method for generating time-series anomalies using AVRAE and mutation; Section 5 thoroughly evaluates the quality of the time-series anomalies generated by the proposed method using widely used anomaly detection ICS time-series datasets; Section 6 discusses several limitations of the proposed method; Finally, in Section 7, we provide conclusions and suggest directions for future research.

2. Related Work

Anomaly detection is a major research topic in various application domains, including cybersecurity. Most studies in this field adopt either one-class classification or binary classification detection strategies, depending on the availability of anomalous data during the training of detection models. In this section, we present existing research related to each approach (Sections 2.1–2.3). Furthermore, since this paper focuses on anomalies observed in time-series data, we discuss recent studies on generating time-series data and anomalous data in Sections 2.4 and 2.5, respectively.

2.1. Statistical Anomaly Detection

The most traditional method to detect an anomaly is to utilize statistical techniques such as calculating the mean and standard deviation of a dataset. By identifying data points that fall outside of a certain threshold, these methods can flag potential outliers.

W. Yu et al. [13] introduces a generalized probabilistic monitoring model (GPMM) designed to handle both random and sequential data for process monitoring. It unifies various probabilistic linear models and establishes connections between different monitoring methods. Using the expectation-maximization (EM) algorithm, the model estimates parameters, derives monitoring statistics, and investigates the equivalence between these statistics and those from classical multivariate methods. The model's effectiveness is demonstrated through numerical examples and application to the Tennessee Eastman process.

W. Yu et al. [14] presents an unsupervised fault detection and diagnosis method called Sparse Distribution Dissimilarity Analytics (SDDA), which combines distribution dissimilarity with a lasso penalty. This method addresses shortcomings in existing techniques by maximizing the dissimilarity between normal and abnormal data distributions, enabling accurate detection and diagnosis of process faults, including those with small magnitudes. The method is validated through both simulations and real industrial processes, showing superior performance compared to traditional methods.

W. Yu et al. [15] presents a novel fault detection method designed for complex industrial systems. The proposed MoniNet framework integrates both temporal and spatial information using a cascaded monitoring network, which enhances the detection accuracy of process anomalies. The method is validated using real industrial data, demonstrating its effectiveness in identifying faults more accurately compared to traditional methods.

2.2. Anomaly Detection in One-Class Classification

As mentioned earlier, anomalous behaviors occurring in enterprise networks or systems are typically very rare. Consequently, most research interprets anomaly detection as a one-class classification problem. L. Shen et al. [4] proposed a temporal hierarchical one-class model and an end-to-end learning method for time-series anomaly detection. This model is designed with a dilated recurrent neural network and incorporates multi-scale clustering to better capture temporal dynamics. The cluster centers are encouraged to be orthogonal.

H. Xu et al. [5] developed a calibrated one-class classifier that learns a more refined normality boundary. The calibration of this model involves penalizing uncertain predictions and discriminating normal samples from simulated abnormal behaviors.

S. Mauceri et al. [16] focused on the representation of time-series data rather than designing a novel classifier. This study represented given time-series data based on their dissimilarities to a set of so-called prototypes. The study evaluated the Cartesian product of 12 dissimilarities and 8 prototypes and used a one-class nearest neighbor classifier to detect anomaly samples.

L. Gjorgiev and S. Gievska [17] explore the use of variational autoencoders (VAEs) combined with Mahalanobis distance for anomaly detection in time-series data. The study evaluates various deep learning architectures on the BATADAL challenge dataset, which focuses on detecting cyber-attacks in water distribution systems. The results indicate that simpler VAE models using Mahalanobis distance can effectively detect anomalies, demonstrating significant promise in time-to-detection performance.

2.3. Anomaly Detection in Binary Classification

While most studies on time-series anomaly detection focus on the one-class classification strategy using only normal data, there have been recent attempts to identify anomalous data through binary classification. Z. Ghrib et al. [6] proposed a hybrid approach to recognize fraudulent credit card transactions. This study generated latent representations of the given data using a long short-term memory (LSTM) [18] based autoencoder pretrained on normal data, and then classified these representations using a support vector machine (SVM) [19].

P. Primus et al. [7] proposed a method for detecting anomalous sounds. Instead of presenting a novel detection model, this study focused on collecting anomalous samples from a given dataset by careful selection of unrelated data to serve as proxy outliers. Then, a detection model based on ResNet [20] was trained as a binary classifier using normal samples and proxy outliers.

I. Ullah et al. [21] proposed an RNN-based model for detecting intrusions in Internet of Things (IoT) networks. The proposed model, designed with LSTM, bidirectional LSTM, or gated recurrent unit (GRU) [22], was evaluated on various IoT datasets. This study trained the detection model as a binary classifier and employed techniques such as weighted loss and borderline SMOTE [23] to overcome the limitations of imbalanced datasets.

K. Gundersen et al. [24] proposed a binary time-series classification model for detecting gas emissions from the ocean. This study adopted a Bayesian convolutional neural network to detect gas leaks and introduced Monte Carlo dropout [25] to maximize generalization.

F. Liu et al. [26] proposed a model for detecting anomalous data in quasi-periodic time-series. This study first split the quasi-time-series into successive quasi-periods through two-level clustering and then detected anomalies using a hybrid attentional LSTM-CNN model.

2.4. Time-Series Data Generation

Many real-world datasets are time-series, which exhibit higher dynamicity and complexity compared to i.i.d. data. Consequently, time-series generation models should address issues arising from temporal dependencies. G. Forestier et al. [27] proposed a time-series generation method based on dynamic time warping (DTW) barycenter averaging (DBA). This method generates new time-series by calculating a weighted average of the time-series within a given dataset. By assigning different weights to each time-series, a variety of rich patterns can be generated. Additionally, this study presented several weight selection methods to ensure diversity in time-series synthesis.

Recently, deep neural network (DNN)-based models have been employed to more effectively capture the temporal dependency and dynamicity in data synthesis. Powerful generative models based on variational inference [10] and generative adversarial networks (GAN) [28] are among these approaches. C. Zhang et al. [29] proposed a GAN-based model for synthesizing power consumption data in smart grids. This study represented power consumption data using two attributes (level and pattern) and conditionally modeled the data probabilistically over users, days, and months, enabling the model to learn temporal attributes.

L. Zhou et al. [30] presents a novel model called LS4, a deep latent state space model for time-series generation. It addresses the limitations of existing ordinary differential equations (ODE)-based models, particularly their struggles with sharp transitions in time-series data and high computational costs. LS4 leverages a convolutional representation to enhance speed and efficiency, significantly outperforming previous models in accuracy and computational efficiency, especially on datasets with irregular sampling and long sequences.

2.5. Pseudo Anomaly Generation

Synthetic data generation plays a crucial role in various domains for augmenting imbalanced datasets and ensuring privacy protection. It is well known that building robust anomaly detection models requires balanced datasets containing both normal and anomalous data [31]. However, to construct high-quality datasets, it is essential to secure relatively rare anomalous data. M. Salem et al. [32] proposed a strategy to transform normal data into anomalous data using Cycle-GAN [33]. Cycle-GAN employs a training method that enables mutual transformation between images from different domains. This study utilized this characteristic to convert data into images and transform template data (normal data) into anomalies. The synthetic anomalies are then appended to the dataset for training detection models.

M. Pourreza et al. [34] introduced G2D, a GAN-based general framework for generating anomalies. This study categorizes synthetic data into three stages based on the learning progress of the generator: random samples, outliers surrounding the normal samples, and samples following the data distribution. Random samples and outliers are considered anomalies and used for training anomaly detection models. As a result, the detection models trained with G2D demonstrate stable performance as the proportion of outliers in the dataset increases.

H. Shen et al. [35] presented a novel method for unsupervised anomaly detection in industrial images. This method involves generating high-quality pseudo-anomaly images and enhancing normal image features. Experiments on various real datasets show performance improvements, specifically by enhancing normal image features to boost the model's prediction accuracy. The method also reduces the uncertainty of single models by integrating various anomaly scores through ensemble detection.

Y. Lin et al. [36] introduced the FastLogAD system, designed for rapid anomaly detection in log data. It uses a mask-guided anomaly generation (MGAG) technique to generate pseudo-abnormal logs and a discriminative abnormality separation (DAS) model for efficient anomaly identification. FastLogAD significantly outperforms existing methods by achieving anomaly detection speeds at least ten times faster and competitive performance metrics, representing a significant advancement in log anomaly detection with an emphasis on speed and efficiency in handling security-related data.

T. Hu et al. [37] introduced AnomalyDiffusion, a new anomaly generation model that enables accurate anomaly detection with limited data. AnomalyDiffusion significantly improves generation accuracy and diversity by integrating anomaly location and appearance information. Experimental results demonstrate that this model outperforms existing methods in both generation accuracy and diversity, showing high performance in downstream anomaly detection tasks.

While numerous studies have proposed methods for generating anomalous data, only a limited number of these focus on time-series data. Most synthetic anomaly generation techniques are confined to i.i.d data, such as images. In contrast, data collected from industrial processes often exhibit time-series characteristics, making i.i.d-based anomaly generation techniques unsuitable for generating time-series anomalous data.

3. Patterns of Time-Series Anomaly

Understanding the characteristics and patterns of anomalous data is as crucial as the techniques for generating time-series or anomalies. Several studies have explored the patterns of time-series anomalies [38–41]. We synthesize the findings of these studies to comprehensively analyze anomaly patterns. Based on this analysis, we design mutation operations in Section 4 to reproduce these patterns. Specifically, we focus on continuous data collected from industrial processes [42,43], rather than discrete data such as log data.

P. Boniol et al. [41] analyzed various publicly available time-series datasets and categorized the anomalous data within these datasets into several patterns. Broadly, this study distinguishes between anomaly patterns occurring at single data points and interval anomaly patterns (collective anomalies) that span multiple data points.

Anomaly patterns for single data points are further divided into point anomalies, which exceed expected value ranges, and contextual anomalies, which do not. Additionally, the concept of multiple anomalies, where several anomalous data points are present, is mentioned. Y. Bao et al. [40] and Z. Tang et al. [39] proposed anomaly detection models for health monitoring data and, as part of their research, analyzed the anomaly patterns within the data. These studies fundamentally consider data that deviate statistically from the norm as anomalies.

In addition to conducting a literature review, we analyzed well-known ICS datasets to examine the anomaly patterns contained within these datasets. Specifically, we analyzed the SWaT [42] and the HIL-based augmented ICS security dataset (HAI) [43]. The secure water treatment (SWaT) [42] dataset is derived from a water treatment testbed designed for ICS and security research. This testbed consists of six processes: raw water intake, chemical dosing, ultrafiltration (UF), reverse osmosis (RO), RO filtration, and UF backwash. In this study, three types of attackers were modeled, performing various attacks such as network packet sniffing and physical access.

The HAI [43] dataset also originates from a testbed primarily for water treatment, consisting of four major processes: the boiler process, turbine process, water treatment process, and hardware-in-the-loop simulator. The dataset was collected over more than ten days, capturing three types of attacks: process variable response prevention, setpoint attack, and control output attack.

Figure 1 illustrates the anomaly patterns found in the HAI and SWaT datasets. The blue and red lines represent normal data and anomalies, respectively. As seen in the figure, the anomaly patterns in both ICS datasets mostly correspond to point anomalies or contextual anomalies as defined by P. Boniol et al. [41]. The SWaT dataset includes some collective anomalies.

Furthermore, according to Figure 1, the collective anomalies in the SWaT dataset can be categorized as minor types, as described by Y. Bao et al. [40] and Z. Tang et al. [39]. Based on our literature review and analysis of the anomaly patterns in ICS datasets, we focus on generating point anomalies, contextual anomalies, and collective anomalies from given normal ICS time-series data.

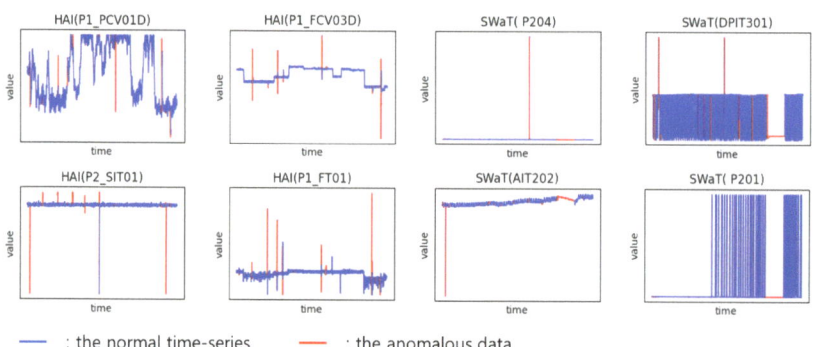

Figure 1. Anomaly patterns in ICS datasets. The leftmost two columns: HAI dataset. The rightmost two columns: SWaT dataset. The title of the subplot consists of the dataset and variable names.

4. Mutation-Based Multivariate Time-Series Anomaly Generation in ICS

This section describes the mutation-based ICS time-series anomaly generation model. Figure 2 illustrates the ICS time-series anomaly generation process. To effectively generate anomalies for ICS time-series data, we adopt an attention-based variational recurrent autoencoder (AVRAE) [44]. AVRAE is fundamentally designed with an RNN architecture and incorporates variational inference and an attention mechanism to better learn the characteristics of the time-series data. In the figure, the blue and red rectangles represent the RNN cells of the encoder and decoder, respectively, while the green circles denote the hidden states produced by the encoder or decoder.

Our anomalous data generation process is divided into two main phases: the training phase (left side of Figure 2) and the generation phase (right side of Figure 2). The training phase aims to train AVRAE as a robust time-series generation model. Each timestep's latent vector produced by AVRAE is forced to follow a well-known probability distribution. Additionally, the attention layers of AVRAE effectively learn the relationships between the hidden states (latent vectors) produced by the encoder and those produced by the decoder. Once AVRAE training is completed, the process moves to the generation phase. In the generation phase, the hidden states generated by the trained encoder of AVRAE are mutated and passed through the attention layers. AVRAE then generates time-series anomalies using the mutated hidden states from the encoder and the hidden states from the decoder, where we define several mutation operators specifically designed to generate point anomalies, contextual anomalies, or collective anomalies.

The remainder of this section is organized as follows. In Section 4.1, we describe the details of AVRAE, including the objective function and attention mechanisms. Section 4.2 presents the mutation operators for generating ICS time-series anomalies. Finally, Section 4.3 proposes an algorithm for ICS time-series anomaly generation that combines AVRAE with the mutation operators.

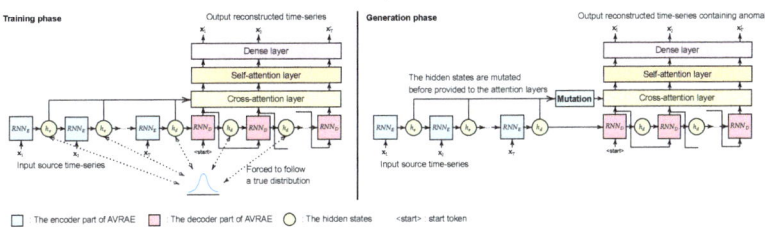

Figure 2. Overview of mutation-based ICS time-series anomaly generation.

4.1. Attention-Based Variational Recurrent Autoencoder

AVRAE is central to our ICS time-series anomaly generation. There are two main reasons for adopting AVRAE for anomalous data generation. First, AVRAE extends variational inference to time-series data, allowing control over the distribution of hidden states produced at each timestep by the RNN. Second, AVRAE's attention mechanism enables the generation of highly plausible time-series by leveraging the relationships between the encoder's and decoder's hidden states.

Since our approach involves applying mutation operations to the hidden states to generate anomalous data, AVRAE, which maps actual data to controllable hidden states, is a highly suitable model. This section formally describes AVRAE's objective function, the time-series evidence lower bound, and the inference process.

4.1.1. Evidence Lower Bound

Variational inference is an approximation method that uses relatively simple distributions to handle complex probability distributions. It is used to optimize a latent variable model for given data, replacing complex distributions with simpler, more computationally feasible ones, thereby reducing computational cost and increasing efficiency. ELBO is a typical objective used in variational inference.

$$\log p(\mathbf{x}) = KL(q(\mathbf{z})||p(\mathbf{z}|\mathbf{x})) + \mathbb{E}_{q(\mathbf{z})}[\log p(\mathbf{z},\mathbf{x})] - \mathbb{E}_{q(\mathbf{z})}[\log q(\mathbf{z})]$$
$$\geq \mathbb{E}_{q(\mathbf{z})}[\log p(\mathbf{z},\mathbf{x})] - \mathbb{E}_{q(\mathbf{z})}[\log q(\mathbf{z})] \qquad (1)$$
$$= ELBO(q)$$

Equation (1) is the derivation of ELBO. Originally, we aim to train the model to maximize the loglikelihood $\log p(\mathbf{x})$, where $\mathbf{x}$ is the observable data and $\mathbf{z}$ is the latent variable. $p(.)$ represents the true distribution, and $q(.)$ represents the variational distribution. The $\log p(\mathbf{x})$ can be decomposed into the Kullback–Leibler divergence (KLD) $KL(q(\mathbf{z})||p(\mathbf{z}|\mathbf{x}))$ and the $ELBO(q)$. Since the KLD $KL(q(\mathbf{z})||p(\mathbf{z}|\mathbf{x}))$ is always non-negative, $\log p(\mathbf{x})$ is always greater than or equal to $ELBO(q)$.

Therefore, variational inference seeks to maximize $ELBO(q)$ instead of directly maximizing $\log p(\mathbf{x})$. This ELBO fundamentally assumes that the data $\mathbf{x}$ is i.i.d. Hence, to handle probability distributions over time-series data with variational inference, ELBO must be extended to time-series.

$$\begin{aligned} ELBO_{ts}(q) &= \mathbb{E}_{q(\mathbf{z},\mathbf{h}_{1:T}|\mathbf{x}_{1:T})}[\log p(\mathbf{z},\mathbf{h}_{1:T},\mathbf{x}_{1:T})] - \mathbb{E}_{q(\mathbf{z},\mathbf{h}_{1:T}|\mathbf{x}_{1:T})}[\log q(\mathbf{z},\mathbf{h}_{1:T}|\mathbf{x}_{1:T})] \\ &= \mathbb{E}_{q(\mathbf{z},\mathbf{h}_{1:T}|\mathbf{x}_{1:T})}[\log p(\mathbf{x}_{1:T}|\mathbf{z})] - KL(q(\mathbf{z}|\mathbf{h}_{1:T})||p(\mathbf{z}|\mathbf{h}_{1:T})) \\ &\quad - KL(q(\mathbf{h}_{1:T}|\mathbf{x}_{1:T})||p(\mathbf{h}_{1:T})) \end{aligned} \quad (2)$$

Equation (2) formulates $ELBO_{ts}(q)$, which is an extended version of ELBO for time-series data. $ELBO_{ts}(q)$ not only extends the data to a time-series but also considers an additional sequential latent variable $\mathbf{h}_{1:T}$ to account for the sequential nature of the data.

Consequently, maximizing $ELBO_{ts}(q)$ is equivalent to maximizing the log-likelihood of the time-series data $\mathbf{x}_{1:T}$ given the latent variable $\mathbf{z}$, while minimizing the Kullback–Leibler divergence between the true distribution and the variational distribution for both the latent variable $\mathbf{z}$ and the sequential latent variable $\mathbf{h}_{1:T}$.

4.1.2. Inference

AVRAE follows an encoder–decoder architecture composed of RNNs. At each timestep, the RNN processes the input data x_t and the hidden state $\mathbf{h}_{t-1}$ from the previous timestep to produce a new hidden state $\mathbf{h}_t$. This hidden state $\mathbf{h}_t$ is propagated to the next timestep, allowing the RNN to reflect the sequential nature of the data. However, basic RNNs perform all inference operations deterministically. Therefore, AVRAE introduces stochasticity into the inference process to enable variational inference.

$$\mathbf{h}_t \sim q_\theta(\mathbf{h}_t|\mathbf{h}_{t-1}, \mathbf{x}_t) \quad (3)$$

Equation (3) represents the stochastic process of the RNN-based encoder at timestep t, where q_θ is the variational distribution parameterized by θ. The hidden state $\mathbf{h}_t$ is sampled from the variational distribution q_θ, which is conditioned on the hidden state $\mathbf{h}_{t-1}$ from the previous timestep and the input data $\mathbf{x}_t$ at the current timestep.

$$\mathbf{h}_t \sim \mathcal{N}(\mu_{\mathbf{h}_t}, \mathrm{diag}(\sigma^2_{\mathbf{h}_t})), \quad \text{where } [\mu_{\mathbf{h}_t}, \sigma_{\mathbf{h}_t}] = \phi(\mathbf{h}_{t-1}, \mathbf{x}_t) \quad (4)$$

Equation (4) describes the sampling process assuming q_θ is a Gaussian distribution. The function $\phi(.)$ uses $\mathbf{h}_{t-1}$ and $\mathbf{x}_t$ to produce the mean $\mu_{\mathbf{h}_t}$ and variance $\sigma_{\mathbf{h}_t}$ of the Gaussian distribution. Then, $\mathbf{h}_t$ is sampled from the Gaussian distribution parameterized by $\mu_{\mathbf{h}_t}$ and $\sigma_{\mathbf{h}_t}$. However, as is well known, sampling is a non-differentiable operation, so the reparameterization trick is typically used in variational inference [10,45,46]. We use a location-scale transformation to ensure that the reparameterized hidden state still follows a Gaussian distribution: $\mathbf{h}_t = \mu_{\mathbf{h}_t} + \sigma_{\mathbf{h}_t} \odot \epsilon \; (\epsilon \sim \mathcal{N}(0, I))$.

The decoder fundamentally mirrors the encoder and thus has similar inference, with three key exceptions. First, the decoder requires the latent vector $\mathbf{z}$ (referred to as context) produced by the encoder. In AVRAE, the hidden state $\mathbf{h}_T$ from the encoder's final timestep is used as $\mathbf{z}$. Second, unlike the encoder, the decoder uses the output from the previous timestep as the input data for the current timestep. The initial piece of input data for the decoder is the start symbol `<start>`. Third, AVRAE processes the decoder's outputs through attention layers to reconstruct the encoder's input data $\mathbf{x}_{1:T}$.

These attention layers include cross-attention and self-attention. Cross-attention combines the encoder's hidden states $\mathbf{h}^e_{1:T}$ and the decoder's hidden states $\mathbf{h}^d_{1:T}$ to calculate attention weights, which are then used to produce the output $\mathbf{o}^c_{1:T}$. Additionally, cross-attention employs a look-ahead mask to prevent future information from being referenced during sequence generation. Next, self-attention takes $\mathbf{o}^c_{1:T}$ as input, calculates attention weights, and produces the output $\mathbf{o}^s_{1:T}$. Finally, AVRAE uses a dense layer to reconstruct $\mathbf{x}_{1:T}$ from $\mathbf{o}^s_{1:T}$, resulting in $\hat{\mathbf{x}}_{1:T}$.

4.1.3. Training

The training of AVRAE is relatively straightforward. AVRAE is trained to maximize Equation (2). More specifically, $\mathbb{E}_{q(\mathbf{z},\mathbf{h}_{1:T}|\mathbf{x}_{1:T})}[\log p(\mathbf{x}_{1:T}|\mathbf{z})]$ is maximized by minimizing the error between the encoder's input $\mathbf{x}_{1:T}$ and the decoder's output $\hat{\mathbf{x}}_{1:T}$. $KL(q(\mathbf{z}|\mathbf{h}_{1:T})||p(\mathbf{z}|\mathbf{h}_{1:T}))$ and $KL(q(\mathbf{h}_{1:T}|\mathbf{x}_{1:T})||p(\mathbf{h}_{1:T}))$ are minimized as the variational distribution becomes closer to the true distribution.

AVRAE adopts the standard normal distribution as the true distribution, so the KLD decreases as the hidden states of the encoder $\mathbf{h}^e_{1:T}$ and the decoder $\mathbf{h}^d_{1:T}$ follow the standard normal distribution more closely.

4.2. Mutation operators

We define three mutation operators to generate ICS time-series anomalies of the type analyzed in Section 3, utilizing the aforementioned characteristics. Algorithms 1–3 are the mutation operators for generating point anomalies, contextual anomalies, and collective anomalies, respectively. All three algorithms are applied to the hidden state sequence $\mathbf{h}^e_{1:T}$ produced by the encoder of AVRAE and return the mutated sequence $\hat{\mathbf{h}}^e_{1:T}$.

Algorithm 1: Mutation operator $\mathcal{M}_p$ for point anomaly generation.

input : the encoder's hidden state sequence $\mathbf{h}^e_{1:T}$
output: the mutated hidden state sequence $\hat{\mathbf{h}}^e_{1:T}$
$t \leftarrow \mathcal{U}(1, T)$;
$\mathbf{v} \leftarrow \mathcal{N}(0, I)$;
$\mathbf{h}^e_{1:T}(t) \leftarrow \mathbf{v}$;
$\hat{\mathbf{h}}^e_{1:T} \leftarrow \mathbf{h}^e_{1:T}$;

Algorithm 2: Mutation operator $\mathcal{M}_{ctx}$ for contextual anomaly generation.

input : the encoder's hidden state sequence $\mathbf{h}^e_{1:T}$
output: the mutated hidden state sequence $\hat{\mathbf{h}}^e_{1:T}$
$t_s \leftarrow \mathcal{U}(1, T)$;
$t_d \leftarrow \mathcal{U}(t_s, T)$;
$\mathbf{v} \leftarrow \mathbf{h}^e_{1:T}(t_s)$;
$\mathbf{h}^e_{1:T}(t_d) \leftarrow \mathbf{v}$;
$\hat{\mathbf{h}}^e_{1:T} \leftarrow \mathbf{h}^e_{1:T}$;

Algorithm 3: Mutation operator $\mathcal{M}_{col}$ for collective anomaly generation.

input : the encoder's hidden state sequence $\mathbf{h}^e_{1:T}$
output: the mutated hidden state sequence $\hat{\mathbf{h}}^e_{1:T}$
$t_s \leftarrow \mathcal{U}(1, T)$;
$t_d \leftarrow \mathcal{U}(t_s, T)$;
$\mathbf{v}_{t_s:t_d} \leftarrow$ a vector of arbitrary value with length $(t_d - t_s)$;
$\mathbf{h}^e_{1:T}(t_s : t_d) \leftarrow \mathbf{v}_{t_s:t_d}$;
$\hat{\mathbf{h}}^e_{1:T} \leftarrow \mathbf{h}^e_{1:T}$;

Algorithm 1 introduces a point anomaly into the given hidden state sequence. First, an index t is randomly selected to specify the element in the hidden state sequence to be altered. Then, a random value $\mathbf{v}$ is sampled from the standard normal distribution to replace the t-th element of the hidden state sequence.

Algorithm 2 is the mutation operator $\mathcal{M}_{ctx}$ for generating contextual anomalies. This algorithm randomly selects two indices t_s and t_d that are smaller than the total length of the sequence T. Then, it replaces the value at the t_d-th position in the hidden state sequence with the value $\mathbf{v}$ from the t_s-th position. The rationale behind this design is that contextual anomalies inherently have values within the normal range but are considered abnormal within a given context. Therefore, Algorithm 2 generates anomalies by altering the context of normal values within the hidden state sequence.

Lastly, Algorithm 3 is the mutation operator $\mathcal{M}_{col}$ for generating collective anomalies. This algorithm first randomly selects two indices t_s and t_d, both less than the total length of the sequence T, to specify the segment to mutate. Then, it replaces the values in this segment of the hidden state sequence with a sequence $\mathbf{v}_{t_s:t_d}$ composed of arbitrary values, generating the mutated sequence $\hat{\mathbf{h}}^e_{1:T}$.

Depending on the method used to generate $\mathbf{v}_{t_s:t_d}$, various types of collective anomalies can be produced. While there are multiple approaches, this study recommends replacing with a sequence of constant vectors, a sequence of random vectors, or a sequence from another segment. The first two methods are the simplest ways to create $\mathbf{v}_{t_s:t_d}$, while the latter extends contextual anomalies into collective anomalies. It is noteworthy that the three algorithms presented so far only mutate the hidden state sequence and do not directly generate actual time-series anomalies.

4.3. Anomaly Generation

As previously mentioned, we generate anomalies by altering the latent space rather than the actual data space. More specifically, we use AVRAE to map ICS time-series data into the latent space. In particular, the encoder of AVRAE produces hidden states at each timestep while processing the time-series. Additionally, since these hidden states follow a well-known probability distribution (in this study, the standard normal distribution), it is easy for us to predict or control the values of the hidden states.

We apply mutations to the hidden states produced by the encoder of AVRAE. This approach has two major advantages. First, the hidden states (the latent vectors) effectively encapsulate the correlations among the features of the observations. Therefore, changing only a part of the latent vector affects all the features of the observations. Second, the hidden states from the encoder are used by the decoder's attention layer (cross-attention) for time-series generation. The attention layer learns the relevance between the elements of the hidden state sequences produced by the encoder and the decoder. Thus, if a segment of the hidden state sequence from the encoder is altered, the subsequent data generated by the decoder are also influenced.

Algorithm 4 outlines the process for generating anomalous ICS time-series proposed in this study. This algorithm is very straightforward. First, the encoder of the trained AVRAE processes $\mathbf{x}_{1:T}$ to produce the hidden state sequence $\mathbf{h}^e_{1:T}$. As mentioned in Section 4.1, we assume the standard normal distribution as the true distribution, so each $\mathbf{h}^e_t$ that makes up $\mathbf{h}^e_{1:T}$ follows the standard normal distribution. Then, one of the three mutation operators $\{\mathcal{M}_p, \mathcal{M}_{ctx}, \mathcal{M}_{col}\}$ presented in Section 4.2 is randomly selected as $\mathcal{M}$. Although $\mathcal{M}$ is chosen randomly in this study, if there is a need to control the type of anomaly to be generated, specifying a particular mutator is allowed. Using $\mathcal{M}$, we generate the mutated sequence $\hat{\mathbf{h}}^e_{1:T}$ from $\mathbf{h}^e_{1:T}$. Finally, the decoder of AVRAE generates the ICS time-series $\hat{\mathbf{x}}_{1:T}$ from $\hat{\mathbf{h}}^e_{1:T}$. Since $\hat{\mathbf{x}}_{1:T}$ is generated from the mutated sequence $\hat{\mathbf{h}}^e_{1:T}$, it contains anomalies. This generated anomalous ICS time-series not only considers the correlations among the features of the actual data but also reflects the temporal dependencies through the attention layers of AVRAE.

Algorithm 4: Mutation-based ICS time-series anomaly generation.

input : the trained AVRAE, the ICS time-series $\mathbf{x}_{1:T}$
output: the anomalous ICS time-series $\hat{\mathbf{x}}_{1:T}$
$\mathbf{h}^e_{1:T} \leftarrow$ produce the hidden state sequence from $\mathbf{x}_{1:T}$ with the AVRAE's encoder;
$\mathcal{M} \leftarrow$ randomly select mutation operator in $\{\mathcal{M}_p, \mathcal{M}_{ctx}, \mathcal{M}_{col}\}$;
$\hat{\mathbf{h}}^e_{1:T} \leftarrow \mathcal{M}(\mathbf{h}^e_{1:T})$;
$\hat{\mathbf{x}}_{1:T} \leftarrow$ product the anomalous ICS time-series from $\hat{\mathbf{h}}^e_{1:T}$ with the AVRAE's decoder;
---

5. Evaluation

In this section, a series of experiments is conducted to evaluate the mutation-based ICS time-series anomaly generation proposed in this paper for the ICS dataset. To our best knowledge, there is no prior research on the generation of anomalous data for time-series. Therefore, instead of comparing performance with other studies, the plausibility of the generated anomalies is assessed, and binary classification is performed using them. From this, two research questions (RQs) are defined as follows:

- RQ1: Are the synthetic ICS time-series anomalies visually and in the embedding space similar to real data?
- RQ2: Does a binary classifier trained on the synthetic ICS time-series anomalies perform better than a one-class classifier?

5.1. Dataset Description

To evaluate the mutation-based ICS time-series anomaly generation proposed in this study, the HAI [43] and SWaT [42] datasets were used. HAI is a testbed (and dataset) collected using a hardware-in-the-loop (HIL) simulator composed of turbines, boilers, and a water treatment system. In this testbed, normal and attack scenarios were repeatedly executed in an unmanned supervised control and data acquisition (SCADA) operating environment, and data were collected accordingly. This testbed has been continuously enhanced since 2017, and the dataset has been updated accordingly.

For our experiments, we used HAI 22.04. This version of the dataset provides six training datasets (each file ranging from 45 MB to 136 MB) and four test datasets (each file ranging from 33 MB to 69 MB). Each dataset consists of 86 features. The training datasets comprise only normal data, while the test datasets include anomaly data along with label information.

The SWaT dataset was collected from a six-stage water treatment process, where each stage is autonomously controlled by PLCs. This testbed is designed to closely mimic a real water treatment system, ensuring that the collected data can be applied to actual systems. In SWaT, communication among sensors, actuators, and PLCs is realized using a combination of wired and wireless channels, allowing for extensive experiments in realistic environments. The SWaT dataset has also been enhanced over time, with corresponding updates to the dataset. For this experiment, datasets collected in 2015 were used. Although the training and test datasets are not explicitly separated, the dataset provides two normal datasets (each file sized 127 MB) and one attack dataset (file sized 113 MB). Excluding the labels, this dataset consists of 51 features.

Furthermore, before presenting the analysis of the experimental results, it is worth noting that various attack methods can be included in actual attack scenarios against ICS. Consequently, the types of anomalies can also be diversified. However, the HAI and SWaT datasets used in this evaluation only categorize the data as either normal or attack. This study does not aim to present a model with high anomaly detection performance. Nonetheless, we conducted anomaly detection experiments to verify that synthetic anomalies help train detection models. Additionally, the primary purpose of these experiments is to distinguish attack data from normal data, rather than categorizing the types of attacks in detail.

5.2. Experimental Settings

All experiments were conducted on the same machine with the following specifications: Intel(R) Core(TM) i9-11900 2.50 GHz, 32 GB RAM, 64-bit Ubuntu 20.04 LTS, and NVIDIA GTX 3080 Titan. The implementation of AVRAE was implemented using Python code, with the deep learning library PyTorch 2.3.0.

Table 1 shows the architecture of AVRAE used in this study. AVRAE has a nearly symmetrical encoder and decoder. The encoder consists of two LSTM layers, with the first layer taking data of size d at each timestep (sequence length of 100) and producing an output of size $100 \times p$. For HAI, p is set to 1024, and for SWaT, it is set to 256. The second layer takes the output of the first layer as input and produces an output of size $100 \times p$.

The decoder uses the hidden state of the last timestep of the encoder as its initial hidden state, taking a vector of size p at each timestep as input and producing an output of size $100 \times p$. Similarly, the second layer of the decoder takes the output of the first layer as input and produces an output of size 100×1024. The reason the input size of the first layer of the decoder is p is that it receives the timestep-wise output of the second layer as feedback.

Then, the cross-attention layer takes the outputs of both the encoder and the decoder as input and produces a sequence of size $100 \times p$. The self-attention layer takes the output of the cross-attention layer as input and outputs a vector sequence of size $100 \times p$. Finally, the output of the self-attention layer is restored to a vector sequence of size $100 \times d$, the same shape as the input to the encoder, by the dense layer.

AVRAE is trained using the Adam optimizer [47]. The Adam optimizer is an adaptive learning rate optimization algorithm designed for training deep learning models, combining the advantages of two other extensions of stochastic gradient descent, namely, AdaGrad [48] and RMSProp [49], to compute individual adaptive learning rates for different parameters. The learning rate was set to 5×10^{-4}, the mini-batch size to 64, and AVRAE was trained for 1024 epochs.

Table 1. The architecture of AVRAE.

Layer	Encoder			Decoder		
	Type	Input Size	Output Size	Type	Input Size	Output Size
Layer 1	LSTM	$100 \times d$	$100 \times p$	LSTM	$100 \times p$	$100 \times p$
Layer 2	LSTM	$100 \times p$	$100 \times p$	LSTM	$100 \times p$	$100 \times p$
Layer 3				Cross-Attention	$100 \times p$, $100 \times p$	$100 \times p$
Layer 4				Self-Attention	$100 \times p$, $100 \times p$	$100 \times p$
Layer 5				Dense	$100 \times p$	$100 \times d$

5.3. Assessment on Quality of Synthetic anomaly

This section assesses the quality of the synthetic ICS time-series anomaly both visually and statistically. Visually inspecting the quality of generated time-series anomaly data is crucial because it allows evaluation of whether an anomaly detection model accurately captures real anomaly situations and whether the data patterns are realistic. This helps in intuitively understanding the detection model's performance and identifying potential areas for improvement.

Figure 3 shows the ICS time-series anomalies generated by the proposed method. In the figure, the blue line represents the real data used as the source for AVRAE to generate anomalous data, and the red line represents the generated anomaly. Each subplot depicts the changes in the values of a variable over time in the dataset (the y-axis represents the variable's value, and the x-axis represents the time sequence). The first row of Figure 3 represents point anomaly generation, the second row represents context anomaly generation, the third row represents collective anomaly generation with a constant value, the fourth row represents collective anomaly generation with a random value, and the fifth row represents collective anomaly generation with swap. The sections where the mutation operation is applied are marked with green circles.

The results of this experiment were extremely interesting. In the case of point anomaly generation, the anomalous values significantly differed from the surrounding context. Additionally, the direction of the outliers varied depending on the variables, which indicates that AVRAE learned the multivariate relationships of the HAI dataset.

The context anomaly generation creates anomalies by swapping the hidden states at two arbitrary timesteps in the embedding space. As a result, the range of anomaly values occurring early did not exceed the surrounding context. In fact, the anomaly values matched the values at the swapped location (i.e., the normal values of the later time). Conversely, the values at the later time remained unchanged, and the exact cause of this phenomenon has not been determined yet, although it is suspected to be due to the influence of the attention layer.

The collective anomaly generations with constant value and random value both exhibited similar effects. Anomalous data ignoring the pattern of the data were placed in a randomly selected interval. Lastly, the collective anomaly generation with swap selects two intervals of the same length at random and swaps their hidden states in the embedding space. Except for the anomaly occurring within the interval, the effect is similar to the context anomaly generation. In this method as well, the anomaly pattern occurring early matched the pattern at the swapped location, while the pattern at the later time remained unchanged. This phenomenon is also suspected to be due to the influence of the attention layer.

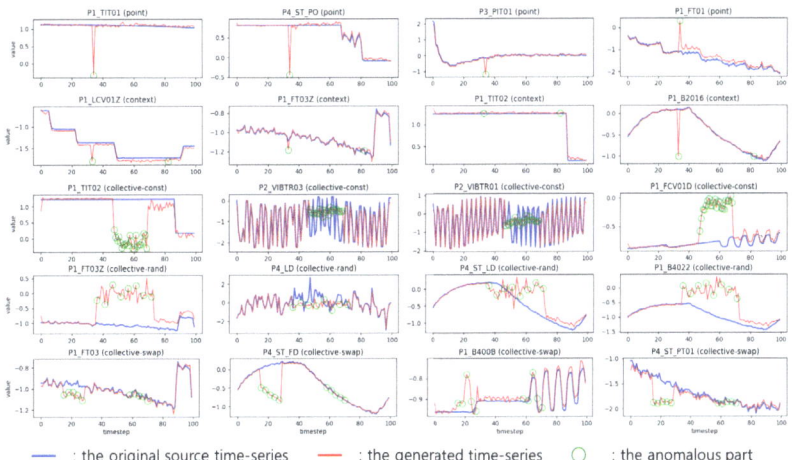

Figure 3. Visual comparison of the original source data for AVRAE and the synthetic anomaly on HAI.

Figure 4 shows the results of ICS time-series anomaly generation using the SWaT dataset. Overall, results similar to the experiments using HAI were observed. However, for SWaT, the quality of the generated time-series was lower compared to HAI. This issue was analyzed as a limitation of AVRAE rather than a problem with the anomaly generation method. The SWaT dataset exhibited much more subtle variations in the values of each variable compared to HAI. This issue appears to have caused a decrease in the data reconstruction performance of the decoder in AVRAE.

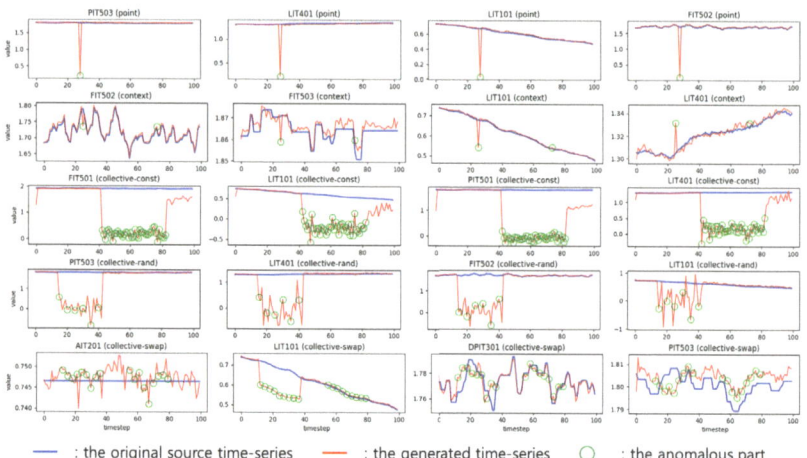

Figure 4. Visual comparison of the original source data for AVRAE and the synthetic anomaly on SWaT.

Figure 5 visualizes the original source data and the synthetic time-series anomalies given to AVRAE in a lower dimension using principal component analysis (PCA) [50] and t-distributed stochastic neighbor embedding (SNE) [51]. Although PCA is not ideally suited for visualizing high-dimensional data, it can be used to examine the data's variance. On the other hand, t-SNE excels at projecting high-dimensional data into a low-dimensional space to reveal local similarities within the data. In the figure, the two subplots on the left represent the HAI dataset, while the two subplots on the right depict the SWaT dataset. In each subplot, blue dots represent the original source data, and red dots represent anomalies. Each dot corresponds to a $100 \times d$ vector, meaning the input to AVRAE's encoder. Additionally, the anomalies used in this figure were generated by the collective anomaly generation method, which produced the greatest variations compared to the original source data.

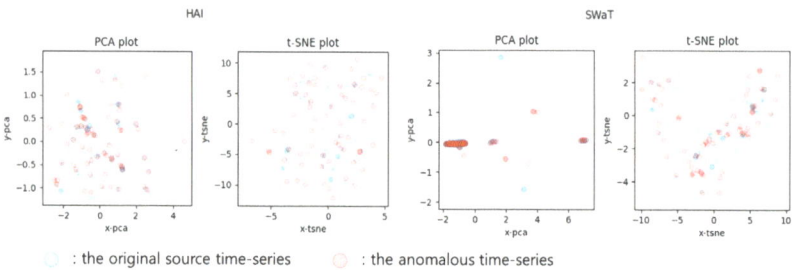

Figure 5. Visual comparison between the original source data and the synthetic anomaly using PCA and t-SNE.

In the HAI dataset, it was confirmed that the original data and the synthetic anomalies had similar distributions in both the PCA and t-SNE plots. This indicates that the synthetic anomalies share structural similarities and variance characteristics with the original data. However, it is evident that the distributions of the two datasets did not completely overlap. This suggests that new variance was introduced during the generation of synthetic anomalies through mutation.

This observation is even more pronounced in the SWaT dataset. The PCA plot shows that most of the data in the SWaT dataset has nearly similar variance characteristics. However, some synthetic anomalies appeared somewhat distinguishable from the original data. Additionally, in the t-SNE plot, the synthetic anomalies exhibited a distribution similar to the original data but were relatively more clustered. These two observations could imply that the anomaly generation method proposed in this study might be less effective for the SWaT dataset compared to the HAI dataset. We interpret this as the differences in the values of the features in the SWaT dataset being very subtle compared to the HAI dataset, which resulted in the mutation-induced changes in hidden states ultimately producing anomalies that differ from the original data.

Figure 6 shows the kernel density estimation (KDE) between the original source data and the synthetic anomaly used as input for AVRAE. In the figure, the first row displays the results for the HAI data, while the second row presents the results for the SWaT dataset. Additionally, the blue area represents the distribution of the original data, and the red area indicates the distribution of the synthetic anomaly. The synthetic anomaly used in Figure 6 was generated through collective anomaly generation, similar to Figure 5. As seen in the figure, the distributions of the original data and the anomaly are almost identical. Table 2 shows the Jensen–Shannon divergence (JSD) for each variable measured using KDE. The upper part of the table presents the results for the HAI dataset, and the lower part shows the results for the SWaT dataset. Furthermore, six variables with the largest JSD values were selected from each dataset.

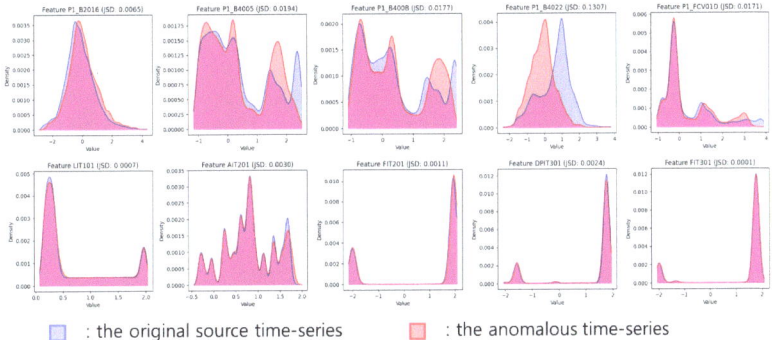

Figure 6. Kernel density estimation between the original source data and the synthetic anomaly.

Table 2. Jensen–Shannon divergence between the original source data and the synthetic anomaly.

Variable (HAI)	P1_B4022	P1_PP04	P2_SIT01	P1_PIT02	P1_FCV03D	P1_FCV01Z
JSD	0.13	0.075	0.065	0.037	0.022	0.02
Variable (SWaT)	FIT503	PIT503	PIT501	FIT501	FIT502	LIT401
JSD	0.138	0.08	0.077	0.034	0.015	0.004

As shown in the table, even the variable with the largest JSD value had a value close to 0. This indicates that the ICS time-series anomaly generated by the proposed method is not only visually similar to the actual anomaly (as shown in Figure 1) but also statistically does not deviate significantly from the original source data.

Nevertheless, it is worth noting from Figure 6 and Table 2 that there is a difference in similarity between the original source time-series and the anomaly depending on the features. For example, in Figure 6, the KDE between the source data and the synthetic anomaly for HAI's P1_B2016 is almost similar, whereas a significant difference is observed in P1_B4022. This observation suggests that the level of realism and indistinguishability may vary depending on the features.

The answer for RQ1. Various experimental results presented in this section confirm that the ICS time-series anomaly generated by mutation-based anomaly generation is visually and statistically quite similar to the actual anomaly. However, as shown in the experiments using the SWaT dataset, the proposed method somewhat depends on the reconstruction performance of AVRAE. Therefore, to improve the performance of the proposed method, it is necessary to enhance the model that maps the original data (such as AVRAE) into the embedding space.

5.4. Comparison between One-Class and Binary Classification

The application of techniques for artificially generating ICS time-series anomalies is clear. When given a dataset containing a small amount of anomalies or even only normal data, augmenting the data with anomalies can help mitigate class imbalance to some extent. Particularly, in the absence of such augmentation techniques, anomaly detection often relies on a one-class classification strategy. Therefore, in this section, the proposed synthetic ICS anomaly is generated to augment the given ICS dataset, and binary classification models are trained and compared with several one-class classification models.

Table 3 shows the anomaly detection performance of several one-class classification models (OC) and binary classification models (BIN) for the HAI and SWaT datasets. The one-class classification models adopted are one-class support vector machine (OCSVM), isolation forest (IF), local outlier factor (LOF), and LSTM-based autoencoder (LSTM-AE). The binary classification models adopted are kernel SVM (k-SVM), random forest (RF), k-nearest neighbor (KNN), and LSTM-based binary classifier (LSTM-BIN). The performance indicators used are accuracy (ACC), recall (REC), precision (PRE), F1 (F1 score), and ROC (ROC-AUC). These models are trained to take the ICS time series of length 100 as input and determine whether an anomaly is present. Specifically, any sequence containing non-normal data for at least one timestep is considered an anomaly.

Table 3. Performance comparison between one-class and binary classification.

Type	Model	HAI					SWaT				
		ACC	REC	PRE	F1	ROC	ACC	REC	PRE	F1	ROC
OC	OCSVM	0.77	0.5	0.04	0.07	0.32	0.61	0.83	0.22	0.35	0.14
	IF	0.94	0.25	0.11	0.14	0.36	0.13	1.0	0.13	0.23	0.18
	LOF	**0.97**	0.31	0.29	0.3	0.35	**0.97**	0.31	0.28	0.29	0.35
	LSTM-AE	0.93	0.22	0.31	0.26	0.69	0.94	0.55	0.99	0.71	0.8
BIN	k-SVM	0.37	0.79	0.06	0.11	0.54	0.86	0.71	0.47	0.57	**0.85**
	RF	0.05	1.0	0.05	0.1	0.47	0.62	0.74	0.22	0.34	0.78
	KNN	0.67	0.35	0.05	0.1	0.53	0.85	0.1	0.24	0.1	0.72
	LSTM-BIN	0.94	0.56	0.44	**0.49**	0.73	0.95	0.81	0.78	**0.79**	0.82

Note that no model selection process was conducted to enhance performance, aiming to confirm the differences in performance among models based on the dataset differences. Additionally, the LSTM-AE and LSTM-BIN were designed to have as similar complexity as possible, specifically the same number of parameters. The LSTM-AE consists of an encoder and decoder, each composed of a single LSTM layer with a hidden state size of 256, with a dense layer added at the end of the decoder for reconstruction of the original input sequence. The LSTM-BIN consists of two LSTM layers with a hidden state size of 256, applying a dense layer to the average of the hidden states from the last LSTM layer to classify the given sequence. Both the LSTM-AE and LSTM-BIN were trained for 2048 epochs.

Last but not least, all one-class classification models were trained on a training set composed only of normal data, while the binary classification models were trained on a dataset where the original normal data, synthetic normal data (no mutation) by AVRAE, and synthetic anomalies were mixed in a 1:1:1 ratio. In other words, the OC models were trained on the standard dataset, while the BIN models were trained on the dataset augmented with synthetic anomalies. Additionally, the standard training sets for HAI and

SWaT do not inherently include anomaly (attack) data. The performance of each model was measured using a test set that did not include any training data and did not contain the synthetic anomalies. Therefore, this experiment not only demonstrates the validity of the binary classifier in anomaly detection but also highlights the effectiveness of the synthetic anomaly.

The results of this experiment were quite intriguing. Basically, accuracy was generally higher for one-class classification models in the case of HAI, while it was higher for binary classification models in the case of SWaT. However, since both HAI and SWaT are imbalanced datasets that overwhelmingly contain normal data, accuracy is not a reliable performance metric for these models. On the other hand, for both HAI and SWaT, the model with the highest F1 score was LSTM-BIN. In fact, most models except for LSTM-BIN exhibited higher recall than precision. This discrepancy is primarily due to the imbalance in the ICS datasets.

Generally, a high recall indicates that the model correctly identifies actual positive samples (anomalies), whereas low precision means that the proportion of actual positives among the samples predicted as positive by the model is low. This suggests that, given the relative scarcity of positive class (anomalies) compared to the negative class (normal data), many samples predicted as positive by the model are likely to be false positives.

Another possible interpretation is that the models, while relatively effectively identifying samples from the positive class, generate many false positives because the differentiation between the negative and positive classes is not pronounced. In other words, while the models successfully detect positive class samples, they frequently confuse them with the negative class, leading to lower precision.

Despite this, LSTM-BIN demonstrated a relatively high F1 score because its recall and precision were not significantly different from each other. This indicates that LSTM-BIN, by using data from both classes, learned an optimal decision boundary that better distinguishes between positive and negative classes. Additionally, LSTM-BIN, being based on a neural network, can learn complex patterns in the data, including non-linearities, allowing it to form a more sophisticated decision boundary compared to other binary classification models. In contrast, LSTM-AE, which is trained only on normal data, learns a less refined decision boundary compared to LSTM-BIN.

The answer for RQ2. Comparing the performance of one-class classification models and binary classification models using the pure ICS dataset and the anomaly-augmented ICS dataset revealed that the neural net-based binary classifier exhibited slightly higher performance. In other words, it was confirmed that dataset augmentation through the generation of ICS time-series anomalies indeed aids in training sophisticated anomaly detection models.

6. Limitations

The mutation-based ICS time-series anomaly generation proposed in this paper has been demonstrated to be effective through various experiments in terms of visual/statistical plausibility and dataset augmentation. This technique is novel, particularly in its application to time-series data, and can be utilized to address imbalances in various time-series datasets beyond ICS datasets. Despite these advantages, the proposed anomaly generation technique has several clear limitations.

- Currently, this study is limited to anomaly generation for numerical time-series data. From a broader perspective, sequential data encompass various forms of data, including text. Although there is potential for this technique to be applied to other types of sequential data, further investigation is required.
- The quality of the synthetic anomaly heavily depends on the performance of the generation model. In this study, AVRAE was adopted as the generation model. While AVRAE is a robust generation model, it still falls short of perfectly capturing the temporal dynamics inherent in time-series datasets.

- The most significant limitation of this technique is its inability to generate scenario-based anomalies. The mutation operation fundamentally relies on randomness. In other words, the generated ICS anomalies do not reflect the causes and consequences of specific cyberattacks. Nevertheless, the proposed technique has sufficient utility because it generates anomalies that consider the correlations between variables in the data through AVRAE.

7. Conclusions

In this paper, a mutation-based ICS time-series anomaly generation method is proposed. This technique first utilizes the encoder of the powerful generation model, AVRAE, to map observations into latent space. Then, it applies carefully designed mutation operations to alter the latent representation. The decoder of AVRAE reconstructs the observations from the mutated latent representations. To design appropriate mutation operations, commonly used ICS datasets were analyzed to derive the types of anomalies they contain. Based on this analysis, mutation operations were proposed to generate point anomalies, contextual anomalies, and collective anomalies. Evaluations using the HAI and SWaT datasets confirmed that the proposed method could generate ICS time-series anomalies that are both visually and statistically plausible.

Furthermore, by using the augmented ICS dataset with synthetic anomalies, various one-class classification models and binary classification models were compared. The results empirically demonstrated that a robust binary classifier could be trained using the augmented dataset. This study presents an effective means to augment ICS datasets, which are often plagued by imbalance issues. The proposed technique is transferable to other time-series datasets with similar characteristics, although its application to sequential datasets of a different nature, such as text, requires further research. Additionally, the method's dependence on the performance of the underlying generation model and its inability to generate scenario-based anomalies were identified as limitations. Consequently, future research will naturally extend to applying the proposed method to various datasets and exploring more powerful anomaly detection models.

Author Contributions: Conceptualization, S.J.; methodology, S.J.; software, S.J.; validation, K.K.; formal analysis, S.J.; investigation, K.K.; resources, J.T.S.; data curation, D.M.; writing—original draft preparation, S.J.; writing—review and editing, J.T.S.; visualization, S.J.; supervision, J.T.S.; project administration, D.M.; funding acquisition, D.M. All authors have read and agreed to the published version of the manuscript.

Funding: This work was supported by Institute of Information & Communications Technology Planning & Evaluation (IITP) grant funded by the Korea Government (MSIT) (No. 2022-0-00961).

Institutional Review Board Statement: Not applicable.

Informed Consent Statement: Not applicable.

Data Availability Statement: The original contributions presented in the study are included in the article, further inquiries can be directed to the corresponding author.

Conflicts of Interest: The authors declare no conflicts of interest.

Abbreviations

The following abbreviations are used in this manuscript:

ICS	Industrial control systems
i.i.d	Independently and identically distributed
ELBO	Evident lower bound
GPMM	Generalized probabilistic monitoring model
EM	Expectation-Maximization
SDDA	Sparse distribution dissimilarity analytics
VAE	Variational autoencoder
RNN	Recurrent neural network

LSTM	Long short-term memory
SVM	Support vector machine
IoT	Internet of Things
GRU	Gated recurrent unit
DTW	Dynamic time warping
DBA	Barycenter averaring
DNN	Deep neural network
GAN	Generative adversarial networks
ODE	Ordinary differential equations
MGAG	Mask-guided anomaly generation
DAS	Discriminative abnormality separation
HAI	HIL based augmented ICS
SWaT	Secure water treatment
UF	Ultrafiltration
RO	Reverse osmosis
AVRAE	Attention-based variational recurrent autoencoder
KLD	Kullback–Leibler divergence
RQ	Research questions
HIL	Hardware-in-the-loop
SCADA	Supervised control and data acquisition
PCA	Principal component analysis
t-SNE	t-distributed stochastic neighbor embedding
KDE	Kernel density estimation
JSD	Jensen-Shannon divergence

References

1. Huang, D.; Mu, D.; Yang, L.; Cai, X. CoDetect: Financial Fraud Detection with Anomaly Feature Detection. *IEEE Access* **2018**, *6*, 19161–19174. [CrossRef]
2. Kravchik, M.; Shabtai, A. Efficient Cyber Attack Detection in Industrial Control Systems Using Lightweight Neural Networks and PCA. *IEEE Trans. Dependable Secur. Comput.* **2022**, *19*, 2179–2197. [CrossRef]
3. Elsayed, M.S.; Le-Khac, N.A.; Dev, S.; Jurcut, A.D. Network Anomaly Detection Using LSTM Based Autoencoder. In Procceddings of the ACM Symposium on QoS and Security for Wireless and Mobile Networks, Alicante, Spain, 16–20 November 2020; pp. 37–45, [CrossRef]
4. Shen, L.; Li, Z.; Kwok, J.T. Timeseries anomaly detection using temporal hierarchical one-class network. In Proceedings of the Advances in Neural Information Processing Systems, Online, 6–12 December 2020; Volume 2020.
5. Xu, H.; Wang, Y.; Jian, S.; Liao, Q.; Wang, Y.; Pang, G. Calibrated One-class Classification for Unsupervised Time Series Anomaly Detection. *IEEE Trans. Knowl. Data Eng.* **2024**, 1–14. [CrossRef]
6. Ghrib, Z.; Jaziri, R.; Romdhane, R. Hybrid approach for Anomaly Detection in Time Series Data. In Proceedings of the International Joint Conference on Neural Networks, Glasgow, UK, 19–24 July 2020. [CrossRef]
7. Primus, P.; Haunschmid, V.; Praher, P.; Widmer, G. Anomalous Sound Detection as a Simple Binary Classification Problem with Careful Selection of Proxy Outlier Examples. *arXiv* **2020**, arXiv:2011.02949. https://doi.org/10.48550/arXiv.2011.02949.
8. Luca, S.; Clifton, D.A.; Vanrumste, B. One-class classification of point patterns of extremes. *J. Mach. Learn. Res.* **2016**, *17*, 1–21.
9. Lee, J.H.; Ji, I.H.; Jeon, S.H.; Seo, J.T. Generating ICS Anomaly Data Reflecting Cyber-Attack Based on Systematic Sampling and Linear Regression. *Sensors* **2023**, *23*, 9855. [CrossRef] [PubMed]
10. Kingma, D.P.; Welling, M. Auto-encoding variational bayes. In Proceedings of the 2nd International Conference on Learning Representations. *arXiv* **2013**, arXiv:1312.6114. https://doi.org/10.48550/arXiv.1312.6114.
11. Zalewski, M. American Fuzzy Lop. 2017. Available online: http://lcamtuf.coredump.cx/afl (accessed on 31 August 2024).
12. Fioraldi, A.; Maier, D.; Eißfeldt, H.; Heuse, M. AFL++: Combining incremental steps of fuzzing research. In Proceedings of the WOOT 2020—14th USENIX Workshop on Offensive Technologies, Online, 11 August 2020.
13. Yu, W.; Wu, M.; Huang, B.; Lu, C. A generalized probabilistic monitoring model with both random and sequential data. *Automatica* **2022**, *144*, 110468. [CrossRef]
14. Yu, W.; Zhao, C.; Huang, B.; Xie, M. An Unsupervised Fault Detection and Diagnosis with Distribution Dissimilarity and Lasso Penalty. *IEEE Trans. Control. Syst. Technol.* **2024**, *32*, 767–779. [CrossRef]
15. Yu, W.; Zhao, C.; Huang, B. MoniNet With Concurrent Analytics of Temporal and Spatial Information for Fault Detection in Industrial Processes. *IEEE Trans. Cybern.* **2022**, *52*, 8340–8351. [CrossRef] [PubMed]
16. Mauceri, S.; Sweeney, J.; McDermott, J. Dissimilarity-based representations for one-class classification on time series. *Pattern Recognit.* **2020**, *100*, 107122. [CrossRef]
17. Gjorgiev, L.; Gievska, S. Time Series Anomaly Detection with Variational Autoencoder Using Mahalanobis Distance. In Proceedings of the Communications in Computer and Information Science, Virtual Event, 8–10 July 2020; Volume 1316. [CrossRef]

18. Hochreiter, S.; Schmidhuber, J. Long Short-Term Memory. *Neural Comput.* **1997**, *9*, 1735–1780. [CrossRef]
19. Cortes, C.; Vapnik, V. Support-Vector Networks. *Mach. Learn.* **1995**, *20*, 273–297. [CrossRef]
20. He, K.; Zhang, X.; Ren, S.; Sun, J. Deep residual learning for image recognition. In Proceedings of the IEEE Computer Society Conference on Computer Vision and Pattern Recognition, Las Vegas, NV, USA, 27–30 June 2016. [CrossRef]
21. Ullah, I.; Mahmoud, Q.H. Design and Development of RNN Anomaly Detection Model for IoT Networks. *IEEE Access* **2022**, *10*, 62722–62750. [CrossRef]
22. Cho, K.; Merriënboer, B.V.; Gulcehre, C.; Bahdanau, D.; Bougares, F.; Schwenk, H.; Bengio, Y. Learning phrase representations using RNN encoder–decoder for statistical machine translation. In Proceedings of the EMNLP 2014 Conference on Empirical Methods in Natural Language Processing, Doha, Qatar, 25–29 October 2014. [CrossRef]
23. Han, H.; Wang, W.Y.; Mao, B.H. Borderline-SMOTE: A new over-sampling method in imbalanced data sets learning. In Proceedings of the Lecture Notes in Computer Science, Istanbul, Turkey, 26–28 October 2005; Volume 3644. [CrossRef]
24. Gundersen, K.; Alendal, G.; Oleynik, A.; Blaser, N. Binary time series classification with bayesian convolutional neural networks when monitoring for marine gas discharges. *Algorithms* **2020**, *13*, 145. [CrossRef]
25. Gal, Y.; Ghahramani, Z. Dropout as a Bayesian approximation: Representing model uncertainty in deep learning. In Proceedings of the 33rd International Conference on Machine Learning, ICML 2016, New York, NY, USA, 19–24 June 2016; Volume 3.
26. Liu, F.; Zhou, X.; Cao, J.; Wang, Z.; Wang, T.; Wang, H.; Zhang, Y. Anomaly Detection in Quasi-Periodic Time Series Based on Automatic Data Segmentation and Attentional LSTM-CNN. *IEEE Trans. Knowl. Data Eng.* **2022**, *34*, 2626–2640. [CrossRef]
27. Forestier, G.; Petitjean, F.; Dau, H.A.; Webb, G.I.; Keogh, E. Generating synthetic time series to augment sparse datasets. In Proceedings of the IEEE International Conference on Data Mining, ICDM, New Orleans, LA, USA 18–21 November 2017; Volume 2017. [CrossRef]
28. Goodfellow, I.J.; Pouget-Abadie, J.; Mirza, M.; Xu, B.; Warde-Farley, D.; Ozair, S.; Courville, A.; Bengio, Y. Generative adversarial nets. In Proceedings of the Advances in Neural Information Processing Systems, Montreal, QC, Canada, 8–13 December 2014.
29. Zhang, C.; Kuppannagari, S.R.; Kannan, R.; Prasanna, V.K. Generative Adversarial Network for Synthetic Time Series Data Generation in Smart Grids. In Proceedings of the 2018 IEEE International Conference on Communications, Control, and Computing Technologies for Smart Grids, SmartGridComm 2018, Aalborg, Denmark, 29–31 October 2018. [CrossRef]
30. Zhou, L.; Poli, M.; Xu, W.; Massaroli, S.; Ermon, S. Deep Latent State Space Models for Time-Series Generation. In Proceedings of the Machine Learning Research, Seattle, WA, USA, 30 November–1 December 2023; Volume 202.
31. Chen, Z.; Duan, J.; Kang, L.; Qiu, G. Supervised Anomaly Detection via Conditional Generative Adversarial Network and Ensemble Active Learning. *IEEE Trans. Pattern Anal. Mach. Intell.* **2023**, *45*, 7781–7798. [CrossRef]
32. Salem, M.; Taheri, S.; Yuan, J.S. Anomaly Generation Using Generative Adversarial Networks in Host-Based Intrusion Detection. In Proceedings of the 2018 9th IEEE Annual Ubiquitous Computing, Electronics and Mobile Communication Conference, UEMCON 2018, New York, NY, USA, 8–10 November 2018. [CrossRef]
33. Zhu, J.Y.; Park, T.; Isola, P.; Efros, A.A. Unpaired Image-to-Image Translation Using Cycle-Consistent Adversarial Networks. In Proceedings of the IEEE International Conference on Computer Vision, Venice, Italy, 22–29 October 2017; Volume 2017. [CrossRef]
34. Pourreza, M.; Mohammadi, B.; Khaki, M.; Bouindour, S.; Snoussi, H.; Sabokrou, M. G2D: Generate to detect anomaly. In Proceedings of the 2021 IEEE Winter Conference on Applications of Computer Vision, WACV 2021, Waikoloa, HI, USA, 5–9 January 2021. [CrossRef]
35. Shen, H.; Wei, B.; Ma, Y.; Gu, X. Unsupervised industrial image ensemble anomaly detection based on object pseudo-anomaly generation and normal image feature combination enhancement. *Comput. Ind. Eng.* **2023**, *182*, 109337. [CrossRef]
36. Lin, Y.; Deng, H.; Li, X. FastLogAD: Log Anomaly Detection with Mask-Guided Pseudo Anomaly Generation and Discrimination. *arXiv* **2024**, arXiv:2404.08750.
37. Hu, T.; Zhang, J.; Yi, R.; Du, Y.; Chen, X.; Liu, L.; Wang, Y.; Wang, C. AnomalyDiffusion: Few-Shot Anomaly Image Generation with Diffusion Model. In Proceedings of the AAAI Conference on Artificial Intelligence, Vancouver, BC, Canada, 20–27 February 2024; pp. 8526–8534. [CrossRef]
38. Choi, K.; Yi, J.; Park, C.; Yoon, S. Deep Learning for Anomaly Detection in Time-Series Data: Review, Analysis, and Guidelines. *IEEE Access* **2021**, *9*, 120043–120065. [CrossRef]
39. Tang, Z.; Chen, Z.; Bao, Y.; Li, H. Convolutional neural network-based data anomaly detection method using multiple information for structural health monitoring. *Struct. Control Health Monit.* **2019**, *26*, e2296. [CrossRef]
40. Bao, Y.; Tang, Z.; Li, H.; Zhang, Y. Computer vision and deep learning–based data anomaly detection method for structural health monitoring. *Struct. Health Monit.* **2019**, *18*, 401–421. [CrossRef]
41. Boniol, P.; Paparrizos, J.; Palpanas, T. New Trends in Time-Series Anomaly Detection. In Proceedings of the Advances in Database Technology-EDBT, Ioannina, Greece, 28–31 March 2023; Volume 26. [CrossRef]
42. Mathur, A.P.; Tippenhauer, N.O. SWaT: A water treatment testbed for research and training on ICS security. In Proceedings of the 2016 International Workshop on Cyber-physical Systems for Smart Water Networks, CySWater 2016, Vienna, Austria, 11 April 2016. [CrossRef]
43. Shin, H.K.; Lee, W.; Yun, J.H.; Kim, H.C. HAI 1.0: HIL-based augmented ICS security dataset. In Proceedings of the CSET 2020-13th USENIX Workshop on Cyber Security Experimentation and Test, Online, 10 August 2020.
44. Jeon, S.; Seo, J.T. A Synthetic Time-Series Generation Using a Variational Recurrent Autoencoder with an Attention Mechanism in an Industrial Control System. *Sensors* **2023**, *24*, 128. [CrossRef]

45. Fabius, O.; van Amersfoort, J.R. Variational recurrent auto-encoders. In Proceedings of the 3rd International Conference on Learning Representations, ICLR 2015, San Diego, CA, USA, 7–9 May 2015.
46. Chung, J.; Kastner, K.; Dinh, L.; Goel, K.; Courville, A.; Bengio, Y. A recurrent latent variable model for sequential data. In Proceedings of the Advances in Neural Information Processing Systems, Montreal, QC, Canada, 7–12 December 2015; Volume 2015.
47. Kingma, D.P.; Ba, J.L. Adam: A method for stochastic optimization. In Proceedings of the 3rd International Conference on Learning Representations, ICLR 2015, San Diego, CA, USA, 7–9 May 2015.
48. Duchi, J.; Hazan, E.; Singer, Y. Adaptive subgradient methods for online learning and stochastic optimization. *J. Mach. Learn. Res.* **2011**, *12*, 2121–2159.
49. Hinton, G.E.; Srivastava, N.; Swersky, K. Neural Networks for Machine Learning Lecture 6a Overview of Mini-Batch Gradient Descent. 2012. Available online: https://www.cs.toronto.edu/~tijmen/csc321/slides/lecture_slides_lec6.pdf (accessed on 31 August 2024).
50. Bro, R.; Smilde, A.K. Principal Component Analysis. 2014. Available online: https://doi.org/10.1039/c3ay41907j (accessed on 31 August 2024).
51. Maaten, L.V.D.; Hinton, G. Visualizing data using t-SNE. *J. Mach. Learn. Res.* **2008**, *9*. Available online: https://jmlr.org/papers/v9/vandermaaten08a.html (accessed on 31 August 2024).

Disclaimer/Publisher's Note: The statements, opinions and data contained in all publications are solely those of the individual author(s) and contributor(s) and not of MDPI and/or the editor(s). MDPI and/or the editor(s) disclaim responsibility for any injury to people or property resulting from any ideas, methods, instructions or products referred to in the content.

Article

Product Demand Prediction with Spatial Graph Neural Networks

Jiale Li [1], Li Fan [2], Xuran Wang [3], Tiejiang Sun [4] and Mengjie Zhou [5,*]

1 Tandon School of Engineering, New York University, New York, NY 10012, USA; jl13249@nyu.edu
2 College of Information Science and Electronic Engineering, Zhejiang University, Hangzhou 310027, China; fanli@ieee.org
3 The Department of Computer and Information Science, The University of Pennsylvania, Philadelphia, PA 19104, USA
4 School of Information Engineering, Chang'an University, Xi'an 710064, China; suntiejiang@st.chd.edu.cn
5 Department of Computer Science, University of Bristol, Bristol BS8 1QU, UK
* Correspondence: ix18497@bristol.ac.uk

Citation: Li, J.; Fan, L.; Wang, X.; Sun, T.; Zhou, M. Product Demand Prediction with Spatial Graph Neural Networks. *Appl. Sci.* 2024, *14*, 6989. https://doi.org/10.3390/app14166989

Academic Editor: Douglas O'Shaughnessy

Received: 2 July 2024
Revised: 30 July 2024
Accepted: 6 August 2024
Published: 9 August 2024

Copyright: © 2024 by the authors. Licensee MDPI, Basel, Switzerland. This article is an open access article distributed under the terms and conditions of the Creative Commons Attribution (CC BY) license (https://creativecommons.org/licenses/by/4.0/).

Abstract: In the rapidly evolving online marketplace, accurately predicting the demand for pre-owned items presents a significant challenge for sellers, impacting pricing strategies, product presentation, and marketing investments. Traditional demand prediction methods, while foundational, often fall short in addressing the dynamic and heterogeneous nature of e-commerce data, which encompasses textual descriptions, visual elements, geographic contexts, and temporal dynamics. This paper introduces a novel approach utilizing the Graph Neural Network (GNN) to enhance demand prediction accuracy by leveraging the spatial relationships inherent in online sales data, named SGNN. Drawing from the rich dataset provided in the fourth Kaggle competition, we construct a spatially aware graph representation of the marketplace, integrating advanced attention mechanisms to refine predictive accuracy. Our methodology defines the product demand prediction problem as a regression task on an attributed graph, capturing both local and global spatial dependencies that are fundamental to accurate predicting. Through attention-aware message propagation and node-level demand prediction, our model effectively addresses the multifaceted challenges of e-commerce demand prediction, demonstrating superior performance over traditional statistical methods, machine learning techniques, and even deep learning models. The experimental findings validate the effectiveness of our GNN-based approach, offering actionable insights for sellers navigating the complexities of the online marketplace. This research not only contributes to the academic discourse on e-commerce demand prediction but also provides a scalable and adaptable framework for future applications, paving the way for more informed and effective online sales strategies.

Keywords: demand prediction; Graph Neural Network; spatial information

1. Introduction

In the vast expanse of today's online marketplace, the ability to effectively sell pre-owned items hinges not just on the inherent qualities of the items themselves but also critically on the nuanced presentation within their descriptions. From vivid imagery to compelling narratives, each element plays a pivotal role in captivating potential buyers. Sellers invest considerable effort into optimizing their listings, yet they frequently encounter a disheartening obstacle: despite a meticulously optimized product listing, the anticipated demand may fail to materialize. This scenario leaves sellers in a quandary, particularly when substantial investments in marketing have been made, underscoring a pressing need for accurate demand prediction.

Navigating the online marketplace demands more than just intuition; it requires a nuanced understanding of a multitude of factors that influence buyer behavior [1]. The challenge of demand prediction lies in its inherent complexity, influenced by a web of interrelated factors, including product descriptions, visual appeal, contextual cues such as geographic location, the presence of competing ads, and the intricate patterns of historical demand. These factors play a significant role in shaping customer behavior [2] and contribute to an environment where traditional sales strategies may fall short, necessitating innovative approaches to predict demand accurately. Besides, advertising demand often follows short-term and long-term patterns, including weekly and seasonal trends, thus requiring models to be able to capture these temporal dynamics [3].

The fourth Kaggle competition, leveraging the Avito dataset (https://www.kaggle.com/competitions/avito-demand-prediction (accessed on 15 June 2024)), exemplifies this complex challenge and highlights the critical importance of accurate demand prediction in the online marketplace. Avito, as Russia's largest classified ads platform, offers a rich and diverse dataset that encapsulates the multifaceted nature of e-commerce, including the very factors mentioned above that influence buyer behavior. This competition not only tasks participants with predicting demand for a wide range of products but also emphasizes the potential impact of such predictions on crucial business decisions, from pricing strategies to marketing investments. By providing a real-world context, the competition creates a unique opportunity to test and validate innovative approaches to demand prediction, directly addressing the need for more sophisticated models in this domain.

However, the path to effective demand prediction in the e-commerce domain is fraught with challenges. The heterogeneous nature of online advertising data, encompassing textual descriptions, images, and contextual information, presents a significant analytical challenge. Traditional statistical methods, while foundational, often lack the flexibility to accommodate the dynamic and multifaceted nature of e-commerce data. Machine learning techniques have introduced a degree of adaptability, yet the quest for models that can fully capture and interpret the complex interplay of factors influencing demand continues.

In response to these challenges, our paper proposes a novel approach utilizing the Graph Neural Network to enhance the accuracy of e-commerce product demand prediction. By constructing a spatially aware graph representation of the marketplace and integrating advanced attention mechanisms, our methodology aims to capture the nuanced relationships and dependencies that shape demand patterns. This approach not only promises to refine demand predictions but also introduces a scalable framework adaptable to the diverse landscape of online sales.

As we delve into this exploration, our paper seeks to make a significant contribution to the domain of e-commerce demand prediction. Through an in-depth examination of the challenges inherent in online sales, a comprehensive review of existing methodologies, and the introduction of an innovative GNN-based approach, we endeavor to equip sellers with a robust tool to navigate the complexities of the online marketplace. In our investigation, we propose the following research questions (RQs) to evaluate the efficacy of our spatial GNN model in the context of geographic product demand prediction: RQ1: How does the performance of the SGNN model in predicting product demand compare to a variety of established baseline models? RQ2: To what extent does each component within the SGNN model contribute to the improvement of product demand prediction accuracy? RQ3: How stable is the SGNN model's predictive accuracy across a range of hyperparameter settings? Our findings validate the effectiveness of our approach and offer actionable insights for optimizing online sales strategies.

In essence, this paper enriches the academic discourse on demand prediction in e-commerce and addresses a critical gap with its pioneering GNN-based methodology. By doing so, it lays the groundwork for future research and practical applications poised to transform the online sales landscape.

2. Related Works

2.1. E-Commerce Demand Prediction

2.1.1. Characteristics of Online Advertising Data

Customers' willingness to purchase on e-commerce platforms is influenced not only by historical data but also significantly by the quality, thoroughness, authenticity, and context of advertisements [1]. This complexity underscores the multifaceted nature of online advertising data. Such data encompass numerical data (e.g., historical demand), image data (e.g., ad visuals), text data (e.g., product descriptions), and location data (e.g., geographic targeting). Detailed descriptions and contextual cues, such as geographic location and the presence of similar ads, play a significant role in shaping customer behavior [2]. Moreover, advertising demand often follows seasonal patterns and short-term and long-term trends, necessitating models that can capture these temporal dynamics [3]. The dynamic nature of online markets introduces volatility and noise, further challenging models to provide accurate predictions amidst these fluctuations. These interconnected characteristics highlight the need for advanced models capable of processing and analyzing diverse and complex data types to enhance demand prediction accuracy.

2.1.2. Demand Prediction Methods

Demand prediction in the context of e-commerce is a relatively novel area of research.

Traditional Statistical Methods. Early efforts in demand prediction for online advertising predominantly employed traditional statistical methods. Levis et al. present a systematic optimization-based approach for customer demand prediction using support vector regression (SVR) [4]. Jain et al. also explore SVR for demand prediction, using a similar three-step algorithm involving nonlinear and linear programming, and a recursive step to adapt to historical sales data for accurate predictions [5]. These traditional statistical models have been widely used due to their simplicity and interoperability.

Machine Learning Techniques. Machine learning techniques offer enhanced flexibility and accuracy in demand prediction for e-commerce. Tugay et al. propose a novel approach that considers market dynamics with multiple sellers offering the same product at different prices [6]. They apply various regression algorithms and a stacked generalization (ensemble learning) technique, showing that the latter yields superior results.

Deep Learning Model. Deep learning models, particularly neural networks, have shown exceptional capability in processing vast amounts of data and identifying complex patterns. Bandara et al. use Long Short-Term Memory (LSTM) networks to exploit non-linear demand relationships in an e-commerce product hierarchy [7]. In domains beyond online advertising, Zhang et al. synthesize research on artificial neural networks (ANNs) in predictions, providing insights into modeling issues and future directions [8]. Kuo et al. compare neural networks with traditional models, highlighting their advantages in handling non-linear relationships [9]. Azzouni et al. propose an LSTM framework for predicting network traffic, demonstrating its effectiveness on real-world data [10].

Ensemble models. Ensemble models combine different techniques to leverage their respective strengths for improved predicting accuracy. Aburto et al. present a hybrid system combining ARIMA models and neural networks for demand prediction, improving accuracy and inventory management in a Chilean supermarket [11]. Irem et al. investigate various classifiers and their combinations, showing that ensemble models outperform single classifiers and simple combinations in predicting accuracy [12].

2.1.3. Spatial Statistics in Demand Prediction

Spatial statistics has long been a cornerstone in understanding and predicting spatially distributed phenomena, including product demand. Traditional spatial statistical methods have provided valuable insights into the geographic aspects of demand prediction, forming a foundation upon which more advanced techniques like our SGNN approach build. Spatial autoregressive (SAR) models [13] have been widely used in econometrics and marketing to capture spatial dependencies in demand patterns. These models assume that the demand in one location is influenced by the demand in neighboring locations, an idea that aligns with our graph-based approach. However, SAR models typically rely on predefined spatial weight matrices and may struggle with non-linear spatial relationships. Geographically Weighted Regression (GWR) [14] extends traditional regression by allowing coefficients to vary over space, considering that the impact of predictors on demand may differ across locations. While GWR provides localized insights, it may not fully capture the complex, non-linear spatial interactions that our SGNN model aims to address. Kriging, or Gaussian process regression [15], has been applied in geostatistics to predict values at unobserved locations based on observed data points. This method excels in interpolation but may face challenges in extrapolation and handling the high-dimensional feature spaces that are common in e commerce data. Our SGNN approach builds upon these foundational spatial statistical methods by leveraging the flexibility of Graph Neural Networks. It allows for learnable, non-linear spatial relationships and can incorporate high-dimensional feature spaces more naturally. Moreover, the attention mechanism in our model provides a data-driven alternative to the fixed spatial weights used in traditional spatial statistics, potentially capturing more nuanced spatial dependencies in demand patterns.

2.2. Graph Neural Network in Modeling Spatial Dynamics Events

Graph Neural Networks offer several advantages over traditional neural networks. They can be trained on datasets that include both input data and pairwise relationships between items, making them particularly effective for modeling spatial dynamics events [16]. Furthermore, demand predicting in online marketplaces also involves spatial dynamics [17], as the location from which products are sold can influence the demand for geographically proximate products.

In this paper, we creatively apply GNN to predict e-commerce product demand by leveraging the geographic information inherent in the data. We construct an adjacency matrix based on the spatial connectivity of administrative regions in Russia, defining a graph where each geographic region is treated as a node, with various features from the dataset serving as attributes for each node. By utilizing this graph structure, GNN effectively integrates location-specific information into the prediction model, capturing spatial dependencies that other neural network models do not consider. This approach not only enhances the accuracy of demand predictions but also provides a more comprehensive understanding of the factors influencing demand across different regions.

3. Methodology

To tackle the complexities of online retail and to accurately predict product demand, our methodology adopts a novel approach based on the model foundation of the Spatial Graph Neural Network (SGNN). This section unfolds our methodological framework, meticulously designed to employ the intricate spatial relationships and rich attribute data inherent in retail locations. We start with the *attributed graph prediction problem formulation*, setting the stage by defining the graph structure that encapsulates the multifaceted nature of retail locations and their interconnections. Following this, we delve into *constructing graph with spatial adjacency*, a critical step that operationalizes the notion that geographic proximity significantly influences demand patterns among retail nodes. The "Attention-Aware Message Propagation" subsection introduces a sophisticated mechanism to dynamically weigh and integrate information from neighboring nodes, ensuring that the most relevant spatial and contextual signals are emphasized in predicting demand. In *node-Level product demand prediction*, we articulate how the model synthesizes the aggregated information to predict demand at individual locations, highlighting the model's capacity to distill both local and global insights. Lastly, the "training objective" outlines our strategy for refining the model's predictions, emphasizing the optimization of a loss function that aligns predicted demands with actual demands, thus encapsulating our comprehensive approach to address the challenge of demand predicting in the digital marketplace. Through this methodological journey, we aim to offer a robust framework that not only enhances the accuracy of demand predictions but also provides actionable insights for retailers operating in the dynamic online marketplace.

3.1. Attributed Graph Prediction Problem Formulation

We define the product demand prediction problem in the context of SGNN as a regression task on an attributed graph $\mathcal{G} = (\mathcal{V}, \mathcal{E}, \mathbf{X})$. Here, $\mathcal{V}$ represents the set of vertices corresponding to different retail locations, and $\mathcal{E} \subseteq \mathcal{V} \times \mathcal{V}$ denotes the set of edges reflecting the spatial connectivity between these locations. The vertex feature matrix is denoted by $\mathbf{X} \in \mathbb{R}^{|\mathcal{V}| \times f}$, encapsulating f-dimensional features that capture each location's attributes relevant to product demand, such as demographic data, store characteristics, and past demand trends.

Each node $v_i \in \mathcal{V}$ is associated with a target variable y_i representing the product demand to be predicted. Our goal is to learn a function $f : \mathcal{G} \rightarrow \mathbb{R}^{|\mathcal{V}|}$ that maps the attributed graph to a vector of predicted product demands. Formally, we define the predicted demand for a node v_i as $\hat{y}_i = f(\mathcal{G}, \mathbf{X})_i$, where f is parameterized by the weights of a GNN.

3.2. Constructing Graph with Spatial Adjacency

In the realm of e-commerce, understanding the spatial dynamics of product demand is crucial for tailoring marketing strategies and optimizing inventory distribution. The geographic location of retail outlets significantly influences consumer behavior, as customers are more likely to purchase from nearby stores due to convenience and lower shipping costs. Furthermore, sociodemographic factors and regional preferences can lead to variations in demand patterns across different areas. Recognizing these spatial dependencies is essential for accurately predicting demand at each retail location. By constructing a graph with spatial adjacency, we can model the complex interplay between geographic proximity and demand similarity, providing a structured framework to capture these nuanced relationships. This approach allows us to not only predict demand more accurately but also to uncover insights into how spatial factors influence consumer preferences and buying behavior. Transitioning from this rationale, the construction of the adjacency matrix $\mathbf{A} \in \mathbb{R}^{|\mathcal{V}| \times |\mathcal{V}|}$ becomes a foundational step in our methodology, enabling us to quantitatively analyze and leverage these spatial relationships for enhanced demand prediction.

The adjacency matrix $\mathbf{A} \in \mathbb{R}^{|\mathcal{V}| \times |\mathcal{V}|}$ is constructed based on spatial proximity among the retail locations, capturing the notion that nearby locations may exhibit similar demand patterns. An edge weight w_{ij} is assigned to each edge $(v_i, v_j) \in \mathcal{E}$, formulated as

$$w_{ij} = \exp\left(-\delta \cdot d(v_i, v_j)\right), \tag{1}$$

where δ is a decay factor and $d(v_i, v_j)$ measures the geographical distance between locations v_i and v_j.

3.3. Attention-Aware Message Propagation

In the intricate landscape of retail, not all interactions between locations bear equal significance in shaping product demand. The influence of one retail location on another can vary dramatically based on a multitude of factors, such as the similarity of the products offered, the competitive dynamics between the stores, or even the demographic characteristics of the surrounding areas. Traditional methods of aggregating information across nodes in a graph often assume uniformity in these relationships, potentially glossing over the subtleties that could inform more nuanced demand predictions. To address this limitation and embrace the complexity of real-world retail networks, it becomes urgent to introduce a mechanism that can discern and weigh the varying degrees of influence between neighboring locations. By implementing an attention-aware message propagation system, we can selectively amplify or attenuate the information flow between nodes, ensuring that the aggregation of features across the network accurately reflects the heterogeneity of inter-node impacts. This approach not only enhances the model's ability to capture the essence of spatial interactions but also fine-tunes the predictive accuracy by focusing on the most relevant signals for demand prediction in each specific location. Following this rationale, the introduction of an attention mechanism becomes a critical advancement in our methodology, allowing for a dynamic and context-sensitive representation of retail locations within the graph.

We introduce an attention mechanism to capture the varying impact that different neighbors have on a node's feature representation. The attention coefficients α_{ij} quantify the importance of node v_j's features to node v_i, computed as

$$\alpha_{ij} = \frac{\exp\left(\text{LeakyReLU}(\mathbf{a}^T[\mathbf{W}\mathbf{h}_i \| \mathbf{W}\mathbf{h}_j])\right)}{\sum_{k \in \mathcal{N}(v_i)} \exp\left(\text{LeakyReLU}(\mathbf{a}^T[\mathbf{W}\mathbf{h}_i \| \mathbf{W}\mathbf{h}_k])\right)}, \quad (2)$$

where $\mathbf{a}$ is a learnable weight vector, $\mathbf{W}$ is a shared linear transformation applied to each node's features, and $\|$ denotes concatenation.

3.4. Node-Level Product Demand Prediction

The process of predicting product demand at the node level, represented by $\hat{y}_i$ for a node v_i, is a sophisticated operation that integrates the core principles of spatial adjacency and attention mechanisms to accurately model demand dynamics. This integration is pivotal, as it allows the model to consider not just the intrinsic attributes of a retail location encapsulated in $\mathbf{h}_i^{(l)}$, but also the complex web of interactions it has with its neighbors. The spatial adjacency construction ensures that the model recognizes the influence of geographic proximity in shaping demand patterns, acknowledging that retail locations situated closer together are more likely to exhibit similar demand characteristics due to shared market conditions and consumer bases. Furthermore, the introduction of attention-aware message propagation enhances the model's ability to discern the varying degrees of relevance among these interactions. By computing attention coefficients α_{ij}, the model dynamically adjusts the influence of neighboring nodes based on the context, ensuring that the aggregated information is tailored to reflect the unique demand landscape of each location. This nuanced approach to information aggregation, where the attention mechanism acts as a filter to prioritize the most impactful signals from the neighborhood, is crucial for capturing the heterogeneity inherent in retail networks.

Following the above analysis, the predicted demand $\hat{y}_i$ for a node v_i that reflects the culmination of feature transformations and attention-weighted information aggregation from its neighborhood is formulated as follows:

$$\hat{y}_i = \sigma\left(\mathbf{w}_o^T\left(\mathbf{h}_i^{(l)} + \sum_{v_j \in \mathcal{N}(v_i)} \alpha_{ij} \mathbf{h}_j^{(l)}\right)\right), \quad (3)$$

where $\mathbf{h}_i^{(l)}$ is the feature representation of node v_i at the l-th layer, $\mathbf{w}_o$ is the output layer's weight vector, and σ is an activation function, typically chosen as the identity function for regression tasks. The final layer's output $\hat{y}_i$ is the demand prediction for product i, and the network is trained to minimize the prediction error over all nodes.

3.5. Training Objective

Building upon the foundational understanding that the predictive accuracy of our model depends on its ability to intricately model the spatial dynamics and attention-driven interactions within the retail network, the training objective of our predictive model takes on a crucial role. The loss function, $\mathcal{L}$, serves as a quantifiable measure of the model's performance, estimating the discrepancy between the predicted demands $\hat{\mathbf{y}}$ and the actual demands $\mathbf{y}$ across the graph. The choice of a mean squared error (MSE) loss function is careful, emphasizing the importance of penalizing larger errors more severely to refine the model's predictive accuracy:

$$\mathcal{L}(\mathbf{y}, \hat{\mathbf{y}}) = \frac{1}{|\mathcal{V}|} \sum_{i=1}^{|\mathcal{V}|} (y_i - \hat{y}_i)^2. \quad (4)$$

This mathematical formulation is underpinned by a deeper strategy aimed at capturing the nuanced interplay of factors influencing product demand. The propagation of features across the layers of the Graph Neural Network is not merely a process of data transformation but a methodical approach to distill both the local and global spatial dependencies that are critical to understanding and predicting demand accurately. These dependencies are revealed through the model's attention mechanisms and the spatial adjacency matrix, enabling a comprehensive analysis of how geographic proximity and contextual relevance between retail locations influence demand patterns.

By meticulously calibrating the parameters of the function f, our objective transcends the minimization of prediction error. We try to shape a predictive model that not only excels in capturing the complex dynamics governing demand across the retail network but also demonstrates an exceptional ability to generalize across diverse nodes and fluctuating demand scenarios. This involves a careful balancing act of ensuring the model remains sensitive to the subtleties of spatial and contextual information while avoiding overfitting to the training data, thereby ensuring its applicability and robustness in real-world settings.

The training phase, therefore, becomes a critical juncture where theoretical concepts and empirical data converge, guiding the model towards achieving a deep, contextual understanding of demand predicting. Through this process, we aim to equip stakeholders in the online marketplace with a powerful analytical tool, capable of handling the intricacies of demand prediction with enough precision and insight. This endeavor not only advances the frontier of research in e-commerce demand prediction but also offers obvious benefits for retailers seeking to optimize their strategies in response to the ever-evolving landscape of consumer preferences and market conditions.

4. Experiments

In our investigation, we answer the research questions (RQs) proposed in Section 1, which aim at evaluating the efficacy of our spatial GNN model in the scenario of geographic product demand prediction. These questions are designed to probe the model's performance, the incremental value of its components, and its robustness across different settings.

4.1. Experiment Setup

4.1.1. Datasets

Overall Introduction

In the experiments, we utilize the Avito Demand Prediction Challenge hosted on Kaggle as the benchmark, which presents participants with a unique opportunity to apply machine learning techniques to predict demand for an extensive range of products listed on Avito's platform. Avito, being Russia's largest classified ads service, encompasses a wide variety of categories, including electronics, real estate, and services, making it a rich source of data for such predictive modeling tasks. The objective of the challenge is to accurately predict the probability of an ad leading to a product transaction, based on the information provided in the ad's description, context, and metadata. This task has profound implications for both sellers by optimizing their ad placements for higher sales, and buyers, by enhancing their shopping experience through the prioritization of listings likely to meet their purchase intent.

Detailed Data Information

The dataset provided by Avito's team contains multiple modalities of information, including images, text, categorical, and continuous features. We provide their details as follows:

- `item id`: Id of a particular advertisement.
- `user id`: Id of a user.
- `region`: The region that Ads belong to.
- `city`: The city that a Ad belongs to.
- `top-level category`: The top-level ad category as classified by Avito's ad model.
- `fine-grain category`: The fine-grain ad category as classified by Avito's ad model.
- `param 1`: The first optional parameter from Avito's ad model.
- `param 2`: The second optional parameter from Avito's ad model.
- `param 3`: The third optional parameter from Avito's ad model.
- `title`: The textual title for the Ad.
- `description`: The multi-sentence textual description for the Ad.
- `price`: The numerical value for the Ad's price.
- `item seq number`: Ad sequential number for the user.
- `activation date`: The date that the Ad was placed onto the platform.
- `user type`: The type of the user, including Private, Company, and Shop.
- `image`: The Id code corresponding to the image which is tied to a jpg file in train jpg. Considering that not every Ad has an image, we don't employ this feature for further analysis.
- `image top 1`: Avito's classification code for the image.
- `deal probability`: The target variable. This is the likelihood that the ad will actually sell the item. It is not possible to verify every transaction with certainty, so the value of this column can be any floating point number from zero to one.

This dataset contains 1,503,424 records, which are randomly divided into train/ validation/test sets according to the 70%/10%/20% ratio.

Data Analysis

Univariate analysis: In the univariate analysis section of our study, we delve into an in-depth examination of six pivotal features deemed to have substantial importance in understanding the dynamics of our dataset. These features include `deal probability`, `price`, `region`, `city`, `top-level category`, and `fine-grain category`. This analysis aims to shed light on the individual characteristics and distributions of these features, providing foundational insights for further multivariate analysis. The distribution histograms for such features have been provided in the Figures 1 and 2. From such figures, we can obtain the following observations:

- `deal probability`: An initial observation from the distribution histograms indicates a pronounced long-tail distribution issue with the `deal probability` feature. Notably, approximately 65% of the ads exhibit a zero deal probability, signifying a substantial portion of ads that do not culminate in a transaction. Conversely, a minimal fraction of ads achieve a deal probability of 1, indicating a successful sale. This distribution suggests a high variance in the likelihood of deals being closed across the dataset.
- `price`: Prior to analysis, the `price` feature undergoes a logarithmic transformation to normalize its distribution. Post-transformation, the `price` distribution approximates a normal distribution, as evidenced by the histograms. This transformation mitigates the skewness originally present in the data, facilitating more meaningful statistical analysis and interpretation.
- `region`: The analysis of the `region` feature reveals a geographical disparity in ad postings. The Krasnodar region emerges as the most prominent area for ad postings, followed closely by the Sverdlovsk and Rostov regions. This distribution highlights

the regional variances in marketplace activity, potentially influenced by factors such as population density and economic conditions.

- `city`: Delving into the `city` feature, we observe that the highest number of ads are posted in Krasnodar and Ekaterinburg cities. Subsequent rankings include Novosibirsk, Rostov-na-Donu, and Nizhny Novgorod cities. This urban-centric distribution underscores the role of major cities as hubs for online marketplace transactions, possibly attributed to their larger populations and higher internet penetration rates.
- `top-level category`: The `top-level category` feature analysis reveals a dominant preference for posting ads in the "Personal things" category, accounting for more than 0.6 million users. Following this, the categories for "Home and Cottages" and "Consumer Electronics" are notable, with approximately 0.2 million users posting ads in each. This distribution indicates a significant inclination towards selling personal belongings, with a notable interest in home-related items and electronics.
- `fine-grain category`: Within the subcategories, "Clothes, shoes, accessories", "Children's clothing and footwear", and "Goods for children and toys" emerge as the top three, each with around 0.3 million postings. This detailed breakdown within the `fine-grain category` feature further elucidates consumer behavior, highlighting a strong market for personal and children-related items.

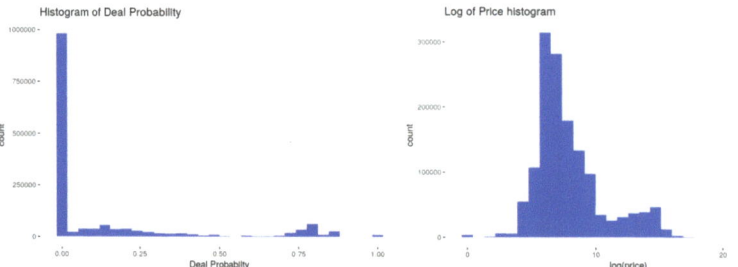

Figure 1. The distribution histogram for the deal probability and log of price over each value range.

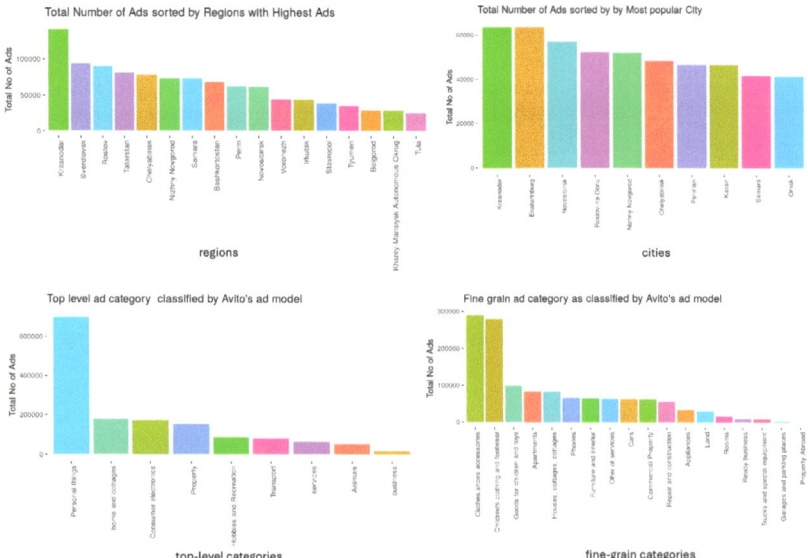

Figure 2. The distribution histogram for the region, city, top-level category, and fine-grain category, correspondingly.

The univariate analysis of these selected features, supported by the distribution histograms in Figures 1 and 2, provides a comprehensive overview of the dataset's characteristics. This foundational understanding paves the way for more intricate multivariate analyses and predictive modeling, with the ultimate goal of enhancing the accuracy and efficiency of product demand prediction in the online marketplace.

Bivariate analysis: In the exploration of bivariate relationships within our dataset, we delve into the interactions between `deal probability` and four critical features: `region`, `city`, `top-level category`, and `user type`. This analysis aims to uncover the nuanced dynamics that these features may have with the likelihood of a deal being closed. By examining the mean deal probability across various groups within these features, we gain insights into how different factors influence transaction outcomes. The findings from this analysis are visualized in Figure 3, facilitating a more intuitive understanding of these relationships.

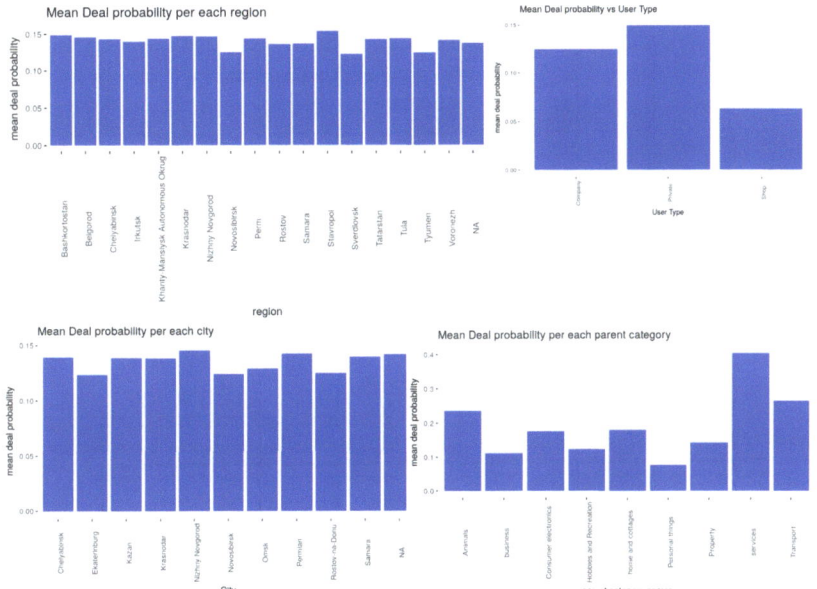

Figure 3. The histograms for mean deal probability in each group of corresponding variables, including region, user type, city, and parent category.

- `deal probability` and `region`: Upon examining the relationship between `deal probability` and `region`, it is observed that the mean deal probability across all regions hovers around 15%. This uniformity suggests that while regional factors may influence the volume of ads, they do not significantly differentiate the likelihood of a deal being closed. This finding could indicate that other factors beyond geographical location play a more pivotal role in influencing deal probability.
- `deal probability` and `city`: Similar to the observation with regions, the analysis of `deal probability` and `city` reveals that all cities also exhibit a mean deal probability of approximately 15%. This consistency across cities further supports the notion that the likelihood of closing a deal is not heavily dependent on specific urban centers, highlighting the importance of looking beyond geographic specifics to understand deal closure dynamics.

- deal probability and top-level category: A more nuanced insight emerges from the relationship between deal probability and top-level category. The "Services" category stands out with the highest mean deal probability at 40%, followed by "Transport" and "Animals" at 25%. This distinction suggests that ads within the "Services" category are significantly more likely to result in a deal, possibly due to the inherent nature of services being in higher demand or more immediately consumable compared to physical goods. This disparity underscores the potential for tailoring strategies based on category-specific demand dynamics.
- deal probability and fine-grain category: The analysis of deal probability and user type reveals a notable difference in mean deal probabilities between Private Users (15%) and Shop Users (5%). This discrepancy suggests that ads posted by private individuals are three times more likely to close a deal than those posted by shops. This could be attributed to a variety of factors, including perceived trustworthiness, pricing differences, or the nature of the goods and services offered by these user types.

4.1.2. Baselines

In our experiments, we benchmark our proposed methodology against a diverse set of representative models that span across three major categories in the domain of product demand prediction. This comparative analysis aims to highlight the strengths and potential of our approach in capturing the complex dynamics of demand prediction. Below is an introduction to each baseline model utilized in our study.

Linear Model:

- Generalized Linear Model(GLM) [18]: A foundational approach in statistical modeling, GLM extends traditional linear regression to support various types of distribution for the target variable, such as binomial and Poisson distributions. This model is pivotal for understanding the linear relationships between the features and the target demand, serving as a baseline to assess the incremental benefits of more complex models.

Tree-based Model:

- XGBoost [19]: A highly efficient and scalable implementation of gradient boosting framework, XGBoost has gained popularity for its performance in various predictive modeling competitions. It leverages an ensemble of decision trees, optimized through gradient boosting, to capture non-linear relationships and interactions among features.
- LightGBM [20]: An advanced gradient boosting model that utilizes a novel tree-growing algorithm to enhance efficiency and scalability. LightGBM is designed to handle large-scale data, offering a faster training process without compromising on model accuracy.
- CatBoost [21]: Another gradient boosting variant, CatBoost is renowned for its handling of categorical features directly, without the need for extensive preprocessing. It provides robust solutions to avoid overfitting, making it highly effective in diverse predictive tasks, including demand prediction.

Deep Model:

- Multiple Layer Perceptron (MLP) [22]: MLP is a class of feedforward artificial neural network (ANN) that consists of at least three layers of nodes: an input layer, a hidden layer, and an output layer. MLP utilizes a backpropagation technique for training, capable of capturing complex non-linear relationships between inputs and outputs.
- LSTM [23]: Long Short-Term Memory networks, a type of recurrent neural network (RNN) architecture, are specifically designed to address the vanishing gradient problem of traditional RNNs. LSTMs are adept at learning long-term dependencies, making them particularly suitable for time-series predicting tasks like demand prediction.
- GRU [24]: Gated Recurrent Units (GRUs) are a variant of RNNs that simplify the LSTM architecture while retaining its capability to capture dependencies over various time spans. GRUs offer a more efficient and equally effective alternative for sequential data modeling.

- CNN [25]: Convolutional Neural Networks, traditionally known for their prowess in image processing, have also been adapted for spatial predicting. By capturing spatial dependencies through their hierarchical structure, CNNs can be utilized to effectively model the geographical information and relationships in demand data.

4.1.3. Evaluation Metrics

In assessing the performance of our product demand prediction models, we employ three key evaluation metrics that offer a comprehensive view of model accuracy and fit. These metrics are essential for quantifying the discrepancy between the actual demand values and the predictions made by our models.

- Mean Absolute Error (MAE): MAE is a straightforward metric that calculates the average absolute difference between the actual demand y_i and the predicted demand $\hat{y}_i$ across all observations. It provides an intuitive measure of the model's accuracy, with lower values indicating better performance. The MAE is defined as

$$\text{MAE} = \frac{1}{N}\sum_{i=1}^{N}|y_i - \hat{y}_i|, \tag{5}$$

where N is the total number of observations. This metric is particularly useful for understanding the magnitude of prediction errors without considering their direction.

- Root Mean Squared Error (RMSE): This metric offers a more sensitive measure of model accuracy by squaring the errors before averaging, thus giving greater weight to larger errors. RMSE is defined as the square root of the average of squared differences between the predicted and actual values:

$$\text{RMSE} = \sqrt{\frac{1}{N}\sum_{i=1}^{N}(y_i - \hat{y}_i)^2}, \tag{6}$$

where N represents the total number of observations. The RMSE is beneficial for identifying when a model might be prone to producing significant errors, as it penalizes larger discrepancies more heavily than smaller ones.

- R-squared (R^2): R-squared, also known as the coefficient of determination, measures the proportion of the variance in the dependent variable that is predictable from the independent variables. It indicates how well the regression predictions approximate the real data points. An R-squared of 1 indicates that the regression predictions perfectly fit the data. The formula for R-squared is

$$R^2 = 1 - \frac{\sum_{i=1}^{N}(y_i - \hat{y}_i)^2}{\sum_{i=1}^{N}(y_i - \bar{y})^2} \tag{7}$$

where $\bar{y}$ is the mean of the actual demand values. R-squared is a relative measure of fit that can be useful when comparing different models' abilities to explain the variability in the data.

4.1.4. Implementation Details

For the implementation phase of our study, we've adopted a rigorous and replicable approach to ensure the reliability of our results. Specifically, we've carried out each experiment a total of five times, each with a unique seed, to ensure the robustness of our findings. The average of these runs is then reported as the final performance metric of our model, providing a solid foundation for the evaluation of our spatial GNN's effectiveness in predicting product demand.

In the detailed setup of each experiment, our model is meticulously trained over a span of 50 epochs. This extensive training period is carefully monitored with an early stopping mechanism in place, a strategic decision aimed at curbing the potential for overfitting and ensuring the model's generalizability to unseen data. Furthermore, we have calibrated the architecture of our spatial GNN to consist of three layers. This specific configuration is chosen to strike a balance between capturing the intricate spatial relationships within the data and avoiding the pitfall of over-smoothing, where the model's output becomes indistinct and loses valuable detail.

The technical execution of our method leverages the powerful capabilities of PyTorch v2.3.0, a choice that facilitates the efficient and flexible development of deep learning models. To harness the computational intensity of training a spatial GNN, our experiments are conducted on a state-of-the-art NVIDIA RTX 4090 GPU manufactured by TSMC in the Hsinchu, Taiwan, equipped with an ample 24 GB of memory. This hardware setup not only accelerates the training process but also enables the handling of complex models and large datasets with ease, ensuring that our implementation is both fast and effective.

4.2. Overall Performance (RQ1)

Addressing Research Question 1, we assess the performance of our Spatial Graph Neural Network model in the realm of product demand prediction, setting it against a spectrum of modeling approaches, including linear, tree-based, and deep learning models. This evaluation leverages metrics such as Mean Absolute Error (MAE), Root Mean Squared Error (RMSE), and R-squared (R^2), providing a comprehensive view of each model's predictive accuracy. As delineated in Table 1, our analysis reveals a clear hierarchy in model performance. The data underscores that both tree-based models (XGBoost, LightGBM, and CatBoost) and deep learning models (encompassing LSTM, GRU, and CNN) surpass the Generalized Linear Model (GLM) in terms of predictive capability. This outcome hints at the limitations of traditional linear models in capturing the intricate and nonlinear relationships inherent in real-world product demand data. While deep learning models such as LSTM and GRU have demonstrated promise across various domains, their edge over sophisticated tree-based models in the context of product demand prediction appears marginal. This observation suggests a need for the further refinement and domain-specific tailoring of deep learning approaches to unlock their full potential in this area. Notably, the CNN model outperforms MLP, LSTM, and GRU, highlighting the pivotal role of spatial information in enhancing demand prediction accuracy. Amidst this competitive landscape, our SGNN model emerges as a standout performer, consistently outshining both the traditional tree-based and contemporary deep learning baselines. This remarkable performance, characterized by lower MAE, RMSE, and higher R^2 scores, underscores the efficacy of our approach in navigating the complexities of product demand prediction. The SGNN model's superior accuracy attests to its capacity to effectively leverage spatial relationships, offering a robust solution that could significantly benefit the online advertisement sector. The findings from our analysis not only validate the innovative design of the SGNN model but also illuminate the path for future advancements in the field of demand predicting. The compelling results achieved by our model on the Avito dataset underscore its potential as a transformative tool for marketers and strategists aiming to optimize their online presence and engagement strategies.

Table 1. The evaluation performance of various baselines and our SGNN on the Avito dataset for product demand prediction.

Method	Avito		
	MAE	RMSE	R^2
GLM	0.3285	0.3172	0.7349
XGBoost	0.2891	0.2587	0.8170
LightGBM	0.2572	0.2312	0.8346
CatBoost	0.2689	0.2563	0.8308
MLP	0.2952	0.2951	0.7652
LSTM	0.2491	0.2286	0.8569
GRU	0.2438	0.2210	0.8625
CNN	0.2347	0.2054	0.8901
SGNN	0.1685	0.1504	0.9234

4.3. Ablation Study (RQ2)

To delve deeper into the intricacies of our Spatial Graph Neural Network model's architecture and to answer Research Question 2 (RQ2), we embarked on an exploratory journey to dissect the influence of individual components within our model. Specifically, we scrutinized the unique contributions of the spatial adjacency and attention-aware message propagation modules by systematically omitting each from the SGNN framework and observing the subsequent impact on prediction accuracy. This methodical approach allowed us to isolate and understand the value added by these critical modules. The results of this analysis are meticulously compiled in Table 2. In this table, "spatial" refers to the module that integrates spatial adjacency information, while "attention" corresponds to the module that facilitates attention-aware message propagation. The comparative performance metrics, including MAE, RMSE, and R^2, serve as clear indicators of each module's significance. Upon reviewing the table, it becomes apparent that the absence of either the spatial or attention module from the SGNN framework results in a marked reduction in predictive performance. This is evidenced by increased values of MAE and RMSE, alongside decreased R^2 scores, signaling a decline in the model's ability to predict product demand accurately. Such findings underscore the indispensable nature of both modules in our predictive framework. The spatial adjacency module, in particular, plays a pivotal role by embedding geographical information into the model, thereby allowing for a nuanced understanding of spatial relationships and their impact on product demand. The noticeable performance drop observed upon the removal of this module underscores its critical contribution to capturing the spatial dynamics integral to accurate demand prediction. Similarly, the attention-aware message-propagation module enriches the model by enabling it to selectively prioritize and learn from the information disseminated across neighboring nodes. This adaptability enhances the model's capacity to discern relevant patterns and relationships, further bolstering its predictive accuracy. In sum, the ablation study not only reaffirms the value of incorporating geographical information into demand prediction models but also highlights the synergistic effect of combining spatial adjacency with attention mechanisms. The discernible performance degradation observed upon excluding these modules validates our initial hypothesis and motivation for their integration, solidifying their status as cornerstone components of our SGNN framework. This insight not only propels our understanding of SGNN's inner workings but also paves the way for future enhancements and optimizations in geographical demand prediction methodologies. To further elucidate the impact of our proposed modules, we also evaluated a stripped-down version of SGNN without both the spatial adjacency and attention-aware message propagation modules. This basic GNN model achieved an MAE of 0.2103, RMSE of 0.2014, and R^2 of 0.8976. These results, which are notably inferior to the full SGNN model, underscore the significant contributions of both modules to the model's predictive performance. Moreover, this baseline provides a useful point of comparison with the various prediction methods discussed in Section 4.2, further highlighting the advantages of our full SGNN approach.

Table 2. The ablation study results for our SGNN model.

Method	Avito		
	MAE	RMSE	R^2
SGNN w/o spatial and attention	0.2103	0.2014	0.8976
SGNN w/o spatial	0.1962	0.1897	0.9045
SGNN w/o attention	0.1876	0.1721	0.9108
SGNN	0.1685	0.1504	0.9234

4.4. Hyperparameter Robustness (RQ3)

In pursuit of answering Research Question 3 (RQ3), our investigation delves into the sensitivity of the Spatial Graph Neural Network model's predictive accuracy to variations in key hyperparameters: the decay factor, batch size, and the number of SGNN layers. This exploration aims to discern the extent to which these parameters influence the model's precision in predicting product demand.

Decay Factor: We initiate our exploration by adjusting the decay factor within our model across a spectrum from 0.1 to 0.9. The empirical findings, encapsulated in Table 3, reveal an intriguing pattern: while the overall performance remains relatively stable across a wide range of decay factor values, we observe a discernible dip in predictive accuracy at the extremities of this range. This phenomenon underscores the delicate balance required in setting the decay factor, as values that are too high or too low can adversely affect the scope of information propagation within the SGNN, thereby impacting learning efficiency.

Table 3. The hyperparameter robustness analysis on the decay factor.

Decay Factor	Avito		
	MAE	RMSE	R^2
0.1	0.1958	0.1792	0.9063
0.3	0.1731	0.1565	0.9187
0.5	0.1685	0.1504	0.9234
0.7	0.1786	0.1592	0.9146
0.9	0.1901	0.1712	0.9084

Batch Size: Further scrutiny is applied to the impact of batch size variations on model performance, with our analysis spanning batch sizes from 1000 to 20,000. As detailed in Table 4, the results showcase an impressive resilience in performance metrics (MAE, RMSE, and R^2) against changes in batch size. Notably, the SGNN model consistently maintains a MAE above the 0.1700 threshold across almost all tested batch sizes, highlighting its robustness and stability in handling varying data volumes during training.

Table 4. The hyperparameter robustness analysis on the batch size.

Batch Size	Avito		
	MAE	RMSE	R^2
1000	0.1702	0.1535	0.9216
2000	0.1685	0.1504	0.9234
5000	0.1674	0.1492	0.9257
10,000	0.1668	0.1487	0.9261
20,000	0.1665	0.1483	0.9273

Layer Number: The final dimension of our hyperparameter analysis focuses on the number of SGNN layers, ranging from 1 to 5. This examination, presented in Table 5, seeks to ascertain whether a deeper SGNN architecture translates to enhanced predictive performance. The findings confirm the model's resilience to variations in layer numbers, with an optimal performance observed at a layer count of 3. Beyond this point, an increase in layers leads to a noticeable decline in performance across all metrics (MAE, RMSE, and R^2), attributed to the over-smoothing issue prevalent in deeper Graph Neural Network models. This observation highlights the criticality of layer number selection in preserving the model's capacity to generate distinct and informative node representations without succumbing to the diluting effects of over-smoothing.

Table 5. The hyperparameter robustness analysis based on the layer number.

Layer Number	Avito		
	MAE	RMSE	R^2
1	0.1923	0.1794	0.9082
2	0.1746	0.1593	0.9175
3	0.1685	0.1504	0.9234
4	0.1891	0.1750	0.9126
5	0.2187	0.2023	0.8927

This comprehensive analysis of hyperparameter sensitivity not only affirms the SGNN model's robustness across a range of configurations but also sheds light on the optimal settings conducive to maximizing predictive accuracy. The insights garnered from this exploration provide valuable guidance for fine-tuning the SGNN framework, ensuring its adaptability and effectiveness in the dynamic landscape of product demand prediction.

5. Conclusions and Future Works

5.1. Conclusions

In this paper, we introduced an innovative approach to product demand prediction through the utilization of the Spatial Graph Neural Network, tailored for the online retail domain. By adopting a novel methodology that intricately models the spatial relationships and attributes of retail locations, we have successfully demonstrated the potential of SGNN in transcending traditional demand prediction methods. Our approach, which constructs a spatially aware graph representation of the marketplace and integrates advanced attention mechanisms, aims to capture the nuanced relationships and dependencies that shape demand patterns.

The comparative analysis against a comprehensive suite of baseline models, spanning linear, tree-based, and deep learning approaches, has underscored the SGNN framework's superior capability in accurately predicting demand. Through rigorous evaluation employing MAE, RMSE, and R^2, our findings reveal the SGNN model's adeptness at providing actionable insights, thereby empowering retailers to navigate the intricacies of the online marketplace with enhanced strategic foresight.

One of the key strengths of our SGNN approach lies in its ability to effectively capture and leverage spatial dependencies in demand patterns. By constructing a graph representation of the marketplace, our model can inherently account for geographical proximity and regional influences on product demand, a feature that traditional methods often struggle to incorporate effectively. This spatial awareness allows for more nuanced predictions that consider the complex interplay between location and demand.

While our SGNN approach demonstrates significant advantages, it is important to acknowledge its limitations. The computational complexity of SGNN models can pose challenges for very large-scale applications, particularly in scenarios with extremely high numbers of retail locations or products. Additionally, the model's performance is dependent on the quality and completeness of the spatial data available, which may not always be consistent across different marketplaces or regions. Furthermore, while our model effectively captures spatial relationships, it may not fully account for temporal dynamics in demand patterns, which could be crucial in certain contexts. These limitations point to potential areas for future research and refinement of the SGNN approach.

5.2. Future Works

In light of the promising results demonstrated by employing the Spatial Graph Neural Network for product demand prediction in online retail, several avenues for future research and development emerge. These potential directions not only aim to refine and extend the current model's capabilities but also seek to explore new applications and methodologies within the realm of SGNN and beyond. below are some detailed insights into possible future work.

- Temporal Dynamics Integration: Incorporating temporal dynamics into the SGNN framework could significantly enhance the model's predictive accuracy. Future work could explore methods for embedding time-series data into the graph structure, allowing the model to capture not only spatial relationships but also temporal patterns in consumer behavior and demand fluctuations.
- Hybrid Models: Combining SGNN with other machine learning techniques, such as reinforcement learning or unsupervised learning algorithms, could lead to hybrid models that leverage the strengths of multiple approaches. For instance, reinforcement learning could optimize inventory levels dynamically based on SGNN demand predictions, offering a comprehensive solution for supply chain management.
- Cross-Domain Adaptation: Exploring the applicability of SGNN in domains beyond retail, such as urban planning, transportation, and social network analysis, could unveil new insights and applications. The spatial and relational modeling capabilities of SGNN hold potential for predicting traffic flow, urban development trends, or information propagation in social networks.
- Advanced Graph Architectures: Investigating more sophisticated Graph Neural Network architectures, including Graph Attention Network and Heterogeneous Graph Neural Network, could provide deeper insights into complex spatial interactions. These advanced models could better capture the heterogeneity in data types and relationships present in retail networks.
- Scalability and Efficiency: Addressing the computational challenges associated with SGNN, particularly for large-scale applications, remains a critical area for future work. Developing more efficient algorithms and leveraging distributed computing frameworks could enhance the scalability and practicality of SGNN for real-world applications.
- Interpretability and Explainability: Enhancing the interpretability of SGNN models is crucial for gaining insights into the underlying factors driving demand predictions. Future work could focus on developing methodologies for visualizing and interpreting graph-based models, providing valuable feedback for decision-makers in retail and other sectors.

Author Contributions: Methodology, X.W. and T.S.; Software, T.S.; Formal analysis, X.W.; Investigation, J.L.; Writing—original draft, J.L.; Writing—review & editing, L.F.and M.Z.; Supervision, M.Z.; Project administration, J.L. All authors have read and agreed to the published version of the manuscript.

Funding: This research received no external funding.

Institutional Review Board Statement: Not applicable.

Informed Consent Statement: Not applicable.

Data Availability Statement: Publicly available datasets were analyzed in this study. This data can be found here: https://www.kaggle.com/competitions/avito-demand-prediction (accessed on 5 August 2024).

Conflicts of Interest: The authors declare no conflicts of interest.

References

1. Kim, J.U.; Kim, W.J.; Park, S.C. Consumer perceptions on web advertisements and motivation factors to purchase in the online shopping. *Comput. Hum. Behav.* **2010**, *26*, 1208–1222. [CrossRef]
2. Rai, S.; Gupta, A.; Anand, A.;Trivedi, A.; Bhadauria, S. Demand prediction for e-commerce advertisements: A comparative study using state-of-the-art machine learning methods. In Proceedings of the 2019 10th International Conference on Computing, Communication and Networking Technologies (ICCCNT), Kanpur, India, 6–8 July 2019; IEEE: Piscataway, NJ, USA.
3. Kin-man To, C. Innovation process management in global fashion businesses: A review of contextual aspects. *Res. J. Text. Appar.* **2003**, *7*, 60–73. [CrossRef]
4. Levis, A.A.; Papageorgiou, L.G. Customer demand forecasting via support vector regression analysis. *Chem. Eng. Res. Des.* **2005**, *83*, 1009–1018. [CrossRef]
5. Jain, A.; Karthikeyan, V.; Sahana, B.; Shambhavi, B.R.; Sindhu, K.; Balaji, S. Demand forecasting for e-commerce platforms. In Proceedings of the 2020 IEEE International Conference for Innovation in Technology (INOCON), Bangluru, India, 6–8 November 2020; IEEE: Piscataway, NJ, USA, 2020.
6. Tugay, R.; Oguducu, S.G. Demand prediction using machine learning methods and stacked generalization. *arXiv* **2020**, arXiv:2009.09756.
7. Bandara, K.; Shi, P.; Bergmeir, C.; Hewamalage, H.; Tran, Q.; Seaman, B. Sales demand forecast in e-commerce using a long short-term memory neural network methodology. In Proceedings of the Neural Information Processing: 26th International Conference, ICONIP 2019, Sydney, NSW, Australia, 12–15 December 2019; Proceedings, Part III 26; Springer International Publishing: Berlin/Heidelberg, Germany, 2019.
8. Zhang, G.; Patuwo, B.E.; Hu, M.Y. Forecasting with artificial neural networks: The state of the art. *Int. J. Forecast.* **1998**, *14*, 35–62. [CrossRef]
9. Kuo, C.; Reitsch, A. Neural networks vs. conventional methods of forecasting. *J. Bus. Forecast.* **1995**, *14*, 17.
10. Azzouni, A.; Pujolle, G. A long short-term memory recurrent neural network framework for network traffic matrix prediction. *arXiv* **2017**, arXiv:1705.05690.
11. Aburto, L.; Weber, R. Improved supply chain management based on hybrid demand forecasts. *Appl. Soft Comput.* **2007**, *7*, 136–144. [CrossRef]
12. Islek, I.; Öğüdücü, S.G. A Decision Support System for Demand Forecasting based on Classifier Ensemble. In *FedCSIS (Communication Papers)*; FedCSIS: Sofia, Bulgaria, 2017.
13. LeSage, J.; Pace, R.K. *Introduction to Spatial Econometrics*; Chapman and Hall/CRC: Boca Raton, FL, USA, 2009.
14. David, O. Geographically weighted regression: The analysis of spatially varying relationships. *Geogr. Anal.* **2003**, *35*, 272–275.
15. Noel, C. The origins of kriging. *Math. Geol.* **1990**, *22*, 239–252.
16. Wu, Z.; Pan, S.; Chen, F.; Long, G.; Zhang, C.; Philip, S.Y. A comprehensive survey on graph neural networks. *IEEE Trans. Neural Netw. Learn. Syst.* **2020**, *32*, 4–24. [CrossRef] [PubMed]
17. Gandhi, A.; Aakanksha; Kaveri, S.; Chaoji, V. Spatio-temporal multi-graph networks for demand forecasting in online marketplaces. In *Joint European Conference on Machine Learning and Knowledge Discovery in Databases*; Springer International Publishing: Cham, Switzerland, 2021.
18. Hastie, T.J.; Pregibon, D. Generalized linear models. In *Statistical Models in S*; Routledge: London, UK, 2017; pp. 195–247.
19. Chen, T.; Guestrin, C. Xgboost: A scalable tree boosting system. In Proceedings of the 22nd acm Sigkdd International Conference on Knowledge Discovery and Data Mining, San Francisco, CA, USA, 13–17 August 2016; pp. 785–794.
20. Ke, G.; Meng, Q.; Finley, T.; Wang, T.; Chen, W.; Ma, W.; Ye, Q.; Liu, T.Y. Lightgbm: A highly efficient gradient boosting decision tree. *Adv. Neural Inf. Process. Syst.* **2017**, *30*, 52.
21. Prokhorenkova, L.; Gusev, G.; Vorobev, A.; Dorogush, A.V.; Gulin, A. CatBoost: Unbiased boosting with categorical features. *Adv. Neural Inf. Process. Syst.* **2018**, *31*.

22. Amalnick, M.S.; Habibifar, N.; Hamid, M.; Bastan, M. An intelligent algorithm for final product demand forecasting in pharmaceutical units. *Int. J. Syst. Assur. Eng. Manag.* **2020**, *11*, 481–493. [CrossRef]
23. Abbasimehr, H.; Shabani, M.; Yousefi, M. An optimized model using LSTM network for demand forecasting. *Comput. Ind. Eng.* **2020**, *143*, 106435. [CrossRef]
24. Shu, W.; Zeng, F.; Ling, Z.; Liu, J.; Lu, T.; Chen, G. Resource demand prediction of cloud workloads using an attention-based GRU model. In Proceedings of the 2021 17th International Conference on Mobility, Sensing and Networking (MSN), Exeter, UK, 13–15 December 2021; IEEE: New York, NY, USA, 2021.
25. Tang, Z.; Ge, Y. CNN model optimization and intelligent balance model for material demand forecast. *Int. J. Syst. Assur. Eng. Manag.* **2022**, *13* (Suppl. S3), 978–986. [CrossRef]

Disclaimer/Publisher's Note: The statements, opinions and data contained in all publications are solely those of the individual author(s) and contributor(s) and not of MDPI and/or the editor(s). MDPI and/or the editor(s) disclaim responsibility for any injury to people or property resulting from any ideas, methods, instructions or products referred to in the content.

Article

Data Analytics for Optimizing and Predicting Employee Performance

Laura Gabriela Tanasescu, Andreea Vines, Ana Ramona Bologa * and Oana Vîrgolici

Department of Computer Science and Cybernetics, Bucharest University of Economic Studies, 010374 Bucharest, Romania; laura.tanasescu@csie.ase.ro (L.G.T.); andreea.vines@csie.ase.ro (A.V.); oanavirgolici2022@gmail.com (O.V.)
* Correspondence: ramona.bologa@ie.ase.ro

Abstract: The need to increase employee performance and productivity has become vital in most companies nowadays, considering the number of changes that processes and people have faced during recent years in many organizations. This becomes even more important as it can sustain the growth of the company, as well as the competitiveness. This work will present multiple methods and comparisons between them for the process of building a machine learning algorithm to predict performance scores for employees in one organization; these methods include pre-processing the data, selecting the best variables, building the best algorithms for the available data, and tuning their hyperparameters. The current research aims to conclude on a collection of practices that will determine the best predictions for the given variables, so that human opinion can become less influential in employee appraisal, increasing objectivity and overall productivity.

Keywords: data mining; data analysis; machine learning; human management; employee performance scores

Citation: Tanasescu, L.G.; Vines, A.; Bologa, A.R.; Virgolici, O. Data Analytics for Optimizing and Predicting Employee Performance. *Appl. Sci.* **2024**, *14*, 3254. https://doi.org/10.3390/app14083254

Academic Editor: Luis Javier Garcia Villalba

Received: 20 March 2024
Revised: 9 April 2024
Accepted: 10 April 2024
Published: 12 April 2024

Copyright: © 2024 by the authors. Licensee MDPI, Basel, Switzerland. This article is an open access article distributed under the terms and conditions of the Creative Commons Attribution (CC BY) license (https://creativecommons.org/licenses/by/4.0/).

1. Introduction

In recent times, organizations have given an increased level of attention to the human resources domain. Starting from, firstly, meticulously selecting the optimal candidates for the needed roles, followed by the process of developing their skills in alignment with the requirements of the organization, and, finally, evaluating them and assessing their performance and abilities, a process that can lead to offering these employees enhanced conditions for their work life, salary increases, or bonuses, which are offered based on performance. Consequently, it becomes highly important for companies to determine and anticipate the capabilities and the performance of their employees, factors that later will contribute to their productivity and organizational development [1].

Evaluating an employee's performance brings challenges, as it implies offering feedback and deciding on their future career development, salary, or promotion. It also involves identifying areas that require updates or modifications. Numerous research studies have explored methodological factors such as academic credentials, technical qualifications, characteristics, and psychological aspects as indicators of employee performance in organizations. However, these factors are applicable only in certain employment domains. It is crucial to explore a multitude of other factors to gain a comprehensive understanding of employee performance [2].

Different elements can contribute to workforce attrition, including low job satisfaction, inappropriate wages, family concerns or a demanding business environment. Poor performance leads to involuntary employee attrition, which will affect, at the same time, the organization's productivity and its progression and development [3,4].

This article initially analyzes employees based on individual factors, as well as job-related ones, in order to gain a better perspective of the employees' behaviors, needs, and preferences. This process of observing the data and identifying correlations leads to a point where employee performance scores can be predicted, based on these elements, using machine learning techniques. Additionally, such an analysis can be useful in optimizing the business-related processes of human resource management, in terms of objectivity, fairness, and resource consumption, by replacing the traditional managerial appraisal with a mixed method. In addition, such predictions can be performed throughout the entire year (and not just at the end of a business year, when performance reviews usually happen) to prevent the other challenges of this sector, such as attrition, a lack of motivation, or a lack of productivity and to introduce other incentives such as promotions, bonuses, or any other benefits.

In the next chapter, the current research on elements/variables that generally contribute to employee performance will be described, as well as the best machine learning algorithms that can help in predicting the dependent variables affecting employee performance scores. While the current state of research in these areas and requirements of future development will be described, this paper will also conduct a study that will determine, in a particular case, the best attributes and algorithms to use to build such a model, and eventually, to predict employee performance scores without or not only by using human intervention. A methodology will be used in order to assure the quality of the research and the results obtained.

2. Background and Related Work

Numerous researchers have investigated the models that can help us predict employee performance. We can identify the fact that, generally, an individual that supervises the employee or are their direct manager is the best person to conduct an employee performance evaluation [5]. It has also been determined that high levels of job satisfaction contribute to the increasing loyalty of the employee, a fact that later can reduce turnover rates [6]. Additionally, a complete evaluation should include static and dynamic elements [7].

Glinow proposes that attaining and maintaining high performance standards emerges as a predominant concern across various types of organizations, including private, public, for-profit, and non-profit entities. According to him, achieving high performance levels, accompanied by positive indicators, enhances the stability of the organization, while ensuring high levels of profitability, quality, productivity, motivation, innovation, and efficiency. Conversely, he asserts that low performance levels entail negative and dysfunctional outcomes for the organization. He argues that instances of low performance indicators are associated with specific circumstances [8].

The most classical sources of performance data generally face limitations in correctly capturing the dynamic nature of performance. Particularly, it is well known that supervisors or managers are the ones who carry out the performance appraisal, with colleagues, subordinates, or even customers providing additional feedback or notes to them [8].

Considering the dynamic nature of organizations, these sources and their ratings are often prone to rapid changes before the moment of the appraisal; therefore, these become unsuitable. Consequently, it also becomes more essential to adopt new methods for analyzing data from discrete sources and to gain a more comprehensive picture of employee performance in more organizational contexts [9].

Recent research applying data mining techniques to predict employee performance scores concludes that the most important goal is to minimize the influence of subjective factors and reduce personal biases as well [10]. Diverse performance attributes can direct the selection of appropriate data mining methods, promoting synchronization across multiple areas like business operations, technology, or information science. As a consequence, the process of performance evaluation tends to become a more scientific approach, lowering the arbitrary nature of artificial scoring. This development contributes to enhanced fairness, authority in assessments, and integrity, as well as simultaneously elevating employee engagement, productivity, and team collaboration [10].

The development of data mining technology is clear and well-known, considering the years spent undertaking research and investigating practical applications, a fact that has provided increasingly complex model types and even mining functions. This maturity enables the provision of decision support in employee performance evaluations by correctly choosing the right index systems and training models [11].

Recent efforts regarding employee performance classification have considered the implementation of various machine learning algorithms. Some studies targeted the exploration of psychological, socioeconomic and creative factors on employee performance and motivation [2,12]. One important research study considered the use of prediction model construction algorithms, such as random forest, logistic regression, support vector machine, artificial neural network or naïve Bayes [13].

Other studies underline the critical importance of employee performance in organizational operations, highlighting it as the central factor in determining survival and competitiveness. Additionally, employee performance significantly influences the rewards system within an organization. Lucy acknowledges that performance is linked to actions related to productivity, innovation, flexibility, production levels, commitment, absenteeism rates, and the overall image of the organization. He categorizes performance into high, moderate, and low levels, emphasizing that low performance is the least desirable state for any organization. He advocates for high performance levels, which correlate with increased productivity, innovation, quality, efficiency, and commitment, recognizing the potential for better prospects for the organization [14].

Liu et al. introduced a method based on artificial intelligence for predicting the employee turnover while using a dataset that was built from state enterprises. Feature extraction was undertaken as well, to determine crucial factors affecting employee performance. For classification purposes, algorithms such as random forest, support vector machine (SVM), and linear regression (LR) were used again, together with AdaBoost, also concluding that there was a direct correlation between the employees' skills and associated performance scores [15]. Another important work focused on correctly and efficiently classifying employee job performance, based on DISC personality ((D)ominance, (i)nfluence, (S)teadiness and (C)onscientiousness). The classification for this personality test is built by comparing an individual personality with the standard personality test that the person took. DISC represents one of the most popular tests in this domain, standing for dominance, influence, steadiness and compliance. They built some models that were tested on a self-made dataset concerning the results of the DISC personality test for 2137 employees. For these models, the authors again used algorithms such as SVM, K-nearest neighbors (KNN), random forest (RF), LR, decision trees or naïve Bayes. Regarding the results, it was concluded that, for the selection chosen, decision trees provided the best performance, with the lowest Hamming loss and the highest accuracy. In addition, as feature selection techniques, the results were better when using multi-label classification with a stacking technique [16].

Jayadi et al. also investigated employee performance predictions using data mining, looking closely into the use of naïve Bayes for a dataset which was based on 310 employees [17]. Ajit et al. focused on an approach based on the eXtreme Gradient Boosting (XGBoost) classifier, again using a self-made dataset with 73,115 labeled data registries. The introduction of feature extraction can also be identified in this last research study, while underlining the impact of turnover [18].

Fallucchi et al. looked closer into machine learning approaches, like K-nearest neighbors, SVM, naïve Bayes, logistic regression, or random forest, regarding leaving the company. Their analysis included objective factors affecting worker wishes about turnover, considering both the correlation matrix for those features and running statistical analysis [19].

Hamidah et al. explored various classification methods such as decision trees (DT), neural networks (NN), and K-nearest neighbors (KNN) for predicting talent outcomes. Their research aimed to identify the most accurate technique for processing Human Resource (HR) data. The findings indicated that the decision tree method was notably effective for talent forecasting within human resource management (HRM), demonstrating the highest level of accuracy. The data utilized in this research were gathered from an academic institution's staff database [20].

Juvitayapun et al. proposed logistic regression, random forest, gradient boosting tree and extreme gradient boosting tree classifiers to identify employees' likelihood of turnover, while Duan et al. suggested logistic regression and XGBoost, with the latter being the better algorithm for the same purpose, outperforming logistic regression [21].

Last, but not least, Sujatha et al. introduced machine learning classifiers such as XGBoost and gradient boosting, while working with a real-time dataset [22]. Obiedat et al. tried to achieve the prediction of productivity performance in the garment sector, offering a hybrid algorithm that combines multiple algorithms for classification such as random forest, naïve Bayes, support vector machine, and multi-layer perceptron. They also tried to incorporate ensemble-learning methods such as AdaBoost and Bagging [23].

3. Methods and Results

The steps followed in the current research are based on the CRISP-DM methodology, which stands for the cross-industry standard process for data mining. This is a generally used approach in guiding and structuring data mining processes, which also provides a comprehensive and organized procedure that helps to extract values, information, and insights from data. Moreover, this way of structuring the overall analysis is designed to be flexible and easy to apply, independent of the industries or the business areas that are under investigation [24]. Lastly, while we will go through each step of this method and detail the ways in which we are applying it to our current paper, it is important to mention as well that this alternative way of organizing the process puts a higher focus on iterative and cyclical development, which also encourage constant improvement and adaptability throughout the whole cycle of this data mining process. We can observe below, in Figure 1, a visual representation of the explained methodology, as well as the flow that will be conducted through the stages of it. It can be observed the process starts with understanding the business needs and the context, and it ends with deployment. All the other steps are critical, to obtain the best results in the end.

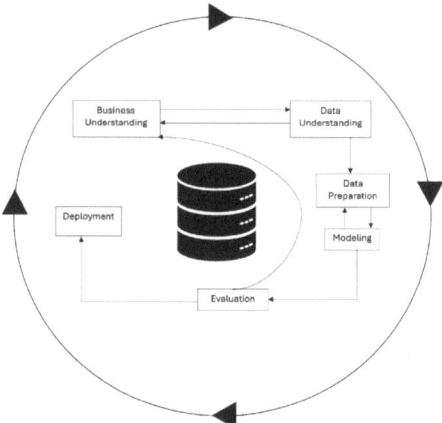

Figure 1. CRISP-DM methodology process (source: https://medium.com/@avikumart_/crisp-dm-framework-a-foundational-data-mining-process-model-86fe642da18c, accessed on 9 April 2024).

From a technical perspective, the code developed for this study was written in Python, using version 3.10.5. Additionally, some of the most important libraries used for this study were pandas, numpy, sklearn, text_normalizer, seaborn, matplotlib, optuna, and tensorflow. Lastly, a business intelligence tool was also used for user-friendly and graphically relevant visualizations, named Oracle Analytics. The purpose of introducing such a tool is to understand, easily and clearly, the insights of the data analyzed, without having to always be connected to code-based methods as this is a drag-and-drop solution.

3.1. Business Understanding

The goal of this research is to identify, firstly, the attributes that affect employee performance, in general. Secondly, using this information, the main objective is to build the algorithm that can best predict employee performance with the highest prediction results. Thus, a company can take advantage of this type of information and closely monitor underperforming staff, reward high-performing staff, or pay more attention to the individual development and skills of those who will become top performers.

3.2. Data Collection

As this kind of test data is very difficult to collect from real organizations, in order to achieve this paper's objective, a dataset found on Kaggle (San Francisco, CA, USA) was used. This dataset, presented in Figure 2, includes several variables needed for our analysis, which include both individual characteristics and work-related ones. We can see below a preview of the dataset used for this current research, which contains inputs from 311 people, meaning that we have 311 rows, representing a good volume for an overall organization analysis, with a good split between the people analyzed, as will be seen later in the study. There are no missing values or outliers, as the considered structured dataset has been specially designed for such an analysis.

Employee_N	EmpID	MarriedID	MaritalStatu	GenderID	EmpStatusID	DeptID	PerfScoreID	FromDiversit	Salary	Termd	PositionID	Position	State	Zip	DOB	Sex	MaritalDesc	CitizenDesc	HispanicLatir	RaceDesc	Da
Adinolfi Wil	10026	0	0	1	1	5	4	0	62506	0	19	Production T	MA	1960	07.10.1983	M	Single	US Citizen	No	White	0
Ait Sidi Kart	10084	1	1	1	5	3	3	0	104437	1	27	Sr. DBA	MA	2148	05.05.1975	M	Married	US Citizen	No	White	3/
Akinkuolie S	10196	1	1	0	5	5	3	0	64955	1	20	Production T	MA	1810	09/19/88	F	Married	US Citizen	No	White	0
Alagbe Trina	10088	1	1	0	1	5	3	0	64991	0	19	Production T	MA	1886	09/27/88	F	Married	US Citizen	No	White	0
Anderson Ca	10069	0	2	0	5	5	3	0	50825	1	19	Production T	MA	2169	09.08.1989	F	Divorced	US Citizen	No	White	0
Anderson Li	10002	0	0	0	1	5	4	0	57568	0	19	Production T	MA	1844	05/22/77	F	Single	US Citizen	No	White	0
Andreola Co	10194	0	0	0	1	4	3	0	95660	0	24	Software En	MA	2110	05/24/79	F	Single	US Citizen	No	White	1
Athwal Sam	10062	0	4	1	1	5	3	0	59365	0	19	Production T	MA	2199	02/18/83	M	Widowed	US Citizen	No	White	9/
Bachiochi Li	10114	0	0	0	3	5	3	1	47837	0	19	Production T	MA	1902	02.11.1970	F	Single	US Citizen	No	Black or Afri	0
Bacong Alej	10250	0	2	1	1	3	3	0	50178	0	14	IT Support	MA	1886	01.07.1988	M	Divorced	US Citizen	No	White	0
Baczenski R.	10252	1	1	0	5	5	3	1	54670	1	19	Production T	MA	1902	01.12.1974	F	Married	US Citizen	Yes	Black or Afri	0
Barbara Tho	10242	1	1	1	5	5	3	1	47211	1	19	Production T	MA	2062	02/21/74	M	Married	US Citizen	Yes	Black or Afri	0
Barbossa He	10012	0	2	1	1	3	4	1	92328	0	9	Data Analyst	TX	78230	07.04.1988	M	Divorced	US Citizen	No	Black or Afri	1
Barone Fran	10265	0	0	1	1	5	3	0	58709	0	19	Production T	MA	1810	07/20/83	M	Single	US Citizen	No	Two or more	2/
Barton Nade	10066	0	2	1	5	5	3	0	52505	1	19	Production T	MA	2747	07/15/77	M	Divorced	US Citizen	No	White	9/
Bates Norm	10061	0	0	1	4	5	3	0	57834	1	19	Production T	MA	2050	10/18/81	M	Single	US Citizen	No	White	2/
Beak Kimbe	10023	1	1	0	2	5	4	0	70131	0	20	Production T	MA	2145	04/17/66	F	Married	US Citizen	No	White	7/
Beatrice Cou	10055	0	0	0	1	5	3	0	59026	0	19	Production T	MA	1915	10/27/70	F	Single	Eligible Non	No	White	0
Becker Rene	10245	0	0	0	4	3	3	0	110000	1	8	Database Ad	MA	2026	04.04.1986	F	Single	US Citizen	Yes	White	0
Becker Scott	10277	0	0	1	3	5	3	0	53250	0	19	Production T	MA	2452	04.06.1979	M	Single	US Citizen	No	Asian	0
Bernstein Se	10046	0	0	1	1	5	3	0	51044	0	19	Production T	MA	2072	12/22/70	M	Single	US Citizen	Yes	White	0
Biden Lowa	10226	0	2	0	1	5	3	0	64919	0	19	Production T	MA	2027	12/27/58	F	Divorced	US Citizen	No	Asian	8/
Billis Helen	10003	1	1	0	1	5	4	0	62910	0	19	Production T	MA	2031	09.01.1989	F	Married	US Citizen	No	White	0
Blount Dian	10294	0	0	0	1	5	2	0	66441	0	20	Production T	MA	2171	09/21/90	F	Single	US Citizen	No	White	0
Bondwell Be	10267	0	0	0	5	5	3	0	57815	1	20	Production T	MA	2210	01/16/67	F	Single	US Citizen	No	White	0
Booth Frank	10199	0	0	1	4	3	3	0	103613	1	30	Enterprise A	CT	6033	07/30/64	M	Single	US Citizen	No	Black or Afri	2/
Boutwell Bo	10081	1	1	0	1	1	3	1	106367	0	26	Sr. Accounta	MA	2468	04.04.1987	F	Married	US Citizen	No	Black or Afri	2/

Figure 2. Dataset sample used for our analysis (source: https://www.kaggle.com/datasets/rhuebner/human-resources-data-set/data, accessed on 9 April 2024).

Considering the businesses' needs, the following variables are included in the analyzed dataset:

(a) Individual attributes: Employee_Name, MarriedID, MaritalStatusID, GenderID, EmpStatusID, DOB, Sex, MaritalDesc, CitizenDesc, HispanicLatino, and RaceDesc.

The above data refer to individual characteristics of the employees, such as their name, marital status, sex, employment status, date of birth, citizenship type, and race. Some of the variables repeat themselves in terms of information provided; therefore, these variables will be handled later in the process.

(b) Geographical-related attributes: State and Zip.

The above data refer to the state where the employee lives and their zip code.

(c) Organizational-related attributes: EmpID, DeptID, FromDiversityJobFairID, Salary, Termd, PositionID, Position, DateofHire, DateofTermination, TermReason, EmploymentStatus, Department, ManagerName, ManagerID, and RecruitmentSource.

The above data refer to job-related data, such as the employee's ID within a specific company, if the recruitment was undertaken through a diversity job fair or not, salary value, termination of the contract (if that is the case), position ID and position name, date when the employee was hired, date of termination (if that is the case), termination reason, employment status in the company, department the employee is part of, their manager's name and ID, and the recruitment source of the specific employee.

(d) Work engagement attributes: EngagementSurvey, SpecialProjectsCount, DaysLate-Last30, and Absences.

The above data refer to the engagement rate that the employee has shown within the organization, how many special projects they has been a part of, how many days the employee has been late in the last 30 days, and how many absences they have had in a respective year.

(e) Performance-related attributes: PerfScoreID, PerformanceScore, EmpSatisfaction, and LastPerformanceReview_Date.

The above data refer to the performance score associated with the employee, employee satisfaction at the workplace, and data regarding their last performance review.

3.3. Data Preparation

First of all, to correctly continue with the data preparation step, we will undertake an overview of the data that are going to be analyzed.

3.3.1. Data Overview

In order to better understand our data, we will have a look at the attributes that are part of this dataset, as well as descriptive statistics based on them.

If we look at some visualizations of the dataset as shown in Figure 3, we can obtain an overview of the analyzed inputs, as follows, with the number of employees (No of emp) being analyzed according to various criteria:

Figure 3. Employee distribution based on recruitment source, sex, race and department (source: authors' own study).

It can be seen that there are 311 employees that are under review and, therefore, 311 distinct registries in our dataset. Looking at the split by recruitment source, we observe that most of these employees were recruited through LinkedIn and Indeed, while others were recruited through Google search, employee referral, diversity job fair, or career builder. The online platforms are the most popular for the analyzed organization.

Moreover, if we look at the sex and race, we can first say that very few are Hispanic, while there is a balanced split between females and males that are part of this research. Lastly, we can conclude that most of our employees are part of the Production department, while another big group come from the Information Technology/Information Systems (IT/IS), Sales, and Admin offices. We can see that very few employees come from the Executive offices or the Software Engineering departments.

In the second set of visualizations, presented in Figure 4, we can see that the average satisfaction score is lowest for the executive officers, and the highest for software engineers. In contrast, if we look at the average salaries for these categories, we can see that the Executive Office department has the highest value; therefore, it seems that not only salaries contribute to overall employee satisfaction. In addition, we can see that females have a slightly higher percentage than males in terms of employee satisfaction, while also having higher salaries on average than males.

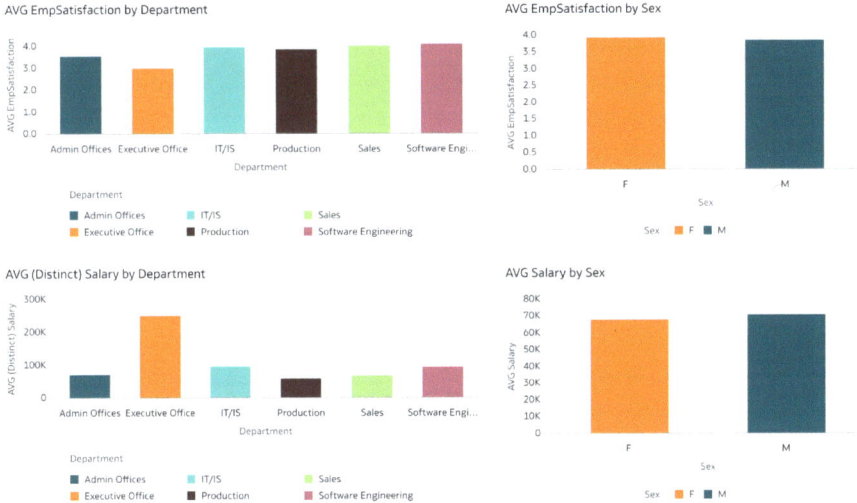

Figure 4. Employee satisfaction and salary distribution based on department and sex (source: authors' own study).

Analyzing the same statistics, as shown in Figure 5, but with negative characteristics such as absences or number of days that employees were late to work, we can see that, on average, the Sales department has the highest number for both categories. Nonetheless, if we look at the Executive Office, we can see that, while they have the lowest satisfaction, they do not have any days in which they were late in the last 30 days, and also have a medium value for the absences taken. If we also return to the previous figure, we see that the Production department has the lowest salaries and low employee satisfaction, a fact that we can understand if we investigate the second chart, in which it is shown that the Production department has high values for both absences and days late at work.

Moreover, if we look at Figure 6, it is easy to observe, using historical data, how performance scores are distributed across departments. While Software Engineers have high levels of satisfaction but are still classified, in terms of performance, as needing improvement, the other departments, like IT/IS, Production, and Sales, have lower levels of satisfaction associated with lower performance scores. In addition, while there are absences for all employees (despite their performance), we can see that days late at work are only present for those with the lowest performance scores. Therefore, we can conclude that performance scores are not fully correlated with satisfaction; however, absences or tardiness in arriving at work are correlated with lower performances.

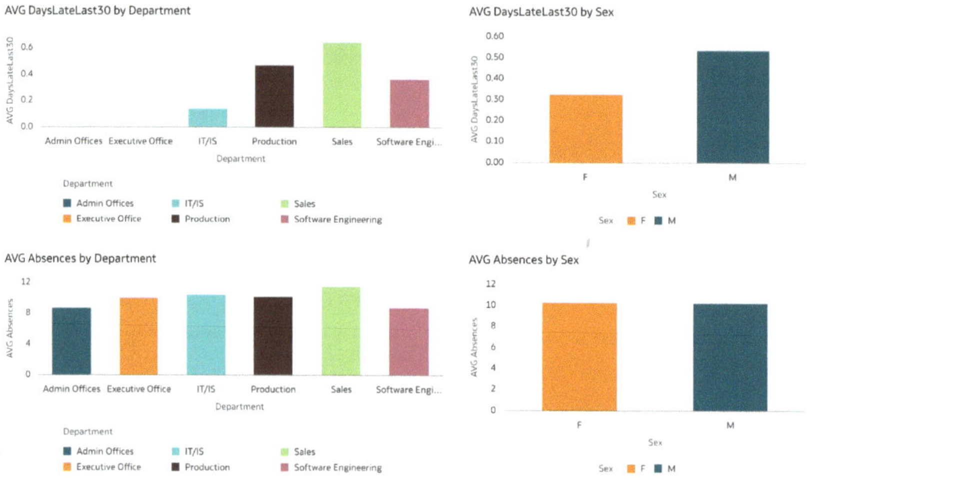

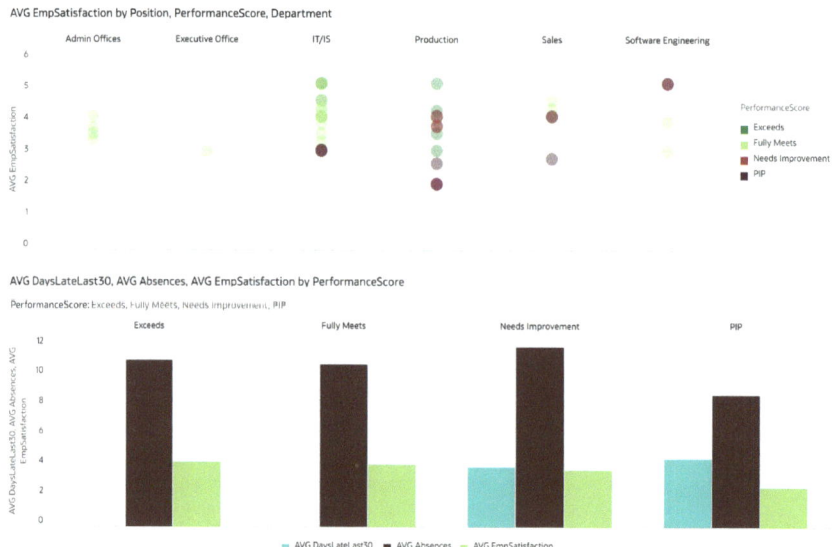

Figure 5. Employee tardiness or absences based on department and sex (source: authors' own study).

Figure 6. Employee satisfaction and performance score distribution based on position and department and also based on days late at work and absences (source: authors' own study).

3.3.2. Data Cleaning and Encoding

Categorical data are frequently encountered in data science and machine learning tasks, presenting unique challenges compared to numerical data. Handling categorical variables requires preprocessing, because many machine learning models operate exclusively on numerical inputs. Thus, it is essential to convert categorical variables into numerical representations, to enable the model to effectively utilize and extract meaningful insights from them. Various encoding techniques exist for this purpose, with one-hot encoding being among the most popular methods. In one-hot encoding, each category level is compared to a chosen reference level, which is particularly useful in scenarios where there is no inherent ordering among the categories. Therefore, this is the solution used for this research study as well, to handle the categorical values [25].

3.3.3. Data Pre-Processing

Feature scaling is a vital part of data pre-processing, so that we can build accurate and optimal machine learning models. Apart from their contributions to the models' performances, these techniques also help to reduce the impact of outliers by avoiding the domination of those attributes which have a larger value. Feature scaling contributes to datasets that have different ranges or even different units of measurement and where variation existing in the attributes can lead to differences in model performance during the learning process. Some important techniques we need to outline for the feature scaling step are standardization, normalization, and min–max scaling.

For this research study, we will continue by applying the standard scaler method, which is a method that resizes the distribution of the data and obtains values that have a mean of zero and a standard deviation of one. This method is suitable when the characteristics of the input dataset differ in their ranges or measurement units [26].

3.3.4. Data Selection

Considering the latest developments in technology, a huge number of computer and Internet applications have generated considerable amounts of data at an extraordinary speed. This kind of data has an important factor in common: high dimensionality, which generally imposes a large challenge for the analysis of data. Therefore, feature selection has been proven to be very effective in both theory and practice, when considering the subject of high-dimensional data analysis and magnifying learning productivity [27]. We can see a detailed process flow of how this feature selection method generally works in Figure 7, as follows:

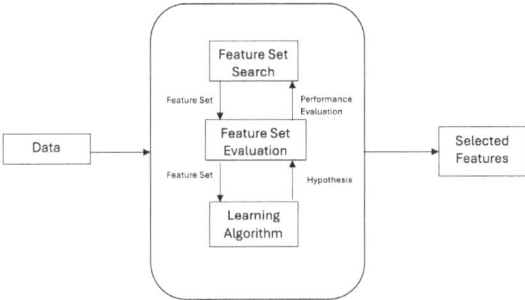

Figure 7. Feature selection process (source: https://www.researchgate.net/figure/A-General-Framework-of-Wrapper-Feature-Selection-Methods_fig8_301856754, accessed on 9 April 2024).

Feature selection is the process of procuring a subgroup from the original dataset, according to certain ways of selecting the considered variables. This contributes enormously to the process of compressing data cleaning, wherein the redundant and unrelated features are removed. Feature selection methods can help to pre-process the learning algorithms, while adequate feature selection outcomes can improve the accuracy of the learning process, reduce the learning time, and simplify the learning results [28]. Therefore, we can consider feature extraction, together with feature selection, as two important means of reducing dimensionality. In contrast with feature selection, feature extraction methods need, generally, to transform the original data into different features, which are characterized by a strong pattern identification ability, in which the original data can be seen as attributes without firm recognition abilities.

Feature selection has been demonstrated to increase the performance of classification across multiple applications. In recent studies, it has been used for a high-dimensional cancer microarray dataset, in the field of Arabic text classification, and in predicting heart diseases using bio-inspired optimization techniques [29,30].

The utilization of feature selection is important, especially in the areas where decision-makers do not have the ability to decide the relevance of each feature for the specific domain.

The literature in the area of feature selection can be categorized into three major areas, organized considering the selection process: filter, wrapper, or embedded methods. Of all these methods, filter techniques have attracted the most attention because of their computational efficiency. Moreover, these are independent of classifiers, therefore making these techniques suitable for problems involving a high number of features [31,32].

To look even closer into the existing types of feature selection methods, below there are some of the examples for each category exemplified:

(a) Filter methods such as univariate feature selection, correlation-based feature selection, and variance thresholding.
(b) Wrapper methods: Wrapper methods are a type of feature selection technique that involves training a model iteratively with different subsets of features and evaluating their impact on the model's performance. One of the most popular techniques for this is recursive feature elimination (RFE).
(c) Embedded methods: A type of feature selection technique that includes feature selection as a vital aspect of the model training process. One example here is related to variable importance feature selection (from tree-based models) [33].

In order to apply, to our particular research, the optimal methods for feature selection and to observe, as well, how they behave, we have chosen some of the most popular ones from each of the categories mentioned above. In this way, we can understand more about how these will work, in which ways they can be applied, and what are the results for the dataset proposed.

A synthesis of the results is presented in Table 1.

Table 1. Feature selection results based on chosen methods.

Method	Univariate Feature Selection	Recursive Feature Elimination	Extra Trees Classifier	Feature Importance Using Decision Tree
Results	FromDiversityJobFairID Salary EmpSatisfaction SpecialProjectsCount DaysLateLast30 Absences EmploymentStatus Position ManagerName RecruitmentSource	Salary EmpSatisfaction DaysLateLast30 Absences EmploymentStatus Position State Sex MaritalDesc RaceDesc	DaysLateLast30 Salary Absences ManagerName EmpSatisfaction RecruitmentSource Position RaceDesc MaritalDesc Sex	Salary EmpSatisfaction ManagerName Absences Sex RecruitmentSource MarriedID MaritalDesc Position RaceDesc

It can be seen in the results above that some attributes are always relevant, regardless of the method used, such as Salary, Position, or EmpSatisfaction. This is completely understandable, because human logic will generally consider that these characteristics can be very important for an employee and could affect their overall performance. Some variables play an important role in three out of four methods, such as DaysLateLast30, RecruitmentSource, and Absences, which again are very critical when we consider the context of analyzing an employee and trying to predict their overall performance. Moreover, we can generally observe the fact that all four methods include, in their selection, variables that are related to both employees as individuals and their performance and behavior in the workplace.

To continue the study and keep this selection as relevant as possible, the first subset of variables will be considered during the data modeling step. Given that the requirement of the business is to predict an employee's performance, the selected features are also some of the most relevant attributes that a person will consider for evaluation.

3.4. Data Modeling

In this chapter, the current work continues by looking deeper into appropriate machine learning algorithms to be used for this classification problem, according to similar research and results in the area of human resource optimization.

Therefore, we will use for our research the algorithms random forest, decision trees, support vector machine, K-nearest neighbors and XGBoost. All of these have been continuously used for classification problems, as also stated previously in this paper, producing good results and consuming an optimal number of resources. Moreover, the selection brings together both very classical and straightforward methods, and more recent and complex ones, if we refer to artificial neural network (ANN) or XGBoost.

Last, but not least, overfitting of the decided models should be always avoided, considering that the final research aims to achieve real-life and objective results. Therefore, apart from simplifying the models and applying feature selection techniques, there will also be additional cross-validation for the models chosen.

3.4.1. Cross-Validating the Models

In the initial step, after having chosen the previously mentioned algorithms, the research study will use the considered dataset to cross-validate these models and observe the results. While there are multiple ways to achieve this, one of the most popular methods used for classification algorithms is the k-fold cross validation technique, together with leave-one-out. When working with bigger datasets, k-fold should be considered as the better option, because the accuracy obtained from the training data is generally too optimistic [34]. When using this option, the method will randomly split a dataset into k separate, roughly equal-sized segments. For each iteration, one segment is used as the test set, while the remaining k − 1 folds are combined to form the training set. A classification algorithm is then applied to this training set to create a model, which is tested on the test set. The algorithm's overall performance is determined by calculating the average accuracy across all k iterations.

For this particular research, the value for k was considered to be five, which is optimally used for similar tests, and the results obtained for all the chosen algorithms can be seen below in Table 2.

Table 2. Cross-validation results for chosen algorithms.

Algorithm	Average Score
Decision trees	73%
Random forest	82%
SVM	78%
KNN	77%
ANN	78%
XGB	79%

Having obtained these results, these will indicate the overall performance that could be achieved by providing more accurate measures of these models' real-world effectiveness.

3.4.2. Building the Models

In order to continue with this process, the dataset spilt will first be considered, as it will help us to obtain a better distribution of data across the training and testing phases. The split will be 80% and 20% for the two categories. The next step is to use the previously mentioned algorithms to build each of the models accordingly. In the next section, each of them will be briefly described, considering that these were chosen for this kind of analysis [35].

- Random Forest

Random forest is one of the most recurrent algorithms used in building predictive models. This algorithm works in a very simple manner, by dividing predictor variables into multiple binary slits in order to predict outcomes. Using a selected dataset as training data together with selected subsets of predictor variables that are randomly selected, this algorithm builds multiple classifications and regression trees. Considering the results of the individual trees, there is a prediction resulting from each observation. In conclusion, random forest offers a higher accuracy than any other decision tree model, maintaining at the same time the same level of benefits specific to tree models [36].

- Decision Tree

Considered to be one of the most popular classification algorithms, the decision tree is a mathematical tool that helps in the decision-making process. This model shows the decision and also possible outcomes, with the help of a flowchart structure that uses nodes and leaves. Multiple nodes build a node network, while those that do not have any incoming edges are generally referred to as commonly. On the other hand, all the other nodes can have outgoing edges and are considered to be internal or tested nodes, or with incoming edges, and are considered to be decision nodes. In order to decide which node should be used, the decision tree algorithm will take into consideration the information received from each node. A root node will be considered a node with the highest gain, while all the other nodes will be set on using the rest of the nodes [36].

- Support Vector Machine (SVM)

Support vector machine is part of the linear classifiers category of algorithms. This works by identifying different classes while separating samples using decision boundaries, commonly known as hyperplane. Linear, together with non-linear, data can be classified with a support vector machine. Nonetheless, it is largely known as the maximum margin classifier, considering the fact that it can maximize the geometric margin while minimizing the empirical classification error [36].

- K-Nearest Neighbors (KNN)

In the current scenario, where there are many algorithms for the purpose of classification, KNN is considered to be one of the simplest. This method involves the action of grouping of unknown data points that have an already known class. Lastly, using the k-value along with the nearest neighbor number of the data points, the nearest neighbor is calculated [37].

- Artificial Neural Network (ANN)

It is thought that artificial neural networks are simulations of our biological brain. They are composed of numerous simple processing units connected through weighted links. These processing units, often referred to as "neurons", only process information available locally, either stored within or received through the weighted connections. Each unit can receive inputs from and transmit outputs to many other units. Individually, a processing unit is not very potent, producing a scalar output—a simple nonlinear function of its inputs. However, the collective operation of many such units, when appropriately combined, unleashes the system's true capability [38].

- XGBoost

    While the previously described algorithms are some of the most classical ones used generally for multi-classification, XGBoost comes as an implementation of grading-boosting decision trees that builds predictive models, combining the predictions of multiple models in an iterative manner. The algorithm sequentially adds weak learners every time to the ensemble, considering that each learning will focus on correcting the errors that were made by the previous one, using gradient descent optimization to minimize a predefined loss function through the training process. One of the most important features for this algorithm consists of handling complex relations in data, regularization methods that can prevent overfitting, and including parallel processing for coherent computation. Finally, this last algorithm is universally used in multiple domains, due to its high predictive performance and adaptability across various datasets [39].

3.4.3. Optimizing the Models

The second step of our data modeling is to optimize the results previously obtained as well, since this can be achieved for each of our algorithms. Based on related works on these kinds of methods, we will discover in the next chapter of the current paper how a hyperparameter can achieve a better performance in general, what kind of methods exist in order to achieve this, and what are the solutions chosen to apply to our research. Hyperparameter tuning is an important factor for machine learning algorithms and their associated processes, and it is also recognized as the best practice for maximizing the results of a successful implementation. This method varies among the different machine learning algorithms due to the variety of parameters existing for each of them, such as discrete, continuous, or even categorical parameters. Nonetheless, this is seen as an expensive implementation, as it also engages the evaluation of multiple combinations and demands a remarkable number of computational resources. Generally, building a productive model is time-consuming, which leads to calls for distinguishing the best model obtained using hyperparameter tuning [40].

Over the last decades, grid search has been the classical approach used for parameter optimization when using machine learning techniques, which introduces a comprehensive search throughout a predefined subset of an algorithm's hyperparameter space used for the learning process. While there are also proposed alternative methods, such as random search, Bayesian optimization or even gradient optimization, grid search remains the most popular one, due to its parallelization capability, lack of difficulty in terms of running it, and flexibility in low-dimensional spaces. Regardless of its simplicity, this method is still expensive in terms of the computational resources needed, mainly when using multiple hyperparameters at different levels, fact that also highlights the exponential growth of the computing cost [41,42].

On another note, there are some other types of optimization in terms of parameters that do not work in the standard way described above. One of these techniques is known as Optuna, and it is a Python library that is dedicated to working on hyperparameter optimization, with origins in Preferred Networks, which is a Japanese organization. This open-source instrument provides a complex and automated way to search the optimal hyperparameters by applying fine-tuning steps to an objective function. In addition, this comes with a very user-friendly design and demonstrates adaptability as well overdiversified machine learning frameworks.

Regarding the way Optuna works, it firstly defines the search space by having users illustrate the range and type of hyperparameters that are going to be used for optimization. Secondly, it also defines the object function that will be in charge of evaluating the model performance, considering a set of hyperparameters. Lastly, Optuna undergoes optimization, by handling iterative evaluations, and updates of the probabilistic model, while the search space will progressively narrow down until adequate parameters are identified [43].

Lastly, since this is a relatively new approach considered for this type of optimization, we can underline some advantages of these methods, such as efficiency, improved performances, automation, and reproducibility. While other standard methods are already well-known and generally applied in similar research, Optuna can actually reduce the time and resources needed for this process; it explores, in a systematic way, the hyperparameter space, which increases the chances of discovering an optimal structure and also provides data mining analysts and developers with the opportunity to focus more on the model, rather than on manually tuning it, since this will mostly be undertaken automatically.

3.5. Evaluation

As explained previously in this current research, multiple classification algorithms that provided the most optimal results for our business case were chosen, so that we could observe how each of these algorithms behaved. Through this process, one could not only see a comparison between them but could also conclude which of these algorithms should be used for further analysis in performance score estimation. In addition, the step of tuning the hyperparameters of the built models was also taken, to achieve even better results.

Consequently, the research will again provide a comparison between the behavior of the chosen algorithms in three different states:

i. without having the hyperparameters tuned;
ii. with a classical way of tuning hyperparameters using grid search;
iii. by introducing Optuna, which is a framework specific to Python libraries that should provide an even better performance and results.

Table 3 presents the results specifically regarding precision, recall, accuracy, and F1 score for all the combinations possible, obtained as described above.

Table 3. Machine learning performance results based on chosen algorithms.

Algorithm	Hyperparameter Tuning	Precision	Recall	Accuracy	F1 Score
Decision trees	No tuning	75%	85%	85%	80%
	Grid search	91%	90%	90%	90%
	Optuna	94%	92%	92%	91%
Random forest	No tuning	83%	89%	89%	85%
	Grid search	83%	89%	89%	85%
	Optuna	83%	89%	89%	85%
SVM	No tuning	83%	89%	89%	85%
	Grid search	73%	86%	86%	79%
	Optuna	83%	90%	90%	87%
KNN	No tuning	72%	78%	78%	75%
	Grid search	83%	89%	89%	85%
	Optuna	73%	86%	86%	79%
ANN	No tuning	51%	71%	71%	60%
	Grid search	63%	79%	79%	70%
	Optuna	77%	88%	88%	82%
XGB	No tuning	88%	86%	86%	86%
	Grid search	83%	89%	89%	85%
	Optuna	94%	92%	92%	91%

In the brief analysis conducted, the research evaluated all the models based on several key metrics: precision, recall, F1 Scores, and balanced accuracies.

Precision is calculated as the number of true positives divided by the sum of true positives and false positives. It is a measure of a model's accuracy in predicting positive cases. The formula is as follows:

$$\text{Precision} = TP/(TP + FP),$$

where TP represents true positive cases and FP represents false positive cases.

Recall assesses the model's ability to correctly identify all actual positives. The formula for recall is as follows:
$$\text{Recall} = TP/(TP + FN),$$
where TP stands for true positive cases and FN stands for false negative cases.

Accuracy reflects the proportion of true results (both true positives and true negatives) among the total number of cases examined. The accuracy formula is as follows:
$$\text{Accuracy} = (TP + TN)/(TP + FP + FN + TN),$$
where TP is true positives, TN is true negatives, FP is false positives, and FN is false negatives [44].

While accuracy is commonly used to assess classification algorithms, it might not always be suitable, especially in cases of imbalanced class distribution. In contexts where minimizing false negatives holds significance, recall gains importance. Conversely, precision takes precedence when the goal is to minimize false positives. Moreover, the F1 score is introduced as a metric that combines precision and recall, offering a balanced assessment. This nuanced approach to model evaluation helps to ensure that the metrics chosen are aligned with the specific objectives and challenges of the classification task at hand [45].

$$F1 = 2 \times (\text{Precision} + \text{Recall})/\text{Precision} \times \text{Recall},$$
where Precision and Recall are described above.

By looking at each of these algorithms, one can immediately observe that decision trees and XGB obtained the best results in terms of performance, with F1 scores of approximately 91%. On the other hand, it can be concluded that KNN and ANN performed worst for our case study, with very low percentages for all the attributes reviewed above.

Moreover, for decision trees, each type of hyperparameter tuning provided better and better results, resulting in Optuna obtaining the best scores. However, for XGB, it is observable that grid search did not provide better results for the scores analyzed compared to the classical model; Optuna managed to obtain, even here, the best result.

On a general note, Optuna provided better and equal scores for accuracy, precision, and F1 score for all the considered algorithms, which can help us conclude that this is indeed a good technique, even for classification algorithms, for achieving a better performance. On the contrary, the same cannot be admitted regarding grid search, which provided even worse results, as we can see in the example obtained for SVM and XGB.

Finally, in order to continue this analysis and follow the step of applying these algorithms to new data, in order to achieve the prediction of performance scores, the firm conclusion is that XGB would be the best solution, considering also the resources used for running this algorithm.

3.6. Deployment

In order to continue with the deployment phase, as was mentioned before, it is clear that XGBoost will provide the best performance while optimizing the computational resources used for this process. Of course, as the best results have been obtained by applying hyperparameter tuning with the Optuna framework, this step will also be included in the deployment phase. Optuna addressed the challenges and offered an enhanced solution through the development of its framework. This innovative method provided a change to its users by dynamically generating a search space, while providing an abundance of tailored sampling, searching, and pruning algorithms for effective implementation. According to the amount of data to be classified, as well as the changes that might appear in the variables considered for training the model, the feature selection methods might vary, as well as the algorithms used for classification.

In order to include this type of analysis in a relatable eco-system, using the batch processing for analyzing data could be considered, since more data as inputs means better results in the end. Moreover, to automate the whole pre-preparation steps needed for every iteration of the training the algorithm, data pipelines could be considered, as well as different platforms used for repetitive steps that could be triggered automatically [46].

Another important step of the deployment phase is the collection of feedback, regarding the results received in comparison to the ones expected. Comparing these periodically and observing the efficiency of the different algorithms, as well as, from time to time, applying the whole selection of algorithms again to understand if the outputs have changed, could lead to an overall improvement in performance. Nonetheless, it is mandatory to also check the associated efficiency coefficients all the time and be aware if any changes appear in the training process.

Last, but not least, as part of this section, it should be considered in the final implementation the biases that could appear. Since the results could highly affect the overall employment process and development, it is crucial to take into consideration the fairness of the results.

4. Discussion

Considering the objective of this research, it is certain that there is a clear focus on developing a machine learning algorithm and providing a method to create a more automatic and objective model for scoring performance. However, it is important not to forget the fact that these kinds of approaches can be dangerous, as, in case something is not working as expected from the start of the process, humans would not be available to correct that [47]. Therefore, as the study has been conducted on a small dataset, this should only be used as a starting point. Humans can supervise or they can also develop similar analyses and the results could be compared, while very different results could be flagged for a second analysis. In this way, not only could this process be improved, but the subjectivity could be lowered.

Moving on to the data that have been used, considering the standard dataset specially created for this kind of analysis, it is much simpler to address the accuracy and balance of the dataset, so that the data can be used at their real value, as opposed to other situations where this can represent a large challenge in the process [48]. Therefore, specifically to address this important step, the first section of the research focused on feature selection, not only as a method to optimize the classification algorithm, but also as a conclusion to understand the best variables for objectively determining performance scores, it was concluded that Salary, Position, and EmpSatisfaction are commonly seen, no matter the method used; however, it proved to us, once again, that compensation, along with work/life balance and additional perks, contribute enormously to overall performance scores. Moreover, variables such as DaysLateLast 30, RecruitmentSource, and Absences also contribute a lot to performance scores for most of the methods. In this area, other studies confirmed that JobTitle, UnivType, and Age can be decisive for employee performance. In addition, other educational factors, such as degree and grade, affected performance scores very little; however, these results were all obtained using classification techniques [49]. On the other hand, even though similar research studies have been presented, they do not underline or reconfirm the most significant attributes that will lead to the best performance in the end [13,17].

Looking at related papers regarding types of classification problems using supervised algorithms, it was determined, once again, that classical algorithms are still the most popular ones used across different datasets and data types. In human resources management, the most classical ones have been chosen for tests, and results have varied. Some decided that naïve Bayes behaves well in terms of some data types and business problems, while others concluded the same for decision tree and XGBoost. However, looking closer, XGBoost has been mostly tested on attrition problems and classification, rather than on determining employee performance scores. Therefore, in addition to the general algorithms used for previous classification problems in predicting performance scores, this research added artificial neural networks and XGBoost. While the former provided some of the worst results, XGBoost managed to provide the opposite. Therefore, the search could confirm that XGBoost could easily be the best solution for classification problems even when talking about predicting employee performance scores, with some of the best results in terms of time and resource consumption as well.

Another important factor added to this study was observing how all these algorithms performed when hyperparameter tuning was added for each of them. Analyzing related works, it can be concluded that grid search was one of the most used and well-known methods for this type of optimization, because of its simple implementation [50]. However, while this is a classic approach, it comes with some downsides as well, especially regarding computational costs. Looking into recent developments in this area, Optuna was discovered, a framework designed to work in a more automatic manner and help with parameter tuning. Despite its novelty, this is already known to work very well and also reduce the number of resources needed. Similar studies show that Optuna, even when compared with other similar frameworks and not with classical approaches of hyperparameter tuning, still provides the best results and takes less computing time than HyperOpt [50]. By applying both methods, it was demonstrated clearly that Optuna provides better results, especially for decision trees and XGBoost. There are indeed some implementations that are not so challenged by introducing this tuning methods; therefore, better results are not generally obtained for random forest. Another important category is the one that includes all the other examples where grid search did not help in any way with performance, but instead provided worse results, even though Optuna managed to maintain the same level of performance. In the end, the most important conclusion is the fact that this research provided a framework in terms of best performances and also for performance prediction, by adding Optuna as the best method for improving the algorithm's performance [51].

5. Conclusions

Human resources represent a vital domain in any organization, especially nowadays, when resources are generally limited and used at their full capacity. As there are multiple changes happening in different domains, industries, and technologies, people start to differentiate from one another, based on their skills and their adaptability capacity. Therefore, as outlined by several other research works in this area, having skilled, flexible, motivated, and productive workers becomes a great challenge for any organization, but, ultimately, a great need [52].

When considering human resources and data mining, several ideas come into discussions for improving businesses and overall performance, such as automating the recruitment process, CV selection, employee turnover, employee satisfaction, yearly reviews, and performance scores. All these areas are connected. This paper has focused on performance scores, and we have understood from previously mentioned related works that poor performance at work leads to involuntary attrition; therefore, it could be considered that one solution can contribute to solving more than one problem. While standard performance scores are generally provided at the end of a working year, this might come too late into the picture, since previous situations or conditions cannot be changed. Therefore, this is the reason why this paper is considering predictions based on previously known factors related to both the work environment and individual characteristics. Since performance reviews are normally performed by direct managers, this also includes the idea that the evaluations might be biased, due to the relationship existing between the two people. Consequently, this gives us another reason to believe that working on a prediction algorithm will not only contribute to the overall mechanism, but it will also transform this process into a more objective one.

One of the main challenges while developing such an analysis can be availability of the data. The variables inside the dataset could also contribute to the end results and overall conclusions; therefore, having so few available datasets make this analysis even harder to perform. On the other hand, it is equally challenging to even be able to introduce such an analysis, as ethical norms should be considered. Therefore, adding to what has been also mentioned in pre-processing steps, for real data, data minimization and anonymization steps should be added. Of course, when extending this analysis into wider optimization for human resources processes, it is mandatory to take into consideration data security and access control, receiving informed consent where this is the case, and following legal regulations. Another important aspect that should be mentioned is related to the fact that this kind of analysis would eventually replace analyses carried out by humans, especially since one of the final objectives is to also optimize, i.e., reduce, resources [53]. However, in such cases, another limitation could extend to bias and a lack of fairness, in the case that the dataset is not correctly built to include all the needed details for such an analysis. While the process develops and the data are trained on new batches of data regularly, a process of comparing human results with prediction could be introduced, at least until the entire process arrives to a maturity and the level of confidence regarding the number of details collected for each employee is high.

Moving forward to the possible extensions of the current research, there are some areas that could benefit and even include this type of study, in the field of human resources. First of all, the results obtained could help to identify talent as part of the hiring process, considering that there are some characteristics that are specific to the best performers, and one organization can look after them. Additionally, it could be used to evaluate the hiring process and resource allocation. When the factors that help a person to perform better as known, it is easier to provide benefits in the early stages of the hiring process that could attract very skilled professionals, as well as offering specific tasks to those that are more skilled in one area than another. Lastly, feedback collection and development are very important domains wherein this research could contribute [54]. Being careful and also warning an employee about their performance in the early stages of the review could lead to collecting more feedback from these employees, so that problems or requests can be reviewed rather sooner than later. In the same manner, knowing someone's intentions, performance, and engagement can also contribute a lot in achieving more accurate and individually adapted development plans.

Finally, this paper managed to provide a set of methods, algorithms, and best practices that need to be applied in order to increase the performance scores of a classification prediction. While similar methods have been used before for other types of data or classification problems (such as attrition), this research has provided the ideal combination for use with the chosen problem. Additionally, it is worth mentioning the challenges faced during this research, which are mainly focused on data availability, collection and volumes. Nonetheless, the means to extend the current paper would include using all the other feature selection results, applying the same steps and comparing the results. In this way, another conclusion could be drawn, related to the best feature selection method to be used when trying to predict performance scores using the given attributes.

Author Contributions: Conceptualization, L.G.T. and A.V.; methodology, L.G.T.; software, L.G.T. and A.V.; data curation, O.V.; writing—original draft preparation, L.G.T. and O.V.; writing—review and editing, A.R.B. and L.G.T.; visualization, L.G.T.; supervision, A.R.B. All authors have read and agreed to the published version of the manuscript.

Funding: This paper was co-financed by The Bucharest University of Economic Studies during the PhD program.

Data Availability Statement: All data used in the analysis were extracted from the following website: https://www.kaggle.com/datasets/rhebner/human-resources-data-set/data (accessed on 9 April 2024). All the information used for the analysis is available at the website mentioned above and can be accessed by creating a free account.

Conflicts of Interest: The authors declare no conflicts of interest.

References

1. Ranjan, J. Data Mining Techniques for better decisions in Human Resource Management Systems. *Int. J. Bus. Inf. Syst.* **2008**, *3*, 464–481. [CrossRef]
2. Thakur, G.S.; Gupta, A.; Gupta, S. Data mining for Prediction of Human Performance Capability in the Software Industry. *Int. J. Data Min. Knowl. Manag. Process* **2015**, *5*, 53–64. [CrossRef]
3. Tanasescu, L.G.; Bologa, A.R. Machine Learning and Data Mining Techniques for Human Resource Optimization Process—Employee Attrition. In *Education, Research and Business Technologies*; Springer: Singapore, 2023. [CrossRef]
4. Jantan, H.; Hamdan, A.R.; Othman, Z.A. Human Talent Prediction in HRM using C4.5 Classification Algorithm. *J. Adv. Trends Comput. Sci. Eng.* **2010**, *2*, 2526–2534.
5. Ali, Z.; Mahmood, B.; Mehreen, A. Linking succession planning to employee performance: The mediating roles of career development and performance appraisal. *Aust. J. Career Dev.* **2019**, *28*, 112–121. [CrossRef]
6. Maulidina, R.; Arini, W.Y.; Damayanti, N.A. Analysis of Employee Performance Appraisal System in Primary Health Care. *Indian J. Public Health Res. Dev.* **2019**, *10*, 1950. [CrossRef]
7. Chahar, B. Performance Appraisal Systems and Their Impact on Employee Performance. *Inf. Resour. Manag. J.* **2020**, *33*, 17–32. [CrossRef]
8. McShane, S.L.; Glinow, M.A.V. *Organizational Behavior: Emerging Knowledge and Practice for the Real World*; McGraw-Hill: New York, NY, USA, 2010.
9. Aguinis, H.; Joo, H.; Gottfredson, R.K. Performance management universals: Think globally and act locally. *Bus. Horiz.* **2012**, *55*, 385–392. [CrossRef]
10. Wang, J. Innovation of Employee Performance Appraisal Model Based on Data Mining. In Proceedings of the International Conference on Cognitive Based Information Processing and Applications, Changzhou, China, 22–23 September 2022; pp. 410–419. [CrossRef]
11. Seers, A. Team-member exchange quality: A new construct for role-making research. *Organ Behav. Hum. Decis. Process* **1989**, *43*, 118–135. [CrossRef]
12. Sangita, G.; Suma, V. Empirical Study on Selection of Team Members for Software Projects—Data Mining Approach. *Int. J. Comput. Sci. Inform.* **2013**, *3*, 97–102. [CrossRef]
13. Lather, A.S.; Malhotra, R.; Saloni, P.; Singh, P.; Mittal, S. Prediction of Employee Performance Using Machine Learning Techniques. In Proceedings of the International Conference on Advanced Information Science and System, Singapore, 15–17 November 2019; Association for Computing Machinery: New York, NY, USA, 2019. [CrossRef]
14. Mponda, J.M.; Biwot, G.K. The effects of deployment practices on employee performance among the public banking institutions in Kenya: A survey of post bank coast region. *Int. J. Sci. Res. Publ.* **2015**, *5*, 534–546.
15. Liu, J.; Long, Y.; Fang, M.; He, R.; Wang, T.; Chen, G. Analyzing Employee Turnover Based on Job Skills. In Proceedings of the International Conference on Data Processing and Applications, Guangdong, China, 12–14 May 2018; Association for Computing Machinery: New York, NY, USA, 2018. [CrossRef]
16. Kamtar, P.; Jitkongchuen, D.; Pacharawongsakda, E. Multi-Label Classification of Employee Job Performance Prediction by DISC Personality. In Proceedings of the 2nd International Conference on Computing and Big Data, Taiwan, China, 18–20 October 2019; Association for Computing Machinery: New York, NY, USA, 2019. [CrossRef]
17. Jayadi, R.; Firmantyo, H.M.; Dzaka, M.T.J.; Suaidy, M.F.; Putra, A.M. Employee performance prediction using naïve bayes. *Int. J. Adv. Trends Comput. Sci. Eng.* **2019**, *8*, 3031–3035. [CrossRef]
18. Punnoose, R.; Ajit, P. Prediction of Employee Turnover in Organizations using Machine Learning Algorithms. *Int. J. Adv. Res. Artif. Intell.* **2016**, *5*. [CrossRef]
19. Fallucchi, F.; Coladangelo, M.; Giuliano, R.; William De Luca, E. Predicting Employee Attrition Using Machine Learning Techniques. *Appl. Sci.* **2022**, *9*, 86. [CrossRef]
20. Jantan, H.; Hamdan, A.R.; Othman, Z.A. Classification Techniques for Talent Forecasting in Human Resource Management. In Proceedings of the 5th International Conference on Advanced Data Mining and Application (ADMA), Beijing, China, 17–19 August 2009; pp. 496–503. [CrossRef]
21. Juvitayapun, T. Employee Turnover Prediction: The impact of employee event features on interpretable machine learning methods. In Proceedings of the 13th International Conference on Knowledge and Smart Technology (KST), Chonburi, Thailand, 21–24 January 2021.
22. Sujatha, P.; Dhivya, R. Ensemble Learning Framework to Predict the Employee Performance. In Proceedings of the Second International Conference on Power, Control and Computing Technologies, Raipur, India, 1–3 March 2022.
23. Obiedat, R.; Toubasi, S.A. A Combined Approach for Predicting Employees' Productivity based on Ensemble Machine Learning Methods. *Informatica* **2022**, *46*, 49–58. [CrossRef]
24. Schäfer, F.; Zeiselmair, C.; Becker, J.; Otten, H. Synthesizing CRISP-DM and Quality Management: A Data Mining Approach for Production Processes. In Proceedings of the 2018 IEEE International Conference on Technology Management, Operations and Decisions (ICTMOD), Marrakech, Morocco, 21–23 November 2018. [CrossRef]

25. Mwamba, K.D.; Inwhee, J. A Deep-Learned Embedding Technique for Categorical Features Encoding. *IEEE Access* **2021**, *9*, 114381–114391. [CrossRef]
26. Cai, J.; Luo, J.; Wang, S.; Yang, S. Feature selection in machine learning: A new perspective. *Neurocomputing* **2018**, *300*, 70–79. [CrossRef]
27. Htun, H.H.; Biehl, M.; Petkov, N. Survey of feature selection and extraction techniques for stock market prediction. *Financ. Innov.* **2023**, *9*, 26. [CrossRef] [PubMed]
28. Al-Mhiqani, M.N.; Ahmad, R.; Abidin, Z.Z.; Yassin, W.; Hassan, A.; Abdulkareem, K.H.; Ali, N.S.; Yunos, Z. A review of insider threat detection: Classification, machine earning techniques, datasets, open challenges, and recommendations. *Appl. Sci.* **2020**, *10*, 5208. [CrossRef]
29. Marie-Sainte, S.L.; Alalyani, N. Firefly algorithm-based feature selection for Arabic text classification. *J. King Saud Univ. Comput. Inf. Sci* **2020**, *32*, 320–328. [CrossRef]
30. Pradhan, M. Cardiac image-based heart disease diagnosis using bio-inspired optimized technique for feature selection to enhance classification accuracy. In *Machine Learning and AI Techniques in Interactive Medical Image Analysis*; IGI Global: Hershey, PA, USA, 2023; pp. 151–166. [CrossRef]
31. Yassine, A.; Mohamed, C.; Zinedine, A. Feature selection based on pairwise evaluation. In Proceedings of the 2017 Intelligent Systems and Computer Vision, Fez, Morocco, 17–19 April 2017; pp. 1–6. [CrossRef]
32. Akhiat, Y.; Asnaoui, Y.; Chahhou, M.; Zinedine, A. A new graph feature selection approach. In Proceedings of the 2020 6th IEEE Congress on Information Science and Technology (CiSt), Agadir–Essaouira, Morocco, 5–12 June 2020. [CrossRef]
33. Pudjihartono, N.; Fadason, T.; Kempa-Liehr, A.W.; O'Sullivan, J.M. A Review of Feature Selection Methods for Machine Learning-Based Disease Risk Prediction. *Front. Bioinform.* **2022**, *2*, 927312. [CrossRef] [PubMed]
34. Wong, T.T. Performance evaluation of classification algorithms by k-fold and leave-one-out cross validation. *Pattern Recognit.* **2015**, *48*, 2839–2846. [CrossRef]
35. Medar, R.; Rajpurohit, V.S.; Rashmi, B.I. Impact of training and testing data splits on accuracy of time series forecasting in machine learning. In Proceedings of the 2017 International Conference on Computing, Communication, Control and Automation (ICCUBEA), Pune, India, 17–18 August 2017. [CrossRef]
36. Iqbal, H.S. Machine Learning: Algorithms, Real-World Applications and Research Directions. *SN Comput. Sci.* **2021**, *2*, 160.
37. Kataria, A.; Singh, M.D. A review of data classification using k-nearest neighbor algorithm. *Int. J. Emerg. Technol. Adv. Eng.* **2013**, *3*, 354–360.
38. Kharde, R.R.; Amit, D.K. Introduction to Artificial Neural Network. *Int. J. Eng. Innov. Technol. IJEIT* **2012**, *2*, 189–194.
39. Amal, A.; Mohamed, K.; Souhaib, A. Enhancing the prediction of student performance based on the machine learning XGBoost algorithm. *Interact. Learn. Environ.* **2021**, *21*, 3360–3379. [CrossRef]
40. Elgeldawi, E.; Sayed, A.; Galal, A.R.; Zaki, A.M. Hyperparameter Tuning for Machine Learning Algorithms Used for Arabic Sentiment Analysis. *Informatics* **2021**, *8*, 79. [CrossRef]
41. Bischl, B.; Binder, M.; Lang, M.; Pielok, T.; Richter, J.; Coors, S.; Thomas, J.; Ullmann, T.; Becker, M.; Boulesteix, A.; et al. Hyperparameter optimization: Foundations, algorithms, best practices, and open challenges. *WIREs Data Min. Knowl. Discov.* **2023**, *13*, e1484. [CrossRef]
42. Belete, D.M.; Manjaiah, D.H. Grid search in hyperparameter optimization of machine learning models for prediction of HIV/AIDS test results. *Int. J. Comput. Appl.* **2021**, *44*, 875–886. [CrossRef]
43. Akiba, T.; Sano, S.; Yanase, T.; Ohta, T.; Koyama, M. Optuna: A Next-generation Hyperparameter Optimization Framework. *arXiv* **2019**, arXiv:1907.10902. [CrossRef]
44. Qiu, G.; He, X.; Zhang, F.; Shi, Y.; Bu, J.; Chen, C. DASA: Dissatisfaction-oriented advertising based on sentiment analysis. *Expert Syst. Appl.* **2010**, *37*, 6182–6191. [CrossRef]
45. Tanasescu, L.G.; Vines, A.; Bologa, A.R.; Vaida, A.C. Big Data ETL Process and Its Impact on Text Mining Analysis for Employees' Reviews. *Appl. Sci.* **2022**, *12*, 7509. [CrossRef]
46. Giovanelli, J.; Bilalli, B.; Abelló, A. Data pre-processing pipeline generation for AutoETL. *Inf. Syst.* **2021**, *108*, 101957. [CrossRef]
47. Eduardo, M.; Pereira, E.; Alonso-Ríos, D.; Bobes-Bascarán, J.; Fernández-Leal, A. Human-in-the-loop machine learning: A state of the art. *Artif. Intell. Rev.* **2023**, *56*, 3005–3054. [CrossRef]
48. Roccetti, M.; Delnevo, G.; Casini, L.; Salomoni, P. A Cautionary Tale for Machine Learning Design: Why we Still Need Human-Assisted Big Data Analysis. *Mob. Netw. Appl.* **2020**, *25*, 1075–10831. [CrossRef]
49. Al-Radaideh, Q.A.; Nagi, E.A. Using Data Mining Techniques to Build a Classification Model for Predicting Employees Performance. *Int. J. Adv. Comput. Sci. Appl.* **2012**, *3*, 144–151. [CrossRef]
50. Shekhar, S.; Bansode, A.; Salim, A. A Comparative study of Hyper-Parameter Optimization Tools. In Proceedings of the 2021 IEEE Asia-Pacific Conference on Computer Science and Data Engineering, Brisbane, Australia, 8–10 December 2021. [CrossRef]
51. Jafar, A.; Lee, M. Comparative Performance Evaluation of State-of-the-Art Hyperparameter Optimization Frameworks. *Trans. Korean Inst. Electr. Eng.* **2023**, *72*, 607–619. [CrossRef]
52. Al-Jedaia, Y.; Mehrez, A. The effect of performance appraisal on job performance in governmental sector: The mediating role of motivation. *Manag. Sci. Lett.* **2020**, *10*, 2077–2088. [CrossRef]

53. Zafar, H. Human resource information systems: Information security concerns for organizations. *Hum. Resour. Manag. Rev.* **2013**, *23*, 105–113. [CrossRef]
54. Lee, J.S.; Akhtar, S. Determinants of employee willingness to use feedback for performance improvement: Cultural and organizational interpretations. *Int. J. Hum. Resour. Manag.* **1996**, *7*, 878–890. [CrossRef]

Disclaimer/Publisher's Note: The statements, opinions and data contained in all publications are solely those of the individual author(s) and contributor(s) and not of MDPI and/or the editor(s). MDPI and/or the editor(s) disclaim responsibility for any injury to people or property resulting from any ideas, methods, instructions or products referred to in the content.

Article

EEG Emotion Classification Based on Graph Convolutional Network

Zhiqiang Fan [1], Fangyue Chen [1], Xiaokai Xia [1,2] and Yu Liu [3,*]

1. Artificial Intelligence Institute of China Electronics Technology Group Corporation, Beijing 100041, China
2. Beijing Institute of System Engineering, Beijing 100101, China
3. State Key Laboratory of Software Development Environment, Beihang University, Beijing 100191, China
* Correspondence: buaa_liuyu@buaa.edu.cn

Citation: Fan, Z.; Chen, F.; Xia, X.; Liu, Y. EEG Emotion Classification Based on Graph Convolutional Network. *Appl. Sci.* **2024**, *14*, 726. https://doi.org/10.3390/app14020726

Academic Editors: Wenjie Zhang and Zhengyi Yang

Received: 1 September 2023
Revised: 23 September 2023
Accepted: 16 October 2023
Published: 15 January 2024

Copyright: © 2024 by the authors. Licensee MDPI, Basel, Switzerland. This article is an open access article distributed under the terms and conditions of the Creative Commons Attribution (CC BY) license (https://creativecommons.org/licenses/by/4.0/).

Abstract: EEG-based emotion recognition is a task that uses scalp-EEG data to classify the emotion states of humans. The study of EEG-based emotion recognition can contribute to a large spectrum of application fields including healthcare and human–computer interaction. Recent studies in neuroscience reveal that the brain regions and their interactions play an essential role in the processing of different stimuli and the generation of corresponding emotional states. Nevertheless, such regional interactions, which have been proven to be critical in recognizing emotions in neuroscience, are largely overlooked in existing machine learning or deep learning models, which focus on individual channels in brain signals. Motivated by this, in this paper, we present RGNet, a model that is designed to learn the regional level representation of EEG signal for accurate emotion recognition. Specifically, after applying preprocessing and feature extraction techniques on raw signals, RGNet adopts a novel region-wise encoder to extract the features of channels located within each region as input to compute the regional level features, enabling the model to effectively explore the regional functionality. A graph is then constructed by considering each region as a node and connections between regions as edges, upon which a graph convolutional network is designed with spectral filtering and learned adjacency matrix. Instead of focusing on only the spatial proximity, it allows the model to capture more complex functional relationships. We conducted experiments from the perspective of region division strategies, region encoders and input feature types. Our model has achieved 98.64% and 99.33% for Deap and Dreamer datasets, respectively. The comparison studies show that RGNet outperforms the majority of the existing models for emotion recognition from EEG signals.

Keywords: electroencephalogram; deep learning; emotion classification

1. Introduction

Emotion recognition has gained increasing prominence in many areas, such as human–computer interaction and healthcare. For instance, developing the ability to recognize emotion can assist in understanding the emotional states of patients. Existing techniques for emotion recognition can be categorized into non-physiological methods and physiological methods. The non-physiological methods involve facial expression, speech, eye movement and so on [1–4]. A main issue with the non-physiological method is its uncertainty and unreliability, as humans can deliberately conceal their true emotions. On the other hand, the physiological methods offer a higher degree of objectivity since they produce uncontrollable physiological responses, providing a potentially more accurate reflection of emotional states. Electroencephalography (EEG), as one of the physiological methods, has been widely used in emotion recognition tasks due to its easy acquisition and high temporal resolution. The collection of EEG signal is carried out by placing the electrodes on a human scalp to record the electrical activity of underlying brain tissues. As the production of emotion tends to have a strong connection with the activity within brain structures that can be captured by electrograms, the investigation of EEG signal can help to explore this functionality, exemplifying the importance of conducting research on emotion recognition using EEG signals. Nowadays, the processing and classification on EEG data still remains challenging. Essentially, EEG signal is the observation of source signal that has been sent from deeper brain regions that varies with time and is transmitted with different intensity. This non-stationary property makes it difficult to be handled by linear methods [5]. Moreover, EEG signal can be contaminated with noise and artifacts produced by the external environment or mixed with other signals. These issues may affect the collection of brain signals, making it challenging to handle emotion classification by naive methods. Therefore, more and more studies are seeking machine learning or deep learning approaches to solve this task.

Earlier studies primarily emphasize how to extract temporal features from an individual channel, where the inter-channel activity was not thoroughly explored [6–8]. Recently, there have been many works proposed to utilize the fused features of multiple channels. For instance, some studies utilizing convolutional neural networks (CNNs) combine the signal with adjacent channels by treating electrodes as equally spaced pixels in images; another widely used approach is graph neural networks (GNNs), which map channels into nodes and relationships into edges to probe the topological characteristics of brain activity. Although these formulations provide a way to describe how activities from different locations occur coherently by channel-level representation, it still does not guarantee to capture the complex functional relationship occurring at the regional level, which has been identified to be an important factor in the elicitation of emotion. Studies in neuroscience reveal that the functionality of brain regions and their interactions are important factors in the process of emotion production [9–12]. Extracting interactions and features frim regions rather than channels allows us to follow the nature of brain structures and has the potential to create the ability to interpret the association between brain activity and emotion states.

Based on such a point, there are several works proposed to tackle emotion recognition from the perspective of brain regions. Ref. [13] uses Bi-LSTM to capture the regional feature and global feature; Refs. [14,15] focus on extracting features for hemisphere. Although these approaches develop effective ways to present regional features, they do not thoroughly investigate the topological structure and interactions among brain regions. Ref. [16] addresses this issue by constructing local and global graphs. However, it takes the assumption that the connection only exists between nodes or regions that have similar characteristics, which limits the scope on investigating the complex structure of regions.

In this study, we propose a model that investigates both the internal and the global activity of brain regions to identify emotions. Our model firstly adopts a preprocessing technique and feature extractions on the input EEG signal. Next, the channels within the same region are grouped together to form regional data. The region encoder is applied to extract the representative features of each region. For the purpose of learning topological structure among different regions, the graph convolutional network (GCN) is employed to learn more discriminative features. The main contributions of our study include:

1. We propose a model that solves emotion recognition based on region-level representation to learn the activity inside and across various brain regions. Such interactions have been proven to be highly relevant to human emotion state from a neurological point of view.
2. To capture the correlation between brain regions, we construct a graph on EEG signals and employ graph spectral filtering with dynamical adjacency matrix. This approach is more applicable to study the interplay of brain areas since it does not limit itself to the notion of geographic closeness and provides flexibility in detecting function-level interactions.
3. To thoroughly investigate how to formulate regional-level characteristics, we conduct a comprehensive experimental study in terms of different region encoders, region division strategies and input features. The results show that our approach outperforms many existing methods on DEAP and Dreamer datasets.

2. Literature Review

Due to the dynamics property and noise presented in an EEG signal, EEG-based emotion recognition has always been a challenging task. Many researchers have employed a wide range of methods to tackle this problem. In this section, we introduce the works that mainly utilize machine learning and deep learning approaches.

2.1. Machine Learning Approach

Machine learning is a widely used approach in EEG emotion recognition. It often starts with preprocessing the raw signal and extracting hand-crafted features. Then, features are fed into a machine learning model, such as a support vector machine, K-nearest neighbor, decision tree, etc., to classify emotion states.

Many studies have been carried out that focus on evaluating the effectiveness of different features. Ref. [17] explores power spectral density, differential asymmetry and rational asymmetry of the paired channels under multiple frequency bands. These features are processed by a support vector machine to recognize emotions. It finds that differential asymmetry is more robust to detect the brain dynamics caused by emotions. Moreover, information provided by the channels from the frontal and parietal lobe is useful to distinguish emotions. Ref. [18] conducts studies on emotion classification with different features as input. During the process, feature dimensionality reduction techniques, such as principal component analysis and linear discriminant analysis, are adopted to improve the efficiency and accuracy. The experiment results indicate that the power spectrum was identified as the most effective amongst all input features and the high frequency band tends to be more useful in emotion classification. These studies show that the choice of input features can largely affect the results.

To compare which classifiers have the best performance, Ref. [6] utilizes statistical data, i.e., min, max, mean and standard deviation, as the input. Then, it adopts a K-nearest neighbor, regression tree, Bayesian network, support vector machine and artificial neural network for classification. The experiments show that the K-nearest neighbor and support vector machine give the best results among all the models. However, it can be challenging for the majority of machine learning methods to work well with large datasets. Ref. [19] employs discrete wavelet transform and spectral features. In the classification stage, it applies a support vector machine with the aid of a radial basis function kernel to process features from 10 channels to do the classification. Ref. [20] employs empirical mode decomposition/intrinsic mode functions and variational mode decomposition to process the raw EEG signal which is widely used in biomedical studies. These methods are used to decompose nonlinear and non-static signals and feed them into VMD to identify low and high frequencies. Then, it extracts two non-linear features: entropy and Higuchi's fractal dimension. Finally, it carries out experiments by using Naive Bayes, K-nearest neighbor, decision tree and convolutional neural networks to recognize emotions. A common observation from these studies is that the support vector machine often generates the best outcomes in emotion classification tasks.

2.2. Deep Learning Approach

Recently, extensive research efforts have been devoted to deep learning techniques for EEG-based emotion identification due to the robustness and low requirement for prior knowledge. These techniques can be generally classified according to the type of network used, as those with similar architectures are prone to follow analogous ideas.

In previous studies, a common class of deep learning model to address EEG-based emotion classification is long-short term memory (LSTM), which is typically designed to capture temporal dependencies with data sequences. Ref. [21] directly inputs EEG signal into the LSTM network by treating channels as features for each time frame. Similarly, Ref. [7] computes the discrete wavelet transform from the raw signal, followed by the extraction of statistical data. These extracted features are then fed into a network architecture that combines LSTM layers with dense layers for each individual channel. Ref. [15] further extends LSTM with a domain adversarial neural network. It involves the extraction of features from each hemisphere using an LSTM-based approach. The domain adversarial network is adopted here to address the challenge of cross-subject variability. These studies demonstrate the strength of LSTM in effectively capturing temporal characteristics from EEG data. A potential drawback of LSTM is that it may hinder the ability to learn the spatial connections among EEG channels.

Another type of network widely adopted in emotion recognition with EEG signal is a convolutional neural network (CNN), which uses a shared-weight kernel to slide over data. It is primarily utilized in the area of image analysis due to its advantages for processing data with grid patterns. Ref. [22] examines the power of CNN in terms of architecture, design and training decisions. The results indicate that CNN is capable of learning highly discriminative features when given the proper conditions. Ref. [23] adopts a 3D convolution layer, which is able to learn spatial and temporal features simultaneously. It requires a 3D input representation for the EEG signal by appending consecutive frames together. Ref. [24] develops a compact convolution architecture for EEG-based brain–computer interfaces (BCI). It introduces separable and depthwise convolution, which can not only give extract interpretable features but also reduces the number of parameters. Ref. [14] uses multi-scale convolutional layers to extract temporal and spatial layers. It specifically considers the asymmetrical property in the frontal area of brain. These studies demonstrate that CNN is capable of processing both temporal and spatial aspects of EEG signals. However, an issue that often comes with CNN is the inflexibility when considering the relationships among channels or areas. As the nature of CNN is to presume the grid pattern of input data, it is challenging for CNN to investigate non-Euclidean connectivity. On the other hand, this problem can be handled by a graph-based approach.

A graph neural network (GNN) is a class of networks that presents data in a graph structure. In EEG signal tasks, a graph is often constructed by treating each channel as a node, while the formulation of edges could vary. One of the options is to utilize the spatial proximity. Ref. [25] builds a 2D matrix to mark the relative position of electrodes. Then, the adjacency matrix is obtained by thresholding the shortest distance between a node and its neighbors. Ref. [26] establishes the connectivity based on the inverse square function of the physical distance. However, argued by [27], these spatial-based formulations may not represent the real functional connection between channels. To address this problem, it proposes a dynamical graph convolutions neural network that can dynamically learn the intrinsic relationship between nodes. In those works that employ GNN, the advantage of exploring topological structure makes it more adaptable to investigate the relationship between channels.

To improve the performance on both the spatial and temporal level, hybrid networks are used that are composed of different types of networks. From the perspective of signal decomposition, Ref. [28] proposes a model that derives the source signal by stack autoencoder (SAE). Next, the sequenced features are fed into the LSTM network to learn the contextual correlation. Ref. [29] proposes a model that first captures spatial features by convolution layers at each timestamp and feeds them into the LSTM layer. The novelty in this work is that it adopts an attention mechanism in both stages to capture which channel or which timestamp contributes more in the process of emotion recognition. Ref. [30] employs a combination of GNN and LSTM, where GNN is responsible for learning static graph-domain features and LSTM extracts effective information from the channel-level relationships in a short range of time. Recently, the study of spatial-temporal graph learning has also been employed in EEG emotion classification. Ref. [31] integrates the spatial graph convolutional network with an attention-enhanced bi-directional LSTM module. This type of model better combines the temporal information to learn the features.

In addition to the aforementioned approach, some other novel methods have emerged in the field of EEG-based emotion classification. The methods provide different directions for advancing the deep learning techniques on EEG emotion classification. One of these methods, Ref. [32], focuses on a real-time method, which employs online learning techniques, including adaptive random forest, streaming random patches and logistic regression. Ref. [33] utilizes a capsule network to extract hierarchical features from the EEG signal, where each emotional capsule associates with an individual task. To enhance the power of multi-task learning, it uses the dynamic routing algorithm to achieve information exchange between primary capsules and emotional capsules. Recently, reinforcement learning has gained attention in EEG emotion classification as well. An example is [34], which is a reinforcement learning-based method that combines the idea of Papez circuit theory and uses EEG signals from the frontal lobe to simulate brain mechanisms. The key contribution in this approach is the utilization of a double dueling deep Q network, which enhances the decision-making process with more informed choices. These various methods have significantly advanced the field of deep learning for EEG emotion classification.

3. Method

In this paper, we propose a deep learning model, RGNet, to address the emotion recognition task. The structure of our model is shown in Figure 1. We firstly present the preprocessing technique in Section 3.1. Next, we introduce the regional feature learning block, which attempts to learn the region functionality in Section 3.2. Finally, to capture the interactions between regions, the graph learning block is proposed in Section 3.3.

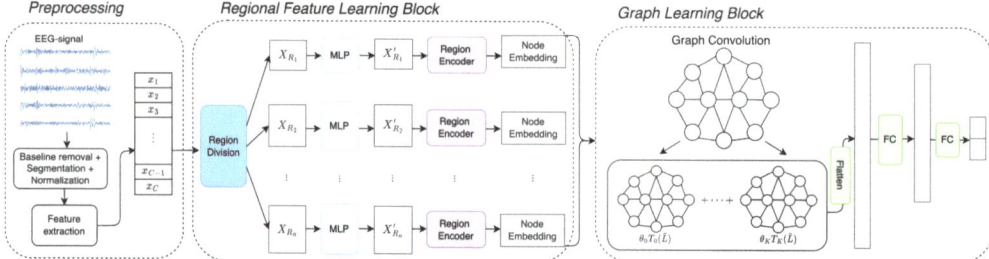

Figure 1. The structure of RGNet.

3.1. Prepocessing

In order to retrieve useful signals that correspond to the emotions elicited by stimuli, we adopt several preprocessing techniques: the baseline signal removal method [35], segmentation and normalization.

Given the trial signal denoted by $\mathbf{X} \in \mathbb{R}^{C \times T}$, where C is the number of channels and T is the time duration, assume the time duration in seconds is t and the frequency of signal is f, then by the definition of frequency, we have $T = t \times f$. It suggests that signal $\mathbf{X}$ can be split up into t segmentations where we denote each segmentation as $X_i \in \mathbb{R}^{C \times f}$. Similarly, the baseline signal $\mathbf{X_b}$ can be segmented into t_b signals where the ith segmentation is referred to as $X_i^b \in \mathbb{R}^{C \times f}$. The mean of baseline signal $\overline{\mathbf{X}}_\mathbf{b}$ can be derived as following:

$$\overline{\mathbf{X}}_\mathbf{b} = \frac{\sum_{i=1}^{t_b} X_i^b}{t_b}. \tag{1}$$

Next, $\overline{\mathbf{X}}_\mathbf{b}$ will be subtracted from each segmentation of the trial signal:

$$X_i = X_i - \overline{\mathbf{X}}_\mathbf{b}. \tag{2}$$

The normalization is then applied, i.e., X_i is subtracted by its mean and divided by the standard deviation. Once the preprocessing is completed, we further extract features for each slice. The details of segmentation and feature extraction are described in Section 4.

3.2. Regional Feature Learning Block

Many studies have argued that individual emotions can be related to activity in multiple brain regions and a single region can be associated with the formulation of multiple emotions [12,36–38]. It is therefore vital to investigate the function that each region plays to determine how the activity of each region helps to recognize different emotions. In this study, we intend to explore the emotional functionality of brain regions by gathering channels within the same region and then feeding them into the corresponding region encoder.

Based on the spatial location of channels, we divide EEG channels into n different regions $R_1, R_2, \cdots, R_n$, where R_i is defined as a set of channels grouped together, i.e., $R_i = \{k_1, k_2, \cdots, k_m\}$, and k_j refers to the channel index. The regional input $X_{R_i} \in \mathbb{R}^{m \times T_s}$ consists of the signals of channels in the same region:

$$X_{R_i} = \{x_{k_j} | x_{k_j} \in \mathbb{R}^{1 \times T_s}, k_j \in R_i\}, \quad (3)$$

where x_{k_j} is the signal of channel k_j. Firstly, we apply a multi-layer perceptron (MLP) to process the raw input signal $X_{R_i} \in \mathbb{R}^{m \times T_s}$:

$$X'_{R_i} = MLP(X_{R_i}). \quad (4)$$

The processed data $X'_{R_i} \in \mathbb{R}^{m \times F_{in}}$ will be taken as the input to be fed into the region encoder f_i:

$$F_{R_i} = f_i(X'_{R_i}), \forall i \in \{1, 2, \cdots, n\}. \quad (5)$$

The structure of region encoder f_i is displayed in the third section in Figure 2. We employ the graph-based network by mapping channels into nodes. The benefit of this approach is its ability to model the underlying patterns of each region since it provides a natural way to explore the relationships between channels, rather than focusing on the integration of individual channel features. In the graph, all nodes are fully connected to each other at the beginning due to the observation that channels in the same region tend to have similar activities. We adopt a graph convolutional network (GCN) to propagate the information among nodes. Finally, the derived node features are flattened and passed into fully connected layers to produce the output F_{R_i}. The detail of the GCN is described in Section 3.3.

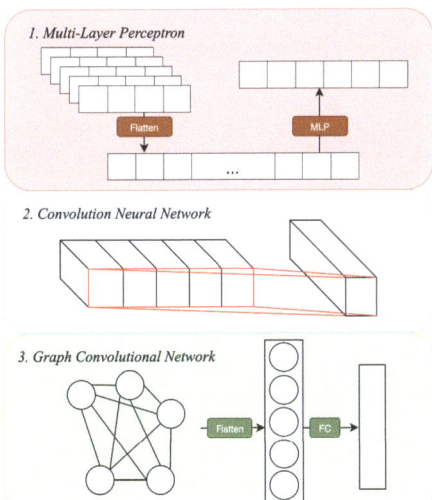

Figure 2. Different types of region encoders.

3.3. Graph Learning Block

Many works suggest that the correlation of regional brain activation plays a critical role in the processing of emotions [12,39]. Thus, with given features of an individual region, we seek a method that allows the study of how these regions relate to one another. In neuroscience research, graph theoretic analyses are frequently employed to investigate functional brain networks from a topological standpoint since they provide a systematic approach to analyze brain structure by mapping neural elements into nodes and their connections into edges [40–42]. Following such an idea, we feed the regional features derived from the region encoder into a graph convolutional network (GCN). We employ the spectral approach to define the convolutional filter instead of spatial approach since it is the more dominant method for dealing with signal processing [43].

The regional features derived from Section 3.2 are used as nodes to formulate a graph $\mathcal{G}$. Then, assume we have the graph $\mathcal{G}$ with adjacency matrix $A \in \mathbb{R}^{n \times n}$ and degree matrix $D \in \mathbb{R}^{n \times n}$. We can derive the Laplacian matrix by $L = D - A$, or the normalized version $\hat{L} = I - D^{\frac{1}{2}} A D^{-\frac{1}{2}}$. Since L will be a real symmetric positive semidefinite matrix, it can be decomposed into

$$L = U \Lambda U^T \tag{6}$$

via singular value decomposition where $\lambda = diag(\lambda_1, \cdots, \lambda_n)$ is the diagonal matrix of the eigenvalues of $\hat{L}$ and U is the Fourier basis. For a given graph data point X, we can derive its graph Fourier transform and inverse graph Fourier transform:

$$\hat{X} = U^T X, \tag{7}$$
$$X = U \hat{X}. \tag{8}$$

Then, the signal filtered by function $g_\theta(\cdot)$ can be expressed by

$$\begin{aligned} Y &= g_\theta(L) X \\ &= g_\theta(U \Lambda U^T) X \\ &= U g_\theta(\Lambda) U^T X, \end{aligned} \tag{9}$$

where $g_\theta(\Lambda)$ can be expressed as:

$$g_\theta(\Lambda) = \begin{bmatrix} g(\lambda_0) & \cdots & 0 \\ \vdots & \ddots & \vdots \\ 0 & \cdots & g(\lambda_{N-1}) \end{bmatrix}. \tag{10}$$

Due to difficulties on the large computation caused directly by learning $g_\theta(\Lambda)$, we additionally adopt Chebyshev expansion [44], which is formulated as following:

$$T_0 = 1, T_1 = x, \tag{11}$$
$$T_k(x) = 2x T_{k-1}(x) - T_{k-2}(x), \tag{12}$$

where $T_k(x)$ is the Chebyshev polynomial with order k. Say we have λ_{max} as the largest eigenvalue of L and $I_n \in \mathbb{R}^{n \times n}$ is the identity matrix, we denote $\tilde{\Lambda} = \frac{2\Lambda}{\lambda_{max}} - I_n$ as a diagonal matrix filled with scaled eigenvalues within $[-1, 1]$. Then, we can make the following estimation based on the Kth order polynomial:

$$g_\theta(\Lambda) = \sum_{k=0}^{K-1} \theta_k T_k(\tilde{\Lambda}) \tag{13}$$

where the parameter $\theta \in \mathbb{R}^K$ presents the Chebyshev coefficients. Similarly, we can derive $g_\theta(L) = \sum_{k=0}^{K-1} \theta_k T_k(\tilde{L})$ with $\tilde{L} = \frac{2L}{\lambda_{max}} - I_n$. Back to the filtering operation, we now have:

$$Y = g_\theta(L)X = \sum_{k=0}^{K-1} \theta_k T_k(\tilde{L}) X. \tag{14}$$

Additionally, to allow the network to learn the connectivity among brain regions in a flexible way, we utilize a dynamical graph convolutional network where the adjacency matrix can be learned.

The detail of the structure of the graph learning block is provided in Figure 3. Finally, the output embedding will generate the final results for predicting the label.

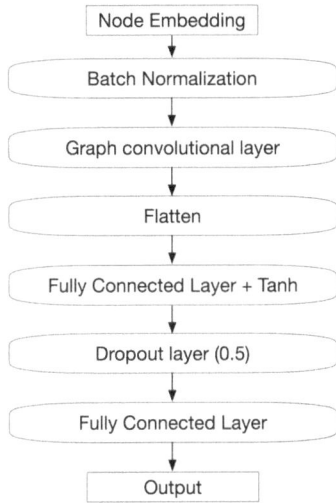

Figure 3. The structure of the graph learning block in Figure 1.

4. Experiments and Discussions

In this section, we present the datasets and discuss the results of experiments that are conducted to investigate the region division strategy, region encoders and different feature types. Lastly, we demonstrate a contrasting study to compare our results with other popular models.

4.1. Dataset

We utilize two public datasets: DEAP [45] and Dreamer [46]. The placement of electrodes in both datasets follows 10–20 systems.

DEAP is a dataset that records the physiological data and corresponding emotion states. It contains the data collected from 32 participants where each participant is required to watch 40 music videos to elicit emotions. Each videos has 3 s baseline data and 60 s trial data. The signal is recorded at 512 Hz. The data of each trial involve 40 channels where the first 32 are EEG channels. The levels of arousal, valence and dominance are rated by each participant on a scale from 1 to 10. The official dataset also provides preprocessed data, where data were downsampled at a rate of 128 Hz. In our study, we make use of the preprocessed data. Following the protocol of [29], each trial is segmented into a set of 3 s slices with a non-overlapping sliding window. The label is categorized into low and high states by a threshold of 5.

Dreamer is a dataset that records EEG and ECG data of 23 participants watching film clips. Each participant is required to watch 18 different videos, which last from 64 s to 393 s. The signals of 14 channels are recorded at a sampling rate of 128 Hz. The levels of arousal, valence and dominance need to be rated by each participant on a scale from 1 to 5. Following the protocol of [47], we segment each recording into a set of 1 s samples with a non-overlapping sliding window. The label is categorized into low and high states by a threshold of 3.

Additionally, we add the SEED dataset [48,49] into our evaluation. The SEED dataset contains data from 15 participants, each of whom participated in 3 sessions. Within each session, there are 15 trials. The signals are recorded with 62 channels and have been downsampled to a frequency of 200 Hz. The emotion label provided by each participant is expressed as either negative, neutral or positive.

4.2. Training Detail

During the training, we set the batch size as 64, number of epochs as 30 and learning rate as 1×10^{-3}. For all the graphs in the network, we chose fully connected edges to capture all the dependencies. In the region encoder, the number of nodes is determined based on the number of channels in the dataset. Specifically, we set the number of nodes to 32 for the Deap dataset, 14 for the Dreamer dataset and 62 for the SEED dataset. In the graph learning block, the number of nodes is determined by the division strategy in Figure 4. Nodes sharing the same color are regarded as a unified region, with the region itself being treated as a single node. The number of nodes is set to be 5 for the first strategy and 14 for the second strategy. As for the third strategy, the number of nodes is consistent with the number of channels proveded by the datasets.

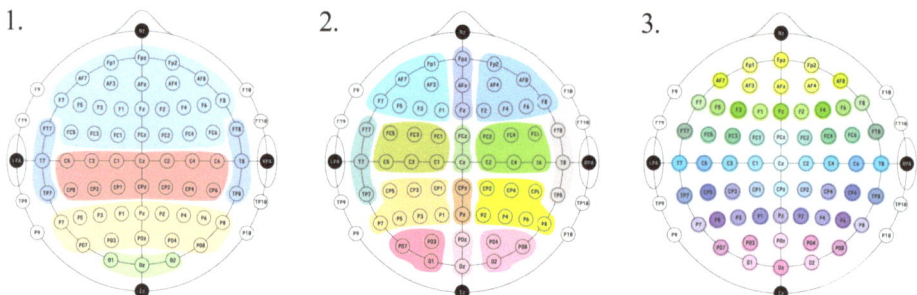

Figure 4. Three different region division strategies constructed based on 10–20 systems. The electrodes in the same group are presented in the same color.

4.3. Evaluation Metric

To align with previous works [29], we conduct 10-fold cross validation experiments. The data of each subject will be randomly shuffled at the beginning and divided into 10 folds. To assess the sensitivity of parameters, we randomly initialize the parameters of the model via a uniform distribution. In the experiments, we present the mean and standard deviation of the results obtained from 10-fold cross validation to evaluate the model's convergence and its ability to generalize across different subsets of data. To provide the result of each fold, we calculate the precision, recall and f1-score as below:

$$\text{precision} = \frac{TP}{TP + FP}, \tag{15}$$

$$\text{recall} = \frac{TP}{TP + FN}, \tag{16}$$

$$\text{f1-score} = \frac{2 \times precision \times recall}{precision + recall}, \tag{17}$$

where TP, FP and FN denote true positive, false positive and false negative.

4.4. Experiment on Region Representation

To study how to generate effective regional features that contribute to emotion recognition, we firstly conduct experiments from the perspective of region encoders and region strategies.

The region encoders utilized in experiments are shown in Figure 2. In addition to the GCN region encoder presented in Section 3.2, we introduce two other types of region encoders for comparison:

- Multi-layer perceptron (MLP) is one of the most common networks. The input X'_{R_i} is firstly flattened into a one-dimensional vector, then the multi-layer perceptron is applied:

$$Y_{R_i} = MLP_{R_i}(Flatten(X'_{R_i})), \qquad (18)$$

to generate the output $Y_{R_i} \in \mathbb{R}^{F_{out}}$.

- Convolutional neural network (CNN) is a class of neural network that is widely used in emotion recognition tasks. It utilizes kernel to move data into a grid pattern. Say the kernel size is m, then we can derive:

$$y_i = g(\sum_j w_{ij} x'_j + b_i), \qquad (19)$$

where x_j is the jth feature; w_{ij} is the kernel weight; b_j is the offset of the jth feature; $g(\cdot)$ is the activation function.

As can be observed in Figure 2, each of the three types of regional encoders has its own specific structure to handle input features from different perspectives. We intend to examine which structure works the best in generating the regional features.

In addition to region encoders, the strategy to define regions is also a critical factor. We provide three different strategies to define the division of brain regions, as shown in Figure 4. Each strategy determines which electrodes are grouped together to form a single region R_i, as stated in Section 3.2. Note that the figure is illustrated based on full 10–20 systems while, in practice, we only consider the electrodes that are given by the dataset. The first one is based on the common division of a human brain [50], where the cortex can be segmented into frontal, temporal, parietal and occipital lobes. Despite the fact that the central lobe does not actually exist in the human brain, we still use it as a distinct region based on 10–20 systems to help identify the location of recorded brain activity more precisely [51]. The other two procedures are further divided into more granular pieces, where, in the second one, left, center and right parts are split into different regions and in the third one only symmetric electrode sites are grouped. We adopt these strategies in accordance with earlier studies implying that the asymmetries in brain activity may have a great impact on emotion identification [52,53]. The main difference between those two strategies is that we set different levels of subdivision to discover which one is best at preserving the distinctive features of asymmetric difference.

The results of applying region strategies on different region encoders are shown in Table 1, which records the average accuracy of valence, arousal and dominance on DEAP and Dreamer datasets. An observation obtained in both datasets is that the second and first strategy achieved the best and worst results, respectively. Such findings suggest that the second strategy gives a proper division where the functionality of each region and the interaction among them can be sufficiently captured by our model. In contrast, the first strategy splits the area in a coarser way, making it difficult to preserve the hemisphere structure, while groups in the third strategy show a more dispersed pattern that resembles channel-wise characteristics rather than region-wise features. For the DEAP dataset, we can see that for the second and third region division strategy, the results derived from the MLP region encoder are usually the lowest and GCN can achieve the best. It demonstrates that compared to MLP and CNN, GCN is better at capturing the regional features by considering the internal topological structure. For the Dreamer dataset, the results imply a similar level of performance on the three region encoders with the same division strategy. The variation among different region encoders is less than 0.3%. A possible explanation is that the Dreamer dataset provides signals from less channels, causing each region to have extremely few electrodes. In this scenario, the structure of each region tends to be relatively simple, which makes the advantages of GCN on capturing internal relationships less useful. Nevertheless, we can still observe that GCN gives the best outcomes in both datasets.

Table 1. The accuracy (%) of region division strategies combined with different region encoders. The first column is the index of the region division strategy.

Region No.	MLP	CNN	GCN
DEAP			
1.	94.11	93.58	94.13
2.	97.48	97.64	98.65
3.	97.05	97.54	98.01
Dreamer			
1.	94.25	94.00	94.29
2.	99.12	99.09	99.15
3.	97.11	96.94	97.03

4.5. Feature Visualization

In this study, we attempt four different types of input features that are often used in EEG-based emotion recognition:

- Raw signal.
- Differential entropy (DE) is a measure of the complexity of a continuous random variable. It can be calculated as following:

$$DE(X) = -\int_{-\infty}^{+\infty} \frac{1}{\sqrt{2\pi\sigma^2}} e^{-\frac{(x-\mu)^2}{2\sigma^2}} \cdot \log\left(\frac{1}{\sqrt{2\pi\sigma^2}} e^{-\frac{(x-\mu)^2}{2\sigma^2}}\right)$$
$$= \frac{1}{2}\log(2\pi e\sigma^2), \quad (20)$$

where μ and σ denote the mean and standard deviation.

- Fast Fourier transform (FFT) is an algorithm that is used to compute the discrete Fourier transform(DFT) of a sequence of data points in an efficient way. It can be defined as:

$$S(f) = \int_{-\infty}^{+\infty} s(t)e^{-j2\pi ft}dt, \quad (21)$$

where f is the frequency; t denotes time; $s(t)$ is the signal in time domain.

- Power spectral density (PSD) refers to the distribution of power of different frequencies in a signal. It is calculated by taking the squared magnitude of Fourier transform of the signal:

$$PSD(f) = \left|\int_{-\infty}^{+\infty} x(\tau)e^{-j2\pi f\tau}d\tau\right|^2. \quad (22)$$

Note that for the frequency-domain features, we decompose the EEG signal into five frequency bands: δ band (1–3 Hz), θ band (4–7 Hz), α band (8–12 Hz), β band (8–12 Hz) and γ band (8–12 Hz). The features are extracted from each band respectively, which indicates the dimension of features for each segment would be five.

To compare learning of models with different input features and region encoders, we visualize the features of the last fully connected layers using the t-SNE visualization tool. The features of data from the same subject are extracted to make a fair comparison. The t-SNE visualization of DEAP is shown in Figure 5. With DE, PSD and FFT as input features, MLP region encoders are unable to distinguish between the two classes, while CNN and GCN have relatively better performance. All the region encoders are able to observe distinct separation with raw signal input.

The features from the Dreamer dataset, as shown in Figure 6, are more variable between low/high classes. We are able to observe that the PSD and FFT features have relatively more outliers for all region encoders. On the other hand, a more distinct boundary can be detected with other features, especially DE.

The differences between observations of DEAP and Dreamer might be attributed to their intrinsic differences as datasets, e.g., stimuli they used or the collection of data and experiment settings. Based on the analysis of features, for the following experiments, we choose the raw signal to be the input for the DEAP dataset and DE as the input for the Dreamer dataset.

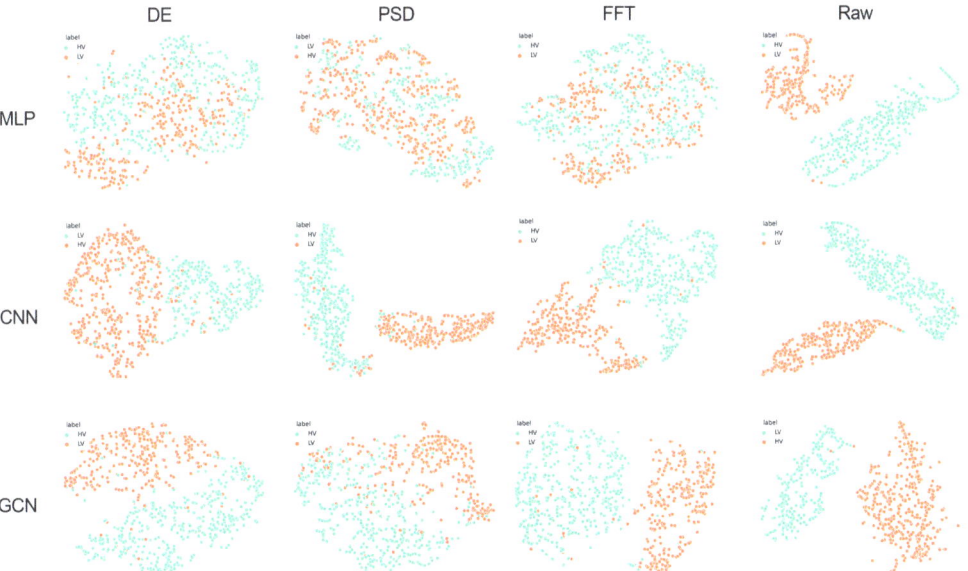

Figure 5. t-SNE visualization of features for DEAP dataset. Row represents region encoder and column represents the type of input features.

4.6. Subject-Wise Results

We plot the subject-wise accuracy and standard deviation of our models with different region encoders and the baseline models for different emotion dimensions. Note that for dominance in the DEAP dataset, we exclude the 27th subject since we can only find low labels in its data. As shown in Figure 7, for the DEAP dataset, our methods achieve higher and more stable results most of the time. Despite the fact that for a few subjects, our models have a relatively big standard deviation, it still can be observed that our approach is able to derive qualified results for the majority of subjects. Among all approaches, RGNet-GCN has shown comparatively superior results due to its high accuracy and low standard deviation. For the Dreamer dataset, as shown in Figure 8, a more stable outcome is demonstrated for both baseline models and our methods. We can observe that the three types of regional encoders have a similar trend on the Dreamer dataset due to the aforementioned problem about the low number of electrodes in each region. The advantages of GCN in terms of capturing internal relationships within regions are suppressed under these circumstances.

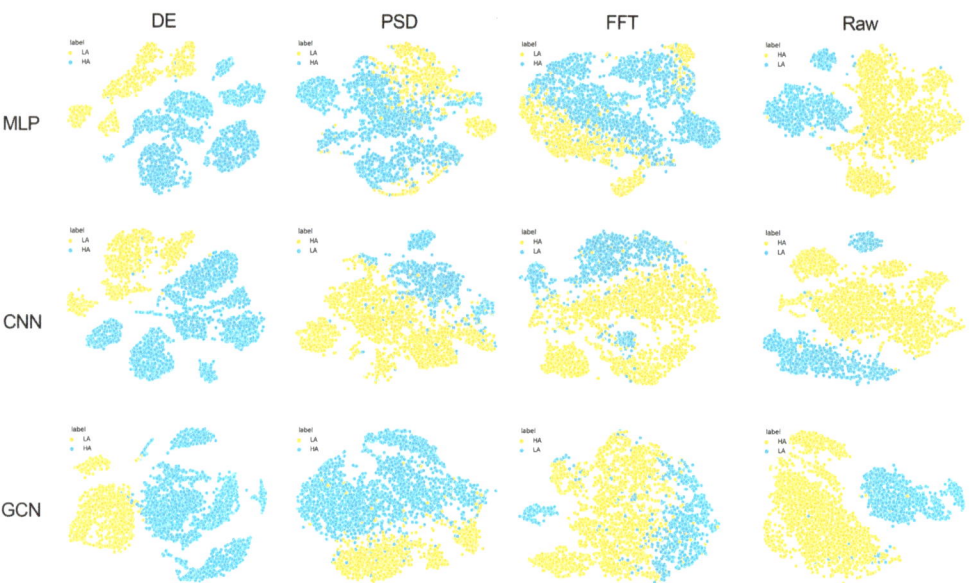

Figure 6. t-SNE visualization of features for Dreamer dataset. Row represents region encoder and column represents the type of input features.

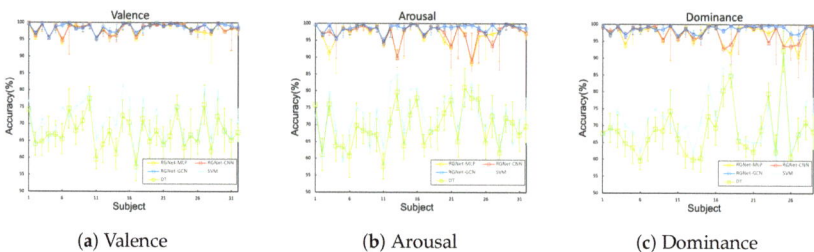

(a) Valence   (b) Arousal   (c) Dominance

Figure 7. Subject-wise average accuracy and standard deviation (%) on DEAP dataset with respect to the classification of valence, arousal and dominance.

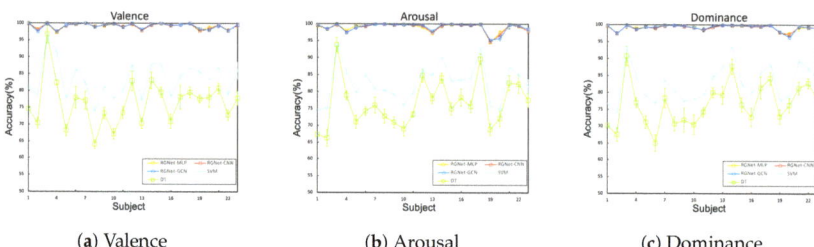

(a) Valence   (b) Arousal   (c) Dominance

Figure 8. Subject-wise average accuracy and standard deviation (%) on Dreamer dataset with respect to the classification of valence, arousal and dominance.

4.7. Comparison of Different Models

In our comparison study, we include two baseline models: decision tree (DT) and support vector machine (SVM), which utilize DE as input. Additionally, we evaluate the outcomes of our approaches using the raw signal and DE as input formulation in comparison to the following models:

- CNN-RNN [35] is a hybrid neural network that combines CNN and RNN to process the spatial and temporal features.
- RACNN [47] is the regional-asymmetric convolutional neural network. It firstly extracts the time-frequency features using 1D CNN. Then, the asymmetrical regional features are captured from 2D CNN.
- ACRNN [29] is an attention-based convolutional recurrent neural network. In the first stage, it applies CNN to extract spatial features where a channel-wise attention mechanism is employed to determine the importance of different channels. Next, the extracted features are fed into the RNN network that has an extended self-attention mechanism to determine the intrinsic importance of each sample.
- DGCNN [27] is a model that utilizes a dynamical graph convolutional network, which maps multi-channel EEG signals into a graph structure by considering each channel as a node and the connection between them as edges. It allows the model to learn the dynamical structure of a graph so that the relationships among nodes are not constrained to geographical proximity.
- CapsNet [33] uses the attention mechanism and capsule network to conduct multi-task learning. The attention mechanism is used to capture the importance of each channel. The capsule network consists of multiple capsule layers that not only learn the characteristics required for individual tasks but also the correlations between them.

The contrasting results of the DEAP dataset are displayed in Table 2. Among our approaches, RGNet-GCN has outperformed all other methods. Additionally, in our approach, it can be observed that the second best results are yielded from RGNet-CNN and the worst ones come from RGNet-MLP. Such results demonstrate that GCN is more capable of learning regional features than CNN and MLP. When compared to other models, firstly, we can observe that each of the deep learning approaches presented in the table is superior to DT and SVM by a margin of at least 17%. The accuracy derived from the majority of models is under 98%, while our model, RGNet-GCN, is able to attain 98.61%, 98.63% and 98.71%, respectively.

For the results of Dreamer dataset shown in Table 3, there is no significant margin between baseline models and some previous deep learning methods. Moreover, the accuracy derived from CNN-RNN is lower than SVM. The highest accuracy achieved by other methods does not exceed 98% for valence and arousal, while the results of our model are over 99% for almost all classes.

Table 2. The comparison of different models on the average accuracy/std(%) of DEAP dataset.

Method	Feature	Valence	Arousal	Dominance
DT	DE	67.52/4.79	69.59/6.09	69.96/9.68
SVM	DE	71.05/6.11	72.18/6.89	71.85/8.38
CNN-RNN	raw signal	89.92/2.96	90.81/2.94	90.90/3.01
ACRNN	raw signal	93.72/3.21	93.38/3.73	-
DGCNN	DE	92.55/3.53	93.50/3.93	93.50/3.69
RACNN	raw signal	96.65/2.65	97.11/2.01	-
MTCA-CapsNet	raw signal	97.24/1.58	97.41/1.47	98.35/1.28
RGNet-MLP	raw signal	98.09/1.66	96.99/2.98	97.36/2.58
RGNet-CNN	raw signal	98.21/1.55	97.21/2.69	97.49/2.35
RGNet-GCN	raw signal	98.61/1.24	98.63/1.26	98.71/1.07

Table 3. The comparison of different models on the average accuracy/std(%) of Dreamer dataset.

Method	Feature	Valence	Arousal	Dominance
DT	DE	76.39/6.69	76.62/6.91	76.59/6.27
SVM	DE	83.36/5.21	82.58/5.41	82.71/5.30
CNN-RNN	raw signal	79.93/6.65	81.48/6.33	80.94/5.66
ACRNN	raw signal	97.93/1.73	97.98/1.92	98.23/1.42
DGCNN	DE	89.59/5.13	88.93/3.93	88.64/5.13
RACNN	raw signal	96.65/2.18	97.01/2.74	-
MTCA-CapsNet	raw signal	94.96/3.60	95.54/3.63	95.52/3.78
RGNet-MLP	DE	99.16/0.75	99.00/1.25	99.20/0.72
RGNet-CNN	DE	99.13/0.82	98.97/1.27	99.18/0.78
RGNet-GCN	DE	99.17/0.85	99.06/1.29	99.23/0.89

We conclude that for both datasets, our approach has the best performance in comparison with other popular models. Furthermore, in our approach, the best results all came from the GCN region encoder. The detailed results from our approach are shown in Tables 4 and 5 for the DEAP and Dreamer dataset, respectively. We further conduct experiments on the SEED dataset. The result in Table 6 reveals that the model exhibits better performance for positive emotion state. However, the prediction ability for the neutral and negative emotion states yielded comparatively lower outcomes. Nevertheless, the overall performance has proven the effectiveness of our method.

Table 4. Detailed performance of RGNet-GCN on DEAP dataset.

	Precision	Recall	F1-Score
Valence	98.65 ± 1.17	98.72 ± 1.61	98.67 ± 1.31
Arousal	98.64 ± 1.33	98.61 ± 1.98	98.60 ± 1.57
Dominance	98.76 ± 1.12	98.85 ± 1.50	98.78 ± 1.19

Table 5. Detailed performance of RGNet-GCN on Dreamer dataset.

	Precision	Recall	F1-Score
Valence	99.05 ± 0.99	98.93 ± 1.11	98.99 ± 1.03
Arousal	99.06 ± 1.36	98.86 ± 1.59	98.96 ± 1.29
Dominance	99.19 ± 0.90	99.35 ± 0.73	99.27 ± 0.80

Table 6. Detailed performance of RGNet-GCN on SEED dataset.

	Precision	Recall	F1-Score
Positive	97.84 ± 2.70	98.28 ± 1.53	97.90 ± 1.97
Neutral	95.72 ± 3.30	94.18 ± 4.55	94.58 ± 3.95
Positive	94.57 ± 6.14	88.50 ± 9.40	90.31 ± 8.19

5. Conclusions

In this study, we propose RGNet, a region-based graph convolutional network, for emotion recognition from EEG signals. Our approach firstly preprocess and extracts features from given EEG signal. Then, the channels are clustered via the region division strategy. Each group of channels is fed into the corresponding region encoder. Next, the produced regional features are treated as node embeddings to be inputted into a graph convolutional network. Finally, the resulting node features are flattened and passed into fully connected layers to produce the classification results. In the experiments, we conducted extensive studies on the region division strategies, region encoders and input feature types to determine the proper regional representation. For the classification of valence, arousal and dominance, our model has achieved 98.61%, 98.63%, 98.61% for the DEAP dataset and 99.17%, 99.06%, 99.23% for the Dreamer dataset. The comparison with other models indicates that our model is able to outperform most of the popular methods for both datasets.

Author Contributions: Conceptualization, Z.F. and X.X.; investigation, Z.F. and F.C.; formal analysis, F.C.; writing, Z.F. and Y.L.; visualization, F.C. and X.X. All authors have read and agreed to the published version of the manuscript.

Funding: This research received no external funding.

Institutional Review Board Statement: Not applicable.

Informed Consent Statement: Not applicable.

Data Availability Statement: The EEG datasets used in this paper are available in [15,16].

Conflicts of Interest: Author Zhiqiang Fan and Fangyue Chen were employed by the Artificial Intelligence Institute of China Electronics Technology Group Corporation. Author Xiaokai Xia was employed by the Artificial Intelligence Institute of China Electronics Technology Group Corporation and Beijing Institute of System Engineering. The remaining authors declare that the research was conducted in the absence of any commercial or financial relationships that could be construed as a potential conflict of interest.

References

1. Zou, S.; Huang, X.; Shen, X.; Liu, H. Improving multimodal fusion with Main Modal Transformer for emotion recognition in conversation. *Knowl.-Based Syst.* **2022**, *258*, 109978. [CrossRef]
2. Wen, G.; Liao, H.; Li, H.; Wen, P.; Zhang, T.; Gao, S.; Wang, B. Self-labeling with feature transfer for speech emotion recognition. *Knowl.-Based Syst.* **2022**, *254*, 109589. [CrossRef]
3. Middya, A.I.; Nag, B.; Roy, S. Deep learning based multimodal emotion recognition using model-level fusion of audio–visual modalities. *Knowl.-Based Syst.* **2022**, *244*, 108580. [CrossRef]
4. Zhang, L.; Mistry, K.; Neoh, S.C.; Lim, C.P. Intelligent facial emotion recognition using moth-firefly optimization. *Knowl.-Based Syst.* **2016**, *111*, 248–267. [CrossRef]
5. Klonowski, W. Everything you wanted to ask about EEG but were afraid to get the right answer. *Nonlinear Biomed. Phys.* **2009**, *3*, 2. [CrossRef] [PubMed]
6. Sohaib, A.T.; Qureshi, S.; Hagelbäck, J.; Hilborn, O.; Jerčić, P. Evaluating Classifiers for Emotion Recognition Using EEG. In *Proceedings of the Foundations of Augmented Cognition*; Lecture Notes in Computer Science; Schmorrow, D.D., Fidopiastis, C.M., Eds.; Springer: Berlin/Heidelberg, Germany, 2013; pp. 492–501.
7. Garg, A.; Kapoor, A.; Bedi, A.K.; Sunkaria, R.K. Merged LSTM Model for emotion classification using EEG signals. In Proceedings of the 2019 International Conference on Data Science and Engineering (ICDSE), Patna, India, 26–28 September 2019; pp. 139–143.
8. Chen, S.; Jin, Q. Multi-modal Dimensional Emotion Recognition using Recurrent Neural Networks. In Proceedings of the 5th International Workshop on Audio/Visual Emotion Challenge, Brisbane, Australia, 26 October 2015; ACM: New York, NY, USA, 2015; pp. 49–56.
9. Davidson, R.J.; Abercrombie, H.; Nitschke, J.B.; Putnam, K. Regional brain function, emotion and disorders of emotion. *Curr. Opin. Neurobiol.* **1999**, *9*, 228–234. [CrossRef]
10. Pessoa, L. Beyond brain regions: Network perspective of cognition-emotion interactions. *Behav. Brain Sci.* **2012**, *35*, 158–159. [CrossRef]
11. Kober, H.; Barrett, L.F.; Joseph, J.; Bliss-Moreau, E.; Lindquist, K.; Wager, T.D. Functional grouping and cortical–subcortical interactions in emotion: A meta-analysis of neuroimaging studies. *NeuroImage* **2008**, *42*, 998–1031. [CrossRef]
12. Lindquist, K.A.; Wager, T.D.; Kober, H.; Bliss-Moreau, E.; Barrett, L.F. The brain basis of emotion: A meta-analytic review. *Behav. Brain Sci.* **2012**, *35*, 121–143. [CrossRef]
13. Li, Y.; Zheng, W.; Wang, L.; Zong, Y.; Cui, Z. From Regional to Global Brain: A Novel Hierarchical Spatial-Temporal Neural Network Model for EEG Emotion Recognition. *IEEE Trans. Affect. Comput.* **2022**, *13*, 568–578. [CrossRef]
14. Ding, Y.; Robinson, N.; Zeng, Q.; Chen, D.; Phyo Wai, A.A.; Lee, T.S.; Guan, C. TSception:A Deep Learning Framework for Emotion Detection Using EEG. In Proceedings of the 2020 International Joint Conference on Neural Networks (IJCNN), Glasgow, UK, 19–24 July 2020; IEEE: Piscataway, NJ, USA, 2020; pp. 1–7.
15. Li, Y.; Zheng, W.; Zong, Y.; Cui, Z.; Zhang, T.; Zhou, X. A Bi-Hemisphere Domain Adversarial Neural Network Model for EEG Emotion Recognition. *IEEE Trans. Affect. Comput.* **2021**, *12*, 494–504. [CrossRef]
16. Ding, Y.; Robinson, N.; Zeng, Q.; Guan, C. LGGNet: Learning from Local-Global-Graph Representations for Brain-Computer Interface. *arXiv* **2022**, arXiv:2105.02786.
17. Lin, Y.P.; Wang, C.H.; Jung, T.P.; Wu, T.L.; Jeng, S.K.; Duann, J.R.; Chen, J.H. EEG-Based Emotion Recognition in Music Listening. *IEEE Trans. Biomed. Eng.* **2010**, *57*, 1798–1806.

18. Wang, X.W.; Nie, D.; Lu, B.L. Emotional state classification from EEG data using machine learning approach. *Neurocomputing* **2014**, *129*, 94–106. [CrossRef]
19. Bazgir, O.; Mohammadi, Z.; Habibi, S.A.H. Emotion Recognition with Machine Learning Using EEG Signals. In Proceedings of the 2018 25th National and 3rd International Iranian Conference on Biomedical Engineering (ICBME), Qom, Iran, 29–30 November 2018; pp. 1–5.
20. Alhalaseh, R.; Alasasfeh, S. Machine-Learning-Based Emotion Recognition System Using EEG Signals. *Computers* **2020**, *9*, 95. [CrossRef]
21. Alhagry, S.; Aly, A.; El-Khoribi, R. Emotion Recognition based on EEG using LSTM Recurrent Neural Network. *Int. J. Adv. Comput. Sci. Appl.* **2017**, *8*, 355–358. [CrossRef]
22. Schirrmeister, R.T.; Springenberg, J.T.; Fiederer, L.D.J.; Glasstetter, M.; Eggensperger, K.; Tangermann, M.; Hutter, F.; Burgard, W.; Ball, T. Deep learning with convolutional neural networks for EEG decoding and visualization: Convolutional Neural Networks in EEG Analysis. *Hum. Brain Mapp.* **2017**, *38*, 5391–5420. [CrossRef] [PubMed]
23. Salama, E.S.; El-Khoribi, R.A.; Shoman, M.E.; Wahby, M.A. EEG-Based Emotion Recognition using 3D Convolutional Neural Networks. *Int. J. Adv. Comput. Sci. Appl.* **2018**, *9*, 329–337. [CrossRef]
24. Lawhern, V.J.; Solon, A.J.; Waytowich, N.R.; Gordon, S.M.; Hung, C.P.; Lance, B.J. EEGNet: A compact convolutional neural network for EEG-based brain–computer interfaces. *J. Neural Eng.* **2018**, *15*, 056013. [CrossRef]
25. Priyasad, D.; Fernando, T.; Denman, S.; Sridharan, S.; Fookes, C. Affect recognition from scalp-EEG using channel-wise encoder networks coupled with geometric deep learning and multi-channel feature fusion. *Knowl.-Based Syst.* **2022**, *250*, 109038. [CrossRef]
26. Zhong, P.; Wang, D.; Miao, C. EEG-Based Emotion Recognition Using Regularized Graph Neural Networks. *IEEE Trans. Affect. Comput.* **2020**, *13*, 1290–1301. [CrossRef]
27. Song, T.; Zheng, W.; Song, P.; Cui, Z. EEG Emotion Recognition Using Dynamical Graph Convolutional Neural Networks. *IEEE Trans. Affect. Comput.* **2020**, *11*, 532–541. [CrossRef]
28. Xing, X.; Li, Z.; Xu, T.; Shu, L.; Hu, B.; Xu, X. SAE+LSTM: A New Framework for Emotion Recognition From Multi-Channel EEG. *Front. Neurorobotics* **2019**, *13*, 37. [CrossRef] [PubMed]
29. Tao, W.; Li, C.; Song, R.; Cheng, J.; Liu, Y.; Wan, F.; Chen, X. EEG-based Emotion Recognition via Channel-wise Attention and Self Attention. *IEEE Trans. Affect. Comput.* **2020**, *14*, 382–393. [CrossRef]
30. Yin, Y.; Zheng, X.; Hu, B.; Zhang, Y.; Cui, X. EEG emotion recognition using fusion model of graph convolutional neural networks and LSTM. *Appl. Soft Comput.* **2021**, *100*, 106954. [CrossRef]
31. Feng, L.; Cheng, C.; Zhao, M.; Deng, H.; Zhang, Y. EEG-based emotion recognition using spatial-temporal graph convolutional LSTM with attention mechanism. *IEEE J. Biomed. Health Inform.* **2022**, *26*, 5406–5417. [CrossRef]
32. Moontaha, S.; Schumann, F.E.F.; Arnrich, B. Online learning for wearable eeg-based emotion classification. *Sensors* **2023**, *23*, 2387. [CrossRef]
33. Li, C.; Wang, B.; Zhang, S.; Liu, Y.; Song, R.; Cheng, J.; Chen, X. Emotion recognition from EEG based on multi-task learning with capsule network and attention mechanism. *Comput. Biol. Med.* **2022**, *143*, 105303. [CrossRef] [PubMed]
34. Li, D.; Xie, L.; Wang, Z.; Yang, H. Brain emotion perception inspired eeg emotion recognition with deep reinforcement learning. *IEEE Trans. Neural Netw. Learn. Syst.* **2023**, 1–14. [CrossRef]
35. Yang, Y.; Wu, Q.; Qiu, M.; Wang, Y.; Chen, X. Emotion Recognition from Multi Channel EEG through Parallel Convolutional Recurrent Neural Network. In Proceedings of the 2018 International Joint Conference on Neural Networks (IJCNN), Rio de Janeiro, Brazil, 8–13 July 2018; IEEE: Piscataway, NJ, USA, 2018; pp. 1–7.
36. Poldrack, R.A. Mapping Mental Function to Brain Structure: How Can Cognitive Neuroimaging Succeed? *Perspect. Psychol. Sci.* **2010**, *5*, 753–761. [CrossRef]
37. Pessoa, L. On the relationship between emotion and cognition. *Nat. Rev. Neurosci.* **2008**, *9*, 148–158. [CrossRef] [PubMed]
38. Scarantino, A. Functional specialization does not require a one-to-one mapping between brain regions and emotions. *Behav. Brain Sci.* **2012**, *35*, 161–162. [CrossRef] [PubMed]
39. Vytal, K.; Hamann, S. Neuroimaging Support for Discrete Neural Correlates of Basic Emotions: A Voxel-based Meta-analysis. *J. Cogn. Neurosci.* **2010**, *22*, 2864–2885. [CrossRef]
40. Fornito, A.; Zalesky, A.; Breakspear, M. Graph analysis of the human connectome: Promise, progress, and pitfalls. *NeuroImage* **2013**, *80*, 426–444. [CrossRef]
41. Bullmore, E.; Sporns, O. Complex brain networks: Graph theoretical analysis of structural and functional systems. *Nat. Rev. Neurosci.* **2009**, *10*, 186–198. [CrossRef]
42. Fair, D.A.; Cohen, A.L.; Power, J.D.; Dosenbach, N.U.F.; Church, J.A.; Miezin, F.M.; Schlaggar, B.L.; Petersen, S.E. Functional Brain Networks Develop from a "Local to Distributed" Organization. *PLoS Comput. Biol.* **2009**, *5*, e1000381. [CrossRef] [PubMed]
43. Shuman, D.I.; Narang, S.K.; Frossard, P.; Ortega, A.; Vandergheynst, P. The emerging field of signal processing on graphs: Extending high-dimensional data analysis to networks and other irregular domains. *IEEE Signal Process. Mag.* **2013**, *30*, 83–98. [CrossRef]
44. Defferrard, M.; Bresson, X.; Vandergheynst, P. Convolutional neural networks on graphs with fast localized spectral filtering. In Proceedings of the NIPS'16: Proceedings of the 30th International Conference on Neural Information Processing Systems, Barcelona, Spain, 5–10 December 2016; Volume 29.

45. Koelstra, S.; Muhl, C.; Soleymani, M.; Lee, J.-S..; Yazdani, A.; Ebrahimi, T.; Pun, T.; Nijholt, A.; Patras, I. DEAP: A Database for Emotion Analysis ;Using Physiological Signals. *IEEE Trans. Affect. Comput.* **2012**, *3*, 18–31. [CrossRef]
46. Katsigiannis, S.; Ramzan, N. DREAMER: A Database for Emotion Recognition Through EEG and ECG Signals From Wireless Low-cost Off-the-Shelf Devices. *IEEE J. Biomed. Health Inform.* **2018**, *22*, 98–107. [CrossRef]
47. Cui, H.; Liu, A.; Zhang, X.; Chen, X.; Wang, K.; Chen, X. EEG-based emotion recognition using an end-to-end regional-asymmetric convolutional neural network. *Knowl.-Based Syst.* **2020**, *205*, 106243. [CrossRef]
48. Duan, R.N.; Zhu, J.Y.; Lu, B.L. Differential entropy feature for EEG-based emotion classification. In Proceedings of the 2013 6th International IEEE/EMBS Conference on Neural Engineering (NER), San Diego, CA, USA, 6–8 November 2013; IEEE: Piscataway, NJ, USA, 2013; pp. 81–84.
49. Zheng, W.L.; Lu, B.L. Investigating critical frequency bands and channels for EEG-based emotion recognition with deep neural networks. *IEEE Trans. Auton. Ment. Dev.* **2015**, *7*, 162–175. [CrossRef]
50. Ribas, G.C. The cerebral sulci and gyri. *Neurosurg. Focus* **2010**, *28*, E2. [CrossRef] [PubMed]
51. Klem, G.; Lüders, H.; Jasper, H.; Elger, C. The ten-twenty electrode system of the International Federation. The International Federation of Clinical Neurophysiology. *Electroencephalogr. Clin. Neurophysiol. Suppl.* **1999**, *52*, 3–6. [PubMed]
52. Dimond, S.J.; Farrington, L.; Johnson, P. Differing emotional response from right and left hemispheres. *Nature* **1976**, *261*, 690–692. [CrossRef]
53. Davidson, R.J.; Ekman, P.; Saron, C.D.; Senulis, J.A.; Friesen, W.V. Approach-withdrawal and cerebral asymmetry: Emotional expression and brain physiology: I. *J. Personal. Soc. Psychol.* **1990**, *58*, 330–341. [CrossRef]

Disclaimer/Publisher's Note: The statements, opinions and data contained in all publications are solely those of the individual author(s) and contributor(s) and not of MDPI and/or the editor(s). MDPI and/or the editor(s) disclaim responsibility for any injury to people or property resulting from any ideas, methods, instructions or products referred to in the content.

Article

A Study of Reciprocal Job Recommendation for College Graduates Integrating Semantic Keyword Matching and Social Networking

Jinping Yao [1,*], Yunhong Xu [1] and Jiaojiao Gao [2]

[1] Faculty of Management and Economics, Kunming University of Science and Technology, Kunming 650093, China; xhyy6681@163.com
[2] Business Administration, Southwest JiaoTong University, Chengdu 611700, China; gaojj66@163.com
* Correspondence: jinpingy287@163.com

Abstract: With the surge in college graduate numbers, a disparity has emerged where the supply of jobs falls short of demand, intensifying employment pressures annually. College graduates, due to their lack of historical employment data compared with job seekers in the broader society, encounter a 'cold start' issue in the job recommendation process. Additionally, the nature of job recommendations, which differs fundamentally from unilateral recommendations, requires consideration of reciprocity between both parties involved. This article introduces a new approach to job recommendations using college graduates as the object of study. In the screening stage, a semantic keyword iterative algorithm is applied to compute the similarity between the resume and recruitment texts. This algorithm enhances the intersectionality of keywords in the calculation process, maximizing the utilization of resume information to enhance the accuracy of text similarity calculations. The ranking phase utilizes in-school data to build a social network between college graduates and graduated students and solves the system's cold-start problem using the social network to recommend jobs for college graduates where graduated students are employed. We introduce a dual-dimensional matching approach that incorporates both specialty and salary, building upon the amalgamated semantic keyword iterative algorithm and the social network job recommendation method, to enhance the reciprocity of job recommendations. The job recommendation method introduced herein outperforms other methods in terms of the average satisfaction rate (AR) and normalized discounted cumulative gain (NDCG), thereby confirming its superior ability to meet the job-seeking preferences of graduates and the recruitment criteria of employers. This job recommendation method offers effective assistance to graduates lacking employment experience and historical employment data, facilitating their search for more suitable job opportunities.

Keywords: job recommendation; semantic keyword matching; reciprocity; social networks; college graduates

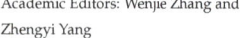

Citation: Yao, J.; Xu, Y.; Gao, J. A Study of Reciprocal Job Recommendation for College Graduates Integrating Semantic Keyword Matching and Social Networking. *Appl. Sci.* **2023**, *13*, 12305. https://doi.org/10.3390/app132212305

Academic Editors: Wenjie Zhang and Zhengyi Yang

Received: 25 October 2023
Revised: 10 November 2023
Accepted: 12 November 2023
Published: 14 November 2023

Copyright: © 2023 by the authors. Licensee MDPI, Basel, Switzerland. This article is an open access article distributed under the terms and conditions of the Creative Commons Attribution (CC BY) license (https://creativecommons.org/licenses/by/4.0/).

1. Introduction

The advancement of higher education has facilitated an expansion in student enrollment within colleges and universities, consequently leading to a yearly increase in the number of graduates. According to statistics, the number of college graduates in China for the year 2023 reached 11.58 million, which represents a year-on-year growth of 820,000. This substantial influx of new graduates has entered the job market, intensifying the competition for employment [1,2]. Concurrently, some graduates encounter challenges due to undefined employment goals, decision-making difficulties, and information overload [3,4]. These factors contribute to a decline in the overall employment rate. To assist graduates in securing employment, colleges offer career guidance; however, tailored recommendations for individual cases are often lacking [5]. Current job search platforms predominantly cater to social job seekers, while the exploration and implementation of personalized recommendations for graduates remain underdeveloped. Additionally, given the multitude of majors and diverse employment fields, providing tailored job recommendations for graduates becomes a more intricate challenge [6]. The following issues afflict the current job recommendation methodology: (a) The content-based approach heavily depends on semantic matching technology, while the current technology still faces limitations in understanding and extracting semantics. This results in poor accuracy when calculating the relevance of resumes to jobs. (b) Collaborative filtering-based methods rely on user behavioral data to model interest preferences, but the sparsity of user data for first-time graduates makes it challenging to accurately capture their interests. (c) The specific group of graduates differs from the richness of historical behavioral data that social users have, and the system faces the cold-start problem, thus limiting the effectiveness of the recommendation model.

In addressing the aforementioned issues, this study proposes an enhanced semantic matching algorithm. This algorithm uses keyword expansion and iterative computation to prevent the loss of semantic information when calculating the similarity between a resume and job text. Building upon this foundation and leveraging the social network relationships among graduates, personalized suggestions are deduced by relying on the recommendation results of similar users. This approach aims to address the cold-start problem in graduate recommendations and provide accurate and reliable recommendation results. The approach integrates information from both semantic and social network dimensions, with the goal of enhancing the performance of graduate job recommendation methods. Moreover, this article emphasizes professional matching and salary matching, aspects of considerable concern for both parties in job search and recruitment. It incorporates the calculation of dimensions related to "professional matching and salary matching," thereby further fortifying the reciprocity of job recommendations.

2. Related Works
2.1. Research on Job Recommendation Based on Keyword Matching

The keyword matching-based job recommendation method is fundamentally a content-based approach. It uncovers job seeker preferences and job recruitment requirements by extracting keywords and calculating the similarity between them, ultimately generating a list of job recommendations. Bansal [7] utilized an LDA model to extract keywords for mining job seekers' preferences and recommending optimal jobs. Lacic [8] used a self-encoder architecture to encode a job seeker's session within the session domain and used k-nearest neighbor methods for inference, analyzing potential jobs to provide recommendations. While keyword matching has advantages over traditional methods, it also faces limitations in semantic matching and effectively processing sparse texts. For instance, the Boolean search-based model utilizes a keyword-matching technique to align job posting requirements with the qualification information from the user's resume. However, this model encounters semantic extraction limitations [9]. Moreover, the limited information in resumes and recruitment texts challenges the effective extraction of job seekers' personality preferences. This has led to the development of behavioral preference models for users, constructed with the collection of their implicit data, and these models are used to recommend jobs that satisfy users' preferences [10]. On this foundation, the development of constructing user profiles by analyzing the behavioral data of job seekers on e-recruitment platforms to extract personality preferences, with the aim of establishing a unidirectional job recommendation model for job seekers, began to unfold [11]. At present, the keyword matching used in job recommendation involves extracting keywords from text for a basic match. However, the information within the job seeker's resume is limited, resulting in the extraction of fewer keywords. This limitation impedes the accurate alignment of resume information with recruitment details, thereby lowering the accuracy and satisfaction levels of job recommendations. In addition, the current keyword matching does not start from semantic matching and reciprocal matching [12].

2.2. Research on Job Recommendations Based on Social Networks

Social networks are essentially the fusion of social elements and network structures, representing virtual networks established with the primary intent of facilitating social interaction [13,14]. In the era of the Internet's evolution, numerous third-party suites have been integrated into social networking platforms, enhancing the diversity and integration of these social platforms. The integration of job recommendations with social networks is intended to assist job seekers in identifying more suitable and satisfying employment opportunities [15–17]. Integrating social networks into the process of generating job recommendations not only diminishes operational costs but also enhances the precision of job recommendations [15]. With his research, Alejandro [18] illustrates that engaging in recruiting and job searching on social networks can effectively address issues such as the low accuracy of job recommendations stemming from sparse user data. Zhao et al. [19] introduced an algorithm that leverages academic social networks to facilitate job transitions by extracting data from publications, a method that not only preserves privacy but also addresses the issue of data sparsity. Job recommendation methods established on career-oriented social networks exhibit superior performance in suggesting satisfactory jobs for job seekers by effectively capturing their preferences [20]. Moreover, disseminating job postings via social networking platforms and suggesting vacancies to friends within social networks can significantly enhance the accuracy of recommendations [21]. The greater the activity level of social network users and the extent of their contacts, the higher the precision of job recommendations [22]. Social networks not only facilitate efficient job searching for job seekers but also assist employers in identifying more suitable candidates for recruitment. Social networks can furnish more dependable hiring references for recruiting employers, as they commonly utilize platforms like Facebook to acquire information about potential candidates [23]. Given that information posted on social networks, such as Facebook, is typically personal rather than professional, employers can form a more precise assessment of a candidate's character [24]. While the integration of social networks can enhance the effectiveness of job recommendations, college graduates, as newcomers in the workplace, often lack a well-established professional social circle. Hence, there is significant research significance in integrating the academic data of college graduates with the employment information of graduated students to establish a social network for college graduates, thereby facilitating the recommendation of satisfactory job opportunities for them.

2.3. Research on Job Recommendations Based on Reciprocity

Reciprocal recommendation is to provide recommendations based on the common preferences of both users [25]. Reciprocal recommendations have been successfully used in various domains, including online dating systems [26], online mentoring systems [26], and online recruitment systems [27]. Reciprocity-based job recommendation implies that the recommended job not only aligns with the preferences of the job seeker but also meets the requirements and preferences of the recruiter [12,28]. To achieve reciprocity in job recommendation, existing research predominantly uses distinct recommendation methods tailored to the characteristics of diverse users. For instance, Malinowski [28] devised two job recommendation systems tailored to the distinct preferences of both job seekers and recruiters, effectively addressing the requirements of each party. Li [29] proposes a job guidance system for college students that integrates ideological and political education with a recommendation algorithm. This algorithm aggregates the preferences and needs of both students and employers to enhance the reciprocity of job recommendations. A job recommender system that utilizes latent factors derived from the explicit profile information of both job seekers and jobs can achieve notable reciprocity [30,31]. Integrating hybrid recommendation methods with reciprocal approaches can further refine the precision of job recommendations. For instance, using Support Vector Machine (SVM) predictive modeling to estimate the likelihood of a company's response to an application, within a hybrid recommendation method that integrates content and collaborative filtering, can enhance the accuracy of job recommendations [32]. These personalized job recommendation systems take into account the mutual preferences of both job seekers and recruiters, overcoming the limitations of reciprocal recommendations and thereby increasing the success rate. However, the evaluation is solely focused on the accuracy of one-way recommendation results and does not provide a side-by-side comparison with other one-way job recommendation methods.

2.4. The Application of Job Recommendation in the Field of Colleges

Currently, established personalized employment platforms, such as 'Wisdom Link Recruitment Network' and '58job', target social users. Nevertheless, the research and application of job recommendations tailored specifically for college graduates are limited. There exist collaborative filtering-based job recommendation algorithms that cluster graduates based on their characteristics and recommend jobs in line with their preferences [33]. Moreover, content-based job recommendation algorithms utilize historical employment data to determine the relevance between graduates and jobs, offering targeted job recommendations [34]. However, these algorithms tend to produce recommendations with a limited focus, which may not be suitable for suggesting a wide range of job types. To address this, Shi [35] proposes to integrate key technologies, such as graduate feature technology, similarity algorithms, and neighbor selection mechanisms, to establish a graduate employment recommendation system, with the aim of broadening the scope of recommendation results. Li [36] combines recommendation and machine learning algorithms to match and optimize job options for college students based on their major types, interests, specialties, preferred employment areas, and other job-related characteristics. This integration improves the diversity and satisfaction of job recommendations simultaneously. Assudani [37] underscores the difficulties in expanding job recommendation diversity and creating a multi-category job database as significant obstacles in the recommendation process. Leveraging existing campus employment portals has become a novel research focus for recommending suitable graduate candidates to companies from the recruiter's perspective. Given that college graduates, as newcomers to the job recommendation system, lack historical behavioral data, the system faces difficulty in capturing graduates' job search preferences [10,35]. Thus, job recommendation research for college graduates could utilize campus data to better understand their job search preferences and suggest more fulfilling employment opportunities.

3. Proposed Job Recommendation Method

The job recommendation model comprises three distinct phases, as illustrated in Figure 1. In the screening stage, a semantic keyword iterative algorithm calculates the text similarity between resumes and job postings, which is then used to filter the pool of potential jobs. The second stage is the ranking stage, in which entropy aggregation is conducted using three dimensions: professional similarity, salary matching, and social network. Based on the calculated values, the set of job recommendations is determined, and subsequently, the jobs are returned to college graduates for scoring. The final evaluation stage measures the satisfaction and reciprocity of the job recommendation results using metrics such as average satisfaction (AR) and normalized discounted cumulative gain (NDCG).

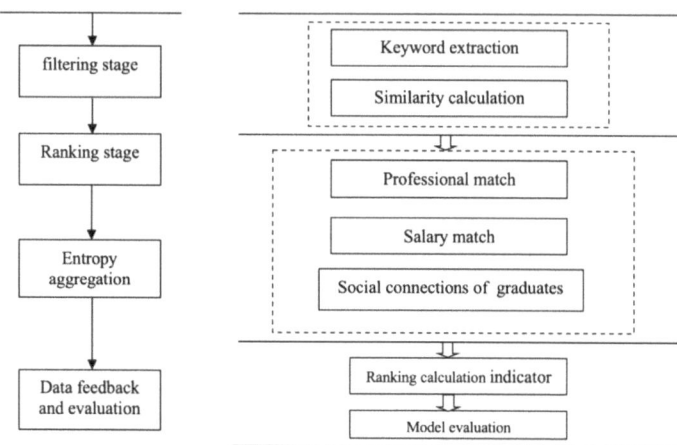

Figure 1. Job recommendation model framework.

3.1. Screening Phase

3.1.1. Text Information Extraction and Processing Filtering Stage

Examples of resume texts of college graduates and job recruitment texts are presented in Tables 1 and 2, respectively. The resume text includes essential information, such as gender, hometown, graduation college, major, research direction, and job preferences. The job recruitment text encompasses details on job positions, workplaces, salary levels, and company nature (state-owned or private enterprises), as well as academic, skill, and professional requirements.

Table 1. Resume information of a logistics graduate.

Logistics Graduate Resume Information	
Name: Zhang	Expected salary CNY: 3000–5000
Gender: Female	Expected work location: Southwest
Graduate school: xx university, logistics engineering	Desired position: engaged in logistics-related work
Research direction: supply chain management supervisor: Li xx	Expected working environment: office environment; corporate culture; work prospects; and so on
Address: Kunming, Yunnan Province	

Table 2. Job recruitment Information.

Job Recruitment Information	
Recruitment company: xxx	Education requirements: graduate degree or above
Salary level CNY: 5000–6000	English level: College English Level 6
Job responsibilities: manage supply chain; cost control	Job requirements: applicants are logistics-related majors, supply chain research direction is preferred, candidates should be skilled in using matlab software, and so on
Working environment: office environment; corporate culture; employment prospects...	
Working location: Kunming, Yunnan	

In this study, the Jieba precise mode was used to perform word segmentation on both the resume and job recruitment texts. To enhance the precision of word segmentation, specialized vocabulary related to a profession was incorporated. We removed punctuation marks and stop words from the texts. Then, Term Frequency-Inverse Document Frequency (TFIDF) values were calculated, and keywords were extracted based on these values.

3.1.2. The Semantic Keyword Iterative Algorithm

Quattrone et al. [38] pointed out that traditional similarity calculation methods, such as cosine similarity, suffer from low utility when dealing with sparse data. Traditional methods rely solely on word frequency to calculate text similarity, making them susceptible to discarding keywords with low frequency, thus resulting in reduced calculation accuracy [38,39]. In light of the sparse data and lack of historical information for college graduates as new users of job recommendation systems, this study uses a semantic keyword iterative algorithm. This algorithm leverages a keyword correlation matrix to calculate text similarity, thereby countering the accuracy issues associated with low-frequency keywords. This approach enhances the accuracy of the job recommendation system, enabling it to provide more reliable recommendations to college graduates, despite their limited historical data.

The keyword correlation matrix is calculated using Equations (1)–(5). First, the TFIDF algorithm was used to calculate the 'keyword-text' matrix, referred to as the KD matrix. KD is an $n_k \times n_d$ matrix, where n_k represents the number of keywords, n_d represents the number of texts, and KD represents the number of times the keyword appears in the text; for example, KD_{im} represents the number of times the keyword k_i appears in the text D_m.

The keyword correlation matrix is calculated based on the KD matrix. The specific calculation process is as follows:

Step 1:

$$sk^0(k_m, k_n) = \theta_{mn}, \ sd^0(d_m, d_n) = \delta_{mn} \qquad (1)$$

The first step is to define the initial similarity value of the keyword $sk^0(k_m, k_n)$ and the text $sd^0(d_m, d_n)$. The principle of definition is that each keyword or text is the same as itself and has certain differences from other keywords and texts. $sk^0(k_m, k_n)$ represents the initial similarity value between keywords k_m and k_n, and $sd^0(d_m, d_n)$ represents the initial similarity value between text d_m and d_n.

Step n:

$$sk^n(k_m, k_n) = \frac{SKK^n(k_m, k_n)}{\sqrt{SKK^n(k_m, k_m)} \cdot \sqrt{SKK^n(k_n, k_n)}} \qquad (2)$$

$$sd^n(d_m, d_n) = \frac{SDD^n(d_m, d_n)}{\sqrt{SDD^n(d_m, d_m)} \cdot \sqrt{SDD^n(d_n, d_n)}} \qquad (3)$$

where $sk^n(k_m, k_n)$ represents the similarity value between keywords k_m and k_n in the nth iteration, and $sd^n(d_m, d_n)$ represents the similarity value between text d_m and d_n in the nth iteration. The definitions of $SKK^n(k_m, k_n)$ and $SDD^n(d_m, d_n)$ are given in Equations (4) and (5):

Where

$$SKK^n(k_m, k_n) = \sum_{i,j=1}^{n_d} KD_{mi} \cdot \varphi_{ij} \cdot sd^{n-1}(d_i, d_j) \cdot KD_{nj} \qquad (4)$$

$$SDD^n(d_m, d_n) = \sum_{i,j=1}^{n_k} KD_{im} \cdot \varphi_{ij} \cdot sk^{n-1}(k_i, k_j) \cdot KD_{jn} \qquad (5)$$

The calculated value of $SKK^n(k_m, k_n)$ in step n must be incorporated into the text similarity calculation of $sd^{n-1}(d_i, d_j)$ in step $(n-1)$. The calculated value of $SDD^n(d_m, d_n)$ in step n must be incorporated into the keyword similarity calculation of $sk^{n-1}(k_i, k_j)$ in step $(n-1)$, and the iterative calculation is carried out in turn. KD_{mi}, KD_{nj}, KD_{im}, and KD_{jn} in Equations (4) and (5) are elements of the KD matrix. φ_{ij} is the mutual reinforcement factor. When keywords k_i and k_j represent the same document, the mutual reinforcement factor $\varphi_{ij} = 1$. In the other cases, the value range of φ_{ij} is (0,1). The value of φ_{ij} was experimentally obtained. In this study, the best result was obtained when $\varphi_{ij} = 0.4$.

To further address the issue of data sparsity, the resume text of graduates was expanded with additional keywords. Specifically, the two most similar keywords, excluding those already present in the resume text, were added to enhance their content. This expanded resume text was then used to match the job recruitment text. A keyword relevance matrix was obtained using the iterative process described above. Finally, the match degree (MD) between the graduates' resume text and the job recruitment text was calculated using Equation (6).

$$MD(s_n, w_m) = \sum_{i=1}^{n_k} TF_{s_n}(k_i) \cdot TF_{w_m}(k_i) \cdot sin(k_i) \tag{6}$$

where n_k indicates the number of extended-resume document keywords. $TF_{ks_n}(i)$ represents the frequency score of keyword i in the nth resume document, and $TF_{kw_m}(i)$ represents the frequency score of keyword i in the mth job document. $sin(i)$ is a parameter used to determine whether the keyword in the resume document is the original keyword. When $sin(i) = 1$, i is the original keyword in the document. When i is a rich keyword, the value of $sin(i)$ is equal to the calculated value of the keyword correlation matrix. The candidate working set was obtained according to the similarity value calculated using the keyword correlation matrix.

3.2. Ranking Stage

In employment, the degree of professional alignment between job seekers and job positions is a crucial factor influencing job search outcomes. With the growing gap between job availability and the demand for skilled workers, employers are emphasizing professional compatibility between job roles and candidates [36]. Rational choice theory posits that individuals are rational decision-makers who weigh the costs and potential benefits when arriving at decisions [40]. Researchers, such as Jung et al. [41], have used the potential Dirichlet distribution method online to extract themes from a substantial volume of employee comments, and their analysis has highlighted salary as a pivotal factor influencing job satisfaction. Hence, salary alignment emerges as a significant determinant affecting the satisfaction of job recommendations. Regular equivalence theory, a fundamental doctrine within communication theory, posits that an individual's behavior is influenced by the information, attitudes, and actions of others within a network [37]. When two individuals share more common social circles, their behavioral preferences tend to exhibit greater similarity, fostering a propensity to establish connections [42]. Thus, this study applies social networks in recommending jobs to recent college graduates, drawing on the employment decisions of alumni to effectively enhance satisfaction and reciprocity in job recommendations.

In the ranking stage, this study used three critical dimensions: professional matching, salary matching, and social network, to perform entropy-based aggregation. The recommended job set is generated by calculating the entropy aggregation. Professional matching assesses the compatibility between college graduates' skills and qualifications and the requirements specified in job postings. Salary matching evaluates the level of correspondence between the expected salary of college graduates and the actual salary offered by the employing companies. Social networks analyze the social connections and relationships between college graduates and other graduate students, taking into consideration potential networking opportunities or affiliations that may influence job recommendations.

3.2.1. Professional Matching

First, random walk probability was used to calculate the connection between graduated students and work, and then the professional matching score between the target and graduated students was calculated. We organized all the professional attributes of the job, job, and graduated students into a graphic $G(V, E)$. Professional job attributes include professional skills. In the figure, V_{pt} represents the set of nodes of the graduated students, V_w represents the set of working nodes, and V_{watt} represents the set of professional attribute nodes of the work, that is, $V = V_{pt} + V_w + V_{watt}$, as shown in Figures 2 and 3.

Figure 2 depicts the initial correlation, which represents the graduated student node and its associated job node without any inserted edges. Starting with wandering, the edges connecting the node $s_p{}'$ of the graduated student and the node w_q of the signed job of this graduate are inserted, as illustrated in Figure 3. The next step is to randomly travel from the graduated student node $s_p{}'$ and, according to the probability ∂, decide whether to continue to travel or stop this travel to return to the starting node s_p'. Based on the above principle, if every job and job specialty attribute node is visited, the probability will converge to a number, and then the edge of the graduated student node to the job node will be removed.

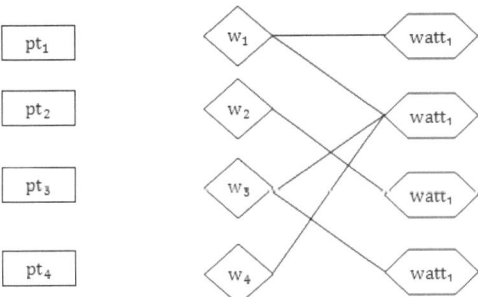

Figure 2. Initial correlation model.

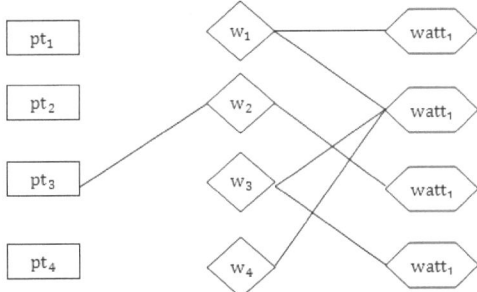

Figure 3. Correlation model.

The algorithm terminates once every starting node s_p' has been visited; if not, the random walk proceeds from the initial graduated student node. In this study, the value of ∂ is set to 0.7 based on experimental findings, and the calculation formula is defined as follows:

$$PR(r) = \begin{cases} \partial \sum_{r' \in in(r)} \frac{PR(r')}{|out(r')|} & (r \neq s_p') \\ (1-\partial) + \partial \sum_{r' \in in(r)} \frac{PR(r')}{|out(r')|} & (r = s_p') \end{cases} \quad (7)$$

where $PR(r)$ denotes the probability of visiting node r, $PR(r')$ denotes the probability of r' being visited, and ∂ denotes the probability of random wandering. $out(r')$ denotes the set of nodes pointing from r', and $in(r)$ denotes the set of nodes pointing to node r. $PR(s_p', w_q)$ denotes the probability that the start node s_p' visits job node w_q. If w_q is a job signed by the graduated student s_p', then $PR(s_p', w_q) = 1$.

The professional matching value between the graduate student s_p' and the graduate s_p is calculated using Equation (8).

$$sim(s_p, s_p') = \frac{|tr_p \cap TR_p|}{|tr_p| + |TR_p|} \quad (8)$$

where $sim(s_p, s_p')$ represents the professional matching value between college graduates and graduate students. tr_p denotes the set of specialized attributes of college graduate p, and TR_p denotes the set of specialized attributes of graduated student s_p'. The wandering probability, starting with the graduate most similar to the college graduate, is considered the specialty match value. For example, if the match value between s_3' and s_2 is the highest, then the wandering probability with graduated students s_3' as the starting node is used as the professional match value for college graduates s_2.

3.2.2. Salary Matching

In this study, salary matching is conducted using a two-dimensional Euclidean metric that considers the job's average and maximum salary against the graduate's desired entry and incentive salary. The average salary is the monthly pay received by an employee, while the maximum salary is the highest amount offered by the company. Entry-level salary refers to the minimum salary required for college graduates, and incentive salary refers to the maximum salary desired by college graduates. The job's average and maximum salaries are viewed as a two-dimensional point $\alpha = (x_w, y_w)$, where x_w represents the average salary for the job, and y_w represents the maximum salary for the job. Similarly, the graduate's entry and incentive salaries are viewed as two-dimensional points $\beta = (x_s, y_s)$, where x_s denotes the entry salary and y_s denotes the incentive salary.

$$dis(\alpha, \beta) = \sqrt[2]{(x_w - x_s)^2 + (y_w - y_s)^2} \tag{9}$$

$$if : (x_w - x_s) < 0, default(x_w - x_s)^2 = 0 \tag{10}$$

$$if : (y_w - y_s) < 0, default(y_w - y_s)^2 = 0 \tag{11}$$

The value of $x_w - x_s$ defaults to zero when the average salary of the job is lower than the entry salary expected by college graduates. Similarly, the value of $y_w - y_s$ defaults to zero when the maximum salary of the job is lower than the incentive salary desired by college graduates. When choosing a job, college graduates look at the average and highest salary of the job with a bias, so when calculating the weight, δ is added to improve the accuracy of the calculation, and the value of δ ranges from 0 to 1. In this study, δ is experimentally set to 0.6, and is calculated as follows:

$$dis(\alpha, \beta) = \sqrt[2]{(x_w - x_s)^2 \cdot \delta + (y_w - y_s)^2 \cdot (1 - \delta)} \tag{12}$$

3.2.3. Social Relationship

Interactive behaviors such as contacting and interacting between college graduates and those who have graduated can constitute a social network structure. In this paper, social networks between college graduates and graduated students are quantified using the "common friend set" and "intersection group" metrics. The common friends set pertains to the friends shared by college graduates and graduated students from the same hometown and college. The common intersection group refers to individuals with the same major and tutor. To account for differences in economic and consumption levels across cities, grouping based on hometown helps minimize variations in the salary requirements of graduates. Moreover, if a college graduate and a graduated student share the same major and mentor, it indicates a high degree of similarity in research interests and, consequently, job search preferences. This study also accounts for the potential impact of the annual economic climate on employment by incorporating the timing of graduation into the job recommendation process.

$$< s_p : f_1, f_2, f_3 \cdots >, < s_p' : f_1', f_2', f_3', \cdots > \tag{13}$$

$$< s_p : g_1, g_2, g_3 \cdots >, < s_p' : g_1', g_2', g_3', \cdots > \tag{14}$$

$$c\left(s_p, s_p'\right) = \left(\sum_{p=1}^{n_f} x_p y_p' + \sum_{q=1}^{n_g} x_q y_q'\right) \cdot \frac{1}{|T - T'|} \tag{15}$$

Equation (13) represents the social network common friend set of college graduate s_p and graduated student s'_p. Equation (14) represents the common intersection group of college graduates s_p and graduated students s'_p. $\sum_{p=1}^{n_f} x_p y'_p$ represents the summation of the number of common friends between college graduates and graduated students, and $\sum_{q=1}^{n_g} x_q y'_q$ represents the summation of the common intersection group of college graduates and graduated students. n_f represents the total number of friends of the college graduates and graduated students. If f_p is a friend of college graduate s_p, x_p equals one; otherwise, it equals zero. If f_p is also a friend of a graduated student s'_p, y'_p equals 1; otherwise, it equals 0. $|T - T'|$ denotes the time difference between graduation time T of college graduates and graduation time T' of graduated students.

3.2.4. Entropy Aggregation

Entropy aggregation is used to convert professional match values, salary match values, and social networks into a decision matrix, which is computed to produce a recommended job set. The calculation process is illustrated in Figure 4.

$$A = \begin{bmatrix} a_{11} & a_{12} & a_{13} \\ a_{21} & a_{22} & a_{23} \\ \vdots & \vdots & \vdots \\ a_{n1} & a_{n2} & a_{n3} \end{bmatrix} \quad (16)$$

where n in the above matrix represents a total of n jobs, and a_{ij} represents the score value of the ith job in the jth column. There are three columns in the matrix: professional, salary, and social relationships. Decision matrix A is obtained using entropy aggregation. The decision matrix is normalized to obtain matrix B. Finally, the entropy values are obtained using Equations (17)–(19).

$$B = \begin{bmatrix} b_{11} & b_{12} & b_{13} \\ b_{21} & b_{22} & b_{23} \\ \vdots & \vdots & \vdots \\ b_{n1} & b_{n2} & b_{n3} \end{bmatrix} \quad (17)$$

$$E_j = -\frac{\left(\sum_{i=1}^{n} b_{ij} \ln b_{ij}\right)}{\ln n} \quad (18)$$

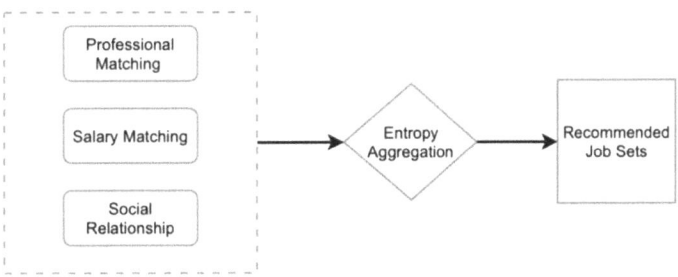

Figure 4. Ranking calculation process.

Let $d_j = 1 - E_j (1 \leq j \leq m)$, where m is the number of column dimensions of the matrix (there are three dimensions in this study: professional matching, salary matching, and social relationship), and the entropy weight of the jth column is obtained using the calculation of Equation (19).

$$w_j = \frac{d_j}{\sum_{j=1}^{m} d_j} \quad (19)$$

Finally, the entropy weights of each column of the work attributes are summarized to obtain the final ranking score FRS_i.

$$FRS_i = \sum_{j=1}^{m} w_j b_{ij} \qquad (20)$$

3.3. Experimental Evaluation

3.3.1. Recommendation Method

To rigorously assess the efficacy of the job recommendation approach proposed in this study, it underwent evaluation and comparison with existing recommendation methods. The description of the recommended method is provided as follows:

TF-C [38]: This method employs cosine similarity to compute the resemblance between the text within a college graduate's resume and the content of the job posting. The system then produces a list of job recommendations based on similarity scores for college graduates to evaluate. The rating scale ranges from 1 (unsatisfactory) to 5 (satisfactory), with a total score of 5.

MS [43]: In the screening stage, a semantic keyword-matching approach is used to evaluate the likeness between the content of the college graduate's resume and the text of the job posting. Subsequently, a list of job recommendations is generated based on similarity and submitted to college graduates for scoring.

GERS [35]: Employment characteristics of graduates are analyzed using a two-dimensional matrix of graduate preferences. Subsequently, the system calculates the similarity between graduates to identify jobs chosen by neighboring graduates, generating a recommendation list.

RSCF [44]: The similarity between graduates' resumes and job descriptions is integrated with a collaborative filtering algorithm based on graduates' similarity to calculate a list of job recommendations. The recommended jobs are then provided to college graduates for scoring.

JRSR: Utilizing the job recommendation method introduced in this paper, the screening stage uses a semantic keyword iterative algorithm to compute the similarity between resume text and recruitment text. In the ranking stage, three dimensions—"professional matching, salary matching, and social network"—are used to generate a set of job recommendations using entropy aggregation. This collection is then returned to college graduates for scoring.

To assess the impact of each dimension of the job recommendation method (JRSR) on the computational method's performance, this study disaggregates the system into its constituent components—semantic keyword matching, professional matching, salary matching, and social networking—and conducts an experimental evaluation of each. RSR omits the semantic keyword-matching method, relying solely on professional alignment, salary comparison, and social network inputs for its calculations. JSR excludes professional alignment, utilizing only semantic keyword matching, salary comparison, and social networks. JRR discards salary comparison, operating with semantic keyword matching, professional alignment, and social networks. In contrast, JRS disregards social networking elements, conducting analyses strictly with semantic keyword matching, professional alignment, and salary matching components. The aforementioned methods were individually applied to the dataset, which comprised 110 target graduates, 320 total graduates, and 280 work samples, to perform calculations, with the recommendation list set at a length of five.

To evaluate the impact of graduates' historical employment information on recommendation performance, this study categorizes the employment data into two sets: one for logistics engineering and another for management and science work samples. Subsequently, the job recommendation method (JRSR) proposed in this study was applied separately to each work sample set, generating two sets of recommendation results. Finally, the performance of the job recommendation method is assessed and compared based on the evaluation results from both sets of work samples.

3.3.2. Evaluation of Indicators

In this study, the recommendation outcomes were evaluated using the average satisfaction rate (AR) and normalized discounted cumulative gain (NDCG). AR was used to assess the average satisfaction of college graduates with recommended jobs. NDCG was used to assess the reciprocity of job referral methods.

The average satisfaction rate (AR) indicator was calculated using the ratings of college graduates for recommended jobs. The calculation formula is as follows:

$$AR@n = \frac{1}{|U|}\sum_{j=1}^{|U|} \frac{1}{|n|}\sum_{i=1}^{n} s_j(i) \tag{21}$$

where $s_j(i)$ represents the rating (on a scale of 1–5) of graduate s_j for job ranked i in the recommendation set. i denotes the ranking of the job in the recommendation set (the rankings are 1, 2, 3, 4, and 5; the value of i is an integer between 1 and 5). N denotes the number of jobs in the recommendation set (the number of recommended jobs in this study was five). $|U|$ is the number of graduates.

The normalized discounted cumulative gain (NDCG) calculates the reciprocity of the recommendation results based on the ranking and rating of the job in the recommendation list. The calculation formula is as follows:

$$NDCG@n = \frac{1}{|U|}\sum_{j=1}^{|U|} \frac{DCG_j@n}{maxDCG_j@n} \tag{22}$$

where

$$DCG_j@n = \sum_{i=1}^{n}\left[\left(2^{s_j(i)} - 1\right)/log(1+i)\right] \tag{23}$$

$$maxDCG_j@n = \sum_{i=1}^{n}\left[\left(2^{s_j(i)} - 1\right)/log(1+e)\right] \tag{24}$$

The i in the equation $DCG_j@n$ represents the rank of the recommended job in the recommendation set; for example, job w_1 is ranked 3 in the recommendation set, and the value of i equals 3. The e in the equation $maxDCG_j@n$ is the ranking from highest to lowest based on the ratings of the college graduates for the recommended jobs. For example, job w_5, where the target graduates rated the lowest and ranked 5; therefore, the value of e is 5. There are a total of five candidate jobs in the recommended list, so the rankings are a total of five places.

4. Analysis and Discussion of Experimental Results

4.1. Experimental Settings

Logistics engineering, management, and science represent a multidisciplinary domain that bridges the realms of management and technology, integrating engineering and scientific principles. It maintains strong connections with fields such as transportation engineering, industrial engineering, computer technology, mechanical engineering, environmental engineering, architecture, and civil engineering. Consequently, this study focuses on graduates in logistics engineering, management, and science, given their versatile qualifications and adaptability. The data on graduates' resumes come from the personal contents of university graduates registered in the university employment program, and the data on job samples come from the information on jobs signed by graduated students at several universities. For the experimental data in this paper, the total number of target graduates is 110, the total number of graduated graduates is 320, and the total number of remaining work samples after screening out the same jobs is 280. All the above data are from the two majors of logistics engineering and management and science. To assess the generalizability of the recommended methods proposed in this paper, additional experimental data is incorporated for comparative evaluation. This paper includes employment data for students who graduated from five colleges in the last five years, encompassing a total of 1200 graduates and 1027 jobs across various majors under the management disciplines of business management, accounting, financial management, marketing, and tourism management.

During the screening stage, a semantic keyword iterative algorithm is used to assess the similarity between the resume text of college graduates and the job recruitment text. In the ranking stage, the top 110 jobs with the highest degree of similarity undergo entropy aggregation, using the three dimensions of "professional matching, salary matching, and social network" to generate a list of job recommendations. Finally, the jobs in the job recommendation list are returned to the college graduates for scoring from 1 (indicating dissatisfaction) to 5 (indicating satisfaction). This rating process serves as the means to evaluate the efficacy of the job recommendation method proposed in this paper.

4.2. Social Network Visualization of Experimental Data

The primary focus of this paper is to investigate the employment situation of students majoring in logistics engineering, management, and science. Therefore, the employment data related to these two majors, including 110 targeted graduates, 320 graduated students, and a total of 280 work samples, were analyzed for data visualization. Figures 5–8 illustrate the percentage distribution of college graduates and graduated hometowns, secondary colleges, majors, and mentors, respectively. The horizontal axis represents the percentage of college graduates in the dataset, while the vertical axis represents the percentage of graduated students in the dataset.

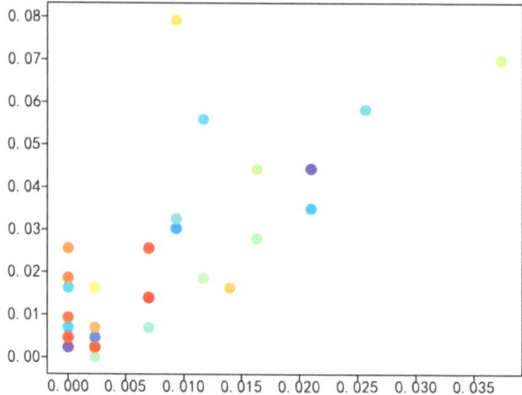

Figure 5. Comparison of high school graduates and graduated students' hometown datasets.

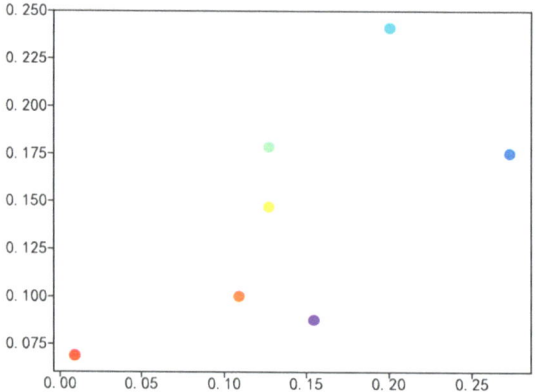

Figure 6. Comparison of high school graduates' and graduated students' secondary college datasets.

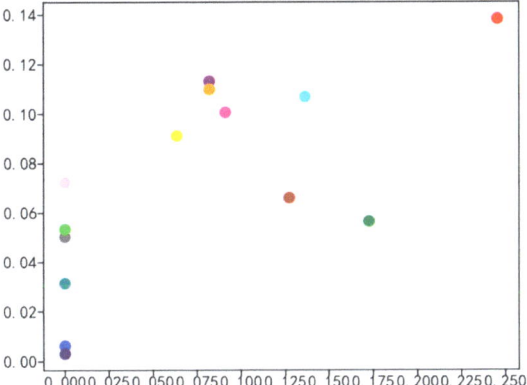

Figure 7. Comparison of high school graduates and graduated students' major datasets.

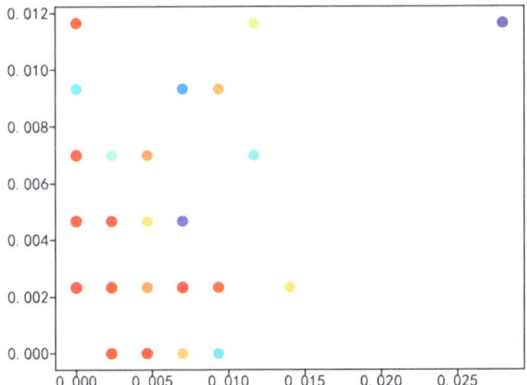

Figure 8. Comparison of high school graduates and graduated students' mentor datasets.

Figures 5–8 illustrate the distribution of hometown, secondary college, major, and advisor proportions for college graduates and graduated students. The horizontal axis represents the percentage of college graduates' hometowns within the dataset of college graduates, while the vertical axis represents the percentage of graduated students' hometowns within the dataset of graduated students. The highest proportion of hometowns in the college graduate dataset is 3.6%, compared with 7% in the graduated student dataset. For the secondary college with the highest proportion in the college graduate dataset, it accounts for 20%, while in the graduated student dataset, it is 24%. The major with the highest proportion in the college graduate dataset is 17.5%, in contrast with 11% in the graduated student dataset. Additionally, the top advisor proportion in the college graduate dataset is 28%, while in the graduated student dataset, it is merely 1.18%. With meticulous data analysis, a notable and substantial social interconnection emerges between college graduates and graduated students, encompassing facets such as hometowns, secondary colleges, majors, and advisors. This interconnectedness serves as the bedrock for cultivating a closely woven social network, which in turn provides the fundamental groundwork for calculating probabilities in the context of random walks.

To analyze the social connections between college graduates and those who already graduated more clearly, this paper subdivides into four dimensions—hometown, secondary college, major, and mentor—to generate a social relationship network, depicted in Figure 9. The analysis demonstrates a strong social connection across the four dimensions of hometowns, secondary colleges, majors, and mentors between college graduates and graduated students. This emphasizes the viability of utilizing social networks to facilitate the recommendation of job opportunities endorsed by graduated students to college graduates.

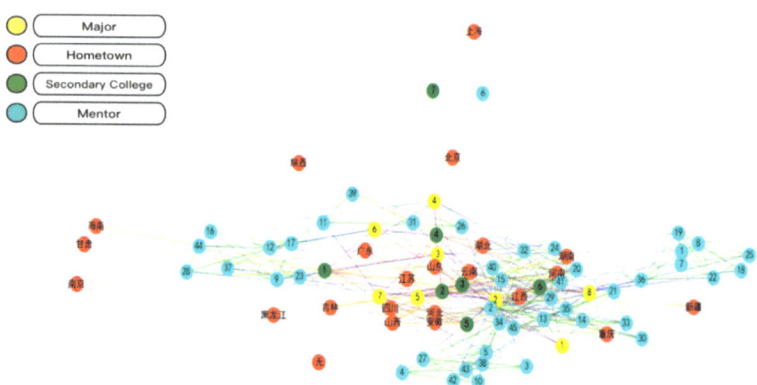

Figure 9. Social network for college graduates and graduated students.

4.3. Result Analysis

This article uses five job recommendation methods (TF-C, MS, GERS, RSCF, JRSR) to compute the recommended work set and subsequently conducts an analysis of the outcomes utilizing evaluation metrics.

4.3.1. Evaluation Analysis of the Average Satisfaction Rate

Figure 10 presents a comparative chart illustrating the average satisfaction rates among the five job recommendation methods. The graph clearly indicates that JRSR attains a notably higher average satisfaction rate when contrasted with the remaining four job recommendation methods. Among these five approaches, TF-C demonstrates the lowest average satisfaction rate, registering at a mere 2.631. Meanwhile, the average satisfaction rates for the other three job recommendation methods, namely, MS, GERS, and RSCF, exhibit relatively close values. The job recommendation method introduced in this paper, JRSR, records an average satisfaction rate of 3.743. In comparison to the four benchmark methods, it showcases a maximum improvement of 1.112 and a minimum improvement of 0.502. This compellingly suggests that the job recommendation method presented in this study, JRSR, excels in discerning the job preferences of college graduates, ultimately resulting in more gratifying job recommendations.

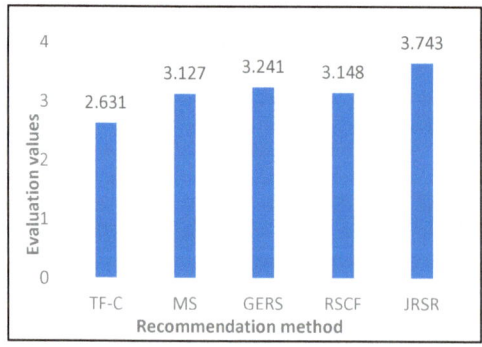

Figure 10. Average satisfaction rate.

The experimental data in this paper were non-normally distributed. To test for a significant difference in the AR@5 assessment values of the JRSR, TF-C, MS, GERS, and RSCF methods, the Wilcoxon signed-rank test was used. As indicated in Table 3 ($p < 0.05$), there is a significant difference between the assessed values of JRSR and the other four methods.

Table 3. Wilcoxon signed rank test for AR@5.

Recommendation Model	TF-C	MS	GERS	RSCF
JRSR	0.000	0.000	0.000	0.000

4.3.2. Evaluation Analysis of Normalized Discounted Cumulative Gain

Figure 11 illustrates the results of normalized discounted cumulative gain (NDCG@5) for the five job recommendation methods. The graph clearly demonstrates that among these methods, JRSR attains the highest NDCG@5 score, reaching 0.938. Among the four benchmark methods, TF-C achieves the lowest NDCG@5 score at 0.675, while GERS reaches the highest score at 0.859. When compared with TF-C and GERS, the proposed JRSR method exhibits a remarkable improvement in NDCG@5, with enhancements of 38.96% and 9.19%, respectively. This emphasizes the effectiveness of the JRSR job recommendation method presented in this paper in aligning the preferences and requirements of college graduates with job opportunities.

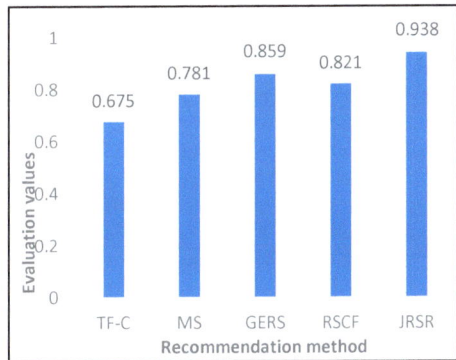

Figure 11. Normalized discounted cumulative gain.

The experimental data were non-normally distributed. In this paper, the Wilcoxon signed-rank test was used to assess whether there was a significant difference in the NDCG@5 assessment values of the JRSR, TF-C, MS, GERS, and RSCF methods. As evident in Table 4, with $p < 0.05$, there is a significant difference between the assessment values of JRSR and the other four methods.

Table 4. Wilcoxon signed rank test for NDCG@5.

Recommendation Model	TF-C	MS	GERS	RSCF
JRSR	0.002	0.001	0.000	0.001

4.3.3. Comparative Analysis of the Recommendation Results under Different Job Sample Sets

To assess the impact of historical employment information on recommendation outcomes, this study categorizes the job placements of graduates into two groups: the "Logistics Engineering Job Sample Set" and the "Management and Science Job Sample Set", as illustrated in Figure 12. The AR@5 evaluation score for the Logistics Engineering sample set is 3.728, surpassing that of the Management and Science sample set by 0.467. This indicates a stronger preference among college graduates for jobs closely aligned with their majors. In terms of NDCG@5, the Logistics Engineering sample set achieves a score of 0.971, while the Management and Science sample set scores 0.866, resulting in a 0.105 higher NDCG@5 score for the Logistics Engineering sample set. This demonstrates the potential for major alignment to enhance the mutual effectiveness of job recommendations.

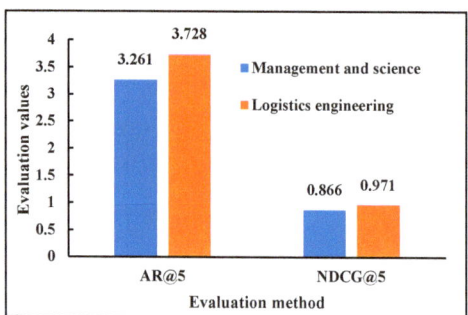

Figure 12. Evaluation results of separate use of historical employment information for the logistics and management section.

4.3.4. Comparative Analysis of Evaluation Values in Different Dimensions

This article dissects each dimension of the job recommendation method (JRSR) to analyze its impact on the system's recommendation performance. The dimensions are individually assessed to calculate the recommendation outcomes, which are then evaluated using the average satisfaction rate and the normalized discounted cumulative gain. Figure 13 reveals that RSR has the lowest average satisfaction rate and normalized discounted cumulative gain, suggesting that dimensionality reduction in the semantic keyword iteration algorithm adversely affects satisfaction and validity. This indicates a superior filtering capability of the semantic keyword iteration algorithm when fully utilized. The data indicate that JRR's average satisfaction rate and normalized discounted cumulative gain are second to last and third to last, respectively, which suggests that salary is a critical concern for graduates during their job search. Conversely, JSR registers the highest values in both average satisfaction rate and normalized discounted cumulative gain, signifying that the alignment of graduates' majors is not a predominant consideration in their employment pursuits.

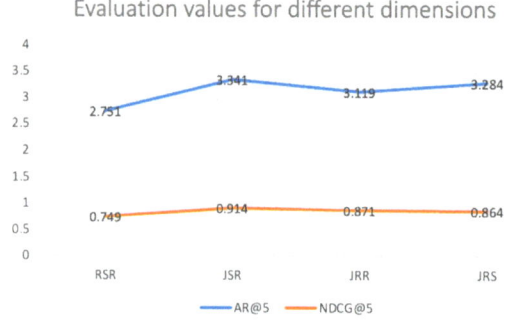

Figure 13. Evaluated values of AR@5 and NDCG@5 for different dimensional approaches.

4.3.5. Comparative Analysis of Evaluated Values for Different Recommendation List Lengths

To assess the performance of job recommendation methods across different sample sizes and recommendation list lengths, this paper expands the experimental sample size and generates recommendation lists of different lengths. The experimental dataset used for this comparative analysis comprises 110 targeted graduates, 1200 graduated students, and 1027 job positions. It encompasses various specializations within the management disciplines, including business management, accounting, financial management, marketing, and tourism management.

By examining Figure 10, Figure 14, and Table 5, it is evident that the assessed values of AR@5 for the five recommended methods exhibited a decline with the augmentation of data. The most substantial decrease occurred in the case of JRSR, dropping from 3.743 to 3.462, which represents a 7.5% reduction. As the length of the recommendation lists increases for the five methods, their AR evaluations correspondingly decrease. In Figure 14, it is evident that the assessed value of AR@20 significantly exceeds that of AR@5, with the MS value-added reaching its peak at 0.301 and the TF-C value-added registering its lowest at 0.114. These findings indicate that both the size of the experimental data sample and the length of the recommendation list directly impact the recommendation satisfaction rate.

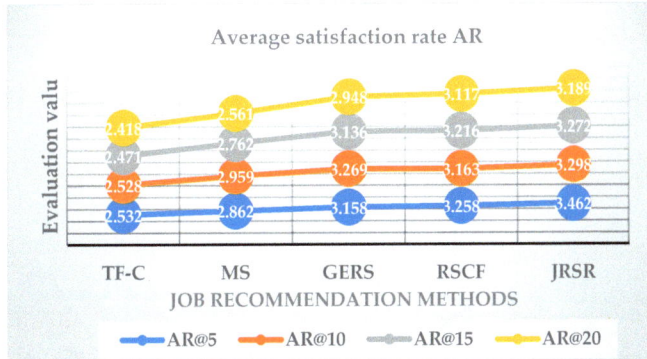

Figure 14. Analysis of AR evaluation values for different recommendation list lengths.

Table 5. AR assessment values for different recommended list lengths.

	AR@5	AR@10	AR@15	AR@20
TF-C	2.532	2.528	2.471	2.418
MS	2.862	2.959	2.762	2.561
GERS	3.158	3.269	3.136	2.948
RSCF	3.258	3.163	3.216	3.117
JRSR	3.462	3.298	3.272	3.189

By examining Figure 11, Figure 15, and Table 6, it is apparent that as the sample size of the experimental data expands, the assessed values of NDCG@5 for the five recommended methods decrease. The most substantial decrease is observed in MS, where it is 0.089, while the smallest decrease is in RSCF, where it is 0.03. Moreover, with the increase in the length of the recommended list, there is a decrease in its NDCG assessment. The most significant decrease is observed for GERS at 12.81%, while the smallest decrease is for MS at 4.9%. These findings indicate that both the size of the experimental data sample and the length of the recommendation list directly impact the normalized discounted cumulative gain assessment value.

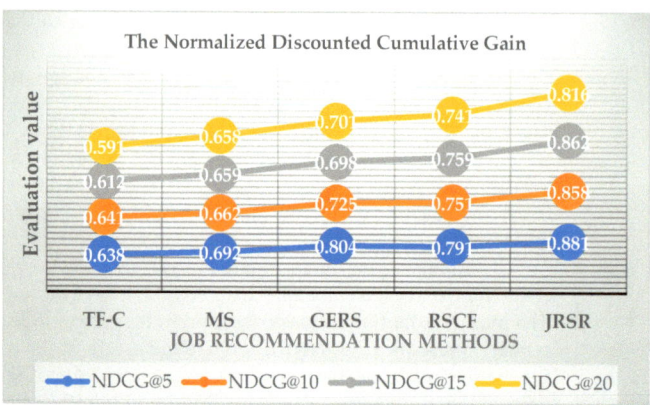

Figure 15. Analysis of NDCG evaluation values for different recommended list lengths.

Table 6. NDCG assessment values for different recommended list lengths.

	NDCG@5	NDCG@10	NDCG@15	NDCG@20
TF-C	0.638	0.641	0.612	0.591
MS	0.692	0.662	0.659	0.658
GERS	0.804	0.725	0.698	0.701
RSCF	0.791	0.751	0.759	0.741
JRSR	0.881	0.858	0.862	0.816

4.4. Discussion

In Figures 10 and 11, both the average satisfaction rate and the normalized discounted cumulative gain (NDCG) of the JRSR job recommendation method, as proposed in this paper, outperform the other four recommendation methods. This robustly underscores the effectiveness and superiority of the JRSR approach in job recommendation. In contrast with the TF-C and MS methods, JRSR uses a keyword iterative calculation approach to determine the similarity between the resume text of college graduates and the job recruitment text. This methodology not only mitigates the problem of neglecting low-frequency keywords but also enhances inter-keyword cross-referencing, resulting in a more robust semantic matching of text similarity. The job recommendation method GERS recommends job selections for graduates by calculating the similarity of employment characteristics among graduates and suggesting the choices of neighboring graduates as pre-recommended items [35]. This method is a collaborative filtering recommendation approach, which narrows down the recommendation scope. However, it simplifies the calculation of similarity in employment characteristics among graduates. In contrast, the JRSR recommendation method, when calculating the similarity in employment characteristics among graduates, establishes a social network based on academic data from graduates. This approach not only effectively computes the similarity in employment characteristics among graduates but also addresses the system cold-start problem caused by a lack of employment data for college graduates. Compared with the recommendation method RSCF, which combines content-based and collaborative filtering approaches [44], the JRSR recommendation method adds dimensions of major matching and salary matching. By using multiple methods and dimensions, JRSR matches the preferences and job requirements of college graduates, thereby enhancing the reciprocity of job recommendations.

The empirical evaluation demonstrates that the job recommendation method introduced in this study exhibits superior performance relative to the benchmark method. Nonetheless, job recommendation for college graduates is a multifaceted and applied discipline, and this study acknowledges certain limitations. (a) While the semantic keyword iterative algorithm enhances the accuracy of text similarity calculations, its iterative nature results in time-consuming processing with large datasets. Future research should, therefore, focus more on improving the scalability of this computational method. (b) The dataset used in this study is not diverse, which limits the consideration of data variability. Consequently, future work will aim to increase the sample size to broaden the assessment indicators. (c) This paper focuses on the two most prevalent employment characteristics, major and salary; future studies should encompass a broader range of employment attributes. (d) This study does not utilize a range of career assessment tools to aid graduates in gaining a more objective and comprehensive understanding of their employment aspirations. Future research could incorporate ideological education to enhance graduates' awareness of their career intentions, thereby improving the overall quality of job recommendations.

5. Conclusions

(a) In response to the issue of low accuracy resulting from the omission of low-frequency keywords during the keyword matching calculation, this study used a text similarity calculation method based on a semantic keyword iteration algorithm during the filtering phase. This method effectively mitigated the problem of discarding low-frequency keywords, thereby enhancing calculation accuracy. This study addressed the issues of major structure matching and salary matching between college graduates and jobs, leading to a significant improvement in job recommendation satisfaction.

(b) For the first time, this study introduces graduate social networks and historical employment information of past graduates. Jobs held by previous graduates are recommended to recent graduates, serving as a strategy to address the cold-start problem of the system. With the augmentation of both the sample size in the experimental data and the length of the job recommendation list, there is a concurrent decrease in the average satisfaction rate (AR) and the normalized discounted cumulative gain (NDCG) of the job recommendation method.

(c) Evaluation based on the average satisfaction rate (AR) and normalized discounted cumulative gain (NDCG) metrics demonstrated that the job recommendation method for college graduates proposed in this study outperforms baseline recommendation methods in terms of recommendation performance.

Author Contributions: Conceptualization, J.Y., Y.X. and J.G.; methodology, J.Y. and Y.X.; software, J.Y.; validation, J.Y., J.G. and Y.X.; formal analysis, J.Y.; investigation, J.Y. and Y.X.; resources, J.Y. and J.G.; data curation, J.Y.; writing—original draft preparation, J.Y.; writing—review and editing, J.Y., J.G. and Y.X.; visualization, J.Y.; supervision, J.Y.; project administration, J.Y. All authors have read and agreed to the published version of the manuscript.

Funding: This work received funding from the National Natural Science Foundation of China (Grant 71861019). This paper solely reflects the views of the authors. The Commission is not responsible for the contents of this paper or any use made thereof.

Institutional Review Board Statement: Not applicable.

Informed Consent Statement: Not applicable.

Data Availability Statement: The datasets generated and analyzed during the current study are available from the corresponding author upon reasonable request.

Conflicts of Interest: The authors declare no conflict of interest.

References

1. Mok, K.H.; Montgomery, C. Remaking higher education for the post-COVID-19 era: Critical reflections on marketization, internationalization and graduate employment. *High. Educ. Q.* **2021**, *75*, 373–380. [CrossRef]
2. Zhao, Y.; He, F.; Feng, Y. Research on the Industrial Structure Upgrading Effect of the Employment Mobility of Graduates from China's "Double First-Class" Colleges and Universities. *Sustainability* **2022**, *14*, 2353. [CrossRef]

3. Liu, H.; Wang, Z. Research on Causes and Countermeasures for the Difference between Employment Expectation and Actual Employment of College Graduates. In Proceedings of the 2016 International Conference on Education, Bangkok, Thailand, 21–22 April 2016.
4. Ntale, P.D.; Ssempebwa, J. Designing Organizations for Collaborative Relationships: The Amenability of Social Capital to Inter-Agency Collaboration in the Graduate Employment Context in Uganda. *Empl. Responsib. Rights J.* **2022**, *34*, 291–318. [CrossRef]
5. Evans, S.; Huxley, P. Factors associated with the recruitment and retention of social workers in Wales: Employer and employee perspectives. *Health Soc. Care Community* **2019**, *17*, 254–266. [CrossRef] [PubMed]
6. Rafter, R.; Bradley, K.; Smyth, B. Personalised Retrieval for Online Recruitment Services. In Proceedings of the BCS/IRSG 22nd Annual Colloquium on Information Retrieval (IRSG 2000), Cambridge, UK, 5–7 April 2000.
7. Bansal, S.; Srivastava, A.; Arora, A. Topic Modeling Driven Content Based Jobs Recommendation Engine for Recruitment Industry. *Procedia Comput. Sci.* **2017**, *122*, 865–872. [CrossRef]
8. Lacic, E.; Reiter-Haas, M.; Kowald, D.; Dareddy, M.R.; Lex, E. Using autoencoders for session-based job recommendations. *User Model. User-Adapt. Interact.* **2020**, *30*, 617–658. [CrossRef]
9. Mostafa, L.; Beshir, S. Job Candidate Rank Approach Using Machine Learning Techniques. In *Advanced Machine Learning Technologies and Applications: Proceedings of AMLTA 2021*; Springer International Publishing: Cham, Switzerland, 2021; pp. 225–233.
10. Reusens, M.; Lemahieu, W.; Baesens, B.; Sels, L. A note on explicit versus implicit information for job recommendation. *Decis. Support Syst.* **2017**, *98*, 26–35. [CrossRef]
11. Rafter, R.; Bradley, K.; Smyth, B. Automated collaborative filtering applications for online recruitment services. In Proceedings of the Adaptive Hypermedia and Adaptive Web-Based Systems: International Conference, AH 2000, Trento, Italy, 28–30 August 2000; Proceedings 1; pp. 363–368.
12. Reusens, M.; Lemahieu, W.; Baesens, B.; Sels, L. Evaluating recommendation and search in the labor market. *Knowl.-Based Syst.* **2018**, *152*, 62–69. [CrossRef]
13. Zhang, Z.J.; Xu, G.W.; Zhang, P.F.; Wang, Y.K. Personalized recommendation algorithm for social networks based on comprehensive trust. *Appl. Intell.* **2017**, *47*, 659–669. [CrossRef]
14. Liu, J.Q.; Fu, L.Y.; Wang, X.B.; Tang, F.L.; Chen, G.H. Joint Recommendations in Multilayer Mobile Social Networks. *IEEE Trans. Mob. Comput.* **2020**, *19*, 2358–2373. [CrossRef]
15. Malherbe, E.; Diaby, M.; Cataldi, M.; Viennet, E.; Aufaure, M.A. Field Selection for Job Categorization and Recommendation to Social Network Users. In Proceedings of the IEEE/ACM International Conference on Advances in Social Networks Analysis and Mining (ASONAM), Beijing, China, 17–20 August 2014; pp. 588–595.
16. Chala, S.; Fathi, M. Job Seeker to Vacancy Matching using Social Network Analysis. In Proceedings of the IEEE International Conference on Industrial Technology (ICIT), Toronto, Canada, 22–25 March 2017; pp. 1250–1255.
17. Urdaneta-Ponte, M.C.; Oleagordia-Ruiz, I.; Mendez-Zorrilla, A. Using LinkedIn Endorsements to Reinforce an Ontology and Machine Learning-Based Recommender System to Improve Professional Skills. *Electronics* **2022**, *11*, 1190. [CrossRef]
18. Corbellini, A.; Mateos, C.; Godoy, D.; Zunino, A.; Schiaffino, S. An architecture and platform for developing distributed recommendation algorithms on large-scale social networks. *J. Inf. Sci. Princ. Pract.* **2015**, *41*, 686–704. [CrossRef]
19. Zhao, R.; Shao, Z.; Zhang, W.; Zhang, J.; Wu, C. A multi-channel multi-tower GNN model for job transfer prediction based on academic social network. *Appl. Soft Comput.* **2023**, *142*, 110300. [CrossRef]
20. Rivas, A.; Channoso, P.; Gonzalez-Briones, A.; Casado-Vara, R.; Manuel Corchado, J. Hybrid job offer recommender system in a social network. *Expert Syst.* **2019**, *36*, e12416. [CrossRef]
21. Van Hoye, G.; Van Hooft, E.A.; Lievens, F. Networking as a job search behaviour: A social network perspective. *J. Occup. Organ. Psychol.* **2009**, *82*, 661–682. [CrossRef]
22. Skeels, M.M.; Grudin, J. When social networks cross boundaries: A case study of workplace use of facebook and linkedin. In Proceedings of the ACM International Conference on Supporting Group Work, Sanibel, FL, USA, 10–13 May 2009; pp. 95–104.
23. Zhitomirsky-Geffet, M.; Bratspiess, Y. Perceived Effectiveness of Social Networks for Job Search. *Libri* **2015**, *65*, 105–118. [CrossRef]
24. Palank, J. Face it:'Book'no secret to employers. *The Washington Times*, 17 July 2006; pp. 1–2.
25. Xia, P.; Liu, B.; Sun, Y.; Chen, C. Reciprocal Recommendation System for Online Dating. In Proceedings of the 2015 IEEE/ACM International Conference on Advances in Social Networks Analysis and Mining, Paris, France, 25–28 August 2015; pp. 234–241.
26. Liu, J.; Li, C.; Huang, Y.; Han, J. An intelligent medical guidance and recommendation model driven by patient-physician communication data. *Front. Public Health* **2023**, *11*, 1098206. [CrossRef]
27. Ullah, Z.; Jamjoom, M. A smart secured framework for detecting and averting online recruitment fraud using ensemble machine learning techniques. *PeerJ Comput. Sci.* **2023**, *9*, e1234. [CrossRef]
28. Jochen, M. Matching people and jobs: A bilateral recommendation approach. In Proceedings of the 39th Annual Hawaii International Conference on System Sciences (HICSS'06), IEEE Computer Society, Kauai, HI, USA, 4–7 January 2006.
29. Huang, L. The Establishment of College Student Employment Guidance System Integrating Artificial Intelligence and Civic Education. *Math. Probl. Eng.* **2022**, *2022*, 3934381. [CrossRef]
30. Jochen, M.; Weitzel, T.; Keim, T. Decision support for team staffing: An automated relational recommendation approach. *Decis. Support Syst.* **2008**, *45*, 429–447.

31. Hong, W.; Zheng, S.; Wang, H.; Shi, J. A job recommender system based on user clustering. *J. Comput.* **2013**, *8*, 1960–1967. [CrossRef]
32. Özcan, G.; Öğüdücü, S.G. Applying different classification techniques in reciprocal job recommender system for considering job candidate preferences. In Proceedings of the 2016 11th International Conference for Internet Technology and Secured Transactions (ICITST), Barcelona, Spain, 5–7 December 2016; IEEE: Piscataway, NJ, USA, 2016; pp. 235–240.
33. Zhou, Q.; Liao, F.L.; Chen, C.; Ge, L. Job recommendation algorithm for graduates based on personalized preference. *CCF Trans. Pervasive Comput. Interact.* **2019**, *1*, 260–274. [CrossRef]
34. Li, S.; Chuancheng, Y.; Hongguo, W.; Yanhui, D. An Employment Recommendation Algorithm Based on Historical Information of College Graduates. In Proceedings of the 2018 9th International Conference on Information Technology in Medicine and Education (ITME), Hangzhou, China, 19–21 October 2018; IEEE: Piscataway, NJ, USA, 2018; pp. 708–711.
35. Shi, S.; Lv, H. A Framework of Graduate Employment Recommendation System and Key Technologies. In Proceedings of the 6th International Conference on Information Engineering for Mechanics & Materials, Huhhot, China, 30–31 July 2016; Atlantis Press: Amsterdam, Netherlands, 2016; pp. 169–174.
36. Li, W. Research on personalised recommendation algorithm for college students' employment. *Appl. Math. Nonlinear Sci.* **2022**. [CrossRef]
37. Assudani, P.J.; Kadu, R.K.; Sheikh, R.; Khanna, T. Smart College Campus Recruitment System. *Int. J. Next-Gener. Comput.* **2022**, *13*, 1280–1285.
38. Quattrone, G.; Capra, L.; De Meo, P.; Ferrara, E.; Ursino, D. Effective retrieval of resources in folksonomies using a new tag similarity measure. In Proceedings of the 20th ACM International Conference on Information and Knowledge Management, Glasgow, UK, 24–28 October 2011; pp. 545–550.
39. Zhang, M.; Ma, J.; Liu, Z.; Sun, J.; Silva, T. A research analytics framework-supported recommendation approach for supervisor selection. *Br. J. Educ. Technol.* **2016**, *47*, 403–420. [CrossRef]
40. Scott, A.J. The Cultural Economy of Cities. *Int. J. Urban Reg. Res.* **2010**, *21*, 323–339. [CrossRef]
41. Jung, Y.; Suh, Y. Mining the voice of employees: A text mining approach to identifying and analyzing job satisfaction factors from online employee reviews. *Decis. Support Syst.* **2019**, *123*, 113074. [CrossRef]
42. Lou, T.; Tang, J.; Hopcroft, J.; Fang, Z.; Ding, X. Learning to predict reciprocity and triadic closure in social networks. *ACM Trans. Knowl. Discov. Data (TKDD)* **2013**, *7*, 1–25. [CrossRef]
43. Ishitani, Y. Model-based information extraction method tolerant of OCR errors for document images. *Int. J. Comput. Process. Orient. Lang.* **2012**, *15*, 165–186. [CrossRef]
44. Zhang, Y.; Yang, C.; Niu, Z. A Research of job recommendation system based on collaborative filtering. In Proceedings of the 2014 Seventh International Symposium on Computational Intelligence and Design, Rome, Italy, 16–18 October 2014; Volume 1, pp. 533–538.

Disclaimer/Publisher's Note: The statements, opinions and data contained in all publications are solely those of the individual author(s) and contributor(s) and not of MDPI and/or the editor(s). MDPI and/or the editor(s) disclaim responsibility for any injury to people or property resulting from any ideas, methods, instructions or products referred to in the content.

Review

Machine Learning Methods in Weather and Climate Applications: A Survey

Liuyi Chen [1], Bocheng Han [1], Xuesong Wang [2], Jiazhen Zhao [3], Wenke Yang [1] and Zhengyi Yang [1,*]

[1] School of Computer Science and Engineering, University of New South Wales, Sydney, NSW 2052, Australia
[2] Commonwealth Scientific and Industrial Research Organisation, Data 61, Sydney, NSW 2015, Australia
[3] Key Laboratory of Meteorological Disaster, Nanjing University of Information Science and Technology, Nanjing 210044, China
* Correspondence: zhengyi.yang@unsw.edu.au

Citation: Chen, L.; Han, B.; Wang, X.; Zhao, J.; Yang, W.; Yang, Z. Machine Learning Methods in Weather and Climate Applications: A Survey. *Appl. Sci.* **2023**, *13*, 12019. https://doi.org/10.3390/app132112019

Academic Editor: Joao Carlos Andrade dos Santos

Received: 9 September 2023
Revised: 22 October 2023
Accepted: 28 October 2023
Published: 3 November 2023

Copyright: © 2023 by the authors. Licensee MDPI, Basel, Switzerland. This article is an open access article distributed under the terms and conditions of the Creative Commons Attribution (CC BY) license (https:// creativecommons.org/licenses/by/ 4.0/).

Abstract: With the rapid development of artificial intelligence, machine learning is gradually becoming popular for predictions in all walks of life. In meteorology, it is gradually competing with traditional climate predictions dominated by physical models. This survey aims to consolidate the current understanding of Machine Learning (ML) applications in weather and climate prediction—a field of growing importance across multiple sectors, including agriculture and disaster management. Building upon an exhaustive review of more than 20 methods highlighted in existing literature, this survey pinpointed eight techniques that show particular promise for improving the accuracy of both short-term weather and medium-to-long-term climate forecasts. According to the survey, while ML demonstrates significant capabilities in short-term weather prediction, its application in medium-to-long-term climate forecasting remains limited, constrained by factors such as intricate climate variables and data limitations. Current literature tends to focus narrowly on either short-term weather or medium-to-long-term climate forecasting, often neglecting the relationship between the two, as well as general neglect of modeling structure and recent advances. By providing an integrated analysis of models spanning different time scales, this survey aims to bridge these gaps, thereby serving as a meaningful guide for future interdisciplinary research in this rapidly evolving field.

Keywords: machine learning; weather prediction; climate prediction; meteorological forecasting; survey

1. Introduction

Weather and climate prediction play an important role in human history. Weather forecasting serves as a critical tool that underpins various facets of human life and social operations, permeating everything from individual decision-making to large-scale industrial planning. Its significance at the individual level is manifested in its capacity to guide personal safety measures, from avoiding hazardous outdoor activities during inclement weather to taking health precautions in extreme temperatures. This decision-making extends into the agricultural realm, where forecasts inform the timing for planting, harvesting, and irrigation, ultimately contributing to maximized crop yields and stable food supply chains [1]. The ripple effect of accurate forecasting also reaches the energy sector, where it aids in efficiently managing demand fluctuations, allowing for optimized power generation and distribution. This efficiency is echoed in the transportation industry, where the planning and scheduling of flights, train routes, and maritime activities hinge on weather conditions. Precise weather predictions are key to mitigating delays and enhancing safety protocols [2]. Beyond these sectors, weather forecasting plays an integral role in the realm of construction and infrastructure development. Adverse conditions can cause project delays and degrade quality, making accurate forecasts a cornerstone of effective project management. Moreover, the capacity to forecast extreme weather events like hurricanes and typhoons is instrumental in disaster management, offering the possibility of early warnings and thereby mitigating loss of life and property [3].

Although climate prediction is often ignored by human beings in the short term, it has a close relationship with Earth's life. Global warming and the subsequent rise in sea levels constitute critical challenges with far-reaching implications for the future of our planet. Through sophisticated climate modeling and forecasting techniques, we stand to gain valuable insights into the potential ramifications of these phenomena, thereby enabling the development of targeted mitigation strategies. For instance, precise estimations of sea-level changes in future decades could inform rational urban planning and disaster prevention measures in coastal cities. On an extended temporal scale, climate change is poised to instigate considerable shifts in the geographical distribution of numerous species, thereby jeopardizing biodiversity. State-of-the-art climate models integrate an array of variables—encompassing atmospheric conditions, oceanic currents, terrestrial ecosystems, and biospheric interactions—to furnish a nuanced comprehension of environmental transformations [4]. This integrative approach is indispensable for the formulation of effective global and regional policies aimed at preserving ecological diversity. Economic sectors such as agriculture, fisheries, and tourism are highly susceptible to the vagaries of climate change. Elevated temperatures may precipitate a decline in crop yields, while an upsurge in extreme weather events stands to impact tourism adversely. Longitudinal climate forecasts are instrumental in guiding governmental and business strategies to adapt to these inevitable changes. Furthermore, sustainable resource management, encompassing water, land, and forests, benefits significantly from long-term climate projections. Accurate predictive models can forecast potential water scarcity in specific regions, thereby allowing for the preemptive implementation of judicious water management policies. Climate change is also implicated in a gamut of public health crises, ranging from the proliferation of infectious diseases to an uptick in heatwave incidents. Comprehensive long-term climate models can equip public health agencies with the data necessary to allocate resources and devise effective response strategies.

Table 1 elucidates the diverse applications of weather forecasting across multiple sectors and time frames. In the short-term context, weather forecasts are instrumental for agricultural activities such as determining the optimal timing for sowing and harvesting crops, as well as formulating irrigation and fertilization plans. In the energy sector, short-term forecasts facilitate accurate predictions of output levels for wind and solar energy production. For transportation, which encompasses road, rail, aviation, and maritime industries, real-time weather information is vital for operational decisions affecting safety and efficiency. Similarly, construction projects rely on short-term forecasts for planning and ensuring safe operations. In the retail and sales domains, weather forecasts enable businesses to make timely inventory adjustments. For tourism and entertainment, particularly those involving outdoor activities and attractions, short-term forecasts provide essential guidance for day-to-day operations. Furthermore, short-term weather forecasts play a pivotal role in environmental and disaster management by providing early warnings for floods, fires, and other natural calamities. In the medium-to-long-term scenario, weather forecasts have broader implications for strategic planning and risk assessment. In agriculture, these forecasts are used for long-term land management and planning. The insurance industry utilizes medium-to-long-term forecasts to prepare for prospective increases in specific types of natural disasters, such as floods and droughts. Real estate sectors also employ these forecasts for evaluating the long-term impact of climate-related factors like sea level rise. Urban planning initiatives benefit from these forecasts for effective water resource management. For the tourism industry, medium-to-long-term weather forecasts are integral for long-term investments and for identifying regions that may become popular tourist destinations in the future. Additionally, in the realm of public health, long-term climate changes projected through these forecasts can inform strategies for controlling the spread of diseases. In summary, weather forecasts serve as a vital tool for both immediate and long-term decision-making across a diverse range of sectors.

Table 1. Applications of Short term and medium-long term weather/climate forecasting in daily life.

Time Scale	Domains	Applications
Short Term	Agriculture	The timing for sowing and harvesting; Irrigation and fertilization plans [5].
	Energy	Predicts output for wind and solar energy [6].
	Transportation	Road traffic safety; Rail transport; Aviation and maritime industries [7].
	Construction	Project plans and timelines; Safe operations [8].
	Retail and Sales	Adjusts inventory based on weather forecasts [9].
	Tourism and Entertainment	Operations of outdoor activities and tourist attractions [10]
	Environment and Disaster Management	Early warnings for floods, fires, and other natural disasters [11].
Medium—Long Term	Agriculture	Long-term land management and planning [12].
	Insurance	Preparations for future increases in types of disasters, such as floods and droughts [13].
	Real Estate	Assessment of future sea-level rise or other climate-related factors [14].
	Urban Planning	Water resource management [15].
	Tourism	Long-term investments and planning, such as deciding which regions may become popular tourist destinations in the future [16].
	Public Health	Long-term climate changes may impact the spread of diseases [17].

Short-term weather prediction. Short-term weather forecasting primarily targets weather conditions that span from a few hours up to seven days, aiming to deliver highly accurate and actionable information that empowers individuals to make timely decisions like carrying an umbrella or postponing outdoor activities. These forecasts typically decrease in reliability as they stretch further into the future. Essential elements of these forecasts include maximum and minimum temperatures, the likelihood and intensity of various forms of precipitation like rain, snow, or hail, wind speed and direction, levels of relative humidity or dew point temperature, and types of cloud cover such as sunny, cloudy, or overcast conditions [18]. Visibility distance in foggy or smoky conditions and warnings about extreme weather events like hurricanes or heavy rainfall are also often included. The methodologies for generating these forecasts comprise numerical simulations run on high-performance computers, the integration of observational data from multiple sources like satellites and ground-based stations, and statistical techniques that involve pattern recognition and probability calculations based on historical weather data. While generally more accurate than long-term forecasts, short-term predictions are not without their limitations, often influenced by the quality of the input data, the resolution of the numerical models, and the sensitivity to initial atmospheric conditions. These forecasts play a crucial role in various sectors, including decision-making processes, transportation safety, and agriculture, despite the inherent complexities and uncertainties tied to predicting atmospheric behavior.

Medium-to-long-term climate prediction. Medium-to-long-term climate forecasting (MLTF) concentrates on projecting climate conditions over periods extending from several months to multiple years, in contrast to short-term weather forecasts, which focus more on immediate atmospheric conditions. The time frame of these climate forecasts can be segmented into medium-term, which generally ranges from a single season up to a year, and long-term, which could span years to decades or even beyond [19]. Unlike weather forecasts, which may provide information on imminent rainfall or snowfall, MLTF centers on the average states or trends of climate variables, such as average temperature and precipitation, ocean-atmosphere interactions like El Niño or La Niña conditions, and the likelihood of extreme weather events like droughts or floods, as well as anticipated hurricane activities [20]. The projection also encompasses broader climate trends, such as global warming or localized climatic shifts. These forecasts employ a variety of methods, including statistical models based on historical data and seasonal patterns, dynamical models that operate on complex mathematical equations rooted in physics, and integrated models that amalgamate multiple data sources and methodologies. However, the accuracy of medium- to long-term climate forecasting often falls short when compared with short-term weather predictions due to the intricate, multi-scale, and multi-process interactions that constitute the climate system, not to mention the lack of exhaustive long-term data. The forecasts' reliability can also be influenced by socio-economic variables, human activities, and shifts in policy. Despite these complexities, medium-to-long-term climate projections serve pivotal roles in areas such as resource management, agricultural planning, disaster mitigation, and energy policy formulation, making them not only a multi-faceted, multi-disciplinary challenge but also a crucial frontier in both climate science and applied research.

Survey Scope. In recent years, machine learning has emerged as a potent tool in meteorology, displaying strong capabilities in feature abstraction and trend prediction. Numerous studies have employed machine learning as the principal methodology for weather forecasting [21,22]. Our survey extends this current understanding by including recent advances in the application of machine learning techniques such as High-Resolution Neural Networks and 3D neural networks, representing the state-of-the-art in this multidisciplinary domain. This survey endeavors to serve as a comprehensive review of machine learning techniques applied in the realms of meteorology and climate prediction. Previous studies have substantiated the efficacy of machine learning methods in short-term weather forecasting [23]. However, there exists a conspicuous dearth of nuanced research in the context of medium-to-long-term climate predictions [24]. The primary objective of this survey is to offer a comprehensive analysis of nearly 20 diverse machine-learning methods applied in meteorology and climate science. It is worth noting that our selection criteria are twofold: we include classic models in the application of machine learning to meteorology, as well as, from a computer science perspective, represent recent state-of-the-art complex models. We categorize these methods based on their temporal applicability: short-term weather forecasting and medium-to-long-term climate predictions. This dual focus uniquely situates our survey as a bridge between immediate weather forecasts and longer climatic trends, thereby filling existing research gaps summarized as follows:

- Limited Scope: Existing surveys predominantly focus either on short-term weather forecasting or medium-to-long-term climate predictions. There is a notable absence of comprehensive surveys that endeavour to bridge these two-time scales. In addition, current investigations tend to focus narrowly on specific methods, such as simple neural networks, thereby neglecting some combination of methods.
- Lack of model details: Many existing studies offer only generalized viewpoints and lack a systematic analysis of the specific model employed in weather and climate prediction. This absence creates a barrier for researchers aiming to understand the intricacies and efficacy of individual methods.
- Neglect of Recent Advances: Despite rapid developments in machine learning and computational techniques, existing surveys have not kept pace with these advancements. The paucity of information on cutting-edge technologies stymies the progression of research in this interdisciplinary field.

By addressing these key motivations, this survey aims to serve as a roadmap for future research endeavors in this rapidly evolving, interdisciplinary field.

Contributions of the Survey. The contributions of this paper are as follows.

- Comprehensive scope: Unlike research endeavors that restrict their inquiry to a singular temporal scale, our survey provides a comprehensive analysis that amalgamates short-term weather forecasting with medium- and long-term climate predictions. In total, 20 models were surveyed, of which a select subset of eight were chosen for in-depth scrutiny. These models are discerned as the industry's avant-garde, thereby serving as invaluable references for researchers. For instance, the PanGu model exhibits remarkable congruence with actual observational results, thereby illustrating the caliber of the models included in our analysis

- In-Depth Analysis: Breaking new ground, this study delves into the intricate operational mechanisms of the eight focal models. We have dissected the operating mechanisms of these eight models, distinguishing the differences in their approaches and summarizing the commonalities in their methods through comparison. This comparison helps readers gain a deeper understanding of the efficacy and applicability of each model and provides a reference for choosing the most appropriate model for a given scenario.
- Identification of Contemporary Challenges and Future Work: The survey identifies pressing challenges currently facing the field, such as the limited dataset of chronological seasons and complex climate change effects, and suggests directions for future work, including simulating datasets and physics-based constraint models. These recommendations not only add a forward-looking dimension to our research but also act as a catalyst for further research and development in climate prediction.

Outline of the paper. This paper consists of six sections. Section 1 describes our motivation and innovations compared with other weather prediction surveys. Section 2 introduces some weather-related background knowledge. Section 3 broadly introduces relevant methods for weather prediction other than machine learning. Section 4 highlights the milestones of forecasting models using machine learning and their categorization. Sections 5 and 6 analyze representative methods on both short-term and medium- and long-term time scales. Sections 7 and 8 summarize the challenges faced, present promising future work, and conclude the paper.

2. Background

In this section, the objective is to provide a thorough understanding of key meteorological principles, tailored to be accessible even to readers outside the meteorological domain. The section commences with an overview of Reanalysis Data, the cornerstone for data inputs in weather forecasting and climate projection models. Following this, the focus shifts to the vital aspect of model output validation. It is necessary to identify appropriate benchmarks and key performance indicators for assessing the model's predictive accuracy. Without well-defined standards, the evaluation of a model's effectiveness remains nebulous. Furthermore, three essential concepts—bias-correction, down-scaling, and emulation—are introduced. These become particularly relevant when discussing the role of machine learning in augmenting physical models. Finally, the text offers an in-depth explanation of predicting extreme events, clearly defining "extreme event" and differentiating them from routine occurrences.

Data source. Observed data undergoes a series of rigorous processing steps before it enters the predictive model (or what is known as the reanalysis data generation process). They are amassed from heterogeneous sources, such as ground-based networks like the Global Historical Climatology Network (GHCN), atmospheric tools like Next-Generation Radar (NEXRAD), and satellite systems like the Geostationary Operational Environmental Satellites (GOES). Oceanic measurements are captured through the specialized ARGO float network, focusing on key parameters like temperature and salinity. These raw datasets are further audited for quality control, spatial and temporal interpolation, and unit standardization.

Despite meticulous preprocessing, observational data exhibit challenges such as spatial-temporal heterogeneity, inherent measurement errors, and discrepancies with numerical models. To mitigate these issues, data assimilation techniques are employed. These techniques synergize observations with model forecasts using mathematical and statistical algorithms like Kalman filtering, Three-Dimensional Variational Analysis (3D-Var), and Four-Dimensional Variational Analysis (4D-Var) [25].

Additionally, data assimilation can be utilized to enhance the initial model conditions and correct systemic model biases. The scope of data assimilation extends beyond singular meteorological models to complex Earth System Models that integrate dynamics from atmospheric, oceanic, and terrestrial subsystems. Post-assimilation, where the model state is updated, leads to the generation of "reanalysis data". Popular reanalysis datasets include ERA5 from the European Centre for Medium-Range Weather Forecasts (ECMWF), NCEP/NCAR Reanalysis from the National Centers for Environmental Prediction and the National Center for Atmospheric Research, JRA-55 from the Japan Meteorological Agency, and MERRA-2 from NASA.

Result evaluation. Result evaluation serves as a critical stage in the iterative process of predictive modeling. It involves comparing forecasted outcomes against observed data to gauge the model's reliability and accuracy. The temporal dimension is a critical factor in result evaluation. Short-term predictive models, like those used in weather forecasting, benefit from near-real-time feedback, which allows for frequent recalibration using machine learning algorithms like Ensemble Kalman Filters. On the other hand, long-term models, such as climate projections based on General Circulation Models (GCMs), are constrained by the absence of an immediate validation period. In weather forecasting, meteorologists employ a variety of numerical models, like the Weather Research and Forecasting (WRF) model, which are evaluated based on short-term observational data. Standard metrics for evaluation include Mean Absolute Error (MAE), Root Mean Square Error (RMSE), and Skill Scores. The high-frequency availability of data from sources like weather radars and satellites facilitates rapid iterations and refinements. In contrast, climate models are scrutinized using different methodologies. Given their long-term nature, climate models are often validated using historical and paleoclimatic data. Statistical techniques like Empirical Orthogonal Functions (EOF) and Principal Component Analysis (PCA) are employed to identify and validate overarching climatic patterns. These models often have to account for high levels of uncertainty and are cross-validated against geological or even astronomical records, making immediate validation impractical. For weather forecasts, predictive accuracy within the scope of hours to days is paramount. Climate models, conversely, are evaluated based on their ability to accurately reproduce decadal and centennial patterns.

Bias correction. In the context of meteorology, climate science, machine learning, and statistical modeling, bias correction (or bias adjustment) refers to a set of techniques used to correct systematic errors (biases) in model simulations or predictions. These biases may arise due to various factors such as model limitations, uncertainties in parameterization, or discrepancies between model assumptions and real-world data. Bias Correction (Bias Adjustment) can be formally defined as the process of modifying the output of predictive models to align more closely with observed data. The primary objective is to minimize the difference between the model's estimates and the observed values, thereby improving the model's accuracy and reliability.

In more formal terms, let M represent the model output and O represent the observed data. Bias B is defined as:

$$B = M - O \qquad (1)$$

The aim of bias-correction is to find a function f such that:

$$f(M) \approx O \qquad (2)$$

Various methods can be employed for bias-correction, including simple linear adjustments, quantile mapping, and more complex machine-learning techniques. The choice of method often depends on the specific characteristics of the data and the overarching objectives of the study.

Emulation. The term emulation is utilized here to denote the approach where machine learning models are employed to simulate or approximate components and processes of the original physical model. In meteorology, physical models are devised based on a comprehensive understanding of atmospheric dynamics, often entailing intricate hydrodynamic equations to elucidate atmospheric motions and interactions. However, to attain high computational efficiency in practical operations, direct resolution of these equations is frequently computationally demanding, particularly when high spatial and temporal resolution simulations are requisite. To alleviate these issues, modelers are already using fast and accurate ML simulations to simulate existing time-consuming parameterizations [26–28]. Machine learning methods are capable of delivering fast and precise approximations of complex physical processes by learning patterns and relationships from historical data or high-precision model runs. For instance, neural networks or other machine learning algorithms can be deployed to deal with Longwave and shortwave radiation parameterization [29,30] and emulate nonlinear wave interactions in wind wave models [31]. Consequently, machine learning models can substitute traditional physical parameterization schemes in prediction models, significantly alleviating the computational burden while preserving or even augmenting the accuracy of predictions.

Down-scaling. Down-scaling in meteorology and climate science is a computational technique employed to bridge the gap between the spatial and temporal resolutions offered by General Circulation Models (GCMs) or Regional Climate Models (RCMs) and the scale at which specific applications, such as local weather predictions or hydrological assessments, operate. Given that GCMs and RCMs typically operate at a coarse resolution—spanning tens or hundreds of kilometers—Down-scaling aims to refine these projections to a more localized level, potentially down to single kilometers or less.

Extreme events. In meteorology, an "extreme event" refers to a rare occurrence within a statistical distribution of a particular weather variable. These events can be extreme high temperatures, heavy precipitation, severe storms, or high winds, among others. These phenomena are considered "extreme" due to their rarity and typically severe impact on ecosystems, infrastructure, and human life.

Symbol definition. Since many formulas are involved in weather and climate prediction methods, we have defined an Abbreviation in the end of paper that summarizes all the common symbols and their definitions.

In standard meteorological models, precipitation is usually represented as a three-dimensional array containing latitude, longitude, and elevation. Each cell in this array contains a numerical value that represents the expected precipitation for that particular location and elevation during a given time window. This data structure allows for straightforward visualization and analysis, such as contour maps or time series plots. Unlike standard precipitation forecasts, which focus primarily on the water content of the atmosphere, extreme events may require tracking multiple variables simultaneously. For example, hurricane modeling may include variables such as wind speed, atmospheric pressure, and sea surface temperature. Given the higher uncertainty associated with extreme events, the output may not be a single deterministic forecast but rather a probabilistic one. An integration approach can be used to generate multiple model runs to capture a range of possible outcomes. Both types of predictions are typically evaluated using statistical metrics; however, for extreme events, more sophisticated measures such as event detection rates, false alarm rates, or skill scores associated with probabilistic predictions can be used.

3. Related Work

This study principally centers on the utilization of machine learning techniques in the realm of climate prediction. However, to furnish a comprehensive perspective, we also elucidate traditional forecasting methodologies—statistical and physical methods—within this section. Historically speaking, the evolution of predictive models in climate science has undergone three distinct phases. Initially, statistical methods were prevalently deployed; however, their limited accuracy led to their gradual supplantation by physical models. While the role of statistical methods has dwindled in terms of standalone application, they are frequently amalgamated with other techniques to enhance predictive fidelity. Subsequently, physical models ascended to become the prevailing paradigm in climate prediction.

Given the current predominance of physical models in the field of climate prediction, they serve as the natural benchmarks against which we evaluate the performance of emerging machine learning approaches. Finally, our focus is on machine learning methods, exploring their potential to mitigate the limitations intrinsic to their historical predecessors.

3.1. Statistical Method

Statistical or empirical forecasting methods have a rich history in meteorology, serving as the initial approach to weather prediction before the advent of computational models. Statistical prediction methodologies serve as the linchpin for data-driven approaches in meteorological forecasting, focusing on both short-term weather patterns and long-term climatic changes. These methods typically harness powerful statistical algorithms, among which Geographically Weighted Regression (GWR) and Spatio-Temporal Kriging (ST-Kriging) stand out as particularly effective [32,33].

GWR is instrumental in adjusting for spatial heterogeneity, allowing meteorological variables to exhibit different relationships depending on their geographical context. ST-Kriging extends this spatial consideration to include the temporal domain, thereby capturing variations in weather and climate that are both location-specific and time-sensitive. Such spatio-temporal modeling is especially pertinent in a rapidly changing environment, where traditional stationary models often fail to capture the dynamism inherent in meteorological systems.

Forecasting using inter-annual increments is now a statistically based forecasting method with better results. The interannual increment of a variable such as precipitation is calculated as:

$$\text{Interannual Increment} = \text{Value}_{year} - \text{Value}_{year-1}$$

Through meticulous analysis of variables correlating with the inter-annual growth rate of the predictive variable, five key predictive factors have been identified. A multivariate linear regression model was developed, employing these selected key predictive factors to estimate the inter-annual increment for future time units. The estimated inter-annual increment is subsequently aggregated with the actual variable value from the preceding year to generate a precise prediction of the total quantity for the current time frame.

However, these statistical models operate on a critical assumption cited in literature [34,35], which posits that the governing laws influencing past meteorological events are consistent and thus applicable to future events as well. While this assumption generally holds for many meteorological phenomena, it confronts limitations when dealing with intrinsically chaotic systems. The Butterfly Effect serves as a prime example of such chaotic behavior, where minuscule perturbations in initial conditions can yield dramatically divergent outcomes. This implies that the reliability of statistical models could be compromised when predicting phenomena susceptible to such chaotic influences.

3.2. Physical Models

Physical models were the predominant method for meteorological forecasting before the advent of Artificial Intelligence (AI) and generally produce more accurate results compared with statistical methods. Physical models are predicated upon a foundational set of physical principles, including but not limited to Newton's laws of motion, the laws of conservation of energy and mass, and the principles of thermodynamics. These governing equations are commonly expressed in mathematical form, with the Navier–Stokes equations serving as a quintessential example for describing fluid dynamics. At the core of these models lies the objective of simulating real-world phenomena in a computational setting with high fidelity. To solve these intricate equations, high-performance computing platforms are typically employed, complemented by specialized numerical methods and techniques such as Computational Fluid Dynamics (CFD) and Finite Element Analysis (FEA).

In the context of atmospheric science, these physical models are especially pivotal for Numerical Weather Prediction (NWP) and climate modeling. NWP primarily focuses on short-to-medium-term weather forecasting, striving for highly accurate meteorological predictions within a span of days or weeks. In contrast, climate models concentrate on long-term changes and predictions, which can span months, years, or even longer time scales. Owing to their rigorous construction based on physical laws, physical models offer a high degree of accuracy and reliability, providing researchers with valuable insights into the underlying mechanisms of weather and climate variations.

As mentioned before, statistical-based methods can analyze past weather data to make predictions, but they may often fail to accurately predict future weather trends [36], and physic-based models, despite being computationally intensive [37], help us understand atmospheric, oceanic, and terrestrial processes in detail. Recently, machine learning methods have begun to be applied to the field of meteorology [38], offering new ways to analyze and predict weather patterns and climate change [39]. Machine learning methods are increasingly being utilized in meteorology for forecasting. Compared to physical models, they offer faster predictions, and compared with statistical methods, they provide more accurate results [40]. Additionally, machine learning can be employed for error correction and Down-scaling, further enhancing its applicability in weather and climate predictions.

In the critical fields of weather forecasting and climate prediction, achieving accuracy and efficiency is of paramount importance. Traditional methods, while foundational, inevitably present limitations, creating a compelling need for innovative approaches. Machine learning has emerged as a promising solution, demonstrating significant potential for enhancing prediction outcomes.

4. Taxonomy of Climate Prediction Applications

In this section, we primarily explore the historical trajectory of machine learning applications within the field of meteorology. We categorize the surveyed methods according to distinct criteria, facilitating a more lucid understanding for the reader.

4.1. Climate Prediction Milestone Based on Machine-Learning

In this subsection, we surveyed almost 20 methods of machine learning applications for weather prediction and climate prediction. These methods are representative and common. We listed them in the following timeline shown in Figure 1. The journey of machine learning applications in climate and weather prediction has undergone significant transformations since their inception.

Climate prediction methods before 2010. The earliest model in this context is the Precipitation Neural Network Prediction Model, published in 1998. This model serves as an archetype of Basic DNN Models, leveraging Artificial Neural Networks to offer short-term forecasts specifically for precipitation in the Middle Atlantic Region. Advancing to the mid-2000s, the realm of medium-to-long-term predictions saw the introduction of ML-Enhanced Non-Deep-Learning Models, exemplified by KNN-Down-scaling in 2005 and SVM-Down-scaling in 2006. These models employed machine learning techniques like K-Nearest Neighbors and Support Vector Machines, targeting localized precipitation forecasts in the United States and India, respectively. In 2009, the field welcomed another medium-to-long-term model, CRF-Down-scaling, which used Conditional Random Fields to predict precipitation in the Mahanadi Basin.

Climate prediction methods from 2010–2019. During the period from 2010 to 2019, the field of weather prediction witnessed significant technological advancements and diversification in modeling approaches. Around 2015, a notable shift back to short-term predictions was observed with the introduction of Hybrid DNN Models, exemplified by ConsvLSTM. This model integrated Long Short-Term Memory networks with Convolutional Neural Networks to provide precipitation forecasts specifically for Hong Kong. As the decade progressed, models became increasingly specialized. For instance, the 2017 Precipitation Convolution prediction model leveraged Convolutional Neural Networks to focus on localized precipitation forecasts in Guang Dong, China. The following year saw the emergence of the Stacked-LSTM-Model, which utilized Long Short-Term Memory networks for temperature predictions in Amsterdam and Eindhoven.

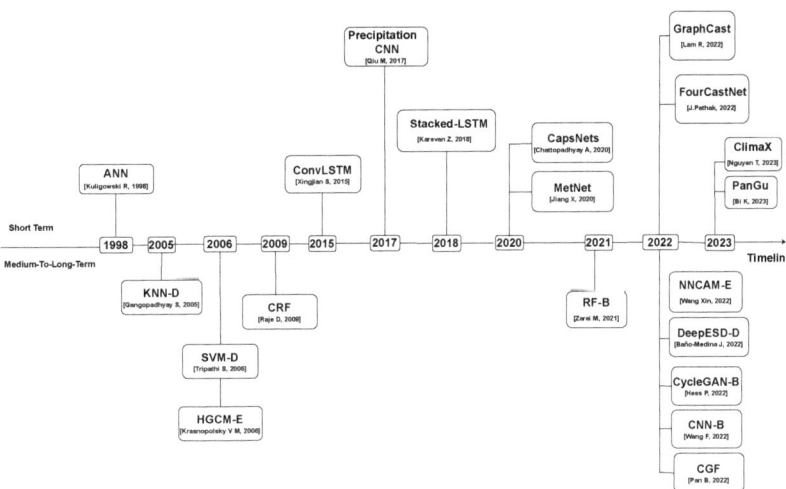

Figure 1. Applications: of machine-learning on climate prediction milestone [41–61].

Climate prediction methods from 2020. Fast forward to 2020, the CapsNet model, a Specific Model, leveraged a novel architecture known as Capsule Networks to predict extreme weather events in North America. By 2021, the scope extended to models like RF-bias-correction and the sea-ice prediction model, focusing on medium-to-long-term predictions. The former employed Random Forests for precipitation forecasts in Iran, while the latter utilized probabilistic deep learning techniques for forecasts in the Arctic region. Recent advancements as of 2022 and 2023 incorporate more complex architectures. Cycle GAN, a 2022 model, utilized Generative Adversarial Networks for global precipitation prediction. PanGu, a 2023 release, employed 3D Neural Networks for predicting extreme weather events globally. Another recent model, FourCastNet, leverages a technique known as AFNO to predict extreme global events. Furthermore, in 2022, this year also witnessed the introduction of DeepESD-Down-scaling and CNN-Bias-correction models, both utilizing Convolutional Neural Networks to predict local temperature scales and perform global bias correction, respectively.

4.2. Classification of Climate Prediction Methods

To provide a deeper level of understanding regarding the various weather prediction methods discussed, we have organized them into classifications in Table 2. These classifications are made according to multiple criteria that encompass Time Scale, Type, Model, Technique, Name, Region, and Event. This structured approach aims to offer readers an easy way to compare and contrast different methods, as well as to gain insights into the specific contexts where each method is most applicable.

Table 2. Classification of models.

Time Scale	Spational Scale	Type	Model	Technology	Name	Event
Short-term weather prediction	Global	ML	Special DNN Models	AFNO	FourCastNet [47]	Extreme Events
				3D Neural Network	PanGu [49]	Temperature & Extreme Event
				Vision Transformers	ClimaX [50]	Temperature & Extreme Event
				SwinTransformer	SwinVRNN [62]	Temperature & Precipitation
				U-Transformer	FuXi [63]	Temperature
				GNN	CLCRN [64]	Temperature
					GraphCast [48]	Extreme Events
				Transformer	FengWu [65]	
	Regional		Single DNNs Model	CNN	CapsNet [45]	Precipitation
					Precipitation Convolution prediction [43]	
				ANN	Precipitation Neural Network prediction [41]	Temperature
				LSTM	Stacked-LSTM-Model [44]	Precipitation
			Hybrid DNNs Model	LSTM + CNN	ConvLSTM [42]	Temperature & Precipitation
					MetNet [46]	Temperature & Extreme Event
				Probabilistic deep learning	Conditional Generative Forecasting [61]	
Medium-to-long-term climate prediction	Global	ML Enhanced	Single DNN models	CNN	CNN-Bias-correction model [60]	Precipitation
				GAN	Cycle GAN [59]	
				NN	Hybrid-GCM-Emulation [53]	
				ResDNN	NNCAM-emulation [57]	Temperature
				CNN	DeepESD-Down-scaling model [58]	
	Regional		Non-Deep-Learning Model	Random forest (RF)	RF-bias-correction model [55]	Precipitation
				Support vector machine (SVM)	SVM-Down-scaling model [52]	
				K-nearest neighbor (KNN)	KNN-Down-scaling model [51]	
				Conditional random field (CRF)	CRF-Down-scaling model [54]	

Time Scale. Models in weather and climate prediction are initially divided based on their temporal range into 'Short-term' and 'Medium-to-long-term'. Short-term weather prediction focuses on the state of the atmosphere in the short term, usually the weather conditions in the next few hours to days. Medium-to-long-term climate prediction focuses on longer time scales, usually the average weather trends over months, years, or decades. Weather forecasts focus on specific weather conditions in the near term, such as temperature, precipitation, humidity, wind speed, and direction. Climate prediction focuses on long-term weather patterns and trends, such as seasonal or inter-annual variations in temperature and precipitation. In the traditional approach, weather forecasting usually utilizes numerical weather prediction models that predict weather changes in the short term by resolving the equations of atmospheric dynamics; climate prediction usually utilizes climate models that incorporate more complex interacting feedback mechanisms and longer-term external drivers, such as greenhouse gas emissions and changes in solar radiation.

Spatial Scale. Regional meteorology concerns a specified geographic area, such as a country or a continent, and aims to provide detailed insights into the weather and climate phenomena within that domain. The finer spatial resolution of regional models allows for a more nuanced understanding of local geographical and topographical influences on weather patterns, which in turn can lead to more accurate forecasts within that particular area. On the other hand, global meteorology encompasses the entire planet's atmospheric conditions, providing a broader yet less detailed view of weather and climate phenomena. The spatial resolution of global models is generally coarser compared with regional models. As such, global forecasts might not capture localized weather events as accurately as regional forecasts. However, global models are crucial for understanding large-scale atmospheric dynamics and providing the boundary conditions necessary for regional models.

ML and ML-Enhanced Types. We categorize models into ML and ML-Enhanced types. In ML type, algorithms are directly applied to climate data for pattern recognition or predictive tasks. These algorithms typically operate independently of traditional physical models, relying instead on data-driven insights garnered from extensive climate datasets. Contrastingly, ML-Enhanced models integrate machine learning techniques into conventional physical models to optimize or enhance their performance. Fundamentally, these approaches still rely on physical models for prediction. However, machine learning algorithms serve as auxiliary tools for parameter tuning, feature engineering, or addressing specific limitations in the physical models, thereby improving their overall predictive accuracy and reliability. In this survey, ML-enhanced was divided into three categories: bias correction, down-scaling, and emulation [66]. **Model.** Within each time scale, models are further categorized by their type. These models include: Specific Models: These are unique or specialized neural network architectures developed for particular applications.

Specific DNN Models: Unique or specialized neural network architectures developed for particular applications.

Hybrid DNN Models: These models use a combination of different neural network architectures, such as LSTM + CNN.

Single DNN Models: These models employ foundational Deep Neural Network architectures like ANNs (Artificial Neural Networks), CNNs (Convolutional Neural Networks), and LSTMs (Long Short-Term Memory networks).

Non-Deep-Learning Models: These models incorporate machine learning techniques that do not rely on deep learning, such as Random Forests and Support Vector Machines.

Technique. This category specifies the underlying machine learning or deep learning technique used in a particular model, for example, CNN, LSTM, Random Forest, Probalistic Deep Learning, and GAN.

CNN. A specific type of ANN is the Convolutional Neural Network (CNN), designed to automatically and adaptively learn spatial hierarchies from data [67]. CNNs comprise three main types of layers: convolutional, pooling, and fully connected [68]. The convolutional layer applies various filters to the input data to create feature maps, identifying spatial hierarchies and patterns. Pooling layers reduce dimensionality, summarizing features in the previous layer [69]. Fully connected layers then perform classification based on the high-level features identified [70]. CNNs are particularly relevant in meteorology for tasks like satellite image analysis, with their ability to recognize and extract spatial patterns [71]. Their unique structure allows them to capture local dependencies in the data, making them robust against shifts and distortions [72].

LSTM. Long Short-Term Memory (LSTM) units are a specialized form of recurrent neural network architecture [42]. Purposefully designed to mitigate the vanishing gradient problem inherent in traditional RNNs, LSTM units manage the information flow through a series of gates, namely the input, forget, and output gates. These gates govern the retention, forgetting, and output of information, allowing LSTMs to effectively capture long-range dependencies and temporal dynamics in sequential data [42]. In the context of meteorological forecasting, the utilization of LSTM contributes to a nuanced understanding of weather patterns as it retains relevant historical information and discards irrelevant details over various time scales [42]. The pioneering design of LSTMs and their ability to deal with nonlinear time dependencies have led to their outstanding robustness, adaptability, and efficiency, making them an essential part of modern predictive models [42].

Random forest. A technique used to adjust or correct biases in predictive models, particularly in weather forecasting or climate modeling. Random Forest (RF) is a machine learning algorithm used for various types of classification and regression tasks. In the context of bias correction, the Random Forest algorithm would be trained to identify and correct systematic errors or biases in the predictions made by a primary forecasting model.

Probabilistic deep learning. Probabilistic deep learning models in weather forecasting aim to provide not just point estimates of meteorological variables but also a measure of uncertainty associated with the predictions. By leveraging complex neural networks, these models capture intricate relationships between various features like temperature, humidity, and wind speed. The probabilistic aspect helps in quantifying the confidence in predictions, which is crucial for risk assessment and decision-making in weather-sensitive industries.

Generative adversarial networks. Generative Adversarial Networks (GANs) are a class of deep learning models composed of two neural networks: a Generator and a Discriminator. The Generator aims to produce data that closely resembles a genuine data distribution, while the discriminator's role is to distinguish between real and generated data. During training, these networks engage in a kind of "cat-and-mouse" game, continually adapting and improving—ultimately with the goal of creating generated data so convincing that the Discriminator can no longer tell it apart from real data.

Graph Neural Network. Graph Neural Network(GNN) are designed to work with graph-structured data, capturing the relationships between connected nodes effectively. They operate by passing messages or aggregating information from neighbors and then updating each node's representation accordingly. This makes GNNs exceptionally good at handling problems like social network analysis, molecular structure analysis, and recommendation systems.

Transformer. A transformer consists of an encoder and a decoder, but its most unique feature is the attention mechanism. This allows the model to weigh the importance of different parts of the input data, making it very efficient for tasks like text summarization, question answering, and language generation.

Name. Some models are commonly cited or recognized under a specific name, such as PanGu or FourCastNet. Some models are named after their technical features.

Event. The type of weather or climatic events that the model aims to forecast is specified under this category. This could range from generalized weather conditions like temperature and precipitation to more extreme weather events.

Selection Rationale. In the next section, we will discuss the related reasons. In the short term, we choose three specific ones (PanGu; GraphCast and FourCastNet) as analysis targets according to the model type. And we also analyze the MetNet, which is a hybrid DNNs Model. The other hybrid DNNs Model (ConsLSTM) is one part of MetNet. In the medium-to-long term, we choose the probabilistic deep learning model (Conditional Generative Forecasting). It has more extensive applicability compared with the other one in the probabilistic deep learning category. The probabilistic deep learning method is also a minority machine learning method that could be used in medium-to-long-term prediction. In addition, we also selected three machine learning-enhanced methods for Down-scaling: bias correction and emulation. In general, our survey includes established models recognized for their utility in applying machine learning to meteorological tasks and cutting-edge complex models viewed from a computer science standpoint as state-of-the-art.

5. Short-Term Weather Forecast

Weather forecasting aims to predict atmospheric phenomena within a short timeframe, generally ranging from one to three days. This information is crucial for a multitude of sectors, including agriculture, transportation, and emergency management. Factors such as precipitation, temperature, and extreme weather events are of particular interest. Forecasting methods have evolved over the years, transitioning from traditional numerical methods to more advanced hybrid and machine-learning models. This section elucidates the working principles, methodologies, and merits and demerits of traditional numerical weather prediction models, MetNet, FourCastNet, and PanGu.

5.1. Model Design

Numerical Weather Model Numerical Weather Prediction (NWP) stands as a cornerstone methodology in the realm of meteorological forecasting, fundamentally rooted in the simulation of atmospheric dynamics through intricate physical models. At the core of NWP lies a set of governing physical equations that encapsulate the holistic behavior of the atmosphere:

- The Navier-Stokes Equations [73]: Serving as the quintessential descriptors of fluid motion, these equations delineate the fundamental mechanics underlying atmospheric flow.

$$\nabla \cdot \mathbf{v} = 0 \quad (3)$$

$$\rho \left(\frac{\partial \mathbf{v}}{\partial t} + \mathbf{v} \cdot \nabla \mathbf{v} \right) = -\nabla p + \mu \nabla^2 \mathbf{v} + \rho \mathbf{g} \quad (4)$$

- The Thermodynamic Equations [74]: These equations intricately interrelate the temperature, pressure, and humidity within the atmospheric matrix, offering insights into the state and transitions of atmospheric energy.

$$\frac{\partial \rho}{\partial t} + \nabla \cdot (\rho \mathbf{v}) = 0 \text{ (Continuity equation)} \quad (5)$$

$$\frac{\partial T}{\partial t} + \mathbf{v} \cdot \nabla T = \frac{q}{c_p} \text{ (Energy equation)} \quad (6)$$

$$\frac{Dp}{Dt} = -\rho c_p \nabla \cdot \mathbf{v} \text{ (Pressure equation)} \quad (7)$$

The model is fundamentally based on a set of time-dependent partial differential equations, which require sophisticated numerical techniques for solving. The resolution of these equations enables the simulation of the inherently dynamic atmosphere, serving as the cornerstone for accurate and predictive meteorological insights. Within this overarching framework, a suite of integral components is embedded to address specific physical interactions that occur at different resolutions, such as cloud formation, radiation, convection, boundary layers, and surface interactions. Each of these components serves a pivotal role:

- The Cloud Microphysics Parameterization Scheme is instrumental for simulating the life cycles of cloud droplets and ice crystals, thereby affecting [75,76] and atmospheric energy balance.
- Shortwave and Longwave Radiation Transfer Equations elucidate the absorption, scattering, and emission of both solar and terrestrial radiation, which in turn influence atmospheric temperature and dynamics.
- Empirical or Semi-Empirical Convection Parameterization Schemes simulate vertical atmospheric motions initiated by local instabilities, facilitating the capture of weather phenomena like thunderstorms.
- Boundary-Layer Dynamics concentrates on the exchanges of momentum, energy, and matter between the Earth's surface and the atmosphere which are crucial for the accurate representation of surface conditions in the model.
- Land Surface and Soil/Ocean Interaction Modules simulate the exchange of energy, moisture, and momentum between the surface and the atmosphere, while also accounting for terrestrial and aquatic influences on atmospheric conditions.

These components are tightly coupled with the core atmospheric dynamics equations, collectively constituting a comprehensive, multi-scale framework. This intricate integration allows for the simulation of the complex dynamical evolution inherent in the atmosphere, contributing to more reliable and precise weather forecasting.

In Numerical Weather Prediction (NWP), a critical tool for atmospheric dynamics forecasting, the process begins with data assimilation, where observational data is integrated into the model to reflect current conditions. This is followed by numerical integration, where governing equations are meticulously solved to simulate atmospheric changes over time. However, certain phenomena, like the microphysics of clouds, cannot be directly resolved and are accounted for through parameterization to approximate their aggregate effects. Finally, post-processing methods are used to reconcile potential discrepancies between model predictions and real-world observations, ensuring accurate and reliable forecasts. This comprehensive process captures the complexity of weather systems and serves as a robust method for weather prediction [77]. While the sophistication of NWP allows for detailed simulations of global atmospheric states, one cannot overlook the intensive computational requirements of such models. Even with the formidable processing capabilities of contemporary supercomputers, a ten-day forecast simulation can necessitate several hours of computational engagement.

MetNet. MetNet [46] is a state-of-the-art weather forecasting model that integrates the functionality of CNN, LSTM, and auto-encoder units. The CNN component conducts a multi-scale spatial analysis, extracting and abstracting meteorological patterns across various spatial resolutions. In parallel, the LSTM component captures temporal dependencies within the meteorological data, providing an in-depth understanding of weather transitions over time [42]. Autoencoders are mainly used in weather prediction for data preprocessing, feature engineering, and dimensionality reduction to assist more complex prediction models in making more accurate and efficient predictions. This combined architecture permits a dynamic and robust framework that can adaptively focus on key features in both spatial and temporal dimensions, guided by an embedded attention mechanism [78,79].

MetNet consists of three core components as shown in Figure 2: Spatial Downsampler, Temporal Encoder (ConvLSTM), and Spatial Aggregator. In this architecture, the Spatial Downsampler acts as an efficient encoder that specializes in transforming complex, high-dimensional raw data into a more compact, low-dimensional, information-intensive form. This process helps with feature extraction and data compression. The Temporal Encoder, using the ConvLSTM (Convolutional Long Short-Term Memory) model, is responsible for processing this dimensionality-reduced data in the temporal dimension. One of the major highlights of ConvLSTM is that it combines the advantages of CNNs and LSTM. The advantage of ConvLSTM is that it combines the advantages of CNN and LSTM, and is able to consider the localization of space in time series analysis simultaneously, increasing the model's ability to perceive complex time and space dependencies. The Spatial Aggregator plays the role of an optimized, high-level decoder. Rather than simply recovering the raw data from its compressed form, it performs deeper aggregation and interpretation of global and local information through a series of axial self-attentive blocks, thus enabling the model to make more accurate weather predictions. These three components work in concert with each other to form a powerful and flexible forecasting model that is particularly well suited to handle meteorological data with a high degree of spatio-temporal complexity.

The operational workflow of MetNet begins with the preprocessing of atmospheric input data, such as satellite imagery and radar information [80]. Spatial features are then discerned through the CNN layers, while temporal correlations are decoded via the LSTM units. This information is synthesized with the attention mechanism strategically emphasizing critical regions and timeframes, leading to short-term weather forecasts ranging from 2 to 12 h [79]. MetNet's strength lies in its precise and adaptive meteorological predictions, blending spatial and temporal intricacies, and thus offering an indispensable tool for refined weather analysis [46].

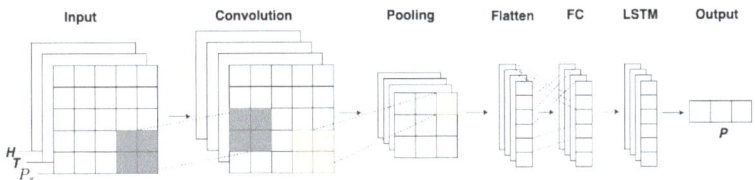

Figure 2. MetNet Structure.

FourCastNet. In response to the escalating challenges posed by global climate change and the increasing frequency of extreme weather phenomena, the demand for precise and prompt weather forecasting has surged. High-resolution weather models serve as pivotal instruments in addressing this exigency, offering the ability to capture finer meteorological features, thereby rendering more accurate predictions [81,82]. Against this backdrop, FourCastNet [47] has been conceived, employing ERA5, an atmospheric reanalysis dataset. This dataset is the outcome of a Bayesian estimation process known as data assimilation, fusing observational results with numerical models' output [83]. FourCastNet leverages the Adaptive Fourier Neural Operator (AFNO), uniquely crafted for high-resolution inputs, incorporating several significant strides within the domain of deep learning.

The essence of AFNO resides in its symbiotic fusion of the Fourier Neural Operator (FNO) learning strategy with the self-attention mechanism intrinsic to Vision Transformers (ViT) [84]. While FNO, through Fourier transforms, adeptly processes periodic data and has proven efficacy in modeling complex systems of partial differential equations, the computational complexity for high-resolution inputs is prohibitive. Consequently, AFNO deploys the Fast Fourier Transform (FFT) in the Fourier domain, facilitating continuous global convolution. This innovation reduces the complexity of spatial mixing to $O(N \log N)$, thus rendering it suitable for high-resolution data [85]. The workflow of AFNO shown in Figure 3 encompasses data preprocessing, feature extraction with FNO, feature processing with ViT, spatial mixing for feature fusion, culminating in prediction output, representing future meteorological conditions such as temperature, pressure, and humidity.

Tailoring AFNO for weather prediction, FourCastNet introduces specific adaptations. Given its distinct application scenario—predicting atmospheric variables utilizing the ERA5 dataset—a dedicated precipitation model is integrated into FourCastNet, predicting six-hour accumulated total precipitation [83]. Moreover, the training paradigm of FourCastNet includes both pre-training and fine-tuning stages. The former learns the mapping from the weather state at one time point to the next, while the latter forecasts two consecutive time steps. The advantages of FourCastNet are manifested in its unparalleled speed—approximately 45,000 times swifter than conventional NWP models—and remarkable energy efficiency—consuming about 12,000 times less energy compared with the IFS model [84]. The model's architectural innovations and its efficient utilization of computational resources position it at the forefront of high-resolution weather modeling.

GraphCast. GraphCast represents a notable advance in weather forecasting, melding machine learning with complex dynamical system modeling to pave the way for more accurate and efficient predictions. It leverages machine learning to model complex dynamical systems and showcases the potential of machine learning in this domain. It's an autoregressive model, built upon graph neural networks (GNNs) and a novel multi-scale mesh representation, trained on historical weather data from the European Centre for Medium-Range Weather Forecasts (ECMWF)'s ERA5 reanalysis archive.

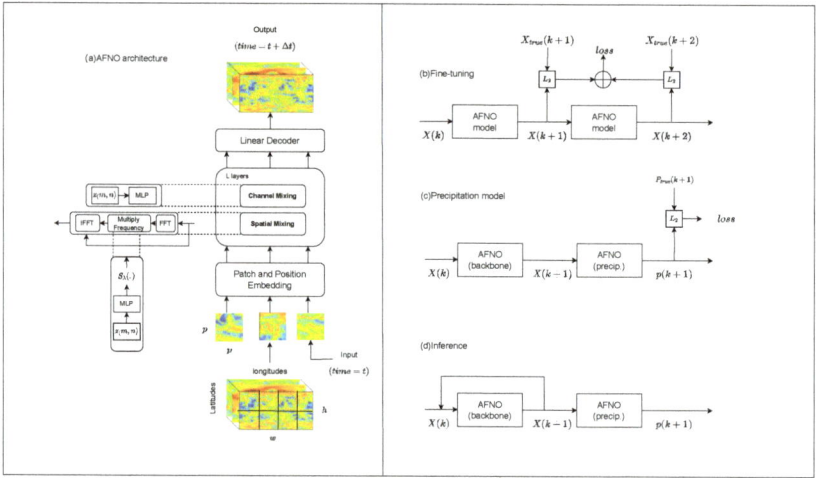

Figure 3. (**a**) The multi-layer transformer architecture; (**b**) two-step fine-tuning; (**c**) backbone model; (**d**) forecast model in free-running autoregressive inference mode.

The structure of GraphCast shown in Figure 4 employs an "encode-process-decode" configuration utilizing GNNs to autoregressively generate forecast trajectories. In detail:

- Encoder: The encoder component maps the local region of the input data (on the original latitude-longitude grid) onto the nodes of the multigrid graphical representation. It maps two consecutive input frames of the latitude-longitude input grid, with numerous variables per grid point, into a multi-scale internal mesh representation. This mapping process helps the model better capture and understand spatial dependencies in the data, allowing for more accurate predictions of future weather conditions.
- Processor: This part performs several rounds of message-passing on the multi-mesh, where the edges can span short or long ranges, facilitating efficient communication without necessitating an explicit hierarchy. More specifically, the section uses a multi-mesh graph representation. It refers to a special graph structure that is able to represent the spatial structure of the Earth's surface in an efficient way. In a multi-mesh graph representation, nodes may represent specific regions of the Earth's surface, while edges may represent spatial relationships between these regions. In this way, models can capture spatial dependencies on a global scale and are able to utilize the power of GNNs to analyze and predict weather changes.
- Decoder: It then maps the multi-mesh representation back to the latitude-longitude grid as a prediction for the next time step.

The workflow of GraphCast begins with the input of weather state(s) defined on a high-resolution latitude-longitude-pressure-levels grid. The encoder processes these inputs into a multi-scale internal mesh representation, which then undergoes many rounds of message-passing in the processor to capture spatio-temporal relationships in the weather data. Finally, the decoder translates the multi-mesh representation back to the latitude-longitude grid to generate predictions for subsequent time steps. It is worth noting that, as shown in the next part, due to the multi-scale mesh mapping property, the model is able to capture both localized weather features on a high-resolution mesh and large-scale weather features on a low-resolution mesh at the same time.

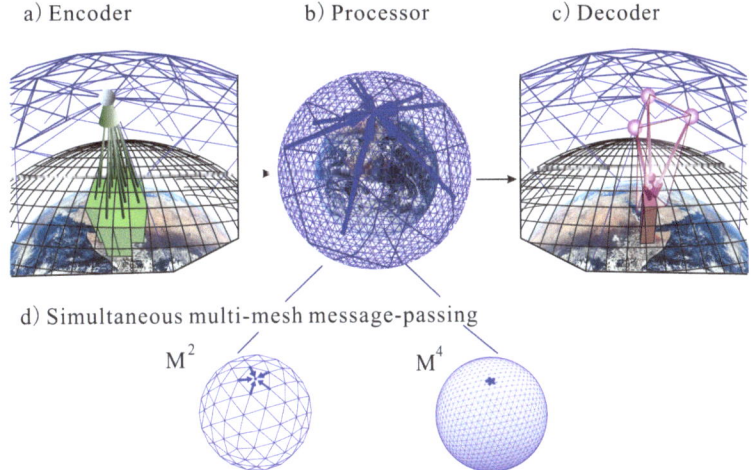

Figure 4. (**a**) The encoder component of the GraphCast architecture maps the input local regions (green boxes) to the nodes of the multigrid graph. (**b**) The processor component uses learned message passing to update each multigrid node. (**c**) The decoder component maps the processed multigrid features (purple nodes) to the grid representation. (**d**) A multi-scale grid set.

In essence, GraphCast encapsulates a pioneering stride in enhancing weather forecasting accuracy and efficiency through the amalgamation of machine learning and complex dynamical system modeling. It uniquely employs an autoregressive model structure underpinned by graph neural networks and a multi-scale mesh representation. The model's "encode-process-decode" configuration, executed through a novel multi-mesh graphical representation, adeptly captures spatial dependencies and facilitates global-scale weather prediction. By processing high-resolution weather data inputs through a systematic workflow of encoding, message-passing, and decoding, GraphCast not only generates precise weather predictions for subsequent time intervals but also exemplifies the profound potential of machine learning in advancing meteorological forecasting methodologies.

PanGu. In the rapidly evolving field of meteorological forecasting, PanGu emerges as a pioneering model shown in Figure 5, predicated on a three-dimensional neural network that transcends traditional boundaries of latitude and longitude. Recognizing the intrinsic relationship between meteorological data and atmospheric pressure, PanGu incorporates a neural network structure that accounts for altitude in addition to latitude and longitude. The initiation of the PanGu model's process involves Block Embedding, where the dataset is parsed into smaller subsets, or blocks. This operation not only mitigates spatial resolution and complexity but also facilitates subsequent data management within the network.

Following block embedding, the PanGu model integrates the data blocks into a 3D cube through a process known as 3D Cube Fusion, thereby enabling data processing within a tri-dimensional space. Swin Encoding [86], a specialized transformer encoder utilized in the deep learning spectrum, applies a self-attention mechanism for data comprehension and processing. This encoder, akin to the Autoencoder, excels at extracting and encoding essential information from the dataset. The ensuing phases include Decoding, which strives to unearth salient information, and Output Splitting, which partitions data into atmospheric and surface variables. Finally, Resolution Restoration reinstates the data to its original spatial resolution, making it amenable for further scrutiny and interpretation.

PanGu's [49] innovative 3D neural network architecture [87] offers a groundbreaking perspective for integrating meteorological data, and its suitability for three-dimensional data is distinctly pronounced. Moreover, PanGu introduces a hierarchical time-aggregation strategy, an advancement that ensures the network with the maximum lead time is consistently invoked, thereby curtailing errors. In juxtaposition with running a model like FourCastNet [47] multiple times, which may accrue errors, this approach exhibits superiority in both speed and precision. Collectively, these novel attributes and methodological advancements position PanGu as a cutting-edge tool in the domain of high-resolution weather modeling, promising transformative potential in weather analysis and forecasting.

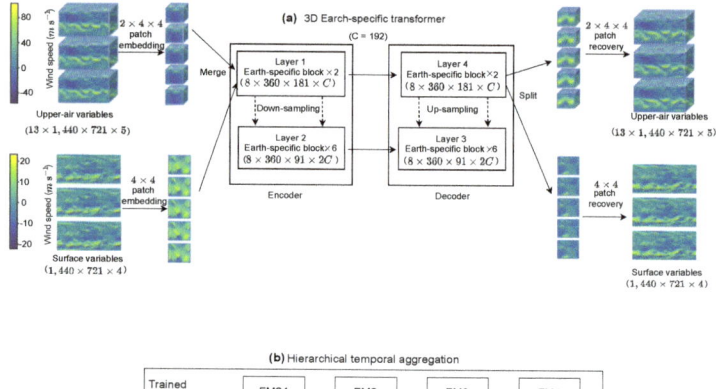

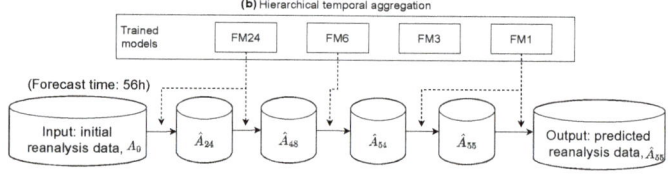

Figure 5. Network training and inference strategies. (**a**) 3DEST architecture. (**b**) Hierarchical temporal aggregation. We use FM1, FM3, FM6 and FM24 to indicate the forecast models with lead times being 1 h, 3 h, 6 h or 24 h, respectively.

MetNet, FourCastNet, GraphCast, and PanGu are state-of-the-art methods in the field of weather prediction, and they share some architectural similarities that can indicate converging trends in this field. All four models initiate the process by embedding or downsampling the input data. FourCastNet uses AFNO, MetNet employs a Spatial Downsampler, and PanGu uses Block Embedding to manage the spatial resolution and complexity of the datasets, while GraphCast maps the input data from the original latitude-longitude grid into a multi-scale internal mesh representation. Spatio-temporal coding is an integral part of all networks; FourCastNet uses pre-training and fine-tuning phases to deal with temporal dependencies, MetNet uses ConvLSTM; PanGu introduces a hierarchical temporal aggregation strategy to manage temporal correlations in the data; and GraphCast employs GNNs to capture and address spatio-temporal dependencies in weather data. Each model employs a specialized approach to understand the spatial relationships within the data. FourCastNet uses AFNO along with Vision Transformers, MetNet utilizes Spatial Aggregator blocks, and PanGu integrates data into a 3D cube via 3D Cube Fusion, while GraphCast translates data into a multi-scale internal mesh. Both FourCastNet and PanGu employ self-attention mechanisms derived from the Transformer architecture for better capturing long-range dependencies in the data. FourCastNet combines FNO with ViT, and PanGu uses Swin Encoding.

5.2. Result Analysis

MetNet: According to the MetNet experiment, at the threshold of 1 mm/h precipitation rate, both MetNet and NWP predictions have high similarity to ground conditions. Evidently, MetNet exhibits a forecasting capability that is commensurate with NWP, distinguished by an accelerated computational proficiency that generally surpasses NWP's processing speed.

FourCastNet: According to the FourCastNet experiment, FourCastNet can predict wind speed 96 h in advance with extremely high fidelity and accurate fine-scale features. In the experiment, the FourCastNet forecast accurately captured the formation and path of the super typhoon Shanzhu, as well as its intensity and trajectory over four days. It also has a high resolution and demonstrates excellent skills in capturing small-scale features. Particularly noteworthy is the performance of FourcastNet in forecasting meteorological phenomena within a 48 h horizon, which has transcended the predictive accuracy intrinsic to conventional numerical weather forecasting methodologies. This constitutes a significant stride in enhancing the veracity and responsiveness of short-term meteorological projections.

GraphCast: According to the GraphCast experiment, GraphCast demonstrates superior performance in tracking weather patterns, substantially outperforming NWP in various forecasting horizons, notably from 18 h to 4.75 days, as depicted in Figure 3b. It excels at predicting atmospheric river behaviors and extreme climatic events, with significant improvement seen in longer-term forecasts of 5 and 10 days. The model's prowess extends to accurately capturing extreme heat and cold anomalies, showcasing not just its forecasting capability but a nuanced understanding of meteorological dynamics, thereby holding promise for more precise weather predictions with contemporary data.

PanGu: According to the PanGu experiment, PanGu can almost accurately predict typhoon trajectories during the tracking of strong tropical cyclones Kong Lei and Yu Tu and is 48 h faster than NWP. The advent of 3D Net further heralds a momentous advancement in weather prediction technology. This cutting-edge model outperforms numerical weather prediction models by a substantial margin and possesses the unprecedented ability to replicate reality with exceptional fidelity. It's not merely a forecasting tool but a near-precise reflection of meteorological dynamics, allowing for a nearly flawless reconstruction of real-world weather scenarios.

In Table 3, "forecast-timeliness" represents the forecasting horizon of each model, indicating their ability to predict weather up to certain future days. In meteorology, z500 refers to the height at the 500 hPa isobaric level, which is critical for understanding atmospheric structures and weather systems. Model evaluation often employs RMSE (Root Mean Square Error) and ACC (Anomaly Correlation Coefficient) to gauge prediction accuracy and correlation with actual observations. Lower RMSE and higher ACC values indicate better model performance. Among GraphCast, PanGu, and IFS, PanGu exhibits the highest accuracy with an ACC of 0.872 for a 7-day forecast timeliness. GraphCast, while having a longer forecast timeliness of 9.75 days, has an ACC of 0.825 and an RMSE of 460, showing a balance between a longer forecasting duration and decent accuracy. Apart from this, introducing GPU data and prediction speed can provide crucial reference information for model selection, especially in scenarios with limited resources or where rapid responses are required. This aids in finding a balance between efficiency and effectiveness, offering support for successful forecasting.

Table 3. Short-term weather forecast model result comparison.

Model	Forecast-Timeliness	Z500 RMSE (7 Days)	Z500 ACC (7 Days)	Training-Complexity	Forecasting-Speed
MetNet [46]	8 h	-	-	256 Google-TPU-accelerators (16-days-training)	Fewer seconds
FourCastNet [47]	7 days	595	0.762	4 A100-GPU	24-h forecast for 100 members in 7 s
GraphCast [48]	9.75 days	460	0.825	32 Cloud-TPU-V4 (21-days-training)	10-days-predication within 1 min
PanGu [49]	7 days	510	0.872	192 V100-GPU (16-days-training)	24-h-global-prediction in 1.4 s for each GPU
IFS [88]	8.5 days	439	0.85	-	-

6. Medium-to-Long-Term Climate Prediction

Medium-to-long-term climate predictions are usually measured in decadal quarters. In the domain of medium-to-long-term climate forecasting, the focal point extends beyond immediate meteorological events to embrace broader, macroscopic elements such as long-term climate change trends, average temperature fluctuations, and mean precipitation levels. This orientation is critical for a wide array of sectors, spanning from environmental policy planning to infrastructure development and agricultural projections. Over time, the forecasting methodologies have experienced significant advancements, evolving from conventional climate models to cutting-edge, computational methods such as Probabilistic Deep Learning for Climate Forecasting (CGF), Machine Learning for Model Down-scaling (DeepESD), and Machine Learning for Result Bias Correction (CycleGAN).

6.1. Model Design

Climate Model. Climate models, consisting of fundamental atmospheric dynamics and thermodynamic equations, focus on simulating Earth's long-term climate system [89]. Unlike NWP, which targets short-term weather patterns, climate models address broader climatic trends. These models encompass Global Climate Models (GCMs), which provide a global perspective but often at a lower resolution, and Regional Climate Models (RCMs), designed for detailed regional analysis [90]. The main emphasis is on the average state and variations rather than transient weather events. The workflow of climate modeling begins with initialization by setting boundary conditions, possibly involving centuries of historical data. Numerical integration follows, using the basic equations to model the long-term evolution of the climate system [91]. Parameterization techniques are employed to represent sub-grid-scale processes like cloud formation and vegetation feedback. The model's performance and uncertainties are then analyzed and validated by comparing them with observational data or other model results [92]. The advantages of climate models lie in their ability to simulate complex climate systems, providing forecasts and insights into future climate changes, thereby informing policy and adaptation strategies. However, they also present challenges such as high computational demands, sensitivity to boundary conditions, and potential uncertainties introduced through parameterization schemes. The distinction between GCMs and RCMs and their integration in understanding both global and regional climate phenomena underscores the sophistication and indispensable role of these models in advancing meteorological studies [93].

Conditional Generative Forecasting [61]. In the intricate arena of medium-to-long-term seasonal climate prediction, the scarcity of substantial datasets since 1979 poses a significant constraint on the rigorous training of complex models like CNNs, thus limiting their predictive efficacy. To navigate this challenge, a pioneering approach to transfer learning has been embraced, leveraging the simulated climate data drawn from CMIP5 (Coupled Model Intercomparison Project Phase 5) [94] to enhance modeling efficiency and accuracy. The process begins with a pre-training phase, where the CNN is enriched with CMIP5 data to comprehend essential climatic patterns and relationships. This foundational insight then transfers seamlessly to observational data without resetting the model parameters, ensuring a continuous learning trajectory that marries simulated wisdom with empirical climate dynamics. The methodology culminates in a fine-tuning phase, during which the model undergoes subtle refinements to align more closely with the real-world intricacies of medium-to-long-term ENSO forecasting [18]. This innovative strategy demonstrates the transformative power of transfer learning in addressing the formidable challenges associated with limited sample sizes in medium-to-long-term climate science.

Leveraging 52,201 years of climate simulation data from CMIP5/CMIP6, which serves to increase the sample size, the method for medium-term forecasting employs CNNs and Temporal Convolutional Neural Networks (TCNNs) to extract essential features from high-dimensional geospatial data. This feature extraction lays the foundation for probabilistic deep learning, which determines an approximate distribution of the target variables, capturing the data's structure and uncertainty [95]. The model's parameters are optimized by maximizing the Evidence Lower Bound (ELBO) within the variational inference framework. The structure is shown in Figure 6. The integration of deep learning techniques with probabilistic modeling ensures accuracy, robustness to sparse data, and flexibility in assumptions, enhancing the precision of forecasts and offering valuable insights into confidence levels and expert knowledge integration.

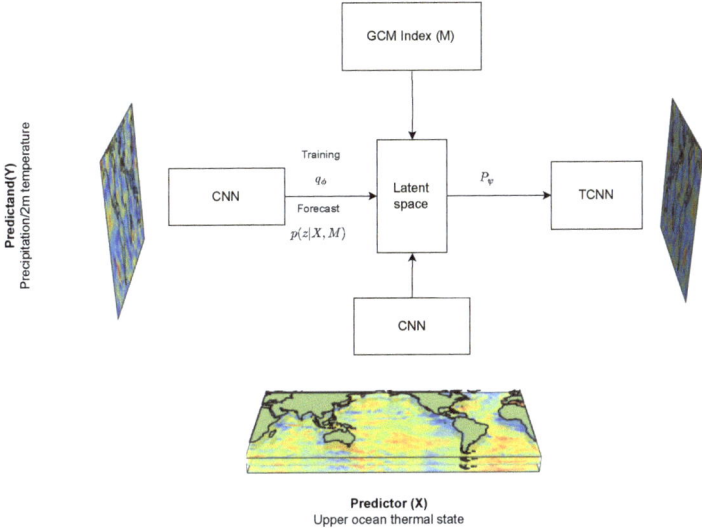

Figure 6. Conditonal Generative Forecasting (CGF) model.

Leveraging advanced techniques in variational inference and neural networks, the method described seeks to approximate the complex distribution $p(Y \mid X, M)$, where Y is the target variable and X and M are predictor and GCM index information, respectively. The process is outlined as follows:

1. *Problem Definition:* The goal is to approximate $p(Y \mid X, M)$, a task challenged by high-dimensional geospatial data, data inhomogeneity, and a large dataset.
2. *Model Specification:*
    - Random Variable z: A latent variable with a fixed standard Gaussian distribution.
    - Parametric Functions p_θ, q_ϕ, p_ψ: Neural networks for transforming z and approximating target and posterior distributions.
    - Objective Function: Maximization of the Evidence Lower Bound (ELBO).

3. *Training Procedure*:
    - Initialize: Define random variable $z \sim N(0,1)$ [96,97] parametric functions $p_\theta(z, X, M), q_\phi(z \mid X, Y, M), p_\psi(Y \mid X, M, z)$.
    - Training Objective (Maximize ELBO) [98]: The ELBO is defined as:

$$\text{ELBO} = \mathbb{E}_{z \sim q_\phi} \left(\log p_\psi(Y \mid X, M, z) \right) - \mathcal{D}_{\text{KL}}(q_\phi \| p(z \mid X, M)) - \mathcal{D}_{\text{KL}}(q_\phi \| p(z \mid X, Y, M)) \qquad (8)$$

    with terms for reconstruction, regularization, and residual error.
    - Optimization: Utilize variational inference, Monte Carlo reparameterization, and Gaussian assumptions.
4. *Forecasting*: Generate forecasts by sampling $p(z \mid X, M)$, the likelihood of p_ψ, and using the mean of p_ψ for an average estimate.

This method embodies a rigorous approach to approximating complex distributions, bridging deep learning and probabilistic modeling to enhance forecasting accuracy and insights.

$$\text{ELBO}(\lambda) = \mathbb{E}_{q(\mathbf{z}|\mathbf{x})} [\log p(\mathbf{x}, \mathbf{z}) - \log q(\mathbf{z}|\mathbf{x})] \text{ (Evidence Lower Bound)} \qquad (9)$$

In summary, the combination of deep learning and probabilistic insights presents a unique and potent method for spatial predictive analytics. The approach is marked by scalability, flexibility, and an ability to learn complex spatial features, even though challenges persist, such as intrinsic complexity in computational modeling and the requirement for a profound statistical and computer science background. Its potential in handling large data sets and adapting to varying scenarios highlights its promising applicability in modern spatial predictive analytics, representing an advanced tool in the arena of seasonal climate prediction.

Cycle-Consistent Generative Adversarial Networks. Cycle-Consistent Generative Adversarial Networks (CycleGANs) have been ingeniously applied to the bias correction of high-resolution Earth System Model (ESM) precipitation fields, such as GFDL-ESM4 [99]. This model includes two generators responsible for translating between simulated and real domains, and two discriminators to differentiate between generated and real observations. A key component of this approach is the cycle consistency loss, which ensures a reliable translation between domains coupled with a constraint to maintain global precipitation values for physical consistency. By framing bias correction as an image-to-image translation task, CycleGANs have significantly improved spatial patterns and distributions in climate projections. The model's utilization of spatial spectral densities and fractal dimension measurements further emphasizes its spatial context awareness, making it a groundbreaking technique in the field of climate science. The CycleGAN model consists of two generators and two discriminators, along with a cycle consistency loss:

- *Two Generators*: The CycleGAN model includes two generators. Generator G learns the mapping from the simulated domain to the real domain, and generator F learns the mapping from the real domain to the simulated domain [100].
- *Two Discriminators*: There are two discriminators, one for the real domain and one for the simulated domain. Discriminator D_x encourages generator G to generate samples that look similar to samples in the real domain, and discriminator D_y encourages generator F to generate samples that look similar to samples in the simulated domain.
- *Cycle Consistency Loss*: To ensure that the mappings are consistent, the model enforces the following condition through a cycle consistency loss: if a sample is mapped from the simulated domain to the real domain and then mapped back to the simulated domain, it should get a sample similar to the original simulated sample. Similarly, if a sample is mapped from the real domain to the simulated domain and then mapped back to the real domain, it should get a sample similar to the original real sample.

$$\mathcal{L}_{\text{cyc}}(G, F) = \mathbb{E}_{x \sim p_{\text{data}}(x)} [\|F(G(x)) - x\|_1] + \mathbb{E}_{y \sim p_{\text{data}}(y)} [\|G(F(y)) - y\|_1] \qquad (10)$$

- *Training Process*: The model is trained to learn the mapping between these two domains by minimizing the adversarial loss and cycle consistency loss between the generators and discriminators.

$$\mathcal{L}_{\text{Gen}}(G,F) = \mathcal{L}_{\text{GAN}}(G,D_y,X,Y) + \mathcal{L}_{\text{GAN}}(F,D_x,Y,X) + \lambda\mathcal{L}_{\text{cyc}}(G,F) \quad (11)$$

- *Application to Prediction*: Once trained, these mappings can be used for various tasks, such as transforming simulated precipitation data into forecasts that resemble observed data.

The bidirectional mapping strategy of Cycle-Consistent Generative Adversarial Networks (CycleGANs) permits the exploration and learning of complex transformation relationships between two domains without reliance on paired training samples. This attribute holds profound significance, especially in scenarios where only unlabeled data are available for training. In its specific application within climate science, this characteristic of CycleGAN enables precise capturing and modeling of the subtle relationships between real and simulated precipitation data. Through this unique bidirectional mapping shown in Figure 7, the model not only enhances the understanding of climatic phenomena but also improves the predictive accuracy of future precipitation trends. This provides a novel, data-driven methodology for climate prediction and analysis, contributing to the ever-expanding field of computational climate science.

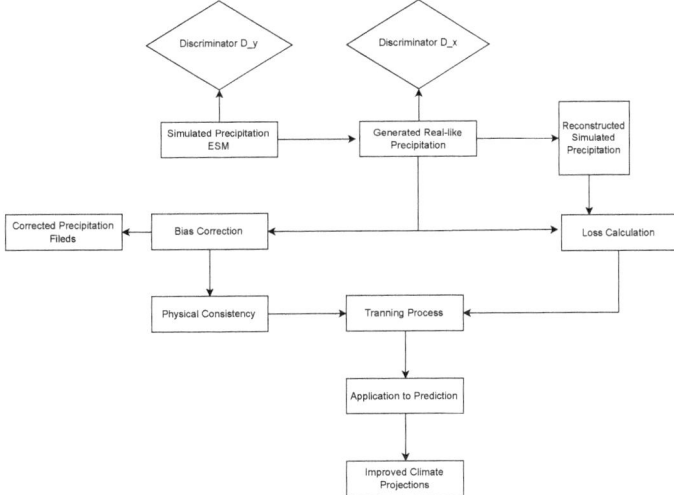

Figure 7. CycleGAN flow chart.

DeepESD. Traditional GCMs, while proficient in simulating large-scale global climatic dynamics [101,102], exhibit intrinsic limitations in representing finer spatial scales and specific regional characteristics. This inadequacy manifests as a pronounced resolution gap at localized scales, restricting the applicability of GCMs in detailed regional climate studies [103,104].

In stark contrast, the utilization of CNNs symbolizes a significant breakthrough [105]. Structurally characterized by hierarchical convolutional layers, CNNs possess the unique ability to articulate complex multi-scale spatial features across disparate scales, commencing with global coarse-grained characteristics and progressively refining to capture intricate regional details. An exemplar implementation of this approach was demonstrated by Baño-Medina et al. [104], wherein a CNN comprised three convolutional layers with spatial kernels of varying counts (50, 25, and 10, respectively). The transformation process began with the recalibration of ERA-Interim reanalysis data to a 2° regular grid, elevating it to 0.5° [106–108]. This configuration allowed the CNN to translate global atmospheric patterns into high-resolution regional specificity [109,110].

The nuanced translation from global to regional scales, achieved through sequential convolutional layers, not only amplifies the spatial resolution but also retains the contextual relevance of climatic variables [111,112]. The first convolutional layer captured global coarse-grained features, with subsequent layers incrementally refining these into nuanced regional characteristics. By the terminal layer, the CNN had effectively distilled complex atmospheric dynamics into a precise, high-resolution grid [113,114].

This enhancement fosters a more robust understanding of regional climatic processes, ushering in an era of precision and flexibility in climate modeling. The deployment of this technology affirms a pivotal advancement in the field, opening new possibilities for more granulated, precise, and comprehensive examination of climatic processes and future scenarios [115–117]. The introduction of CNNs thus represents a transformative approach shown in Figure 8 to bridging the resolution gap inherent to traditional GCMs, with substantial implications for future climate analysis and scenario planning.

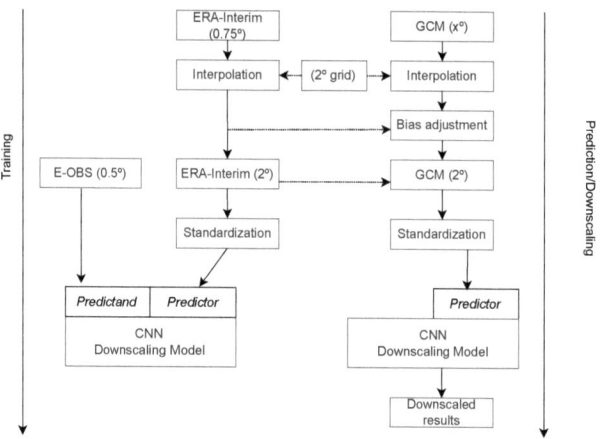

Figure 8. DeepESD structure.

NNCAM. The design and implementation of the Neural Network Community Atmosphere Model (NNCAM) are architected to leverage advancements in machine learning for improved atmospheric simulations. The architecture is a nuanced blend of traditional General Circulation Models (GCMs), specifically the Super-Parameterized Community Atmosphere Model (SPCAM), and cutting-edge machine learning techniques like Residual Deep Neural Networks (ResDNNs).

- Reference Model: SPCAM. SPCAM serves as the foundational GCM and is embedded with Cloud-Resolving Models (CRMs) to simulate microscale atmospheric processes like cloud formation and convection. SPCAM is employed to generate "target simulation data", which serves as the training baseline for the neural networks. The use of CRMs is inspired by recent advancements in data science, demonstrating that machine learning parameterizations can potentially outperform traditional methods in simulating convective and cloud processes.

- Neural Networks: ResDNNs, a specialized form of deep neural networks, are employed for their ability to approximate complex, nonlinear relationships. The network comprises multiple residual blocks, each containing two fully connected layers with Rectified Linear Unit (ReLU) activations. ResDNNs are designed to address the vanishing and exploding gradient problems in deep networks through residual connections, offering a stable and effective gradient propagation mechanism. This makes them well-suited for capturing the complex and nonlinear nature of atmospheric processes.

- Subgrid-Scale Physical Simulator. Traditional parameterizations often employ simplified equations to model subgrid-scale processes, which might lack accuracy. In contrast, the ResDNNs are organized into a subgrid-scale physical simulator that operates independently within each model grid cell. This simulator takes atmospheric states as inputs and outputs physical quantities at the subgrid scale, such as cloud fraction and precipitation rate.

In the NNCAM model, the core workflow is divided into several key steps to achieve efficient and accurate climate simulations. First, the dynamic core, which serves as the base component of the model, is responsible for solving the underlying hydrodynamic equations and calculating the current climate state, e.g., temperature, pressure, and humidity, as well as the environmental forcings, e.g., wind and solar radiation. These calculations are then transmitted to the NN-GCM coupler. Upon receiving these data, the coupler further passes them to the neural network parameterization module. This module utilizes pre-trained neural networks, specifically ResDNNs, for faster and more accurate parameterization of the climate. Upon completion of the predictions, these results are fed back to the host GCM, i.e., NNCAM. The host GCM then uses the predictions generated by these neural networks to update the climate state in the model, and based on these updates, it performs the simulation at the next time step.

Overall, the host GCM, as the core of the whole simulation, is not only responsible for the basic climate simulation but also efficiently interacts with the dynamic core and neural network parameterization modules to achieve higher simulation accuracy and computational efficiency. This hierarchical architecture ensures both computational efficiency and high simulation fidelity. It allows for seamless integration and synchronization of the model states and predictions, thereby enabling continuous and efficient operation of NNCAM. The proposed framework represents a significant stride in the realm of atmospheric science, offering a harmonious integration of machine learning and physical simulations to achieve unprecedented accuracy and computational efficiency.

CGF, DeepESD, and CycleGAN are very different in their uses and implementations, but there are also some levels of similarity. All three approaches focus on mapping from one data distribution to another. Furthermore, they focus more on the mechanisms of climate change than previous models for weather forecasting. CycleGAN specifically emphasizes the importance of not only mapping from distribution A to B but also the inverse mapping capability from B to A, which is to some extent what CGF and DeepESD are concerned with. NNCAM realizes the mapping from physical parameterization to machine learning parameterization. This mapping can be viewed as a functional mapping that replaces parameterized functions in the physical process with functions learned and inferred by the machine learning model.

6.2. Result Analysis

CGF: In the utilization of deep probabilistic machine learning techniques, the figure compares the performance of the CGF model using both simulated samples and actual data against the traditional climate model, Cancm4. The findings illustrate that our model outperforms the conventional climate modeling approach in terms of accuracy, irrespective of the employment of simulated or real data sets. This distinction emphasizes the enhanced predictive capability of our method and underlines its potential superiority in handling complex meteorological phenomena.

CycleGANs: In the context of long-term climate estimation, the application of deep learning for model correction has yielded promising results. As illustrated in the accompanying figure, the diagram delineates the mean absolute errors of different models relative to the W5E5v2 baseline facts. Among these, the error correction technique utilizing Generative Adversarial Networks (GANs) in conjunction with the ISIMIP3BASD physical model has demonstrated the lowest discrepancy. This evidence underscores the efficacy of sophisticated deep-learning methodologies in enhancing the precision of long-term climate estimations, thereby reinforcing their potential utility in climatological research and forecasting applications.

DeepESD: In the conducted study, deep learning has been employed to enhance resolution, resulting in a model referred to as DeepESD. The following figure portrays the Probability Density Functions (PDFs) of precipitation and temperature for the historical period from 1979 to 2005, as expressed by the General Circulation Model (GCM) in red, the Regional Climate Model (RCM) in blue, and DeepESD in green. These are contextualized across regions such as the Alps, the Iberian Peninsula, and Eastern Europe as defined by the PRUDENCE area. In the diagram, solid lines represent the overall mean, while the shaded region includes two standard deviations. Dashed lines depict the distribution mean of each PDF. A clear observation from the graph illustrates that DeepESD maintains higher consistency with observed data in comparison to the other models.

NNCAM: NNCAM has demonstrated proficient simulation of strong precipitation centers across maritime continental tropical regions, Asian monsoon areas, South America, and the Caribbean. The model maintains the spatial pattern and global average of precipitation over the subsequent 5 years in its simulation, showcasing its long-term stability. Overall, in terms of the spatial distribution of multi-annual summer precipitation, NNCAM results are closer to the standard values compared with those from CAM5, with smaller root mean square errors and global average deviations. Additionally, NNCAM operates at a speed that is 30 times faster than traditional models, marking a significant stride in enhancing computational efficiency.

In Table 4, MAE is a metric commonly used to measure the magnitude of forecast errors. It calculates the average of the absolute errors between the actual and predicted values. This metric was selected because it provides a clear, intuitive way to understand the accuracy of model predictions. A low MAE value indicates better prediction accuracy, while a high MAE value indicates a larger prediction error. The Euclidean Distance to Observations in the Probability Density Function (PDF) is utilized to evaluate the performance of the model by comparing the distance difference in the PDFs between the predicted and actual observed data. This metric was selected because it provides a means of quantifying how well a model's predicted distribution aligns with the actual observed distribution, enabling the evaluation of model performance in complex systems, particularly when dealing with systems that possess inherent uncertainty and variability. While these four methods address different problems and, thus, a direct comparison is not feasible in this study, it is evident that they all exhibit significant improvements compared with traditional earth system models.

Table 4. Medium-to-long term climate prediction model result comparison.

Name	Categories	Metrics	ESM	This Model
CycleGAN [59]	Bias correction	MAE	0.241	0.068
DeepESD [58]	Down-scaling	Euclidean Distance to Observations in PDF	0.5	0.03
CGF [61]	Prediction	ACC	0.31	0.4
NNCAM [57]	Emulation	Speed	1	30 times speed-up

From the results, it can be discerned that although the utilization of machine learning has significantly diminished in medium-to-long-term climate forecasting, our findings demonstrate that by judiciously addressing the challenge of scarce sample sizes and employing appropriate machine learning techniques, superior results can still be achieved compared with those derived from physical models. This observation underscores the potential of machine learning methodologies to enhance prediction accuracy in climate science, even in situations constrained by data limitations. In the context of climate estimation, it is observable that the utilization of neural networks for predicting climate variations has become less prevalent among meteorologists. However, the adoption of machine learning techniques to aid and optimize climate modeling has emerged as a complementary strategy. As evidenced by the two preceding figures, climate models that have been enhanced through the application of machine learning demonstrate superior predictive capabilities when compared with other conventional models.

7. Discussion

Weather forecasting and climate prediction are closely related to people's lives and provide important information and support for social and economic activities. For example, governments and relief organizations rely on accurate weather forecasts to warn of and respond to natural disasters, thereby mitigating their impact on people's lives and property. At the same time, the energy industry also relies heavily on climate forecasts to predict energy demand and optimize energy distribution, thereby ensuring the stability and efficiency of energy supply. Our research purpose, the examination of machine learning in meteorological forecasting, is situated within a rich historical context, charting the evolution of weather prediction methodologies. Starting from simple statistical methods to complex deterministic modeling, the field has witnessed a paradigm shift with the advent of machine learning techniques.

7.1. Overall Comparison

In this section of our survey, we delineate key differences between our study and existing surveys, thereby underscoring the unique contribution of our work. We contrast various time scales—short-term versus medium-to-long-term climate predictions—to substantiate our rationale for focusing on these particular temporal dimensions. Additionally, we draw a comparative analysis between machine learning approaches and traditional models in climate prediction. This serves to highlight our reason for centering our survey on machine learning techniques for climate forecasting. Overall, this section not only amplifies the distinctiveness and relevance of our survey but also frames it within the larger scientific discourse.

Comparison to existing surveys. Compared to existing literature, our survey takes a unique approach by cohesively integrating both short-term weather forecasting and medium-to-long-term climate predictions—a dimension often underrepresented. While other surveys may concentrate on a limited range of machine learning methods, ours extends to nearly 20 different techniques. However, we recognize our limitations, particularly the challenge of providing an exhaustive analysis due to the complexity of machine learning algorithms and their multifaceted applications in meteorology. This signals an opportunity for future research to delve deeper into specialized machine-learning techniques or specific climatic variables. In contrast to many generalized surveys, our study ventures into the technical nuances of scalability, interpretability, and applicability for each method. We also make a conscious effort to incorporate the most recent advances in the field, although we acknowledge that the pace of technological change inevitably leaves room for further updates. In sum, while our survey provides a more comprehensive and technically detailed roadmap than many existing reviews, it also highlights gaps and opportunities for future work in this rapidly evolving interdisciplinary domain.

Short-term weather prediction vs. medium-to-long-term climate predication. Short-term weather predictions focus on immediate atmospheric conditions within a time span of hours to days. This is a contrast to medium-to-long-term climate predictions, which aim to forecast broader patterns in weather, temperature trends, and precipitation averages over extended timeframes of months to decades. The goals underlying these two forms of prediction also diverge significantly. Short-term forecasts are usually operational in nature, aimed at immediate public safety or aiding sectors like agriculture and industry, whereas medium-to-long-term predictions typically inform strategic and policy-oriented planning for various societal sectors, including agriculture, energy, and urban development.

This comparison extends to the variables considered in the predictive models. Short-term weather predictions often hone in on localized states like temperature, humidity, wind speed, and precipitation. On the other hand, medium-to-long-term climate predictions scrutinize a wider array of variables, such as average temperature shifts, sea-level rise, and the general patterns of extreme weather events, often on a global or regional scale.

Regarding methodologies, machine learning techniques such as neural networks, random forests, and support vector machines are frequently deployed in the realm of short-term weather prediction, owing to their prowess in swiftly analyzing large datasets. In contrast, for medium-to-long-term climate predictions, machine learning generally complements traditional physics-based models, serving a supplementary role to handle the complexities and uncertainties inherent in longer-range forecasts.

Finally, each type of prediction comes with its own set of challenges. Short-term forecasts grapple with issues related to the accuracy and granularity of the data and the speed of its dissemination to the public. Medium-to-long-term climate predictions, however, face challenges related to the scarcity of quality long-term datasets and the intricacies associated with interdependent climatic variables. Yet, there are challenges that are common to both, exemplified by the nonlinearity inherent in weather and climate prediction models, which underscore the complex dynamic relationships among atmospheric variables, necessitating techniques adept at capturing such intricate interactions. Furthermore, the assessment of model uncertainties is arduous as they emanate from various facets, demanding algorithms that can quantify, accommodate, and ideally mitigate these uncertainties to augment the reliability and accuracy of predictions.

Machine-learning models vs. traditional models. In terms of computational speed, machine learning algorithms—particularly those based on deep learning—have the capability to process extensive datasets at a far quicker rate compared with traditional methodologies. When it comes to prediction accuracy, the machine learning algorithms stand out for their superior feature extraction capabilities, often yielding more precise outcomes in short-term weather forecasting scenarios. Additionally, the adaptability of machine learning models enables them to evolve and improve over time. This flexibility makes them particularly useful tools that can be fine-tuned as climate data and observational technologies continue to advance.

While machine learning models can excel at generating rapid and sometimes more accurate forecasts, their lack of interpretability can be a barrier to gaining deeper scientific insights. Machine learning models, especially complex ones like deep neural networks, are often considered "black boxes", meaning their internal workings are not easily understandable. This is a significant drawback during meteorological application. Understanding the underlying mechanisms of weather and climate variability is crucial across all temporal scales, serving as the bedrock upon which all predictive methods are built. For instance, in short-term weather forecasting, an in-depth grasp of these mechanisms assists researchers in selecting the most relevant datasets. For example, when forecasting precipitation, it would be ineffective to merely input precipitation data as a training set. Instead, one must understand the specific meteorological factors that influence precipitation in a given region. This necessity becomes even more pronounced for medium-to-long-term forecasts, which are inherently more complex. To construct accurate and reliable models, it is imperative to identify the factors that interact with each other, eventually leading to variations in the target predictive elements for a particular region. Thus, a nuanced understanding of these mechanisms not only enhances the precision of our models but also broadens the scope for comprehensive climatic analysis and future scenario planning.

7.2. Challenge

Although we found extensive work on machine learning frameworks that succeed in short-term weather prediction and even outperform traditional methods, climate prediction in the medium-to-long term mainly relies on traditional methods. The main challenges can be attributed to the limited data size and complex climate change effects.

Dataset. The scarcity of seasonal meteorological data, particularly evident from the era around 1979, poses significant challenges for applying machine learning to climate prediction. While data from this period may be adequate for short-term weather forecasting, it falls short for medium-to-long-term climate models. This data limitation impacts machine learning algorithms, which rely on large, quality datasets for robust training. Consequently, the lack of seasonal data affects not only the model's performance and reliability but also complicates validation procedures. This makes it challenging to assess the model's generalizability and accuracy. Additionally, the sparse data hampers the effective fusion of machine learning with traditional physics-based models, affecting the overall reliability of climate predictions. Therefore, the limitations of historical meteorological data significantly constrain the application of machine learning in long-term climate studies.

Complex climate change effect. A certain climate change may be related to hundreds or thousands of variables. It's difficult for us to use machine learning to capture their correlation. The intricate nature of climate change, influenced by hundreds or even thousands of interrelated variables, presents a daunting challenge for machine learning applications in climate prediction. Unlike simpler systems, where causal relationships between variables are straightforward, climate systems embody complex, non-linear interactions that are difficult to model. Machine learning algorithms, though powerful, often require clearly defined feature sets and labels for effective training, a condition seldom met in the realm of climate science. The sheer number of variables can lead to issues of dimensionality, where the complexity of the model grows exponentially, making it computationally intensive and difficult to interpret. Furthermore, capturing long-term dependencies between these myriad variables is particularly challenging, given the current state-of-the-art in machine learning techniques. This complexity often results in models that, while mathematically sophisticated, lack the interpretability necessary for scientific validation and policy implications.

7.3. Future Work

For these challenges and the disadvantages of machine-learning prediction methods in meteorology, we propose the following future work:

- Simulate the dataset using statistical methods or physical methods.
- Combining statistical knowledge with machine learning methods to enhance the interpretability of patterns.
- Consider the introduction of physics-based constraints into deep learning models to produced more accurate and reliable results.
- Accelerating Physical Model Prediction with machine learning knowledge.

Simulating Datasets: One promising avenue for future work is to simulate datasets using either statistical or physical methods. Such synthetic datasets can provide a controlled environment to test and validate predictive models. Utilizing methods like Monte Carlo simulations or employing first-principle equations to generate realistic data, this approach promises to enhance model robustness by enabling better generalizability testing.

Enhancing Interpretability: The issue of interpretability is a well-known drawback of machine learning models. A future research direction could be the fusion of statistical methodologies with machine learning algorithms. Incorporating statistical tests for feature selection or Bayesian methods for uncertainty quantification can render the inherently opaque machine learning models more interpretable, thereby making their results more actionable in critical fields like meteorology.

Physics-Based Constraints: A particularly vital frontier for research is the integration of atmospheric physics-based constraints into deep learning architectures. Traditional machine learning models, when unconstrained, might produce forecasts that, although statistically plausible, violate fundamental principles of atmospheric physics and dynamics. To mitigate this, it would be beneficial to incorporate terms or constraints that reflect the known interactions among meteorological elements such as temperature, pressure, and humidity. This can be done through methods like Physics-Informed Neural Networks (PINNs) or physics-based regularization terms. Such an approach would be invaluable for complex meteorological applications like severe weather forecasting, where both the accuracy and physical plausibility of predictions are of utmost importance.

Accelerating Physical Models: Lastly, the intersection of machine learning with traditional physical models offers significant potential. Physical models are often computationally intensive; however, machine learning can expedite these calculations. Techniques such as model parallelization or simpler surrogate models developed via machine learning could dramatically speed up real-time analysis and forecasting, a critical need in time-sensitive applications.

Machine Learning (ML), a subset of Artificial Intelligence (AI), holds a distinctive prowess in discerning patterns from large datasets, yet it does not possess the capability to replace physical models, including the NWP and the Global Climate Model. This limitation predominantly stems from ML's inherent "black box" nature, which lacks explicability, in contrast to the physical models based on atmosphere principles. The symbiotic alliance between ML and physical models unveils a plethora of enhancements in weather forecasting. Specifically, ML significantly augments physical models in areas like bias correction, parameterization, and Down-scaling, where the fusion of data-driven insights with physical models tends to yield more accurate and efficient forecasts. On the flip side, physical models enrich ML by imparting robust physical constraints that guide the learning process towards physically plausible solutions. The inextricable synergy between ML and NWP models is underscored by their irreplaceable strengths, heralding a future where their collaborative integration could unlock new horizons in advancing meteorological science and forecasting accuracy. This harmonious coexistence not only propels the forecasting capabilities to new heights but also bridges the interpretability gap, thereby fostering a more comprehensive understanding and enhanced trust in predictive modeling within the meteorological community.

8. Conclusions

In conclusion, this study offers an extensive look into the transformative role of machine learning in meteorological forecasting. It uniquely amalgamates short-term weather forecasting with medium- and long-term climate predictions, covering a total of 20 models and providing an in-depth introduction to eight select models that stand at the forefront of the industry. Our rigorous survey helps distinguish the operational mechanisms of these eight models, serving as a reference for model selection in various contexts. Furthermore, this work identifies current challenges, like the limited dataset of chronological seasons, and suggests future research directions, including data simulation and the incorporation of physics-based constraints. Thus, the survey not only provides a comprehensive current view but also outlines a roadmap for future interdisciplinary work in this burgeoning field. While the research acknowledges its limitations in providing an exhaustive analysis, it delineates a promising direction for future exploration.

Author Contributions: Conceptualization, L.C., Z.Y. and B.H.; methodology, L.C. and Z.Y.; validation, L.C., Z.Y., B.H., J.Z. and X.W.; formal Analysis, Z.Y., L.C., B.H. and W.Y.; resources, J.Z. and L.C.; data curation, L.C. and B.H.; writing—original draft preparation, L.C.; writing—review & editing, L.C., Z.Y. and B.H.; proof reading L.C., Z.Y., B.H., X.W., J.Z. and W.Y.; supervision, Z.Y., X.W. and J.Z.; project administration, Z.Y. and X.W.; funding acquisition, Z.Y. and X.W. All authors have read and agreed to the published version of the manuscript.

Funding: This research received no external funding.

Institutional Review Board Statement: Not applicable.

Informed Consent Statement: Not applicable.

Data Availability Statement: Not applicable.

Conflicts of Interest: The authors declare no conflict of interest.

Abbreviations

Commonly used symbols and definitions:

Symbol	Definition
v	velocity vector
t	time
ρ	fluid density
p	pressure
μ	dynamic viscosity
g	gravitational acceleration vector
$\mathbb{E}_{q(\mathbf{z}\|\mathbf{x})}$	expectation under the variational distribution $q(\mathbf{z}\|\mathbf{x})$
$\mathbf{z}$	latent variable
$\mathbf{x}$	observed data
$p(\mathbf{x}, \mathbf{z})$	joint distribution of observed and latent variables
$q(\mathbf{z}\|\mathbf{x})$	variational distribution
G, F	Generators for mappings from simulated to real domain and vice versa.
D_x, D_y	Discriminators for real and simulated domains.
$\mathcal{L}_{\text{cyc}}$, $\mathcal{L}_{\text{GAN}}$	Cycle consistency loss and Generative Adversarial Network loss.
X, Y	Data distributions for simulated and real domains.
λ	Weighting factor for the cycle consistency loss.

References

1. Abbe, C. The physical basis of long-range weather. *Mon. Weather Rev.* **1901**, *29*, 551–561.
2. Zheng, Y.; Capra, L.; Wolfson, O.; Yang, H. Urban computing: Concepts, methodologies, and applications. *Acm Trans. Intell. Syst. Technol. TIST* **2014**, *5*, 1–55.
3. Gneiting, T.; Raftery, A.E. Weather forecasting with ensemble methods. *Science* **2005**, *310*, 248–249.
4. Agapiou, A. Remote sensing heritage in a petabyte-scale: Satellite data and heritage Earth Engine applications. *Int. J. Digit. Earth* **2017**, *10*, 85–102.
5. Bendre, M.R.; Thool, R.C.; Thool, V.R. Big data in precision agriculture: Weather forecasting for future farming. In Proceedings of the 2015 1st International Conference on Next Generation Computing Technologies (NGCT), Dehradun, India, 4–5 September 2015; pp. 744–750.
6. Zavala, V.M.; Constantinescu, E.M.; Krause, T. On-line economic optimization of energy systems using weather forecast information. *J. Process Control* **2009**, *19*, 1725–1736.
7. Nurmi, V.; Perrels, A.; Nurmi, P.; Michaelides, S.; Athanasatos, S.; Papadakis, M. Economic value of weather forecasts on transportation–Impacts of weather forecast quality developments to the economic effects of severe weather. EWENT FP7 Project. 2012; Volume 490. Available online: http://virtual.vtt.fi/virtual/ewent/Deliverables/D5/D5_2_16_02_2012_revised_final.pdf (accessed on 8 September 2023).
8. Russo, J.A., Jr. The economic impact of weather on the construction industry of the United States. *Bull. Am. Meteorol. Soc.* **1966**, *47*, 967–972.
9. Badorf, F.; Hoberg, K. The impact of daily weather on retail sales: An empirical study in brick-and-mortar stores. *J. Retail. Consum. Serv.* **2020**, *52*, 101921.
10. de Freitas, C.R. Tourism climatology: Evaluating environmental information for decision making and business planning in the recreation and tourism sector. *Int. J. Biometeorol.* **2003**, *48*, 45–54.
11. Smith, K. *Environmental Hazards: Assessing Risk and Reducing Disaster*; Routledge: London, UK, 2013.
12. Hammer, G.L.; Hansen, J.W.; Phillips, J.G.; Mjelde, J.W.; Hill, H.; Love, A.; Potgieter, A. Advances in application of climate prediction in agriculture. *Agric. Syst.* **2001**, *70*, 515–553.
13. Guedes, G.; Raad, R.; Raad, L. Welfare consequences of persistent climate prediction errors on insurance markets against natural hazards. *Estud. Econ. Sao Paulo* **2019**, *49*, 235–264.
14. McNamara, D.E.; Keeler, A. A coupled physical and economic model of the response of coastal real estate to climate risk. *Nat. Clim. Chang.* **2013**, *3*, 559–562.
15. Kleerekoper, L.; Esch, M.V.; Salcedo, T.B. How to make a city climate-proof, addressing the urban heat island effect. *Resour. Conserv. Recycl.* **2012**, *64*, 30–38.
16. Kaján, E.; Saarinen, J. Tourism, climate change and adaptation: A review. *Curr. Issues Tour.* **2013**, *16*, 167–195.
17. Dessai, S.; Hulme, M.; Lempert, R.; Pielke, R., Jr. Climate prediction: A limit to adaptation. *Adapt. Clim. Chang. Threshold. Values Gov.* **2009**, *64*, 78.
18. Ham, Y.-G.; Kim, J.-H.; Luo, J.-J. Deep Learning for Multi-Year ENSO Forecasts. *Nature* **2019**, *573*, 568–572. [CrossRef].
19. Howe, L.; Wain, A. *Predicting the Future*; Cambridge University Press: Cambridge, UK, 1993; Volume V, pp. 1–195.

20. Hantson, S.; Arneth, A.; Harrison, S.P.; Kelley, D.I.; Prentice, I.C.; Rabin, S.S.; Archibald, S.; Mouillot, F.; Arnold, S.R.; Artaxo, P.; et al. The status and challenge of global fire modelling. *Biogeosciences* **2016**, *13*, 3359–3375.
21. Racah, E.; Beckham, C.; Maharaj, T.; Ebrahimi Kahou, S.; Prabhat, M.; Pal, C. ExtremeWeather: A large-scale climate dataset for semi-supervised detection, localization, and understanding of extreme weather events. *Adv. Neural Inf. Process. Syst.* **2017**, *30*, 3402–3413.
22. Gao, S.; Zhao, P.; Pan, B.; Li, Y.; Zhou, M.; Xu, J.; Zhong, S.; Shi, Z. A nowcasting model for the prediction of typhoon tracks based on a long short term memory neural network. *Acta Oceanol. Sin.* **2018**, *37*, 8–12.
23. Ren, X.; Li, X.; Ren, K.; Song, J.; Xu, Z.; Deng, K.; Wang, X. Deep Learning-Based Weather Prediction: A Survey. *Big Data Res.* **2021**, *23*, 100178.
24. Reichstein, M.; Camps-Valls, G.; Stevens, B.; Jung, M.; Denzler, J.; Carvalhais, N.; Prabhat, F. Deep learning and process understanding for data-driven Earth system science. *Nature* **2019**, *566*, 195–204.
25. Stockhause, M.; Lautenschlager, M. CMIP6 data citation of evolving data. *Data Sci. J.* **2017**, *16*, 30.
26. Hsieh, W.W. *Machine Learning Methods in the Environmental Sciences: Neural Networks and Kernels*; Cambridge University Press: Cambridge, UK, 2009.
27. Krasnopolsky, V.M.; Fox-Rabinovitz, M.S.; Chalikov, D.V. New Approach to Calculation of Atmospheric Model Physics: Accurate and Fast Neural Network Emulation of Longwave Radiation in a Climate Model. *Mon. Weather Rev.* **2005**, *133*, 1370–1383.
28. Krasnopolsky, V.M.; Fox-Rabinovitz, M.S.; Belochitski, A.A. Using ensemble of neural networks to learn stochastic convection parameterizations for climate and numerical weather prediction models from data simulated by a cloud resolving model. *Adv. Artif. Neural Syst.* **2013**, *2013*, 485913.
29. Chevallier, F.; Morcrette, J.-J.; Chéruy, F.; Scott, N.A. Use of a neural-network-based long-wave radiative-transfer scheme in the ECMWF atmospheric model. *Q. J. R. Meteorol. Soc.* **2000**, *126*, 761–776.
30. Krasnopolsky, V.M.; Fox-Rabinovitz, M.S.; Hou, Y.T.; Lord, S.J.; Belochitski, A.A. Accurate and fast neural network emulations of model radiation for the NCEP coupled climate forecast system: Climate simulations and seasonal predictions. *Mon. Weather Rev.* **2010**, *138*, 1822–1842.
31. Tolman, H.L.; Krasnopolsky, V.M.; Chalikov, D.V. Neural network approximations for nonlinear interactions in wind wave spectra: Direct mapping for wind seas in deep water. *Ocean. Model.* **2005**, *8*, 253–278.
32. Markakis, E.; Papadopoulos, A.; Perakakis, P. Spatiotemporal Forecasting: A Survey. *arXiv* **2018**, arXiv:1808.06571.
33. Box, G.E.; Jenkins, G.M.; Reinsel, G.C.; Ljung, G.M. *Time Series Analysis: Forecasting and Control*; John Wiley & Sons: Hoboken, NJ, USA, 2015.
34. He, Y.; Kolovos, A. Spatial and Spatio-Temporal Geostatistical Modeling and Kriging. In *Wiley StatsRef: Statistics Reference Online*; John Wiley & Sons: Hoboken, NJ, USA, 2015.
35. Lu, H.; Fan, Z.; Zhu, H. Spatiotemporal Analysis of Air Quality and Its Application in LASG/IAP Climate System Model. *Atmos. Ocean. Sci. Lett.* **2011**, *4*, 204–210.
36. Chatfield, C. *The Analysis of Time Series: An Introduction*, 7th ed.; CRC Press: Boca Raton, FL, USA, 2016.
37. Stull, R. *Meteorology for Scientists and Engineers*, 3rd ed.; Brooks/Cole: Pacific Grove, CA, USA, 2015.
38. Yuval, J.; O'Gorman, P.A. Machine Learning for Parameterization of Moist Convection in the Community Atmosphere Model. *Proc. Natl. Acad. Sci. USA* **2020**, *117*, 12–20.
39. Gagne, D.J.; Haupt, S.E.; Nychka, D.W. Machine Learning for Spatial Environmental Data. *Meteorol. Monogr.* **2020**, *59*, 9.1–9.36.
40. Xu, Z.; Li, Y.; Guo, Q.; Shi, X.; Zhu, Y. A Multi-Model Deep Learning Ensemble Method for Rainfall Prediction. *J. Hydrol.* **2020**, *584*, 124579.
41. Kuligowski, R.J.; Barros, A.P. Localized precipitation forecasts from a numerical weather prediction model using artificial neural networks. *Weather. Forecast.* **1998**, *13*, 1194–1204.
42. Shi, X.; Chen, Z.; Wang, H.; Yeung, D.Y.; Wong, W.K.; Woo, W.C. Convolutional LSTM Network: A Machine Learning Approach for Precipitation Nowcasting. *arXiv* **2015**, arXiv:1506.04214.
43. Qiu, M.; Zhao, P.; Zhang, K.; Huang, J.; Shi, X.; Wang, X.; Chu, W. A short-term rainfall prediction model using multi-task convolutional neural networks. In Proceedings of the 2017 IEEE International Conference on Data Mining (ICDM), New Orleans, LA, USA, 18–21 November 2017; IEEE: New York, NY, USA, 2017; pp. 395–404.
44. Karevan, Z.; Suykens, J.A. Spatio-temporal stacked lstm for temperature prediction in weather forecasting. *arXiv* **2018**, arXiv:1811.06341.
45. Chattopadhyay, A.; Nabizadeh, E.; Hassanzadeh, P. Analog Forecasting of extreme-causing weather patterns using deep learning. *J. Adv. Model. Earth Syst.* **2020**, *12*, e2019MS001958.
46. Sønderby, C.K.; Espeholt, L.; Heek, J.; Dehghani, M.; Oliver, A.; Salimans, T.; Alchbrenner, N. MetNet: A Neural Weather Model for Precipitation Forecasting. *arXiv* **2020**, arXiv:2003.12140.
47. Pathak, J.; Subramanian, S.; Harrington, P.; Raja, S.; Chattopadhyay, A.; Mardani, M.; Anandkumar, A. FourCastNet: A Global Data-Driven High-Resolution Weather Model Using Adaptive Fourier Neural Operators. *arXiv* **2022**, arXiv:2202.11214.
48. Lam, R.; Sanchez-Gonzalez, A.; Willson, M.; Wirnsberger, P.; Fortunato, M.; Pritzel, A.; Battaglia, P. GraphCast: Learning skillful medium-range global weather forecasting. *arXiv* **2022**, arXiv:2212.12794.
49. Bi, K.; Xie, L.; Zhang, H.; Chen, X.; Gu, X.; Tian, Q. Accurate Medium-Range Global Weather Forecasting with 3D Neural Networks. *Nature* **2023**, *619*, 533–38.

50. Nguyen, T.; Brandstetter, J.; Kapoor, A.; Gupta, J.K.; Grover, A. ClimaX: A foundation model for weather and climate. *arXiv* **2023**, arXiv:2301.10343.
51. Gangopadhyay, S.; Clark, M.; Rajagopalan, B. Statistical Down-scaling using K-nearest neighbors. In *Water Resources Research*; Wiley Online Library: Hoboken, NJ, USA, 2005; Volume 41.
52. Tripathi, S.; Srinivas, V.V.; Nanjundiah, R.S. Down-scaling of precipitation for climate change scenarios: A support vector machine approach. *J. Hydrol.* **2006**, *330*, 621–640.
53. Krasnopolsky, V.M.; Fox-Rabinovitz, M.S. Complex hybrid models combining deterministic and machine learning components for numerical climate modeling and weather prediction. *Neural Netw.* **2006**, *19*, 122–134
54. Raje, D.; Mujumdar, P.P. A conditional random field–based Down-scaling method for assessment of climate change impact on multisite daily precipitation in the Mahanadi basin. In *Water Resources Research*; Wiley Online Library: Hoboken, NJ, USA, 2009; Volume 45.
55. Zarei, M.; Najarchi, M.; Mastouri, R. Bias correction of global ensemble precipitation forecasts by Random Forest method. *Earth Sci. Inform.* **2021**, *14*, 677–689.
56. Andersson, T.R.; Hosking, J.S.; Pérez-Ortiz, M.; Paige, B.; Elliott, A.; Russell, C.; Law, S.; Jones, D.C.; Wilkinson, J.; Phillips, T.; et al. Seasonal Arctic Sea Ice Forecasting with Probabilistic Deep Learning. *Nat. Commun.* **2021**, *12*, 5124.
57. Wang, X.; Han, Y.; Xue, W.; Yang, G.; Zhang, G. Stable climate simulations using a realistic general circulation model with neural network parameterizations for atmospheric moist physics and radiation processes. *Geosci. Model Dev.* **2022**, *15*, 3923-3940
58. Baño-Medina, J.; Manzanas, R.; Cimadevilla, E.; Fernández, J.; González-Abad, J.; Cofiño, A.S.; Gutiérrez, J.M. Down-scaling Multi-Model Climate Projection Ensembles with Deep Learning (DeepESD): Contribution to CORDEX EUR-44. *Geosci. Model Dev.* **2022**, *15*, 6747–6758.
59. Hess, P.; Lange, S.; Boers, N. Deep Learning for bias-correcting comprehensive high-resolution Earth system models. *arXiv* **2022**, arXiv:2301.01253.
60. Wang, F.; Tian, D. On deep learning-based bias correction and Down-scaling of multiple climate models simulations. *Clim. Dyn.* **2022**, *59*, 3451–3468.
61. Pan, B.; Anderson, G.J.; Goncalves, A.; Lucas, D.D.; Bonfils, C.J.W.; Lee, J. Improving Seasonal Forecast Using Probabilistic Deep Learning. *J. Adv. Model. Earth Syst.* **2022**, *14*, e2021MS002766.
62. Hu, Y.; Chen, L.; Wang, Z.; Li, H. SwinVRNN: A Data-Driven Ensemble Forecasting Model via Learned Distribution Perturbation. *J. Adv. Model. Earth Syst.* **2023**, *15*, e2022MS003211.
63. Chen, L.; Zhong, X.; Zhang, F.; Cheng, Y.; Xu, Y.; Qi, Y.; Li, H. FuXi: A cascade machine learning forecasting system for 15-day global weather forecast. *arXiv* **2023**, arXiv:2306.12873.
64. Lin, H.; Gao, Z.; Xu, Y.; Wu, L.; Li, L.; Li, S.Z. Conditional local convolution for spatio-temporal meteorological forecasting. *Proc. Aaai Conf. Artif. Intell.* **2022**, *36*, 7470–7478
65. Chen, K.; Han, T.; Gong, J.; Bai, L.; Ling, F.; Luo, J.J.; Chen, X.; Ma, L.; Zhang, T.; Su, R.; et al. FengWu: Pushing the Skillful Global Medium-range Weather Forecast beyond 10 Days Lead. *arXiv* **2023**, arXiv:2304.02948.
66. de Burgh-Day, C.O.; Leeuwenburg, T. Machine Learning for numerical weather and climate modelling: A review. *EGUsphere* **2023**, *2023*, 1–48.
67. LeCun, Y.; Bottou, L.; Bengio, Y.; Haffner, P. Gradient-based learning applied to document recognition. *Proc. IEEE* **1998**, *86*, 2278–2324.
68. Krizhevsky, A.; Sutskever, I.; Hinton, G.E. ImageNet classification with deep convolutional neural networks. *Adv. Neural Inf. Process. Syst.* **2012**, *25*, 1097–1105.
69. Scherer, D.; Müller, A.; Behnke, S. Evaluation of pooling operations in convolutional architectures for object recognition. In Proceedings of the International Conference on Artificial Neural Networks 2010, Thessaloniki, Greece, 15–18 September 2010; pp. 92–101.
70. LeCun, Y.; Bengio, Y.; Hinton, G. Deep learning. *Nature* **2015**, *521*, 436–444.
71. Liu, Y.; Racah, E.; Correa, J.; Khosrowshahi, A.; Lavers, D.; Kunkel, K.; Wehner, M.; Collins, W. Application of deep convolutional neural networks for detecting extreme weather in climate datasets. *arXiv* **2016**, arXiv:1605.01156.
72. Goodfellow, I.; Warde-Farley, D.; Mirza, M.; Courville, A.; Bengio, Y. Maxout networks. In Proceedings of the International Conference on Machine Learning, Atlanta, GA, USA, 16–21 June 2013; pp. 1319–1327.
73. Marion, M.; Roger, T. Navier-Stokes equations: Theory and approximation. *Handb. Numer. Anal.* **1998**, *6*, 503–689.
74. Iacono, M.J.; Mlawer, E.J.; Clough, S.A.; Morcrette, J.-J. Impact of an improved longwave radiation model, RRTM, on the energy budget and thermodynamic properties of the NCAR community climate model, CCM3. *J. Geophys. Res. Atmos.* **2000**, *105*, 14873–14890.
75. Guo, Y.; Shao, C.; Su, A. Comparative Evaluation of Rainfall Forecasts during the Summer of 2020 over Central East China. *Atmosphere* **2023**, *14*, 992.
76. Guo, Y.; Shao, C.; Su, A. Investigation of Land–Atmosphere Coupling during the Extreme Rainstorm of 20 July 2021 over Central East China. *Atmosphere* **2023**, *14*, 1474.
77. Bauer, P.; Thorpe, A.; Brunet, G. The Quiet Revolution of Numerical Weather Prediction. *Nature* **2015**, *525*, 47–55.
78. Vaswani, A.; Shazeer, N.; Parmar, N.; Uszkoreit, J.; Jones, L.; Gomez, A.N.; Kaiser, Ł.; Polosukhin, I. Attention is All You Need. In Proceedings of the NeurIPS, Long Beach, CA, USA, 4–9 December 2017.

79. Wang, H.; Zhu, Y.; Green, B.; Adam, H.; Yuille, A.; Chen, L.C. Axial-DeepLab: Stand-Alone Axial-Attention for Panoptic Segmentation. *arXiv* **2019**, arXiv:2003.07853.
80. Schmit, T.J.; Griffith, P.; Gunshor, M.M.; Daniels, J.M.; Goodman, S.J.; Lebair, W.J. A closer look at the ABI on the GOES-R series. *Bull. Am. Meteorol. Soc.* **2017**, *98*, 681–698.
81. Li, Z.; Kovachki, N.; Azizzadenesheli, K.; Liu, B.; Bhattacharya, K.; Stuart, A.; Anandkumar, A. Fourier Neural Operator for Parametric Partial Differential Equations. In Proceedings of the International Conference on Learning Representations (ICLR), Virtual Event, 3–7 May 2021.
82. Guibas, J.; Mardani, M.; Li, Z.; Tao, A.; Anandkumar, A.; Catanzaro, B. Adaptive Fourier Neural Operators: Efficient token mixers for transformers. In Proceedings of the International Conference on Representation Learning, Virtual Event, 25–29 April 2022.
83. Rasp, S.; Thuerey, N. Purely data-driven medium-range weather forecasting achieves comparable skill to physical models at similar resolution. *arXiv* **2020**, arXiv:2008.08626.
84. Weyn, J.A.; Durran, D.R.; Caruana, R.; Cresswell-Clay, N. Sub-seasonal forecasting with a large ensemble of deep-learning weather prediction models. *arXiv* **2021**, arXiv:2102.05107.
85. Rasp, S.; Dueben, P.D.; Scher, S.; Weyn, J.A.; Mouatadid, S.; Thuerey, N. Weatherbench: A benchmark data set for data-driven weather forecasting. *J. Adv. Model. Earth Syst.* **2020**, *12*, e2020MS002203.
86. Liu, Z.; Lin, Y.; Cao, Y.; Hu, H.; Wei, Y.; Zhang, Z.; Lin, S.; Guo, B. Swin transformer: Hierarchical vision transformer using shifted windows. In Proceedings of the International Conference on Computer Vision, Virtual, 11–17 October 2021; IEEE: New York, NY, USA, 2021; pp. 10012–10022.
87. Dosovitskiy, A.; Beyer, L.; Kolesnikov, A.; Weissenborn, D.; Zhai, X.; Unterthiner, T.; Dehghani, M.; Minderer, M.; Heigold, G.; Gelly, S.; et al. An image is worth 16x16 words: Transformers for image recognition at scale. *arXiv* **2020**, arXiv:2010.11929.
88. Váňa, F.; Düben, P.; Lang, S.; Palmer, T.; Leutbecher, M.; Salmond, D.; Carver, G. Single precision in weather forecasting models: An evaluation with the IFS. *Mon. Weather Rev.* **2017**, *145*, 495–502.
89. IPCC. *Climate Change 2013: The Physical Science Basis. Contribution of Working Group I to the Fifth Assessment Report of the Intergovernmental Panel on Climate Change*; Cambridge University Press: Cambridge, UK; New York, NY, USA, 2013.
90. Flato, G.; Marotzke, J.; Abiodun, B.; Braconnot, P.; Chou, S.C.; Collins, W.; Cox, P.; Driouech, F.; Emori, S.; Eyring, V.; et al. Evaluation of Climate Models. In *Climate Change 2013: The Physical Science Basis. Contribution of Working Group I to the Fifth Assessment Report of the Intergovernmental Panel on Climate Change*; Cambridge University Press: Cambridge, UK; New York, NY, USA, 2013.
91. Washington, W.M.; Parkinson, C.L. *An Introduction to Three-Dimensional Climate Modeling*; University Science Books: Beijing, China, 2005.
92. Giorgi, F.; Gutowski, W.J. Regional Dynamical Down-scaling and the CORDEX Initiative. *Annu. Rev. Environ. Resour.* **2015**, *40*, 467–490.
93. Randall, D.A.; Wood, R.A.; Bony, S.; Colman, R.; Fichefet, T.; Fyfe, J.; Kattsov, V.; Pitman, A.; Shukla, J.; Srinivasan, J.; et al. Climate Models and Their Evaluation. In *Climate Change 2007: The Physical Science Basis. Contribution of Working Group I to the Fourth Assessment Report of the Intergovernmental Panel on Climate Change*; Cambridge University Press: Cambridge, UK; New York, NY, USA, 2007.
94. Taylor, K.E.; Stouffer, R.J.; Meehl, G.A. An overview of CMIP5 and the experiment design. *Bull. Am. Meteorol. Soc.* **2012**, *93*, 485–498.
95. Miao, C.; Shen, Y.; Sun, J. Spatial–temporal ensemble forecasting (STEFS) of high-resolution temperature using machine learning models. *J. Adv. Model. Earth Syst.* **2019**, *11*, 2961–2973.
96. Mukkavilli, S.; Perone, C.S.; Rangapuram, S.S.; Müller, K.R. Distribution regression forests for probabilistic spatio-temporal forecasting. In Proceedings of the International Conference on Machine Learning (ICML), Vienna, Austria, 12–18 July 2020.
97. Walker, G.; Charlton-Perez, A.; Lee, R.; Inness, P. Challenges and progress in probabilistic forecasting of convective phenomena: The 2016 GFE/EUMETSAT/NCEP/SPC severe convective weather workshop. *Bull. Am. Meteorol. Soc.* **2016**, *97*, 1829–1835.
98. Kingma, D.P.; Welling, M. Auto-encoding variational bayes. *arXiv* **2013**, arXiv:1312.6114.
99. Krasting, J.P.; John, J.G.; Blanton, C.; McHugh, C.; Nikonov, S.; Radhakrishnan, A.; Zhao, M. NOAA-GFDL GFDL-ESM4 model output prepared for CMIP6 CMIP. *Earth Syst. Grid Fed.* **2018**, *10*. [CrossRef]
100. Zhu, J.-Y.; Park, T.; Isola, P.; Efros, A.A. Unpaired image-to-image translation using cycle-consistent adversarial networks. In Proceedings of the IEEE International Conference on Computer Vision, Venice, Italy, 22–29 October 2017; pp. 2223–2232.
101. Brands, S.; Herrera, S.; Fernández, J.; Gutiérrez, J.M. How well do CMIP5 Earth System Models simulate present climate conditions in Europe and Africa? *Clim. Dynam.* **2013**, *41*, 803–817.
102. Vautard, R.; Kadygrov, N.; Iles, C. Evaluation of the large EURO-CORDEX regional climate model ensemble. *J. Geophys. Res.-Atmos.* **2021**, *126*, e2019JD032344.
103. Boé, J.; Somot, S.; Corre, L.; Nabat, P. Large discrepancies in summer climate change over Europe as projected by global and regional climate models: Causes and consequences. *Clim. Dynam.* **2020**, *54*, 2981–3002.
104. Baño-Medina, J.; Manzanas, R.; Gutiérrez, J.M. Configuration and intercomparison of deep learning neural models for statistical Down-scaling. *Geosci. Model Dev.* **2020**, *13*, 2109–2124.
105. Lecun, Y.; Bengio, Y. Convolutional Networks for Images, Speech, and Time-Series. *Handb. Brain Theory Neural Netw.* **1995**, *336*, 1995.

106. Dee, D.P.; Uppala, S.M.; Simmons, A.J.; Berrisford, P.; Poli, P.; Kobayashi, S.; Andrae, U.; Balmaseda, M.A.; Balsamo, G.; Bauer, D.P.; et al. The ERA-Interim reanalysis: Configuration and performance of the data assimilation system. *Q. J. Roy Meteor. Soc.* **2011**, *137*, 553–597.
107. Cornes, R.C.; van der Schrier, G.; van den Besselaar, E.J.M.; Jones, P.D. An Ensemble Version of the E-OBS Temperature and Precipitation Data Sets. *J. Geophys. Res.-Atmos.* **2018**, *123*, 9391–9409.
108. Baño-Medina, J.; Manzanas, R.; Gutiérrez, J.M. On the suitability of deep convolutional neural networks for continentalwide Down-scaling of climate change projections. *Clim. Dynam.* **2021**, *57*, 1–11.
109. Maraun, D.; Widmann, M.; Gutiérrez, J.M.; Kotlarski, S.; Chandler, R.E.; Hertig, E.; Wibig, J.; Huth, R.; Wilcke, R.A. VALUE: A framework to validate Down-scaling approaches for climate change studies. *Earths Future* **2015**, *3*, 1–14.
110. Vrac, M.; Ayar, P. Influence of Bias Correcting Predictors on Statistical Down-scaling Models. *J. Appl. Meteorol. Clim.* **2016**, *56*, 5–26.
111. Williams, P.M. Modelling Seasonality and Trends in Daily Rainfall Data. In *Advances in Neural Information Processing Systems 10, Proceedings of the Neural Information Processing Systems (NIPS). Denver, Colorado, USA, 1997*, MIT Press: Cambridge, MA, USA, 1998; pp. 985–991, ISBN 0-262-10076-2.
112. Cannon, A.J. Probabilistic Multisite Precipitation Down-scaling by an Expanded Bernoulli–Gamma Density Network. *J. Hydrometeorol.* **2008**, *9*, 1284–1300.
113. Schoof, J.T. and Pryor, S.C. Down-scaling temperature and precipitation: A comparison of regression-based methods and artificial neural networks. *Int. J. Climatol.* **2001**, *21*, 773–790.
114. Maraun, D.; Widmann, M. *Statistical Down-Scaling and Bias Correction for Climate Research*; Cambridge University Press: Cambridge, UK, 2018; ISBN 9781107588783.
115. Vrac, M.; Stein, M.; Hayhoe, K.; Liang, X.-Z. A general method for validating statistical Down-scaling methods under future climate change. *Geophys. Res. Lett.* **2007**, *34*, L18701.
116. San-Martín, D.; Manzanas, R.; Brands, S.; Herrera, S.; Gutiérrez, J.M. Reassessing Model Uncertainty for Regional Projections of Precipitation with an Ensemble of Statistical Down-scaling Methods. *J. Clim.* **2017**, *30*, 203–223.
117. Quesada-Chacón, D.; Barfus, K.; Bernhofer, C. Climate change projections and extremes for Costa Rica using tailored predictors from CORDEX model output through statistical Down-scaling with artificial neural networks. *Int. J. Climatol.* **2021**, *41*, 211–232.

Disclaimer/Publisher's Note: The statements, opinions and data contained in all publications are solely those of the individual author(s) and contributor(s) and not of MDPI and/or the editor(s). MDPI and/or the editor(s) disclaim responsibility for any injury to people or property resulting from any ideas, methods, instructions or products referred to in the content.

Review

AI Fairness in Data Management and Analytics: A Review on Challenges, Methodologies and Applications

Pu Chen [1], Linna Wu [2] and Lei Wang [1,*]

[1] College of Communication Engineering, PLA Army Engineering University, Nanjing 210007, China; puchen0127@163.com
[2] Aerospace System Engineering Shanghai, Shanghai 201109, China; wulinna1214@sina.com
* Correspondence: iponly@126.com

Citation: Chen, P.; Wu, L.; Wang, L. AI Fairness in Data Management and Analytics: A Review on Challenges, Methodologies and Applications. *Appl. Sci.* **2023**, *13*, 10258. https://doi.org/10.3390/app131810258

Academic Editors: Wenjie Zhang and Zhengyi Yang

Received: 29 July 2023
Revised: 31 August 2023
Accepted: 1 September 2023
Published: 13 September 2023

Copyright: © 2023 by the authors. Licensee MDPI, Basel, Switzerland. This article is an open access article distributed under the terms and conditions of the Creative Commons Attribution (CC BY) license (https://creativecommons.org/licenses/by/4.0/).

Abstract: This article provides a comprehensive overview of the fairness issues in artificial intelligence (AI) systems, delving into its background, definition, and development process. The article explores the fairness problem in AI through practical applications and current advances and focuses on bias analysis and fairness training as key research directions. The paper explains in detail the concept, implementation, characteristics, and use cases of each method. The paper explores strategies to reduce bias and improve fairness in AI systems, reviews challenges and solutions to real-world AI fairness applications, and proposes future research directions. In addition, this study provides an in-depth comparative analysis of the various approaches, utilizing cutting-edge research information to elucidate their different characteristics, strengths, and weaknesses. The results of the comparison provide guidance for future research. The paper concludes with an overview of existing challenges in practical applications and suggests priorities and solutions for future research. The conclusions provide insights for promoting fairness in AI systems. The information reviewed in this paper is drawn from reputable sources, including leading academic journals, prominent conference proceedings, and well-established online repositories dedicated to AI fairness. However, it is important to recognize that research nuances, sample sizes, and contextual factors may create limitations that affect the generalizability of the findings.

Keywords: AI fairness; bias analysis; data analytics

1. Introduction

1.1. Background

With recent advances in artificial intelligence (AI), decision making has gradually shifted from rule-based systems to machine learning-based developments (e.g., [1–3]), learning patterns from data and performing pattern recognition, inference, or prediction. Although such a new methodological trend is derived from the bias brought by human rules, this bias and unfairness are gradually permeating artificial intelligence in another form, as humans are still involved in collecting the datasets used to train machine learning in the new system [4,5].

Artificial intelligence fairness (AI Fairness) is an issue proposed in response to this status quo, which is intended to prevent different harms (or benefits) to different subgroups, thereby providing a system that both quantifies prejudice and mitigates discrimination against subgroups [6,7]. Questions about AI Fairness are practical and affect the lives around us in many ways. Some decision support systems for credit applications tend to favor certain sociodemographic groups, resulting in people living in certain areas, and people of certain ethnic backgrounds or genders having a certain selection preference for loan approval, which is difficult to make completely objective and fair [8–11]. Meanwhile, disability information is highly sensitive and cannot be shared, thus exacerbating this unfairness due to the opaqueness of the information [12]. Companies may miss out on many potential talents due to an AI-based recruiting engine that is biased against region, gender, and ethnicity, and even cause the company's team composition to gradually become homogenized in biased elements, thereby losing the advantages of diversity [13,14].

It can be seen that the study of this issue has broad social, political, and economic significance. Once the AI misunderstands the intended task, the problem of value misalignment often ensues, and many social issues and responsibilities will arise.

1.2. Directions

Based on the works in recent years, the conceptual development of AI Fairness has focused on the following directions:

- Fairness and bias [15–17]: Introduction of widely used fairness metrics, such as disparate impact, equal opportunity, and statistical parity. Evaluation of their applicability and limitations in different contexts, contributing to a nuanced understanding of group fairness assessment.
- Algorithmic bias mitigation [18–20]: Exploration of techniques, like pre-processing, in-processing, and post-processing, to mitigate algorithmic biases. Critical analysis of their effectiveness in different scenarios, offering insights into the trade-offs between bias reduction and model performance.
- Fair representation learning [21–23]: Introduction of techniques for learning fair representations, including adversarial debiasing and adversarial learning frameworks. Investigation into their potential for producing fair and informative representations, fostering a deeper comprehension of their role in mitigating biases, understanding the true sources of disparities, aiding in the design of more targeted interventions.

Based on the above conceptual directions, we condense and analyze the methodology and technical analysis involved, and focus on the major key elements in this paper, including definition and problem formulation, bias analysis, fair training, and corresponding applications and practices.

This article undertakes a comprehensive exploration of the critical subject of fairness issues within artificial intelligence (AI) systems. The overarching scope of this survey is to provide an in-depth analysis of the multifaceted landscape of AI fairness, covering its foundational aspects, developmental trajectory, practical applications, and emerging research directions. By delving into these dimensions, the survey aims to shed light on the complex challenges linked to fairness in AI, while offering insights into potential remedies and avenues for future exploration.

1.3. Scope

This article mainly collects the research with the details of the corresponding research plan and methodological route, providing a comprehensive survey of the advancements in the domain of AI Fairness. The scope of this survey is expansive and encompasses diverse facets of AI fairness. It begins by elucidating the foundational background and definition of fairness within the realm of AI systems. Subsequently, the survey ventures into the dynamic landscape of fairness concerns, exploring practical applications and recent advancements. Of particular significance are the domains of bias analysis and fairness training, which are delved into as crucial research directions aimed at ameliorating biases and fostering equitable AI outcomes. The survey encompasses meticulous explanations of the concepts, implementations, characteristics, and practical use cases of each method, thereby providing a comprehensive understanding of their nuances.

Encompassing a retrospective spectrum, the covered literature spans from the most recent contributions (e.g., [24–26]) to the initial inception of pertinent theories, extending as far back as 1993 (e.g., [27–29]). A meticulous curation process led to the inclusion of 310 papers from an extensive pool of 1083 pieces of materials. The selection criteria entailed a thorough assessment of factors, such as the intrinsic significance, perceptible impact, novelty, ingenuity, and citation prevalence of the respective works. These works were methodically categorized and subjected to thorough examination within the manuscript.

The ensuing textual discourse encompasses not only analysis but also the deliberation and the derivation of insightful perspectives.

1.4. Contributions

This article offers an extensive and comparative analysis of diverse approaches, leveraging contemporary research to expound upon their distinct attributes, strengths, and limitations. This comparative exploration not only guides researchers but also informs practitioners, providing them with a nuanced understanding of available methods and aiding their decision making.

Additionally, the survey enriches the discourse on AI fairness by contextualizing its practical implications. By exploring strategies to mitigate bias and enhance fairness in AI systems, it bridges the gap between theoretical foundations and real-world challenges. The survey further discusses the critical subject of challenges and solutions in real-world AI fairness applications, offering insights into the current limitations and potential remedies.

Furthermore, this survey contributes by acknowledging the dynamic nature of the AI fairness landscape and the evolving nature of research and advancements. It underscores the evolving nature of the field and the limitations associated with the evidence derived from reputable sources. While these limitations stem from factors such as research nuances, sample sizes, and contextual intricacies, the survey remains committed to fostering the continuous exploration and understanding of AI fairness.

In essence, this survey encompasses a wide-ranging scope, delving into the genesis, evolution, applications, and challenges of AI fairness. Its multifaceted contributions aim to advance the understanding of fairness in AI, providing valuable insights for both academia and industry in their pursuit of equitable and unbiased AI systems.

1.5. Organization of This Article

The organization of the article is organized as follows. Section 2 introduces the background and definition of AI fairness, and Section 3 formulates the definitions and problems of fairness in AI systems. The main directions of the research of addressing AI fairness, bias analysis, and fair training are reviewed in Sections 4 and 5 with details of corresponding methodologies. Section 6 discusses the measures of migrating the bias and improving fairness in the AI system. Section 7 reviews the related issues and solutions in the practical applications of AI fairness, and corresponding future works are discussed and given. Section 8 concludes the paper.

2. Preliminary

2.1. Status Quo

Although the study of fairness in machine learning is a relatively new topic, it has attracted extensive attention. IBM launched AI Fairness 360 [30–32], which can help detect and mitigate unwanted bias in machine learning models and datasets. It provides around 70 fairness metrics to test for bias and 11 algorithms to reduce bias in datasets and models, thereby reducing software bias and improving its fairness (e.g., [33]).

Facebook has also developed the Fairness Flow tool to detect bias in AI, which works by detecting forms of statistical bias in some of Facebook's commonly used models and data labels, enabling the analysis of how certain types of AI models perform across different groups [34–36]. It defines "bias" as the systematic application of different standards to different groups of people. Given a dataset containing predictions, labels, group membership (for example, gender or age), and other information, Fairness Flow can divide the data used by the model into subsets and estimate its performance.

In 2019, Google also embedded the Fairness Indicators component in a series of AI tools it developed, resulting in tools built on top of TensorFlow model analysis that can regularly calculate and visualize fairness indicators for binary and multi-class classification [37–39].

Although the above work provides tools and theoretical analysis, due to the short research time of this problem and still in the preliminary exploratory stage, there is no mature standard for how to quantify the risk of AI fairness and little insights in how to make decisions in the case of consensus and controversy with the commonly accepted solutions to the risks.

2.2. Review Methodology

2.2.1. Materials

Aiming at the topic along with the issues above, we collected a variety of current academic and technical materials on AI equity and conducted a synthesis study. The information synthesized in this study comes from a variety of reliable sources. These sources include recent publications in prestigious academic journals, distinguished conference proceedings, and well-established online repositories dedicated to the fairness of AI.

Our comprehensive search strategy includes systematic searches of respected academic databases, including IEEE Xplore, ScienceDirect, ACM Digital Library, Springer, Wiley Library, etc. In addition, we carefully reviewed relevant conference proceedings and authoritative organization websites to ensure research inclusiveness. In a robust and diverse collection, we conducted a meticulous review process that encompassed a wide range of sources. We extensively searched through various databases, culminating in the compilation of 1083 materials, comprising Proceedings, Miscellaneous, Articles, Tech Reports, Books, Ph.D. theses, and Collections. To filter the literature and complete the review, the review process was multifaceted and involved several key criteria.

2.2.2. Criteria

The inclusion and exclusion criteria we use in selecting sources of information are carefully thought out to ensure the relevance and quality of the studies included in our analysis. Our criteria included peer-reviewed academic articles, conference papers, and authoritative reports that explicitly address the fairness of AI in data management and analytics. During the synthesis process, we thoughtfully grouped studies based on thematic affinity, methodology, and the nature of the fairness challenges to be addressed. This grouping strategy facilitates a coherent and well-organized synthesis of the different perspectives in the literature. Our criteria for selecting materials are carefully considered and include the following factors, including the following:

- Duplication: We strive to offer diverse and original content to our audience. To avoid redundancy, we review submissions to ensure that the material we publish does not duplicate the existing content in our collection.
- Ineligible content: Our selection process also involves evaluating whether the submitted content meets our eligibility criteria, including adhering to our guidelines and standards.
- Publishing time: We value timeliness and relevance. We prioritize materials that are current and align with the most recent developments and trends in the respective field.
- Quality of publication: Ensuring the quality of the content we publish is of utmost importance. We assess the accuracy, credibility, and overall value of the material to ensure it meets our quality standards.
- Accessibility: Our goal is to make information accessible to a wide range of readers. We select materials that are well structured, clear, and easily understandable, catering to readers with varying levels of expertise.
- Similarity of content: While covering a broad spectrum of topics, we also strive for variety and distinctiveness in our content selection. We aim to present diverse perspectives and insights to enrich the reader experience.

We adopted PRISMA (Preferred Reporting Items for Systematic Reviews and Meta-Analyses) in our review, which meticulously outlines the systematic progression of the study identification, screening, eligibility, and inclusion phases, thereby increasing the reproducibility and rigor of the review process. The PRISMA procedure is shown in Figure 1 as a flowchart. After the procedure, reference lists of selected articles in the field are reviewed intensively while identifying potential studies.

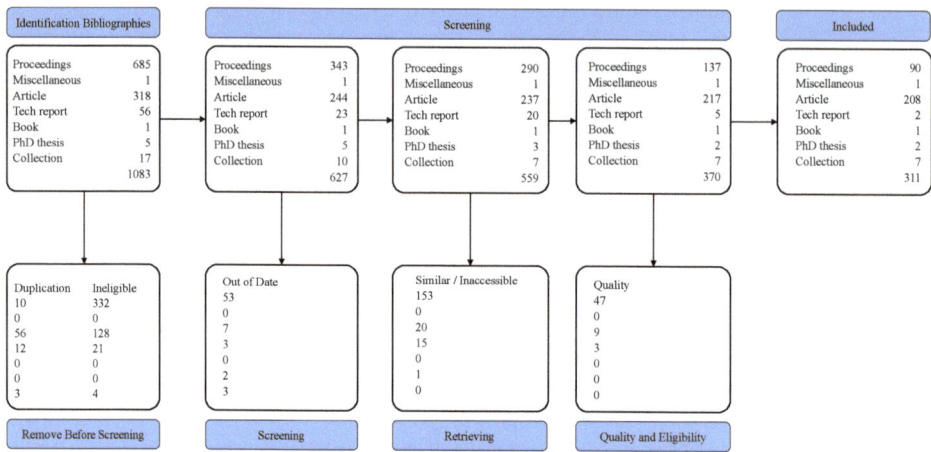

Figure 1. Procedure of preferred reporting items for systematic reviews and meta-analyses.

2.3. Limitations

It is important to recognize that while these sources have contributed significantly to our understanding, there are limitations to the evidence they provide. These limitations stem primarily from nuances in research methodology, sample size, and context, which may affect the generalizability of the conclusions drawn from individual studies. The landscape of AI fairness is dynamic, with research and advancements continually shaping our understanding of its complexities. While our current coverage might have limitations due to the rapid pace of change and ongoing research, please know that we are committed to further studying and exploring this crucial subject. Despite these inherent limitations, our review endeavors to provide a comprehensive and balanced overview of the current state of research related to the fairness of AI. We are dedicated to providing accurate and comprehensive information to readers with the notice of the need to stay engaged with emerging topics like AI fairness.

3. Definition and Problems

3.1. Definition

As AI technologies continue to permeate all aspects of society, ensuring fairness in their decision-making processes is crucial to avoid perpetuating bias and inequality. However, defining what constitutes fairness in AI is a complex and multifaceted task. So far, there are mainly seven types of definitions, including individual fairness [40,41], group fairness [42], equality of opportunity [11], disparate treatment [43], fairness through unawareness [44,45], disparate impact [46], and subgroup fairness [47].

Fairness in AI can be approached through different conceptual lenses. Individual fairness emphasizes equitable treatment for similar individuals, while group fairness aims to avoid disparate treatment based on demographic attributes. Equality of opportunity focuses on consistent predictive accuracy and error rates across various groups, regardless of outcomes.

An alternative approach is fairness through unawareness, achieved by ignoring sensitive attributes in decision making. Despite its intentions, this method might indirectly perpetuate bias present in data. Disparate impact examines whether AI systems disproportionately harm certain groups, irrespective of intent. It aims to uncover biases in outcomes, intentional or not.

To address complex interactions, subgroup fairness evaluates fairness at the intersection of multiple protected attributes, ensuring equitable experiences for diverse subgroups. These conceptions contribute to a comprehensive understanding of fairness in AI and underscore the multifaceted nature of achieving equitable outcomes.

Table 1 summarizes these approaches to fairness in AI. Individual fairness prioritizes personalized treatment, while group fairness targets demographic equity. Fairness through unawareness and equality of opportunity tackle fairness differently—ignoring attributes vs. ensuring equal chances based on qualifications. Disparate impact assesses negative effects, disparate treatment detects unequal treatment. Subgroup fairness navigates complex attribute interactions for equitable outcomes. These concepts collectively enrich the understanding of fairness in AI systems.

Table 1. Fairness definition.

Data Bias	Definition	Main Cause	References
Individual Fairness	Similarity at the individual level	Treat similar individuals similarly	[40,41,48,49]
Group Fairness	Equitable outcomes for demographic groups	Avoid disparities among groups	[42,50,51]
Fairness through Unawareness	Ignoring sensitive attributes	Treat individuals as if attributes are unknown	[44,45,52]
Equality of Opportunity	Equal chances for similar qualifications	Ensure equal chances for outcomes	[11,53,54]
Disparate Impact	Disproportionate negative effects	Evaluate disparities in outcomes	[6,46,55]
Disparate Treatment	Explicit unequal treatment	Detect explicit biases in treatment	[43,56,57]
Subgroup Fairness	Fairness at the intersection of multiple attributes	Consider fairness for multiple groups	[47,58]

3.2. Problems

The risks with AI systems mainly come from data accountability [24,59] and algorithm accountability [60–62]. The connotation of data accountability mainly includes data ownership, storage, use, and sharing, while algorithm accountability emphasizes determining who is responsible for the output of AI algorithms. The interplay of these two risks also raises the question of mission inclusivity [63–65], which mainly focuses on whether the AI system is effective for diverse user populations. Bias effects in machine learning are shown in Figure 2.

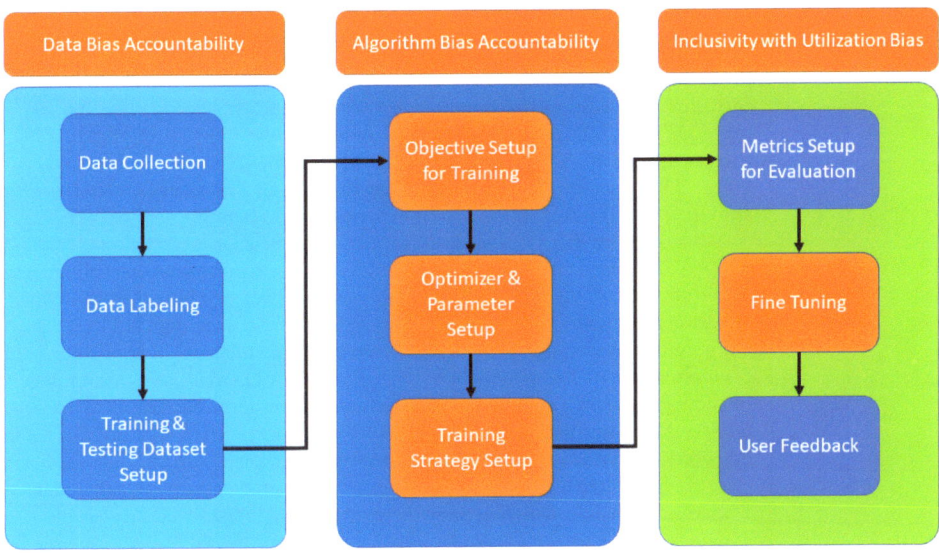

Figure 2. Bias effects in machine learning.

Biases in AI models can arise from data collection, labeling, and partitioning, affecting data integrity. Human factors during training, including optimization objectives and parameter configurations also contribute to bias. Inclusivity applications involve tuning and updates guided by user feedback, which holds substantial influence. Techniques like K-fold mitigate dataset bias, but original bias persists, highlighting the importance of robust data accountability. Subjective optimization objective design exacerbates bias effects. Addressing these issues requires comprehensive strategies for data and model development.

Feedback bias in AI model tuning can arise if participants providing feedback are disproportionately represented in specific communities or feature sets. This concentration can lead to model adjustments aligning more closely with the preferences of that group. Grouping can be based on experimental settings or attributes, aiding the analysis of cognitive and labeling differences' impact on bias patterns. Statistical features synthesized from group evaluations can influence machine learning model outcomes.

The inclusivity of intelligent computing services relies on data and algorithm accountability to mitigate bias and ensure fairness in machine learning processes. While industry practices often exclude sensitive attributes to address fairness concerns, this approach overlooks the potential influence of non-sensitive attributes in reflecting bias. Additionally, evaluating fairness using static test sets poses challenges, including potential incompleteness and inherent bias carried over from existing systems.

Moreover, the feedback loop between machine learning system outputs and inputs can perpetuate and reinforce biases, necessitating the analysis of algorithms in dynamic systems. Label noise further complicates the picture, as large datasets essential for deep network training can inadvertently incorporate incorrect labels, undermining model accuracy and performance.

Addressing these challenges, ongoing research focuses on detecting and mitigating bias while designing fair machine learning mechanisms and intelligent systems. Bias analysis and fair training emerge as critical areas, aiming to enhance the technical understanding and current status of each direction.

4. Bias Analysis

4.1. Data Bias

Data bias is a critical concern in artificial intelligence (AI) systems, as biased data can lead to unfair and discriminatory outcomes. It arises when the training data used to develop AI models are skewed, leading to biased predictions or decisions [66,67]. Biased data can perpetuate historical prejudices and result in discriminatory outcomes. There are five main types bias, including selection bias [68–71], sampling bias [25,72,73], labeling bias [26,74–77], temporal bias [78–81], aggregation bias [82–86], historical bias [52,87–89], measurement bias [4,90–92], confirmation bias, proxy bias, cultural bias, under-representation bias [93–95], and homophily bias [96–98]. Table 2 shows the comparison of the different types of data biases.

Bias in AI models can stem from various data-related sources. Selection bias arises from skewed data representation due to biased collection or incomplete sampling. Aggregation bias results when data from different sources with varying biases are combined without proper consideration. Sampling bias emerges when training data fail to represent the target population adequately. Labeling bias occurs due to errors in annotation, introducing bias into training. Measurement bias originates from inaccuracies during data collection, impacting the model's ability to learn accurately. Temporal and historical biases arise from reflecting outdated societal biases. Unconscious biases, such as cultural bias, lead to biased decisions for diverse groups. Proxy bias uses correlated proxy variables, indirectly introducing bias. Homophily bias reinforces existing patterns in prediction, potentially intensifying bias. Understanding and mitigating these biases are crucial for equitable AI systems.

Table 2. Comparison on data biases.

Data Bias	Definition	Main Cause	Impact on AI	References
Selection Bias	Certain groups are over/under-represented	Biased data collection process	AI models may not be representative, leading to biased decisions	[68–71]
Sampling Bias	Data are not a random sample	Incomplete or biased sampling	Poor generalization to new data, biased predictions	[25,72,73]
Labeling Bias	Errors in data labeling	Annotators' biases or societal stereotypes	AI models learn and perpetuate biased labels	[26,74–76]
Temporal Bias	Historical societal biases	Outdated data reflecting past biases	AI models may reinforce outdated biases	[78–81]
Aggregation Bias	Data combined from multiple sources	Differing biases in individual sources	AI models may produce skewed outcomes due to biased data	[82–85]
Historical Bias	Training data reflect past societal biases	Biases inherited from historical societal discrimination	Model may perpetuate historical biases and reinforce inequalities	[52,87–89]
Measurement Bias	Errors or inaccuracies in data collection	Data collection process introduces measurement errors	Model learns from flawed data, leading to inaccurate predictions	[4,90–92]
Confirmation Bias	Focus on specific patterns or attributes	Data collection or algorithmic bias towards specific features	Model may overlook relevant information and reinforce existing biases	[27,99–102]
Proxy Bias	Indirect reliance on sensitive attributes	Use of correlated proxy variables instead of sensitive attributes	Model indirectly relies on sensitive information, leading to biased outcomes	[42,103–105]
Cultural Bias	Data reflect cultural norms and values	Cultural influences in data collection or annotation	Model predictions may be biased for individuals from different cultural backgrounds	[72,106,107]
Under-representation Bias	Certain groups are significantly underrepresented	Low representation of certain groups in the training data	Model performance is poorer for underrepresented groups	[93–95]
Homophily Bias	Predictions based on similarity between instances	Tendency of models to make predictions based on similarity	Model may reinforce existing patterns and exacerbate biases	[96–98]

4.2. Algorithmic Bias

Algorithmic bias refers to biases inherent in the design and structure of AI models [108,109]. These biases may be unintentionally introduced during the development process, leading to unequal treatment of different groups. The main algorithmic biases include prejudice bias, sampling bias, feedback loop bias, lack of diversity bias, and automation bias.

Prejudice bias arises from biased training data, perpetuating societal stereotypes. Sampling bias stems from data misrepresentation, causing poor generalization. Feedback loop bias is a self-reinforcing cycle, where biased AI predictions lead to biased feedback. Lack of diversity bias emerges from inadequate dataset representation, affecting underrepresented groups. Automation bias involves over-reliance on AI decisions without scrutiny, potentially amplifying underlying biases.

Table 3 summarizes the comparison of different types of algorithmic bias in AI systems, highlighting their definitions and main implications. Prejudice bias originates from biased data collection, reinforcing discrimination. Sampling bias results from non-representative data, causing biased predictions. Feedback loop bias is a self-reinforcing cycle driven by biased predictions and feedback. Lack of diversity bias emerges from homogeneous training datasets, affecting underrepresented groups. Automation bias is the uncritical reliance on AI decisions, amplifying underlying biases.

Table 3. Algorithmic bias comparison.

Algorithmic Bias	Definition	Main Cause	Impact on AI	References
Prejudice Bias	AI models trained on biased data	Biased training data and societal prejudices	Reinforces biases, leads to discriminatory outcomes	[76,110–112]
Sampling Bias	Data do not represent the target population	Incomplete or skewed sampling methods	Poor generalization, biased predictions	[85,113–115]
Feedback Loop Bias	Self-reinforcing bias cycle in AI predictions	Biased predictions influencing biased feedback	Amplifies biases, perpetuates discrimination	[116–120]
Lack of Diversity Bias	Training on limited or homogeneous datasets	Insufficient representation of diverse groups	Performs poorly for underrepresented groups	[40,121–125]
Automation Bias	Human over-reliance on AI decisions	Blind trust in AI without critical evaluation	Perpetuates biases without human intervention	[126–131]

4.3. User Interaction Bias

User interaction bias occurs when AI systems adapt their behavior based on user feedback, potentially reinforcing and amplifying existing biases [67,132]. It manifests in various forms, each contributing to biased decision making and unequal outcomes in AI systems. Table 4 summarizes the typical user interaction biases, including user feedback bias, underrepresented or biased user data bias, and automation bias.

Table 4. User interaction bias comparison.

Bias Type	Definition	Main Cause	Impact on AI	Reference
User Feedback Bias	User Feedback Bias occurs when biased user feedback or responses influence the behavior of AI systems.	Biased user feedback or responses can be influenced by users' subjective preferences, opinions, or prejudices. The AI system learns from this feedback and incorporates it into its decision-making process.	AI models may generate biased predictions and decisions based on the biased feedback, potentially leading to unequal treatment of certain user groups. User satisfaction and trust in the AI system can be affected by biased outputs.	[116–118]
Biases from Underrepresented or Biased User Data	This bias arises when the data collected from users lack diversity or contain inherent biases, which can lead to biased model predictions and decisions that disproportionately affect certain user groups.	Lack of diversity or inherent biases in user data can result from biased data collection practices, data preprocessing, or historical biases reflected in the data.	AI systems trained on biased user data may produce unfair outcomes, disproportionately impacting specific user groups. Biases in data can lead to the perpetuation and amplification of existing inequalities.	[133–135]
Automation Bias in Human–AI Interaction	Automation bias refers to biased decision making by users when utilizing AI systems, potentially influencing the AI system's outcomes and recommendations.	Automation bias can occur when users over-rely on AI recommendations without critically evaluating or verifying the results. Human trust in AI systems and the perceived authority of the AI can contribute to automation bias.	Automation bias can lead to the uncritical acceptance of AI-generated outputs, even when they are biased or inaccurate. It may result in erroneous or unfair decisions based on AI recommendations. Awareness of automation bias is crucial to avoid blindly accepting AI decisions without human oversight.	[126,128,129]

User feedback bias and bias from underrepresented or biased user data contribute to user interaction biases, influencing AI system behavior and predictions. The interaction between humans and AI, rooted in automation bias, further affects these biases. Notably, user interaction bias and algorithmic bias overlap, as biases from human–computer interaction data impact industrial intelligence models, highlighting their interconvertibility.

5. Fair Training

5.1. Fair Training Methods

In response to the above bias analysis, we hope to be able to develop an AI system without bias by conducting fair training so that we can avoid perpetuating inequalities due to discriminatory appearances caused by biases. Fairness training aims to reduce these biases and promote fair decision making. There are several fair training methods that are currently in common use, including pre-processing fairness [136], in-processing fairness [137], post-processing fairness [46], regularization-based fairness [43], counterfactual fairness [41,45,138].

Pre-processing, in-processing, and post-processing fairness techniques address bias in AI systems from different angles. Pre-processing involves modifying training data to balance group representation. In-processing modifies learning algorithms to integrate fairness. Post-processing adjusts model predictions to align with fairness goals. Additionally, regularization-based methods introduce fairness constraints in optimization, aiming to minimize disparities, while counterfactual fairness measures fairness by assessing outcome consistency for similar individuals across sensitive attributes.

Fair training techniques, as depicted in Table 5, strive to mitigate biases in AI systems by integrating fairness considerations into the training process. Through the incorporation of sensitive attributes and fairness constraints, these methods aim to diminish the impact of such attributes on model predictions, guarding against biased outcomes that could disproportionately affect marginalized groups. The challenge lies in striking a balance between fairness and accuracy, avoiding the compromise of model performance while enhancing fairness.

Table 5. Fair training method comparison.

Fair Training Method	Definition	Implementation	Key Features	References
Pre-processing Fairness	Modifying training data before feeding into the model	Re-sampling, re-weighting, data augmentation	Addresses bias at the data level	[136,139,140]
In-processing Fairness	Modifying learning algorithms or objective functions	Adversarial training, adversarial debiasing	Simultaneously optimizes for accuracy and fairness	[137,141,142]
Post-processing Fairness	Adjusting the model's predictions after training	Re-ranking, calibration	Does not require access to the model's internals	[46,143–145]
Regularization-based Fairness	Adding fairness constraints to the optimization process	Penalty terms in the loss function	Can be combined with various learning algorithms	[43,146,147]
Counterfactual Fairness	Measuring fairness based on changes in sensitive attributes	Counterfactual reasoning	Focuses on individual-level fairness	[45,148,149]

5.2. Pre-Processing Fairness

Preprocessing fairness applications involve modifying training data before feeding them into an AI model to reduce bias and promote fairness. These techniques focus on addressing biases in the data themselves, which can lead to fairer model results. Common methods include resampling, reweighting, data augmentation, fairness-aware clustering, and synthetic oversampling techniques.

Resampling techniques, such as oversampling and undersampling, adjust data distribution to alleviate bias by equalizing group representation. Reweighting assigns higher weights to underrepresented instances during model training, reducing bias against marginalized groups. Data augmentation generates synthetic data to bolster underrepresented groups, enhancing fairness. Fairness-aware clustering ensures equitable grouping, while the Synthetic Minority Oversampling Technique (SMOTE) generates synthetic samples to balance class distribution, promoting fairness in classification tasks. These methods collectively counteract bias and enhance fairness in AI models.

In Table 6, it can be seen that re-sampling techniques handle class imbalance, reweighting adjusts data importance, data augmentation enhances diversity, attribute swapping equalizes sensitive attributes, fairness-aware clustering ensures equitable grouping, and SMOTE addresses class imbalance. By selecting and applying the appropriate preprocessing fairness method based on the specific dataset and fairness goals, AI practitioners can develop models that prioritize fairness and equitable outcomes. Continued research and experimentation with these techniques will advance the pursuit of unbiased AI applications across various domains.

Table 6. Pre-processing fairness comparison.

Pre-Processing Fairness Method	Features	Pros	Cons	References
Re-sampling Techniques	Balance representation of different groups	Simple and easy to implement	May lead to loss of information and increased computation	[150–153]
Re-weighting Techniques	Assign higher weights to underrepresented groups	Does not alter the original dataset	Requires careful selection of appropriate weights	[154–159]
Data Augmentation	Generate synthetic data to increase representation	Increases the diversity of the training dataset	Synthetic data may not fully represent real-world samples	[160–163]
Fairness-aware Clustering	Cluster data points while maintaining fairness	Incorporates fairness constraints during clustering	May not guarantee perfect fairness in all clusters	[164–167]
Synthetic Minority Over-sampling Technique (SMOTE)	Generate synthetic samples for the minority class	Addresses class imbalance	May result in overfitting or noisy samples	[168–171]

5.3. In Processing Fairness

In-processing fairness refers to modifying the learning algorithm or objective function during model training to explicitly incorporate fairness constraints. These techniques aim to simultaneously optimize accuracy while reducing bias and promoting fairness. Their main approaches include adversarial training [172–176], adversarial debiasing [137,177–179], equalized odds post-processing [11,144,177,180], fair causal learning [45,181–184], and meta-fairness [163,185,186].

Table 7 summarizes the comparison of the methods above. Adversarial training and adversarial debiasing introduce an adversarial component to the learning process, aiming to minimize the influence of sensitive attributes on model predictions. These methods have been applied across tasks like natural language processing, computer vision, and recommendation systems to enhance fairness and reduce bias. Causal learning methods focus on understanding causal relationships within data and addressing confounding factors that lead to biased predictions. This approach has been implemented in domains such as healthcare and criminal justice to ensure fairer and more interpretable outcomes. Meta Fairness involves learning a fairness-aware optimization algorithm that dynamically adjusts the balance between fairness and accuracy during model training. It is particularly valuable when fairness requirements vary across user groups or over time.

Table 7. In-processing fairness comparison.

In-Processing Fairness Method	Features	Pros	Cons	References
Adversarial Training	Adversarial component to minimize bias impact	Enhances model's fairness while maintaining accuracy	Sensitive to adversarial attacks, requires additional computational resources	[172–176]
Adversarial Debiasing	Adversarial network to remove sensitive attributes	Simultaneously reduces bias and improves model's fairness	Adversarial training challenges, potential loss of predictive performance	[137,177–179]
Equalized Odds Post-processing	Adjust model predictions to ensure equalized odds	Guarantees fairness in binary classification tasks	May lead to suboptimal trade-offs between fairness and model performance	[11,144,177,180]
Causal Learning for Fairness	Focus on causal relationships to adjust for bias	Addresses confounding factors to achieve fairer predictions	Requires causal assumptions, may be limited by data availability	[45,181–184]
Meta Fairness	Learns fairness-aware optimization algorithm	Adapts fairness-accuracy trade-off to changing requirements	Complexity in learning the optimization algorithm, potential increased complexity	[163,185,186]

Adapting to different biases and trade-offs between fairness and performance, these methods provide valuable tools for equitable AI. Choosing the appropriate method hinges on factors such as the application context and bias type.

5.4. Post-Processing Fairness

Post-processing fairness methods focus on adjusting or post-processing the output of trained AI models to ensure fairness and reduce bias after the model has made its predictions. These techniques are applied after the model has made a decision to align the results with the fairness goal and mitigate any potential bias present in the predictions. Some common post-processing fairness methods include equalized odds post-processing [11,144,177,180], calibration post-processing [187–190], rejected options classification (ROC) post-processing [144,191–193], priority sampling post-processing [194–196], threshold optimization post-processing [197–200], and regularization post-processing [201–204]. Table 8 summarizes the features, pros and cons with the comparison of these methods.

Equalized odds post-processing is employed post-model training to align predictions, ensuring equal false alarm and omission rates across different groups. Calibration refines predicted probabilities to accurately reflect event likelihood. Reject option classification introduces a "reject" option to avoid biased predictions in sensitive situations. Preferential sampling post-processing reshapes training data distribution for enhanced fairness. Threshold optimization post-processing adjusts decision thresholds for a balanced fairness–accuracy trade-off. Regularization post-processing employs regularization techniques to encourage fairness during model optimization. These techniques offer ways to enhance fairness in AI predictions and are particularly useful in contexts like credit scoring and hiring decisions.

The effectiveness and suitability of post-processing fairness methods vary with the AI application and fairness goals. While valuable in certain contexts, these techniques might not entirely resolve root biases. A holistic AI fairness approach should combine pre-processing, in-processing, and post-processing methods, alongside continuous monitoring and evaluation, to ensure equitable outcomes.

Table 8. Post-processing fairness comparison.

Post-Processing Fairness Method	Features	Pros	Cons	References
Equalized Odds Post-processing	Adjust model predictions to ensure equalized odds	Ensures equalized false positive and true positive rates across groups	May lead to suboptimal trade-offs between fairness and model performance	[11,144,177,180]
Calibration Post-processing	Calibrates model's predicted probabilities	Improves fairness by aligning confidence scores with true likelihood	Calibration may not entirely remove bias from the model	[187–190]
Reject Option Classification (ROC) Post-processing	Introduces a "reject" option in classification decisions	Allows the model to abstain from predictions in high fairness concern cases	May lead to lower accuracy due to abstaining from predictions	[144,191–193]
Preferential Sampling Post-processing	Modifies the training data distribution by resampling instances	Improves fairness by adjusting the representation of different groups	May not address the root causes of bias in the model	[194–196]
Threshold Optimization Post-processing	Adjusts decision thresholds for fairness and accuracy trade-off	Allows fine-tuning of fairness and performance balance	May not fully eliminate all biases in the model	[197–200]
Regularization Post-processing	Applies fairness constraints during model training	Encourages fairness during the optimization process	Fairness constraints might impact model performance	[201–204]

5.5. Regularization Based Fairness

Regularization-based fairness methods are emerging as a promising approach to mitigate biases in machine learning models. Regularization techniques aim to enforce fairness constraints during the model training process, ensuring that the model's predictions are less influenced by sensitive attributes and promote equitable outcomes. Table 9 summarizes and compares different regularization methodologies for AI fairness, including adversarial regularization [205–208], demographic parity regularization [201,204,209–211], equalized odds regularization [201,212,213], covariate leveling regularization [214,215], and mixture density network regularization [216–218].

Table 9. Regularization-based fairness comparison.

Regularization-Based Fairness Method	Features	Pros	Cons	References
Adversarial Regularization	Introduces adversarial component	Encourages disentanglement of sensitive attributes	Computationally expensive	[205–208]
Demographic Parity Regularization	Enforces similar distributions across groups	Addresses group fairness	May lead to accuracy trade-offs	[201,204,209–211]
Equalized Odds Regularization	Ensures similar false/true positive rates	Emphasizes fairness in both rates	May lead to accuracy trade-offs	[201,212,213]
Covariate Shift Regularization	Reduces impact of biased/underrepresented subgroups	Addresses bias due to distributional differences	Sensitive to noise in the data	[214,215]
Mixture Density Network Regularization	Models uncertainty in predictions	Provides probabilistic approach to fairness regularization	Requires larger amount of data to estimate probability distributions	[216–218]

Regularization-based fairness methods introduce additional components to the model training process to mitigate bias in AI predictions. Adversarial regularization aims to minimize model dependence on sensitive attributes by introducing an adversarial component. Demographic parity regularization enforces similar prediction distributions across sensitive attribute groups. Equalized odds regularization maintains consistent false alarm and true alarm rates among these groups. Covariate leveling regularization adapts predictions to diverse data distributions. Mixture density network regularization models prediction uncertainty through probability density functions. Each approach offers distinct benefits and trade-offs in addressing bias.

5.6. Counterfactual Fairness

Counterfactual fairness is an approach that seeks to address bias in AI models by considering counterfactual scenarios, where sensitive attributes are altered while keeping other features fixed. The idea is to evaluate fairness by examining how the model's predictions would change if an individual belonged to a different demographic group, allowing for a more nuanced understanding of biases. Table 10 summarizes and compares different regularization methodologies for AI fairness, including individual fairness [40,168,196,219], equal opportunity fairness [220–222], reweighted counterfactual fairness [223–225], and oblivious training [226–228].

Table 10. Counterfactual fairness methods comparison.

Counterfactual Fairness Method	Features	Pros	Cons	References
Individual Fairness	Focuses on treating similar individuals similarly based on their features	Considers fairness at the individual level, promoting personalized fairness	Defining similarity metrics and enforcing individual fairness can be challenging	[40,196,219]
Equal Opportunity Fairness	Minimizes disparate impact on true positive rates across sensitive attribute groups	Targets fairness in favor of historically disadvantaged groups	May neglect other fairness concerns, such as false positive rates or overall accuracy	[220–222]
Equalized Odds Fairness	Aims for similar false positive and true positive rates across sensitive attribute groups	Addresses fairness in both false positives and false negatives	May lead to accuracy trade-offs between groups	[229–231]
Reweighted Counterfactual Fairness	Assigns different weights to instances based on similarity to counterfactual scenarios	Provides better fairness control by adjusting instance weights	Determining appropriate weights and balancing fairness and accuracy can be challenging	[223–225]
Oblivious Training	Trains the model to be ignorant of certain sensitive attributes during learning	Offers a simple and effective way to mitigate the impact of sensitive attributes	May result in lower model performance when sensitive attributes are relevant to the task	[226–228]

Individual fairness focuses on treating similar individuals equally despite their protected attributes. It promotes personalized fairness at the individual level, emphasizing fine-grained treatment. Equal opportunity fairness ensures similar true positive rates across different groups to prevent disparate impact in binary classification. Reweighted counterfactual fairness adjusts data weights during training to mitigate bias and can be combined with fairness-aware algorithms. Oblivious training trains models on both original and counterfactual data to promote fairness without explicit labels.

These methods address different fairness concerns, considering both individual and group fairness aspects, each with their computational and implementation considerations. Each fairness method has strengths and limitations, potentially impacting areas like model performance and interpretability. The method chosen should align with specific fairness criteria and application contexts, as certain methods may be better suited for particular domains than others.

In medical data collection, informed consent methods are employed to clarify data usage and potential risks. Privacy techniques like anonymization protect individuals' identities. Data minimization reduces privacy risks by collecting only necessary information, though this may limit insights. Transparency communicates data collection processes, building trust while potentially raising privacy concerns. Data security measures include encryption and access controls to prevent unauthorized access. Accuracy and accountability methods involve auditing for reliable data and research outcomes. These approaches enhance data quality and accountability but may require resource allocation. Balancing these strategies is essential for ethical and effective data collection in scientific research.

6. Discussion

6.1. Fair Data Collection

To guarantee the fairness in data collection, we summarize the different methods with the comparison in Table 11 between informed consent, privacy and anonymity, privacy and anonymization, accuracy and accountability, data security, data minimization, and transparency approach.

Table 11. Fair data collection fairness methods comparison.

Method Category	Features	Pros	Cons	References
Informed Consent	Obtain explicit consent from participants	Respects individual autonomy	May lead to selection bias	[232–234]
Informed Consent	Clear explanation of data collection purpose	Builds trust with participants	Consent may not always be fully informed	[235,236]
Informed Consent	Informed of potential risks		Difficulties with complex research studies	[237–239]
Privacy and Anonymity	Data anonymization, aggregation, de-identification	Protects participant privacy	Reduced utility of anonymized data	[240,241]
Privacy and Anonymity	Prevents re-identification of individuals	Minimizes risk of data breaches	Challenges in preserving data utility	[242–244]
Data Minimization	Collect only necessary data	Reduces data collection and storage costs	Limited data for certain analyses	[28,245,246]
Data Minimization	Avoid gathering excessive/inappropriate data	Mitigates privacy risks	Potential loss of insights	[247,248]
Transparency	Clear communication of data collection process	Builds trust with data subjects	May lead to privacy concerns	[249–251]
Transparency	Information on methods and data use	Increases data sharing and collaboration	Difficulties in balancing transparency	[249–251]
Data Security	Encryption, access controls, security audits	Protects data from unauthorized access	Implementation costs	[252–254]
Data Security	Safeguards data from breaches	Prevents data manipulation and tampering	Potential usability impact	[252–254]
Accuracy and Accountability	Processes for data accuracy and accountability	Ensures reliability of data	Requires resource allocation for auditing	[24,255,256]

6.2. Regular Auditing and Monitoring

The continuous monitoring and auditing of AI systems are crucial to identify and address emerging biases throughout the AI lifecycle. Regular auditing and monitoring are crucial aspects of ensuring AI fairness in real-world applications. Table 12 summarizes different methods for auditing and monitoring AI fairness, including disparate impact analysis, fairness-aware performance metrics, bias detection techniques, algorithmic fairness dashboards, model explanation and interpretability, and continual bias monitoring.

Table 12. Regular auditing and monitoring comparison.

Method	Features	Pros	Cons	References
Disparate Impact Analysis	Measures disparate impact ratios	Easy to implement and interpret	Only captures one aspect of fairness (impact ratios)	[6,257,258]
Fairness-aware Performance Metrics	Simultaneously evaluates accuracy and fairness	Provides a holistic view of model performance and fairness	Choice of fairness metric may not fully capture desired notions of fairness	[259–261]
Bias Detection Techniques	Identifies biases in data or model predictions	Alerts to potential fairness issues early	May require domain expertise for interpreting and addressing identified biases	[71,262,263]
Algorithmic Fairness Dashboards	Real-time visualizations and metrics for monitoring	Enables continuous fairness monitoring	Complexity in designing comprehensive dashboards	[264–266]
Model Explanation and Interpretability	Provides insights into decision-making	Facilitates understanding of model behavior and potential biases	May not fully capture complex interactions in the model, leading to limited interpretability	[267–270]
Continual Bias Monitoring	Ongoing and regular assessment	Detects and addresses emerging fairness issues over time	May require significant resources for continuous monitoring	[47,271,272]

7. AI Fairness in Practice

AI fairness has a large number of real-world applications in a variety of fields, where it is critical to ensure that machine learning models do not perpetuate or amplify bias and discrimination. The areas where the current research and application work are more focused are AI-based social infrastructure and management and business applications. Tables 13 and 14 summarize common applications and case studies with a comparison of the approaches and challenges, respectively, including education [273–277] health care [52,278–280] criminal justice and sentencing [88,281–283], hiring and recruiting [284–286], lending and credit decisions [287–292], online advertising [8,293–295], customer service and chatbots [296–303].

7.1. Social Administration

Artificial intelligence (AI) has become an integral part of all industries, changing the way decisions and processes are managed. In recent years, the concept of AI fairness has gained prominence, especially in the field of social management. AI systems are increasingly being used in areas such as criminal justice, healthcare, and education. Table 13 summarizes the typical applications, including issues, mechanisms, opportunities and challenges.

7.1.1. Health Care

AI fairness can also be applied to healthcare diagnosis and treatment recommendation systems to reduce bias and ensure fairness in healthcare delivery, as some healthcare AI systems have been found to differ in the diagnosis of certain diseases among different racial groups [52,278]. The use of a fairness-aware algorithm improves the performance of the model and provides a fairer diagnosis for all patients [279,280].

Table 13. AI fairness in social administration practices.

Application	Issues	Mechanism	Opportunities	Challenges
Health Care	Racial and gender biases in diagnosis and treatment. Unequal healthcare due to socioeconomic factors.	diversifying representative datasets. Personalized treatment plans based on individual characteristics.	Enhancing healthcare access and outcomes for all individuals. Reducing healthcare disparities.	Ensuring patient privacy and data security. Addressing biases in data collection and data sources.
Education	Bias in admissions and resource allocation. Unequal access to quality education.	Fair criteria for admissions and resource allocation. Personalized learning for individual needs. Identifying and assisting at-risk students.	Reducing educational disparities. Enhancing learning outcomes for all students.	ethical considerations regarding data privacy in educational settings. avoiding undue focus on standardized testing.
Criminal Justice and Sentencing	Racial Bias in predictive policing and sentencing. Unfair allocation of resources for crime prevention.	focus on rehabilitation with regular auditing and updating the models with transparency in decision-making.	Reducing biased arrests and sentencing. Allocating resources more efficiently.	The ethical implications of using AI in criminal justice. Ensuring model accountability and avoiding "tech-washing".

AI applications in healthcare face challenges of interpretability, trust, data privacy, and security. Privacy concerns hinder data sharing, while complex AI models lack interpretability, impacting trust. Transparent and responsible data management is needed for data sharing while protecting privacy. Explainable AI can enhance trust by making AI recommendations understandable [304]. Aligning with healthcare governance measures can ensure trustworthy AI use. Addressing these issues can revolutionize medical decision making, improve outcomes, and foster equitable and patient-centered healthcare.

7.1.2. Education

Artificial intelligence fairness is applied to education technology to ensure equal opportunity for students regardless of their background [273]. This is because in reality, AI-powered tutoring systems exhibit biases when assigning tasks to students [274,275]. Therefore with the incorporation of fairness awareness, the system can adjust the recommendations to treat all students fairly [276,277].

AI algorithms in college admissions and resource allocation may unintentionally perpetuate biases, impacting opportunities and diversity. Personalized learning platforms might worsen educational disparities, particularly for marginalized students. Testing and assessment bias can lead to unfair evaluations, affecting self-esteem and prospects. Future work should design fairness-conscious admissions models and AI systems optimizing fairness to mitigate bias. Transparency and accountability measures should guide AI-based educational decisions. Incorporating equity in personalized learning algorithms and diverse educational content can promote equitable support. Culturally responsive education and diverse resources can also aid in reducing bias in assessments.

7.1.3. Criminal Justice and Sentencing

Utilizing AI fairness to address bias in risk assessment tools ensures that criminal sentencing decisions are fair [88,281]. In the criminal justice system, some AI-based risk assessment tools have been found to be racially biased, resulting in harsher sentences for some minorities [282]. Implementation of fairness awareness training resulted in a significant reduction in system bias [283].

Current research predominantly addresses racial, socioeconomic, and recidivism prediction biases. Data-driven disparities may lead to biased arrests, bail decisions, and sentencing. Biased recidivism prediction algorithms misclassify groups as high risk, perpetuating unfair treatment and higher incarceration rates for marginalized groups.

Future efforts should gather diverse, representative training data to mitigate bias. Fairness-aware algorithms and AI models optimizing fairness should be developed to prevent differential treatment based on race or socioeconomic status. Transparent risk assessment models can enhance interpretability, aiding defendants and legal professionals. Regular model audits are essential to identify and rectify potential biases in model deployment.

7.2. Business

Another important application area for AI Fairness is business. More and more AI technologies are also being continuously introduced into commercial applications, and Table 14 summarizes and compares several trending widely used scenarios.

Table 14. AI fairness in business practices.

Application	Issues	Mechanism	Opportunities	Challenges
Recruiting	Bias in job ads and candidate selection. Lack of diversity in hiring.	Debiasing job descriptions, candidate screening and removing identifiable information, diversifying training data.	Increasing workforce diversity. Reducing hiring discrimination.	Balancing fairness and competence. Ensuring fairness across different demographics.
Lending and Credit Decisions	Discrimination in loan approvals. Lack of transparency in decision making.	Implementing fairness-aware algorithms, explaining model decisions, alternative data to creditworthiness.	Expanding access to credit for marginalized groups. Improving overall lending practices.	Striking a balance between fairness and risk assessment. Handling potential adversarial attacks on models.
Online Advertising	Targeting ads based on sensitive attributes. Reinforcing stereotypes through ad delivery.	Differential privacy to protect privacy, biased message screening, providing users preference controls.	Improving user experience and privacy protection. Fostering a positive brand image.	The balance between targeted ads and user privacy. Identifying and Addressing hidden biases in ad delivery.
Customer Service and Chatbots	biased responses and inappropriate interactions. Lack of understanding diverse linguistic expressions.	Training chatbots on inclusive and diverse datasets with reinforcement learning to improve interactions with feedback on bot behavior.	Enhancing user experience and customer satisfaction. Scaling customer support efficiently.	Minimizing harmful or offensive responses. Dealing with novel inputs and out-of-distribution data.

7.2.1. Hiring and Recruiting

The integration of artificial intelligence (AI) in human resource management (HRM) introduces transformative enhancements. Figure 3 shows a recruitment process supported by AI throughout. AI-driven algorithms streamline CV screening and candidate profiling, while proctored assessments ensure secure remote testing. AI optimizes interview scheduling and personalizes HR training. Behavior tracking and personality analysis provide insights into candidate dynamics, and AI aids in appraisal monitoring through performance metric analysis. These applications collectively reshape HRM practices, enhancing efficiency and informed decision making.

In the applications of AI system in HRM, artificial intelligence fairness is applied to mitigate bias in automated hiring systems, ensuring equitable and non-discriminatory candidate selection [305,306]. Many AI-driven recruitment tools have exhibited biases, favoring specific candidates and overlooking job requisites [307,308]. Utilizing AI fairness techniques rectifies these model biases, fostering impartial hiring decisions independent of attributes unrelated to job proficiency [309]. Tackling these challenges and future endeavors in AI fairness is pivotal to harnessing the potential of AI for equitable recruitment, fostering diversity and inclusivity in workforce dynamics.

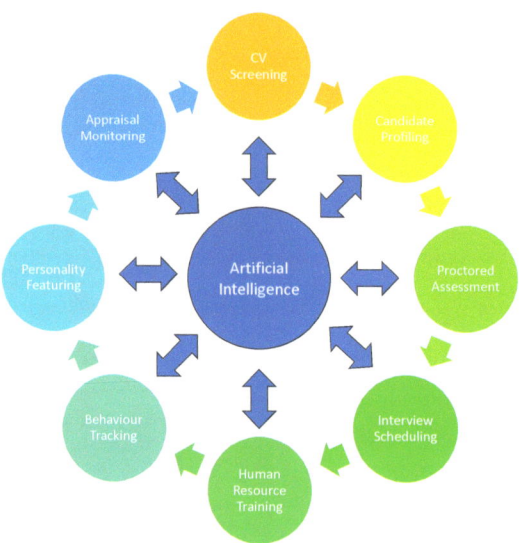

Figure 3. Tasks with artificial intelligence for hiring and recruiting in human resources.

7.2.2. Loan and Credit Decisions

AI applications in loan and credit decision making aim to improve decision accuracy, speed, and fairness while maintaining prudent risk management. As shown in Figure 4, AI applications in loan and credit decision making involve leveraging artificial intelligence techniques to assess creditworthiness, streamline lending processes, and enhance risk management. These applications use AI algorithms to analyze various data sources, such as financial records, transaction histories, and alternative data, to make more accurate and efficient lending decisions. This aids in automating and optimizing the loan approval process, reducing human bias, and increasing access to credit for underserved populations. AI assists in fraud detection, predicting default risks, and personalizing loan terms based on individual borrower profiles.

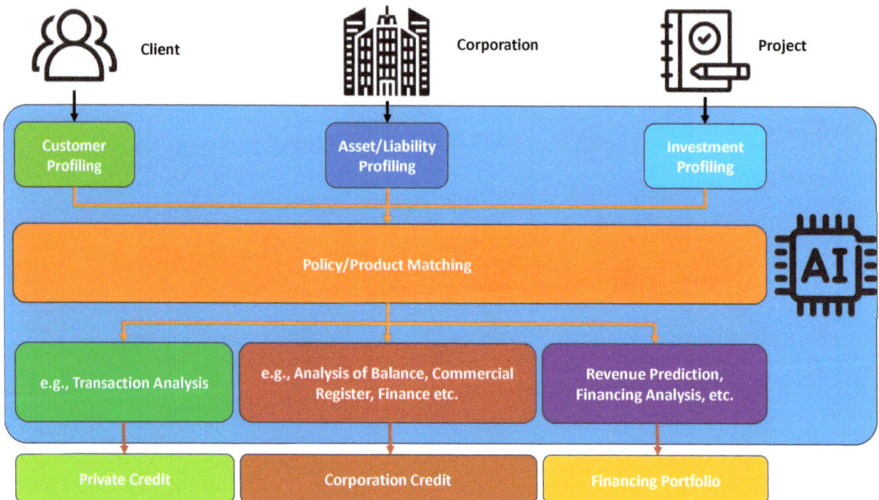

Figure 4. Tasks with artificial intelligence for hiring and recruiting in human resources.

7.2.3. Online Advertising

To counteract bias in credit-scoring models and ensure equitable access to loans and credit opportunities for all individuals, AI fairness is applied with bias migration strategies [287,288]. Certain AI-driven credit scoring models have exhibited potential bias towards specific demographic groups [288,289]. Implementing bias mitigation techniques enhances model fairness, leading to more impartial lending determinations [290–292]. Looking ahead, future efforts should focus on integrating diverse data sources like rental histories or utility payments into credit assessments while maintaining fairness. Designing AI models capable of adapting to various data distributions, including non-traditional data, can also sustain fairness and accuracy. Incorporating fairness-aware explanations into AI models offers insight into achieving equitable credit decisions with transparency. Through these applications and ongoing research, the aim is to foster inclusive and just lending practices by minimizing bias and promoting unbiased access to credit [287,288,290–292].

AI systems have a substantial role in online advertising, including targeted ad delivery, content censorship and related design. Figure 5 shows an example of AI applications according to the hierarchical taxonomy of online advertising. It can be seen that the AI support can enhance ad relevance and user experience, while also mitigating inappropriate content. However, challenges related to biases in ad targeting and content moderation necessitate the development of fairness-aware approaches to ensure equitable outcomes. In this context, AI technologies both facilitate and necessitate ongoing efforts to maintain fairness and effectiveness in online advertising practices.

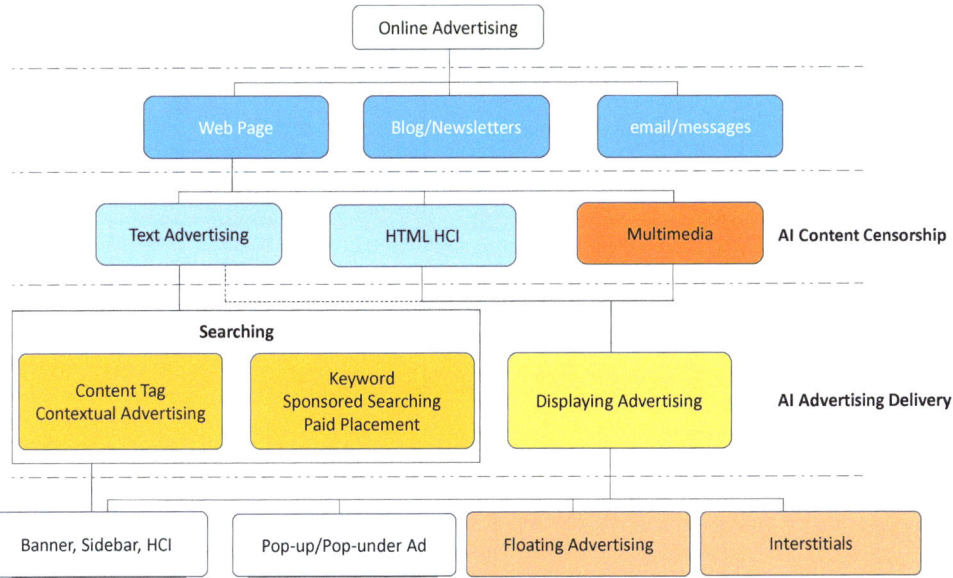

Figure 5. An example of AI support corresponding to the taxonomy of online advertising.

To address the issue above, AI fairness is used for ad targeting to avoid promoting discriminatory or biased content to users based on their attributes [293]. Some online advertising platforms have experienced problems with certain ads being disproportionately shown to users from specific demographic groups [8,294]. By incorporating fairness constraints, the platform achieved more balanced ad targeting across all users [295]. AI algorithms in advertising may unintentionally yield biased ad targeting and content due to biased training data and content generation. Future work should center on fairness-aware targeting, bias audits, diverse data, and inclusive content to ensure fairness and inclusivity in ad delivery.

7.2.4. Customer Service

Artificial intelligence is also introduced into customer service, or the customer relationship management (CRM) system [296], which enhances customer interactions and support. As shown in Figure 6, the chatbots utilize natural language processing and sentiment analysis to understand customer queries and provide accurate, timely responses. They enable automated, efficient, and personalized customer interactions, improving user experience. AI-driven chatbots handle routine inquiries, offer real-time support, and gather insights for businesses to enhance their services. This technology aims to streamline customer service operations while ensuring effective and satisfactory customer interactions.

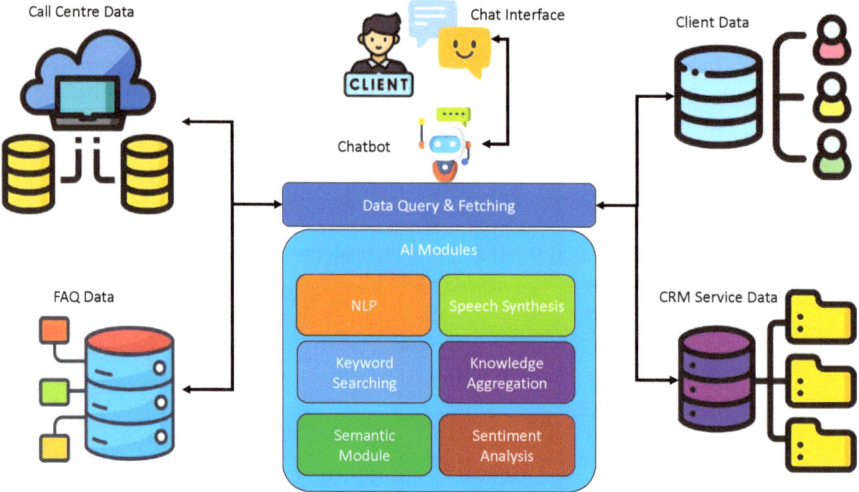

Figure 6. An example of AI support chatbot system for CRM.

However, some customer service chatbots show biased responses to users who speak certain language dialects [297–299]. Aiming at this, AI fairness is used in chatbot design to avoid biased responses or inappropriate behavior towards users [300,301]. After implementing fairness checks, the chatbot provides culturally sensitive and fair interactions [302,303].

The current challenge in the customer service bot domain pertains to mitigating uncertain biased and inappropriate responses. Chatbots often unknowingly offer biased or offensive replies due to training data exposure, leading to customer dissatisfaction and reputational harm. Additionally, limitations in comprehending diverse linguistic expressions hinder accurate responses to various language forms, including slang. Further, inadequacies in addressing sensitive topics and emotional responses lead to inappropriate interactions in some customer service bots.

In prospective research, countering the aforementioned concerns requires embedding bias detection and mitigation mechanisms to identify and address biased language and responses in chatbot interactions. Mitigating biased replies can be achieved by adopting inclusive training data representing diverse user demographics and employing natural language processing techniques to enhance language comprehension. Continuous learning is essential for customer service bots to adapt and comprehend various language styles through user interactions.

8. Conclusions

This article introduces the study of fairness in artificial intelligence, detailing the background and definition of this concept. The article introduces the development process of the fairness problem in AI systems from the perspectives of practical applications and the current state of development, and reviews and discusses the main research directions for solving the fairness problem in AI—bias analysis and fairness training—respectively. In the course of the review, the ideas and implementations of each method are explained in detail, and their respective characteristics and occasions of use are compared. The article also explores measures to reduce bias and improve fairness in AI systems, reviews relevant problems and solutions in practical applications of AI fairness, and discusses possible future research directions. On the basis of the theoretical foundations and methodology of AI fairness, the paper also explores scenarios and application examples in practical applications, thus contributing to the current discussion on fair and unbiased AI systems.

This paper also provides an in-depth comparison of the characteristics, advantages, and disadvantages of each of the different methods, based on the collation of the state-of-the-art research. The results of the comparison will provide advisory support for future research and development. At the same time, this paper also summarizes some of the existing problems in existing applications and proposes some focuses and solution ideas for future research work. These summaries will provide ideas for the further development of fairness in future AI systems.

The information synthesized in this study comes from a variety of reliable sources. These sources include recent publications in prestigious academic journals, distinguished conference proceedings, and well-established online repositories dedicated to the fairness of AI. It is important to recognize that while these sources have contributed significantly to our understanding, there are limitations to the evidence they provide. These limitations stem primarily from nuances in the research methodology, sample size, and context, which may affect the generalizability of conclusions drawn from individual studies. The landscape of AI fairness is dynamic, with research and advancements continually shaping our understanding of its complexities. While our current coverage might have limitations due to the rapid pace of change and ongoing research, please know that we are committed to further studying and exploring this crucial subject.

Author Contributions: The idea of this paper came from P.C., who also arranged the division of labor for this paper. Our work focuses are as follows: P.C. is responsible for introducing the background and definition of AI fairness; reviewing the main research directions of addressing AI fairness, including the related methods of bias analysis and fair training. L.W. (Lei Wang) is responsible for explaining the fairness problem and evaluation methods in AI systems, as well as the measures to reduce bias and improve fairness. L.W. (Linna Wu) is responsible for evaluating the related issues and solutions in practical applications. All authors have read and agreed to the published version of the manuscript.

Funding: This research received no external funding.

Conflicts of Interest: The authors declare no conflict of interest.

References

1. Angerschmid, A.; Zhou, J.; Theuermann, K.; Chen, F.; Holzinger, A. Fairness and explanation in AI-informed decision making. *Mach. Learn. Knowl. Extr.* **2022**, *4*, 556–579. [CrossRef]
2. Kratsch, W.; Manderscheid, J.; Röglinger, M.; Seyfried, J. Machine learning in business process monitoring: A comparison of deep learning and classical approaches used for outcome prediction. *Bus. Inf. Syst. Eng.* **2021**, *63*, 261–276. [CrossRef]
3. Kraus, M.; Feuerriegel, S.; Oztekin, A. Deep learning in business analytics and operations research: Models, applications and managerial implications. *Eur. J. Oper. Res.* **2020**, *281*, 628–641. [CrossRef]
4. Varona, D.; Suárez, J.L. Discrimination, bias, fairness, and trustworthy AI. *Appl. Sci.* **2022**, *12*, 5826. [CrossRef]
5. Saghiri, A.M.; Vahidipour, S.M.; Jabbarpour, M.R.; Sookhak, M.; Forestiero, A. A survey of Artificial Intelligence challenges: Analyzing the definitions, relationships, and evolutions. *Appl. Sci.* **2022**, *12*, 4054. [CrossRef]
6. Barocas, S.; Selbst, A.D. Big data's disparate impact. *Calif. Law Rev.* **2016**, *104*, 671–732. [CrossRef]
7. Corsello, A.; Santangelo, A. May Artificial Intelligence Influence Future Pediatric Research?—The Case of ChatGPT. *Children* **2023**, *10*, 757. [CrossRef] [PubMed]
8. Von Zahn, M.; Feuerriegel, S.; Kuehl, N. The cost of fairness in AI: Evidence from e-commerce. *Bus. Inf. Syst. Eng.* **2021**, *64*, 335–348. [CrossRef]
9. Liu, L.T.; Dean, S.; Rolf, E.; Simchowitz, M.; Hardt, M. Delayed impact of fair machine learning. In Proceedings of the International Conference on Machine Learning, PMLR, Stockholm, Sweden, 10–15 July 2018; pp. 3150–3158.
10. Cathy, O. *How Big Data Increases Inequality and Threatens Democracy*; Crown Publishing Group: New York, NY, USA, 2016.
11. Hardt, M.; Price, E.; Srebro, N. Equality of opportunity in supervised learning. *Adv. Neural Inf. Process. Syst.* **2016**, *29*, 3323–3331.

12. Trewin, S. AI fairness for people with disabilities: Point of view. *arXiv* **2018**, arXiv:1811.10670.
13. Kodiyan, A.A. An overview of ethical issues in using AI systems in hiring with a case study of Amazon's AI based hiring tool. *Researchgate Prepr.* **2019**, 1–19.
14. Righetti, L.; Madhavan, R.; Chatila, R. Unintended consequences of biased robotic and Artificial Intelligence systems [ethical, legal, and societal issues]. *IEEE Robot. Autom. Mag.* **2019**, *26*, 11–13. [CrossRef]
15. Garg, P.; Villasenor, J.; Foggo, V. Fairness metrics: A comparative analysis. In Proceedings of the 2020 IEEE International Conference on Big Data (Big Data), Atlanta, GA, USA, 10–13 December 2020; IEEE: Piscataway, NJ, USA, 2020; pp. 3662–3666.
16. Mehrotra, A.; Sachs, J.; Celis, L.E. Revisiting Group Fairness Metrics: The Effect of Networks. *Proc. Acm Hum. Comput. Interact.* **2022**, *6*, 1–29. [CrossRef]
17. Ezzeldin, Y.H.; Yan, S.; He, C.; Ferrara, E.; Avestimehr, A.S. Fairfed: Enabling group fairness in federated learning. In Proceedings of the AAAI Conference on Artificial Intelligence, Washington, DC, USA, 7–14 February 2023; Volume 37, pp. 7494–7502.
18. Hooker, S. Moving beyond "algorithmic bias is a data problem". *Patterns* **2021**, *2*, 100241. [CrossRef]
19. Amini, A.; Soleimany, A.P.; Schwarting, W.; Bhatia, S.N.; Rus, D. Uncovering and mitigating algorithmic bias through learned latent structure. In Proceedings of the 2019 AAAI/ACM Conference on AI, Ethics, and Society, Honolulu, HI, USA, 27–28 January 2019; pp. 289–295.
20. Yang, J.; Soltan, A.A.; Eyre, D.W.; Yang, Y.; Clifton, D.A. An adversarial training framework for mitigating algorithmic biases in clinical machine learning. *NPJ Digit. Med.* **2023**, *6*, 55. [CrossRef]
21. Li, S. Towards Trustworthy Representation Learning. In Proceedings of the 2023 SIAM International Conference on Data Mining (SDM), Minneapolis, MN, USA, 27–29 April 2023; SIAM: Philadelphia, PA, USA, 2023; pp. 957–960.
22. Creager, E.; Madras, D.; Jacobsen, J.H.; Weis, M.; Swersky, K.; Pitassi, T.; Zemel, R. Flexibly fair representation learning by disentanglement. In Proceedings of the International Conference on Machine Learning, PMLR, Long Beach, CA, USA, 10–15 June 2019; pp. 1436–1445.
23. McNamara, D.; Ong, C.S.; Williamson, R.C. Costs and benefits of fair representation learning. In Proceedings of the 2019 AAAI/ACM Conference on AI, Ethics, and Society, Honolulu, HI, USA, 27–28 January 2019; pp. 263–270.
24. Sahlgren, O. The politics and reciprocal (re) configuration of accountability and fairness in data-driven education. *Learn. Media Technol.* **2023**, *48*, 95–108. [CrossRef]
25. Ravishankar, P.; Mo, Q.; McFowland III, E.; Neill, D.B. Provable Detection of Propagating Sampling Bias in Prediction Models. *Proc. AAAI Conf. Artif. Intell.* **2023**, *37*, 9562–9569. [CrossRef]
26. Park, J.; Ellezhuthil, R.D.; Isaac, J.; Mergerson, C.; Feldman, L.; Singh, V. Misinformation Detection Algorithms and Fairness across Political Ideologies: The Impact of Article Level Labeling. In Proceedings of the 15th ACM Web Science Conference 2023, Austin, TX, USA, 30 April–1 May 2023; pp. 107–116.
27. Friedrich, J. Primary error detection and minimization (PEDMIN) strategies in social cognition: A reinterpretation of confirmation bias phenomena. *Psychol. Rev.* **1993**, *100*, 298. [CrossRef] [PubMed]
28. Frincke, D.; Tobin, D.; McConnell, J.; Marconi, J.; Polla, D. A framework for cooperative intrusion detection. In Proceedings of the 21st NIST-NCSC National Information Systems Security Conference, Arlington, VA, USA, 2–8 April 1998; pp. 361–373.
29. Estivill-Castro, V.; Brankovic, L. Data swapping: Balancing privacy against precision in mining for logic rules. In *International Conference on Data Warehousing and Knowledge Discovery*; Springer: Berlin/Heidelberg, Germany, 1999; pp. 389–398.
30. Bellamy, R.K.; Dey, K.; Hind, M.; Hoffman, S.C.; Houde, S.; Kannan, K.; Lohia, P.; Martino, J.; Mehta, S.; Mojsilovic, A.; et al. AI Fairness 360: An extensible toolkit for detecting, understanding, and mitigating unwanted algorithmic bias. *arXiv* **2018**, arXiv:1810.01943.
31. Zhang, Y.; Bellamy, R.K.; Singh, M.; Liao, Q.V. Introduction to AI fairness. In Proceedings of the Extended Abstracts of the 2020 CHI Conference on Human Factors in Computing Systems, Yokohama, Japan, 8–13 May 2020; pp. 1–4.
32. Mahoney, T.; Varshney, K.; Hind, M. *AI Fairness*; O'Reilly Media Incorporated: Sebastopol, CA, USA, 2020.
33. Mosteiro, P.; Kuiper, J.; Masthoff, J.; Scheepers, F.; Spruit, M. Bias discovery in machine learning models for mental health. *Information* **2022**, *13*, 237. [CrossRef]
34. Wing, J.M. Trustworthy AI. *Commun. ACM* **2021**, *64*, 64–71. [CrossRef]
35. Percy, C.; Dragicevic, S.; Sarkar, S.; d'Avila Garcez, A. Accountability in AI: From principles to industry-specific accreditation. *AI Commun.* **2021**, *34*, 181–196. [CrossRef]
36. Benjamins, R.; Barbado, A.; Sierra, D. Responsible AI by design in practice. *arXiv* **2019**, arXiv:1909.12838.
37. Dignum, V. The myth of complete AI-fairness. In Proceedings of the Artificial Intelligence in Medicine: 19th International Conference on Artificial Intelligence in Medicine, AIME 2021, Virtual, 15–18 June 2021; Springer: Cham, Switzerland, 2021; pp. 3–8.
38. Silberg, J.; Manyika, J. *Notes from the AI Frontier: Tackling Bias in AI (and in Humans)*; McKinsey Global Institute: San Francisco, CA, USA, 2019; Volume 1.
39. Bird, S.; Kenthapadi, K.; Kiciman, E.; Mitchell, M. Fairness-aware machine learning: Practical challenges and lessons learned. In Proceedings of the Twelfth ACM International Conference on Web Search and Data Mining, Melbourne, Australia, 11–15 February 2019; pp. 834–835.
40. Dwork, C.; Hardt, M.; Pitassi, T.; Reingold, O.; Zemel, R. Fairness through awareness. In Proceedings of the 3rd Innovations in Theoretical Computer Science Conference, Cambridge, MA, USA, 8–10 January 2012; pp. 214–226.

41. Islam, R.; Keya, K.N.; Pan, S.; Sarwate, A.D.; Foulds, J.R. Differential Fairness: An Intersectional Framework for Fair AI. *Entropy* **2023**, *25*, 660. [CrossRef] [PubMed]
42. Barocas, S.; Hardt, M.; Narayanan, A. Fairness in machine learning. *Nips Tutor.* **2017**, *1*, 2017.
43. Zafar, M.B.; Valera, I.; Rogriguez, M.G.; Gummadi, K.P. Fairness constraints: Mechanisms for fair classification. In Proceedings of the Artificial Intelligence and Statistics, PMLR, Ft. Lauderdale, FL, USA, 20–22 April 2017; pp. 962–970.
44. Cornacchia, G.; Anelli, V.W.; Biancofiore, G.M.; Narducci, F.; Pomo, C.; Ragone, A.; Di Sciascio, E. Auditing fairness under unawareness through counterfactual reasoning. *Inf. Process. Manag.* **2023**, *60*, 103224. [CrossRef]
45. Kusner, M.J.; Loftus, J.; Russell, C.; Silva, R. Counterfactual fairness. *Adv. Neural Inf. Process. Syst.* **2017**, *30*.
46. Feldman, M.; Friedler, S.A.; Moeller, J.; Scheidegger, C.; Venkatasubramanian, S. Certifying and removing disparate impact. In Proceedings of the 21th ACM SIGKDD International Conference on Knowledge Discovery and Data Mining, Sydney, Australia, 11–14 August 2015; pp. 259–268.
47. Kearns, M.; Neel, S.; Roth, A.; Wu, Z.S. Preventing fairness gerrymandering: Auditing and learning for subgroup fairness. In Proceedings of the International Conference on Machine Learning, PMLR, Stockholm, Sweden, 10–15 July 2018; pp. 2564–2572.
48. Fleisher, W. What's fair about individual fairness? In Proceedings of the 2021 AAAI/ACM Conference on AI, Ethics, and Society, New York, NY, USA, 19–21 May 2021; pp. 480–490.
49. Mukherjee, D.; Yurochkin, M.; Banerjee, M.; Sun, Y. Two simple ways to learn individual fairness metrics from data. In Proceedings of the International Conference on Machine Learning, PMLR, Copenhagen, Denmark, 16–19 December 2020; pp. 7097–7107.
50. Dwork, C.; Ilvento, C. Group fairness under composition. In Proceedings of the 2018 Conference on Fairness, Accountability, and Transparency (FAT* 2018), New York, NY, USA, 23–24 February 2018; Volume 3.
51. Binns, R. On the apparent conflict between individual and group fairness. In Proceedings of the 2020 Conference on Fairness, Accountability, and Transparency, Barcelona, Spain, 27–30 January 2020; pp. 514–524.
52. Chen, R.J.; Wang, J.J.; Williamson, D.F.; Chen, T.Y.; Lipkova, J.; Lu, M.Y.; Sahai, S.; Mahmood, F. Algorithmic fairness in Artificial Intelligence for medicine and healthcare. *Nat. Biomed. Eng.* **2023**, *7*, 719–742. [CrossRef]
53. Sloan, R.H.; Warner, R. Beyond bias: Artificial Intelligence and social justice. *Va. Law Technol.* **2020**, *24*, 1. [CrossRef]
54. Feuerriegel, S.; Dolata, M.; Schwabe, G. Fair AI: Challenges and opportunities. *Bus. Inf. Syst. Eng.* **2020**, *62*, 379–384. [CrossRef]
55. Bing, L.; Pettit, B.; Slavinski, I. Incomparable punishments: How economic inequality contributes to the disparate impact of legal fines and fees. *RSF Russell Sage Found. J. Soc. Sci.* **2022**, *8*, 118–136. [CrossRef] [PubMed]
56. Wang, L.; Zhu, H. How are ML-Based Online Content Moderation Systems Actually Used? Studying Community Size, Local Activity, and Disparate Treatment. In Proceedings of the 2022 ACM Conference on Fairness, Accountability, and Transparency, Seoul, Republic of Korea, 21–24 June 2022; pp. 824–838.
57. Tom, D.; Computing, D. *Eliminating Disparate Treatment in Modeling Default of Credit Card Clients*; Technical Report; Center for Open Science: Charlottesville, VA, USA, 2023.
58. Shui, C.; Xu, G.; Chen, Q.; Li, J.; Ling, C.X.; Arbel, T.; Wang, B.; Gagné, C. On learning fairness and accuracy on multiple subgroups. *Adv. Neural Inf. Process. Syst.* **2022**, *35*, 34121–34135.
59. Mayernik, M.S. Open data: Accountability and transparency. *Big Data Soc.* **2017**, *4*, 2053951717718853. [CrossRef]
60. Zhou, N.; Zhang, Z.; Nair, V.N.; Singhal, H.; Chen, J.; Sudjianto, A. Bias, Fairness, and Accountability with AI and ML Algorithms. *arXiv* **2021**, arXiv:2105.06558.
61. Shin, D. User perceptions of algorithmic decisions in the personalized AI system: Perceptual evaluation of fairness, accountability, transparency, and explainability. *J. Broadcast. Electron. Media* **2020**, *64*, 541–565. [CrossRef]
62. Sokol, K.; Hepburn, A.; Poyiadzi, R.; Clifford, M.; Santos-Rodriguez, R.; Flach, P. Fat forensics: A python toolbox for implementing and deploying fairness, accountability and transparency algorithms in predictive systems. *arXiv* **2022**, arXiv:2209.03805.
63. Gevaert, C.M.; Carman, M.; Rosman, B.; Georgiadou, Y.; Soden, R. Fairness and accountability of AI in disaster risk management: Opportunities and challenges. *Patterns* **2021**, *2*, 100363. [CrossRef]
64. Morris, M.R. AI and accessibility. *Commun. ACM* **2020**, *63*, 35–37. [CrossRef]
65. Israni, S.T.; Matheny, M.E.; Matlow, R.; Whicher, D. Equity, inclusivity, and innovative digital technologies to improve adolescent and young adult health. *J. Adolesc. Health* **2020**, *67*, S4–S6. [CrossRef]
66. Ntoutsi, E.; Fafalios, P.; Gadiraju, U.; Iosifidis, V.; Nejdl, W.; Vidal, M.E.; Ruggieri, S.; Turini, F.; Papadopoulos, S.; Krasanakis, E.; et al. Bias in data-driven Artificial Intelligence systems—An introductory survey. *Wiley Interdiscip. Rev. Data Min. Knowl. Discov.* **2020**, *10*, e1356. [CrossRef]
67. Baeza-Yates, R. Bias on the web. *Commun. ACM* **2018**, *61*, 54–61. [CrossRef]
68. Pessach, D.; Shmueli, E. Improving fairness of Artificial Intelligence algorithms in Privileged-Group Selection Bias data settings. *Expert Syst. Appl.* **2021**, *185*, 115667. [CrossRef]
69. Wang, Y.; Singh, L. Analyzing the impact of missing values and selection bias on fairness. *Int. J. Data Sci. Anal.* **2021**, *12*, 101–119. [CrossRef]
70. Russell, G.; Mandy, W.; Elliott, D.; White, R.; Pittwood, T.; Ford, T. Selection bias on intellectual ability in autism research: A cross-sectional review and meta-analysis. *Mol. Autism* **2019**, *10*, 1–10. [CrossRef]
71. Bolukbasi, T.; Chang, K.W.; Zou, J.Y.; Saligrama, V.; Kalai, A.T. Man is to computer programmer as woman is to homemaker? debiasing word embeddings. *Adv. Neural Inf. Process. Syst.* **2016**, *29*.

72. Mehrabi, N.; Morstatter, F.; Saxena, N.; Lerman, K.; Galstyan, A. A survey on bias and fairness in machine learning. *ACM Comput. Surv. (CSUR)* **2021**, *54*, 1–35. [CrossRef]
73. Torralba, A.; Efros, A.A. Unbiased look at dataset bias. In Proceedings of the CVPR, Colorado Springs, CO, USA, 20–25 June 2011; IEEE: Piscataway, NJ, USA, 2011; pp. 1521–1528.
74. Liao, Y.; Naghizadeh, P. The impacts of labeling biases on fairness criteria. In Proceedings of the 10th International Conference on Learning Representations, ICLR, Virtually, 25–29 April 2022; pp. 25–29.
75. Paulus, J.K.; Kent, D.M. Predictably unequal: Understanding and addressing concerns that algorithmic clinical prediction may increase health disparities. *NPJ Digit. Med.* **2020**, *3*, 99. [CrossRef]
76. Zhao, J.; Wang, T.; Yatskar, M.; Ordonez, V.; Chang, K.W. Men also like shopping: Reducing gender bias amplification using corpus-level constraints. *arXiv* **2017**, arXiv:1707.09457.
77. Yang, N.; Yuan, D.; Liu, C.Z.; Deng, Y.; Bao, W. FedIL: Federated Incremental Learning from Decentralized Unlabeled Data with Convergence Analysis. *arXiv* **2023**, arXiv:2302.11823.
78. Tripathi, S.; Musiolik, T.H. Fairness and ethics in Artificial Intelligence-based medical imaging. In *Research Anthology on Improving Medical Imaging Techniques for Analysis and Intervention*; IGI Global: Hershey, PA, USA, 2023; pp. 79–90.
79. Mashhadi, A.; Kyllo, A.; Parizi, R.M. Fairness in Federated Learning for Spatial-Temporal Applications. *arXiv* **2022**, arXiv:2201.06598.
80. Zhao, D.; Yu, G.; Xu, P.; Luo, M. Equivalence between dropout and data augmentation: A mathematical check. *Neural Netw.* **2019**, *115*, 82–89. [CrossRef] [PubMed]
81. Chun, J.S.; Brockner, J.; De Cremer, D. How temporal and social comparisons in performance evaluation affect fairness perceptions. *Organ. Behav. Hum. Decis. Process.* **2018**, *145*, 1–15. [CrossRef]
82. Asiedu, M.N.; Dieng, A.; Oppong, A.; Nagawa, M.; Koyejo, S.; Heller, K. Globalizing Fairness Attributes in Machine Learning: A Case Study on Health in Africa. *arXiv* **2023**, arXiv:2304.02190.
83. Hutiri, W.T.; Ding, A.Y. Bias in automated speaker recognition. In Proceedings of the 2022 ACM Conference on Fairness, Accountability, and Transparency, Seoul, Republic of Korea, 21–24 June 2022; pp. 230–247.
84. Makhlouf, K.; Zhioua, S.; Palamidessi, C. Machine learning fairness notions: Bridging the gap with real-world applications. *Inf. Process. Manag.* **2021**, *58*, 102642. [CrossRef]
85. Kallus, N.; Zhou, A. Residual unfairness in fair machine learning from prejudiced data. In Proceedings of the International Conference on Machine Learning, PMLR, Stockholm, Sweden, 10–15 July 2018; pp. 2439–2448.
86. Yang, N.; Yuan, D.; Zhang, Y.; Deng, Y.; Bao, W. Asynchronous Semi-Supervised Federated Learning with Provable Convergence in Edge Computing. *IEEE Netw.* **2022**, *36*, 136–143. [CrossRef]
87. So, W.; Lohia, P.; Pimplikar, R.; Hosoi, A.; D'Ignazio, C. Beyond Fairness: Reparative Algorithms to Address Historical Injustices of Housing Discrimination in the US. In Proceedings of the 2022 ACM Conference on Fairness, Accountability, and Transparency, Seoul, Republic of Korea, 21–24 June 2022; pp. 988–1004.
88. Alikhademi, K.; Drobina, E.; Prioleau, D.; Richardson, B.; Purves, D.; Gilbert, J.E. A review of predictive policing from the perspective of fairness. *Artif. Intell. Law* **2022**, *30*, 1–17. [CrossRef]
89. Rajkomar, A.; Hardt, M.; Howell, M.D.; Corrado, G.; Chin, M.H. Ensuring fairness in machine learning to advance health equity. *Ann. Intern. Med.* **2018**, *169*, 866–872. [CrossRef]
90. Woo, S.E.; LeBreton, J.M.; Keith, M.G.; Tay, L. Bias, fairness, and validity in graduate-school admissions: A psychometric perspective. *Perspect. Psychol. Sci.* **2023**, *18*, 3–31. [CrossRef]
91. Weerts, H.; Pfisterer, F.; Feurer, M.; Eggensperger, K.; Bergman, E.; Awad, N.; Vanschoren, J.; Pechenizkiy, M.; Bischl, B.; Hutter, F. Can Fairness be Automated? Guidelines and Opportunities for Fairness-aware AutoML. *arXiv* **2023**, arXiv:2303.08485.
92. Hauer, K.E.; Park, Y.S.; Bullock, J.L.; Tekian, A. "My Assessments Are Biased!" Measurement and Sociocultural Approaches to Achieve Fairness in Assessment in Medical Education. *Acad. Med. J. Assoc. Am. Med. Coll.* **2023**, *online ahead of print*.
93. Chen, Y.; Mahoney, C.; Grasso, I.; Wali, E.; Matthews, A.; Middleton, T.; Njie, M.; Matthews, J. Gender bias and under-representation in natural language processing across human languages. In Proceedings of the 2021 AAAI/ACM Conference on AI, Ethics, and Society, New York, NY, USA, 19–21 May 2021; pp. 24–34.
94. Chai, J.; Wang, X. Fairness with adaptive weights. In Proceedings of the International Conference on Machine Learning, PMLR, Baltimore, MD, USA, 17–23 July 2022; pp. 2853–2866.
95. Zhou, Q.; Mareček, J.; Shorten, R. Fairness in Forecasting of Observations of Linear Dynamical Systems. *J. Artif. Intell. Res.* **2023**, *76*, 1247–1280. [CrossRef]
96. Spinelli, I.; Scardapane, S.; Hussain, A.; Uncini, A. Fairdrop: Biased edge dropout for enhancing fairness in graph representation learning. *IEEE Trans. Artif. Intell.* **2021**, *3*, 344–354. [CrossRef]
97. Yu, C.; Liao, W. Professionalism and homophily bias: A study of Airbnb stay choice and review positivity. *Int. J. Hosp. Manag.* **2023**, *110*, 103433. [CrossRef]
98. Lerchenmueller, M.; Hoisl, K.; Schmallenbach, L. Homophily, biased attention, and the gender gap in science. In *Academy of Management Proceedings*; Academy of Management Briarcliff Manor: New York, NY, USA, 2019; Volume 2019, p. 14784.
99. Vogrin, M.; Wood, G.; Schmickl, T. Confirmation Bias as a Mechanism to Focus Attention Enhances Signal Detection. *J. Artif. Soc. Soc. Simul.* **2023**, *26*, 2. [CrossRef]

100. Kulkarni, A.; Shivananda, A.; Manure, A. Actions, Biases, and Human-in-the-Loop. In *Introduction to Prescriptive AI: A Primer for Decision Intelligence Solutioning with Python*; Springer: Berkeley, CA, USA, 2023; pp. 125–142.
101. Gwebu, K.L.; Wang, J.; Zifla, E. Can warnings curb the spread of fake news? The interplay between warning, trust and confirmation bias. *Behav. Inf. Technol.* **2022**, *41*, 3552–3573. [CrossRef]
102. Miller, A.C. Confronting confirmation bias: Giving truth a fighting chance in the information age. *Soc. Educ.* **2016**, *80*, 276–279.
103. Ghazimatin, A.; Kleindessner, M.; Russell, C.; Abedjan, Z.; Golebiowski, J. Measuring fairness of rankings under noisy sensitive information. In Proceedings of the 2022 ACM Conference on Fairness, Accountability, and Transparency, Seoul, Republic of Korea, 21–24 June 2022; pp. 2263–2279.
104. Warner, R.; Sloan, R.H. Making Artificial Intelligence transparent: Fairness and the problem of proxy variables. *Crim. Justice Ethics* **2021**, *40*, 23–39. [CrossRef]
105. Mazilu, L.; Paton, N.W.; Konstantinou, N.; Fernandes, A.A. Fairness in data wrangling. In Proceedings of the 2020 IEEE 21st International Conference on Information Reuse and Integration for Data Science (IRI), Las Vegas, NV, USA, 11–13 August 2020; IEEE: Piscataway, NJ, USA, 2020; pp. 341–348.
106. Caliskan, A.; Bryson, J.J.; Narayanan, A. Semantics derived automatically from language corpora contain human-like biases. *Science* **2017**, *356*, 183–186. [CrossRef] [PubMed]
107. Helms, J.E. Fairness is not validity or cultural bias in racial-group assessment: A quantitative perspective. *Am. Psychol.* **2006**, *61*, 845. [CrossRef]
108. Danks, D.; London, A.J. Algorithmic Bias in Autonomous Systems. *Ijcai* **2017**, *17*, 4691–4697.
109. Kordzadeh, N.; Ghasemaghaei, M. Algorithmic bias: Review, synthesis, and future research directions. *Eur. J. Inf. Syst.* **2022**, *31*, 388–409. [CrossRef]
110. Shen, X.; Plested, J.; Caldwell, S.; Gedeon, T. Exploring biases and prejudice of facial synthesis via semantic latent space. In Proceedings of the 2021 International Joint Conference on Neural Networks (IJCNN), Shenzhen, China, 18–22 July 2021; IEEE: Piscataway, NJ, USA, 2021; pp. 1–8.
111. Garcia, M. Racist in the Machine. *World Policy J.* **2016**, *33*, 111–117. [CrossRef]
112. Heffernan, T. Sexism, racism, prejudice, and bias: A literature review and synthesis of research surrounding student evaluations of courses and teaching. *Assess. Eval. High. Educ.* **2022**, *47*, 144–154. [CrossRef]
113. Prabhu, A.; Dognin, C.; Singh, M. Sampling bias in deep active classification: An empirical study. *arXiv* **2019**, arXiv:1909.09389.
114. Cortes, C.; Mohri, M. Domain adaptation and sample bias correction theory and algorithm for regression. *Theor. Comput. Sci.* **2014**, *519*, 103–126. [CrossRef]
115. Griffith, G.J.; Morris, T.T.; Tudball, M.J.; Herbert, A.; Mancano, G.; Pike, L.; Sharp, G.C.; Sterne, J.; Palmer, T.M.; Davey Smith, G.; et al. Collider bias undermines our understanding of COVID-19 disease risk and severity. *Nat. Commun.* **2020**, *11*, 5749. [CrossRef]
116. Kleinberg, J.; Mullainathan, S.; Raghavan, M. Inherent trade-offs in the fair determination of risk scores. *arXiv* **2016**, arXiv:1609.05807.
117. Mansoury, M.; Abdollahpouri, H.; Pechenizkiy, M.; Mobasher, B.; Burke, R. Feedback loop and bias amplification in recommender systems. In Proceedings of the 29th ACM International Conference on Information & Knowledge Management, Virtual, 19–23 October 2020; pp. 2145–2148.
118. Pan, W.; Cui, S.; Wen, H.; Chen, K.; Zhang, C.; Wang, F. Correcting the user feedback-loop bias for recommendation systems. *arXiv* **2021**, arXiv:2109.06037.
119. Taori, R.; Hashimoto, T. Data feedback loops: Model-driven amplification of dataset biases. In Proceedings of the International Conference on Machine Learning, PMLR, Honolulu, HI, USA, 23–29 July 2023; pp. 33883–33920.
120. Vokinger, K.N.; Feuerriegel, S.; Kesselheim, A.S. Mitigating bias in machine learning for medicine. *Commun. Med.* **2021**, *1*, 25. [CrossRef]
121. Kuhlman, C.; Jackson, L.; Chunara, R. No computation without representation: Avoiding data and algorithm biases through diversity. *arXiv* **2020**, arXiv:2002.11836.
122. Raub, M. Bots, bias and big data: Artificial Intelligence, algorithmic bias and disparate impact liability in hiring practices. *Ark. L. Rev.* **2018**, *71*, 529.
123. Norori, N.; Hu, Q.; Aellen, F.M.; Faraci, F.D.; Tzovara, A. Addressing bias in big data and AI for health care: A call for open science. *Patterns* **2021**, *2*, 100347. [CrossRef]
124. Kafai, Y.; Proctor, C.; Lui, D. From theory bias to theory dialogue: Embracing cognitive, situated, and critical framings of computational thinking in K-12 CS education. *ACM Inroads* **2020**, *11*, 44–53. [CrossRef]
125. Celi, L.A.; Cellini, J.; Charpignon, M.L.; Dee, E.C.; Dernoncourt, F.; Eber, R.; Mitchell, W.G.; Moukheiber, L.; Schirmer, J.; Situ, J.; et al. Sources of bias in Artificial Intelligence that perpetuate healthcare disparities—A global review. *PLoS Digit. Health* **2022**, *1*, e0000022. [CrossRef] [PubMed]
126. Schemmer, M.; Kühl, N.; Benz, C.; Satzger, G. On the influence of explainable AI on automation bias. *arXiv* **2022**, arXiv:2204.08859.
127. Alon-Barkat, S.; Busuioc, M. Human–AI interactions in public sector decision making: "Automation bias" and "selective adherence" to algorithmic advice. *J. Public Adm. Res. Theory* **2023**, *33*, 153–169. [CrossRef]
128. Jones-Jang, S.M.; Park, Y.J. How do people react to AI failure? Automation bias, algorithmic aversion, and perceived controllability. *J. Comput. Mediat. Commun.* **2023**, *28*, zmac029. [CrossRef]

129. Strauß, S. Deep automation bias: How to tackle a wicked problem of ai? *Big Data Cogn. Comput.* **2021**, *5*, 18. [CrossRef]
130. Raisch, S.; Krakowski, S. Artificial Intelligence and management: The automation–augmentation paradox. *Acad. Manag. Rev.* **2021**, *46*, 192–210. [CrossRef]
131. Lyons, J.B.; Guznov, S.Y. Individual differences in human–machine trust: A multi-study look at the perfect automation schema. *Theor. Issues Ergon. Sci.* **2019**, *20*, 440–458. [CrossRef]
132. Nakao, Y.; Stumpf, S.; Ahmed, S.; Naseer, A.; Strappelli, L. Toward involving end-users in interactive human-in-the-loop AI fairness. *ACM Trans. Interact. Intell. Syst. (TiiS)* **2022**, *12*, 1–30. [CrossRef]
133. Yarger, L.; Cobb Payton, F.; Neupane, B. Algorithmic equity in the hiring of underrepresented IT job candidates. *Online Inf. Rev.* **2020**, *44*, 383–395. [CrossRef]
134. Zhou, Y.; Kantarcioglu, M.; Clifton, C. On Improving Fairness of AI Models with Synthetic Minority Oversampling Techniques. In Proceedings of the 2023 SIAM International Conference on Data Mining (SDM), Minneapolis, MN, USA, 27–29 April 2023; SIAM: Philadelphia, PA, USA, 2023; pp. 874–882.
135. Obermeyer, Z.; Powers, B.; Vogeli, C.; Mullainathan, S. Dissecting racial bias in an algorithm used to manage the health of populations. *Science* **2019**, *366*, 447–453. [CrossRef]
136. Calmon, F.; Wei, D.; Vinzamuri, B.; Natesan Ramamurthy, K.; Varshney, K.R. Optimized pre-processing for discrimination prevention. *Adv. Neural Inf. Process. Syst.* **2017**, *30*.
137. Zhang, B.H.; Lemoine, B.; Mitchell, M. Mitigating unwanted biases with adversarial learning. In Proceedings of the 2018 AAAI/ACM Conference on AI, Ethics, and Society, New Orleans, LA, USA, 2–3 February 2018; pp. 335–340.
138. Chiappa, S. Path-specific counterfactual fairness. *AAAI Conf. Artif. Intell.* **2019**, *33*, 7801–7808. [CrossRef]
139. Sun, Y.; Haghighat, F.; Fung, B.C. Trade-off between accuracy and fairness of data-driven building and indoor environment models: A comparative study of pre-processing methods. *Energy* **2022**, *239*, 122273. [CrossRef]
140. Sun, Y.; Fung, B.C.; Haghighat, F. The generalizability of pre-processing techniques on the accuracy and fairness of data-driven building models: A case study. *Energy Build.* **2022**, *268*, 112204. [CrossRef]
141. Wan, M.; Zha, D.; Liu, N.; Zou, N. In-processing modeling techniques for machine learning fairness: A survey. *ACM Trans. Knowl. Discov. Data* **2023**, *17*, 1–27. [CrossRef]
142. Sun, Y.; Fung, B.C.; Haghighat, F. In-Processing fairness improvement methods for regression Data-Driven building Models: Achieving uniform energy prediction. *Energy Build.* **2022**, *277*, 112565. [CrossRef]
143. Petersen, F.; Mukherjee, D.; Sun, Y.; Yurochkin, M. Post-processing for individual fairness. *Adv. Neural Inf. Process. Syst.* **2021**, *34*, 25944–25955.
144. Lohia, P.K.; Ramamurthy, K.N.; Bhide, M.; Saha, D.; Varshney, K.R.; Puri, R. Bias mitigation post-processing for individual and group fairness. In Proceedings of the Icassp 2019—2019 IEEE International Conference on Acoustics, Speech and Signal Processing (ICASSP), Brighton, UK, 12–17 May 2019; IEEE: Piscataway, NJ, USA, 2019; pp. 2847–2851.
145. Putzel, P.; Lee, S. Blackbox post-processing for multiclass fairness. *arXiv* **2022**, arXiv:2201.04461.
146. Jung, S.; Park, T.; Chun, S.; Moon, T. Re-weighting Based Group Fairness Regularization via Classwise Robust Optimization. *arXiv* **2023**, arXiv:2303.00442.
147. Lal, G.R.; Geyik, S.C.; Kenthapadi, K. Fairness-aware online personalization. *arXiv* **2020**, arXiv:2007.15270.
148. Wu, Y.; Zhang, L.; Wu, X. Counterfactual fairness: Unidentification, bound and algorithm. In Proceedings of the Twenty-Eighth International Joint Conference on Artificial Intelligence, Macao, China, 10–16 August 2019.
149. Cheong, J.; Kalkan, S.; Gunes, H. Counterfactual fairness for facial expression recognition. In *European Conference on Computer Vision*; Springer: Cham, Switzerland, 2022; pp. 245–261.
150. Wang, X.; Li, B.; Su, X.; Peng, H.; Wang, L.; Lu, C.; Wang, C. Autonomous dispatch trajectory planning on flight deck: A search-resampling-optimization framework. *Eng. Appl. Artif. Intell.* **2023**, *119*, 105792. [CrossRef]
151. Xie, S.M.; Santurkar, S.; Ma, T.; Liang, P. Data selection for language models via importance resampling. *arXiv* **2023**, arXiv:2302.03169.
152. Khushi, M.; Shaukat, K.; Alam, T.M.; Hameed, I.A.; Uddin, S.; Luo, S.; Yang, X.; Reyes, M.C. A comparative performance analysis of data resampling methods on imbalance medical data. *IEEE Access* **2021**, *9*, 109960–109975. [CrossRef]
153. Ghorbani, R.; Ghousi, R. Comparing different resampling methods in predicting students' performance using machine learning techniques. *IEEE Access* **2020**, *8*, 67899–67911. [CrossRef]
154. He, E.; Xie, Y.; Liu, L.; Chen, W.; Jin, Z.; Jia, X. Physics Guided Neural Networks for Time-Aware Fairness: An Application in Crop Yield Prediction. *AAAI Conf. Artif. Intell.* **2023**, *37*, 14223–14231. [CrossRef]
155. Wang, S.; Wang, B.; Zhang, Z.; Heidari, A.A.; Chen, H. Class-aware sample reweighting optimal transport for multi-source domain adaptation. *Neurocomputing* **2023**, *523*, 213–223. [CrossRef]
156. Song, P.; Li, P.; Dai, L.; Wang, T.; Chen, Z. Boosting R-CNN: Reweighting R-CNN samples by RPN's error for underwater object detection. *Neurocomputing* **2023**, *530*, 150–164. [CrossRef]
157. Jin, M.; Ju, C.J.T.; Chen, Z.; Liu, Y.C.; Droppo, J.; Stolcke, A. Adversarial reweighting for speaker verification fairness. *arXiv* **2022**, arXiv:2207.07776.
158. Kieninger, S.; Donati, L.; Keller, B.G. Dynamical reweighting methods for Markov models. *Curr. Opin. Struct. Biol.* **2020**, *61*, 124–131. [CrossRef]

159. Zhou, X.; Lin, Y.; Pi, R.; Zhang, W.; Xu, R.; Cui, P.; Zhang, T. Model agnostic sample reweighting for out-of-distribution learning. In Proceedings of the International Conference on Machine Learning, PMLR, Baltimore, MD, USA, 17–23 July 2022; pp. 27203–27221.
160. Khalifa, N.E.; Loey, M.; Mirjalili, S. A comprehensive survey of recent trends in deep learning for digital images augmentation. *Artif. Intell. Rev.* **2022**, *55*, 2351–2377. [CrossRef]
161. Pastaltzidis, I.; Dimitriou, N.; Quezada-Tavarez, K.; Aidinlis, S.; Marquenie, T.; Gurzawska, A.; Tzovaras, D. Data augmentation for fairness-aware machine learning: Preventing algorithmic bias in law enforcement systems. In Proceedings of the 2022 ACM Conference on Fairness, Accountability, and Transparency, Seoul, Republic of Korea, 21–24 June 2022; pp. 2302–2314.
162. Kose, O.D.; Shen, Y. Fair node representation learning via adaptive data augmentation. *arXiv* **2022**, arXiv:2201.08549.
163. Zhang, Y.; Sang, J. Towards accuracy-fairness paradox: Adversarial example-based data augmentation for visual debiasing. In Proceedings of the 28th ACM International Conference on Multimedia, Seattle, WA, USA, 12–16 October 2020; pp. 4346–4354.
164. Zheng, L.; Zhu, Y.; He, J. Fairness-aware Multi-view Clustering. In Proceedings of the 2023 SIAM International Conference on Data Mining (SDM), Minneapolis, MN, USA, 27–29 April 2023; SIAM: Philadelphia, PA, USA, 2023; pp. 856–864.
165. Le Quy, T.; Friege, G.; Ntoutsi, E. A Review of Clustering Models in Educational Data Science Toward Fairness-Aware Learning. In *Educational Data Science: Essentials, Approaches, and Tendencies: Proactive Education based on Empirical Big Data Evidence*; Springer: Singapore, 2023; pp. 43–94.
166. Chierichetti, F.; Kumar, R.; Lattanzi, S.; Vassilvitskii, S. Fair clustering through fairlets. *Adv. Neural Inf. Process. Syst.* **2017**, *30*.
167. Kamishima, T.; Akaho, S.; Asoh, H.; Sakuma, J. Fairness-aware classifier with prejudice remover regularizer. In Proceedings of the Machine Learning and Knowledge Discovery in Databases: European Conference, ECML PKDD 2012, Bristol, UK, 24–28 September 2012; Springer: Berlin/Heidelberg, Germany, 2012; pp. 35–50.
168. Chakraborty, J.; Majumder, S.; Menzies, T. Bias in machine learning software: Why? how? what to do? In Proceedings of the 29th ACM Joint Meeting on European Software Engineering Conference and Symposium on the Foundations of Software Engineering, Athens, Greece, 23–28 August 2021; pp. 429–440.
169. Blagus, R.; Lusa, L. SMOTE for high-dimensional class-imbalanced data. *BMC Bioinform.* **2013**, *14*, 106. [CrossRef] [PubMed]
170. Blagus, R.; Lusa, L. Evaluation of smote for high-dimensional class-imbalanced microarray data. In Proceedings of the 2012 11th International Conference on Machine Learning and Applications, Boca Raton, FL, USA, 12–15 December 2012; IEEE: Piscataway, NJ, USA, 2012; Volume 2, pp. 89–94.
171. Chawla, N.V.; Bowyer, K.W.; Hall, L.O.; Kegelmeyer, W.P. SMOTE: Synthetic minority over-sampling technique. *J. Artif. Intell. Res.* **2002**, *16*, 321–357. [CrossRef]
172. Zhao, W.; Alwidian, S.; Mahmoud, Q.H. Adversarial Training Methods for Deep Learning: A Systematic Review. *Algorithms* **2022**, *15*, 283. [CrossRef]
173. Bai, T.; Luo, J.; Zhao, J.; Wen, B.; Wang, Q. Recent advances in adversarial training for adversarial robustness. *arXiv* **2021**, arXiv:2102.01356.
174. Wong, E.; Rice, L.; Kolter, J.Z. Fast is better than free: Revisiting adversarial training. *arXiv* **2020**, arXiv:2001.03994.
175. Andriushchenko, M.; Flammarion, N. Understanding and improving fast adversarial training. *Adv. Neural Inf. Process. Syst.* **2020**, *33*, 16048–16059.
176. Shafahi, A.; Najibi, M.; Ghiasi, M.A.; Xu, Z.; Dickerson, J.; Studer, C.; Davis, L.S.; Taylor, G.; Goldstein, T. Adversarial training for free! *Adv. Neural Inf. Process. Syst.* **2019**, *32*.
177. Lim, J.; Kim, Y.; Kim, B.; Ahn, C.; Shin, J.; Yang, E.; Han, S. BiasAdv: Bias-Adversarial Augmentation for Model Debiasing. In Proceedings of the IEEE/CVF Conference on Computer Vision and Pattern Recognition, Vancouver, BC, Canada, 18–22 June 2023; pp. 3832–3841.
178. Hong, J.; Zhu, Z.; Yu, S.; Wang, Z.; Dodge, H.H.; Zhou, J. Federated adversarial debiasing for fair and transferable representations. In Proceedings of the 27th ACM SIGKDD Conference on Knowledge Discovery & Data Mining, Singapore, 14–18 August 2021; pp. 617–627.
179. Darlow, L.; Jastrzębski, S.; Storkey, A. Latent adversarial debiasing: Mitigating collider bias in deep neural networks. *arXiv* **2020**, arXiv:2011.11486.
180. Mishler, A.; Kennedy, E.H.; Chouldechova, A. Fairness in risk assessment instruments: Post-processing to achieve counterfactual equalized odds. In Proceedings of the 2021 ACM Conference on Fairness, Accountability, and Transparency, Virtual Event/Toronto, ON, Canada, 3–10 March 2021; pp. 386–400.
181. Roy, S.; Salimi, B. Causal inference in data analysis with applications to fairness and explanations. In *Reasoning Web. Causality, Explanations and Declarative Knowledge: 18th International Summer School 2022, Berlin, Germany, 27–30 September 2022*; Springer: Cham, Switzerland, 2023; pp. 105–131.
182. Madras, D.; Creager, E.; Pitassi, T.; Zemel, R. Fairness through causal awareness: Learning causal latent-variable models for biased data. In Proceedings of the Conference on Fairness, Accountability, and Transparency, Atlanta, GA, USA, 29–31 January 2019; pp. 349–358.
183. Loftus, J.R.; Russell, C.; Kusner, M.J.; Silva, R. Causal reasoning for algorithmic fairness. *arXiv* **2018**, arXiv:1805.05859.
184. Hinnefeld, J.H.; Cooman, P.; Mammo, N.; Deese, R. Evaluating fairness metrics in the presence of dataset bias. *arXiv* **2018**, arXiv:1809.09245.

185. Modén, M.U.; Lundin, J.; Tallvid, M.; Ponti, M. Involving teachers in meta-design of AI to ensure situated fairness. *Proceedings* **2022**, *1613*, 0073.
186. Zhao, C.; Li, C.; Li, J.; Chen, F. Fair meta-learning for few-shot classification. In Proceedings of the 2020 IEEE International Conference on Knowledge Graph (ICKG), Nanjing, China, 9–11 August 2020; IEEE: Piscataway, NJ, USA, 2020; pp. 275–282.
187. Hsu, B.; Chen, X.; Han, Y.; Namkoong, H.; Basu, K. An Operational Perspective to Fairness Interventions: Where and How to Intervene. *arXiv* **2023**, arXiv:2302.01574.
188. Salvador, T.; Cairns, S.; Voleti, V.; Marshall, N.; Oberman, A. Faircal: Fairness calibration for face verification. *arXiv* **2021**, arXiv:2106.03761.
189. Noriega-Campero, A.; Bakker, M.A.; Garcia-Bulle, B.; Pentland, A. Active fairness in algorithmic decision making. In Proceedings of the 2019 AAAI/ACM Conference on AI, Ethics, and Society, Honolulu, HI, USA, 27–28 January 2019; pp. 77–83.
190. Pleiss, G.; Raghavan, M.; Wu, F.; Kleinberg, J.; Weinberger, K.Q. On fairness and calibration. *Adv. Neural Inf. Process. Syst.* **2017**, *30*.
191. Tahir, A.; Cheng, L.; Liu, H. Fairness through Aleatoric Uncertainty. *arXiv* **2023**, arXiv:2304.03646.
192. Tubella, A.A.; Barsotti, F.; Koçer, R.G.; Mendez, J.A. Ethical implications of fairness interventions: What might be hidden behind engineering choices? *Ethics Inf. Technol.* **2022**, *24*, 12. [CrossRef]
193. Kamishima, T.; Akaho, S.; Asoh, H.; Sakuma, J. Model-based and actual independence for fairness-aware classification. *Data Min. Knowl. Discov.* **2018**, *32*, 258–286. [CrossRef]
194. Kasmi, M.L. Machine Learning Fairness in Finance: An Application to Credit Scoring. Ph.D. Thesis, Tilburg University, Tilburg, The Netherlands, 2021.
195. Zhang, T.; Zhu, T.; Li, J.; Han, M.; Zhou, W.; Philip, S.Y. Fairness in semi-supervised learning: Unlabeled data help to reduce discrimination. *IEEE Trans. Knowl. Data Eng.* **2020**, *34*, 1763–1774. [CrossRef]
196. Caton, S.; Haas, C. Fairness in machine learning: A survey. *arXiv* **2020**, arXiv:2010.04053.
197. Small, E.A.; Sokol, K.; Manning, D.; Salim, F.D.; Chan, J. Equalised Odds is not Equal Individual Odds: Post-processing for Group and Individual Fairness. *arXiv* **2023**, arXiv:2304.09779.
198. Jang, T.; Shi, P.; Wang, X. Group-aware threshold adaptation for fair classification. *AAAI Conf. Artif. Intell.* **2022**, *36*, 6988–6995. [CrossRef]
199. Nguyen, D.; Gupta, S.; Rana, S.; Shilton, A.; Venkatesh, S. Fairness improvement for black-box classifiers with Gaussian process. *Inf. Sci.* **2021**, *576*, 542–556. [CrossRef]
200. Iosifidis, V.; Fetahu, B.; Ntoutsi, E. Fae: A fairness-aware ensemble framework. In Proceedings of the 2019 IEEE International Conference on Big Data (Big Data), Los Angeles, CA, USA, 9–12 December 2019; IEEE: Piscataway, NJ, USA, 2019; pp. 1375–1380.
201. Zhong, M.; Tandon, R. Learning Fair Classifiers via Min-Max F-divergence Regularization. *arXiv* **2023**, arXiv:2306.16552.
202. Nandy, P.; Diciccio, C.; Venugopalan, D.; Logan, H.; Basu, K.; El Karoui, N. Achieving Fairness via Post-Processing in Web-Scale Recommender Systems. In Proceedings of the 2022 ACM Conference on Fairness, Accountability, and Transparency, Seoul, Republic of Korea, 21–24 June 2022; pp. 715–725.
203. Boratto, L.; Fenu, G.; Marras, M. Interplay between upsampling and regularization for provider fairness in recommender systems. *User Model. User Adapt. Interact.* **2021**, *31*, 421–455. [CrossRef]
204. Yao, S.; Huang, B. Beyond parity: Fairness objectives for collaborative filtering. *Adv. Neural Inf. Process. Syst.* **2017**, *30*.
205. Yu, B.; Wu, J.; Ma, J.; Zhu, Z. Tangent-normal adversarial regularization for semi-supervised learning. In Proceedings of the IEEE/CVF Conference on Computer Vision and Pattern Recognition, Long Beach, CA, USA, 15–20 June 2019; pp. 10676–10684.
206. Sato, M.; Suzuki, J.; Kiyono, S. Effective adversarial regularization for neural machine translation. In Proceedings of the 57th Annual Meeting of the Association for Computational Linguistics, Florence, Italy, 28 July–2 August 2019; pp. 204–210.
207. Nasr, M.; Shokri, R.; Houmansadr, A. Machine learning with membership privacy using adversarial regularization. In Proceedings of the 2018 ACM SIGSAC Conference on Computer and Communications Security, Toronto, ON, Canada, 15–19 October 2018; pp. 634–646.
208. Mertikopoulos, P.; Papadimitriou, C.; Piliouras, G. Cycles in adversarial regularized learning. In Proceedings of the Twenty-Ninth Annual ACM-SIAM Symposium on Discrete Algorithms, New Orleans, LA, USA, 7–10 January 2018; SIAM: Philadelphia, PA, USA, 2018; pp. 2703–2717.
209. Du, M.; Yang, F.; Zou, N.; Hu, X. Fairness in deep learning: A computational perspective. *IEEE Intell. Syst.* **2020**, *36*, 25–34. [CrossRef]
210. Horesh, Y.; Haas, N.; Mishraky, E.; Resheff, Y.S.; Meir Lador, S. Paired-consistency: An example-based model-agnostic approach to fairness regularization in machine learning. In Proceedings of the Machine Learning and Knowledge Discovery in Databases: International Workshops of ECML PKDD 2019, Würzburg, Germany, 16–20 September 2019; Springer: Cham, Switzerland, 2020; pp. 590–604.
211. Lohaus, M.; Kleindessner, M.; Kenthapadi, K.; Locatello, F.; Russell, C. Are Two Heads the Same as One? Identifying Disparate Treatment in Fair Neural Networks. *Adv. Neural Inf. Process. Syst.* **2022**, *35*, 16548–16562.
212. Romano, Y.; Bates, S.; Candes, E. Achieving equalized odds by resampling sensitive attributes. *Adv. Neural Inf. Process. Syst.* **2020**, *33*, 361–371.
213. Cho, J.; Hwang, G.; Suh, C. A fair classifier using mutual information. In Proceedings of the 2020 IEEE International Symposium on Information Theory (ISIT), Los Angeles, CA, USA, 21–26 June 2020; IEEE: Piscataway, NJ, USA, 2020; pp. 2521–2526.

214. Wieling, M.; Nerbonne, J.; Baayen, R.H. Quantitative social dialectology: Explaining linguistic variation geographically and socially. *PLoS ONE* **2011**, *6*, e23613. [CrossRef]
215. Bhanot, K.; Qi, M.; Erickson, J.S.; Guyon, I.; Bennett, K.P. The problem of fairness in synthetic healthcare data. *Entropy* **2021**, *23*, 1165. [CrossRef]
216. Brusaferri, A.; Matteucci, M.; Spinelli, S.; Vitali, A. Probabilistic electric load forecasting through Bayesian mixture density networks. *Appl. Energy* **2022**, *309*, 118341. [CrossRef]
217. Errica, F.; Bacciu, D.; Micheli, A. Graph mixture density networks. In Proceedings of the International Conference on Machine Learning, PMLR, Virtual, 18–24 July 2021; pp. 3025–3035.
218. Makansi, O.; Ilg, E.; Cicek, O.; Brox, T. Overcoming limitations of mixture density networks: A sampling and fitting framework for multimodal future prediction. In Proceedings of the IEEE/CVF Conference on Computer Vision and Pattern Recognition, Long Beach, CA, USA, 15–20 June 2019; pp. 7144–7153.
219. John, P.G.; Vijaykeerthy, D.; Saha, D. Verifying individual fairness in machine learning models. In Proceedings of the Conference on Uncertainty in Artificial Intelligence, PMLR, Virtual, 3–6 August 2020; pp. 749–758.
220. Han, X.; Baldwin, T.; Cohn, T. Towards equal opportunity fairness through adversarial learning. *arXiv* **2022**, arXiv:2203.06317.
221. Shen, A.; Han, X.; Cohn, T.; Baldwin, T.; Frermann, L. Optimising equal opportunity fairness in model training. *arXiv* **2022**, arXiv:2205.02393.
222. Verma, S.; Rubin, J. Fairness definitions explained. In Proceedings of the International Workshop on Software Fairness, Gothenburg, Sweden, 29 May 2018; pp. 1–7.
223. Balashankar, A.; Wang, X.; Packer, B.; Thain, N.; Chi, E.; Beutel, A. Can we improve model robustness through secondary attribute counterfactuals? In Proceedings of the 2021 Conference on Empirical Methods in Natural Language Processing, Virtual, 7–11 November 2021; pp. 4701–4712.
224. Dong, Z.; Zhu, H.; Cheng, P.; Feng, X.; Cai, G.; He, X.; Xu, J.; Wen, J. Counterfactual learning for recommender system. In Proceedings of the 14th ACM Conference on Recommender Systems, Virtual Event, Brazil, 22–26 September 2020; pp. 568–569.
225. Veitch, V.; D'Amour, A.; Yadlowsky, S.; Eisenstein, J. Counterfactual invariance to spurious correlations in text classification. *Adv. Neural Inf. Process. Syst.* **2021**, *34*, 16196–16208.
226. Chang, Y.C.; Lu, C.J. Oblivious polynomial evaluation and oblivious neural learning. In Proceedings of the Advances in Cryptology—ASIACRYPT 2001: 7th International Conference on the Theory and Application of Cryptology and Information Security Gold Coast, Australia, 9–13 December 2001; Springer: Berlin/Heidelberg, Germany, 2001; pp. 369–384.
227. Meister, M.; Sheikholeslami, S.; Andersson, R.; Ormenisan, A.A.; Dowling, J. Towards distribution transparency for supervised ML with oblivious training functions. In Proceedings of the Workshop MLOps Syst, Austin, TX, USA, 2–4 March 2020; pp. 1–3.
228. Liu, J.; Juuti, M.; Lu, Y.; Asokan, N. Oblivious neural network predictions via minionn transformations. In Proceedings of the 2017 ACM SIGSAC Conference on Computer and Communications Security, Dallas, TX, USA, 30 October–3 November 2017; pp. 619–631.
229. Goel, N.; Yaghini, M.; Faltings, B. Non-discriminatory machine learning through convex fairness criteria. In Proceedings of the 2018 AAAI/ACM Conference on AI, Ethics, and Society, New Orleans, LA, USA, 2–3 February 2018; p. 116.
230. Makhlouf, K.; Zhioua, S.; Palamidessi, C. Survey on causal-based machine learning fairness notions. *arXiv* **2020**, arXiv:2010.09553.
231. Gölz, P.; Kahng, A.; Procaccia, A.D. Paradoxes in fair machine learning. *Adv. Neural Inf. Process. Syst.* **2019**, *32*.
232. Ferryman, K.; Pitcan, M. *Fairness in Precision Medicine*; Data and Society Research Institute: New York, NY, USA, 2018.
233. Dempsey, W.; Foster, I.; Fraser, S.; Kesselman, C. Sharing begins at home: How continuous and ubiquitous FAIRness can enhance research productivity and data reuse. *Harv. Data Sci. Rev.* **2022**, *4*, 10–11. [CrossRef]
234. Durand, C.M.; Segev, D.; Sugarman, J. Realizing HOPE: The ethics of organ transplantation from HIV-positive donors. *Ann. Intern. Med.* **2016**, *165*, 138–142. [CrossRef]
235. Rubinstein, Y.R.; McInnes, P. NIH/NCATS/GRDR® Common Data Elements: A leading force for standardized data collection. *Contemp. Clin. Trials* **2015**, *42*, 78–80. [CrossRef]
236. Frick, K.D. Micro-costing quantity data collection methods. *Med. Care* **2009**, *47*, S76. [CrossRef] [PubMed]
237. Rothstein, M.A. Informed consent for secondary research under the new NIH data sharing policy. *J. Law Med. Ethics* **2021**, *49*, 489–494. [CrossRef] [PubMed]
238. Greely, H.T.; Grady, C.; Ramos, K.M.; Chiong, W.; Eberwine, J.; Farahany, N.A.; Johnson, L.S.M.; Hyman, B.T.; Hyman, S.E.; Rommelfanger, K.S.; et al. Neuroethics guiding principles for the NIH BRAIN initiative. *J. Neurosci.* **2018**, *38*, 10586. [CrossRef] [PubMed]
239. Nijhawan, L.P.; Janodia, M.D.; Muddukrishna, B.; Bhat, K.M.; Bairy, K.L.; Udupa, N.; Musmade, P.B. Informed consent: Issues and challenges. *J. Adv. Pharm. Technol. Res.* **2013**, *4*, 134.
240. Elliot, M.; Mackey, E.; O'Hara, K.; Tudor, C. *The Anonymisation Decision-Making Framework*; UKAN: Manchester, UK, 2016; p. 171.
241. Rosner, G. De-Identification as Public Policy. *J. Data Prot. Priv.* **2019**, *3*, 1–18.
242. Moretón, A.; Jaramillo, A. Anonymisation and re-identification risk for voice data. *Eur. Data Prot. L. Rev.* **2021**, *7*, 274. [CrossRef]
243. Rumbold, J.M.; Pierscionek, B.K. A critique of the regulation of data science in healthcare research in the European Union. *BMC Med. Ethics* **2017**, *18*, 27. [CrossRef] [PubMed]
244. Stalla-Bourdillon, S.; Knight, A. Anonymous data v. personal data-false debate: An EU perspective on anonymization, pseudonymization and personal data. *Wis. Int'l LJ* **2016**, *34*, 284.

245. Ilavsky, J. Nika: Software for two-dimensional data reduction. *J. Appl. Crystallogr.* **2012**, *45*, 324–328. [CrossRef]
246. Fietzke, J.; Liebetrau, V.; Günther, D.; Gürs, K.; Hametner, K.; Zumholz, K.; Hansteen, T.; Eisenhauer, A. An alternative data acquisition and evaluation strategy for improved isotope ratio precision using LA-MC-ICP-MS applied to stable and radiogenic strontium isotopes in carbonates. *J. Anal. At. Spectrom.* **2008**, *23*, 955–961. [CrossRef]
247. Gwynne, S. *Conventions in the Collection and Use of Human Performance Data*; National Institute of Standards and Technology: Gaithersburg, MD, USA, 2010; pp. 10–928.
248. Buckleton, J.S.; Bright, J.A.; Cheng, K.; Budowle, B.; Coble, M.D. NIST interlaboratory studies involving DNA mixtures (MIX13): A modern analysis. *Forensic Sci. Int. Genet.* **2018**, *37*, 172–179. [CrossRef] [PubMed]
249. Sydes, M.R.; Johnson, A.L.; Meredith, S.K.; Rauchenberger, M.; South, A.; Parmar, M.K. Sharing data from clinical trials: The rationale for a controlled access approach. *Trials* **2015**, *16*, 104. [CrossRef] [PubMed]
250. Abdul Razack, H.I.; Aranjani, J.M.; Mathew, S.T. Clinical trial transparency regulations: Implications to various scholarly publishing stakeholders. *Sci. Public Policy* **2022**, *49*, 951–961. [CrossRef]
251. Alemayehu, D.; Anziano, R.J.; Levenstein, M. Perspectives on clinical trial data transparency and disclosure. *Contemp. Clin. Trials* **2014**, *39*, 28–33. [CrossRef]
252. Force, J.T.; Initiative, T. Security and privacy controls for federal information systems and organizations. *NIST Spec. Publ.* **2013**, *800*, 8–13.
253. Plans, B.E.A. Assessing security and privacy controls in federal information systems and organizations. *NIST Spec. Publ.* **2014**, *800*, 53A.
254. Dempsey, K.; Witte, G.; Rike, D. *Summary of NIST SP 800-53, Revision 4: Security and Privacy Controls for Federal Information Systems and Organizations*; Technical Report; National Institute of Standards and Technology: Gaithersburg, MD, USA, 2014.
255. Passi, S.; Jackson, S.J. Trust in data science: Collaboration, translation, and accountability in corporate data science projects. *Proc. ACM Hum. Comput. Interact.* **2018**, *2*, 1–28. [CrossRef]
256. Hutt, E.; Polikoff, M.S. Toward a framework for public accountability in education reform. *Educ. Res.* **2020**, *49*, 503–511. [CrossRef]
257. Carle, S.D. A social movement history of Title VII Disparate Impact analysis. *Fla. L. Rev.* **2011**, *63*, 251. [CrossRef]
258. Griffith, D.; McKinney, B. Using Disparate Impact Analysis to Develop Anti-Racist Policies: An Application to Coronavirus Liability Waivers. *J. High. Educ. Manag.* **2021**, *36*, 104–116.
259. Liu, S.; Ge, Y.; Xu, Y.; Zhang, Y.; Marian, A. Fairness-aware federated matrix factorization. In Proceedings of the 16th ACM Conference on Recommender Systems, Seattle, WA, USA, 18–22 September 2022; pp. 168–178.
260. Gao, R.; Ge, Y.; Shah, C. FAIR: Fairness-aware information retrieval evaluation. *J. Assoc. Inf. Sci. Technol.* **2022**, *73*, 1461–1473. [CrossRef]
261. Zhang, W.; Ntoutsi, E. Faht: An adaptive fairness-aware decision tree classifier. *arXiv* **2019**, arXiv:1907.07237.
262. Serna, I.; DeAlcala, D.; Morales, A.; Fierrez, J.; Ortega-Garcia, J. IFBiD: Inference-free bias detection. *arXiv* **2021**, arXiv:2109.04374.
263. Li, B.; Peng, H.; Sainju, R.; Yang, J.; Yang, L.; Liang, Y.; Jiang, W.; Wang, B.; Liu, H.; Ding, C. Detecting gender bias in transformer-based models: A case study on BERT. *arXiv* **2021**, arXiv:2110.15733.
264. Constantin, R.; Dück, M.; Alexandrov, A.; Matošević, P.; Keidar, D.; El-Assady, M. How Do Algorithmic Fairness Metrics Align with Human Judgement? A Mixed Initiative System for Contextualized Fairness Assessment. In Proceedings of the 2022 IEEE Workshop on TRust and EXpertise in Visual Analytics (TREX), Oklahoma City, OK, USA, 16 October 2022; IEEE: Piscataway, NJ, USA, 2022; pp. 1–7.
265. Goel, Z. Algorithmic Fairness Final Report.
266. Bird, S.; Dudík, M.; Edgar, R.; Horn, B.; Lutz, R.; Milan, V.; Sameki, M.; Wallach, H.; Walker, K. Fairlearn: A toolkit for assessing and improving fairness in AI. *Microsoft Tech. Rep.* **2020**.
267. Jethani, N.; Sudarshan, M.; Aphinyanaphongs, Y.; Ranganath, R. Have We Learned to Explain?: How Interpretability Methods Can Learn to Encode Predictions in their Interpretations. In Proceedings of the International Conference on Artificial Intelligence and Statistics, PMLR, Virtual, 13–15 April 2021; pp. 1459–1467.
268. Stiglic, G.; Kocbek, P.; Fijacko, N.; Zitnik, M.; Verbert, K.; Cilar, L. Interpretability of machine learning-based prediction models in healthcare. *Wiley Interdiscip. Rev. Data Min. Knowl. Discov.* **2020**, *10*, e1379. [CrossRef]
269. Moraffah, R.; Karami, M.; Guo, R.; Raglin, A.; Liu, H. Causal interpretability for machine learning-problems, methods and evaluation. *ACM SIGKDD Explor. Newsl.* **2020**, *22*, 18–33. [CrossRef]
270. Jacovi, A.; Swayamdipta, S.; Ravfogel, S.; Elazar, Y.; Choi, Y.; Goldberg, Y. Contrastive explanations for model interpretability. *arXiv* **2021**, arXiv:2103.01378.
271. Jeffries, A.C.; Wallace, L.; Coutts, A.J.; McLaren, S.J.; McCall, A.; Impellizzeri, F.M. Athlete-reported outcome measures for monitoring training responses: A systematic review of risk of bias and measurement property quality according to the COSMIN guidelines. *Int. J. Sport. Physiol. Perform.* **2020**, *15*, 1203–1215. [CrossRef] [PubMed]
272. Oliveira-Rodrigues, C.; Correia, A.M.; Valente, R.; Gil, Á.; Gandra, M.; Liberal, M.; Rosso, M.; Pierce, G.; Sousa-Pinto, I. Assessing data bias in visual surveys from a cetacean monitoring programme. *Sci. Data* **2022**, *9*, 682. [CrossRef]
273. Memarian, B.; Doleck, T. Fairness, Accountability, Transparency, and Ethics (FATE) in Artificial Intelligence (AI), and higher education: A systematic review. *Comput. Educ. Artif. Intell.* **2023**, *5*, 100152. [CrossRef]

274. Marcinkowski, F.; Kieslich, K.; Starke, C.; Lünich, M. Implications of AI (un-) fairness in higher education admissions: The effects of perceived AI (un-) fairness on exit, voice and organizational reputation. In Proceedings of the 2020 Conference on Fairness, Accountability, and Transparency, Barcelona, Spain, 27–30 January 2020; pp. 122–130.
275. Kizilcec, R.F.; Lee, H. Algorithmic fairness in education. In *The Ethics of Artificial Intelligence in Education*; Routledge: Boca Raton, FL, USA, 2022; pp. 174–202.
276. Mashhadi, A.; Zolyomi, A.; Quedado, J. A Case Study of Integrating Fairness Visualization Tools in Machine Learning Education. In Proceedings of the CHI Conference on Human Factors in Computing Systems Extended Abstracts, New Orleans, LA, USA, 29 April–5 May 2022; pp. 1–7.
277. Fenu, G.; Galici, R.; Marras, M. Experts' view on challenges and needs for fairness in artificial intelligence for education. In *International Conference on Artificial Intelligence in Education*; Springer: Cham, Switzerland, 2022; pp. 243–255.
278. Chen, R.J.; Chen, T.Y.; Lipkova, J.; Wang, J.J.; Williamson, D.F.; Lu, M.Y.; Sahai, S.; Mahmood, F. Algorithm fairness in ai for medicine and healthcare. *arXiv* **2021**, arXiv:2110.00603.
279. Gichoya, J.W.; McCoy, L.G.; Celi, L.A.; Ghassemi, M. Equity in essence: A call for operationalising fairness in machine learning for healthcare. *BMJ Health Care Inform.* **2021**, *28*, e100289. [CrossRef]
280. Johnson, K.B.; Wei, W.Q.; Weeraratne, D.; Frisse, M.E.; Misulis, K.; Rhee, K.; Zhao, J.; Snowdon, J.L. Precision medicine, AI, and the future of personalized health care. *Clin. Transl. Sci.* **2021**, *14*, 86–93. [CrossRef]
281. Chiao, V. Fairness, accountability and transparency: Notes on algorithmic decision-making in criminal justice. *Int. J. Law Context* **2019**, *15*, 126–139. [CrossRef]
282. Angwin, J.; Larson, J.; Mattu, S.; Kirchner, L. Machine bias. In *Ethics of Data and Analytics*; Auerbach Publications: Boca Raton, FL, USA, 2022; pp. 254–264.
283. Berk, R.; Heidari, H.; Jabbari, S.; Kearns, M.; Roth, A. Fairness in criminal justice risk assessments: The state of the art. *Sociol. Methods Res.* **2021**, *50*, 3–44. [CrossRef]
284. Mujtaba, D.F.; Mahapatra, N.R. Ethical considerations in AI-based recruitment. In Proceedings of the 2019 IEEE International Symposium on Technology and Society (ISTAS), Medford, MA, USA, 15–16 November 2019; IEEE: Piscataway, NJ, USA, 2019; pp. 1–7.
285. Hunkenschroer, A.L.; Luetge, C. Ethics of AI-enabled recruiting and selection: A review and research agenda. *J. Bus. Ethics* **2022**, *178*, 977–1007. [CrossRef]
286. Nugent, S.E.; Scott-Parker, S. Recruitment AI has a Disability Problem: Anticipating and mitigating unfair automated hiring decisions. In *Towards Trustworthy Artificial Intelligent Systems*; Springer: Cham, Swizeraland, 2022; pp. 85–96.
287. Hurlin, C.; Pérignon, C.; Saurin, S. The fairness of credit scoring models. *arXiv* **2022**, arXiv:2205.10200.
288. Gemalmaz, M.A.; Yin, M. Understanding Decision Subjects' Fairness Perceptions and Retention in Repeated Interactions with AI-Based Decision Systems. In Proceedings of the 2022 AAAI/ACM Conference on AI, Ethics, and Society, Oxford, UK, 19–21 May 2021; pp. 295–306.
289. Genovesi, S.; Mönig, J.M.; Schmitz, A.; Poretschkin, M.; Akila, M.; Kahdan, M.; Kleiner, R.; Krieger, L.; Zimmermann, A. Standardizing fairness-evaluation procedures: Interdisciplinary insights on machine learning algorithms in creditworthiness assessments for small personal loans. *AI Ethics* **2023**, 1–17. [CrossRef]
290. Hiller, J.S. Fairness in the eyes of the beholder: Ai; fairness; and alternative credit scoring. *W. Va. L. Rev.* **2020**, *123*, 907.
291. Kumar, I.E.; Hines, K.E.; Dickerson, J.P. Equalizing credit opportunity in algorithms: Aligning algorithmic fairness research with us fair lending regulation. In Proceedings of the 2022 AAAI/ACM Conference on AI, Ethics, and Society, Oxford, UK, 19–21 May 2021; pp. 357–368.
292. Moldovan, D. Algorithmic decision making methods for fair credit scoring. *IEEE Access* **2023**, *11*, 59729–59743. [CrossRef]
293. Rodgers, W.; Nguyen, T. Advertising benefits from ethical Artificial Intelligence algorithmic purchase decision pathways. *J. Bus. Ethics* **2022**, *178*, 1043–1061. [CrossRef]
294. Yuan, D. Artificial Intelligence, Fairness and Productivity. Ph.D. Thesis, University of Pittsburgh, Pittsburgh, PA, USA, 2023.
295. Bateni, A.; Chan, M.C.; Eitel-Porter, R. AI fairness: From principles to practice. *arXiv* **2022**, arXiv:2207.09833.
296. Rossi, F. Building trust in Artificial Intelligence. *J. Int. Aff.* **2018**, *72*, 127–134.
297. Bang, J.; Kim, S.; Nam, J.W.; Yang, D.G. Ethical chatbot design for reducing negative effects of biased data and unethical conversations. In Proceedings of the 2021 International Conference on Platform Technology and Service (PlatCon), Jeju, Republic of Korea, 23–25 August 2021; IEEE: Piscataway, NJ, USA, 2021; pp. 1–5.
298. Følstad, A.; Araujo, T.; Law, E.L.C.; Brandtzaeg, P.B.; Papadopoulos, S.; Reis, L.; Baez, M.; Laban, G.; McAllister, P.; Ischen, C.; et al. Future directions for chatbot research: An interdisciplinary research agenda. *Computing* **2021**, *103*, 2915–2942. [CrossRef]
299. Lewicki, K.; Lee, M.S.A.; Cobbe, J.; Singh, J. Out of Context: Investigating the Bias and Fairness Concerns of "Artificial Intelligence as a Service". In Proceedings of the 2023 CHI Conference on Human Factors in Computing Systems, Hamburg, Germany, 23–28 April 2023; pp. 1–17.
300. Chen, Q.; Lu, Y.; Gong, Y.; Xiong, J. Can AI chatbots help retain customers? Impact of AI service quality on customer loyalty. *Internet Res.* **2023**. [CrossRef]
301. Chen, Y.; Jensen, S.; Albert, L.J.; Gupta, S.; Lee, T. Artificial Intelligence (AI) student assistants in the classroom: Designing chatbots to support student success. *Inf. Syst. Front.* **2023**, *25*, 161–182. [CrossRef]

302. Simbeck, K. FAccT-Check on AI regulation: Systematic Evaluation of AI Regulation on the Example of the Legislation on the Use of AI in the Public Sector in the German Federal State of Schleswig-Holstein. In Proceedings of the 2022 ACM Conference on Fairness, Accountability, and Transparency, Seoul, Republic of Korea, 21–24 June 2022; pp. 89–96.
303. Srivastava, B.; Rossi, F.; Usmani, S.; Bernagozzi, M. Personalized chatbot trustworthiness ratings. *IEEE Trans. Technol. Soc.* **2020**, *1*, 184–192. [CrossRef]
304. Hulsen, T. Explainable Artificial Intelligence (XAI): Concepts and Challenges in Healthcare. *AI* **2023**, *4*, 652–666. [CrossRef]
305. Chen, Z. Collaboration among recruiters and Artificial Intelligence: Removing human prejudices in employment. *Cogn. Technol. Work.* **2023**, *25*, 135–149. [CrossRef] [PubMed]
306. Rieskamp, J.; Hofeditz, L.; Mirbabaie, M.; Stieglitz, S. Approaches to improve fairness when deploying ai-based algorithms in hiring—Using a systematic literature review to guide future research. In Proceedings of the 56th Hawaii International Conference on System Sciences, HICSS 2023, Maui, HI, USA, 3–6 January 2023.
307. Hunkenschroer, A.L.; Kriebitz, A. Is AI recruiting (un) ethical? A human rights perspective on the use of AI for hiring. *AI Ethics* **2023**, *3*, 199–213. [CrossRef] [PubMed]
308. Dastin, J. Amazon scraps secret AI recruiting tool that showed bias against women. In *Ethics of Data and Analytics*; Auerbach Publications: Boca Raton, FL, USA, 2022; pp. 296–299.
309. Hunkenschroer, A.L.; Lütge, C. How to improve fairness perceptions of AI in hiring: The crucial role of positioning and sensitization. *AI Ethics J.* **2021**, *2*, 1–19. [CrossRef]

Disclaimer/Publisher's Note: The statements, opinions and data contained in all publications are solely those of the individual author(s) and contributor(s) and not of MDPI and/or the editor(s). MDPI and/or the editor(s) disclaim responsibility for any injury to people or property resulting from any ideas, methods, instructions or products referred to in the content.

Article

Machine Learning-Based Label Quality Assurance for Object Detection Projects in Requirements Engineering

Neven Pičuljan * and Željka Car

Faculty of Electrical Engineering and Computing, University of Zagreb, 10000 Zagreb, Croatia; zeljka.car@fer.hr
* Correspondence: neven.piculjan@fer.hr

Featured Application: Our machine learning-based label quality assurance demo showcases the potential of our approach to improve object detection projects within the data requirement stage of requirements engineering. The accompanying API enables easy integration with existing platforms. This approach reduces the resources needed for label quality assurance.

Abstract: In recent years, the field of artificial intelligence has experienced significant growth, which has been primarily attributed to advancements in hardware and the efficient training of deep neural networks on graphics processing units. The development of high-quality artificial intelligence solutions necessitates a strong emphasis on data-centric approaches that involve the collection, labeling and quality-assurance of data and labels. These processes, however, are labor-intensive and often demand extensive human effort. Simultaneously, there exists an abundance of untapped data that could potentially be utilized to train models capable of addressing complex problems. These raw data, nevertheless, require refinement to become suitable for machine learning training. This study concentrates on the computer vision subdomain within artificial intelligence and explores data requirements within the context of requirements engineering. Among the various data requirement activities, label quality assurance is crucial. To address this problem, we propose a machine learning-based method for automatic label quality assurance, especially in the context of object detection use cases. Our approach aims to support both annotators and computer vision project stakeholders while reducing the time and resources needed to conduct label quality assurance activities. In our experiments, we trained a neural network on a small set of labeled data and achieved an accuracy of 82% in differentiating good and bad labels on a large set of labeled data. This demonstrates the potential of our approach in automating label quality assurance.

Keywords: artificial intelligence; computer vision; data requirements; data-centric artificial intelligence; deep learning; label quality assurance; machine learning; object detection; requirements engineering

Citation: Pičuljan, N.; Car, Ž. Machine Learning-Based Label Quality Assurance for Object Detection Projects in Requirements Engineering. *Appl. Sci.* **2023**, *13*, 6234. https://doi.org/10.3390/app13106234

Academic Editors: Wenjie Zhang and Zhengyi Yang

Received: 29 April 2023
Revised: 15 May 2023
Accepted: 17 May 2023
Published: 19 May 2023

Copyright: © 2023 by the authors. Licensee MDPI, Basel, Switzerland. This article is an open access article distributed under the terms and conditions of the Creative Commons Attribution (CC BY) license (https://creativecommons.org/licenses/by/4.0/).

1. Introduction

Modern artificial intelligence has come to rely heavily on artificial neural networks, which are predominantly trained through supervised learning with labeled data. A variety of neural network architectures have emerged to tackle diverse problems, and their performance is often dependent on the quality of the underlying labeled data. Large language models (LLMs), such as GPT-3 [1], have gained widespread popularity due to their impressive capabilities. The labeling tasks required for training models such as GPT-3 are relatively simple, facilitating easy scaling. These autoregressive models predict future words based on past words, and labels can be programmatically generated from vast text corpora. However, to harness more specific outputs from these models, fine-tuning of specially labeled data is necessary [2]. In contrast, generating inexpensive, high-quality labels for images is a more challenging process, even for pretraining large computer vision models. Labels, in the context of supervised learning, are the desired outputs or target values associated with the input data. They are used to guide the learning process of the neural network by providing a reference to the correct output. In object detection tasks, labels are the annotations that provide information about the location and category of objects within an image. For object detection, labels typically consist of two main components: bounding boxes and class labels. Bounding boxes are rectangular boxes drawn around each object of interest in the image. A bounding box is usually represented by the coordinates of its top–left and bottom–right corners, which define the position and size of the box. Class labels are the categories or classes assigned to each object within the bounding boxes. For example, if an object is a cat, its class label would be "cat". Another example of a task is to generate photo-realistic images from textual inputs, as demonstrated by models such as DALL·E 2 [3] and Stable Diffusion [4]. These models require datasets that contain both images and their corresponding textual descriptions. Labels play a crucial role in ensuring the quality of the generated images. Errors or inaccuracies in the textual descriptions can lead to the generation of images that do not align with the intended content.

This research paper concentrates on the computer vision subfield within the broader context of modern artificial intelligence. Computer vision enables machines to extract meaning or semantics from images or videos, thereby allowing them to understand the contents. There are three popular tasks in computer vision: detection, recognition and segmentation. Three sample images from the Microsoft Common Objects in Context (MS COCO) dataset [5] are showcased, each demonstrating one of these tasks with a cat as the target object. Detection involves generating a bounding box around the object [6] (Figure 1), recognition involves assigning a tag to describe the object in the image [7] (Figure 2), and segmentation involves classifying pixels at the individual level [8] (Figure 3). Segmentation is the most comprehensive task, as detection and recognition can usually be derived from it.

Figure 1. Detection: cat enclosed by a bounding box.

Figure 2. Recognition: cat identified and tag is assigned to the image.

Figure 3. Segmentation: cat and background pixels distinguished.

In our research, we address problems related to data requirements for computer vision, with a particular focus on quality assurance of data labels. We propose a comprehensive framework for data collection, labeling and quality assurance of data and labels for machine learning projects. Furthermore, we provide a detailed explanation of our machine learning-based label quality assurance method to assess whether the ground truth assigned for a specific task and image is indeed accurate. This method allows us to determine if the labeled data accurately represent the ground truth, ensuring the reliability of the training data for machine learning models. Our method aims to reduce the time and resources needed for label quality assurance activity by offering immediate estimates of label quality to annotators and computer vision project stakeholders. While we focus on object detection as an example, our method can be extended to other tasks and artificial intelligence subfields.

In order to provide a clear overview of the paper's structure, we present an article map outlining the content of each section.

- **Related Work**: This section explores the crucial role of data requirements in artificial intelligence projects, distinguishes them from traditional software engineering needs and surveys various methodologies for label quality assurance, such as manual review, inter-annotator agreement, deep active learning and algorithmic approaches.
- **Proposed Process for Data Requirements within Requirements Engineering**: This section outlines a proposed process for incorporating data requirements within requirements engineering for artificial intelligence projects, placing the "Data Requirements" phase between "Requirements Elicitation" and "Requirements Analysis" activities.
- **Machine Learning-Based Label Quality Assurance**: This section discusses a machine learning-based label quality assurance method that involves a series of steps to build a quality assurance model that classifies object detection labels as good or bad, helping annotators focus on samples with potentially incorrect labels.
- **Results and Discussion**: This section details the performance of a machine learning-based label quality assurance model utilizing ResNet-18 components and a fully connected neural network that attains 82% accuracy in discerning good and bad labels for object detection tasks, even when trained on a small dataset.
- **Conclusions**: This section underscores the significance of data requirements for artificial intelligence development and underlines a pioneering machine learning methodology for automating label quality assurance, which, while demonstrated for object detection, offers flexibility for adaptation across a variety of computer vision tasks and other machine learning subfields.

2. Related Work

In this section, we discuss the related work in two areas: data requirements in the context of requirements engineering and approaches to label quality assurance. We explore how requirements engineering has been adapted to accommodate the unique needs of artificial intelligence projects. Furthermore, we examine various methods for ensuring label quality, ranging from manual review to deep active learning. This review of related work provides a foundation for understanding the significance of data requirements and label quality assurance in the development of artificial intelligence solutions.

2.1. Data Requirements in the Context of Requirements Engineering

Software requirements are the needs and constraints placed on a software product that contribute to finding a solution for a specific real-world problem. The systematic handling of requirements is referred to as "requirements engineering" [9]. Common phases in requirements engineering include requirements elicitation, requirements analysis, requirements specification and requirements validation.

The field of artificial intelligence has expanded considerably in recent years. Projects in this domain differ significantly from traditional software engineering projects due to their heavy reliance on data. There have been attempts to adapt requirements engineering for artificial intelligence projects to accommodate these unique characteristics. In computer vision projects, the goal is to automatically process images to extract hidden knowledge, creating both value and experience for users. Outputs of the project are a trained instance of a neural network (or model), extracted knowledge, generated images, etc., and their quality depends on the data.

A few papers discuss the need to refine requirements engineering to support the needs of artificial intelligence projects. One paper suggests that training data are an integral part of any machine learning system. The authors argue that data requirements may play a larger role in specifying machine learning systems than in conventional systems, potentially introducing a new class of requirements called data requirements [10]. Another paper posits that to find a suitable technical solution, data requirements must be clarified. Business owners should provide data sources and examine potential data ethics issues. Domain experts should confirm the appropriate use of data. Data scientists should closely examine data completeness, sample distribution and the assumption that the data are independent and identically distributed, among other factors. It is mentioned that about 80% of the time in machine learning application development is spent preparing data. As coding is not as challenging, data requirements should likely dominate the cost [11]. The authors of a related paper emphasize the importance of collaboration between software engineers and data scientists to harness big data analytics during the software development process [12]. They propose a new requirements engineering model that enables both parties to work together in discovering hidden business values through data mining and analytics. This approach ensures that software systems are developed to fully exploit existing and newly generated data, ultimately leading to more effective and evidence-based decision making.

A study on modern deep learning systems addresses the challenges of determining the appropriate amount and type of data needed for optimal performance [13]. The researchers propose a novel paradigm for modeling the data collection workflow as a formal optimal data collection problem, enabling designers to specify performance targets, collection costs, a time horizon and penalties for not meeting the targets. This approach reduces the risks of failing to meet performance targets in various tasks, such as classification, segmentation and detection, while keeping total collection costs low. A different paper proposes a new approach to estimate the number of samples needed for a model to achieve the targeted performance, overcoming the limitations of the power law when extrapolating from small datasets [14]. The authors utilize a random forest regressor trained via meta-learning, which generalizes across various tasks and architectures. This method significantly improves performance estimation across classification and detection datasets while also reducing over-estimation of data. Another paper addresses the critical question of determining how much additional data are needed to reach a target performance given a small training dataset and a learning algorithm, particularly in applications where data collection is expensive and time-consuming [15]. The authors systematically investigate a family of functions that generalize the power law function to better estimate data requirements across various computer vision tasks. By incorporating a tuned correction factor and collecting data over multiple rounds, their approach significantly improves data estimators' performance, ultimately saving development time and data acquisition costs.

One of the examined papers highlights that the current focus of the artificial intelligence industry is on machine learning as a data-driven approach due to the information technology (IT) infrastructural developments available today, such as fast processing power and inexpensive data storage [16]. The authors state that healthcare is one of the areas most attractive for artificial intelligence applications, yet it faces notable obstacles such as the lack of mandatory standards or continuous data exchange. By properly understanding data requirements activities, these problems can be resolved, and engineers can proceed with building artificial intelligence solutions once requirements specifications, with an emphasis on data requirements, are finalized. This specific healthcare case can be addressed by understanding HIPAA [17] and GDPR [18] regulations and FHIR [19] and DICOM [20] standards used for handling sensitive patient medical data.

2.2. Approaches to Label Quality Assurance

The most effective method for ensuring label quality is to manually review samples and flag those with bad-quality labels for reannotation. However, this approach can be time-consuming and tedious for human reviewers, and it may become less accurate if they lose concentration while working on a monotonous task.

An alternative approach is to assign multiple annotators to the same image and calculate inter-annotator agreement [21,22]. Low inter-annotator agreement indicates that the image likely needs to be reannotated. This approach has some challenges, such as defining a suitable inter-annotator agreement measure for different machine learning tasks. Various authors have proposed methods for assessing the quality of suggested dataset labels in the context of human labeling [23–25]. Another issue with inter-annotator agreement is handling specific cases wherein not all annotators annotated all samples [26]. In a relevant study, the authors explore the inter-annotator agreement among multiple expert annotators when segmenting lesions and abnormalities on medical images, which is crucial for the performance of artificial intelligence-based medical computer vision algorithms [27]. They propose the use of three metrics for qualitative and quantitative assessment. The experiments demonstrate the consistency of the inter-annotator reliability assessment and highlight the importance of combining different metrics to avoid biased evaluations. In a study focusing on lung ultrasounds for detecting COVID-19 manifestations, the authors investigated the agreement among physicians when identifying signs associated with the disease [28]. In a separate study that concentrates on manual segmentation of gliomas using magnetic resonance imaging (MRI), the authors scrutinized the level of agreement between novices and experts at different stages of the disease. MRI is a non-invasive medical imaging technique that employs strong magnets, radio waves and a computer to generate detailed images of the body's internal structures with the intention of diagnosis [29]. The authors found that the inter-rater agreement varied depending on the stage of the disease, with higher agreement generally observed between experts than between novices, particularly for non-glioblastoma cases. A different study presents a quality control protocol using an automated tool for assessing functional MRI data quality and assesses the inter-rater reliability of four independent raters [30]. The authors suggest several approaches to increase rater agreement and reduce disagreement for uncertain cases, ultimately aiming to improve classification consistency in data quality assessments.

Label quality assurance can also be achieved using a form of deep active learning [31–33]. Deep active learning focuses on a continuous loop between the model being trained and the human annotator. This approach requires a neural network architecture that can already produce reasonably accurate predictions for the target task and a large amount of high-quality labels. For example, to implement deep active learning for an object detection task, the entire pipeline for building the object detection model must be set up with a model capable of providing predictions of a certain quality. Samples requiring attention are identified by the model and subsequently directed for reannotation.

Platforms such as Amazon Mechanical Turk enable crowdsourcing of data and labels [34]. Annotators from various parts of the world and with different backgrounds participate, making it challenging to ensure the quality of large-scale labeling tasks. It is important to note that not only human reviewers or annotators can perform label quality assurance. Various algorithms can flag suspicious samples based on specific heuristics. Machine learning approaches such as deep active learning can be employed to flag low-quality labels. Filters based on label dimensions, shape or color of the annotated region can be applied to address certain issues. Images that should not be labeled at all can be filtered using heuristics or machine learning approaches as part of data quality assurance activity. A blur detector [35] can be used to remove overly blurry images. Width and height information about an image can be employed to eliminate images that are too small or too large and thus immediately unsuitable for further labeling tasks.

3. Proposed Process for Data Requirements within Requirements Engineering

We propose a process for incorporating data requirements within requirements engineering for artificial intelligence projects. The typical requirements engineering activities include "Requirements Elicitation", "Requirements Analysis", "Requirements Specification" and "Requirements Validation". Our proposed "Data Requirements" phase is inserted between the "Requirements Elicitation" and "Requirements Analysis" activities and consists of "Legal and Regulatory Data Requirements", "Production-like Image Data Acquisition", "Data Quality Assurance", "Data Labeling" and "Label Quality Assurance" activities. Figure 4 illustrates the general requirements engineering activities with the addition of the data requirements activities.

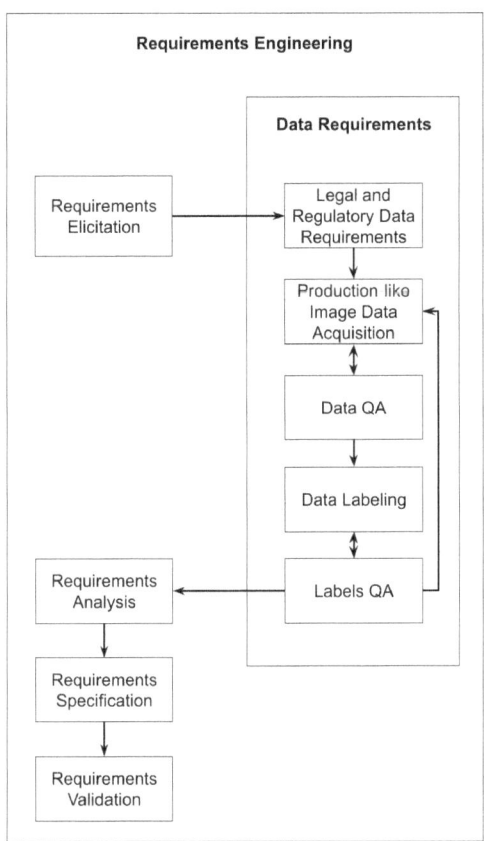

Figure 4. Requirements engineering process with data requirements activities for machine learning projects. "QA" stands for "Quality Assurance".

During the requirements elicitation activity, which is the initial phase of understanding the problem that the software must address, it is essential to determine whether a continuous stream of similar data is available and whether these data will be accessible once the project is completed. This consideration is specifically tied to artificial intelligence projects because the performance and effectiveness of machine learning models heavily rely on the availability and quality of data. Ensuring that there is a consistent flow of relevant data for training, validation and testing purposes allows the model to adapt and improve over time, leading to better overall performance and long-term viability of the artificial intelligence solution. The effort required to extract knowledge from the data, whether human or programmatic, must also be assessed. Additionally, it is crucial to identify any issues related to the speed, accuracy or cost of this effort. If a significant investment is being made, the next question to answer is whether the task can be framed as a segmentation, recognition or detection task with a fixed number of predefined classes. Examples of such tasks include detecting abnormalities in MRI scans, classifying traffic lights, detecting cats or creating a visual substitution system for blind people.

Following the requirements elicitation activity, the data requirements phase begins. During the legal and regulatory data requirements activity, any relevant regulations are identified and steps are taken to ensure compliance. For example, with medical images, HIPAA and GDPR regulations require patient consent or data de-identification [36]. Once regulatory compliance is understood, production-like image data acquisition can commence. Data should be from the same distribution as the data in production. This means that the data used during the project should closely resemble the real-world data the model will ultimately process when deployed. Further, maintaining a connection to the data source throughout the project's life cycle is crucial. Data sources can include raw camera photos or MRI scans from specific MRI scanners. It is also important to remove any irrelevant data and to ensure a balanced dataset. Data ready for machine learning processes can be stored in commercial storage solutions such as Amazon S3 on Amazon Web Services [37], Azure Blob Storage on Microsoft Azure [38] or Cloud Storage on Google Cloud [39].

Subsequently, data quality assurance is performed by checking structural attributes such as image width, height and pixel histograms and visually inspecting the data's semantics. If any issues with the data are found (e.g., images being too small, too large or containing excessive noise), the production-like image data acquisition activity should be repeated. The frequency of repeating the production-like image data acquisition activity depends on data quality and project requirements. A representative subset of the collected data should be assessed, and if significant issues are found, the process may be repeated for all or affected images. Decisions should consider the project's needs, resources and timeline.

The next step is to label the data according to the defined classes. Labels should correspond to the expected output of the trained model, and in some cases, expert knowledge may be necessary. The amount of labeled data needed for training a machine learning model on image data depends on the variance in factors such as content, lighting, image quality, backgrounds and camera angles. High-variance image datasets require more labeled data to help the model generalize better, while low-variance datasets with simpler patterns may need less labeled data to achieve good performance.

The labels quality assurance activity follows, during which the quality and distribution of labels (proportions of different objects or classes within the labeled dataset, as well as the spatial distribution of these objects in the images) are checked. If the quality is bad, the data labeling activity should be repeated. This work further elaborates on what constitutes good or bad label quality in Section 4.3. If there are many outliers in the labels and the reason is related to the data content, it may be necessary to return to the production-like image data acquisition activity. The final product is computer vision software that generates predictions, such as a cat detector system, face recognition system or other similar applications.

There are certain assumptions about the project. Although this work focuses on detection, recognition and segmentation tasks in computer vision and presents a machine learning-based label quality assurance method for object detection tasks, the approach can be extended to other computer vision tasks and other machine learning domains, ranging from natural language processing to tabular data analysis. The software can be cloud-based. Security, privacy, types of cloud resources, cost and other aspects are not discussed in this work, as it is assumed that industry standards are followed. The response time of the system is also not discussed, but it is assumed to be reasonable—not in real-time, but not taking several minutes either. A response time in the range of seconds is expected. Some limitations are present in the proposed data requirements process. Over-regulation can be an issue, as highly regulated data for solving specific tasks can potentially halt the project. Moreover, if there is high variance in a large dataset or a multitude of different labels, creating a model with the current state of technology may be impossible (e.g., a general object detection model).

In the following section, a novel machine learning-based label quality assurance method is presented. It uses a small amount of carefully annotated data to build a model that can solve the binary classification task of estimating whether a label for a given image is of good or bad quality. By automating the process of determining label quality, the need for manual inspection and validation of labels is reduced, saving time and resources.

4. Machine Learning-Based Label Quality Assurance

Demo is accessible at https://label-qa.piculjantechnologies.ai/. The accompanying API can be found at https://label-qa.piculjantechnologies.ai/?view=api (accessed on 16 May 2023).

In this section, we describe the proposed machine learning-based label quality assurance method. To contextualize this within the proposed process for data requirements within requirements engineering, let us assume that during the "Requirements Elicitation" activity, the objective is to build an object detection computer vision software product capable of detecting objects in images belonging to 80 classes (e.g., "apple", "banana", "person", "umbrella" and so on). It is assumed that the "Legal and Regulatory Data Requirements" activity is completed, as well as the "Production-like Image Data Acquisition" activity, which a dataset that accurately represents the problem is collected. For the "Data Quality Assurance" activity, we assume that all images are of acceptable sizes and qualities.

The method starts with labeling a small random subset (approximately 5% of the full collected dataset) carefully to ensure that the labels are of very high quality. Let us call this the *small set,* and the remaining approximately 95% of the full collected dataset is the *large set*. For the purpose of this work and for building and evaluating the machine learning-based label quality assurance method, we rely on a publicly available labeled object detection dataset.

Using the ground truth label information about a carefully annotated *small set*, large amounts of good and bad labels for every sample can be created to train a machine learning-based label quality assurance model. With this model, there is no need to assign a reviewer to examine all remaining samples from the *large set* and find the ones with bad labels or to assign multiple annotators to all samples from the *large set* to perform inter-annotator agreement. Instead, the model can determine whether a label is good or bad by being trained on a large number of good and bad labels. Once it has learned the patterns and features that distinguish good labels from bad ones, it can then evaluate the quality of new labels. Consequently, a single annotator can annotate one sample from the *large set*, and the trained model can assess the label quality, streamlining the annotation process and ensuring higher-quality labeled data. There is also no need to set up a full machine learning pipeline with a larger amount of labeled data of good quality to perform a deep active learning approach.

Each image from *large set* receives labels from a single annotator, which may be a machine learning model that generates labels, a program or a human. The label quality assurance neural network can immediately determine if a label is good or not and notify the annotator to pay more attention to the sample if it is classified as a bad sample. If the label quality assurance neural network produces a false negative prediction, the annotator can confirm that they have inspected the sample carefully and their confirmation serves as a strong signal that the sample is outside the *small set* distribution used for training the model. The creation of a machine learning-based label quality assurance neural network within the proposed data requirements process is illustrated in Figure 5.

Subsequently in the development process, the *small set* is utilized by machine learning engineers and researchers as a validation set, while the *large set* serves as a training set for the primary task being addressed: in this case, the creation of an object detection model. The percentages for set cutoffs are determined based on the typical data splits used in machine learning projects. Further details are illustrated in Figure 6.

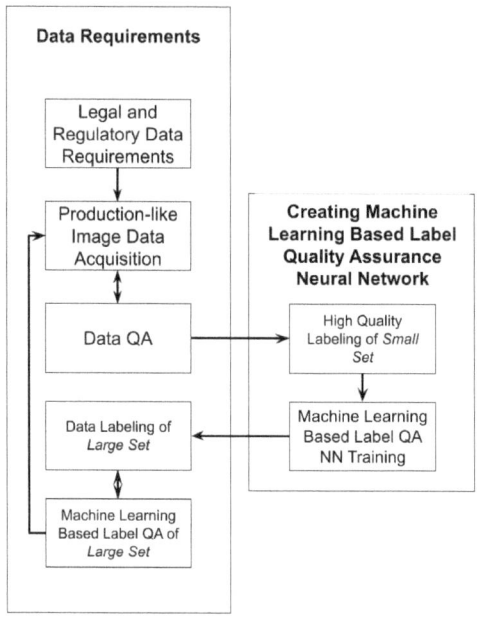

Figure 5. Developing a machine learning-based label quality assurance neural network. "QA" represents "Quality Assurance", and "NN" denotes "Neural Network".

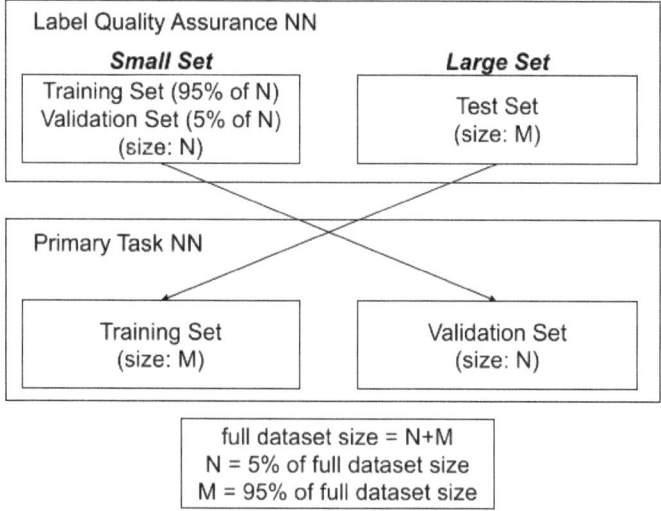

Figure 6. The training set used to create the label quality assurance neural network validation set is used to solve the primary task (object detection), and the test set used to create the label quality assurance neural network is the training set used to create the neural network for the primary task. "NN" stands for "Neural Network".

4.1. Machine Learning-Based Label Quality Assurance Method

In this section, we outline the algorithmic steps for creating a machine learning-based label quality assurance model that can be utilized to streamline the annotation process and improve label quality for various computer vision tasks.

1. Collect a dataset that accurately represents the problem to be solved. This dataset should be large enough to train a machine learning model for the primary task (e.g., object detection).
2. Split the dataset into two parts: a *small set* (approximately 5% of the full dataset) and a *large set* (approximately 95% of the full dataset).
3. Carefully annotate the *small set* with high-quality labels. This can be done by assigning multiple annotators to each sample and checking inter annotator agreement or by assigning one or more annotators per sample, followed by reviewers checking the quality of all labels.
4. Generate large amounts of good and bad labels for every sample in the *small set* based on the ground truth label information.
5. Train a machine learning-based label quality assurance model using the generated good and bad labels from the *small set*.
6. Use the trained label quality assurance model to classify the quality of labels from the *large set*, which are created by a machine learning model that generates labels, a program or a human. Notify annotators to pay more attention to samples classified as having bad labels.
7. If there are false-negative or false-positive predictions from the model, which occur when the model incorrectly predicts the presence or absence of certain labels, have annotators confirm that they have carefully inspected the sample. Their confirmation serves as a strong signal that the sample is outside the *small set* distribution.
8. Use the *small set* as a validation set for the primary task and the *large set* as a training set.

These steps outline the process for creating a machine learning-based label quality assurance model that can be adapted and extended to various computer vision tasks and other machine learning subfields with appropriate label representation and uncertainty region ranges. By implementing this approach, researchers can enhance the efficiency and quality of the data labeling process, ultimately improving the performance of their primary task models.

4.2. Dataset for Machine Learning-Based Label Quality Assurance Method Verification

The dataset employed for the machine learning-based label quality assurance method experiments is Microsoft Common Objects in Context (MS COCO) [40]. MS COCO is a widely used dataset containing a diverse collection of images for various tasks, including object detection, segmentation, key-point detection and captioning. For the purpose of these experiments, we focus on the object detection task, where the goal is to identify bounding boxes surrounding objects in the images. The MS COCO dataset comprises a training set of 118,287 images and a validation set of 5000 images, each with labeled bounding boxes. Some labels carry an "iscrowd = 1" flag, indicating that large groups of objects are annotated using a single bounding box. We exclude these samples, resulting in a filtered training set of 109,172 samples and a filtered validation set of 4589 samples. The MS COCO dataset contains 80 predefined classes, with each annotated bounding box for the object detection task belonging to one of these classes based on the object it surrounds. The classes include: "airplane", "apple", "backpack", "banana", "baseball bat", "baseball glove", "bear", "bed", "bench", "bicycle", "bird", "boat", "book", "bottle", "bowl", "broccoli", "bus", "cake", "car", "carrot", "cat", "cell phone", "chair", "clock", "couch", "cow", "cup", "dining table", "dog", "donut", "elephant", "fire hydrant", "fork", "frisbee", "giraffe", "hair drier", "handbag", "horse", "hot dog", "keyboard", "kite", "knife", "laptop", "microwave", "motorcycle", "mouse", "orange", "oven", "parking meter", "person", "pizza", "potted plant", "refrigerator", "remote", "sandwich", "scissors", "sheep", "sink", "skateboard", "skis", "snowboard", "spoon", "sports ball", "stop sign", "suitcase", "surfboard", "teddy bear", "tennis racket", "tie", "toaster", "toilet", "toothbrush", "traffic light", "train", "truck", "TV", "umbrella", "vase", "wine glass" and "zebra".

In this study, we consider the MS COCO validation set as a *small set*, which is used as the training and validation set for constructing the label quality assurance model. The MS COCO training set is treated as a test set for evaluating the label quality assurance model. Figure 7 presents a labeled sample from the label quality assurance training set (a subset of the MS COCO validation set):

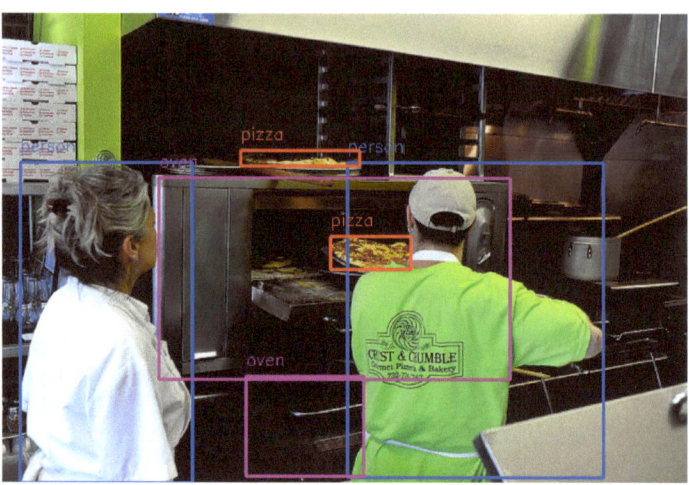

Figure 7. A labeled sample from MS COCO belonging to the training set used for building the label quality assurance model.

4.3. Uncertainty Regions for Determining Good and Bad Labels

During the training process, the machine learning-based label quality assurance neural network is exposed to both positive and negative samples. Positive samples comprise a pair of the original image and a good label, while negative samples consist of the original image and a bad label. To comprehend the distinction between good and bad labels, we first introduce the concept of uncertainty regions. These regions represent the area surrounding ground truth labels, delineating the space where all acceptable labels for a given object can reside. Figure 8 illustrates the ground truth label for a given image.

Given that $x1$ and $y1$ denote the top–left coordinates of the ground truth bounding box label and $x2$ and $y2$ represent the bottom–right coordinates, the uncertainty region for coordinate $x1$ is defined as follows:

$$[x1 - width \times 0.2, x1 + width \times 0.0], \quad (1)$$

for $y1$:

$$[y1 - height \times 0.2, y1 + height \times 0.0], \quad (2)$$

for $x2$:

$$[x2 + width \times 0.2, x2 - width \times 0.0], \quad (3)$$

and for $y2$:

$$[y2 + height \times 0.2, y2 - height \times 0.0], \quad (4)$$

where *width* and *height* are the width and height of the input image, and $x1$, $y1$, $x2$ and $y2$ are absolute coordinates; $x1$ and $x2$ are in the $[0, width]$ range, and $y1$ and $y2$ in the $[0, height]$ range.

Throughout the training process, positive and negative samples are randomly generated from a single pair of raw image and the ground truth label. A good label is fully enclosed within the uncertainty region, i.e., inside the outer (red) bounding box and outside the inner (green) bounding box, as illustrated in Figure 9. All bounding box coordinates must be located within their corresponding uncertainty region ranges.

Figure 8. Ground truth for the object "elephant" in the image.

Figure 9. Uncertainty region for the object "elephant" in the image.

Figure 10 displays an example of a good label situated within the outer bounding box and outside the inner bounding box, as indicated in blue.

Figure 10. Example of a good bounding box label for object "elephant" inside the uncertainty region.

In contrast, a bad label is any label that lies partially or entirely outside the uncertainty region: either outside the red bounding box or inside the green bounding box, as shown in Figure 11. At least one of the bounding box coordinates must fall outside its corresponding uncertainty region range.

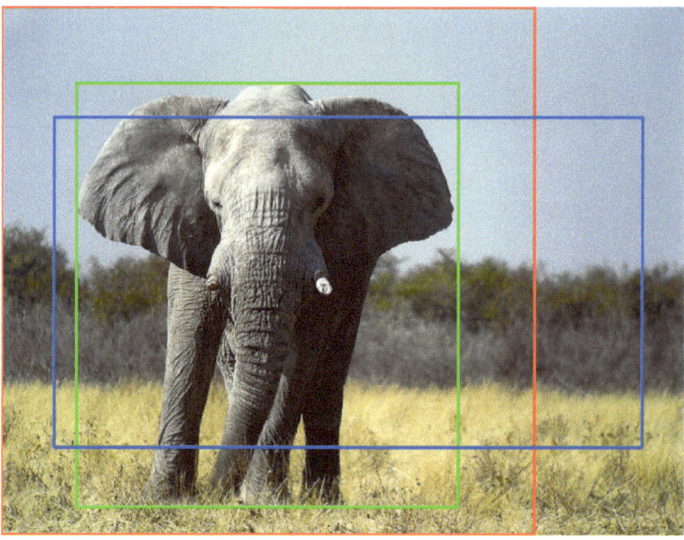

Figure 11. Example of a bad bounding box label for object "elephant" outside the uncertainty region.

It is crucial to note that one uncertainty region corresponds to a single bounding box label. If multiple bounding boxes are labeled and are intended to be fully enclosed within a single uncertainty region, that sample is considered a negative sample containing a bad label. Furthermore, if a sample contains multiple labeled bounding boxes and at least one of them is a bad bounding box, it is deemed a negative sample. The MS COCO dataset provides annotated bounding boxes, with each bounding box belonging to one of 80 classes.

Each uncertainty region is associated with a specific class. The space for bad bounding box labels is extensive. To manage this vastness, error types are introduced to systematically cover the most common errors annotators may make. Error types are divided into two major categories: Type A, which includes labels placed inside uncertainty regions that are damaged or manipulated; and Type B, which involves the creation of new labels outside of uncertainty regions. Table 1 displays the subtypes A1, A2, A3, B1 and B2 of the two major types: Type A (damage to labels inside uncertainty regions) and Type B (creation of new labels outside of uncertainty regions). Figure 12 presents examples of Type A errors, and Figure 13 displays examples of Type B errors. Images on the left side show ground truth labels, while the ones on the right side show labels with errors.

A1

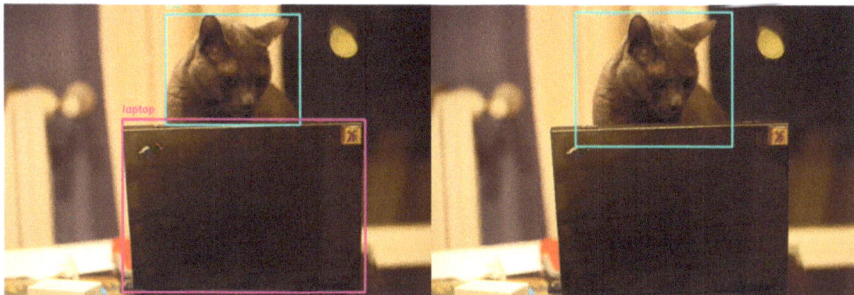

A2

A3

Figure 12. Error types A.

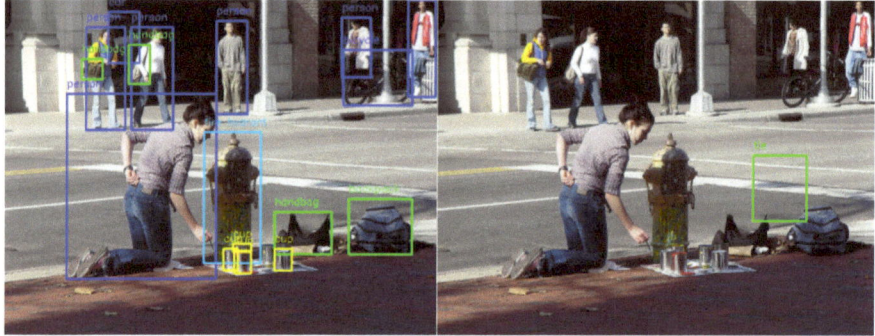

Figure 13. Error types B.

Table 1. Error subtypes with descriptions.

A1	erase one or multiple label(s) from uncertainty regions
A2	distort label that is inside uncertainty region to become outside of uncertainty region
A3	swap classes of labels from uncertainty regions
B1	add new labels to ground truth classes, outside of any uncertainty region
B2	add new labels to classes that do not belong to any ground truth classes, outside of any uncertainty region

4.4. Neural Network Architecture for Machine Learning-Based Label Quality Assurance

The neural network is designed to accept both the image and its corresponding label, performing classification to determine if the label is good (outputting 1) or bad (outputting 0). All images are resized to 640 × 640, maintaining their aspect ratio, as the maximum width and height in the training set are both 640. Black padding is added if the width and/or height are smaller. Labels are represented as 640 × 640 images with 80 channels, where pixels representing the border of the labeled bounding box are set to 1 and all other pixels are set to 0. For the padded image in Figure 14, the label representation is shown in Figure 15 (displaying only the image planes corresponding to the classes present in the image: class "sink" and class "bottle"; the remaining 78 image planes are black).

Figure 14. Padded image that goes to the label quality assurance neural network.

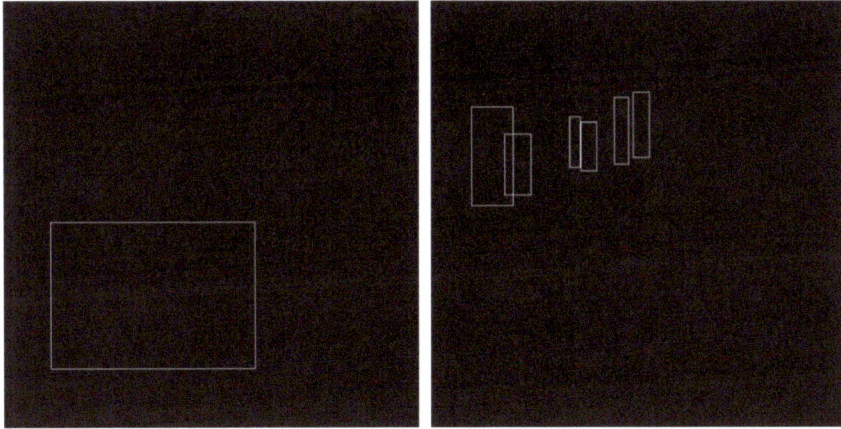

Figure 15. Representation of the labels for objects "sink" and "bottle" that goes to the label quality assurance neural network. Other planes are all black because there are no other MS COCO classes annotated for this particular image.

Figure 16 illustrates the neural network architecture being utilized.

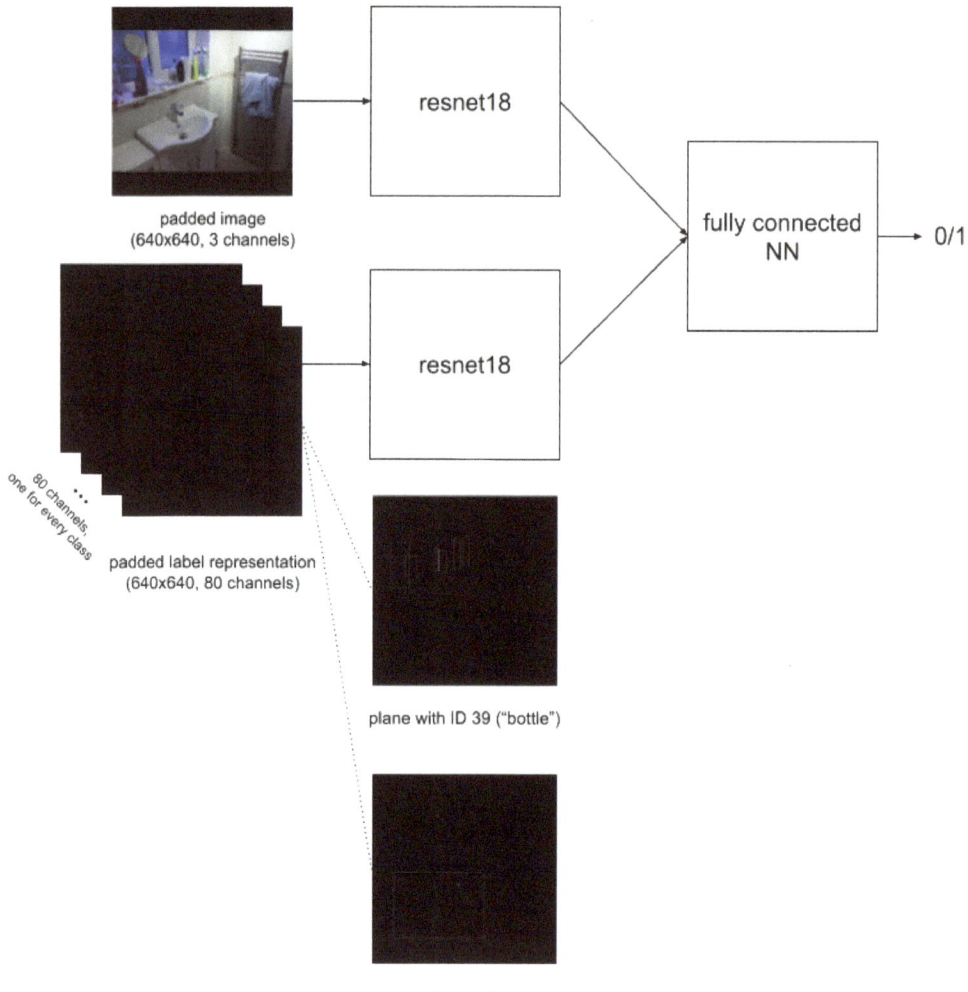

Figure 16. Label quality assurance neural network architecture. The ellipsis displayed on the image signifies the existence of 80 channels, which are not visually presented. "NN" stands for "Neural Network".

In this study, a neural network is employed as the feature extractor. The images are input into the neural network in their original format, while the labels are provided using the aforementioned label representation method. It is worth noting that some studies suggest that incorporating wavelet transform-based feature extraction techniques could potentially enhance the accuracy of neural networks [41]. This is an area that warrants further exploration in future research. Additionally, there are a few studies that discuss the integration of wavelet transforms and neural networks, which presents promising avenues for improving the effectiveness of neural networks in machine learning-based label quality assurance tasks [42,43]. Furthermore, alternative traditional machine learning algorithms, such as support vector machines (SVMs), random forests and others could also be employed for this task. Feature extraction techniques, such as gray-level co-occurrence matrix (GLCM), can be utilized in conjunction with these algorithms to further improve classification performance.

5. Results and Discussion

We employed ResNet-18 [44] components and a fully connected neural network [45] with random initialization for our classification task. Optimization was carried out using the cross-entropy loss function and the Adam optimizer [46], featuring a learning rate of 1×10^{-3}, betas set to (0.9, 0.999), eps of 1×10^{-8} and weight decay of 0. Training was executed on a single NVIDIA A100 GPU with 40GB of GPU memory [47] using a batch size of 64 to maximize GPU memory utilization. The model was trained for 250 epochs, with each epoch involving a full pass through all training images. Samples were dynamically determined as positive or negative with equal probabilities. The ground truth label from the MS COCO dataset was utilized to generate good or bad labels. To create a negative sample, a single error type and subtype were introduced to the ground truth label. There was a 50% probability of choosing either major Type A or major Type B for generating a negative sample. If major Type A was selected, there was a 33.3% chance that A1, A2 or A3 would be performed. If major Type B was chosen, there was a 50% chance that either B1 or B2 would be performed. These probabilities were designed to ensure that both major Types A and B as well as their subtypes had equal chances of being selected.

Table 2 displays the performance metrics for the trained model [48] on the test set. The MS COCO training set serves as the test set for the machine learning-based label quality assurance model, with good and bad labels generated for testing and each having an equal probability of occurrence. The classification report on the test set indicates that the trained model can effectively differentiate between good-labeled and bad-labeled samples. A baseline random classifier, which provides random good or bad predictions for labeled samples, would have an accuracy of approximately 50%. In comparison, our classifier achieves an accuracy of 82%, correctly identifying the quality of labels for 82% of the samples. The support metric reveals that Class 0 (bad label) contains 54,473 samples, while Class 1 (good label) consists of 54,699 samples. Since there is an equal chance of a sample being assigned a good or bad label, these numbers are closely matched. The total number of test samples is 109,172. The classification report displays class-wise precision, recall, F1-score, macro and weighted averages, along with overall accuracy, precision and recall. Metrics demonstrate the predictive power of the machine learning-based quality assurance model. Figure 17 presents the training loss, validation loss and validation accuracy plots, with the epoch number on the x-axis and loss or accuracy on the y-axis. The decreasing trend in both training and validation losses, combined with the increasing validation accuracy, indicates that the neural network is effectively learning from the data and is able to distinguish between good and bad labels.

Table 2. Test classification report.

Class	Precision	Recall	F-Score	Support
0	0.86	0.75	0.80	54,473
1	0.78	0.88	0.83	54,699
accuracy			0.82	109,172
macro avg	0.82	0.82	0.82	109,172
weighted avg	0.82	0.82	0.82	109,172
accuracy	0.8166			
precision	0.8222			
recall	0.8166			

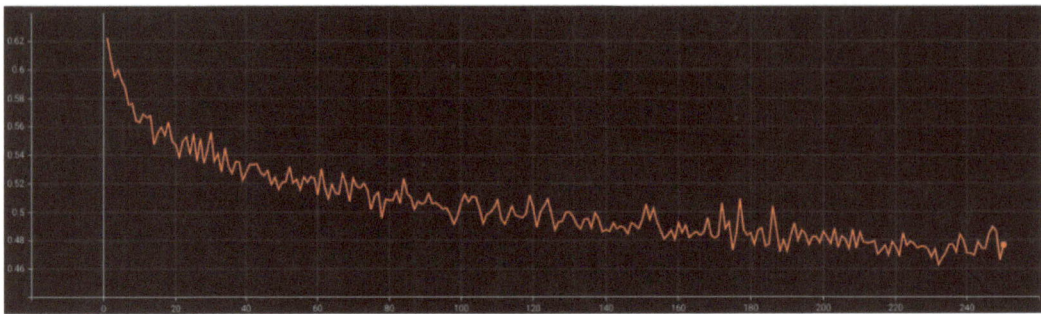
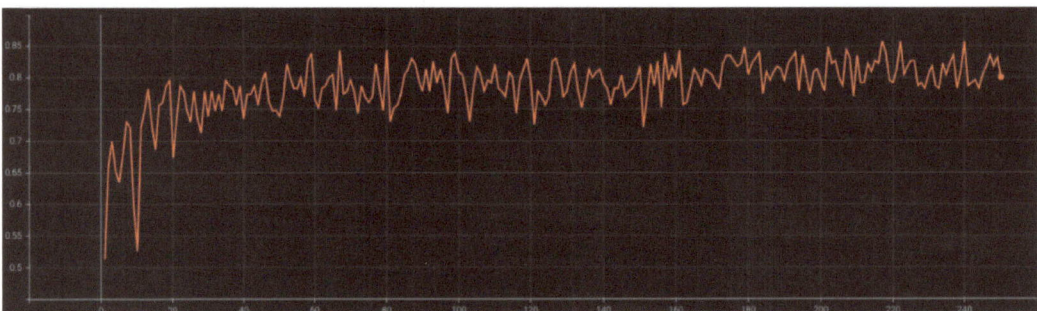
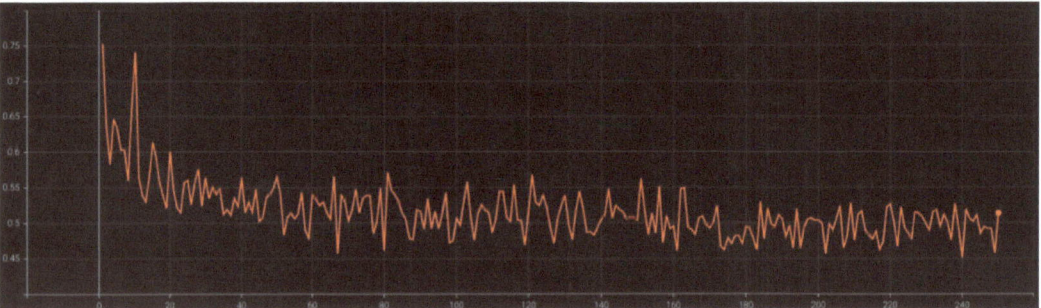

Figure 17. Training loss, validation accuracy and validation loss plots.

We also examined the impact of neural network size on the classification accuracy by training smaller neural networks. This was accomplished by reducing the number of layers in the fully connected part of the neural network and removing the last layers within the ResNet-18 components. The analysis of our findings is presented below in Table 3. Our results indicate that increasing the size of the neural network may lead to further improvements in classification accuracy. This suggests that there is potential for enhancing model performance by exploring larger and deeper architectures in future studies. Figure 18 presents the architecture of the large neural network employed in our study, while Figure 19 depicts the architectures of the medium and small neural networks that we also utilized. These architectural diagrams were generated using Netron [49].

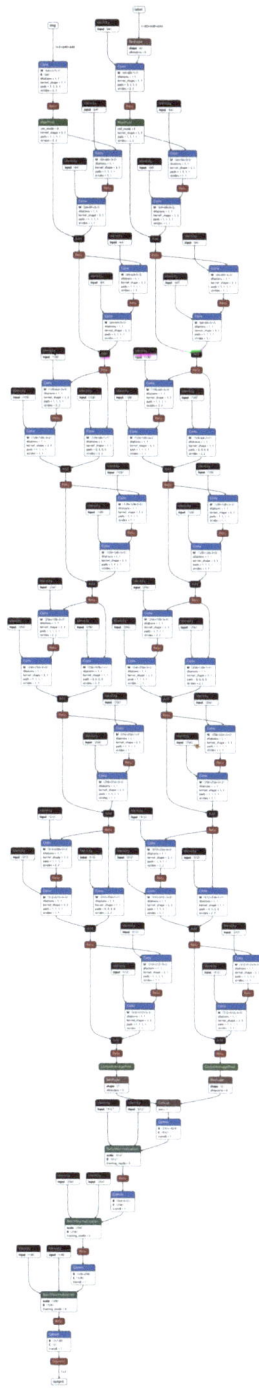

Figure 18. Large neural network architecture for machine learning-based label quality assurance.

Table 3. The relationship between the number of learnable parameters and the accuracy of a machine learning-based label quality assurance neural network.

Size	Number of Learnable Parameters	Accuracy
small	564,994	0.79
medium	1,641,026	0.80
large	23,285,570	**0.82**

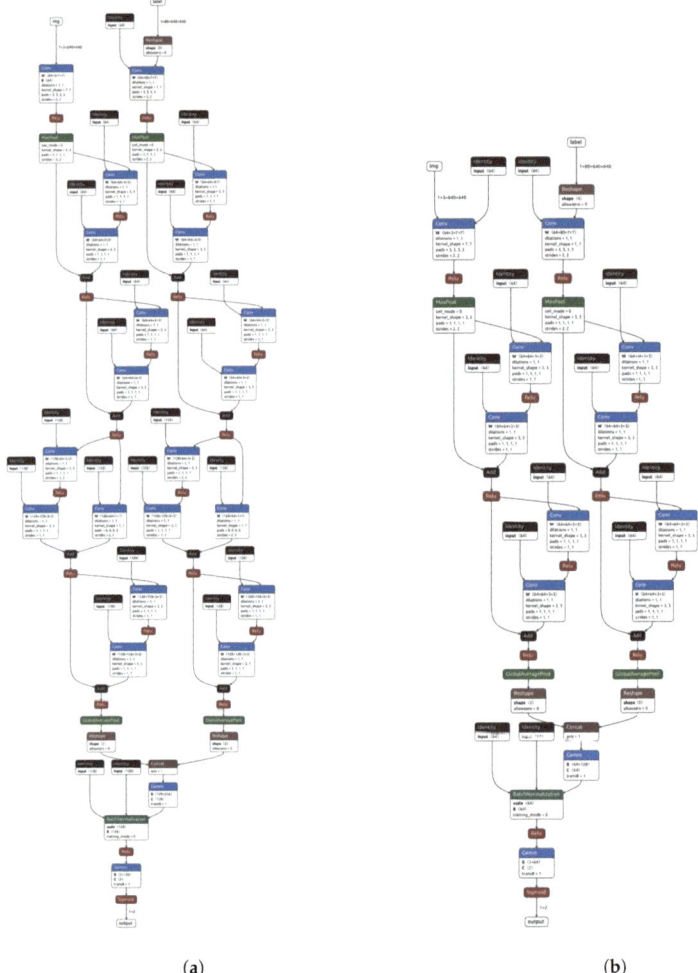

(a)   (b)

Figure 19. Smaller neural network architectures for machine learning-based label quality assurance. (**a**) Medium neural network architecture. (**b**) Small neural network architecture.

Figure 20 displays several examples for which the model accurately predicts that the labels are good and the corresponding labels are, in fact, of high quality.

Figure 20. Examples of true positives.

Figure 21 presents a selection of examples for which the model correctly identifies the labels as bad and the corresponding labels are indeed of bad quality.

Figure 21. Examples of true negatives.

Figure 22 showcases two instances where the model incorrectly predicts the labels as bad when they are actually good. These samples are likely outside the distribution of the *small set* used for training the label quality assurance neural network.

Figure 23 presents two examples for which the model erroneously predicts the labels as good when they are actually bad. Similar to the false negatives mentioned earlier, false-positive predictions are likely to be outside the distribution of the *small set* used for training the label quality assurance neural network.

Figure 22. Examples of false negatives.

During training, only one of the error subtypes (A1, A2, A3, B1, or B2) is applied to the label if the sample is chosen to be negative. Further analysis involving different error types and subtypes and testing on specific combinations is conducted and presented in Table 4. The order of operations is important, and meaningful orders are shown. For instance, A1A2 means that A1 is first performed on the ground truth label, followed by A2 on the already modified ground truth label. There is an equal chance for a sample to be classified as positive or negative. If a sample is positive, labels are created within uncertainty regions, and if it is negative, a combination of error subtypes is performed on ground truth labels. The evaluation is performed using 1000 random samples from the test set 10 times for every combination. The mean and standard deviation for 10 runs per combination are shown. The label quality assurance neural network performs the worst on the A2 error subtype (distorting labels inside uncertainty regions to become outside of them), which is reasonable, as it can be challenging even for a human to determine if a bounding box with a good class is entirely inside the uncertainty region or not. The neural network best detects the B2 and B1B2 combinations (B1: adding new labels to ground truth classes outside any uncertainty region; B2: adding new labels to classes that do not belong to any ground truth classes, outside any uncertainty region). This outcome makes sense because these errors involve adding entirely new bounding boxes that do not belong to any uncertainty region.

Table 4. Mean ± standard deviation for accuracy per error combination.

Error Combination	Mean ± Std
A1	0.71 ± 0.01
A2	0.65 ± 0.02
A3	0.71 ± 0.02
A1A2	0.77 ± 0.01
A1A3	0.78 ± 0.01
A2A3	0.78 ± 0.01
A1A2A3	0.83 ± 0.01
B1	0.91 ± 0.01
B2	0.92 ± 0.01
B1B2	0.92 ± 0.01
A1B1	0.77 ± 0.01
A2B1	0.74 ± 0.01
A3B1	0.77 ± 0.01
A1A2B1	0.81 ± 0.01
A1A3B1	0.83 ± 0.01
A2A3B1	0.81 ± 0.01
A1A2A3B1	0.85 ± 0.01
A1B2	0.77 ± 0.02
A2B2	0.74 ± 0.01
A3B2	0.79 ± 0.01
A1A2B2	0.83 ± 0.01
A1A3B2	0.83 ± 0.01
A2A3B2	0.83 ± 0.01
A1A2A3B2	0.87 ± 0.01
A1B1B2	0.82 ± 0.01
A2B1B2	0.8 ± 0.01
A3B1B2	0.83 ± 0.01
A1A2B1B2	0.86 ± 0.01
A1A3B1B2	0.86 ± 0.01
A2A3B1B2	0.87 ± 0.01
A1A2A3B1B2	0.88 ± 0.01

Figure 23. Examples of false positives.

The results indicate that training a reasonably effective neural network for label quality evaluation is achievable using a *small set*. Once trained, this neural network can be applied to a *large set*, automatically assessing whether the labels are of good quality or not. To recapitulate label quality assurance from a requirements engineering perspective, let us review Figure 4 for the "Production-like Image Data Acquisition" activity. In this activity, relevant data are collected. The subsequent activity, "Data Quality Assurance", involves manual visual inspection of a random subset for a sanity check, along with statistics about widths, heights, pixel histograms and semantic similarity analysis. The "Data Labeling" activity follows, which includes careful and high-quality labeling of a *small set* of collected data by the internal team. A rule of thumb for the size of the subset is approximately 5% of the full dataset. This work uses 4.2% of all relevant data for training the label quality assurance model. Once the label quality assurance model is complete, the remaining unlabeled data from the *large set* can be distributed among multiple annotators, and the model will immediately alert annotators if a label is suspicious.

The quantitative parameters that demonstrate the efficacy of this approach include an accuracy of 82%, precision of 82% and recall of 82%, as shown in the test classification report (Table 2). For qualitative parameters, the paper presents various examples of true positives, true negatives, false positives and false negatives (Figures 20–23). These examples help illustrate the model's ability to correctly identify good and bad labels as well as highlight cases where the model makes incorrect predictions, providing a visual assessment of the label quality assurance performance.

In summary, our findings demonstrate the effectiveness of the machine learning-based label quality assurance model by differentiating between good and bad labels with an accuracy of 82%. The model performs particularly well in detecting B2 and B1B2 error combinations, while it faces challenges in detecting the A2 error subtype. The approach we proposed enables efficient and accurate label quality assurance in object detection tasks, allowing for rapid evaluation of labels in large datasets. This method can greatly reduce the time and effort spent on manual review, ultimately improving the overall quality and reliability of the labeled data used for training computer vision models.

The proposed approach has several advantages. First, it automates the label quality assurance process, saving significant time and effort that would have been spent on manual review. Second, it allows for the rapid assessment of label quality in large datasets, which can be crucial for developing high-performance computer vision models. Finally, the approach is adaptable and can be extended to other tasks beyond detection, such as segmentation, with appropriate modifications to the representation of the label and uncertainty region ranges. However, there are some limitations to our study. One limitation is that the label quality assurance model may struggle to detect certain error subtypes, such as the A2 error subtype. This can be addressed by exploring different neural network architectures or training strategies or incorporating additional features to improve the model's ability to distinguish between subtle differences in label quality. Another limitation is that our approach relies on a *small set* for training the label quality assurance model. The performance of the model may be sensitive to the quality and diversity of this *small set*, which should be carefully curated to ensure its representativeness of the entire dataset. Future research could focus on the investigation of more advanced techniques to improve the detection of challenging error subtypes, such as incorporating additional context information or improving the neural network architecture. Additionally, the approach could be extended and adapted to a wider range of computer vision tasks. By exploring future directions, our approach can pave the way for more efficient, accurate and reliable labeling processes in artificial intelligence projects, ultimately leading to the development of higher-quality and more robust machine learning models.

In this paper, we emphasize the importance of data requirements for object detection projects within the field of requirements engineering because it heavily relies on image data with labeled object bounding boxes. We introduce a process for integrating data requirements into the requirements engineering process, with a particular emphasis on label quality assurance, a critical component of the overall data requirements process for creating modern artificial intelligence solutions. Our study presents a unique machine learning-based approach to perform label quality assurance automatically, providing immediate feedback to annotators and project stakeholders about the quality of the labeling work and significantly improving the efficiency of the process. Our approach can be extended to various computer vision tasks and other machine learning subfields by adjusting label representation and setting suitable uncertainty region ranges. To the best of our knowledge, this is the first machine learning-based label quality assurance method for object detection projects, setting our work apart from previous research that relied on manual review, inter-annotator agreement and deep active learning approaches.

6. Conclusions

In this study, we emphasized the importance of data requirements for building effective object detection solutions within the context of requirements engineering. We proposed a process for integrating data requirements into the requirements engineering process, specifically focusing on the challenges of label quality assurance. This aspect is often sensitive, expensive and time-consuming, making it a critical component of the overall data requirements process for creating modern artificial intelligence solutions. To address these challenges, we demonstrated how machine learning can be employed to create a model that can perform label quality assurance automatically. This model provides immediate feedback to annotators and project stakeholders about the quality of the labeling work, significantly improving the efficiency of the process. Using the object detection task as an example, we showcased the effectiveness of our approach, achieving an accuracy of 82% in differentiating between good and bad labels. The proposed approach is not limited to object detection tasks and can be extended to various computer vision tasks as well as other machine learning subfields. By adjusting the label representation and setting suitable uncertainty region ranges, our method can be adapted to a wide range of applications. For instance, in the case of segmentation tasks, polygons could be used as an alternative to bounding boxes. The problem solver is responsible for determining the appropriate label representation and uncertainty region ranges based on the specific task at hand. In conclusion, our work contributes to the development of more efficient, accurate and reliable labeling processes in object detection projects, which is crucial for the creation of high-quality and robust machine learning models. By integrating our approach into the requirements engineering process, we can significantly enhance the overall performance of artificial intelligence solutions and empower practitioners, engineers and scientists to tackle a wide array of real-world challenges. Future research should focus on addressing the limitations of our study, such as improving the detection of challenging error subtypes and ensuring the representativeness of the *small set* used as a training set. Additionally, researchers could explore the potential of our approach in a broader range of computer vision tasks and machine learning subfields, as well as investigate the synergy between automated label quality assurance and other quality control techniques. By building on the foundation established in this work, we can continue to drive the field of artificial intelligence forward.

Author Contributions: Conceptualization, N.P.; Methodology, N.P.; Software, N.P.; Validation, N.P.; Investigation, N.P.; Resources, N.P.; Data curation, N.P.; Writing—original draft, N.P.; Writing—review & editing, Ž.C.; Visualization, N.P.; Supervision, Ž.C. All authors have read and agreed to the published version of the manuscript.

Funding: This research received no external funding.

Institutional Review Board Statement: Not applicable.

Informed Consent Statement: Not applicable.

Data Availability Statement: Publicly available dataset was analyzed in this study. This data can be found here: https://cocodataset.org/#home.

Conflicts of Interest: The authors declare no conflict of interest.

References

1. Brown, T.; Mann, B.; Ryder, N.; Subbiah, M.; Kaplan, J.D.; Dhariwal, P.; Neelakantan, A.; Shyam, P.; Sastry, G.; Askell, A.; et al. Language models are few-shot learners. *Adv. Neural Inf. Process. Syst.* **2020**, *33*, 1877–1901.
2. Ouyang, L.; Wu, J.; Jiang, X.; Almeida, D.; Wainwright, C.L.; Mishkin, P.; Zhang, C.; Agarwal, S.; Slama, K.; Ray, A.; et al. Training language models to follow instructions with human feedback. *arXiv* **2022**, arXiv:2203.02155.
3. Ramesh, A.; Pavlov, M.; Goh, G.; Gray, S.; Voss, C.; Radford, A.; Chen, M.; Sutskever, I. Zero-shot text-to-image generation. In Proceedings of the International Conference on Machine Learning, Virtual, 18–24 July 2021; pp. 8821–8831.
4. Rombach, R.; Blattmann, A.; Lorenz, D.; Esser, P.; Ommer, B. High-resolution image synthesis with latent diffusion models. In Proceedings of the IEEE/CVF Conference on Computer Vision and Pattern Recognition, New Orleans, LA, USA, 18–24 June 2022; pp. 10684–10695.
5. Lin, T.Y.; Maire, M.; Belongie, S.; Hays, J.; Perona, P.; Ramanan, D.; Dollár, P.; Zitnick, C.L. Microsoft coco: Common objects in context. In Proceedings of the Computer Vision–ECCV 2014: 13th European Conference, Zurich, Switzerland, 6–12 September 2014; Proceedings, Part V 13; Springer International Publishing: Cham, Switzerland, 2014; pp. 740–755.
6. Zaidi, S.S.A.; Ansari, M.S.; Aslam, A.; Kanwal, N.; Asghar, M.; Lee, B. A survey of modern deep learning based object detection models. *Digit. Signal Process.* **2022**, *126*, 103514. [CrossRef]
7. Zhu, Z.; Xie, L.; Yuille, A.L. Object recognition with and without objects. *arXiv* **2016**, arXiv:1611.06596.
8. Hafiz, A.M.; Bhat, G.M. A survey on instance segmentation: State of the art. *Int. J. Multimed. Inf. Retr.* **2020**, *9*, 171–189. [CrossRef]
9. Borque, P.; Fairley, R. *Guide to the Software Engineering Body of Knowledge Version 3.0*; IEEE Computer Society: Washington, DC, USA, 2014.
10. Vogelsang, A.; Borg, M. Requirements engineering for machine learning: Perspectives from data scientists. In Proceedings of the 2019 IEEE 27th International Requirements Engineering Conference Workshops (REW), Jeju Island, Republic of Korea, 23–27 September 2019; pp. 245–251.
11. Pei, Z.; Liu, L.; Wang, C.; Wang, J. Requirements Engineering for Machine Learning: A Review and Reflection. In Proceedings of the 2022 IEEE 30th International Requirements Engineering Conference Workshops (REW), Virtual, 15–19 August 2022; pp. 166–175.
12. Altarturi, H.H.; Ng, K.Y.; Ninggal, M.I.H.; Nazri, A.S.A.; Ghani, A.A.A. A requirement engineering model for big data software. In Proceedings of the 2017 IEEE Conference on Big Data and Analytics (ICBDA), Kuching, Malaysia, 16–17 November 2017; pp. 111–9117.
13. Mahmood, R.; Lucas, J.; Alvarez, J.M.; Fidler, S.; Law, M. Optimizing data collection for machine learning. *Adv. Neural Inf. Process. Syst.* **2022**, *35*, 29915–29928.
14. Jain, A.; Swaminathan, G.; Favaro, P.; Yang, H.; Ravichandran, A.; Harutyunyan, H.; Achille, A.; Dabeer, O.; Schiele, B.; Swaminathan, A.; et al. A Meta-Learning Approach to Predicting Performance and Data Requirements. *arXiv* **2023**, arXiv:2303.01598.

15. Mahmood, R.; Lucas, J.; Acuna, D.; Li, D.; Philion, J.; Alvarez, J.M.; Yu, Z.; Fidler, S.; Law, M.T. How Much More Data Do I Need? Estimating Requirements for Downstream Tasks. In Proceedings of the IEEE/CVF Conference on Computer Vision and Pattern Recognition, New Orleans, LA, USA, 18–24 June 2022; pp. 275–284.
16. Belani, H.; Vukovic, M.; Car, Ž. Requirements engineering challenges in building AI-based complex systems. In Proceedings of the 2019 IEEE 27th International Requirements Engineering Conference Workshops (REW), Jeju Island, Republic of Korea, 23–27 September 2019; pp. 252–255.
17. Asghar, M.R.; Lee, T.; Baig, M.M.; Ullah, E.; Russello, G.; Dobbie, G. A review of privacy and consent management in healthcare: A focus on emerging data sources. In Proceedings of the 2017 IEEE 13th International Conference on e-Science (e-Science), Auckland, New Zealand, 24–27 October 2017; pp. 518–522.
18. Linden, T.; Khandelwal, R.; Harkous, H.; Fawaz, K. The privacy policy landscape after the GDPR. *Proc. Priv. Enhanc. Technol.* **2020**, *2020*, 47–64. [CrossRef]
19. Ayaz, M.; Pasha, M.F.; Alzahrani, M.Y.; Budiarto, R.; Stiawan, D. The Fast Health Interoperability Resources (FHIR) standard: Systematic literature review of implementations, applications, challenges and opportunities. *JMIR Med. Inform.* **2021**, *9*, e21929.
20. DICOM. Available online: https://www.dicomstandard.org/ (accessed on 15 May 2023).
21. Ribeiro, V.; Avila, S.; Valle, E. Handling inter-annotator agreement for automated skin lesion segmentation. *arXiv* **2019**, arXiv:1906.02415.
22. Lampert, T.A.; Stumpf, A.; Gançarski, P. An empirical study into annotator agreement, ground truth estimation, and algorithm evaluation. *IEEE Trans. Image Process.* **2016**, *25*, 2557–2572. [CrossRef] [PubMed]
23. Braylan, A.; Alonso, O.; Lease, M. Measuring Annotator Agreement Generally across Complex Structured, Multi-object, and Free-text Annotation Tasks. In Proceedings of the ACM Web Conference 2022, Lyon, France, 25–29 April 2022; pp. 1720–1730.
24. DiPietro, D.M.; Hazari, V. DiPietro-Hazari Kappa: A Novel Metric for Assessing Labeling Quality via Annotation. *arXiv* **2022**, arXiv:2209.08243.
25. Nassar, J.; Pavon-Harr, V.; Bosch, M.; McCulloh, I. Assessing data quality of annotations with Krippendorff alpha for applications in computer vision. *arXiv* **2019**, arXiv:1912.10107.
26. Nørregaard, J.; Derczynski, L. Sparse Probability of Agreement. *arXiv* **2022**, arXiv:2208.06161.
27. Yang, F.; Zamzmi, G.; Angara, S.; Rajaraman, S.; Aquilina, A.; Xue, Z.; Jaeger, S.; Papagiannakis, E.; Antani, S.K. Assessing Inter-Annotator Agreement for Medical Image Segmentation. *IEEE Access* **2023**, *11*, 21300–21312. [CrossRef]
28. Herraiz, J.L.; Freijo, C.; Camacho, J.; Muñoz, M.; González, R.; Alonso-Roca, R.; Álvarez-Troncoso, J.; Beltrán-Romero, L.M.; Bernabeu-Wittel, M.; Blancas, R.; et al. Inter-Rater Variability in the Evaluation of Lung Ultrasound in Videos Acquired from COVID-19 Patients. *Appl. Sci.* **2023**, *13*, 1321. [CrossRef]
29. Visser, M.; Müller, D.M.J.; van Duijn, R.J.M.; Smits, M.; Verburg, N.; Hendriks, E.J.; Nabuurs, R.J.A.; Bot, J.C.J.; Eijgelaar, R.S.; Witte, M.; et al. Inter-rater agreement in glioma segmentations on longitudinal MRI. *NeuroImage Clin.* **2019**, *22*, 101727. [CrossRef]
30. Williams, B.; Hedger, N.; McNabb, C.B.; Rossetti, G.M.; Christakou, A. Inter-rater reliability of functional MRI data quality control assessments: A standardised protocol and practical guide using pyfMRIqc. *Front. Neurosci.* **2023**, *17*, 1070413. [CrossRef]
31. Takezoe, R.; Liu, X.; Mao, S.; Chen, M.T.; Feng, Z.; Zhang, S.; Wang, X. Deep Active Learning for Computer Vision: Past and Future. *arXiv* **2022**, arXiv:2211.14819.
32. Ren, P.; Xiao, Y.; Chang, X.; Huang, P.Y.; Li, Z.; Gupta, B.B.; Chen, X.; Wang, X. A survey of deep active learning. *ACM Comput. Surv. (CSUR)* **2021**, *54*, 1–40. [CrossRef]
33. Wu, M.; Li, C.; Yao, Z. Deep Active Learning for Computer Vision Tasks: Methodologies, Applications, and Challenges. *Appl. Sci.* **2022**, *12*, 8103. [CrossRef]
34. Kovashka, A.; Russakovsky, O.; Li, F.-F.; Grauman, K. Crowdsourcing in computer vision. *Found. Trends® Comput. Graph. Vis.* **2016**, *10*, 177–243. [CrossRef]
35. Xiao, X.; Yang, F.; Sadovnik, A. Msdu-net: A multi-scale dilated u-net for blur detection. *Sensors* **2021**, *21*, 1873. [CrossRef] [PubMed]
36. Diaz, O.; Kushibar, K.; Osuala, R.; Linardos, A.; Garrucho, L.; Igual, L.; Radeva, P.; Prior, F.; Gkontra, P.; Lekadir, K. Data preparation for artificial intelligence in medical imaging: A comprehensive guide to open-access platforms and tools. *Phys. Med.* **2021**, *83*, 25–37. [CrossRef] [PubMed]
37. Cloud Object Storage—Amazon S3—Amazon Web Services. Available online: https://aws.amazon.com/s3/ (accessed on 15 May 2023).
38. Azure Blob Storage | Microsoft Azure. Available online: https://azure.microsoft.com/en-us/products/storage/blobs/ (accessed on 15 May 2023).
39. Cloud Storage | Google Cloud. Available online: https://cloud.google.com/storage (accessed on 15 May 2023).
40. COCO Dataset | Papers With Code. Available online: https://paperswithcode.com/dataset/coco (accessed on 15 May 2023).
41. Fortuna-Cervantes, J.M.; Ramírez-Torres, M.T.; Martínez-Carranza, J.; Murguía-Ibarra, J.S.; Mejía-Carlos, M. Object detection in aerial navigation using wavelet transform and convolutional neural networks: A first approach. *Program. Comput. Softw.* **2020**, *46*, 536–547. [CrossRef]
42. Vakharia, V.; Kiran, M.B.; Dave, N.J.; Kagathara, U. Feature extraction and classification of machined component texture images using wavelet and artificial intelligence techniques. In Proceedings of the 2017 8th International Conference on Mechanical and Aerospace Engineering (ICMAE), Prague, Czech Republic, 22–25 July 2017; pp. 140–144.

43. Alaba, S.Y.; Ball, J.E. Wcnn3d: Wavelet convolutional neural network-based 3d object detection for autonomous driving. *Sensors* **2022**, *22*, 7010. [CrossRef] [PubMed]
44. He, K.; Zhang, X.; Ren, S.; Sun, J. Deep residual learning for image recognition. In Proceedings of the IEEE Conference on Computer Vision and Pattern Recognition, Las Vegas, NV, USA, 27–30 June 2016; pp. 770–778.
45. Scabini, L.F.; Bruno, O.M. Structure and performance of fully connected neural networks: Emerging complex network properties. *Phys. A Stat. Mech. Its Appl.* **2023**, *615*, 128585. [CrossRef]
46. Kingma, D.P.; Ba, J. Adam: A method for stochastic optimization. *arXiv* **2014**, arXiv:1412.6980.
47. NVIDIA A100 | NVIDIA. Available online: https://www.nvidia.com/en-us/data-center/a100/ (accessed on 15 May 2023).
48. Gösgens, M.; Zhiyanov, A.; Tikhonov, A.; Prokhorenkova, L. Good classification measures and how to find them. *Adv. Neural Inf. Process. Syst.* **2021**, *34*, 17136–17147.
49. Roeder, L. Netron. GitHub Repository. 2017. Available online: https://github.com/lutzroeder/netron (accessed on 15 May 2023).

Disclaimer/Publisher's Note: The statements, opinions and data contained in all publications are solely those of the individual author(s) and contributor(s) and not of MDPI and/or the editor(s). MDPI and/or the editor(s) disclaim responsibility for any injury to people or property resulting from any ideas, methods, instructions or products referred to in the content.

Article

Implicit Bias of Deep Learning in the Large Learning Rate Phase: A Data Separability Perspective

Chunrui Liu [1], Wei Huang [2,*] and Richard Yi Da Xu [3]

[1] School of Computer Science, Faculty of Engineering and IT, University of Technology Sydney, Ultimo, NSW 2007, Australia
[2] RIKEN Center for Advanced Intelligence Project (AIP), 1-4-1 Nihonbashi, Chuo-ku, Tokyo 103-0027, Japan
[3] Department of Mathematics, Hong Kong Baptist University, Kowloon Tong, Hong Kong
* Correspondence: wei.huang.vr@riken.jp

Abstract: Previous literature on deep learning theory has focused on implicit bias with small learning rates. In this work, we explore the impact of data separability on the implicit bias of deep learning algorithms under the large learning rate. Using deep linear networks for binary classification with the logistic loss under the large learning rate regime, we characterize the implicit bias effect with data separability on training dynamics. From a data analytics perspective, we claim that depending on the separation conditions of data, the gradient descent iterates will converge to a flatter minimum in the large learning rate phase, which results in improved generalization. Our theory is rigorously proven under the assumption of degenerate data by overcoming the difficulty of the non-constant Hessian of logistic loss and confirmed by experiments on both experimental and non-degenerated datasets. Our results highlight the importance of data separability in training dynamics and the benefits of learning rate annealing schemes using an initial large learning rate.

Keywords: data separability; data complexity; deep learning theory; catapult phase; neural tangent kernel

Citation: Liu, C.; Huang, W.; Xu, R.Y.D. Implicit Bias of Deep Learning in the Large Learning Rate Phase: A Data Separability Perspective. *Appl. Sci.* **2023**, *13*, 3961. https://doi.org/10.3390/app13063961

Academic Editors: Wenjie Zhang and Zhengyi Yang

Received: 4 February 2023
Revised: 12 March 2023
Accepted: 16 March 2023
Published: 20 March 2023

Copyright: © 2023 by the authors. Licensee MDPI, Basel, Switzerland. This article is an open access article distributed under the terms and conditions of the Creative Commons Attribution (CC BY) license (https://creativecommons.org/licenses/by/4.0/).

1. Introduction

Deep neural networks have proven to be highly effective in both supervised and unsupervised learning tasks. Theoretical understanding of the mechanisms underlying deep learning's power is continuously evolving and expanding. Recent progress in deep learning theory has shown that over-parameterized networks can achieve very low or zero training error through gradient descent-based optimization [1–6]. Surprisingly, these over-parameterized networks can also generalize well to the test set, a phenomenon known as double descent [7]. One promising explanation for this phenomenon is implicit bias [8] or implicit regularization [9], which is characterized by maximum margin. A large family of works has studied exponential tailed losses, such as logistic and exponential loss, and reported implicit regularization of maximum margin [8,10–13].

However, the current theoretical understanding of the optimization and generalization properties of deep learning models is limited due to the assumption of small learning rates in existing theoretical results on implicit bias. In practice, using a large initial learning rate in a learning rate annealing scheme has been shown to result in improved performance. The relationship between data separability and implicit bias during the large learning rate phase remains unclear [14,15]. To address this gap, we examine the effect of the large learning rate on deep linear networks with logistic and exponential loss.

Ref. [16] shed light on the large learning rate phase by observing a distinct phenomenon that the local curvature of the loss landscape drops significantly in the large learning rate phase and thus typically can obtain the best performance. By following [16], we characterize the gradient descent training in terms of three learning rate regimes or phases. (i) Lazy phase $\eta < \eta_0$, when the learning rate is small, the dynamics of a neural network under a linearized dynamics regime, where a model converges to a nearby point in parameter space called lazy training and characterized by the neural tangent kernel [1–3,17–19]. (ii) Catapult phase $\eta_0 < \eta < \eta_1$, the loss grows at the beginning and then drops until it converges to the solution with a flatter minimum. (iii) Divergent phase $\eta > \eta_1$, the loss diverges and the model does not train. The importance of the catapult phase increases because the lazy phase is generally detrimental to generalization and does not explain the practically observed power of deep learning [20,21].

While the phenomenon of the three learning rate phases is reported in a regression setting with mean-squared-error (MSE) loss, it remains unclear whether this can be extended to cross-entropy (logistic) loss along with the data separability. To fill this gap, we examine the effect of a large learning rate on deep linear networks with logistic and exponential loss. Contrary to MSE loss, the characterization of gradient descent with logistic loss concerning learning rate is associated with separation conditions of the data. In addition, the major difficulty is that a non-constant Hessian makes it difficult to draw the boundaries of the catapult phase in the classification settings. Meanwhile, the changes in dynamics have become more complicated, making it difficult to analyse. Our results are different from [16] in many aspects. First, a non-constant Hessian brings more technical challenges. Second, the appearance the catapult phase under logistic loss depends on the separability of the dataset, while squared loss has no such condition. Third, we observed oscillations in the dynamics of training loss in Figure 1, which is not observed in MSE loss. Finally, we summarize our contribution as follows:

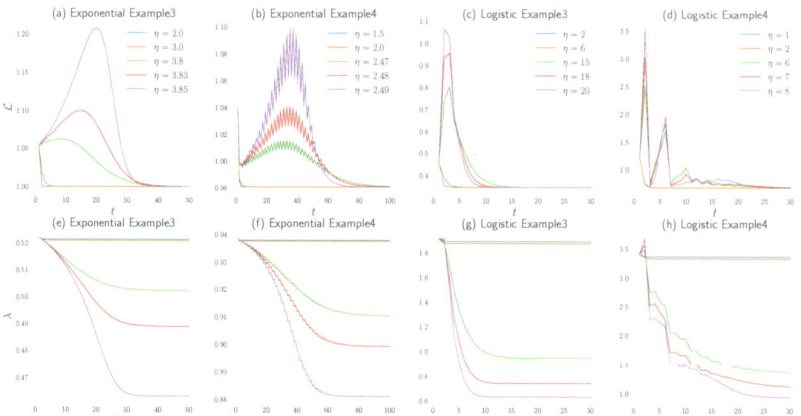

Figure 1. Dependence of dynamics of training loss and maximum eigenvalue of the NTK on the learning rate for a one-hidden-layer linear network, with (**a**,**b**,**e**,**f**) exponential loss and (**c**,**d**,**g**,**h**) logistic loss in Examples 3 and 4. (**a**–**d**) In a large learning rate regime (the catapult phase), the loss increases at the beginning and converges to a global minimum. (**e**–**h**) The maximum eigenvalue of the NTK decreases rapidly to a fixed value which is lower than its initial position in the large learning regime (the catapult phase).

- According to the separation conditions of the data, we characterize the dynamics of gradient descent with logistic and exponential loss corresponding to the learning rate. We find that the gradient descent iterates converge to a flatter minimum in the catapult phase when the data is non-separable. The above three learning rate phases do not apply to the linearly separable data since the optimum is towards infinity.
- Our theoretical analysis ranges from a linear predictor to a one-hidden-layer network. By comparing the convex optimization characterized by Theorem 1 and non-convex optimization characterized by Theorem A2 in terms of the learning rate, we show that the catapult phase is a unique phenomenon for non-convex optimizations.

- We find that in practical classification tasks, the best generalization results tend to occur in the catapult phase. Given the fact that the infinite-width analysis (lazy training) does not fully explain the empirical power of deep learning, our results can be used to partially fill this gap.
- Our theoretical findings were supported by extensive experimentation on the MNIST [22], CIFAR-10 [23] and CIFAR-100 datasets [24] with label noise, and the WebVision dataset [25].

2. Related Work

2.1. Implicit Bias of Gradient Methods

Since the seminal work from [8], implicit bias has led to a fruitful line of research. Works along this line have treated linear predictors [10,11,26,27]; deep linear networks with a single output [28–30] and multiple outputs [31,32]; homogeneous networks (including ReLU, max pooling activation) [12,13,33]; ultra wide networks [34–36]; and matrix factorization [31]. Notably, these studies adopt gradient flow (infinitesimal learning rate) or a sufficiently small learning rate.

2.2. Data Separability

In a recent review of data complexity measures, ref. [37] listed various measures for classification difficulty, including those based on the geometrical complexity of class boundaries. In a later survey by [38], most complexity measures were categorized into six groups: feature-based, linearity, neighbourhood, network, dimensionality, and class imbalance measures. Ref. [39] introduced the distance-based Ssparability index (DSI) to independently evaluate the data separability of the classifier model. The DSI indicates the degree to which data from different classes have similar distributions, which can make separation particularly challenging for classifiers. There has been limited attention given to combining data separability and the theory of implicit bias in deep learning. The noisy features can also impact data separability. The feature selection process is a type of dimensionality reduction that seeks to identify the most important features while discarding irrelevant or noisy features. Ref. [40] summarized how swarm intelligence-based feature selection methods are applied in different applications. Ref. [41] proposed the AGNMF-AN method seeking to improve upon existing methods for community detection by incorporating attribute information and using an adaptive affinity matrix.

2.3. Neural Tangent Kernel

Recently, we have witnessed exciting theoretical developments in understanding the optimization of ultra-wide networks, known as the neural tangent kernel (NTK) [1–3,5,17–19,42]. It is shown that in the infinite-width limit, NTK converges to an explicit limiting kernel, and it stays constant during training. Further, ref. [43] show that gradient descent dynamics of the original neural network fall into its linearized dynamics regime in the NTK regime. In addition, the NTK theory has been extended to various architectures such as orthogonal initialization [44], convolutions [17,45], graph neural networks [46,47], attention [48], PAC-Bayesian learning [6] and batch normalization [49] (see [50] for a summary). The constant property of NTK during training can be regarded as a special case of implicit bias, and importantly, it is only valid in the small learning rate regime.

2.4. Large Learning Rate and Logistic Loss

A large learning rate with SGD training is often set initially to achieve good performance in deep learning empirically [14,15,51]. The existing theoretical explanation of the benefit of the large learning rate contributes to two classes. One is that a large learning rate with SGD leads to flat minima [16,52,53], and the other is that the large learning rate acts as a regularizer [54]. Especially, [16] find a large learning rate phase can result in flatter minima without the help of SGD for mean squared loss. In this work, we ask whether the large learning rate still has this advantage with logistic loss. We expect a different outcome because the logistic loss is sensitive to the separation conditions of the data, and the loss surface is different from that of MSE loss [55].

3. Background

3.1. Setup

Consider a dataset $\{x_i, y_i\}_{i=1}^n$, with inputs $x_i \in \mathbb{R}^d$ and binary labels $y_i \in \{-1, 1\}$. The empirical risk of the classification task follows the form,

$$\mathcal{L} = \frac{1}{n} \sum_{i=1}^n \ell(f(x_i)y_i), \qquad (1)$$

where $f(x_i)$ is the output of the model corresponding to the input x_i, $\ell(\cdot)$ is the loss function, and $\mathcal{L}$ is the empirical loss. Refer to Table 1 for the symbol description. In this work, we study two exponential tail losses which are exponential loss $\ell_{\exp}(u) = \exp(-u)$ and logistic loss $\ell_{\log}(u) = \log(1 + \exp(-u))$. The reason we look at these two losses together is that they are jointly considered in the realm of implicit bias by default [8]. We adopt gradient descent (GD) updates with learning rate η to minimize empirical risk,

$$w_{t+1} = w_t - \eta \nabla \mathcal{L}(w_t) = w_t - \eta \sum_{i=1}^n \ell'(f(x_i)y_i), \qquad (2)$$

where w_t is the parameter of the model at time step t.

Table 1. Key symbols and their definition.

Symbol	Definition
x	Input
y	Label
η	Learning rate
$\ell(\cdot)$	Loss function
$\mathcal{L}$	Empirical loss
w_t	Parameters of the model at time step t
β	β-smooth convexity
α	α-strongly convexity
$\Theta_{\alpha\beta}$	Neural Tangent Kernel

3.2. Separation Conditions of Dataset

It is known that landscapes of cross-entropy loss on linearly separable and non-separable data are different. Thus, the separation condition plays a crucial role in understanding the dynamics of gradient descent in terms of the learning rate. To build towards this, we define the two classes of separation conditions and review existing results for loss landscapes of a linear predictor in terms of separability.

Assumption 1. *The dataset is linearly separable, i.e., there exists a separator w_* such that $\forall i : w_*^T x_i y_i > 0$.*

Assumption 2. *The dataset is non-separable, i.e., there is no separator w_* such that $\forall i : w_*^T x_i y_i > 0$.*

Linearly separable. Consider the data under Assumption 1, one can examine that the loss of a linear predictor, i.e., $f(x) = w^T x$, is β-smooth convex with respect to w, and the global minimum is at infinity. The implicit bias of gradient descent with a sufficient small learning rate ($\eta < \frac{2}{\beta}$) in this phase was studied by [8]. They showed that the predictor converges to the direction of the maximum margin (hard margin SVM) solution, which implies the gradient descent method itself will find a proper solution with an implicit regularization instead of picking up a random solver. If one increases the learning rate until it exceeds

$\eta < \frac{2}{\beta}$, then the result of converging to the maximum margin is not guaranteed, though loss can still converge to a global minimum.

Non-separable. Suppose we consider the data under Assumption 2, which is not linearly separable. The empirical risk of a linear predictor on these data are α-strongly convex, and the global minimum is finite. In this case, given an appropriate small learning rate ($\eta < \frac{2}{\beta}$), the gradient descent converges towards the unique finite solution. When the learning rate is large enough, i.e., $\eta > \frac{2}{\alpha}$, we can rigorously show that gradient descent updates with this large learning rate leading to risk exploding or saturating.

We formally construct the relationship between loss surfaces and learning dynamics of gradient descent with respect to different learning rates on the two classes of data through the following proposition,

Proposition 1. *For a linear predictor $f = w^T x$, along with a loss $\ell \in \{\ell_{\exp}, \ell_{\log}\}$.*

1. *Under Assumption 1, the empirical loss is β-smooth. Then the gradient descent with constant learning rate $\eta < \frac{2}{\beta}$ never increases the risk, and empirical loss will converge to zero:*

$$\mathcal{L}(w_{t+1}) - \mathcal{L}(w_t) \leq 0, \quad \lim_{t \to \infty} \mathcal{L}(w_t) = 0, \quad \text{with} \quad \eta < \frac{2}{\beta}.$$

2. *Under Assumption 2, the empirical loss is β-smooth and α-strongly convex, where $\alpha \leq \beta$. Then the gradient descent with a constant learning rate $\eta < \frac{2}{\beta}$ never increases the risk, and empirical loss will converge to a global minimum. On the other hand, the gradient descent with a constant learning rate $\eta > \frac{2}{\alpha}$ never decreases the risk, and empirical loss will explode or saturate:*

$$\mathcal{L}(w_{t+1}) - \mathcal{L}(w_t) \leq 0, \quad \lim_{t \to \infty} \mathcal{L}(w_t) = G_0, \quad \text{with} \quad \eta < \frac{2}{\beta},$$

$$\mathcal{L}(w_{t+1}) - \mathcal{L}(w_t) \geq 0, \quad \lim_{t \to \infty} \mathcal{L}(w_t) = G_1, \quad \text{with} \quad \eta > \frac{2}{\alpha},$$

where G_0 is the value of a global minimum while $G_1 = \infty$ for exploding situation or $G_0 < G_1 < \infty$ when saturating.

4. Theoretical Results

4.1. Convex Optimization

It is known that the Hessian of the logistic and exponential loss with respect to the linear predictor is non-constant. Moreover, the estimated β-smooth convexity and α-strongly convexity vary across different finite-bounded subspaces. As a result, the learning rate threshold in Proposition A1 is not detailed in terms of optimization trajectory. However, we can obtain more elaborate thresholds of the learning rate for a linear predictor by considering the degeneracy assumption:

Assumption 3. *The dataset contains two data points that have the same feature and opposite label, that is*

$$(x_1 = 1, y_1 = 1) \quad \text{and} \quad (x_2 = 1, y_2 = -1).$$

We call this assumption the degeneracy assumption since the features from opposite label degenerate. Without loss of generality, we simplify the dimension of data and fix the position of the feature. Note that this assumption can be seen as a special case of non-separable data. Theoretical work has characterized general non-separable data [11], and we leave the analysis of this setting for the large learning rate to future work. Thanks to the symmetry of the risk function in space at the basis of degeneracy assumption, we can construct the exact dynamics of empirical risk with respect to the whole learning rate space.

Theorem 1. *For a linear predictor $f = w^T x$ equipped with an exponential (logistic) loss under Assumption 3, there is a critical learning rate that separates the whole learning rate space into two (three) regions. The critical learning rate satisfies*

$$\mathcal{L}'(w_0) = -\mathcal{L}'(w_0 - \eta_{\text{critical}} \mathcal{L}'(w_0)),$$

where w_0 is the initial weight. Moreover,

1. *For exponential loss, the gradient descent with a constant learning rate $\eta < \eta_{\text{critical}}$ never increases loss, and the empirical loss converges to the global minimum. On the other hand, the gradient descent with learning rate $\eta = \eta_{\text{critical}}$ oscillates. Finally, when the learning rate $\eta > \eta_{\text{critical}}$, the training process never decreases the loss and the empirical loss will explode to infinity:*

$$\mathcal{L}(w_{t+1}) - \mathcal{L}(w_t) < 0, \quad \lim_{t \to \infty} \mathcal{L}(w_t) = 1, \quad \text{with} \quad \eta < \eta_{\text{critical}},$$
$$\mathcal{L}(w_{t+1}) - \mathcal{L}(w_t) = 0, \quad \lim_{t \to \infty} \mathcal{L}(w_t) = \mathcal{L}(w_0), \quad \text{with} \quad \eta = \eta_{\text{critical}},$$
$$\mathcal{L}(w_{t+1}) - \mathcal{L}(w_t) > 0, \quad \lim_{t \to \infty} \mathcal{L}(w_t) = \infty, \quad \text{with} \quad \eta > \eta_{\text{critical}}.$$

2. *For logistic loss, the critical learning rate satisfies the condition: $\eta_{\text{critical}} > 8$. The gradient descent with a constant learning rate $\eta < 8$ never increases the loss, and the loss converges to the global minimum. On the other hand, the loss along with a learning rate $8 \leq \eta < \eta_{\text{critical}}$ does not converge to the global minimum but oscillates. Finally, when the learning rate $\eta > \eta_{\text{critical}}$, gradient descent never decreases the loss, and the loss saturates:*

$$\mathcal{L}(w_{t+1}) - \mathcal{L}(w_t) < 0, \quad \lim_{t \to \infty} \mathcal{L}(w_t) = \log(2), \quad \text{with} \quad \eta < 8,$$
$$\mathcal{L}(w_{t+1}) - \mathcal{L}(w_t) \leq 0, \quad \lim_{t \to \infty} \mathcal{L}(w_t) = \mathcal{L}(w_*) < \mathcal{L}(w_0), \quad \text{with} \quad 8 \leq \eta < \eta_{\text{critical}},$$
$$\mathcal{L}(w_{t+1}) - \mathcal{L}(w_t) \geq 0, \quad \lim_{t \to \infty} \mathcal{L}(w_t) = \mathcal{L}(w_*) \geq \mathcal{L}(w_0), \quad \text{with} \quad \eta \geq \eta_{\text{critical}}.$$

where w_* satisfies $-w_* = w_* - \frac{\eta}{2} \frac{\sinh(w_*)}{1+\cosh(w_*)}$.

Remark 1. *The difference between the two losses is due to the monotonicity of the loss. For exponential loss, the function $|\mathcal{L}'(w_t)/w_t|$ is monotonically increasing with respect to $|w_t|$, while it is monotonically decreasing for logistic loss.*

We demonstrate the gradient descent dynamics with the degenerate and non-separable case through the following example.

Example 1. *Consider optimizing $\mathcal{L}(w)$ with dataset $\{(x_1 = 1, y_1 = 1) \text{ and } (x_2 = 1, y_2 = -1).\}$ using gradient descent with constant learning rates. Figure 2a,c shows the dependence of different dynamics on the learning rate η for exponential and logistic loss, respectively.*

Example 2. *Consider optimizing $\mathcal{L}(w)$ with dataset $\{(x_1 = 1, y_1 = 1), (x_2 = 2, y_2 = -1) \text{ and } (x_3 = -1, y_3 = 1).\}$ using gradient descent with constant learning rates. Figure 2b,d shows the dependence of different dynamics on the learning rate η for exponential and logistic loss, respectively.*

Remark 2. *The dataset considered here is an example of a non-separable case, and the dynamics of loss behave similarly to those in Example 1. We use this example to show that our theoretical results on the degenerate data can be extended empirically to the non-separable data.*

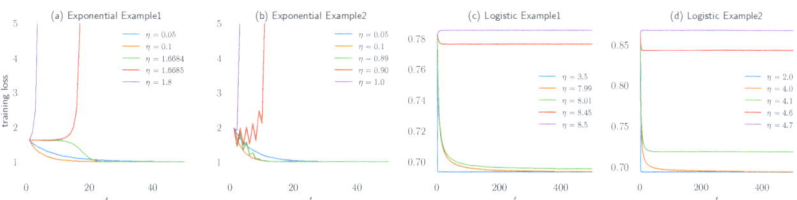

Figure 2. Showing the dependence of the dynamics of the training loss on the learning rate for linear predictors using both exponential and logistic loss functions. Examples 1 and 2 were used to test the performance of the linear predictors. The sub-graphs (**a**,**c**) show the experimental learning curves for separable data, consistent with the theoretical predictions. The critical learning rates were found to be $\eta_{\text{critical}} = 1.66843$ and $\eta_{\text{critical}} = 8.485$ for the exponential and logistic loss functions, respectively. Sub-graphs (**b**,**d**) show the dynamics of the training loss for non-separable data. The dynamics of training loss regarding the learning rate for non-separable data are similar to those of degenerate cases. Hence, the critical learning rates can be approximated by $\eta_{\text{critical}} = 0.895$ and $\eta_{\text{critical}} = 4.65$, respectively.

4.2. Non-Convex Optimization

To investigate the relationship between the dynamics of gradient descent and the learning rate for deep linear networks, we consider linear networks with one hidden layer, and the information propagation in these networks is governed by,

$$f(x) = m^{-1/2} w^{(2)} w^{(1)} x, \tag{3}$$

where m is the width, i.e., the number of neurons in the hidden layer, $w^{(1)} \in \mathbb{R}^{m \times d}$ and $w^{(2)} \in \mathbb{R}^m$ are the parameters of the model. Taking the exponential loss as an example, the gradient descent equations at training step t are,

$$\begin{aligned} w^{(1)}_{t+1} &= w^{(1)}_t - \frac{1}{n}\frac{\eta}{m^{1/2}}(-e^{-y_\alpha f_t(x_\alpha)}) w^{(2)}_t x_\alpha y_\alpha, \\ w^{(2)}_{t+1} &= w^{(2)}_t - \frac{1}{n}\frac{\eta}{m^{1/2}}(-e^{-y_\alpha f_t(x_\alpha)}) w^{(1)}_t x_\alpha y_\alpha, \end{aligned} \tag{4}$$

where we use the Einstein summation convention to simplify the expression and apply this convention in the following derivation.

We introduce the neural tangent kernel, an essential element for the evolution of output function in Equation 8. The neural tangent kernel (NTK) originates from [1] and is formulated as,

$$\Theta_{\alpha\beta} = \frac{1}{m}\sum_{p=1}^{P} \frac{\partial f(x_\alpha)}{\partial \theta_p} \frac{\partial f(x_\beta)}{\partial \theta_p}. \tag{5}$$

where P is the number of parameters. For a two-layer linear neural network, the NTK can be written as,

$$\Theta_{\alpha\beta} = \frac{1}{mn}\left((w^{(1)} x_\alpha)(w^{(1)} x_\beta) + (w^{(2)})^2 (x_\alpha x_\beta)\right). \tag{6}$$

Here we use normalized NTK which is divided by the number of samples n. Under the degeneracy Assumption 3, the loss function becomes $\mathcal{L} = \cosh(m^{-1/2} w^{(2)} w^{(1)})$. Then Equation (4) reduces to

$$\begin{aligned} w^{(1)}_{t+1} &= w^{(1)}_t - \frac{\eta}{m^{1/2}} w^{(2)}_t \sinh(m^{-1/2} w^{(2)}_t w^{(1)}_t), \\ w^{(2)}_{t+1} &= w^{(2)}_t - \frac{\eta}{m^{1/2}} w^{(1)}_t \sinh(m^{-1/2} w^{(2)}_t w^{(1)}_t). \end{aligned} \tag{7}$$

The updates of output function f_t and the eigenvalue of NTK λ_t, which are both scalars in our setting:

$$f_{t+1} = f_t - \eta \lambda_t \tilde{f}_{t_{\exp}} + \frac{\eta^2}{m} f_t \tilde{f}_{t_{\exp}}^2,$$
$$\lambda_{t+1} = \lambda_t - \frac{4\eta}{m} f_t \tilde{f}_{t_{\exp}} + \frac{\eta^2}{m} \lambda_t \tilde{f}_{t_{\exp}}^2. \tag{8}$$

where $\tilde{f}_{t_{\exp}} := \sinh(f_t)$ while $\tilde{f}_{t_{\log}} := \frac{\sinh(f_t)}{1+\cosh(f_t)}$ for logistic loss.

We have previously introduced the catapult phase where the loss grows at the beginning and then drops until it converges to a global minimum. In the following theorem, we prove the existence of the catapult phase on the degenerate data with exponential and logistic loss.

Theorem 2. *Under appropriate initialization and Assumption 3, there exists a catapult phase for both the exponential and logistic loss. More precisely, when η belongs to this phase, $T > 0$ exists such that the output function f_t and the eigenvalue of NTK λ_t update in the following way:*

1. *$\mathcal{L}_t$ keeps increasing when $t < T$.*
2. *After the T step and its successors, the loss decreases, which is equivalent to:*

$$|f_{T+1}| > |f_{T+2}| \geq |f_{T+3}| \geq \ldots.$$

3. *The eigenvalue of NTK keeps dropping after the T steps:*

$$\lambda_{T+1} > \lambda_{T+2} \geq \lambda_{T+3} \geq \ldots.$$

Moreover, we have the inverse relationship between the learning rate and final eigenvalue of the NTK: $\lambda_\infty \leq \lim_{t\to\infty} \frac{4 f_t}{\eta \tilde{f}_{t_{\exp}}}$ with exponential loss, or $\lambda_\infty \leq \lim_{t\to\infty} \frac{4 f_t}{\eta \tilde{f}_{t_{\log}}}$ with logistic loss.

We demonstrate that the catapult phase can be found in both degenerate and non-separable data through the following examples. The weight matrix is initialized by iid Gaussian distribution, i.e., $w^{(1)}, w^{(2)} \sim \mathcal{N}(0, \sigma_w^2)$. For exponential loss, we adopt the setting of $\sigma_w^2 = 0.5$ and $m = 1000$ while we set $\sigma_w^2 = 1.0$ and $m = 100$ for logistic loss.

Example 3. *Consider optimizing $\mathcal{L}(w)$ using a one-hidden-layer linear network with dataset $\{(x_1 = [1, 0], y_1 - 1)$ and $(x_2 = [1, 0], y_2 = -1)\}$ and exponential (logistic) loss using gradient descent with a constant learning rate. Figure 1a,c,e,g shows how the different choices of learning rate η change the dynamics of the loss function with exponential and logistic loss.*

Example 4. *Consider optimizing $\mathcal{L}(w)$ using a one-hidden-layer linear network with dataset $\{(x_1 = [1, 1], y_1 = -1), (x_2 = [1, -1], y_1 = 1), (x_3 = [-1, -2], y_1 = 1)$ and $(x_4 = [-1, 1], y_4 = 1).\}$ and exponential (logistic) loss using gradient descent with a constant learning rate. Figure 1b,d,f,h shows how the different choices of learning rate η change the dynamics of the loss function with exponential and logistic loss.*

As Figure 1 shows, in the catapult phase, the eigenvalue of the NTK decreases to a lower value than its initial point, while it remains unchanged in the lazy phase where the learning rate is small. For MSE loss, the lower value of the NTK indicates a flatter curvature given the training loss is low [16]. Yet, it is unknown whether the aforementioned conclusion can be applied to exponential and logistic loss. Through the following corollary, we show that the Hessian is equivalent to the NTK when the loss converges to a global minimum for degenerate data.

Corollary 1. *Consider optimizing $\mathcal{L}(w)$ with a one-hidden-layer linear network under Assumption 3 and exponential (logistic) loss using gradient descent with a constant learning rate. For any learning rate that loss can converge to the global minimum, the larger the learning rate, the flatter* curvature the gradient descent will achieve at the end of training (see Corollary A1 in Appendix A for detail).

We demonstrate that the flatter curvature can be achieved in the catapult phase through Examples 3 and 4, using the code provided by [56] to measure the Hessian, as shown in Figure 3. In the lazy phase, both the curvature and eigenvalue of the NTK are independent of the learning rate at the end of training. In the catapult phase, however, the curvature decreases to a value smaller than that in the lazy phase. In conclusion, the NTK and Hessian have similar behaviours at the end of training on non-separable data.

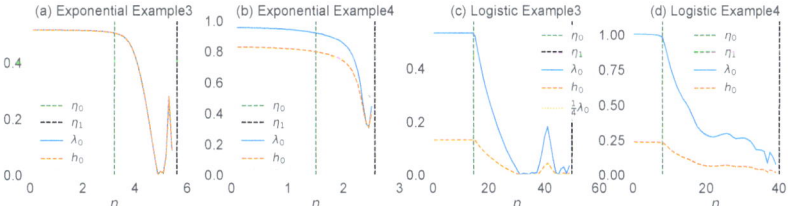

Figure 3. Top eigenvalue of the NTK (λ_0) and Hessian (h_0) measured at $t = 100$ as a function of the learning rate, with (**a**,**b**) exponential loss and (**c**,**d**) logistic loss in Examples 3 and 4. The green dashed line $\eta = \eta_0$ represents the boundary between the lazy and catapult phases, while the black dashed line $\eta = \eta_1$ separates the catapult and divergent phases. We adopt the settings of $\sigma_w^2 = 0.5$ and $m = 100$ for exponential loss, and the settings for logistic loss are $\sigma_w^2 = 0.5$ and $m = 200$. (**a**,**c**) The curves of the maximum eigenvalue of the NTK and Hessian coincide as predicted by the Corollary A1. (**b**,**d**) For non-separable data, the trend of the two eigenvalue curves is consistent with the change in the learning rate.

Finally, we compare our results from the catapult phase to the results with MSE loss and show the summary in Table 2.

Table 2. A summary of the relationship between separation conditions of the data and the catapult phase for different losses.

Separation Condition	Linear Separable	Degenerate	Non-Separable
Exponential loss (this work)	✗	✓	✓
Logistic loss (this work)	✗	✓	✓
Squared loss ([16])	✓	✓	✓

5. Experiment

5.1. Experimental Results

In this section, we present our experimental results of linear networks with the logistic loss on CIFAR-10 to examine whether flatter minima achieved in the catapult phase can lead to better generalization in real applications. We selected two ("cars" and "dogs") of the ten categories from the CIFAR-10 dataset to form a binary classification problem. Training is performed on a server with a CPU with 32 cores, and an 8 GB Nvidia 3060 GPU. The results will be illustrated by comparing the generalization performance with respect to different learning rates.

Figure 4 shows the performance of the two linear networks, one has one hidden layer without bias, and the other has two hidden layers of linear network with bias, trained on CIFAR-10. We present the results using two different stopping conditions. Firstly, we fix the training time for all learning rates, the learning rates within the catapult phase have the advantage of obtaining a higher test accuracy, as shown in Figure 4a,c. However, adopting a fixed training time will result in a bias in favour of large learning rates, since the large learning rate naturally runs faster. To ensure a fair comparison, we then used a fixed physical time, defined as $t_{\text{phy}} = t_0 \eta$, where t_0 is a constant. In this setting, as shown in Figure 4b,d, the performance of the large learning rate phase is even worse than that of the small learning phase. Nevertheless, we find this is achieved in the catapult phase when adopting the learning rate annealing strategy.

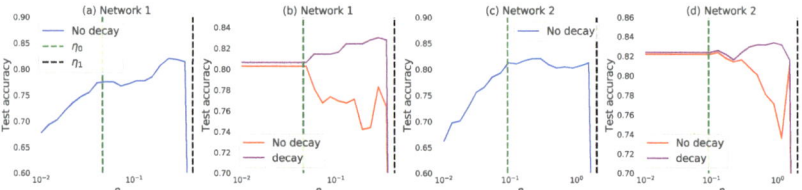

Figure 4. Test performance on the CIFAR-10 dataset with respect to different learning rate phases. The data size is of $n_{\text{train}} = 2048$ and $n_{\text{test}} = 512$. (**a**,**b**) A two-layer linear network without bias of $\sigma_w^2 = 0.5$ and $m = 500$. (**c**,**d**) A three-layer linear network with the bias of $\sigma_w^2 = 0.5$, $\sigma_b^2 = 0.01$, and $m = 500$. (**a**,**c**) The test accuracy is measured at the time step $t = 500$ and $t = 300$, respectively. The optimal performance is obtained when the learning rate is in the catapult phase. (**b**,**d**) The test accuracy is measured at the physical time step (red curve), after which it continues to evolve for a period of time at a small learning rate (purple): $t_{\text{phy}} = 50/\eta$ and extra time $t = 500$ at $\eta = 0.01$ for the decaying case. Although the results in the catapult phase do not perform as well as the lazy phase when there is no decay, the best performance can be found in the catapult phase when adopting learning rate annealing.

To explain the above experimental results, we refer to Theorem 2 in [30]. According to this theorem, the data can be uniquely partitioned into the linearly separable and non-separable parts. When we tune the learning rate to the large learning rate regime, the algorithm quickly iterates to a flat minimum in a space spanned by non-separable data. At the same time, for linearly separable data, the gradient descent cannot achieve the maximum margin due to the large learning rate. As a result, for this part of the data, the generalization performance is suppressed. This explains why when we fix the physical steps, the performance in the large learning rate regime is worse than that of the small learning rate phase. On the other hand, when we adopt the strategy of learning rate annealing, for non-separable data, since the large learning rate has learned a flat curvature, the subsequent small learning rate will not affect this result. For data with linearly separable parts, reducing the learning rate can restore the maximum margin. Therefore, we can see that under this strategy, the best performance can be found in the phase of a large learning rate.

5.2. Effectiveness on Synthetic and Real-World Datasets

To further evaluate the impact of learning rate annealing strategies on model performance, we conducted experiments using two different annealing strategies powered by the learning rate scheduler in PyTorch: one-step annealing and exponential annealing. In the one-step annealing strategy, we started with a relatively large learning rate of 1 and then reduced it by a decay factor of 0.01 after 30 training steps. In the exponential annealing strategy, we started with a large learning rate of 1 and then reduced it exponentially with a learning rate decay rate of 0.98 over time. We evaluated the performance of these two annealing strategies on both synthetic and real-world datasets using convolutional neural networks. Specifically, we measured the accuracy of the models trained with each annealing strategy.

Creating synthetic data with label noise can help represent the separability of the data by simulating a more realistic scenario in which data points may not be perfectly separable. We synthesize the label noise on three public datasets MNIST, CIFAR-10 and CIFAR-100 following previous works [57–59]. Symmetric noise was generated by randomly flipping the labels of each class to incorrect labels from other classes. Asymmetric noise was generated by flipping the labels within a specific set of classes to a certain incorrect class. For example, for CIFAR-10, flipping "truck" → "automobile", "bird" → "airplane", "deer" → "horse", "cat" ↔ "dog". In CIFAR-100, the 100 classes were grouped into 20 super-classes, each with 5 sub-classes, and each class was flipped to the next class in a circular fashion within the same super-class. The noise rate $\tau \in [0.1, 0.4]$ for both symmetric and asymmetric noise. Regarding the models a four-layer CNN for MNIST, an eight-layer CNN for CIFAR-10 and a ResNet-34 for CIFAR-100. We train the networks for 50, 120 and 200 epochs for MNIST, CIFAR-10, and CIFAR-100, respectively. For all training, we used a SGD optimizer with no momentum, cross-entropy loss, and three different learning rate schedules. Typical data augmentations including random width/height shift and horizontal flip were applied.

The classification accuracies under symmetric label noise are reported in Table 3. As can be seen, the learning rate annealing methods achieved better results across all datasets. The superior performance of the learning rate annealing methods is more pronounced when the noise rates are extremely high and the dataset is more complex. Results for asymmetric noise are reported in Table 4. Comparing the results in both Tables 3 and 4, we find that learning rate annealing is quite consistent across different noise types and rates. Overall, this demonstrates a consistently strong performance across different datasets.

Table 3. Test accuracy (%) of different methods on benchmark datasets with clean or symmetric label noise ($\tau \in [0.1, 0.4]$). The results (mean±std) are reported over three random runs. SL refers to a training schedule with a small learning rate that remains constant throughout the training process. OS (one-step) denotes a training schedule where the learning rate starts at a high value and then drops to a smaller value after a specified number of training steps. Exp refers to a training schedule where the learning rate decreases exponentially as the training progresses.

Datasets	Methods	Clean ($\tau = 0.0$)	Symmetric Noise Rate (τ)			
			0.1	0.2	0.3	0.4
MNIST	SL	99.09 ± 0.02	98.60 ± 0.04	98.29 ± 0.08	97.88 ± 0.12	97.57 ± 0.09
	OS	99.33 ± 0.04	99.22 ± 0.57	98.71 ± 0.10	98.34 ± 0.07	97.96 ± 0.16
	EXP	99.40 ± 0.03	98.85 ± 0.21	98.84 ± 0.10	98.63 ± 0.20	98.48 ± 0.03
CIFAR-10	SL	86.37 ± 0.05	82.01 ± 0.19	78.70 ± 0.29	75.83 ± 0.28	71.58 ± 0.08
	OS	91.38 ± 0.07	86.87 ± 0.15	83.95 ± 0.24	81.72 ± 0.08	78.70 ± 0.25
	EXP	91.63 ± 0.15	85.52 ± 0.22	82.94 ± 0.32	81.57 ± 0.99	79.66 ± 2.20
CIFAR-100	SL	48.10 ± 0.14	42.31 ± 0.44	38.10 ± 0.65	34.10 ± 0.25	31.21 ± 1.01
	OS	70.50 ± 1.07	62.66 ± 1.51	57.31 ± 2.09	52.08 ± 1.63	47.22 ± 0.88
	EXP	70.14 ± 0.82	63.67 ± 0.26	55.70 ± 0.24	49.67 ± 1.95	43.39 ± 1.11

To further enhance our theoretical finding and complement the effectiveness of the general annealing methods, we conducted experiments on the large-scale real-world dataset WebVision [25] as it is a large-scale dataset of images that has been specifically designed to evaluate the performance of computer vision algorithms under noise. We followed the "Mini" setting in [24,59] that only takes the first 50 classes of the resized Google image subset. We evaluated the trained networks on the same 50 classes of the WebVision validation set, considered as a clean validation.

We trained a ResNet-50 [14] using SGD for 250 epochs with a Nesterov momentum of 0.9, a weight decay of 3×10^{-5}, and a batch size of 512. We resized the images to 224×224. Typical data augmentations, including random width/height shift, colour jittering and random horizontal flip, were applied. The accuracies on the clean WebVision validation set (e.g., only the first 50 classes) are reported in Table 5. As a result, the large learning rate annealing methods (one-step annealing and exponential learning rate annealing) provided better generalization.

Table 4. Test accuracy (%) of different methods on benchmark datasets with clean or asymmetric label noise ($\tau \in [0.1, 0.4]$). The results (mean±std) are reported over three random runs. SL refers to a training schedule with a small learning rate that remains constant throughout the training process. OS (one-step) denotes a training schedule where the learning rate starts at a high value and then drops to a smaller value after a specified number of training steps. Exp refers to a training schedule where the learning rate decreases exponentially as the training progresses.

Datasets	Methods	Clean (τ = 0.0)	Asymmetric Noise Rate (τ)			
			0.1	0.2	0.3	0.4
MNIST	SL	99.09 ± 0.02	98.52 ± 0.07	98.25 ± 0.01	97.89 ± 0.16	97.45 ± 0.01
	OS	99.33 ± 0.04	98.86 ± 0.16	98.98 ± 0.71	98.35 ± 0.14	98.24 ± 0.17
	EXP	99.40 ± 0.03	98.85 ± 0.09	98.63 ± 0.09	98.46 ± 0.13	98.24 ± 0.15
CIFAR-10	SL	86.37 ± 0.05	81.91 ± 0.25	78.87 ± 0.11	75.85 ± 0.17	72.02 ± 0.59
	OS	91.38 ± 0.07	86.61 ± 0.32	83.90 ± 0.41	81.41 ± 0.41	78.77 ± 0.40
	EXP	91.63 ± 0.15	85.26 ± 0.79	83.53 ± 0.37	81.38 ± 1.05	78.82 ± 0.45
CIFAR-100	SL	48.10 ± 0.14	42.15 ± 0.13	37.93 ± 0.95	34.80 ± 0.28	30.97 ± 0.54
	OS	70.50 ± 1.07	62.65 ± 0.91	57.66 ± 0.97	50.42 ± 1.06	47.07 ± 1.74
	EXP	70.14 ± 0.82	63.51 ± 1.20	56.35 ± 0.55	48.09 ± 0.44	44.34 ± 0.40

Table 5. Test accuracies (%) on the clean WebVision validation set of ResNet-50 models trained on WebVision. SL refers to a training schedule with a small learning rate that remains constant throughout the training process. OS (one-step) denotes a training schedule where the learning rate starts at a high value and then drops to a smaller value after a specified number of training steps. Exp refers to a training schedule where the learning rate decreases exponentially as the training progresses.

Loss	SL	OS	EXP
Acc	60.38	66.04	65.92

In terms of computational complexity, the actual process of changing the magnitude of the learning rate during training is typically straightforward and computationally inexpensive. The real computational cost of learning rate annealing comes from the additional training iterations required to allow the model to converge more precisely towards the optimal solution. Overall, the actual computational cost of learning rate annealing can depend on a variety of factors, including the size of the dataset, the complexity of the model, and the specific annealing schedule used. However, in general, the computational cost of learning rate annealing is relatively small compared to the overall cost of training a deep learning model.

6. Discussion

In this work, we characterized the dynamics of deep linear networks for binary classification trained with gradient descent in a large learning rate regime, inspired by the seminal work by [16]. We present a catapult effect in the large learning rate phase depending on separation conditions associated with logistic and exponential loss. According to our theoretical analysis, the loss in the catapult phase can converge to the global minimum like the lazy phase. However, from the perspective of the Hessian, the minimum achieved in the catapult phase is flatter. We empirically show that even without SGD optimization, the best generalization performance can be achieved in the catapult stage phase for linear networks, while this works in the large learning rate for linear networks in binary classification, there are several remaining open questions. For non-linear networks, the effect of a large learning rate is not clear in theory. In addition, the stochastic gradient descent algorithm also needs to be explored when the learning rate is large. We leave these unsolved problems for future work.

Future work could investigate the theoretical impact of data separability on a wider range of deep learning models, including convolutional neural networks or recurrent neural networks, and for different types of loss functions. Additionally, it would be beneficial to explore the effect of data separability on the design of neural network architectures, such as varying the number of layers, hidden unit size, or connectivity patterns. Furthermore, our study assumes degenerate data, which simplifies the analysis. As new mathematical analytical methods become available, future research could extend the results to non-degenerate datasets and explore how the relationship between data separability and training dynamics/model performance changes in this setting. Finally, practical applications of this research could be explored, such as utilizing data separability to guide the design of neural networks or the development of learning rate annealing schemes.

Author Contributions: Conceptualization, C.L. and W.H.; methodology, W.H.; software, C.L.; formal analysis, C.L. and W.H.; data curation, C.L.; writing—original draft preparation, C.L. and W.H.; writing—review and editing, C.L. and W.H.; visualization, C.L.; supervision, R.Y.D.X. and C.L. All authors have read and agreed to the published version of the manuscript.

Funding: This research received no external funding.

Institutional Review Board Statement: Not applicable.

Informed Consent Statement: Not applicable.

Data Availability Statement: The data used in this paper are published as open-source data available at https://data.vision.ee.ethz.ch/cvl/webvision/dataset2017.html (accessed on 2 February 2023) and https://www.cs.toronto.edu/~kriz/cifar.html (accessed on 2 February 2023).

Conflicts of Interest: The authors declare no conflict of interest.

Appendix A

This appendix is dedicated to proving the key results of this paper, namely Proposition A1, Theorems A1 and A2, and Corollary A1 which describe the dynamics of gradient descent with logistic and exponential loss in different learning rate phase.

Proposition A1. *For a linear predictor $f = w^T x$, along with a loss $\ell \in \{\ell_{\exp}, \ell_{\log}\}$.*

1. *Under Assumption 1, the empirical loss is β-smooth. Then the gradient descent with constant learning rate $\eta < \frac{2}{\beta}$ never increases the risk, and empirical loss will converge to zero:*

$$\mathcal{L}(w_{t+1}) - \mathcal{L}(w_t) \leq 0, \quad \lim_{t \to \infty} \mathcal{L}(w_t) = 0, \quad \text{with} \quad \eta < \frac{2}{\beta}$$

2. *Under Assumption 2, the empirical loss is β-smooth and α-strongly convex, where $\alpha \leq \beta$. Then the gradient descent with a constant learning rate $\eta < \frac{2}{\beta}$ never increases the risk, and empirical loss will converge to a global minimum. On the other hand, the gradient descent with a constant learning rate $\eta > \frac{2}{\alpha}$ never decreases the risk, and empirical loss will explode or saturate:*

$$\mathcal{L}(w_{t+1}) - \mathcal{L}(w_t) \leq 0, \quad \lim_{t \to \infty} \mathcal{L}(w_t) = G_0, \quad \text{with} \quad \eta < \frac{2}{\beta}$$

$$\mathcal{L}(w_{t+1}) - \mathcal{L}(w_t) \geq 0, \quad \lim_{t \to \infty} \mathcal{L}(w_t) = G_1, \quad \text{with} \quad \eta > \frac{2}{\alpha}$$

where G_0 is the value of a global minimum while $G_1 = \infty$ for exploding situation or $G_0 < G_1 < \infty$ when saturating.

Proof. 1 We first prove that empirical loss $\mathcal{L}(u)$ regrading data-scaled weight $u_i \equiv w^T x_i y_i$ for the linearly separable dataset is smooth. The empirical loss can be written as $\mathcal{L} = \sum_{i=1}^{n} \ell(u_i)$, then the second derivatives of logistic and exponential loss are,

$$\mathcal{L}''_{\exp} = \sum_{i=1}^{n} \ell''_{\exp}(u_i) = \sum_{i=1}^{n} \exp''(-u_i) = \sum_{i=1}^{n} \exp(-u_i)$$

$$\mathcal{L}''_{\log} = \sum_{i=1}^{n} \ell''_{\log}(u_i) = \sum_{i=1}^{n} \log''(1+\exp(-u_i)) = \sum_{i=1}^{n} \frac{\exp(-u_i)}{(1+\exp(-u_i))^2}$$

when w_t is limited, there will be a β such that $\mathcal{L}'' < \beta$. Furthermore, because there exists a separator w_* such that $\forall i : w_*^T x_i y_i > 0$, the second derivative of empirical loss can be arbitrarily close to zero. This implies that the empirical loss function is not strongly convex.

Recalling a property of the β-smooth function f [60],

$$f(y) \leq f(x) + (\nabla_x f)^T (y-x) + \frac{1}{2}\beta \|y-x\|^2$$

Taking the gradient descent into consideration,

$$\mathcal{L}(w_{t+1}) \leq \mathcal{L}(w_t) + \left(\nabla_{w_t}\mathcal{L}(w_t)\right)^T (w_{t+1} - w_t) + \frac{1}{2}\beta \|w_{t+1} - w_t\|^2$$

$$= \mathcal{L}(w_t) + \left(\nabla_{w_t}\mathcal{L}(w_t)\right)^T \left(-\eta \nabla_{w_t}\mathcal{L}(w_t)\right) + \frac{1}{2}\beta \|-\eta \nabla_{w_t}\mathcal{L}\|^2$$

$$= \mathcal{L}(w_t) + \left(\nabla_{w_t}\mathcal{L}(w_t)\right)^T \left(-\eta \nabla_{w_t}\mathcal{L}(w_t)\right) + \frac{1}{2}\beta \|-\eta \nabla_{w_t}\mathcal{L}\|^2$$

$$= \mathcal{L}(w_t) - \eta (1 - \frac{\eta \beta}{2}) \|\nabla_{w_t}\mathcal{L}\|^2$$

when $1 - \frac{\eta \beta}{2} > 0$, that is $\eta < \frac{2}{\beta}$, we have,

$$\mathcal{L}(w_{t+1}) \leq \mathcal{L}(w_t) - \eta (1 - \frac{\eta \beta}{2}) \|\nabla_{w_t}\mathcal{L}\|^2 \leq \mathcal{L}(w_t)$$

We now prove that empirical loss will converge to zero with learning rate $\eta < \frac{2}{\beta}$. We changing the form of the above inequality,

$$\frac{\mathcal{L}(w_t) - \mathcal{L}(w_{t+1})}{\eta (1 - \frac{\eta \beta}{2})} \geq \|\nabla_{w_t}\mathcal{L}(w_t)\|^2$$

this implies,

$$\sum_{t=0}^{T} \|\nabla_{w_t}\mathcal{L}(w_t)\|^2 \leq \sum_{t=0}^{T} \frac{\mathcal{L}(w_t) - \mathcal{L}(w_{t+1})}{\eta (1 - \frac{\eta \beta}{2})} = \frac{\mathcal{L}(w_0) - \mathcal{L}(w_T)}{\eta (1 - \frac{\eta \beta}{2})} < \infty$$

therefore, we have $\lim_{t \to \infty} \|\nabla_{w_t}\mathcal{L}(w_t)\| = 0$.

2 When the data is not linear separable, there is no w_* such that $\forall i : w_*^T x_i y_i > 0$. Thus, at least one $w_*^T x_i y_i$ is negative when the other terms are positive. This implies that the solution of the loss function is finite and the empirical loss is both α-strongly convex and β-smooth.

Recalling a property of the α-strongly convex function f [60],

$$f(y) \geq f(x) + (\nabla_x f)^T (y-x) + \frac{1}{2}\alpha \|y-x\|^2$$

Taking the gradient descent into consideration,

$$\mathcal{L}(w_{t+1}) \geq \mathcal{L}(w_t) + \left(\nabla_{w_t}\mathcal{L}(w_t)\right)^T (w_{t+1} - w_t) + \frac{1}{2}\alpha\|w_{t+1} - w_t\|^2$$

$$= \mathcal{L}(w_t) + \left(\nabla_{w_t}\mathcal{L}(w_t)\right)^T \left(-\eta\nabla_{w_t}\mathcal{L}(w_t)\right) + \frac{1}{2}\alpha\|-\eta\nabla_{w_t}\mathcal{L}\|^2$$

$$= \mathcal{L}(w_t) - \eta(1 - \frac{\eta\alpha}{2})\|\nabla_{w_t}\mathcal{L}\|^2$$

when $1 - \frac{\eta\alpha}{2} < 0$, that is $\eta > \frac{2}{\alpha}$, we have,

$$\mathcal{L}(w_{t+1}) \geq \mathcal{L}(w_t) - \eta(1 - \frac{\eta\alpha}{2})\|\nabla_{w_t}\mathcal{L}\|^2 \geq \mathcal{L}(w_t).$$

□

Theorem A1. *For a linear predictor $f = w^T x$ equipped with exponential (logistic) loss under Assumption 3, there is a critical learning rate that separates the whole learning rate space into two (three) regions. The critical learning rate satisfies*

$$\mathcal{L}'(w_0) = -\mathcal{L}'(w_0 - \eta_{\text{critical}}\mathcal{L}'(w_0)),$$

where w_0 is the initial weight. Moreover,

1. *For exponential loss, the gradient descent with a constant learning rate $\eta < \eta_{\text{critical}}$ never increases loss, and the empirical loss will converge to the global minimum. On the other hand, the gradient descent with learning rate $\eta = \eta_{\text{critical}}$ will oscillate. Finally, when the learning rate $\eta > \eta_{\text{critical}}$, the training process never decreases the loss and the empirical loss will explode to infinity:*

$$\mathcal{L}(w_{t+1}) - \mathcal{L}(w_t) < 0, \quad \lim_{t\to\infty}\mathcal{L}(w_t) = 1, \quad \text{with} \quad \eta < \eta_{\text{critical}},$$

$$\mathcal{L}(w_{t+1}) - \mathcal{L}(w_t) = 0, \quad \lim_{t\to\infty}\mathcal{L}(w_t) = \mathcal{L}(w_0), \quad \text{with} \quad \eta = \eta_{\text{critical}},$$

$$\mathcal{L}(w_{t+1}) - \mathcal{L}(w_t) > 0, \quad \lim_{t\to\infty}\mathcal{L}(w_t) = \infty, \quad \text{with} \quad \eta > \eta_{\text{critical}}.$$

2. *For logistic loss, the critical learning rate satisfies a condition: $\eta_{\text{critical}} > 8$. The gradient descent with a constant learning rate $\eta < 8$ never increases the loss, and the loss will converge to the global minimum. On the other hand, the loss along with a learning rate $8 \leq \eta < \eta_{\text{critical}}$ will not converge to the global minimum but oscillate. Finally, when the learning rate $\eta > \eta_{\text{critical}}$, gradient descent never decreases the loss, and the loss will saturate:*

$$\mathcal{L}(w_{t+1}) - \mathcal{L}(w_t) < 0, \quad \lim_{t\to\infty}\mathcal{L}(w_t) = \log(2), \quad \text{with} \quad \eta < 8,$$

$$\mathcal{L}(w_{t+1}) - \mathcal{L}(w_t) \leq 0, \quad \lim_{t\to\infty}\mathcal{L}(w_t) = \mathcal{L}(w_*) < \mathcal{L}(w_0), \quad \text{with} \quad 8 \leq \eta < \eta_{\text{critical}},$$

$$\mathcal{L}(w_{t+1}) - \mathcal{L}(w_t) \geq 0, \quad \lim_{t\to\infty}\mathcal{L}(w_t) = \mathcal{L}(w_*) \geq \mathcal{L}(w_0), \quad \text{with} \quad \eta \geq \eta_{\text{critical}}.$$

where w_* satisfies $-w_* = w_* - \frac{\eta}{2}\frac{\sinh(w_*)}{1+\cosh(w_*)}$.

Proof. 1 Under the degeneracy assumption, the risk is given by the hyperbolic function $\mathcal{L}(w_t) = \cosh(w_t)$. The update function for the single weight is,

$$w_{t+1} = w_t - \eta\sinh(w_t).$$

To compare the norm of the gradient $\|\sinh(w_t)\|$ and the norm of loss, we introduce the following function:

$$\phi(x) = \eta \mathcal{L}'(x) - 2x = \eta \sinh(x) - 2x, \text{ for } x \geq 0. \tag{A1}$$

Then it is easy to see that

$$\mathcal{L}(w_{t+1}) > |\mathcal{L}(w_t)| \iff \phi(|w_t|) > 0.$$

In this way, we have transformed the problem into studying the iso-surface of $\phi(x)$. Define Phase$_1$ by

$$\text{Phase}_1 = \{x | \phi(x) < 0\}.$$

Let Phase$_2$ be the complementary set of Phase$_1$ in $[0, +\infty)$. Since $\frac{\sin x}{x}$ is monotonically increasing, we know that Phase$_2$ is connected and contains $+\infty$.

Suppose $\eta > \eta_{\text{critical}}$, then $\phi(w_0) > 0$, which implies that

$$\mathcal{L}(w_1) > \mathcal{L}(w_0) \text{ and } |w_1| > |w_0|.$$

Thus, the first step becomes trapped in Phase$_2$:

$$\phi(w_1) > 0.$$

By induction, we can prove that $\phi(w_t) > 0$ for arbitrary $t \in \mathbb{N}$, which is equivalent to

$$\mathcal{L}(w_t) > \mathcal{L}(w_{t-1}).$$

Similarly, we can prove the theorem under another toe initial conditions: $\eta = \eta_{\text{critical}}$ and $\eta < \eta_{\text{critical}}$.

2 Under the degeneracy assumption, the risk is governed by the hyperbolic function $\mathcal{L}(w_t) = \frac{1}{2}\log(2 + 2\cosh(w_t))$. The update function for the single weight is,

$$w_{t+1} = w_t - \frac{\eta}{2}\frac{\sinh(w_t)}{1 + \cosh(w_t)}.$$

Thus,

$$\phi(x) = \eta \mathcal{L}'(x) - 2x = \frac{\eta}{2}\frac{\sinh(x)}{1 + \cosh(x)} - 2x, \text{ for } x \geq 0. \tag{A2}$$

Unlike the exponential loss, $\frac{\sinh(x)}{x(1+\cosh(x))}$ is monotonically decreasing, which means that Phase$_2$ of $\phi(x)$ does not contain $+\infty$ (see Figure A1).

Suppose $8 < \eta < \eta_{\text{critical}}$, then w_0 lies in Phase$_2$. In this situation, we denote the critical point that separates Phase$_1$ and Phase$_2$ by w_*. That is

$$-w_* = w_* - \eta\frac{\sinh(w_*)}{1 + \cosh(w_*)}.$$

Then it is obvious that before w_t arrives at w_*, it keeps decreasing and will eventually become trapped at w_*:

$$\lim_{t \to \infty} w_t = w_*,$$

and we have $\lim_{t \to \infty} \mathcal{L}(w_t) - \mathcal{L}(w_{t-1}) = 0$. When $\eta < 8$, Phase$_2$ is empty. In this case, we can prove by induction that $\phi(w_t) > 0$ for arbitrary $t \in \mathbb{N}$, which is equivalent to $\mathcal{L}(w_t) > \mathcal{L}(w_{t-1})$.

□

Theorem A2. *Under appropriate initialization and Assumption 3, there exists a catapult phase for both the exponential and logistic loss. More precisely, when η belongs to this phase, there exists a $T > 0$ such that the output function f_t and the eigenvalue of the NTK λ_t update in the following way:*

1. $\mathcal{L}_t$ keeps increasing when $t < T$.
2. After the T step and its successors, the loss decreases, which is equivalent to:

$$|f_{T+1}| > |f_{T+2}| \geq |f_{T+3}| \geq \dots.$$

3. The eigenvalue of NTK keeps dropping after the T steps:

$$\lambda_{T+1} > \lambda_{T+2} \geq \lambda_{T+3} \geq \dots.$$

Moreover, we have the inverse relation between the learning rate and the final eigenvalue of the NTK: $\lambda_\infty \leq \lim_{t \to \infty} \frac{4 f_t}{\eta \tilde{f}_{t_{\exp}}}$ *with exponential loss, or* $\lambda_\infty \leq \lim_{t \to \infty} \frac{4 f_t}{\eta \tilde{f}_{t_{\log}}}$ *with logistic loss.*

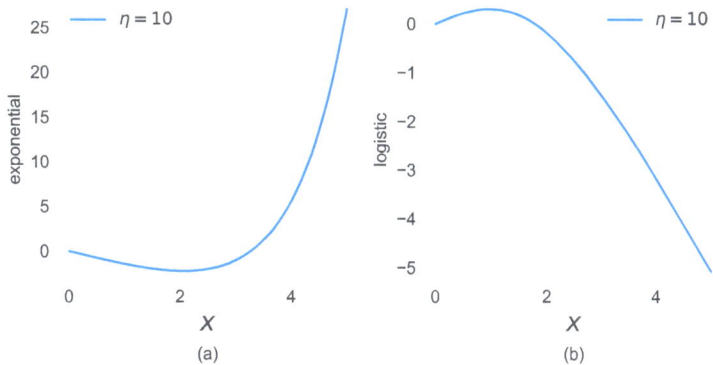

Figure A1. Graph of $\phi(x)$ for the two losses. (**a**) Exponential loss with learning rate $\eta = 10$. (**b**) Logistic loss with learning rate $\eta = 10$.

Proof. Exponential loss

$\tilde{f}_{\exp}$ satisfies:

1. $|\tilde{f}_{\exp}(x)| = |\tilde{f}_{\exp}(-x)|$.
2. $\lim_{x \to 0} \frac{\tilde{f}_{\exp}(x)}{x} = 1$.
3. $\tilde{f}_{\exp}(x)$ has exponential growth as $x \to \infty$.

By the definition of the normalized NTK, we automatically obtain

$$\lambda_t \geq 0.$$

From the numerical experiment, we observe that at the ending phase of training, λ_t does not increase. Thus, λ_t must converge to a non-negative value, which satisfies

$$\frac{\eta^2}{m} \lambda f_t^2 - \frac{4\eta}{m} f_t \tilde{f}_t \leq 0. \tag{A3}$$

Thus, $\lambda \leq \lim_{t \to \infty} \frac{4 f_t}{\eta \tilde{f}_t}$.

Since the output f converges to the global minimum, a larger learning rate will lead to a lower limiting value of the NTK. As it was pointed out in [16], a flatter NTK corresponds to a smaller generalization error in the experiment. However, we still need to verify that a large learning rate exists.

Note that during training, the loss function curve may experience more than one wave of uphill and downhill. To give a precise definition of a large learning rate, it should satisfy the following two conditions:

1. $|f_{T+1}| > |f_T|$, this implies that
$$\mathcal{L}_{T+1} > \mathcal{L}_T.$$

For the $T+1$ step and its successors,
$$|f_{T+1}| > |f_{T+2}| \geq |f_{T+3}| \geq \ldots.$$

2. The norm of the NTK keeps dropping after T steps:
$$\lambda_T > \lambda_{T+1} \geq \lambda_{T+2} \geq \ldots.$$

If we already know that the loss keeps decreasing after $T+1$ step, then
$$\Delta \lambda = \frac{\eta}{m} \tilde{f} \cdot (\eta \lambda \tilde{f} - 4f). \tag{A4}$$

Since $\frac{|\tilde{f}|}{|f|} \geq 1$ and is monotonically increasing when $\tilde{f} = \sinh f$, we automatically have
$$\lambda_T > \lambda_{T+1} > \lambda_{T+2} \geq \ldots,$$

If
$$\lambda_T < \frac{4f_T}{\eta \tilde{f}_T} \text{ and } \lambda_{T+1} < \frac{4f_{T+1}}{\eta \tilde{f}_{T+1}}.$$

This condition holds if the parameters are initially close to zero.

To check Condition (1), the following function which plays an essential role as in the non-hidden layer case:
$$\phi_\lambda(x) = \eta \lambda \sinh(x) - \frac{\eta^2}{m} x \sinh^2(x) - 2x, \text{ for } x \geq 0.$$

Notice that an extra parameter λ emerges with the appearance of the hidden layer. We call this the control parameter of the function $\phi(x)$.

For a fixed λ, since now $\phi(x)$ becomes linear, the whole $[0, +\infty)$ is divided into three phases (see Figure A2):

Phase$_1$:= the connected component of $\{x|\ \phi_\lambda(x) < 0\}$ that contains 0;
Phase$_2$:= $\{x|\ \phi_\lambda(x) > 0\}$;
Phase$_3$:= the connected component of $\{x|\ \phi_\lambda(x) < 0\}$ that contains $+\infty$.

It is easy to see that $\mathcal{L}_{\exp}(f_{T+1}) > \mathcal{L}_{\exp}(f_T)$ if, and only if,
$$\phi_{\lambda_T}(f_T) > 0.$$

That is, f_T lies in Phase$_2$ of ϕ_{λ_T}. Similarly,
$$\mathcal{L}_{\exp}(f_{T+2}) < \mathcal{L}_{\exp}(f_{T+1}) \iff \phi_{\lambda_{T+1}}(f_{T+1}) < 0.$$

That is, f_{T+1} jumps into Phase$_1$ of $\phi_{\lambda_{T+1}}$. Denote the point that separates Phase$_1$ and Phase$_2$ by x_*, then form the graph of $\phi_\lambda(x)$ with different λ, we know that
$$x_*(\lambda') > x_*(\lambda) \text{ if } \lambda' < \lambda.$$

Therefore, Condition (1) is satisfied if
$$x_*(\lambda_{T+1}) > f_T + \phi_{\lambda_T}(f_T) \tag{A5}$$

and at the same time,
$$\lambda_{T+1} - \lambda_T > 0.$$
For simplicity, we reset T as our initial step, and write the output function f_t as
$$f_{t+1} = f_t(1 + \mathcal{A}_t), \tag{A6}$$
where $\mathcal{A}_t = \frac{\eta^2}{m}\tilde{f}_t^2 - \eta \lambda_t \tilde{f}_t / f_t$. Thus, $\phi_{\lambda_0}(f_0) > 0$ is equivalent to $\mathcal{A}_0 < -2$.
Similarly, write the update function for λ_t as
$$\lambda_{t+1} = \lambda_t(1 + \mathcal{B}_t), \tag{A7}$$
where $\mathcal{B}_t = \frac{\eta^2}{m}\tilde{f}_t^2 - \frac{4\eta}{m}\tilde{f}_t f_t / \lambda_t$. To fulfil the above condition on the NTK, we need
$$\mathcal{B}_0 < 0.$$
To check (A5), let the initial output f_0 be close to $X_*(\lambda_0)$ (this can be performed by adjusting w_0):
$$0 < f_0 - X_* < \epsilon.$$
Then by the mean value theorem,
$$x_*(\lambda_1) - x_*(\lambda_0) = \frac{\partial x_*}{\partial \lambda_*}(\lambda_*) \cdot \Delta \lambda.$$
The derivative $\frac{\partial x_*}{\partial \lambda_*}$ can be calculated by the implicit function theorem:
$$\frac{\partial x_*}{\partial \lambda} = -\frac{\partial \phi_\lambda(x_*)}{\partial \lambda} / \frac{\partial \phi_\lambda(x_*)}{\partial x_*}$$
$$= -\eta \sinh(x_*) / \frac{\partial \phi_\lambda(x_*)}{\partial x_*}.$$
It is easy to see that $|\frac{\partial x_*}{\partial \lambda}|$ is bounded away from zero if the initial output is in Phase$_2$ and near x_* of $\phi_{\lambda_0}(x)$ (see Figure A2).
On the other hand, we have the freedom to move f_0 towards x_* of $\phi_{\lambda_0}(x)$ without breaking the $\Delta \lambda < 0$ condition. Since
$$|\frac{\eta \lambda \tilde{f}}{4f}| < |\frac{\eta \lambda \tilde{f}'}{4f'}| \quad \text{if } f < f'.$$
Therefore, we can always find $\epsilon > 0$ such that $0 < f_0 - x_* < \epsilon$ and (A5) is satisfied. Combining the above, we have demonstrated the existence of the catapult phase for the exponential loss.

logistic loss

When considering the degeneracy case for the logistic loss, the loss will be
$$\mathcal{L} = \frac{1}{2}\log(2 + 2\cosh(m^{-1/2}w^{(2)}w^{(1)})). \tag{A8}$$
Much of the argument is similar. For example, Equation (A3) still holds if we replace $\tilde{f}_{\exp}$ by
$$\tilde{f}_{\log}(x) := \frac{\sinh(x)}{1 + \cosh(x)}.$$
$\tilde{f}_{\log}$ satisfies

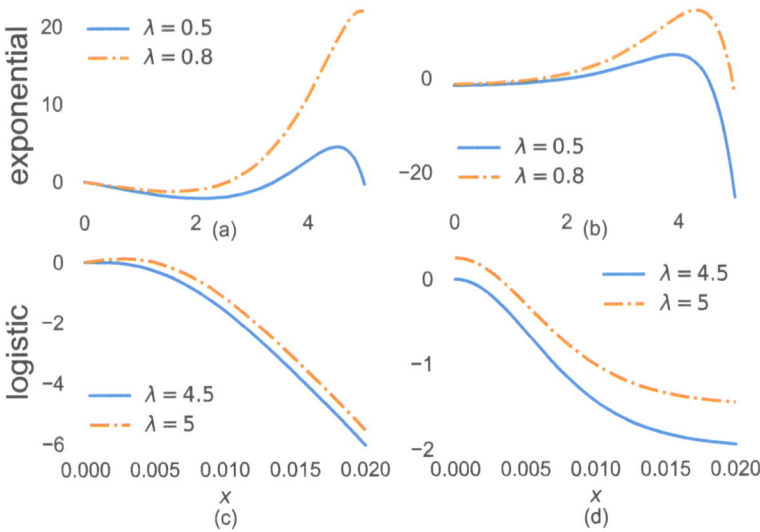

Figure A2. Different colours represent different λ(NTK) values. (**a**) Graph of $\phi_\lambda(x)$ equipped with the exponential loss. (**b**) Graph of the derivative of $\phi_\lambda(x)$ equipped with the exponential loss. (**c**) Graph of $\phi_\lambda(x)$ equipped with the logistic loss. (**d**) Graph of the derivative of $\phi_\lambda(x)$ equipped with the logistic loss. Notice that the critical point of the exponential loss moves to the right as λ decreases.

1. $|\tilde{f}_{\log}(x)| = |\tilde{f}_{\log}(-x)|$.
2. $|\tilde{f}_{\log}(x)| \leq 1$ for $x \in (-\infty, \infty)$.

This implies that
$$\left|\frac{\tilde{f}}{f}\right| \leq \frac{1}{2}.$$

Then by (A4), we have $\Delta\lambda < 0$ if $\lambda \leq \frac{8}{\eta}$. Thus, Condition 2 is satisfied for both loss functions. Now, $\phi_\lambda(x)$ becomes:

$$\phi_\lambda(x) := \eta\lambda \frac{\sinh(x)}{1+\cosh(x)} - \frac{\eta^2}{m} x \frac{\sinh^2(x)}{(1+\cosh(x))^2} - 2x,$$

along with its derivative:

$$\phi'_\lambda(x) := \eta\lambda \frac{\cosh(x)}{1+\cosh(x)} - \frac{\eta\lambda \sinh^2(x)}{(1+\cosh(x))^2} - 2$$
$$- 2\frac{\eta^2}{m} \frac{\sinh(x)}{1+\cosh(x)} \left[\frac{\cosh(x)}{1+\cosh(x)} - \frac{\sinh^2(x)}{(1+\cosh(x))^2}\right]$$
$$- \frac{\eta^2}{m} \frac{\sinh^2(x)}{(1+\cosh(x))^2}.$$

The method of verifying Condition 1 is similar with the exponential case, except that $\phi_\lambda(x)$ has only Phase$_1$ and Phase$_2$ (see Figure A2). As the NTK λ decreases, Phase$_1$ will disappear and at that moment, and the loss will keep decreasing. Let λ_* be the value such that $\phi'_{\lambda_*}(x) = 0$, then
$$\lambda_* = 4/\eta.$$

During the period when $4/\eta < \lambda_t < 8/\eta$, the NTK keeps dropping and the loss may oscillate around x_*. However, we may encounter the scenario where both the loss and λ_t are increases before dropping down simultaneously (see the first three steps in Figure A2).

Theoretically, it corresponds to the jump from Phase$_2$ to Phase$_3$ and then to Phase$_1$ of $\phi_{\lambda_1}(x)$ in the first two steps. This is possible since $\tilde{f}_{\log}$ is decreasing when $x > 0$. This implies that

$$|\frac{\eta\lambda\tilde{f}'}{4f'}| < |\frac{\eta\lambda\tilde{f}}{4f}| \text{ if } f < f'.$$

So an increase in the output will cause the NTK to drop faster. □

Corollary A1. *Consider optimizing $\mathcal{L}(w)$ with a one-hidden-layer linear network under Assumption 3 and exponential (logistic) loss using gradient descent with a constant learning rate. For any learning rate that loss can converge to the global minimum, the larger the learning rate, the flatter curvature the gradient descent will achieve at the end of training.*

Proof. The Hessian matrix is defined as the second derivative of the loss with respect to the parameters,

$$H_{\alpha\beta} = \frac{\partial^2 \mathcal{L}}{\partial \theta_\alpha \partial \theta_\beta}$$

where $\theta_\alpha, \theta_\beta \in \{w^{(1)}, w^{(2)}\}$ for our linear network settings. For logistic loss,

$$H_{\alpha\beta} = \frac{1}{n}\sum_i \frac{\partial^2 \exp(-y_i f_i)}{\partial \theta_\alpha \partial \theta_\beta}$$

$$= \frac{1}{n}\sum_i [\frac{\partial^2 f_i}{\partial \theta_\alpha \partial \theta_\beta}\exp(-y_i f_i)(-y_i) + \frac{\partial f_i}{\partial \theta_\alpha}\frac{\partial f_i}{\partial \theta_\beta}\exp(-y_i f_i)]$$

We want to make a connection from the Hessian matrix to the NTK. Note that the second term contains $\frac{\partial f_i}{\partial \theta_\alpha}\frac{\partial f_i}{\partial \theta_\beta}$, which can be written as JJ^T, where $J = \text{vec}[\frac{\partial f_i}{\partial \theta_j}]$, while the NTK can be expressed as $J^T J$. It is known that they have the same eigenvalue. Furthermore, under Assumption 3, we have $n = 2$ and $f_1 = f_2$, thus,

$$H_{\alpha\beta} = \frac{1}{n}\sum_i [\frac{\partial^2 f_i}{\partial \theta_\alpha \partial \theta_\beta}\frac{\partial \mathcal{L}}{\partial f_\theta} + \frac{\partial f_i}{\partial \theta_\alpha}\frac{\partial f_i}{\partial \theta_\beta}\mathcal{L}]$$

Suppose at the end of gradient descent training we can achieve a global minimum. Then we have, $\frac{\partial \mathcal{L}}{\partial f_\theta} = 0$, and $\mathcal{L} = 1$. Thus, the Hessian matrix reduces to,

$$H_{\alpha\beta} = \frac{1}{n}\sum_i \frac{\partial f_i}{\partial \theta_\alpha}\frac{\partial f_i}{\partial \theta_\beta}$$

In this case, the eigenvalues of the Hessian matrix are equal to those of the NTK. Combine with Theorem A2, we can prove the result.

For logistic loss,

$$H_{\alpha\beta} = \frac{1}{n}\sum_i \frac{\partial^2 \log(1+\exp(-y_i f_i))}{\partial \theta_\alpha \partial \theta_\beta}$$

$$= \frac{1}{n}\sum_i [\frac{\partial^2 f_i}{\partial \theta_\alpha \partial \theta_\beta}\frac{\exp(-y_i f_i)(-y_i)}{1+\exp(-y_i f_i)} + \frac{\partial f_i}{\partial \theta_\alpha}\frac{\partial f_i}{\partial \theta_\beta}\frac{\exp(-y_i f_i)}{(1+\exp(-y_i f_i))^2}]$$

Under Assumption 3, we have $n = 2$ and $f_1 = f_2$, thus,

$$H_{\alpha\beta} = \frac{1}{n}\sum_i [\frac{\partial^2 f_i}{\partial \theta_\alpha \partial \theta_\beta} \frac{\partial \mathcal{L}}{\partial f_\theta} + \frac{\partial f_i}{\partial \theta_\alpha} \frac{\partial f_i}{\partial \theta_\beta} \frac{\exp(-y_i f_i)}{(1+\exp(-y_i f_i))^2}]$$

Suppose at the end of gradient descent training we can achieve a global minimum. Then we have, $\frac{\partial \mathcal{L}}{\partial f_\theta} = 0$, and $f_i = 0$. Thus, the Hessian matrix reduces to,

$$H_{\alpha\beta} = \frac{1}{4n}\sum_i \frac{\partial f_i}{\partial \theta_\alpha} \frac{\partial f_i}{\partial \theta_\beta}$$

In this case, the eigenvalues of the Hessian matrix and NTK have the relation $\frac{1}{4}\lambda_{\text{NTK}} = \lambda_{\text{Hessian}}$.

□

References

1. Jacot, A.; Gabriel, F.; Hongler, C. Neural tangent kernel: Convergence and generalization in neural networks. In Proceedings of the Advances in Neural Information Processing Systems, Red Hook, NY, USA, 3–8 December 2018; pp. 8571–8580.
2. Allen-Zhu, Z.; Li, Y.; Song, Z. A convergence theory for deep learning via over-parameterization. In Proceedings of the International Conference on Machine Learning. PMLR, Long Beach, CA, USA, 9–15 June 2019; pp. 242–252.
3. Du, S.S.; Lee, J.D.; Li, H.; Wang, L.; Zhai, X. Gradient descent finds global minima of deep neural networks. *arXiv* **2018**, arXiv:1811.03804.
4. Chizat, L.; Bach, F. On the global convergence of gradient descent for over-parameterized models using optimal transport. In Proceedings of the Advances in Neural Information Processing Systems, Red Hook, NY, USA, 3–8 December 2018; pp. 3036–3046.
5. Zou, D.; Cao, Y.; Zhou, D.; Gu, Q. Stochastic gradient descent optimizes over-parameterized deep ReLU networks. *arXiv* **2018**, arXiv:1811.08888.
6. Huang, W.; Liu, C.; Chen, Y.; Liu, T.; Da Xu, R.Y. Demystify Optimization and Generalization of Over-parameterized PAC-Bayesian Learning. *arXiv* **2022**, arXiv:2202.01958
7. Nakkiran, P.; Kaplun, G.; Bansal, Y.; Yang, T.; Barak, B.; Sutskever, I. Deep double descent: Where bigger models and more data hurt. *arXiv* **2019**, arXiv:1912.02292.
8. Soudry, D.; Hoffer, E.; Nacson, M.S.; Gunasekar, S.; Srebro, N. The implicit bias of gradient descent on separable data. *J. Mach. Learn. Res.* **2018**, *19*, 2822–2878.
9. Neyshabur, B.; Tomioka, R.; Srebro, N. In search of the real inductive bias: On the role of implicit regularization in deep learning. *arXiv* **2014**, arXiv:1412.6614.
10. Gunasekar, S.; Lee, J.; Soudry, D.; Srebro, N. Characterizing implicit bias in terms of optimization geometry. *arXiv* **2018**, arXiv:1802.08246.
11. Ji, Z.; Telgarsky, M. The implicit bias of gradient descent on nonseparable data. In Proceedings of the Conference on Learning Theory, Phoenix, AZ, USA, 25–28 June 2019; pp. 1772–1798.
12. Nacson, M.S.; Gunasekar, S.; Lee, J.D.; Srebro, N.; Soudry, D. Lexicographic and depth-sensitive margins in homogeneous and non-homogeneous deep models. *arXiv* **2019**, arXiv:1905.07325.
13. Lyu, K.; Li, J. Gradient descent maximizes the margin of homogeneous neural networks. *arXiv* **2019**, arXiv: 1906.05890.
14. He, K.; Zhang, X.; Ren, S.; Sun, J. Deep residual learning for image recognition. In Proceedings of the IEEE Conference on Computer Vision and Pattern Recognition, Las Vegas, NV, USA, 26 June–1 July 2016; pp. 770–778.
15. Zagoruyko, S.; Komodakis, N. Wide residual networks. *arXiv* **2016**, arXiv:1605.07146.
16. Lewkowycz, A.; Bahri, Y.; Dyer, E.; Sohl-Dickstein, J.; Gur-Ari, G. The large learning rate phase of deep learning: the catapult mechanism. *arXiv* **2020**, arXiv:2003.02218.
17. Arora, S.; Du, S.S.; Hu, W.; Li, Z.; Salakhutdinov, R.R.; Wang, R. On exact computation with an infinitely wide neural net. In Proceedings of the Advances in Neural Information Processing Systems, Vancouver, BC, Canada, 8–14 December 2019; pp. 8141–8150.
18. Yang, G. Scaling limits of wide neural networks with weight sharing: Gaussian process behavior, gradient independence, and neural tangent kernel derivation. *arXiv* **2019**, arXiv:1902.04760.
19. Huang, J.; Yau, H.T. Dynamics of deep neural networks and neural tangent hierarchy. *arXiv* **2019**, arXiv:1909.08156.
20. Allen-Zhu, Z.; Li, Y. What Can ResNet Learn Efficiently, Going Beyond Kernels? In Proceedings of the Advances in Neural Information Processing Systems, Vancouver, BC, Canada, 8–14 December 2019; pp. 9017–9028.
21. Chizat, L.; Oyallon, E.; Bach, F. On lazy training in differentiable programming. In Proceedings of the Advances in Neural Information Processing Systems, Vancouver, BC, Canada, 8–14 December 2019; pp. 2937–2947.

22. Cohen, G.; Afshar, S.; Tapson, J.; Van Schaik, A. EMNIST: Extending MNIST to handwritten letters. In Proceedings of the 2017 international joint conference on neural networks (IJCNN), Anchorage, AK, USA, 14–19 May 2017; pp. 2921–2926.
23. Ho-Phuoc, T. CIFAR10 to compare visual recognition performance between deep neural networks and humans. *arXiv* **2018**, arXiv:1811.07270.
24. Jiang, L.; Zhou, Z.; Leung, T.; Li, L.J.; Fei-Fei, L. MentorNet: Learning Data-Driven Curriculum for Very Deep Neural Networks on Corrupted Labels. In Proceedings of the ICML, Stockholm, Sweden, 10–15 July 2018.
25. Li, W.; Wang, L.; Li, W.; Agustsson, E.; Van Gool, L. Webvision database: Visual learning and understanding from web data. *arXiv* **2017**, arXiv:1708.02862.
26. Ali, A.; Dobriban, E.; Tibshirani, R.J. The Implicit Regularization of Stochastic Gradient Flow for Least Squares. *arXiv* **2020**, arXiv:2003.07802.
27. Mousavi-Hosseini, A.; Park, S.; Girotti, M.; Mitliagkas, I.; Erdogdu, M.A. Neural Networks Efficiently Learn Low-Dimensional Representations with SGD. *arXiv* **2022**, arXiv:2209.14863.
28. Nacson, M.S.; Lee, J.D.; Gunasekar, S.; Savarese, P.H.; Srebro, N.; Soudry, D. Convergence of gradient descent on separable data. *arXiv* **2018**, arXiv:1803.01905.
29. Gunasekar, S.; Lee, J.D.; Soudry, D.; Srebro, N. Implicit bias of gradient descent on linear convolutional networks. In Proceedings of the Advances in Neural Information Processing Systems, Red Hook, NY, USA, 3–8 December 2018; pp. 9461–9471.
30. Ji, Z.; Telgarsky, M. Gradient descent aligns the layers of deep linear networks. *arXiv* **2018**, arXiv:1810.02032.
31. Razin, N.; Cohen, N. Implicit Regularization in Deep Learning May Not Be Explainable by Norms. *arXiv* **2020**, arXiv:2005.06398.
32. Smith, S.L.; Dherin, B.; Barrett, D.G.; De, S. On the origin of implicit regularization in stochastic gradient descent. *arXiv* **2021**, arXiv:2101.12176.
33. Ji, Z.; Telgarsky, M. Directional convergence and alignment in deep learning. *arXiv* **2020**, arXiv:2006.06657.
34. Chizat, L.; Bach, F. Implicit bias of gradient descent for wide two-layer neural networks trained with the logistic loss. *arXiv* **2020**, arXiv:2002.04486.
35. Oymak, S.; Soltanolkotabi, M. Overparameterized nonlinear learning: Gradient descent takes the shortest path? *arXiv* **2018**, arXiv:1812.10004.
36. Nguyen, T.; Novak, R.; Xiao, L.; Lee, J. Dataset distillation with infinitely wide convolutional networks. *Adv. Neural Inf. Process. Syst.* **2021**, *34*, 5186–5198.
37. Ho, T.K.; Basu, M. Complexity measures of supervised classification problems. *IEEE Trans. Pattern Anal. Mach. Intell.* **2002**, *24*, 289–300.
38. Lorena, A.C.; Garcia, L.P.; Lehmann, J.; Souto, M.C.; Ho, T.K. How complex is your classification problem? a survey on measuring classification complexity. *ACM Comput. Surv. (CSUR)* **2019**, *52*, 1–34. [CrossRef]
39. Guan, S.; Loew, M.; Ko, H. Data separability for neural network classifiers and the development of a separability index. *arXiv* **2020**, arXiv:2005.13120.
40. Rostami, M.; Berahmand, K.; Nasiri, E.; Forouzandeh, S. Review of swarm intelligence-based feature selection methods. *Eng. Appl. Artif. Intell.* **2021**, *100*, 104210. [CrossRef]
41. Berahmand, K.; Mohammadi, M.; Saberi-Movahed, F.; Li, Y.; Xu, Y. Graph regularized nonnegative matrix factorization for community detection in attributed networks. *IEEE Trans. Netw. Sci. Eng.* **2022**, *10*, 372–385. [CrossRef]
42. Bietti, A.; Bruna, J.; Sanford, C.; Song, M.J. Learning Single-Index Models with Shallow Neural Networks. *arXiv* **2022**, arXiv:2210.15651.
43. Lee, J.; Xiao, L.; Schoenholz, S.; Bahri, Y.; Novak, R.; Sohl-Dickstein, J.; Pennington, J. Wide neural networks of any depth evolve as linear models under gradient descent. In Proceedings of the Advances in Neural Information Processing Systems, Vancouver, BC, Canada, 8–14 December 2019; pp. 8570–8581.
44. Huang, W.; Du, W.; Da Xu, R.Y. On the Neural Tangent Kernel of Deep Networks with Orthogonal Initialization. *arXiv* **2020**, arXiv:2004.05867.
45. Li, Z.; Wang, R.; Yu, D.; Du, S.S.; Hu, W.; Salakhutdinov, R.; Arora, S. Enhanced convolutional neural tangent kernels. *arXiv* **2019**, arXiv:1911.00809.
46. Du, S.S.; Hou, K.; Salakhutdinov, R.R.; Poczos, B.; Wang, R.; Xu, K. Graph neural tangent kernel: Fusing graph neural networks with graph kernels. In Proceedings of the Advances in Neural Information Processing Systems, Vancouver, BC, Canada, 8–14 December 2019; pp. 5723–5733.
47. Huang, W.; Li, Y.; Du, W.; Yin, J.; Da Xu, R.Y.; Chen, L.; Zhang, M. Towards deepening graph neural networks: A GNTK-based optimization perspective. *arXiv* **2021**, arXiv:2103.03113.
48. Hron, J.; Bahri, Y.; Sohl-Dickstein, J.; Novak, R. Infinite attention: NNGP and NTK for deep attention networks. *arXiv* **2020**, arXiv:2006.10540.
49. Jacot, A.; Gabriel, F.; Hongler, C. Freeze and chaos for dnns: An NTK view of batch normalization, checkerboard and boundary effects. *arXiv* **2019**, arXiv:1907.05715.
50. Yang, G. Tensor Programs II: Neural Tangent Kernel for Any Architecture. *arXiv* **2020**, arXiv:2006.14548.
51. Krizhevsky, A.; Sutskever, I.; Hinton, G.E. Imagenet classification with deep convolutional neural networks. In Proceedings of the Advances in neural information processing systems, Lake Tahoe, NV, USA, 3–6 December 2012; pp. 1097–1105.

52. Keskar, N.S.; Mudigere, D.; Nocedal, J.; Smelyanskiy, M.; Tang, P.T.P. On large-batch training for deep learning: Generalization gap and sharp minima. *arXiv* **2016**, arXiv:1609.04836.
53. Jiang, Y.; Neyshabur, B.; Mobahi, H.; Krishnan, D.; Bengio, S. Fantastic generalization measures and where to find them. *arXiv* **2019**, arXiv:1912.02178.
54. Li, Y.; Wei, C.; Ma, T. Towards explaining the regularization effect of initial large learning rate in training neural networks. In Proceedings of the Advances in Neural Information Processing Systems, Vancouver, BC, Canada, 8–14 December 2019; pp. 11674–11685.
55. Nitanda, A.; Chinot, G.; Suzuki, T. Gradient Descent can Learn Less Over-parameterized Two-layer Neural Networks on Classification Problems. *arXiv* **2019**, arXiv:1905.09870.
56. Nilsen, G.K.; Munthe-Kaas, A.Z.; Skaug, H.J.; Brun, M. Efficient computation of hessian matrices in tensorflow. *arXiv* **2019**, arXiv:1905.05559.
57. Patrini, G.; Rozza, A.; Krishna Menon, A.; Nock, R.; Qu, L. Making deep neural networks robust to label noise: A loss correction approach. In Proceedings of the IEEE Conference on Computer Vision and Pattern Recognition, Honolulu, HI, USA, 21–26 July 2017; pp. 1944–1952.
58. Ma, X.; Wang, Y.; Houle, M.E.; Zhou, S.; Erfani, S.M.; Xia, S.T.; Wijewickrema, S.; Bailey, J. Dimensionality-Driven Learning with Noisy Labels. In Proceedings of the ICML, Stockholm, Sweden, 10–15 July 2018.
59. Ma, X.; Huang, H.; Wang, Y.; Romano, S.; Erfani, S.; Bailey, J. Normalized loss functions for deep learning with noisy labels. In Proceedings of the International Conference on Machine Learning, Atlanta, GA, USA, 16–21 June 2013; PMLR: New York, NY, USA, 2020; pp. 6543–6553.
60. Bubeck, S. Convex optimization: Algorithms and complexity. *arXiv* **2014**, arXiv:1405.4980.

Disclaimer/Publisher's Note: The statements, opinions and data contained in all publications are solely those of the individual author(s) and contributor(s) and not of MDPI and/or the editor(s). MDPI and/or the editor(s) disclaim responsibility for any injury to people or property resulting from any ideas, methods, instructions or products referred to in the content.

MDPI AG
Grosspeteranlage 5
4052 Basel
Switzerland
Tel.: +41 61 683 77 34

Applied Sciences Editorial Office
E-mail: applsci@mdpi.com
www.mdpi.com/journal/applsci

Disclaimer/Publisher's Note: The title and front matter of this reprint are at the discretion of the Guest Editors. The publisher is not responsible for their content or any associated concerns. The statements, opinions and data contained in all individual articles are solely those of the individual Editors and contributors and not of MDPI. MDPI disclaims responsibility for any injury to people or property resulting from any ideas, methods, instructions or products referred to in the content.

www.ingramcontent.com/pod-product-compliance
Lightning Source LLC
LaVergne TN
LVHW072320090526
838202LV00019B/2320